BUSINESS ANALYSIS AND VALUATION

IFRS EDITION

BUSINESS ANALYSIS AND VALUATION

IFRS EDITION   TEXT ONLY

KRISHNA G. PALEPU

PAUL M. HEALY

VICTOR L. BERNARD

ERIK PEEK

Australia • Canada • Mexico • Singapore • Spain • United Kingdom • United States

THOMSON

Business Analysis and Valuation: IFRS Edition
Text Only
Krishna G. Palepu, Paul M. Healy, Victor L. Bernard, and Erik Peek

| **Publishing Director** | **Publisher** | **Development Editor** |
| John Yates | Patrick Bond | Rachael Sturgeon |

| **Production Editor** | **Manufacturing Manager** | **Editorial Assistant** |
| Fiona Freel | Helen Mason | Alice Rodgers |

| **Typesetter** | **Production Controller** | **Marketing Manager** |
| Saxon Graphics Ltd, Derby | Maeve Healy | Leo Stanley |

| **Cover Design** | **Text Design** | **Cover Design Controller** |
| Adam Renvoize | Design Deluxe Ltd, Bath, UK | Jackie Wrout |

Printer
Canale & C., Italy

CONTENTS

PREFACE

Financial statements are the basis for a wide range of business analyses. Managers use them to monitor and judge their firms' performance relative to competitors, to communicate with external investors, to help judge what financial policies they should pursue, and to evaluate potential new businesses to acquire as part of their investment strategy. Securities analysts use financial statements to rate and value companies they recommend to clients. Bankers use them in deciding whether to extend a loan to a client and to determine the loan's terms. Investment bankers use them as a basis for valuing and analyzing prospective buyouts, mergers, and acquisitions. And consultants use them as a basis for competitive analysis for their clients. Not surprisingly, therefore, there is a strong demand among business students for a course that provides a framework for using financial statement data in a variety of business analysis and valuation contexts. The purpose of this book is to provide such a framework for business students and practitioners.

THIS EDITION

This IFRS edition is a European adaptation of the successful U.S. edition – authored by Krishna G. Palepu, Paul M. Healy, and Victor L. Bernard – that has been used in Accounting and Finance departments in universities around the world. The European business environment has its own unique character. In addition, the recent requirement that public corporations in the European Union prepare their financial statements in accordance with International Financial Reporting Standards (IFRS) has changed the European reporting environment substantially. These factors more than justify writing this European IFRS edition. Particular features of this edition are the following:

- A large number of examples support the discussion of business analysis and valuation throughout the chapters. The examples are from European companies that students will generally be familiar with, such as Alcatel, AstraZeneca, British American Tobacco, British Petroleum, Carlsberg, easyGroup, Finnair, GlaxoSmithKline, Porsche, Royal Dutch Shell, and Volkswagen.

- We substantially revised the chapters dealing with accounting analysis (Chapters 3 and 4) to better prepare European students for the task of analyzing IFRS-based financial statements. All numerical examples of accounting adjustments in Chapter 4 describe adjustments to IFRS-based financial statements. Further, throughout the book we discuss various topics that are particularly relevant to understanding IFRS-based European financial reports, such as: the classification of expenses by nature and by function; a principles-based approach versus a rules-based approach to standard setting; the first-time adoption of IFRS; cross-country differences and similarities in external auditing and public enforcement, and cross-country differences in financing structures.

■ The terminology that we use throughout the chapters is consistent with the terminology that is used in the IFRS.

■ Throughout the chapters, we describe the average performance and growth ratios, the average time-series behavior of these ratios, and average financing policies of a sample of close to 7,000 firms that have been listed on European public exchanges between 1989 and 2005.

■ This IFRS edition includes 13 new cases, which are all about European companies. Ten of these new cases make use of IFRS-based financial statements. However, we also retained several popular cases from the previous (U.S.) edition because they have proved to be very effective for many instructors.

KEY FEATURES

This book differs from other texts in business and financial analysis in a number of important ways. We introduce and develop a framework for business analysis and valuation using financial statement data. We then show how this framework can be applied to a variety of decision contexts.

Framework for analysis

We begin the book with a discussion of the role of accounting information and intermediaries in the economy, and how financial analysis can create value in well-functioning markets. We identify four key components of effective financial statement analysis:

■ Business strategy analysis
■ Accounting analysis
■ Financial analysis
■ Prospective analysis

The first of the components, business strategy analysis, involves developing an understanding of the business and competitive strategy of the firm being analyzed. Incorporating business strategy into financial statement analysis is one of the distinctive features of this book. Traditionally, this step has been ignored by other financial statement analysis books. However, we believe that it is critical to begin financial statement analysis with a company's strategy because it provides an important foundation for the subsequent analysis. The strategy analysis section discusses contemporary tools for analyzing a company's industry, its competitive position and sustainability within an industry, and the company's corporate strategy.

Accounting analysis involves examining how accounting rules and conventions represent a firm's business economics and strategy in its financial statements, and, if necessary, developing adjusted accounting measures of performance. In the accounting analysis section, we do not emphasize accounting rules. Instead we develop general approaches to analyzing assets, liabilities, entities, revenues, and expenses. We believe that such an approach enables students to effectively evaluate a company's accounting choices and accrual estimates, even if students have only a basic knowledge of accounting rules and standards. The material is also designed to allow students to make accounting adjustments rather than merely identify questionable accounting practices.

Financial analysis involves analyzing financial ratio and cash flow measures of the operating, financing, and investing performance of a company relative to either key competitors or historical performance. Our distinctive approach focuses on using financial analysis to evaluate the effectiveness of a company's strategy and to make sound financial forecasts.

Finally, under prospective analysis we show how to develop forecasted financial statements and how to use these to make estimates of a firm's value. Our discussion of valuation includes traditional discounted cash flow models as well as techniques that link value directly to accounting numbers. In discussing accounting-based valuation models, we integrate the latest academic research with traditional approaches such as earnings and book value multiples that are widely used in practice.

While we cover all four components of business analysis and valuation in the book, we recognize that the extent of their use depends on the user's decision context. For example, bankers are likely to use business strategy analysis, accounting analysis, financial analysis, and the forecasting portion of prospective analysis. They are less likely to be interested in formally valuing a prospective client.

Application of the framework to decision contexts

The next section of the book shows how our business analysis and valuation framework can be applied to a variety of decision contexts:

- Securities analysis
- Credit analysis
- Corporate financing policies analysis
- Merger and acquisition analysis
- Governance and communication analysis

For each of these topics we present an overview to provide a foundation for the class discussions. Where possible we discuss relevant institutional details and the results of academic research that are useful in applying the analysis concepts developed earlier in the book. For example, the chapter on credit analysis shows how banks and rating agencies use financial statement data to develop analysis for lending decisions and to rate public debt issues. This chapter also presents academic research on how to determine whether a company is financially distressed.

CASE APPROACH

We have found that teaching a course in business analysis and valuation is significantly enhanced, both for teachers and students, by using cases as a pedagogical tool. Students want to develop "hands-on" experience in business analysis and valuation so that they can apply the concepts in decision contexts similar to those they will encounter in the business world. Cases are a natural way to achieve this objective by presenting practical issues that might otherwise be ignored in a traditional classroom exercise. Our cases all present business analysis and valuation issues in a specific decision context, and we find that this makes the material more interesting and exciting for students.

To provide both guidance and flexibility in the choice of cases, we include one case at the end of each chapter, especially chosen for applying the concepts in that chapter.

USING THE BOOK

We designed the book so that it is flexible for courses in financial statement analysis for a variety of student audiences – MBA students, Masters in Accounting students, Executive Program participants, and undergraduates in Accounting or Finance. Depending upon the audience, the instructor can vary the manner in which the conceptual materials in the chapters, end-of-chapter questions, and case examples are used.

Prerequisites

To get the most out of the book, students should have completed basic courses in financial accounting, finance, and either business strategy or business economics. The text provides a concise overview of some of these topics, primarily as background for preparing the cases. But it would probably be difficult for students with no prior knowledge in these fields to use the chapters as stand-alone coverage of them. We have integrated only a small amount of business strategy into each case and do not include any cases that focus exclusively on business strategy analysis.

The extent of accounting knowledge required for the cases varies considerably. Some require only a basic understanding of accounting issues, whereas others require a more detailed knowledge at the level of a typical intermediate financial accounting course. However, we have found it possible to teach even these more complex cases to students without a strong accounting background by providing additional reading on the topic.

How to use the text and case materials

The materials can be used in a variety of ways. If the book is used for students with prior working experience or for executives, the instructor can use almost a pure case approach, adding relevant lecture sections as needed. When teaching students with little work experience, a lecture class can be presented first, followed by an appropriate case. It is also possible to use the book primarily for a lecture course and include some of the cases as in-class illustrations of the concepts discussed in the book.

Alternatively, lectures can be used as a follow-up to cases to more clearly lay out the conceptual issues raised in the case discussions. This may be appropriate when the book is used in undergraduate capstone courses. In such a context, cases can be used in course projects that can be assigned to student teams.

We have designed the cases so that they can be taught at a variety of levels. For students who need more structure to work through a case, the Instructor's Manual includes a set of detailed questions that the instructor can hand out before class. For students who need less structure, there are recommended questions at the end of each case.

Companion website

A companion website accompanies this book. This website contains the following valuable material for instructors and students:

- Instructions for how to easily produce standardized financial statements in Excel.
- Spreadsheets containing: (1) the reported and standardized financial statements of Volkswagen and Porsche; (2) calculations of Volkswagen's and Porsche's ratios

(presented in Chapter 5); (3) Porsche's forecasted financial statements (presented in Chapter 6); and (4) valuations of Porsche's shares (presented in Chapter 8). Using these spreadsheets students can easily replicate the analyses presented in Chapters 5 through 8 and perform "what-if" analyses – i.e., to find out how the reported numbers change as a result of changes to the standardized statements or forecasting assumptions.

■ Spreadsheets containing case material.

■ Answers to the discussion questions and case instructions (for instructors only).

ACKNOWLEDGMENTS

We thank the following colleagues who gave us feedback as we wrote this IFRS edition: Sanjay Bissessur (University of Amsterdam); Ignace De Beelde (Ghent University); Lakshmanan Shivakumar (London Business School); and Shifei Lisa Liu (The University of Liverpool Management School). We are also very grateful to Pat Bond, Rachael Sturgeon, and the rest of the publishing team at Thomson Learning for their help and assistance throughout the production of this edition.

AUTHORS

KRISHNA G. PALEPU is the Ross Graham Walker Professor of Business Administration and Senior Associate Dean for International Development at the Harvard Business School. During the past 20 years, Professor Palepu's research has focused on corporate strategy, governance, and disclosure. Professor Palepu is the winner of the American Accounting Association's Notable Contributions to Accounting Literature Award (in 1999) and the Wildman Award (in 1997).

PAUL HEALY is the James R. Williston Professor of Business Administration and Head of the Accounting and Management Unit at the Harvard Business School. Professor Healy's research has focused on corporate governance and disclosure, mergers and acquisitions, earnings management, and management compensation. He has previously worked at the MIT Sloan School of Management, ICI Ltd., and Arthur Young in New Zealand. Professor Healy has won the Notable Contributions to Accounting Literature Award (in 1990 and 1999) and the Wildman Award (in 1997) for contributions to practice.

VIC BERNARD, who passed away November 14, 1995, was a CPA and held a PhD from the University of Illinois. He was the Price Waterhouse Professor of Accounting and Director of the Paton Accounting Center at the University of Michigan and Director of Research for the American Accounting Association. His research examined issues in financial reporting, financial statement analysis, and financial economics. He received the Notable Contributions to Accounting Literature Award in 1991, 1993, and 1999, the Outstanding Accounting Educator Award in 1997, and the Wildman Award in 1997.

ERIK PEEK is Associate Professor of Financial Accounting at Maastricht University, The Netherlands. He is a CFA charterholder and holds a PhD from the Vrije Universiteit Amsterdam. Professor Peek's research has focused on international accounting, earnings management, and management compensation.

FRAMEWORK

A Framework for Business Analysis and Valuation Using Financial Statements

This chapter outlines a comprehensive framework for financial statement analysis. Because financial statements provide the most widely available data on public corporations' economic activities, investors and other stakeholders rely on financial reports to assess the plans and performance of firms and corporate managers.

A variety of questions can be addressed by business analysis using financial statements, as shown in the following examples:

- A security analyst may be interested in asking: "How well is the firm I am following performing? Did the firm meet my performance expectations? If not, why not? What is the value of the firm's stock given my assessment of the firm's current and future performance?"

- A loan officer may need to ask: "What is the credit risk involved in lending a certain amount of money to this firm? How well is the firm managing its liquidity and solvency? What is the firm's business risk? What is the additional risk created by the firm's financing and dividend policies?"

- A management consultant might ask: "What is the structure of the industry in which the firm is operating? What are the strategies pursued by various players in the industry? What is the relative performance of different firms in the industry?"

- A corporate manager may ask: "Is my firm properly valued by investors? Is our investor communication program adequate to facilitate this process?"

- A corporate manager could ask: "Is this firm a potential takeover target? How much value can be added if we acquire this firm? How can we finance the acquisition?"

- An independent auditor would want to ask: "Are the accounting policies and accrual estimates in this company's financial statements consistent with my understanding of this business and its recent performance? Do these financial reports communicate the current status and significant risks of the business?"

In the past century, we have seen two distinct models for channeling savings into business investments. Communist and socialist market economies have used central planning and government agencies to pool national savings and to direct investments in business enterprises. The failure of this model is evident from the fact that most of these economies have abandoned it in favor of the second model – the market model. In almost all countries in the world today, capital markets play an important role in channeling financial resources from savers to business enterprises that need capital.

Financial statement analysis is a valuable activity when managers have complete information on a firm's strategies, and a variety of institutional factors make it unlikely that they fully disclose this information. In this setting outside analysts attempt to create "inside information" from analyzing financial statement data, thereby gaining valuable insights about the firm's current performance and future prospects.

To understand the contribution that financial statement analysis can make, it is important to understand the role of financial reporting in the functioning of capital markets and the institutional forces that shape financial statements. Therefore we present first a brief description of these forces; then we discuss the steps that an analyst must perform to extract information from financial statements and provide valuable forecasts.

THE ROLE OF FINANCIAL REPORTING IN CAPITAL MARKETS

A critical challenge for any economy is the allocation of savings to investment opportunities. Economies that do this well can exploit new business ideas to spur innovation and create jobs and wealth at a rapid pace. In contrast, economies that manage this process poorly dissipate their wealth and fail to support business opportunities.

Figure 1.1 provides a schematic representation of how capital markets typically work. Savings in any economy are widely distributed among households. There are usually many new entrepreneurs and existing companies that would like to attract these savings to fund their business ideas. While both savers and entrepreneurs would like to do business with each other, matching savings to business investment opportunities is complicated for at least two reasons. First, entrepreneurs typically have better information than savers on the value of business investment opportunities. Second, communication by entrepreneurs to investors is not completely credible because investors know entrepreneurs have an incentive to inflate the value of their ideas.

These information and incentive issues lead to what economists call the "lemons" problem, which can potentially break down the functioning of the capital market.[1] It works like this. Consider a situation where half the business ideas are "good" and the other half are "bad." If investors cannot distinguish between the two types of business ideas, entrepreneurs with "bad" ideas will try to claim that their ideas are as valuable as the "good" ideas. Realizing this possibility, investors value both good and bad ideas at an average level. Unfortunately, this penalizes good ideas, and entrepreneurs with good ideas find the terms on which they can get financing to be unattractive. As these entrepreneurs leave the capital market, the proportion of bad ideas in the market increases. Over time, bad ideas "crowd out" good ideas, and investors lose confidence in this market.

The emergence of intermediaries can prevent such a market breakdown. Intermediaries are like a car mechanic who provides an independent certification of a used car's quality to help a buyer and seller agree on a price. There are two types of intermediaries in the capital markets. Financial intermediaries, such as venture capital firms, banks, collective investment funds, pension funds, and insurance companies, focus on aggregating funds from individual investors and analyzing different investment alternatives to make investment decisions. Information intermediaries,

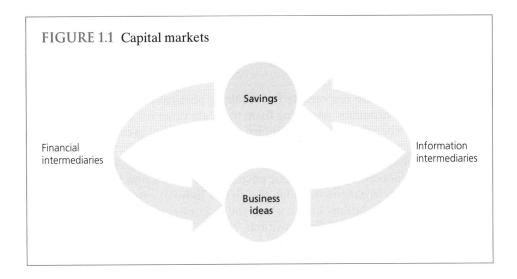

FIGURE 1.1 Capital markets

such as auditors, financial analysts, credit-rating agencies, and the financial press, focus on providing information to investors (and to financial intermediaries who represent them) on the quality of various business investment opportunities. Both these types of intermediaries add value by helping investors distinguish "good" investment opportunities from the "bad" ones.

The relative importance of financial intermediaries and information intermediaries varies from country to country for historical reasons. In countries where individual investors traditionally have had strong legal rights to discipline entrepreneurs who invest in "bad" business ideas, such as in the U.K., individual investors have been more inclined to make their own investment decisions. In these countries, the funds that entrepreneurs attract may come from a widely dispersed group of individual investors and be channeled through public stock exchanges. Information intermediaries consequently play an important role in supplying individual investors with the information that they need to distinguish between "good" and "bad" business ideas. In contrast, in countries where individual investors traditionally have had weak legal rights to discipline entrepreneurs, such as in many Continental European countries, individual investors have been more inclined to rely on the help of financial intermediaries. In these countries, financial intermediaries, such as banks, tend to supply most of the funds to entrepreneurs and can get privileged access to entrepreneurs' private information.

Over the past decade, many countries in Europe have been moving towards a model of strong protection of investors' rights to discipline entrepreneurs and well-developed stock exchanges. In this model, financial reporting plays a critical role in the functioning of both the information intermediaries and financial intermediaries. Information intermediaries add value by either enhancing the credibility of financial reports (as auditors do), or by analyzing the information in the financial statements (as analysts and the rating agencies do). Financial intermediaries rely on the information in the financial statements to analyze investment opportunities, and supplement this information with other sources of information. In the following section, we discuss key aspects of the financial reporting system design that enable it to play effectively this vital role in the functioning of the capital markets.

FROM BUSINESS ACTIVITIES TO FINANCIAL STATEMENTS

Corporate managers are responsible for acquiring physical and financial resources from the firm's environment and using them to create value for the firm's investors. Value is created when the firm earns a return on its investment in excess of the return required by its capital suppliers. Managers formulate business strategies to achieve this goal, and they implement them through business activities. A firm's business activities are influenced by its economic environment and its own business strategy. The economic environment includes the firm's industry, its input and output markets, and the regulations under which the firm operates. The firm's business strategy determines how the firm positions itself in its environment to achieve a competitive advantage.

As shown in Figure 1.2, a firm's financial statements summarize the economic consequences of its business activities. The firm's business activities in any time period are too numerous to be reported individually to outsiders. Further, some of the activities undertaken by the firm are proprietary in nature, and disclosing these activities in detail could be a detriment to the firm's competitive position. The firm's accounting system provides a mechanism through which business activities are selected, measured, and aggregated into financial statement data.

Intermediaries using financial statement data to do business analysis have to be aware that financial reports are influenced both by the firm's business activities and by its accounting system. A key aspect of financial statement analysis, therefore, involves understanding the influence of the accounting system on the quality of the financial statement data being used in the analysis. The institutional features of accounting systems discussed next determine the extent of that influence.

Accounting system feature 1: Accrual accounting

One of the fundamental features of corporate financial reports is that they are prepared using accrual rather than cash accounting. Unlike cash accounting, accrual accounting distinguishes between the recording of costs and benefits associated with economic activities and the actual payment and receipt of cash. Net profit is the primary periodic performance index under accrual accounting. To compute net profit, the effects of economic transactions are recorded on the basis of *expected*, not necessarily *actual*, cash receipts and payments. Expected cash receipts from the delivery of products or services are recognized as revenues, and expected cash outflows associated with these revenues are recognized as expenses.

The need for accrual accounting arises from investors' demand for financial reports on a periodic basis. Because firms undertake economic transactions on a continual basis, the arbitrary closing of accounting books at the end of a reporting period leads to a fundamental measurement problem. Because cash accounting does not report the full economic consequence of the transactions undertaken in a given period, accrual accounting is designed to provide more complete information on a firm's periodic performance.

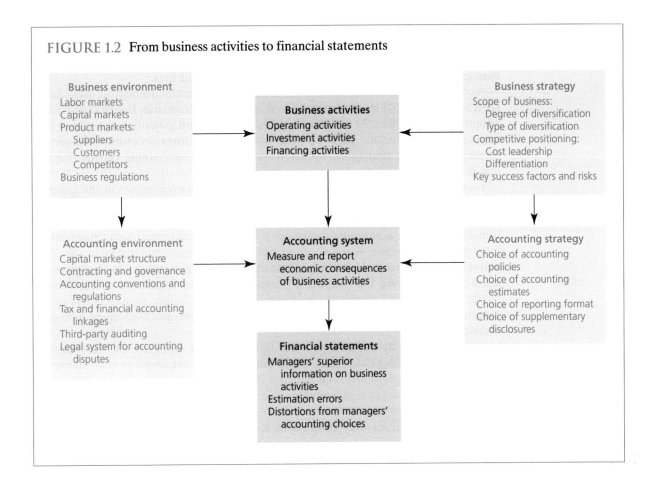

FIGURE 1.2 From business activities to financial statements

Accounting system feature 2: Accounting standards and auditing

The use of accrual accounting lies at the center of many important complexities in corporate financial reporting. Because accrual accounting deals with *expectations* of future cash consequences of current events, it is subjective and relies on a variety of assumptions. Who should be charged with the primary responsibility of making these assumptions? A firm's managers are entrusted with the task of making the appropriate estimates and assumptions to prepare the financial statements because they have intimate knowledge of their firm's business.

The accounting discretion granted to managers is potentially valuable because it allows them to reflect inside information in reported financial statements. However, because investors view profits as a measure of managers' performance, managers have incentives to use their accounting discretion to distort reported profits by making biased assumptions. Further, the use of accounting numbers in contracts between the firm and outsiders provides another motivation for management manipulation of accounting numbers. Earnings management distorts financial accounting data, making them less valuable to external users of financial statements. Therefore, the delegation of financial reporting decisions to corporate managers has both costs and benefits.

A number of accounting conventions have evolved to ensure that managers use their accounting flexibility to summarize their knowledge of the firm's business activities, and not to disguise reality for self-serving purposes. For example, the measurability and conservatism conventions are accounting responses to concerns about distortions from managers' potentially optimistic bias. Both these conventions attempt to limit managers' optimistic bias by imposing their own pessimistic bias.

Accounting standards, such as International Financial Reporting Standards (IFRS), promulgated by the International Accounting Standards Board (IASB) and adopted by more than 70 countries worldwide, also limit potential distortions that managers can introduce into reported numbers.[2] Uniform accounting standards attempt to reduce managers' ability to record similar economic transactions in dissimilar ways, either over time or across firms.

Increased uniformity from accounting standards, however, comes at the expense of reduced flexibility for managers to reflect genuine business differences in their firm's financial statements. Rigid accounting standards work best for economic transactions whose accounting treatment is not predicated on managers' proprietary information. However, when there is significant business judgment involved in assessing a transaction's economic consequences, rigid standards that prevent managers from using their superior business knowledge would be dysfunctional. Further, if accounting standards are too rigid, they may induce managers to expend economic resources to restructure business transactions in order to achieve a desired accounting result.

Auditing, broadly defined as a verification of the integrity of the reported financial statements by someone other than the preparer, ensures that managers use accounting rules and conventions consistently over time, and that their accounting estimates are reasonable. Therefore auditing improves the quality of accounting data.

Third-party auditing may also reduce the quality of financial reporting because it constrains the kind of accounting rules and conventions that evolve over time. For example, the IASB considers the views of auditors in the standard-setting process. Auditors are likely to argue against accounting standards producing numbers that are difficult to audit, even if the proposed rules produce relevant information for investors.

The legal environment in which accounting disputes between managers, auditors, and investors are adjudicated can also have a significant effect on the quality of reported numbers. The threats of lawsuits and resulting penalties, which vary greatly in strength across countries, have the beneficial effect of improving the accuracy of disclosure. However, the potential for a significant legal liability might also discourage managers and auditors from supporting accounting proposals requiring risky fore-casts, such as forward-looking disclosures.

Accounting system feature 3: Managers' reporting strategy

Because the mechanisms that limit managers' ability to distort accounting data add noise, it is not optimal to use accounting regulation to eliminate managerial flexibility completely. Therefore real-world accounting systems leave considerable room for managers to influence financial statement data. A firm's reporting strategy – that is, the manner in which managers use their accounting discretion – has an important influence on the firm's financial statements.

Corporate managers can choose accounting and disclosure policies that make it more or less difficult for external users of financial reports to understand the true economic picture of their businesses. Accounting rules often provide a broad set of alternatives from which managers can choose. Further, managers are entrusted with making a range of estimates in implementing these accounting policies. Accounting regulations usually prescribe *minimum* disclosure requirements, but they do not restrict managers from *voluntarily* providing additional disclosures.

A superior disclosure strategy will enable managers to communicate the underlying business reality to outside investors. One important constraint on a firm's disclosure strategy is the competitive dynamics in product markets. Disclosure of proprietary information about business strategies and their expected economic consequences may hurt the firm's competitive position. Subject to this constraint, managers can use financial statements to provide information useful to investors in assessing their firm's true economic performance.

Managers can also use financial reporting strategies to manipulate investors' perceptions. Using the discretion granted to them, managers can make it difficult for investors to identify poor performance on a timely basis. For example, managers can choose accounting policies and estimates to provide an optimistic assessment of the firm's true performance. They can also make it costly for investors to understand the true performance by controlling the extent of information that is disclosed voluntarily.

The extent to which financial statements are informative about the underlying business reality varies across firms and across time for a given firm. This variation in accounting quality provides both an important opportunity and a challenge in doing business analysis. The process through which analysts can separate noise from information in financial statements, and gain valuable business insights from financial statement analysis, is discussed next.

FROM FINANCIAL STATEMENTS TO BUSINESS ANALYSIS

Because managers' insider knowledge is a source both of value and distortion in accounting data, it is difficult for outside users of financial statements to separate true information from distortion and noise. Not being able to undo accounting distortions completely, investors "discount" a firm's reported accounting performance. In doing so, they make a probabilistic assessment of the extent to which a firm's reported numbers reflect economic reality. As a result, investors can have only an imprecise assessment of an individual firm's performance. Financial and information intermediaries can add value by improving investors' understanding of a firm's current performance and its future prospects.

Effective financial statement analysis is valuable because it attempts to get at managers' inside information from public financial statement data. Because intermediaries do not have direct or complete access to this information, they rely on their knowledge of the firm's industry and its competitive strategies to interpret financial statements. Successful intermediaries have at least as good an understanding of the industry economics as do the firm's managers, as well as a reasonably good understanding of the firm's competitive strategy. Although outside analysts have an information disadvantage relative to the firm's managers, they are more objective in evaluating the economic consequences of the firm's investment and operating decisions. Figure 1.3 provides a schematic overview of how business intermediaries use financial statements to accomplish four key steps: (1) business strategy analysis, (2) accounting analysis, (3) financial analysis, and (4) prospective analysis.

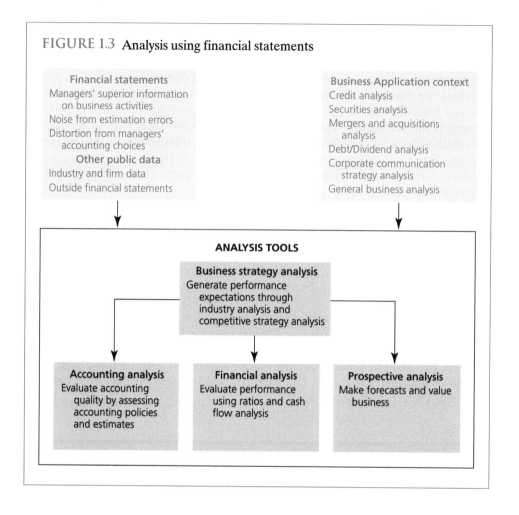

FIGURE 1.3 Analysis using financial statements

Financial statements
Managers' superior information on business activities
Noise from estimation errors
Distortion from managers' accounting choices

Other public data
Industry and firm data
Outside financial statements

Business Application context
Credit analysis
Securities analysis
Mergers and acquisitions analysis
Debt/Dividend analysis
Corporate communication strategy analysis
General business analysis

ANALYSIS TOOLS

Business strategy analysis
Generate performance expectations through industry analysis and competitive strategy analysis

Accounting analysis
Evaluate accounting quality by assessing accounting policies and estimates

Financial analysis
Evaluate performance using ratios and cash flow analysis

Prospective analysis
Make forecasts and value business

Analysis step 1: Business strategy analysis

The purpose of business strategy analysis is to identify key profit drivers and business risks, and to assess the company's profit potential at a qualitative level. Business strategy analysis involves analyzing a firm's industry and its strategy to create a sustainable competitive advantage. This qualitative analysis is an essential first step because it enables the analyst to frame the subsequent accounting and financial analysis better. For example, identifying the key success factors and key business risks allows the identification of key accounting policies. Assessment of a firm's competitive strategy facilitates evaluating whether current profitability is sustainable. Finally, business analysis enables the analyst to make sound assumptions in forecasting a firm's future performance. We discuss business strategy analysis in further detail in Chapter 2.

Analysis step 2: Accounting analysis

The purpose of accounting analysis is to evaluate the degree to which a firm's accounting captures the underlying business reality. By identifying places where there is accounting flexibility, and by evaluating the appropriateness of the firm's accounting policies and estimates, analysts can assess the degree of distortion in a firm's accounting numbers. Another important step in accounting analysis is to "undo" any accounting distortions by recasting a firm's accounting numbers to create unbiased accounting data. Sound accounting analysis improves the reliability of conclusions from financial analysis, the next step in financial statement analysis. Accounting analysis is the topic in Chapters 3 and 4.

Analysis step 3: Financial analysis

The goal of financial analysis is to use financial data to evaluate the current and past performance of a firm and to assess its sustainability. There are two important skills related to financial analysis. First, the analysis should be systematic and efficient. Second, the analysis should allow the analyst to use financial data to explore business issues. Ratio analysis and cash flow analysis are the two most commonly used financial tools. Ratio analysis focuses on evaluating a firm's product market performance and financial policies; cash flow analysis focuses on a firm's liquidity and financial flexibility. Financial analysis is discussed in Chapter 5.

Analysis step 4: Prospective analysis

Prospective analysis, which focuses on forecasting a firm's future, is the final step in business analysis. (This step is explained in Chapters 6, 7, and 8.) Two commonly used techniques in prospective analysis are financial statement forecasting and valuation. Both these tools allow the synthesis of the insights from business analysis, accounting analysis, and financial analysis in order to make predictions about a firm's future.

While the value of a firm is a function of its future cash flow performance, it is also possible to assess a firm's value based on the firm's current book value of equity, and its future return on equity (ROE) and growth. Strategy analysis, accounting analysis, and financial analysis, the first three steps in the framework discussed here, provide an excellent foundation for estimating a firm's intrinsic value. Strategy analysis, in addition to enabling sound accounting and financial analysis, also helps in assessing potential changes in a firm's competitive advantage and their implications for the firm's future ROE and growth. Accounting analysis provides an unbiased estimate of a firm's current book value and ROE. Financial analysis facilitates an in-depth understanding of what drives the firm's current ROE.

The predictions from a sound business analysis are useful to a variety of parties and can be applied in various contexts. The exact nature of the analysis will depend on the context. The contexts that we will examine include securities analysis, credit evaluation, mergers and acquisitions, evaluation of debt and dividend policies, and assessing corporate communication strategies. The four analytical steps described above are useful in each of these contexts. Appropriate use of these tools, however, requires a familiarity with the economic theories and institutional factors relevant to the context.

There are several ways in which financial statement analysis can add value, even when capital markets are reasonably efficient. First, there are many applications of financial statement analysis whose focus is outside the capital market context – credit analysis, competitive benchmarking, analysis of mergers and acquisitions, to name a few. Second, markets become efficient precisely because some market participants rely on analytical tools such as the ones we discuss in this book to analyze information and make investment decisions.

PUBLIC VERSUS PRIVATE CORPORATIONS

This book focuses primarily on public corporations. In some countries, financial statements of (unlisted) private corporations are also widely available. For example, the member states of the European Union (E.U.) require that privately held corporations prepare their financial statements under a common set of rules and make their financial statements publicly available. All corporations must prepare at least single company financial statements, while parent corporations of large groups must also prepare consolidated financial statements.[3] Consolidated financial statements are typically more appropriate for use in business analysis and valuation because these statements report the combined assets, liabilities, revenues, and expenses of the parent company and its subsidiaries. Single company financial statements report the assets, liabilities, revenues, and expenses of the parent company only and therefore provide little insight into the activities of subsidiaries.

E.U. law also requires that private corporations' financial statements be audited by an external auditor, although member states may exempt small corporations from this requirement.[4] The way in which private corporations in the E.U. make their financial statements available to the public is typically by filing these with a local public register that is maintained by agencies such as the companies register, the chamber of commerce, or the national bank.[5]

Private corporations' financial statements can be, and are being, used for business analysis and valuation. For example, venture capitalists, which provide equity funds to mostly private start-up companies, can use financial statements to evaluate potential investments. Nevertheless, although private corporations' financial statements are also subject to accounting standards, their usefulness in business analysis and valuation is less than that of public corporations' financial statements for the following reasons.[6] First, information and incentive problems are smaller in private corporations than in public corporations. Investors and managers of private corporations maintain close relationships and communicate their information through other means than public financial reports, such as personal communication or ad hoc reports. Because public reporting plays only a small role in communication, managers of private corporations have little incentive to make their public financial statements informative about the underlying business reality. Second, private corporations often produce one set of financial statements that meets the requirements of both tax rules and accounting rules. Tax rules grant managers less discretion in their assumptions than, for example, IFRS. Under tax rules, the recording of costs and benefits is also typically more associated with the payment and receipt of cash than with the underlying economic activities. Consequently, when private corporations' financial statements also comply with tax rules, they are less useful in assessing the corporations' true economic performance.[7]

SUMMARY

Financial statements provide the most widely available data on public corporations' economic activities; investors and other stakeholders rely on them to assess the plans and performance of firms and corporate managers. Accrual accounting data in financial statements are noisy, and unsophisticated investors can assess firms' performance only imprecisely. Financial analysts who understand managers' disclosure strategies have an opportunity to create inside information from public data, and they play a valuable role in enabling outside parties to evaluate a firm's current and prospective performance.

This chapter has outlined the framework for business analysis with financial statements, using the four key steps: business strategy analysis, accounting analysis, financial analysis, and prospective analysis. The remaining chapters in this book describe these steps in greater detail and discuss how they can be used in a variety of business contexts.

DISCUSSION QUESTIONS

1. Matti, who has just completed his first finance course, is unsure whether he should take a course in business analysis and valuation using financial statements since he believes that financial analysis adds little value, given the efficiency of capital markets. Explain to Matti when financial analysis can add value, even if capital markets are efficient.

2. Accounting statements rarely report financial performance without error. List three types of errors that can arise in financial reporting.

3. Juan Perez argues that "learning how to do business analysis and valuation using financial statements is not very useful, unless you are interested in becoming a financial analyst." Comment.

4. Four steps for business analysis are discussed in the chapter (strategy analysis, accounting analysis, financial analysis, and prospective analysis). As a financial analyst, explain why each of these steps is a critical part of your job and how they relate to one another.

NOTES

1. G. Akerlof, "The Market for 'Lemons': Quality Uncertainty and the Market Mechanism," *Quarterly Journal of Economics* (August 1970): 488–500.
2. Other countries have similar standard-setting bodies. For example, in the U.S., accounting standards are called Generally Accepted Accounting Principles (U.S. GAAP) and are promulgated by the Financial Accounting Standards Board (FASB). The FASB and IASB cooperate to eliminate differences between U.S. GAAP and IFRS and to develop new common standards.
3. The Seventh E.U. Company Law Directive, which governs the preparation of consolidated financial statements in the E.U., defines large groups as those meeting at least two of the following three criteria in two consecutive years: (1) total assets above €14.6 million, (2) annual turnover above €29.2 million, and (3) more than 250 employees.
4. The Fourth E.U. Company Law Directive, which governs corporations' financial reporting in the E.U., defines small corporations as those failing to meet two of the following three criteria in two consecutive years: (1) total assets above €3.65 million, (2) annual turnover above €7.3 million, and (3) more than 50 employees.
5. It should be noted that although the E.U. regulations have partly harmonized private corporations' accounting, the accessibility of public registers varies greatly and private corporations' financial statements are therefore in practice not equally available across the E.U.
6. See R. Ball and L. Shivakumar, "Earnings Quality in UK Private Firms: Comparative Loss Recognition Timeliness," *Journal of Accounting and Economics* 39 (2005): 83–128, and

D. Burgstahler, L. Hail and C. Leuz, "The Importance of Reporting Incentives: Earnings Management in European Private and Public Firms," *The Accounting Review* (forthcoming).

7. The influence of tax rules is particularly strong on single company financial statements, which in many countries are the basis for tax computations. Although the influence of tax rules on consolidated financial statements is less direct, tax considerations may still affect the preparation of these statements. For example, companies may support their aggressive tax choices by having the consolidated statements conform to the single company statements.

APPENDIX: DEFINING EUROPE

At various places in this book we refer to "Europe" and "European companies" without intending to imply that all European countries and companies are exactly alike. Because Europe's richness in diversity makes it impossible to describe the institutional details of each European country in detail, this book discusses primarily the commonalities between the countries that have chosen to harmonize the differences among their accounting systems. These countries are the 25 member states of the European Union as well as the three members of the European Economic Area (Iceland, Norway, and Liechtenstein), which are also committed to following E.U. accounting Directives. Of particular importance to the topic of this book is that, since 2005, companies from these 28 countries that have their shares publicly traded on a stock exchange are required to prepare their financial statements in accordance with IFRS. A special position is occupied by Switzerland, which is neither a member of the E.U. nor of the European Economic Area. Many of the issues that we address in this book also apply to a large group of Swiss listed companies, because Switzerland requires its listed companies with international operations to prepare IFRS-based financial statements.

In some of the chapters in this book we summarize the financial ratios, stock returns, and operational characteristics of a representative sample of listed European companies for illustrative purposes. This sample is composed of all domestic companies that were listed on one of the largest seven European stock exchanges (or their predecessors) between April 1989 (labeled the start of fiscal year 1989) and April 2006 (labeled the end of fiscal year 2005). Table 1.1 displays the seven largest European stock exchanges at the end of December 2005 and their countries of operation. The sample contains observations from 6,951 European companies operating in non-financial industries.

TABLE 1.1 European stock exchanges

Country	Stock exchange	Total market capitalization of domestic companies at December 2005 (in € billions)
Belgium	Euronext Brussels	244.6
Denmark	OMX Exchanges (combined)	680.4
Finland	OMX Exchanges (combined)	680.4
France	Euronext Paris	1,490.9
Germany	Deutsche Börse	1,035.3
Italy	Borsa Italiana	676.6
Netherlands	Euronext Amsterdam	528.1
Portugal	Euronext Lisbon	53.1
Spain	Bolsa y Mercados Españoles (BME)	813.8
Sweden	OMX Exchanges (combined)	680.4
Switzerland	SWX Swiss Exchange	793.1
United Kingdom	London Stock Exchange	2,599.4

Source: Eurostat and the World Federation of Exchanges. Euronext is a Pan-European exchange that was formed from the merger of the exchanges of Amsterdam, Brussels, Lisbon, and Paris. OMX Exchanges includes the exchanges of Copenhagen, Helsinki, Stockholm, Tallinn, Riga, and Vilnius. The reported market capitalizations of the Euronext segments represent the sizes of the individual segments. The reported market capitalization of the OMX Exchanges represents the total sum of the sizes of the individual segments.

The role of capital market intermediaries in the dot-com crash of 2000

The rise and fall of the internet consultants

In the summer of 1999, a host of Internet consulting firms made their debut on the Nasdaq. Scient Corporation, which had been founded less than two years earlier in March 1997, went public in May 1999 at an IPO price of $20 per share ($10 on a pre-split basis). Its close on the first day of trading was $32.63. Other Internet consulting companies that went public that year included Viant Corporation, IXL Enterprises, and US Interactive (see Exhibit 1).

The main value proposition of these companies was that they would be able to usher in the new Internet era by lending their information technology and web expertise to traditional "old economy" companies that wanted to gain Web-based technology, as well as to the emerging dot-com sector. Other companies like Sapient Corporation and Cambridge Technology Partners had been doing IT consulting for years, but this new breed of companies was able to capitalize on the burgeoning demand for Internet expertise.

Over the following months, the stock prices of the Internet consultants rose dramatically. Scient traded at a high of $133.75 in March 2000. However, this was after a 2–1 split, so each share was actually worth twice this amount on a pre-split basis. This stock level represented a 1238 percent increase from its IPO price and a valuation of 62 times the company's revenues for the fiscal year 2000. Similar performances were put in by the other companies in this group. However, these valuation levels proved to be unsustainable. The stock prices of web consulting firms dropped sharply in April 2000 along with many others in the Internet sector, following what was afterwards seen as a general "correction" in the Nasdaq. The prices of the Web consultants seemed to stabilize for a while, and many analysts continued to write favorably about their prospects and maintained buy ratings on their stocks. But starting early in September 2000, after some bad news from Viant Corporation and many subsequent analyst downgrades, the stocks went into a free-fall. All were trading in the single digits by February of 2001, representing a greater than 95 percent drop from their peak valuations (see Exhibit 2).

The dramatic rise and fall of the stock prices of the Web consultants, along with many others in the Internet sector, caused industry observers to wonder how this could have happened in a relatively sophisticated capital market like that of the United States. Several well-respected venture capitalists, investment banks, accounting firms, financial analysts, and money management companies were involved in bringing these companies to market and rating and trading their shares (see Exhibit 3). Who, if anyone, caused the Internet stock price bubble? What, if anything, could be done to avoid the recurrence of such stock market bubbles?

Gillian Elcock, MBA '01, prepared this case under the supervision of Professor Krishna Palepu. The case is intended solely as the basis for class discussion and is not intended to serve as an endorsement, source of primary data, or illustration of effective or ineffective management. Copyright © 2001 by the President and Fellows of Harvard College. HBS Case 9–103–083.

Context: *The technology bull market*

The 1980s and 1990s marked the beginning of a global technology revolution that started with the personal computer (PC) and led to the Internet era. Companies like Apple, Microsoft, Intel, and Dell Computer were at the forefront of this new wave of technology that promised to enhance productivity and efficiency through the computerization and automation of many processes.

The capital markets recognized the value that was being created by these companies. Microsoft, which was founded in 1975, had a market capitalization of over $600 billion by the beginning of 2000, making it the world's most valuable company, and its founder, Bill Gates, one of the richest men in the world. High values were also given to many of the other blue-chip technology firms such as Intel and Dell (Exhibit 4).

The 1990s ushered in a new group of companies that were based on information networks. These included AOL, Netscape, and Cisco. Netscape was a visible symbol of the emerging importance of the Internet: its browser gave regular users access to the World Wide Web, whereas previously the Internet had been mostly the domain of academics and experts. In March 2000, Cisco Systems, which made the devices that routed information across the Internet, overtook Microsoft as the world's most valuable company (based on market capitalization). This seemed further evidence of the value shift that was taking place from PC-focused technologies and companies to those that were based on the global information network.

It appeared obvious that the Internet was going to profoundly change the world through greater computing power, ease of communication, and the host of technologies that could be built upon it. Opportunities to build new services and technologies were boundless, and they were global in scale. The benefits of the Internet were expected to translate into greater economic productivity through the lowering of communication and transaction costs. It also seemed obvious that someone would be able to capitalize upon these market opportunities and that "the next Microsoft" would soon appear. No one who missed out on the original Microsoft wanted to do so the second time around.

A phrase that became popularized during this time was the "new economy." New economy companies, as opposed to old economy ones (exemplified by companies in traditional manufacturing, retail, and commodities), based their business models around exploiting the Internet. They were usually small compared to their old economy counterparts, with little need for their real-world "bricks and mortar" structures, preferring to outsource much of the capital intensive parts of the business and concentrate on the higher value-added, information-intensive elements. Traditional companies, finding their market shares and business models attacked by a host of nimble, specialized dot-com start-ups, lived in danger of "being Amazoned." To many, the new economy was the future and old economy companies would become less and less relevant.

The capital markets seemed to think similarly. From July 1999 to February 2000, as the Nasdaq Composite Index (which was heavily weighted with technology and Internet stocks) rose by 74.4 percent, the Dow Jones Industrial Average (which was composed mainly of old economy stocks) fell by 7.7 percent. Investors no longer seemed interested in anything that was not new economy.

Internet gurus and economists predicted the far-reaching effects of the Internet. The following excerpts represent the mood of the time:

> *Follow the personal computer and you can reach the pot of gold. Follow anything else and you will end up in a backwater. What the Model T was to the industrial era … the PC is to the information age. Just as people who rode the wave of automobile technology – from tire makers to fast food franchisers – prevailed in the industrial*

era, so the firms that prey on the passion and feed on the force of the computer community will predominate in the information era.[1]

George Gilder, 1992

* * * * *

Due to technological advances in PC-based communications, a new medium – with the Internet, the World Wide Web, and TCP/IP at its core – is emerging rapidly. The market for Internet-related products and services appears to be growing more rapidly than the early emerging markets for print publishing, telephony, film, radio, recorded music, television, and personal computers. … Based on our market growth estimates, we are still at the very early stages of a powerful secular growth cycle.[2]

Mary Meeker, Morgan Stanley Dean Witter, February 1996

* * * * *

The easy availability of smart capital – the ability of entrepreneurs to launch potentially world-beating companies on a shoestring, and of investors to intelligently spread risk – may be the new economy's most devastating innovation. At the same time, onrushing technological change requires lumbering dinosaurs to turn themselves into clever mammals overnight. Some will. But for many others, the only thing left to talk about is the terms of surrender.[3]

The Wall Street Journal, April 17, 2000

In the new economy, gaining market share was considered key because of the benefits of network effects. In addition, a large customer base was needed to cover the high fixed costs often associated with doing business. Profitability was of a secondary concern, and Netscape was one of the first of many Internet companies to go public without positive earnings. Some companies deliberately operated at losses because it was essential to spend a lot early to gain market share, which would presumably translate at a later point into profitability. This meant that revenue growth was the true measure of success for many Internet companies. Of course there were some dissenting voices, warning that this was just a period of irrational exuberance and the making of a classic stock market bubble. But for the most part, investors seemed to buy into the concept, as evidenced by the values given to several loss-making dot-coms (Exhibit 5).

Scient Corporation

The history of Scient, considered a leader in the Internet consulting space, is representative of what happened to the entire industry. The firm was founded in November 1997. Its venture capital backers included several leading firms such as Sequoia Capital and Benchmark Capital (see Exhibit 3).

Scient described itself as "a leading provider of a new category of professional services called eBusiness systems innovation" that would "rapidly improve a client's competitive position through the development of innovative business strategies

---

1. *Mary Meeker and Chris DePuy, "U.S. Investment Research, Technology/New Media, The Internet Report"* (*Excerpt from* Life After Television *by George Gilder, 1992), Morgan Stanley Dean Witter, February 1996.*
2. *Mary Meeker and Chris DePuy, "U.S. Investment Research, Technology/New Media, The Internet Report," Morgan Stanley Dean Witter, February 1996.*
3. *John Browning and Spencer Reiss, "For the New Economy, the End of the Beginning,"* The Wall Street Journal, *April 17, 2000.*

enabled by the integration of emerging and existing technologies."[4] Its aim was to provide services in information technology and systems design as well as high-level strategy consulting, previously the domain of companies such as McKinsey and The Boston Consulting Group.

The company grew quickly to almost 2,000 people within three years, primarily organically. Its client list included AT&T, Chase Manhattan, Johnson & Johnson, and Homestore.com.[5] As with any consulting firm, its ability to attract and retain talented employees was crucial, since they were its main assets.

By the fiscal year ending in March 2000, Scient had a net loss of $16 million on revenues of $156 million (see financial statements in Exhibit 6). These revenues represented an increase of 653 percent over the previous year. Analysts wrote glowingly about the firm's prospects. In February 2000, when the stock was trading at around $87.25, a Deutsche Bank Alex Brown report stated:

> We have initiated research coverage of Scient with a BUY investment rating on the shares. In our view Scient possesses several key comparative advantages: (1) an outstanding management team; (2) a highly scalable and leverageable operating model; (3) a strong culture, which attracts the best and the brightest; (4) a private equity portfolio, which enhances long-term relationships and improves retention; and (5) an exclusive focus on the high-end systems innovation market with eBusiness and industry expertise, rapid time-to-market and an integrated approach…. Scient shares are currently trading at roughly 27x projected CY00 revenues, modestly ahead of pure play leaders like Viant (24x) and Proxicom (25x), and ahead of our interactive integrator peer group average of just over 16x. Our 12-month price target is $120. It is a stock we would want to own.[6]

And in March 2000, when the stock was at $77.75, Morgan Stanley, which had given Scient an "outperform" rating, wrote:

> All said we believe Scient continues to effectively execute on what is a very aggressive business plan…. While shares of SCNT trade at a premium valuation to its peer group, we continue to believe that such level is warranted given the company's high-end market focus, short but impressive record of execution, and deep/experienced management team. As well, in our view there is a high probability of meaningful upward revisions to Scient's model.[7]

Scient's stock reached a high of $133.75 in March 2000 but fell to $44 by June as part of the overall drop in valuation of most of the technology sector. In September the company announced it had authorized a stock repurchase of $25 million. But in December 2000 it lowered its revenue and earnings expectations for the fourth quarter due to the slowdown in demand for Internet consulting services. The company also announced plans to lay off 460 positions worldwide (over 20 percent of its workforce) as well as to close two of its offices, and an associated $40–$45 million restructuring charge. By February 2001 the stock was trading at $2.94.

Most of the analysts that covered Scient had buy or strong buy ratings on the company as its stock rose to its peak and even after the Nasdaq correction in April 2000. Then in September a warning by Viant Corporation of results that would come

---

4. *Scient Corporation Prospectus, May 1999. Available from Edgar Online.*

5. *Scient Corporation website, <http://www.scient.com/non/content/clients/client_list/index.asp>*

6. *F. Mark D'Annolfo, William S. Zinsmeister and Jeffrey A. Buchbinder, "Scient Corporation Premier Builder of eBusinesses," Deutsche Bank Alex Brown, February 14, 2000.*

7. *Michael A. Sherrick and Mary Meeker, "Scient Corporation Quarter Update," Morgan Stanley Dean Witter, March 2, 2000.*

in below expectations, due to a slowdown in e-business spending from large corporate clients, prompted many analysts to downgrade most of the companies in the sector, including Scient. Several large mutual fund companies were holders of Scient as its stock rose, peaked, and fell (see Exhibit 7).

As the major technology indices continued their slump during late 2000 and early 2001, and the stock prices of the Internet consulting firms floundered in the single digits, they received increasing attention from the press:

> *Examining the downfall of the eConsultants provides an excellent case study of failed business models. Rose-colored glasses, a lack of a sustainable competitive advantage, and a "me too" mentality are just some of the mistakes these companies made… . The eConsultants failed to do the one thing that they were supposed to be helping their clients do – build a sustainable business model … many eConsultants popped up and expected to be able to take on the McKinseys and Booz Allens of the world. Now they are discovering that the relationships firmly established by these old economy consultants are integral to building a sustainable competitive advantage.*[8]

* * * * *

> *Seems like everything dot-com is being shunned by investors these days. But perhaps no other group has experienced quite the brutality that Web consultancies have. Once the sweethearts of Wall Street, their stocks are now high-tech whipping boys. Even financial analysts, who usually strive to be positive about companies they cover, seem to have given up on the sector. … Many of these firms were built on the back of the dot-com boom. Now these clients are gone. At the same time, pressure on bricks-and-mortar companies to build online businesses has lifted, leading to the cancellation or delay of Web projects.*[9]

The analysts who were formerly excited about Scient's prospects and had recommended the stock when it was trading at almost $80 per share now seemed much less enthusiastic. In January 2001, with the stock around $3.44, Morgan Stanley wrote:

> *We maintain our Neutral rating due to greater than anticipated market weakness, accelerating pricing pressure, the potential for increased turnover and management credibility issues. While shares of SCNT trade at a depressed valuation, we continue to believe that turnover and pricing pressure could prove greater than management's assumptions. While management indicated it would be "aggressive" to maintain its people, we still believe it will be difficult to maintain top-tier talent in the current market and company specific environment.*[10]

Performance of the Nasdaq

The performance of the stock prices of Scient and its peers mirrored that of many companies in the Internet sector. So dramatic was the drop in valuation of these companies that this period was subsequently often referred to as the "dot-com crash."

In the months following the crash, the equity markets essentially closed their doors to the Internet firms. Several once high-flying dot-coms, operating at losses and starved for cash, filed for bankruptcy or closed down their operations (see Exhibit 8).

---

8. *Todd N. Lebor, "The Downfall of Internet Consultants," Fool's Den, Fool.com, December 11, 2000.*
9. *Amey Stone, "Streetwise: Who'll Help the Web Consultants?" BusinessWeek Online, February 15, 2001.*
10. *Michael A. Sherrick, Mary Meeker, and Douglas Levine, "Scient Corporation. Outlook Remains Cloudy, Adjusting Forecasts," Morgan Stanley Dean Witter, January 18, 2001.*

The Nasdaq, which had reached a high of 5,132.52 in March of 2000 closed at 2,470.52 in December 2000, a drop of 52 percent from its high. As of February 2001 it had not recovered, closing at 2,151.83.

Capital market intermediaries

The role of intermediaries in a well functioning market

In a capitalist economy, individuals and institutions have savings that they want to invest, and companies need capital to finance and grow their businesses. The capital markets provide a way for this to occur efficiently. Companies issue debt or equity to investors who are willing to part with their cash now because they expect to earn an adequate return in the future for the risk they are taking.

However, there is an information gap between investors and companies. Investors usually do not have enough information or expertise to determine the good investments from the bad ones. And companies do not usually have the infrastructure and know-how to directly receive capital from investors. Therefore, both parties rely on intermediaries to help them make these decisions. These intermediaries include accountants, lawyers, regulatory bodies (such as the SEC in the United States), investment banks, venture capitalists, money management firms, and even the media (see Exhibit 9). The focus of this case is on the equity markets in the United States.

In a well functioning system, with the incentives of intermediaries fully aligned in accordance with their fiduciary responsibility, public markets will correctly value companies such that investors earn a normal "required" rate of return. In particular, companies that go public will do so at a value which will give investors this fair rate of investment.

The public market valuation will have a trickle down effect on all intermediaries in the investment chain. Venture capitalists, who typically demand a very high return on investment, and usually exit their portfolio companies through an IPO, will do their best to ensure these companies have good management teams and a sustainable business model that will stand the test of time. Otherwise, the capital markets will put too low a value on the companies when they try to go public. Investment bankers will provide their expertise in helping companies to go public or to make subsequent offerings, and introducing them to investors.

On the other side of the process, portfolio managers, acting on behalf of investors will only buy companies that are fairly priced, and will sell companies if they become overvalued, since buying or holding an overvalued stock will inevitably result in a loss. Sell-side analysts, whose clients include portfolio managers and therefore investors, will objectively monitor the performance of public companies and determine whether or not their stocks are good or bad investments at any point in time. Accountants audit the financial statements of companies, ensuring that they comply with established standards and represent the true states of the firms. This gives investors and analysts the confidence to make decisions based on these financial documents.

The integrity of this process is critical in an economy because it gives investors the confidence they need to invest their money into the system. Without this confidence, they would not plow their money back into the economy but instead keep it under the proverbial mattress.

What happened during the dot-com bubble?

Many observers believed that something went wrong with the system during the dot-com bubble. In April 2001, *BusinessWeek* wrote about "The Great Internet Money

Game. How America's top financial firms reaped billions from the Net boom, while investors got burned."[11] The following month, *Fortune* magazine's cover asked "Can we ever trust Wall Street again?"[12] referring to the way in which, in some people's opinions, Wall Street firms had led investors and companies astray before and after the dot-com debacle.

The implications of the Internet crash were far reaching. Many companies that needed to raise capital for investment found the capital markets suddenly shut to them. Millions of investors saw a large portion of their savings evaporate. This phenomenon was a likely contributor to the sharp drop in consumer confidence that took place in late 2000 and early 2001. In addition, the actual decrease in wealth threatened to dampen consumer spending. These factors, along with an overall slowing of the U.S. economy, threatened to put the United States into recession for the first time in over 10 years.

On a more macro level, the dot-coms used up valuable resources that could have been more efficiently allocated within the economy. The people who worked at failed Internet firms could have spent their time and energy creating lasting value in other endeavors, and the capital that funded the dot-coms could have been plowed into viable, lasting companies that would have benefited the overall economy. However, it could be argued that there were benefits as well, and that the large investment in the technology sector positioned the United States to be a world leader in the future.

Nevertheless, the question remained: how could the dot-com bubble occur in a sophisticated capital market system like that of the United States? Why did the market allow the valuations of many Internet companies to go so high? What was the role of the intermediaries in the process that gave rise to the stock market bubble?

Key intermediaries

One way to try to answer some of these questions is to look more closely at some of the players in the investing chain. Much of the material in the following sections is derived from interviews with representatives from each sector.

Venture capitalists

Venture capitalists (VCs) provided capital for companies in their early stages of development. They sought to provide a very high rate of return to their investors for the associated risk. This was typically accomplished by selling their stake in their portfolio companies either to the public through an IPO, or to another company in a trade sale.

The partners in a VC firm typically had a substantial percentage of their net worth tied up in their funds, which aligned their interests with their investors. Their main form of compensation was a large share of profits (typically 20 percent) in addition to a relatively low fee based on the assets under management.

A large part of a VC's job was to screen good business ideas and entrepreneurial teams from bad ones. Partners at a VC firm were typically very experienced, savvy business people who worked closely with their portfolio companies to both monitor and guide them to a point where they have turned a business idea into a well managed, fully functional company that could stand on its own. In a sense, their role was to nurture the companies until they reached a point where they were ready to face the

---

11. Peter Elstrom, "The Great Internet Money Game. How America's top financial firms reaped billions from the Net boom while investors got burned," BusinessWeek e.biz, April 16, 2001.
12. Fortune, May 14, 2001.

scrutiny of the public capital markets after an IPO. Typically, companies would not go public until they had shown profits for at least three quarters.[13]

After the dot-com crash, some investors and the media started pointing fingers at the venture capitalists that had invested in many of the failed dot-coms. They blamed them for being unduly influenced by the euphoria of the market, and knowingly investing in and bringing public companies with questionable business models, or that had not yet proven themselves operationally. Indeed, many of the dot-coms went public within record time of receiving VC funding – a study of venture-backed initial public offerings showed that companies averaged 5.4 years in age when they went public in 1999, compared with 8 years in 1995.[14]

Did the venture capital investing process change in a way that contributed to the Internet bubble of 2000? According to a partner at a venture capital firm that invested in one of the Internet consulting companies, the public markets had a tremendous impact on the way VCs invested during the late 1990s.[15] He felt that, because of expectations of high stock market valuations, VC firms invested in companies during the late 1990s that they would not have invested in under ordinary circumstances. He also believed that the ready availability of money affected the business strategies and attitudes of the Internet companies: "If the [management] team knows $50 million is available, it acts differently, i.e., 'go for market share.'"

The VC partner acknowledged that VCs took many Internet companies public very early, but he felt that the responsibility of scrutinizing these companies lay largely with the investors that subscribed to the IPOs: "If a mutual fund wants to invest in the IPO of a company that has no track record, profitability, etcetera but sees it as a liquidity event, it has made a decision to become a VC. Lots of mutual funds thought 'VC is easy, I want a piece of it.'"

Investment bank underwriters

Entrepreneurs relied on investment banks (such as Goldman Sachs, Morgan Stanley Dean Witter and Credit Suisse First Boston) in the actual process of doing an initial public offering, or "going public." Investment banks provided advisory financial services, helped the companies price their offerings, underwrite the shares, and introduce them to investors, often in the form of a road show.

Investment banks were paid a commission based on the amount of money that the company manages to raise in its offering, typically of the order of 7 percent.[16] Several blue-chip firms were involved in the capital-raising process of the Internet consultants (see Exhibit 3), and they also received a share of the blame for the dot-com crash in the months that followed it. In an article entitled "Just Who Brought Those Duds to Market?," the *New York Times* wrote:

> … *many Wall Street investment banks, from top-tier firms like Goldman, Sachs … to newer entrants like Thomas Weisel Partners … have reason to blush. In one blindingly fast riches-to-rags story, Pets.com filed for bankruptcy just nine months after Merrill Lynch took it public.*

---

13. Peter Elstrom, *"The Great Internet Money Game. How America's top financial firms reaped billions from the Net boom while investors got burned,"* BusinessWeek e.biz, April 16, 2001.
14. Shawn Neidorf, *"Venture-Backed IPOs Make a Comeback,"* Venture Capital Journal, *August 1, 1999.*
15. *Limited partners are the investors in a venture capital fund; the venture capital firm itself usually serves as the general partner.*
16. *Source: case writer interview.*

Of course, investment banks that took these underperforming companies public may not care. They bagged enormous fees, a total of more than $600 million directly related to initial public offerings involving just the companies whose stocks are now under $1.

… How did investment banks, paid for their expert advice, pick such lemons?[17]

Sell-side analysts

Sell-side analysts worked at investment banks and brokerage houses. One of their main functions was to publish research on public companies. Each analyst typically followed 15 to 30 companies in a particular industry, and his or her job involved forming relationships with and talking to the managements of the companies, following trends in the industry, and ultimately making buy or sell recommendations on the stocks. The recommendations analysts made could be very influential with investors. If a well respected analyst downgraded a stock, the reaction from the market could be severe and swift, resulting in a same-day drop in the stock price. Sell-side analysts typically interacted with buy-side analysts and portfolio managers at money management companies (the buy-side) to market or "sell" their ideas. In addition, they usually provided support during a company's IPO process, providing research to the buy-side before the company actually went public. Sell-side analysts were usually partly compensated based on the amount of trading fees and investment banking revenue they helped the firm to generate through their research.

In the months following the dot-com crash, sell-side technology and Internet analysts found themselves the target of criticism for having buy ratings on companies that had subsequently fallen drastically in price. Financial cable TV channel CNBC ran a report called "Analyzing the Analysts," addressing the issue of whether or not they were to blame for their recommendations of tech stocks. A March 2001 article in *The Wall Street Journal* raised similar issues after it was reported that J.P. Morgan Chase's head of European research sent out a memo requiring all the company's analysts to show their stock recommendation changes to the company involved and to the investment banking division.[18] The previously mentioned issue of *Forbes* featured an article criticizing Mary Meeker, a prominent Internet analyst.[19] And a *Financial Times* article entitled "Shoot all the analysts" made a sweeping criticism of their role in the market bubble:

… instead of forecasting earnings per share, they were now in the business of fore-casting share prices themselves. And those prices were almost always very optimistic. Now, at last, they have had their comeuppance. Much of what many of them have done in the past several years has turned out to be worthless. High-flying stocks that a year ago were going to be cheap at twice the price have halved or worse – and some analysts have been putting out buy recommendations all the way down. … They should learn a little humility and get back to analysis.[20]

Responding to the media criticism of financial analysts, Karl Keirstead, a Lehman Brothers analyst who followed Internet consulting firms, stated:

It is too easy as they do on CNBC to slam the analysts for recommending stocks when they were very expensive. In the case of the Internet consulting firms, looking

17. Andrew Ross Sorkin, "Just Who Brought Those Duds to Market?" New York Times, April 15, 2001.
18. Wade Lambert and Jathon Sapsford, "J.P. Morgan Memo to Analysts Raises Eyebrows," The Wall Street Journal, March 22, 2001.
19. Peter Elkind, "Where Mary Meeker Went Wrong," Fortune, May 14, 2001.
20. "Shoot all the analysts," Financial Times, March 20, 2001.

back before the correction in April 2000, the fundamentals were "nothing short of pristine." The companies were growing at astronomical rates, and it looked as though they would continue to do so for quite a while. Under these assumptions, if you modeled out the financials for these companies and discounted them back at a reasonable rate, they did not seem all that highly valued. [21]

Keirstead also pointed out that there were times when it was legitimate to have a buy rating on a stock that was "overvalued" based on fundamentals:

The future price of a stock is not always tied to the discounted value of cash flow or earnings, it is equal to what someone is willing to pay. This is especially true in periods of tremendous market liquidity and huge interest in young companies with illiquid stocks and steep growth curves that are difficult to project. The valuation may seem too high, but if the fundamentals are improving and Street psychology and hype are building, the stock is likely to rally. Stock pickers must pay as much attention to these factors as the company and industry fundamentals.

When asked his view on why the buy-side institutions went along with the high valuations that these companies were trading for, Keirstead commented, "A lot of buy-side analysts and portfolio managers became momentum investors in disguise. They claimed in their mutual fund prospectus that they made decisions based on fundamental analysis. Truth is, they played the momentum game as well."

Keirstead also commented on the criticism analysts had received for being too heavily influenced by the possibility of banking deals when making stock recommendations. He stated that this claim was "completely over-rated." Though there was some legitimacy to the argument and some of analysts' compensation did come from investment banking fees, it was a limited component. Analysts also got significant fees from the trading revenue they generated and from their published rankings.[22] He pointed out that critics' arguments were ludicrous because if analysts only made decisions based on banking fees, it would jeopardize their rankings and credibility with their buy-side clients. However, he did note that the potential deal flow could have distorted the view of some technology analysts during the boom.

Finally, Keirstead described the bias that was present on the sell side to be bullish:

To be negative when you are a sell-side analyst is to be a contrarian, to stick your neck out. You take a lot of heat, it's tough. And it would have been the wrong call for the last four years. Had I turned short in 1999 when these stocks seemed overvalued, I would have missed a 200 percent increase in the stocks. My view was: I can't be too valuation-sensitive. The stocks are likely to rise as long as the fundamentals hold, and that's the position a lot of analysts took.

Consistent with this optimistic bias, there were very few sell recommendations from analysts during the peak of the Internet stock bubble. According to financial information company First Call, more than 70 percent of the 27,000 plus recommendations outstanding on some 6,000 stocks in November 2000 were strong buys or buys, while fewer than 1percent were sells or strong sells.[23]

---

21. Source: case writer interview.

22. Several financial journals publish analyst rankings. The most prominent is Institutional Investor magazine, which publishes annual rankings of sell-side analysts by industry. These rankings are very influential in the analyst and investment community.

23. Walter Updegrave, "The ratings game," Money, January 2001.

Capital market intermediaries in the dot-com crash

Buy-side analysts and portfolio managers

The "buy-side" refers to institutions that do the actual buying and selling of public securities, such as mutual fund companies, insurance companies, hedge funds, and other asset managers.

There were two main roles on the buy side: analysts and portfolio managers. Buy-side analysts had some of the same duties as their sell-side counterparts. They were usually assigned to a group of companies within a certain industry and were responsible for doing industry research, talking to the companies' management teams, coming up with earning estimates, doing valuation analysis, and ultimately rating the stock prices of the companies as either "buys" or "sells." The analyst's job was not yet complete, however. Though they did not publish their research, buy-side analysts needed to convince the portfolio managers within their company to follow their recommendations.

Portfolio managers were the ones who actually managed money, whether it was a retail mutual fund or an institutional account. Though they listened to the recommendations of the analysts, they were the ones who were ultimately responsible for buying or selling securities.

The compensation of the buy-side analysts was often linked to how well their stock recommendations did, and in the case of portfolio managers, compensation was determined by the performance of their funds relative to an appropriate benchmark return. These compensation schemes were designed to align the incentives of buy-side analysts and portfolio managers with the interests of investors.

Why then, did so many buy-side firms buy and hold on to the Internet consulting firms during the market bubble? Did they really believe the companies were worth what they were trading for? Or did they know they were overvalued, but invest in them anyway for other reasons?

According to a former associate at a large mutual fund company, many people within his company knew that most of the Internet companies were overvalued before the market correction, but they felt pressure to invest anyway:

> *My previous employer is known as a value investor, growth at a reasonable price. At first the general impression in the firm was that a lot of the Internet firms would blow up, that they didn't deserve these valuations. But articles were written about my company … that it was being left behind because it was not willing to invest in the Internet companies. Some of the analysts at the firm began to recommend companies simply because they knew that the stock prices would go up, even though they were clearly overvalued. And portfolio managers felt that if they didn't buy the stocks, they would lag their benchmarks and their competitors – they are rewarded on a one-year term horizon and three-year horizon. It is very important to meet their benchmark, it makes up a material part of their compensation. In addition, they compare against the performance of their peers for marketing purposes.* [24]

The role of information

The accounting profession

Independent accountants audited the financial statements of public companies to verify their accuracy and freedom from fraud. If they were reasonably satisfied, they provided an unqualified opinion statement which was attached to the company's

---

24. Source: case writer interview.

public filings. If auditors were not fully satisfied, this was noted as well. Investors usually took heed of the auditor's opinion as it provided an additional level of assurance of the quality of the information they were receiving from companies.

In the year 2000, the accounting profession in the United States was dominated by five major accounting firms, collectively referred to as "The Big Five" (PriceWaterhouseCoopers, Deloitte & Touche, KPMG, Ernst & Young, and Arthur Andersen). The top 100 accounting firms had roughly a 50 percent share of the market and the Big Five account for about 84 percent of the revenues of the top 100.[25] However, the Big Five made up an even larger percentage of the auditing activity of Internet IPOs. Of the 410 Internet services and software IPOs between January 1998 and December 2000, 373 of them, or 91 percent, were audited by one of the Big Five accountants.[26]

During the aftermath of the dot-com crash, these firms came under some criticism for not adequately warning investors about the precarious financial position of some of the companies. *The Wall Street Journal* wrote an article addressing the fact that many dot-coms that went bankrupt were not given "going concern" clauses by their auditors. A going concern clause was included by an auditor if it had a substantial doubt that the company would be able to remain in operation for another 12 months:

> *In retrospect, critics say, there were early signs that the businesses weren't sustainable, including their reliance on external financing, rather than money generated by their own operations, to stay afloat. You wonder where some of the skepticism was... critics say many auditors appear to have presumed the capital markets would remain buoyant. For anybody to have assumed a continuation of those aberrant, irrational conditions was in itself irrational and unjustifiable whether it was an auditor, a board member or an investor....*[27]

However, in the same article, accountants defended their actions by noting that going concern judgments were subjective, and that they were not able to predict the future any better than the capital markets.

Dr. Howard Schilit, founder and CEO of CFRA, an independent financial research organization,[28] believed that accountants certainly had to take a part of the blame for what happened. In his opinion, they "looked the other way when they could have been more rigorous in doing their work."[29] However, he noted that the outcome may not have been materially different even if they did.

One particular criticism he had was that many accountants didn't look closely enough at the substance of transactions and didn't do enough questioning of the circumstances surrounding sales contracts. His hope was that accountants "go back and learn what the basic rules are of when revenues should be booked. The rules haven't changed whether this is the new economy or old economy."

FASB: A regulator

The Financial Accounting Standards Boards (FASB) was an independent regulatory body in the United States whose mission was to "establish and improve standards of

Capital market intermediaries in the dot-com crash

---

25. *"Accounting Today Top 100 Survey Shows All Is Well,"* The CPA Journal, *May 1999.*
26. *Information extracted from IPO web site <http://www.ipo.com>*
27. *Johnathan Weil, "'Going Concerns': Did Accountants Fail to Flag Problems at Dot-Com Casualties?"* The Wall Street Journal, *February 9, 2001.*
28. *CFRA's mission is to warn investors and creditors about companies experiencing operational problems and particularly those that employ unusual or aggressive accounting practices to camouflage such problems.*
29. *Source: case writer interview.*

financial accounting and reporting for the guidance and education of the public, including issuers, auditors, and users of financial information."[30] FASB standards were recognized by the Securities and Exchange Commission (SEC), which regulates the financial reporting of public companies in the United States.

The accounting practices of some new economy firms posed challenges for auditors and investors, and though some observers felt that the accountants were not doing a good enough job, others thought that the accounting rules themselves were too ambiguous, and this fact lent itself to exploitation by the companies.

Specific examples included the treatment of barter revenues in the case of companies that exchanged on-line advertising space, the practice of booking gross rather than net revenues in commission-based businesses (e.g., Priceline.com), and the issue of when to recognize revenues from long-term contracts (e.g., MicroStrategy Inc.). Given that the valuations of many Internet firms were driven by how quickly they grew revenues, there was a lot of incentive to inflate this number. In fact, the accounting practices of dot-coms became so aggressive that the SEC had to step in:

> *The Securities & Exchange Commission's crackdown on the aggressive accounting practices that have taken off among many dot-com firms really began … when it quietly issued new guidelines to refocus corporate management and investors…. To rein in what it saw as an alarming trend in inflated revenue reports, the SEC required companies using lax accounting practices to restate financial results by the end of their next fiscal year's quarter….*
>
> *The SEC has also directed the Financial Accounting Standards Board to review a range of Internet company accounting practices that could boost revenues or reduce costs unfairly. Under the scrutiny, more companies are likely to issue restatements of financial results….*[31]

In another spin on the issue, some questioned whether the accounting rules set out by the regulatory bodies had in fact become obsolete for the new economy. In July 2000, leaders in the accounting community told a Senate banking subcommittee that the United States needed "a new accounting model for the New Economy." A major concern of theirs was that the current rules did not allow companies to report the value of intangible assets on their balance sheets, such as customers, employees, suppliers and organization.[32] Others argued that the accounting rules caused Internet firms to appear unprofitable when they were actually making money. This was because old economy firms were allowed to capitalize their major investments such as factories, plants and equipment, whereas the rules did not allow capitalization of expenditures on R&D and marketing, which created value for many dot-com companies:

> *While Internet stocks may not be worth what they are selling for, the movement in their prices may not be as crazy as it seems. Many of these companies reporting losses actually make money – lots of it. It all has to do with accounting. Old-economy companies get to capitalize their most important investments, while new economy ones do not. While Amazon.com announces a loss almost every quarter, when it capitalizes its investments in intangibles that loss turns into a $400 million profit.*[33]

30. *FASB web site: <http: //accounting.rutgers.edu/raw/fasb/>*
31. *Catherine Yang, "Earth to Dot-Com Accountants,"* BusinessWeek, *April 3, 2000.*
32. *Stephen Barlas, "New accounting model demanded,"* Strategic Finance, *September 2000.*
33. *Geoffrey Colvin, "The Net's hidden profits,"* Fortune, *April 17, 2000.*

Retail investors

The role of the general public in the dot-com craze cannot be ignored. In addition to the people who poured money into mutual funds, many retail investors began trading on their own, often electronically. A group of avid day traders grew up, some of whom quit their regular jobs to devote all their time and energy to trading stocks. Analysts estimated that they made up almost 18 percent of the trading volume of the NYSE and Nasdaq in 2000.[34] Sites such as Yahoo Finance grew in popularity, while chat rooms devoted to stocks and trading proliferated.

The number of accounts of Internet stock brokers like Etrade and Ameritrade grew rapidly (Etrade grew from 544 thousand brokerage accounts in 1998 to 3 million in 2000 and Ameritrade grew from 98 thousand accounts in 1997 to 1.2 million in 2000) as they slashed their commissions, some to as low as $8/trade compared to the $50–$300[35] charged by traditional brokerage firms. These companies were dot-coms themselves and they were able to slash prices partly because they were operating at losses that they were not penalized for by the capital markets. This gave rise to an interesting positive feedback loop: the Etrades of the world, funded by the dot-com frenzied capital markets, slashed their prices and therefore encouraged more trading, which continued to fuel the enthusiasm of investors for the markets.

The financial press also became increasingly visible during this period. Several publications like *Barrons* and *The Wall Street Journal* had always been very influential in the financial community. However, a host of other information sources, often on the web, sprang up to support the new demand for information. CNBC and CNNfn, major network channels devoted to the markets, often featured analysts and portfolio managers making stock recommendations or giving their views on the market.

Many of the retail investors did not know much about finance or valuation, and often didn't understand much about the companies whose shares they were buying. They were therefore likely to be heavily influenced by some of the intermediaries previously described, especially the financial press, and the sell-side analysts that publicly upgraded and downgraded companies.

These investors were pointed to by some as having had a large role in driving Internet valuations to the levels they went to. The reasoning was that other more sophisticated buyers such as the institutional money managers may have bought over-valued companies because they thought they could easily sell them later at even higher valuations to "dumb retail investors."

The companies themselves

The entrepreneurs who founded the Internet consulting companies, and the management teams who ran them, could almost be described as bystanders to the process that took the stock prices of their companies to such lofty highs and then punishing lows. However, they were profoundly affected by these changes in almost every aspect of their businesses.

Obviously there were many benefits to having a high stock price. According to a managing director (MD) at one of the Internet consultants, the company was facing a very competitive labor market while trying to grow organically, and having a stock that

Capital market intermediaries in the dot-com crash

---

34. *Amy S. Butte, "Day Trading and Beyond. A New Niche Is Emerging," Bear Stearns Equity Research, April 2000.*
35. *Lee Patterson, "If you can't beat 'em…," Forbes, August 23, 1999.*

was doing well helped with recruiting people since the option part of the compensation package was attractive.[36] He also explained that people were proud to be a part of the firm, partly because the stock was doing so well.

As the stock price of the company continued to rise higher and higher, the MD admitted that he did become afraid that the market was overvaluing the company, and that this doubt probably went all the way up to the CEO. As he put it, "We were trading at just absurd levels."

When asked about his thoughts on his firm's current stock price, the MD thought that the market had over-reacted and gone to the other extreme. He remarked that investors were worried that the Internet consulting firms were facing renewed competition from companies like IBM, the Big Five accounting firms, and the strategy consulting firms. Overall, though the rise and fall of the company's stock price was in many ways a painful experience, this MD thought that the market bubble presented a good opportunity that the company was able to capitalize upon. It was able to do a secondary offering at a high price and now had lots of cash on its balance sheet. His view was that "If you look at competitive sustainability [in this business], it could boil down to the company with the best balance sheet wins."

The blame game

In the aftermath of the dot-com crash, many tried to pinpoint whose fault it was that the whole bubble occurred in the first place. As mentioned previously, sell-side analysts, often the most visible group in the investment community, came under frequent attack in the media, as did to some extent venture capitalists, investment bankers, and even the accounting industry. Company insiders (including the founder of Scient) were also scrutinized for selling large blocks of shares when the stock prices of their companies were near their peaks.[37]

A *Wall Street Journal* article entitled "Investors, Entrepreneurs All Play the Blame Game" described how these various players were trying to blame each other for what happened:

> *With the tech-heavy Nasdaq Composite Index dancing close to the 2,000 mark –*
> *down from over 5,000 – Internet entrepreneurs and venture capitalists have stepped*
> *up their finger-pointing about just who's at fault for the technology meltdown, which*
> *continues to topple businesses and once-cushy lifestyles…. Fingers pointed right and*
> *left – from entrepreneurs to venture capitalists, from analysts to day traders to share-*
> *holders – and back around again.[38]*

The Internet stock market bubble was certainly not the first to occur. Other notable instances include the Tulip Craze of the seventeenth century and the Nifty Fifty boom of the 1970s. In these cases market valuations went to unsustainably high levels and ended with a sharp decrease in valuation that left many investors empty-handed.

But the question of what happened in this latest bubble remained: who, if anyone, could be blamed for the dot-com rise and crash? How did the various intermediaries described here affect or cause what happened? Was there really a misalignment of incentives in the system? If so, could it be fixed so that this sort of thing did not

---

36. Source: case writer interview.

37. Mark Maremont and John Hechinger, "If Only You'd Sold Some Stock Earlier – Say $100 Million Worth," The Wall Street Journal, *March 22, 2001.*

38. Rebecca Buckman, "Investors, Entrepreneurs All Play the Blame Game," The Wall Street Journal, *March 5, 2001.*

happen in the future? Or were market bubbles an inevitable part of the way the economy functioned?

Questions

1. What is the intended role of each of the institutions and intermediaries discussed in the case for the effective functioning of capital markets?

2. Are their incentives aligned properly with their intended role? Whose incentives are most misaligned?

3. Who, if anyone, was primarily responsible for the Internet stock bubble?

4. What are the costs of such a stock market bubble? As a future business professional, what lessons do you draw from the bubble?

Capital market intermediaries in the dot-com crash

EXHIBIT 1 Timeline of the internet consultants: Founding and IPO

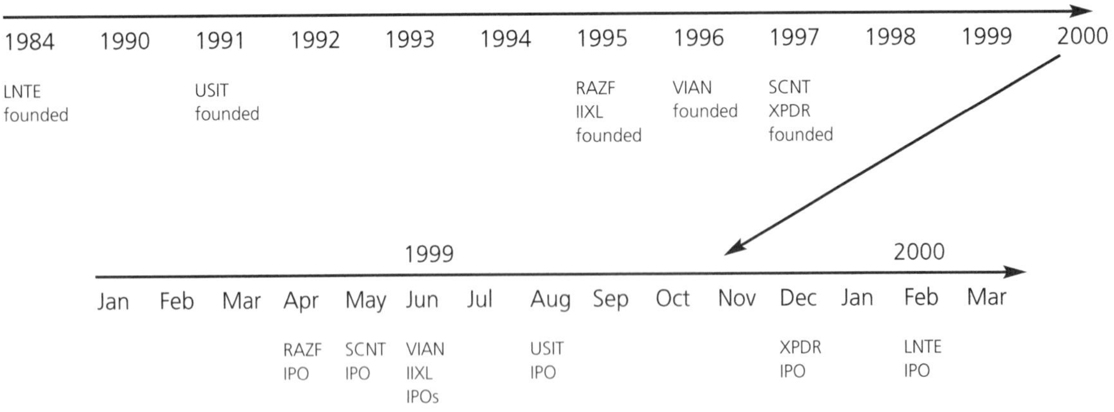

Sources: Edgar Online, Marketguide.com.

EXHIBIT 2 Internet consultants: Stock price highs and lows

Company	IPO price[a]	Peak price	% Change IPO to peak	Date of peak	Price at end of Feb 2001	% Change from peak
Scient	10	133.75	1,238%	10-Mar-00	2.94	−97.8%
Viant	8	63.56	695%	14-Dec-99	3.06	−95.2%
IXL Enterprises	12	58.75	390%	20-Jan-00	1.25	−97.9%
Lante	20	87.50	338%	29-Feb-00	1.81	−97.9%
Razorfish	8	56.94	612%	14-Feb-00	1.16	−98.0%
US Interactive	10	83.75	738%	4-Jan-00	0.56[b]	−99.3%
Xpedior	19	34.75	83%	10-Jan-00	0.69	−98.0%

Sources: Thomson Datastream.

a. Split adjusted.

b. Last trade on January 11, 2001. Filed for bankruptcy under Chapter 11 in January 2001.

EXHIBIT 3 Intermediaries in the capital-raising process of the internet consultants

Company	Venture capital stage investors	Investment bank underwriters	Auditors[a]	Analyst coverage	Selected institutional holders	Venture funding ($M)	IPO amount raised ($M)[b]	IPO underwriting fee ($M)	Percent institutional ownership[c]
Scient	Sequoia Capital, Benchmark Capital, Stanford Univ., Capital Research, Morgan Stanley Venture Partners, Amerindo Investment Advisors, Palantir Capital	Morgan Stanley Dean Witter, Hambrecht & Quist, Thomas Weisel Partners	PWC	Merrill Lynch, Morgan Stanley Dean Witter, CSFB, Lehman Brothers, UBS Warburg, SG Cowen, others	Capital Research, Putnam, Janus, Vanguard, Wellingon, State Street	31.2	60	4.2	34% (66% of float)
Viant	Kleiner Perkins Caufield & Byers, Mohr Davidow Ventures, Information Associates, Trident Capital, BancBoston Capital, General Motors, Technology Crossover Ventures	Goldman Sachs, Credit Suisse First Boston, WIT Capital Corporation	PWC	Goldman Sachs, Merrill Lynch, Lehman Brothers, CSFB, Wasserstein Perella, Bear Stearns, others	Fidelity, T Rowe Price, Putnam, Franklin, State Street, Vanguard, American Century, Goldman Sachs Asset Management	32.2	48	3.4	34% (67% of float)
IXL	Greylock Mgmt., Chase Capital Partners, Flatiron Partners, GE Capital, Kelso & Co., TTC Ventures, CB Capital, Portage Venture Partners, Transamerica Technology Finance	Merrill Lynch, BancBoston Robertson Stephens, DLJ, SG Cowen	PWC	Merrill Lynch, Robinson Humphrey, First Union Capital, others	Capital Research, State Street, Vanguard, Goldman Sachs Asset Management, GE Asset Management	91.0	72	5.0	29% (108% of float)
Lante	Frontenac Co., Dell Ventures, MSD Capital	Credit Suisse First Boston, Deutsche Bank Alex Brown, Thomas Weisel Partners	PWC	CSFB, Deutsche Bank, Thomas Weisel Partners, others	Fidelity, State Street, Vanguard, Goldman Sachs Asset Management	26.8	80	5.6	3% (21% of float)
Razorfish	N/A	Credit Suisse First Boston, BancBoston Robertson Stephens, Deutsche Bank Alex Brown, Lehman Brothers	AA, PWC	CSFB, Lehman Brothers, SG Cowen, others	Janus, Capital Research, Fidelity, Vanguard, Goldman Sachs Asset Management	N/A	48	3.4	8% (14% of float)
US Interactive	Safeguard Scientific, Technology Leaders	Lehman Brothers, Hambrecht & Quist, Adams Harkness & Hill	KPMG	Lehman Brothers, Hambrecht & Quist, Deutsche Bank Alex Brown, others	T Rowe Price, Prudential, JP Morgan Investment Management, Credit Suisse Asset Mgmt.	N/A	46	2.0	4% (6% of float)
Xpedior	N/A	DLJ, First Union Securities, JP Morgan, The Robinson-Humphrey Group	E&Y	DLJ, First Union Securities, Robinson-Humphrey, others	Capital Research, T Rowe Price, Franklin, Vanguard, John Hancock	N/A	162	11.4	2% (10% of float)

Sources: VentureSource, Edgar Online, Thomson Datastream, Quicken.com, Lionshares.com.

a. PWC stands for PriceWaterhouseCoopers; AA for Arthur Anderson; E&Y for Ernst & Young.

b. Includes underwriting fee.

c. As of April 2001.

Capital market intermediaries in the dot-com crash

EXHIBIT 4 **Market capitalization of major technology companies, January 2000**

Company	Market capitalization ($ billions)[a]	Stock Price (January 3, 2000)
Microsoft	603	116.56
Intel	290	87.00
IBM	218	116.00
Dell Computer	131	50.88
Hewlett Packard	117	117.44
Compaq Computer	53	31.00
Apple Computer	18	111.94

Sources: Thomson Datastream, Edgar Online.

a. Based on share price close on January 3, 2000, and reported shares outstanding.

EXHIBIT 5 **Market valuations given to loss-making dot-coms**

Company	Net income ('99/'00)[a] ($ millions)	Market capitalization ($ billions)[b]	Stock price (January 3, 2000)
Amazon.com	−720	30.8	89.38
DoubleClick	−56	30.1	268.00
Akamai Technologies	−58	29.7	321.25
VerticalNet	−53	12.4	172.63
Priceline.com	−1,055	8.4	51.25
E*Trade	−57	7.1	28.06
EarthLink	−174	5.2	44.75
Drugstore.com	−116	1.6	37.13

Sources: Thomson Datastream, Edgar Online.

a. As of end of 1999 or early 2000, depending on fiscal year end.

b. Based on share price close on January 3, 2000, and reported shares outstanding.

EXHIBIT 6 **Scient: Consolidated financial statements**

INCOME STATEMENT
(in thousands except per-share amounts)

	November 7, 1997 (inception) through March 31, 1998	Year ended March 31,	
		1999	2000
Revenues	$179	$20,675	$155,729
Operating expenses:			
Professional services	102	10,028	70,207
Selling, general and administrative	1,228	15,315	90,854
Stock compensation	64	7,679	15,636
Total operating expenses	1,394	22,022	176,697
Loss from operations	(1,215)	(12,347)	(20,968)
Interest income and other, net	56	646	4,953
Net loss	$(1,159)	$(11,701)	$(16,015)
Net loss per share:			
Basic and diluted	$(0.10)	$(0.89)	$(0.29)
Weighted average shares	11,894	13,198	54,590

Capital market intermediaries in the dot-com crash

BALANCE SHEET
(in thousands except per-share amounts)

	March 31, 1999	March 31, 2000
ASSETS		
Current assets:		
Cash and cash equivalents	$11,261	$108,102
Short-term investments	16,868	121,046
Accounts receivable, net	5,876	56,021
Prepaid expenses	811	4,929
Other	318	4,228
Total current assets	35,134	294,326
Long-term investments	—	3,146
Property and equipment, net	3,410	16,063
Other	268	219
	$38,812	$313,754
LIABILITIES AND STOCKHOLDERS' EQUITY		
Current liabilities:		
Bank borrowings, current	$413	$1,334
Accounts payable	832	5,023
Accrued compensation and benefits	2,554	33,976
Accrued expenses	2,078	9,265
Deferred revenue	524	6,579
Capital lease obligations, current	625	2,624
Total current liabilities	7,026	58,801
Capital lease obligations, long-term	680	2,052
	8,835	61,718
Commitments and contingencies (Note 5)		
Stockholders' equity:		
Convertible preferred stock; issuable in series, $.0001 par value; 10,000 shares authorized; 9,012 and no shares issued and outstanding, respectively	1	—
Common stock: $.0001 par value; 125,000 shares authorized; 33,134 and 72,491 shares issues and outstanding, respectively	3	7
Additional paid-in capital	70,055	297,735
Accumulated other comprehensive loss	—	(47)
Unearned compensation	(27,222)	(16,784)
Accumulated deficit	(12,860)	(28,875)
Total stockholders' equity	29,977	252,036
	$38,812	$313,754

Sources: Scient Corporation 10-K; Edgar Online <http: //www.freedgar.com> (May 11, 2001).

EXHIBIT 7 **Selected institutional holders of Scient Corporation, 1999–2000**

Institution	*June 1999*	*September 1999*	*December 1999*	*March 2000*	*June 2000*	*September 2000*	*December 2000*
				Quarter ended:			
Capital Research	—	—	—	265	1,079,911	586,442	586,706
Putnam Investments	5,000	—	625,900	2,209,200	4,800,800	5,749,200	—
Wellington Management	—	—	—	—	—	—	803,000
State Street	—	12,450	38,167	52,867	89,667	180,668	672,352
Janus	267,300	273,915	483,730	775,085	1,359,700	4,382,250	—

Source: Edgar Online (SEC).

Capital market intermediaries in the dot-com crash

EXHIBIT 8 **Dot-coms that filed for bankruptcy or closed operations** *(selected list)*

August 2000
Auctions.com
Hardware.com
Living.com
SaviShopper.com
GreatCoffee

September 2000
Clickmango.com
Pop.com
FreeScholarships.com
RedLadder.com
DomainAuction.com
Gazoontite.com
Surfing2Cash.com
Affinia.com

October 2000
FreeInternet.com
Chipshot.com
Stockpower.com
The Dental Store
More.com
WebHouse
UrbanFetch.com
Boxman.com
RedGorilla.com
Eve.com
MyLackey.com
BigWords.com
Mortgage.com
MotherNature.com
Ivendor
TeliSmart.com

November 2000
Pets.com
Caredata.com
Streamline.com
Garden.com
Furniture.com
TheMan.com
Ibelieve.com
eSociety
UrbanDesign.com
HalfthePlanet.com
Productopia.com
BeautyJungle.com
ICanBuy.com
Bike.com
Mambo.com
Babystripes.com
Thirsty.com
Checkout.com

December 2000
Quepasa.com
Finance.com
BizBuyer.com
Desktop.com
E-pods.com
Clickabid.com
HeavenlyDoor.com
ShoppingList.com
Babygear.com
HotOffice.com
Goldsauction.com
AntEye.com
EZBid
Admart
I-US.com
Riffage.com

January 2001
MusicMaker.com
Mercata
Send.com
CompanyLeader.com
Zap.com
Savvio.com
News Digital Media
TravelNow.com
Foodline.com
LetsBuyIt.com
e7th.cm
CountryCool.com
Ibetcha.com
Fibermarket.com
Dotcomix
New Digital Media
GreatEntertaining.com
AndysGarage.com
Lucy.com
US Interactive

Sources: Johnathan Weil, "'Going Concerns': Did Accountants Fail to Flag Problems at Dot-Com Casualties?" *Wall Street Journal*, February 2001; Jim Battey, "Dot-com details: The numbers behind the year's e-commerce shake-out," *Infoworld*, March 2001.

EXHIBIT 9   **Capital flows from investors to companies**

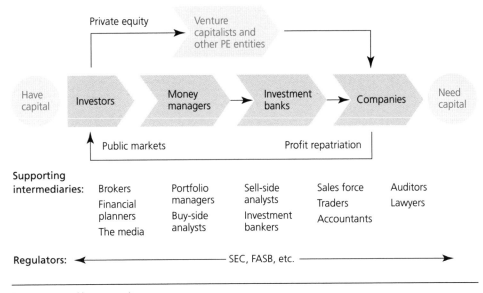

Source: created by case writer

BUSINESS ANALYSIS AND VALUATION TOOLS

Strategy Analysis

Strategy analysis is an important starting point for the analysis of financial statements. Strategy analysis allows the analyst to probe the economics of a firm at a qualitative level so that the subsequent accounting and financial analysis is grounded in business reality. Strategy analysis also allows the identification of the firm's profit drivers and key risks. This in turn enables the analyst to assess the sustainability of the firm's current performance and make realistic forecasts of future performance.

A firm's value is determined by its ability to earn a return on its capital in excess of the cost of capital. What determines whether or not a firm is able to accomplish this goal? While a firm's cost of capital is determined by the capital markets, its profit potential is determined by its own strategic choices: (1) the choice of an industry or a set of industries in which the firm operates (industry choice), (2) the manner in which the firm intends to compete with other firms in its chosen industry or industries (competitive positioning), and (3) the way in which the firm expects to create and exploit synergies across the range of businesses in which it operates (corporate strategy). Strategy analysis, therefore, involves industry analysis, competitive strategy analysis, and corporate strategy analysis.[1] In this chapter, we will briefly discuss these three steps and use the European airline industry, IKEA and the easyGroup, respectively, to illustrate the application of the steps.

INDUSTRY ANALYSIS

In analyzing a firm's profit potential, an analyst has to first assess the profit potential of each of the industries in which the firm is competing because the profitability of various industries differs systematically and predictably over time. For example, the ratio of earnings before interest and taxes to the book value of assets for European listed companies between 1989 and 2005 was 2.9 percent. However, the average returns varied widely across specific industries: for the cleaning and maintenance industry, the profitability ratio was 15 percentage points greater than the population average, and for the gold and silver ore mining industry it was 38 percentage points less than the population average.[2] What causes these profitability differences?

There is a vast body of research in industrial organization on the influence of industry structure on profitability.[3] Relying on this research, strategy literature suggests that the average profitability of an industry is influenced by the "five forces" shown in Figure 2.1.[4] According to this framework, the intensity of competition determines the potential for creating abnormal profits by the firms in an industry. Whether or not the potential profits are kept by the industry is determined by the relative

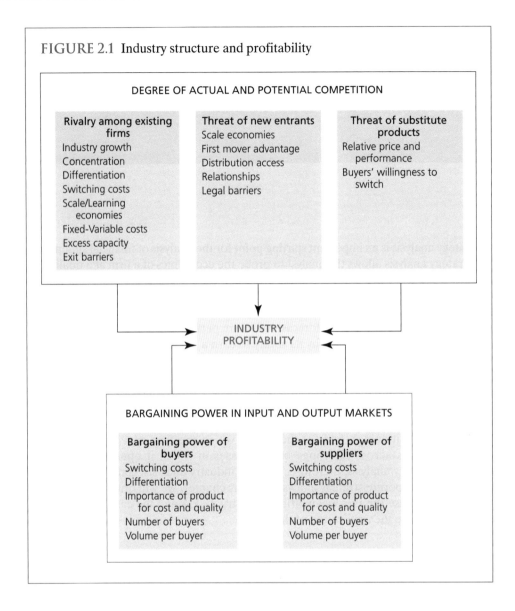

FIGURE 2.1 Industry structure and profitability

bargaining power of the firms in the industry and their customers and suppliers. We will discuss each of these industry profit drivers in more detail below.

Degree of actual and potential competition

At the most basic level, the profits in an industry are a function of the maximum price that customers are willing to pay for the industry's product or service. One of the key determinants of the price is the degree to which there is competition among suppliers of the same or similar products. At one extreme, if there is a state of perfect competition in the industry, micro-economic theory predicts that prices will be equal to marginal cost, and there will be few opportunities to earn supernormal profits. At the other extreme, if the industry is dominated by a single firm, there will be potential to earn monopoly profits. In reality, the degree of competition in most industries is somewhere in between perfect competition and monopoly.

There are three potential sources of competition in an industry: (1) rivalry between existing firms, (2) threat of entry of new firms, and (3) threat of substitute products or services. We will discuss each of these competitive forces in the following paragraphs.

Competitive force 1: Rivalry among existing firms

In most industries the average level of profitability is primarily influenced by the nature of rivalry among existing firms in the industry. In some industries firms compete aggressively, pushing prices close to (and sometimes below) the marginal cost. In other industries firms do not compete aggressively on price. Instead, they find ways to coordinate their pricing, or compete on nonprice dimensions such as innovation or brand image. Several factors determine the intensity of competition between existing players in an industry:

Industry growth rate If an industry is growing very rapidly, incumbent firms need not grab market share from each other to grow. In contrast, in stagnant industries the only way existing firms can grow is by taking share away from the other players. In this situation one can expect price wars among firms in the industry.

Concentration and balance of competitors The number of firms in an industry and their relative sizes determine the degree of concentration in an industry.[5] The degree of concentration influences the extent to which firms in an industry can coordinate their pricing and other competitive moves. For example, if there is one dominant firm in an industry (such as Microsoft in the operating systems industry in the 1990s), it can set and enforce the rules of competition. Similarly, if there are only two or three equal-sized players (such as Boeing and Airbus in the large commercial aircraft industry), they can implicitly cooperate with each other to avoid destructive price competition. If an industry is fragmented, price competition is likely to be severe.

Degree of differentiation and switching costs The extent to which firms in an industry can avoid head-on competition depends on the extent to which they can differentiate their products and services. If the products in an industry are very similar, customers are ready to switch from one competitor to another purely on the basis of price. Switching costs also determine customers' propensity to move from one product to another. When switching costs are low, there is a greater incentive for firms in an industry to engage in price competition.

Scale/learning economies and the ratio of fixed to variable costs If there is a steep learning curve or there are other types of scale economies in an industry, size becomes an important factor for firms in the industry. In such situations, there are incentives to engage in aggressive competition for market share. Similarly, if the ratio of fixed to variable costs is high, firms have an incentive to reduce prices to utilize installed capacity. The airline industry, where price wars are quite common, is an example of this type of situation.

Excess capacity and exit barriers If capacity in an industry is larger than customer demand, there is a strong incentive for firms to cut prices to fill capacity. The problem of excess capacity is likely to be exacerbated if there are significant barriers for firms to exit the industry. Exit barriers are high when the assets are specialized or if there are regulations that make exit costly.

Competitive force 2: Threat of new entrants

The potential for earning abnormal profits will attract new entrants to an industry. The very threat of new firms entering an industry potentially constrains the pricing of existing firms within it. Therefore the ease with which new firms can enter an industry is a key determinant of its profitability. Several factors determine the height of barriers to entry in an industry:

Economies of scale When there are large economies of scale, new entrants face the choice of having either to invest in a large capacity which might not be utilized right away or to enter with less than the optimum capacity. Either way, new entrants will at least initially suffer from a cost disadvantage in competing with existing firms. Economies of scale might arise from large investments in research and development (the pharmaceutical or jet engine industries), in brand advertising (sportswear industry), or in physical plant and equipment (telecommunications industry).

First mover advantage Early entrants in an industry may deter future entrants if there are first mover advantages. For example, first movers might be able to set industry standards, or enter into exclusive arrangements with suppliers of cheap raw materials. They may also acquire scarce government licenses to operate in regulated industries. Finally, if there are learning economies, early firms will have an absolute cost advantage over new entrants. First mover advantages are also likely to be large when there are significant switching costs for customers once they start using existing products. For example, switching costs faced by the users of Microsoft's Windows operating system make it difficult for software companies to market a new operating system.

Access to channels of distribution and relationships Limited capacity in the existing distribution channels and high costs of developing new channels can act as powerful barriers to entry. For example, a new entrant into the auto industry is likely to face formidable barriers because of the difficulty of developing a dealer network. Similarly, new consumer goods manufacturers find it difficult to obtain supermarket shelf space for their products. Existing relationships between firms and customers in an industry also make it difficult for new firms to enter an industry. Industry examples of this include auditing, investment banking, and advertising.

Legal barriers There are many industries in which legal barriers such as patents and copyrights in research-intensive industries limit entry. Similarly, licensing regulations limit entry into taxi services, medical services, broadcasting, and telecommunications industries.

Competitive force 3: Threat of substitute products

The third dimension of competition in an industry is the threat of substitute products or services. Relevant substitutes are not necessarily those that have the same form as the existing products but those that perform the same function. For example, airlines and high-speed rail systems might be substitutes for each other when it comes to travel over short distances. Similarly, plastic bottles and metal cans substitute for each other as packaging in the beverage industry. In some cases, threat of substitution comes not from customers' switching to another product but from utilizing technologies that allow them to do without, or use less of, the existing products. For example, energy-conserving technologies allow customers to reduce their consumption of electricity and fossil fuels.

The threat of substitutes depends on the relative price and performance of the competing products or services and on customers' willingness to substitute. Customers' perception of whether two products are substitutes depends to some extent on whether they perform the same function for a similar price. If two products perform an identical function, then it would be difficult for them to differ from each other in price. However, customers' willingness to switch is often the critical factor in making this competitive dynamic work. For example, even when tap water and bottled water serve the same function, many customers may be unwilling to substitute the former for the latter, enabling bottlers to charge a price premium. Similarly, designer label clothing commands a price premium even if it is not superior in terms of basic functionality because customers place a value on the image offered by designer labels.

While the degree of competition in an industry determines whether there is *potential* to earn abnormal profits, the *actual profits* are influenced by the industry's bargaining power with its suppliers and customers. On the input side, firms enter into transactions with suppliers of labor, raw materials and components, and finances. On the output side, firms either sell directly to the final customers or enter into contracts with intermediaries in the distribution chain. In all these transactions, the relative economic power of the two sides is important to the overall profitability of the industry firms.

Competitive force 4: Bargaining power of buyers

Two factors determine the power of buyers: price sensitivity and relative bargaining power. Price sensitivity determines the extent to which buyers care to bargain on price; relative bargaining power determines the extent to which they will succeed in forcing the price down.[6]

Price sensitivity Buyers are more price sensitive when the product is undifferentiated and there are few switching costs. The sensitivity of buyers to price also depends on the importance of the product to their own cost structure. When the product represents a large fraction of the buyers' cost (for example, the packaging material for soft-drink producers), the buyer is likely to expend the resources necessary to shop for a lower-cost alternative. In contrast, if the product is a small fraction of the buyers' cost (for example, windshield wipers for automobile manufacturers), it may not pay to expend resources to search for lower-cost alternatives. Further, the importance of the product to the buyers' own product quality also determines whether or not price becomes the most important determinant of the buying decision.

Relative bargaining power Even if buyers are price sensitive, they may not be able to achieve low prices unless they have a strong bargaining position. Relative bargaining power in a transaction depends, ultimately, on the cost to each party of not doing business with the other party. The buyers' bargaining power is determined by the number of buyers relative to the number of suppliers, volume of purchases by a single buyer, number of alternative products available to the buyer, buyers' costs of switching from one product to another, and the threat of backward integration by the buyers. For example, in the automobile industry, car manufacturers have considerable power over component manufacturers because auto companies are large buyers with several alternative suppliers to choose from, and switching costs are relatively low. In contrast, in the personal computer industry, computer makers have low bargaining power relative to the operating system software producers because of high switching costs.

Competitive force 5: Bargaining power of suppliers

The analysis of the relative power of suppliers is a mirror image of the analysis of the buyers' power in an industry. Suppliers are powerful when there are only a few companies and few substitutes available to their customers. For example, in the soft-drink industry, Coke and Pepsi are very powerful relative to the bottlers. In contrast, metal can suppliers to the soft-drink industry are not very powerful because of intense competition among can producers and the threat of substitution of cans by plastic bottles. Suppliers also have a lot of power over buyers when the suppliers' product or service is critical to buyers' business. For example, airline pilots have a strong bargaining power in the airline industry. Suppliers also tend to be powerful when they pose a credible threat of forward integration. For example, insurance companies are powerful relative to insurance intermediaries because of their own presence in the insurance-selling business.

APPLYING INDUSTRY ANALYSIS: THE EUROPEAN AIRLINE INDUSTRY

Let us consider the above concepts of industry analysis in the context of the European airline industry. In the early 1980s, the European airline industry was highly regulated. Bilateral agreements between European governments severely restricted competition by determining which airlines could operate which routes at what fares. During the ten years from 1987 to 1997, the European Union (E.U.) gradually liberalized the industry, and reduced government intervention. The industry exhibited steady growth. While the four largest European airlines carried 54 million passengers in 1980, the same airlines carried 147 million passengers in 2000.[7] Despite the steady growth in passenger traffic, however, many of the large European airlines, such as Alitalia, British Airways, KLM, Lufthansa, and SAS, reported poor performance in the early 2000s and were forced to undergo internal restructuring. Other national carriers, such as Sabena and Swissair, went bankrupt. What accounted for this low profitability? What was the effect of liberalization on competition? What was the European airline industry's future profit potential?

Competition in the European airline industry

The competition was very intense for a number of reasons:

- *Rivalry – industry growth.* Between 1995 and 2004, the average annual industry growth was a moderate 5 percent. The industry growth was negative, at minus 5 percent, in the year immediately following the September 11, 2001 terrorist attacks, compared with a range from 7 to 10 percent in the years before 2001.[8]
- *Rivalry – concentration.* The industry was fragmented. While several new airlines had entered the industry after the liberalization period, inefficient and loss-making national carriers, which were often state owned or state controlled, did not leave the industry because they were kept from bankruptcy through state subsidies and loans.
- *Rivalry – differentiation and switching costs.* Services delivered by different airlines on short-haul flights, within Europe, were virtually identical, and, with the possible exception of frequent flyer programs, there were few opportunities to differentiate the products. Switching costs across different airlines were also low because in

some areas airports were geographically close and code-sharing agreements increased the number of alternatives that passengers could consider.

■ *Rivalry – excess capacity.* The European airlines had a structural excess capacity problem. Between 1995 and 2004, the average annual passenger load factor, which measures the percentage of passenger seats filled, was 72 percent. Because airlines lacked the opportunity to differentiate, they engaged in price competition in an attempt to fill the empty seats.

■ *Threat of new entrants – access to distribution channels/legal barriers.* The system that most of the large European airports used to allocate their time slots among the airlines could have created barriers to entry. Slots are the rights to land at, or take off from, an airport at a particular date and time. In the twice-yearly allocation of time slots, priority was given to airlines that had slots in the previous season. After 1993, however, E.U. regulation promoted the entry of new airlines to the European market by requiring that at least 50 percent of the slots that became available were allocated to new entrants. New airlines also successfully managed to enter the European market by using alternative, smaller airports in the vicinity of those used by the established airlines. Most of these new entrants focused on offering low-fare, no-frills flights. Early new entrants were low-cost carriers easyJet and Ryanair, which experienced explosive growth and forced the incumbent airlines to start competing on price. In fact, the number of weekly passengers that new entrants in the low-fare, no-frills segment carried during the summer season increased from about 300,000 passengers in 1999 to 2.6 million passengers in 2005.

■ *Threat of new entrants.* New entrants had easy access to capital. Purchased aircraft served to securitize loans, or aircraft could be leased. Further, second-hand aircraft became cheap during industry downturns, when troubled airlines disposed of excess capacity.

■ *Threat of new entrants – legal barriers.* After 1997, European airlines faced no legal barriers to enter European markets outside their domestic market. Measures taken by the E.U. to deregulate the industry made it possible for the airlines to freely operate on any route within the E.U., instead of having to conform to bilateral agreements between countries.

■ *Threat of substitute products.* High-speed rail networks were being expanded and provided a potential, not yet fully exploited, substitute for air travel over shorter distances.

The power of suppliers and buyers

Suppliers and buyers had significant power over firms in the industry for these reasons:

■ *Suppliers' bargaining power.* Airlines' primary costs for operating passenger flights were airport fees and handling charges, aircraft depreciation and maintenance, fuel, and labor. Ninety percent of the aircraft that European airlines had acquired or leased came from two commercial aircraft manufacturers, Airbus and Boeing. The strong dependence of European airlines on only two aircraft suppliers impaired airlines' bargaining power. Further, during the 1990s, ground handling agents at several European airports were monopolist and charged higher handling fees than agents at airports with competition. Liberalization measures taken by the E.U. promoted competition among ground handling agents, but in the early 2000s, still very few airports had more than two competing agents. In addition, although competition among jet fuel suppliers helped to ensure that the fuel prices that suppliers charged to the airlines did not deviate much from market prices, the fluctuations in fuel market prices were beyond airlines' control. Finally, European airline employees had significant power over their employers since their job security tended to be well-protected and the threat of a strike was an efficient bargaining tool in labor negotiations.

■ *Buyers' bargaining power.* Buyers gained more power because of the development of web booking systems, which made market prices transparent. Buyers were price sensitive since they increasingly viewed air travel as a commodity. Being able to easily compare prices across different airlines substantially increased their bargaining power.

As a result of the intense rivalry and low barriers to entry in the European airline industry, there was severe price competition among different airlines. Further, government interference kept the national carriers from entering into mergers. Instead, they created alliances that did not sufficiently reduce or reallocate capacity. These factors led to a low profit potential in the industry. The power of suppliers and buyers reduced the profit potential further.

There were some indications of change in the basic structure of the European airline industry. First, most of the established airlines cut capacity in 2002, which led to an overall improvement in the passenger load factor (75 percent, on average, compared to less than 70 percent in the 1990s). Second, in 2003, the merger between two established airlines, Air France and KLM, was one of the first signs of consolidation in the industry. Third, the E.U. was mandated to negotiate an "open skies" agreement with the U.S., which should substitute for all the bilateral agreements between European governments and the U.S., and open up a new market for European airlines. As a result, the profitability of the European airline industry may improve in the near future.

Limitations of industry analysis

A potential limitation of the industry analysis framework discussed in this chapter is the assumption that industries have clear boundaries. In reality, it is often not easy to clearly demarcate industry boundaries. For example, in analyzing the European airline industry, should one focus on the short-haul flight segment or the airline industry as a whole? Should one include charter flights and cargo transport in the industry definition? Should one consider only the airlines domiciled in Europe or also the airlines from other continents that operate flights to Europe? Inappropriate industry definition will result in incomplete analysis and inaccurate forecasts.

COMPETITIVE STRATEGY ANALYSIS

The profitability of a firm is influenced not only by its industry structure but also by the strategic choices it makes in positioning itself in the industry. While there are many ways to characterize a firm's business strategy, as Figure 2.2 shows, there are two generic competitive strategies: (1) cost leadership and (2) differentiation.[9] Both these strategies can potentially allow a firm to build a sustainable competitive advantage. Strategy researchers have traditionally viewed cost leadership and differentiation as mutually exclusive strategies. Firms that straddle the two strategies are considered to be "stuck in the middle" and are expected to earn low profitability.[10] These firms run the risk of not

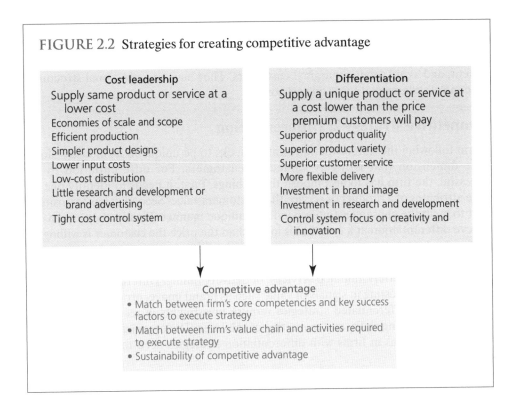

FIGURE 2.2 Strategies for creating competitive advantage

Cost leadership
Supply same product or service at a lower cost
Economies of scale and scope
Efficient production
Simpler product designs
Lower input costs
Low-cost distribution
Little research and development or brand advertising
Tight cost control system

Differentiation
Supply a unique product or service at a cost lower than the price premium customers will pay
Superior product quality
Superior product variety
Superior customer service
More flexible delivery
Investment in brand image
Investment in research and development
Control system focus on creativity and innovation

Competitive advantage
• Match between firm's core competencies and key success factors to execute strategy
• Match between firm's value chain and activities required to execute strategy
• Sustainability of competitive advantage

being able to attract price conscious customers because their costs are too high; they are also unable to provide adequate differentiation to attract premium price customers.

Sources of competitive advantage

Cost leadership enables a firm to supply the same product or service offered by its competitors at a lower cost. Differentiation strategy involves providing a product or service that is distinct in some important respect valued by the customer. As an example in food retailing, U.K.-based Sainsbury's competes on the basis of differentiation by emphasizing the high quality of its food and service, and by operating an online grocery store. In contrast, Germany-based Aldi and Lidl are discount retailers competing purely on a low-cost basis.

Competitive strategy 1: Cost leadership

Cost leadership is often the clearest way to achieve competitive advantage. In industries where the basic product or service is a commodity, cost leadership might be the only way to achieve superior performance. There are many ways to achieve cost leadership, including economies of scale and scope, economies of learning, efficient production, simpler product design, lower input costs, and efficient organizational processes. If a firm can achieve cost leadership, then it will be able to earn above-average profitability by merely charging the same price as its rivals. Conversely, a cost leader can force its competitors to cut prices and accept lower returns, or to exit the industry. For example, the entrance of low-cost carriers to the European airline industry at the end of the 1990s forced the incumbent airlines to change their strategy and focus more on competing through price.

Firms that achieve cost leadership focus on tight cost controls. They make investments in efficient scale plants, focus on product designs that reduce manufacturing costs, minimize overhead costs, make little investment in risky research and development, and avoid serving marginal customers. They have organizational structures and control systems that focus on cost control.

Competitive strategy 2: Differentiation

A firm following the differentiation strategy seeks to be unique in its industry along some dimension that is highly valued by customers. For differentiation to be successful, the firm has to accomplish three things. First, it needs to identify one or more attributes of a product or service that customers value. Second, it has to position itself to meet the chosen customer need in a unique manner. Finally, the firm has to achieve differentiation at a cost that is lower than the price the customer is willing to pay for the differentiated product or service.

Drivers of differentiation include providing superior intrinsic value via product quality, product variety, bundled services, or delivery timing. Differentiation can also be achieved by investing in signals of value such as brand image, product appearance, or reputation. Differentiated strategies require investments in research and development, engineering skills, and marketing capabilities. The organizational structures and control systems in firms with differentiation strategies need to foster creativity and innovation.

While successful firms choose between cost leadership and differentiation, they cannot completely ignore the dimension on which they are not primarily competing. Firms that target differentiation still need to focus on costs so that the differentiation can be achieved at an acceptable cost. Similarly, cost leaders cannot compete unless they achieve at least a minimum level on key dimensions on which competitors might differentiate, such as quality and service.

Achieving and sustaining competitive advantage

The choice of competitive strategy does not automatically lead to the achievement of competitive advantage. To achieve competitive advantage, the firm has to have the capabilities needed to implement and sustain the chosen strategy. Both cost leadership and differentiation strategy require that the firm makes the necessary commitments to acquire the core competencies needed, and structures its value chain in an appropriate way. Core competencies are the economic assets that the firm possesses, whereas the value chain is the set of activities that the firm performs to convert inputs into outputs. The uniqueness of a firm's core competencies and its value chain and the extent to which it is difficult for competitors to imitate them determines the sustainability of a firm's competitive advantage.[11]

To evaluate whether a firm is likely to achieve its intended competitive advantage, the analyst should ask the following questions:

- What are the key success factors and risks associated with the firm's chosen competitive strategy?
- Does the firm currently have the resources and capabilities to deal with the key success factors and risks?
- Has the firm made irreversible commitments to bridge the gap between its current capabilities and the requirements to achieve its competitive advantage?

- Has the firm structured its activities (such as research and development, design, manufacturing, marketing and distribution, and support activities) in a way that is consistent with its competitive strategy?

- Is the company's competitive advantage sustainable? Are there any barriers that make imitation of the firm's strategy difficult?

- Are there any potential changes in the firm's industry structure (such as new technologies, foreign competition, changes in regulation, changes in customer requirements) that might dissipate the firm's competitive advantage? Is the company flexible enough to address these changes?

Applying competitive strategy analysis

Let us consider the concepts of competitive strategy analysis in the context of IKEA. In 2005, Sweden-based IKEA was one of the world's largest furniture retailers. The company, founded by Ingvar Kamprad as a mail-order company, bought its first furniture factory and showroom in 1953. During the 1960s, IKEA started to develop the operating concept that the company is still renowned for: selling flat-packed furniture through large warehouse stores. In those years, IKEA also started to expand internationally.

While continuously expanding its worldwide store base, IKEA firmly established itself in the furniture retailing industry by following a low-cost strategy. For the fiscal year ending August 31, 2005, IKEA achieved €15.2 billion in revenues. IKEA's average annual growth rate during the six years between 1999 and 2005 was approximately 11 percent. Although the company did not reveal its profit margin because of its private status, industry analysts estimated this at 10 percent.[12] This margin was well above those of some of IKEA's larger competitors, such as U.S.-based Target (7.7 percent). IKEA was one of the most successful and, presumably, one of the most profitable furniture retailers in the industry. How did IKEA achieve such performance?

IKEA's superior performance was based on a low-cost competitive strategy that consisted of the following key elements: [13]

- *Global strategy*. IKEA followed a purely global strategy. In each of the 33 countries where the retailer operated its stores, it targeted the same customer group – young families and young couples – and offered virtually the same selection of furniture. This strategy of strong economic integration and low responsiveness to national cultures helped the company to achieve economies of scale.

- *Sourcing of production*. IKEA did not own any production facilities other than Swedwood, which supplied 10 percent of its furniture. Instead, the company outsourced its production to manufacturers located throughout the world. Because IKEA had developed a network of 1,300 suppliers in 53 countries, the company could choose among a large number of manufacturers. Often, the company was a manufacturer's sole customer. Consequently, IKEA had substantial bargaining power in its dealings with its suppliers, which kept input costs to a minimum.

- *Economic designs*. Although IKEA outsourced its production, the company kept tight control of the design of its furniture. Its designers worked two to three years ahead of production to have sufficient time to find the most economic design solutions and review potential suppliers.

- *Logistics*. IKEA incorporated logistics into its strategy. The company operated large warehouse stores on relatively cheap locations outside the city centers. These warehouse stores sold furniture in flat-pack format that customers assembled at home. The integration of stores and warehouses and the use of flat-packs helped IKEA to economize on costs for storage and transportation.

■ *Sales.* IKEA stores were able to employ a lower amount of sales staff than other stores because customers needed little assistance. All warehouse stores were designed such that customers, after having made their choice, picked the flat-packs from the shelves and paid for their purchases at a central location in the store. IKEA also provided its customers with limited after-sales service. Through this strategy, the company was able to keep personnel expenses to a minimum.

As a result of the above strategy, IKEA achieved a significant cost advantage over its competitors in the furniture retailing industry. Consequently, IKEA was able to continuously cut prices and maintain the price difference with its competitors. Because, over the years, the company had made large investments in knowledge of low-cost furniture design, store design, and logistics, the business model was difficult to replicate, making its competitive advantage sustainable. Although IKEA's brand image varied greatly across countries, in some countries it had become a cult brand. In 2005, Interbrand Corp. estimated the value of the IKEA brand at €7.8 billion. This value was similar to the values of brands such as Apple and Google. The strength of the retailer's brand name, the diversity in its assortment, and the distinctiveness of its designs illustrate that IKEA's strategy also exhibited some characteristics of a differentiation strategy.[14] However, the company's continuous focus on cost control was most likely the main driver of success. IKEA's success inspired some local competitors, such as France-based Fly, to attempt to replicate parts of its strategy. However no competitor to date has been able to replicate the business model on a similar scale.

CORPORATE STRATEGY ANALYSIS

So far in this chapter we have focused on the strategies at the individual business level. While some companies focus on only one business, many companies operate in multiple businesses. For example, of all companies that were listed on the seven largest European exchanges at the end of 2005, 41 percent operated in more than two business segments.[15] In the 1990s and 2000s, there has been an attempt by U.S. and western European companies to reduce the diversity of their operations and focus on a relatively few "core" businesses. However, multibusiness organizations continue to dominate the economic activity in many countries in the world.

When analyzing a multibusiness organization, an analyst has to not only evaluate the industries and strategies of the individual business units but also the economic consequences – either positive or negative – of managing all the different businesses under one corporate umbrella. For example, General Electric has been very successful in creating significant value by managing a highly diversified set of businesses ranging from aircraft engines to light bulbs. In contrast, during the first half of the 2000s, shareholders of several German conglomerates, such as MAN and Siemens, pressured their companies to improve profitability by spinning off their "noncore" divisions.

Sources of value creation at the corporate level

Economists and strategy researchers have identified several factors that influence an organization's ability to create value through a broad corporate scope. Economic theory suggests that the optimal activity scope of a firm depends on the relative transaction cost of performing a set of activities inside the firm versus using the market mechanism.[16] Transaction cost economics implies that the multiproduct firm is an efficient choice of organizational form when coordination among independent, focused firms is costly due to market transaction costs.

Transaction costs can arise out of several sources. They may arise if the production process involves specialized assets such as human capital skills, proprietary technology, or other organizational know-how that is not easily available in the marketplace. Transaction costs also may arise from market imperfections such as information and incentive problems. If buyers and sellers cannot solve these problems through standard mechanisms such as enforceable contracts, it will be costly to conduct transactions through market mechanisms.

For example, as discussed in Chapter 1, public capital markets may not work well when there are significant information and incentive problems, making it difficult for entrepreneurs to raise capital from investors. Similarly, if buyers cannot ascertain the quality of products being sold because of lack of information, or cannot enforce warranties because of poor legal infrastructure, entrepreneurs will find it difficult to break into new markets. Finally, if employers cannot assess the quality of applicants for new positions, they will have to rely more on internal promotions rather than external recruiting to fill higher positions in an organization. Emerging economies often suffer from these types of transaction costs because of poorly developed intermediation infrastructure.[17] Even in many advanced economies, examples of high transaction costs can be found. For example, in many countries other than the U.S. and western European nations, the venture capital industry is not highly developed, making it costly for new businesses in high technology industries to attract financing. Even in Europe and the U.S., transaction costs may vary across economic sectors. For example, until recently electronic commerce was hampered by consumer concerns regarding the security of credit card information sent over the internet.

Transactions inside an organization may be less costly than market-based transactions for several reasons. First, communication costs inside an organization are reduced because confidentiality can be protected and credibility can be assured through internal mechanisms. Second, the headquarters office can play a critical role in reducing costs of enforcing agreements between organizational subunits. Third, organizational subunits can share valuable nontradable assets (such as organizational skills, systems, and processes) or nondivisible assets (such as brand names, distribution channels, and reputation).

There are also forces that increase transaction costs inside organizations. Top management of an organization may lack the specialized information and skills necessary to manage businesses across several different industries. This lack of expertise reduces the possibility of actually realizing economies of scope, even when there is potential for such economies. This problem can be remedied by creating a decentralized organization, hiring specialist managers to run each business unit, and providing these managers with proper incentives. However, decentralization will also potentially decrease goal congruence among subunit managers, making it difficult to realize economies of scope.

Whether or not a multibusiness organization creates more value than a comparable collection of focused firms is, therefore, context dependent.[18] Analysts should ask the following questions to assess whether an organization's corporate strategy has the potential to create value:

- Are there significant imperfections in the product, labor, or financial markets in the industries (or countries) in which a company is operating? Is it likely that transaction costs in these markets are higher than the costs of similar activities inside a well-managed organization?

- Does the organization have special resources such as brand names, proprietary know-how, access to scarce distribution channels, and special organizational processes that have the potential to create economies of scope?

- Is there a good fit between the company's specialized resources and the portfolio of businesses in which the company is operating?

- Does the company allocate decision rights between the headquarters office and the business units optimally to realize all the potential economies of scope?

- Does the company have internal measurement, information, and incentive systems to reduce agency costs and increase coordination across business units?

Empirical evidence suggests that creating value through a multibusiness corporate strategy is hard in practice. Several researchers have documented that diversified companies trade at a discount in the stock market relative to a comparable portfolio of focused companies.[19] Studies also show that acquisitions of one company by another, especially when the two are in unrelated businesses, often fail to create value for the acquiring companies.[20] Finally, there is considerable evidence that value is created when multibusiness companies increase corporate focus through divisional spin-offs and asset sales.[21]

There are several potential explanations for the above diversification discount. First, managers' decisions to diversify and expand are frequently driven by a desire to maximize the size of their organization rather than to maximize shareholder value. Second, diversified companies often suffer from incentive misalignment problems leading to suboptimal investment decisions and poor operating performance. Third, capital markets find it difficult to monitor and value multi-business organizations because of inadequate disclosure about the performance of individual business segments.

In summary, while companies can theoretically create value through innovative corporate strategies, there are many ways in which this potential fails to get realized in practice. Therefore, it pays to be skeptical when evaluating companies' corporate strategies.

Applying corporate strategy analysis

Let us apply the concepts of corporate strategy analysis to easyGroup, a privately-owned company that licenses the "easy" brand name to, and holds shares in, various no-frills, low-cost businesses. easyGroup's first and primary holding, easyJet, started operations as a low-fare short-haul airline company in 1995 and five years later placed 28 percent of its shares on the London Stock Exchange at an amount of £224 million. The company grew rapidly and began to pose a serious threat in the short-haul segment to the dominance of leading European airlines like Air France, British Airways, and Lufthansa. EasyJet's revenues increased from £46 million in 1997 to £1,341 million in 2005.

Flush with his success in selling cheap short-haul flights, Stelios Haji-Ioannou, the founder of easyJet and private owner of easyGroup, stretched the "easy" brand name to other industries. The new ventures that easyGroup started had a few common characteristics. They primarily sold services with high fixed costs and exploited the fact that the demand for a service could be highly elastic to its price. In fact, when demand was low, the ventures sold their services at often drastically reduced prices. Because the easyGroup ventures consistently offered their services through the internet and rewarded customers for booking in advance, they were able to flexibly adjust prices to demand. Further, because of the no-frills character of services and the bypassing of intermediaries in industries such as the travel industry, the ventures were able to keep tight control over their costs. Following this strategy, easyGroup expanded into car rental, pizza delivery, bus transport, cruise travel, cinemas, and hotels. In an interview, Haji-Ioannou emphasized his unique position: "Brand extension is very tricky. It's like starting another company, all the time. This is the privilege of entrepreneurs spending their own money."[22]

EasyGroup's diversification into unrelated businesses was not without risks. Haji-Ioannou claimed that easyGroup could create value through its broad corporate focus for the following reasons:[23]

- Through easyJet's rapid growth, its marketing strategy, and the innovations that the airline company had brought to the European airline industry, Haji-Ioannou had gained much exposure for his "easy" brand throughout Europe. Making use of easyJet's valuable brand name and its established reputation in offering no-frills services at low prices, Haji-Ioannou could economize on transaction costs in his new ventures. Customers are likely to have greater trust in new businesses that operate under a familiar brand name. Further, brand-stretching can help to economize on advertising. In fact, Haji-Ioannou admitted on occasions that, without the airline, the other businesses were not likely to survive.

- EasyGroup had been able to acquire critical expertise in flexible pricing and online selling. This is a general competency that can be exploited in many industries.

- EasyGroup's revenues came from licensing the "easy" brand and holding financial stakes in easyJet and the new ventures. Haji-Ioannou planned to take a venture public when it had proven to be successful, as he had done with easyJet. Because the easyGroup did not produce the services itself, the company shared the risks of production with the ventures' other stakeholders.

There were also signs that easyGroup was expanding too rapidly and that its diversification beyond air travel was likely to fail. Very few of the easyGroup's new business ventures were profitable during their first years of operation. For example, at the end of 2003, the losses incurred by easyGroup's internet café chain added up to an estimated £100 million. In many of the industries that easyGroup entered, incumbent companies also had valuable brand names, execution capabilities, and customer loyalty. Therefore these companies were likely to offer formidable competition to easyGroup's individual business lines. EasyGroup's critics also pointed out that expanding rapidly into so many different areas is likely to confuse customers, dilute easyGroup's brand value, and increase the chance of poor execution.

An interesting question to examine is whether there are systematic reasons to believe that a company such as easyGroup can succeed in pursuing a wide focus because its business model – online selling of no-frills services under one common brand – somehow allows it to manage this diversity in a fundamentally different manner than a traditional company would be able to. EasyGroup's poor financial performance during the early 2000s cast doubts on whether it can succeed as a diversified company.

SUMMARY

Strategy analysis is an important starting point for the analysis of financial statements because it allows the analyst to probe the economics of the firm at a qualitative level. Strategy analysis also allows the identification of the firm's profit drivers and key risks, enabling the analyst to assess the sustainability of the firm's performance and make realistic forecasts of future performance.

Whether a firm is able to earn a return on its capital in excess of its cost of capital is determined by its own strategic choices: (1) the choice of an industry or a set of industries in which the firm operates (industry choice), (2) the manner in which the firm intends to compete with other firms in its chosen industry or industries (competitive positioning), and (3) the way in which the firm expects to create and exploit synergies across the range of businesses in which it operates (corporate strategy). Strategy analysis involves analyzing all three choices.

Industry analysis consists of identifying the economic factors that drive the industry profitability. In general, an industry's average profit potential is influenced by the degree of rivalry among existing competitors, the ease with which new firms can enter the industry, the availability of substitute products, the power of buyers, and the power of suppliers. To perform industry analysis, the analyst has to assess the current strength of each of these forces in an industry and make forecasts of any likely future changes.

Competitive strategy analysis involves identifying the basis on which the firm intends to compete in its industry. In general, there are two potential strategies that could provide a firm with a competitive advantage: cost leadership and differentiation. Cost leadership involves offering at a lower cost the same product or service that other firms offer. Differentiation involves satisfying a chosen dimension of customer need better than the competition, at an incremental cost that is less than the price premium that customers are willing to pay. To perform strategy analysis, the analyst has to identify the firm's intended strategy, assess whether the firm possesses the competencies required to execute the strategy, and recognize the key risks that the firm has to guard against. The analyst also has to evaluate the sustainability of the firm's strategy.

Corporate strategy analysis involves examining whether a company is able to create value by being in multiple businesses at the same time. A well-crafted corporate strategy reduces costs or increases revenues from running several businesses in one firm relative to the same businesses operating independently and transacting with each other in the marketplace. These cost savings or revenue increases come from specialized resources that the firm has that help it to exploit synergies across these businesses. For these resources to be valuable, they must be nontradable, not easily imitated by competition, and nondivisible. Even when a firm has such resources, it can create value through a multibusiness organization only when it is managed so that the information and agency costs inside the organization are smaller than the market transaction costs.

The insights gained from strategy analysis can be useful in performing the remainder of the financial statement analysis. In accounting analysis the analyst can examine whether a firm's accounting policies and estimates are consistent with its stated strategy. For example, a firm's choice of functional currency in accounting for its international operations should be consistent with the level of integration between domestic and international operations that the business strategy calls for. Similarly, a firm that mainly sells housing to low-income customers should have higher than average bad debt expenses.

Strategy analysis is also useful in guiding financial analysis. For example, in a cross-sectional analysis the analyst should expect firms with cost leadership strategy to have lower gross margins and higher asset turnover than firms that follow differentiated strategies. In a time series analysis, the analyst should closely monitor any increases in expense ratios and asset turnover ratios for low-cost firms, and any decreases in investments critical to differentiation for firms that follow differentiation strategy.

Business strategy analysis also helps in prospective analysis and valuation. First, it allows the analyst to assess whether, and for how long, differences between the firm's performance and its industry (or industries) performance are likely to persist. Second, strategy analysis facilitates forecasting investment outlays the firm has to make to maintain its competitive advantage.

DISCUSSION QUESTIONS

1. Judith, an accounting student, states, "Strategy analysis seems to be an unnecessary detour in doing financial statement analysis. Why can't we just get straight to the accounting issues?" Explain to Judith why she might be wrong.

2. What are the critical drivers of industry profitability?

3. One of the fastest growing industries in the last 20 years is the memory chip industry, which supplies memory chips for personal computers and other electronic devices. Yet the average profitability for this industry has been very low. Using the industry analysis framework, list all the potential factors that might explain this apparent contradiction.

4. Examples of European firms that operate in the pharmaceutical industry are GlaxoSmithKline and Bayer. Examples of European firms that operate in the tour operating industry are Thomas Cook and TUI. Rate the pharmaceutical and tour operating industries as high, medium, or low on the following dimensions of industry structure: (1) Rivalry, (2) Threat of new entrants, (3) Threat of substitute products, (4) Bargaining power of suppliers, and (5) Bargaining power of buyers. Given your ratings, which industry would you expect to earn the highest returns?

5. Joe argues, "Your analysis of the five forces that affect industry profitability is incomplete. For example, in the banking industry, I can think of at least three other factors that are also important; namely, government regulation, demographic trends, and cultural factors." His classmate Jane disagrees and says, "These three factors are important only to the extent that they influence one of the five forces." Explain how, if at all, the three factors discussed by Joe affect the five forces in the banking industry.

6. In 2005, Puma was a very profitable sportswear company. Puma did not produce most of the shoes, apparel and accessories that it sold. Instead, the company entered into contracts with independent manufacturers, primarily in Asia. Puma also licensed independent companies throughout the world to design, develop, produce and distribute a selected range of products under its brand name. Use the five-forces framework and your knowledge of the sportswear industry to explain Puma's high profitability in 2005.

7. In response to the deregulation of the European airline industry during the 1980s and 1990s, European airlines followed their U.S. peers in starting frequent flyer programs as a way to differentiate themselves from others. Industry analysts, however, believe that frequent flyer programs had only mixed success. Use the competitive advantage concepts to explain why.

8. What are the ways that a firm can create barriers to entry to deter competition in its business? What factors determine whether these barriers are likely to be enduring?

9. Explain why you agree or disagree with each of the following statements:

   a. It's better to be a differentiator than a cost leader, since you can then charge premium prices.

   b. It's more profitable to be in a high technology than a low technology industry.

   c. The reason why industries with large investments have high barriers to entry is because it is costly to raise capital.

10. There are very few companies that are able to be both cost leaders and differentiators. Why? Can you think of a company that has been successful at both?

11. Many consultants are advising diversified companies in emerging markets such as India, Korea, Mexico, and Turkey to adopt corporate strategies proven to be of value in advanced economies like the U.S. and western Europe. What are the pros and cons of this advice?

NOTES

1. The discussion presented here is intended to provide a basic background in strategy analysis. For a more complete discussion of the strategy concepts, see, for example, *Contemporary Strategy Analysis* by Robert M. Grant (Oxford: Blackwell Publishers, 2005); *Economics of Strategy* by David Besanko, David Dranove, and Mark Shanley (New York: John Wiley & Sons, 2004); *Strategy and the Business Landscape* by Pankaj Ghemawat (London: Pearson Education, 2005); and *Corporate Strategy: Resources and the Scope of the Firm* by David J. Collis and Cynthia Montgomery (Burr Ridge, IL: Irwin/McGraw-Hill, 1997).
2. The data to calculate these statistics come from Thomson Financial's Worldscope. The statistics apply to all companies that were listed between April 1989 and April 2006 on one of the seven largest European stock exchanges (see the appendix to Chapter 1 for more details about the sample of European companies).
3. For a summary of this research, see *Industrial Market Structure and Economic Performance*, second edition, by F. M. Scherer (Chicago: Rand McNally College Publishing Co., 1980).
4. See *Competitive Strategy* by Michael E. Porter (New York: The Free Press, 1980).
5. The four-firm concentration ratio is a commonly used measure of industry concentration; it refers to the market share of the four largest firms in an industry.
6. While the discussion here uses the buyer to connote industrial buyers, the same concepts also apply to buyers of consumer products. Throughout this chapter we use the terms buyers and customers interchangeably.
7. The industry statistics in this section are drawn from the Association of European Airlines (AEA) yearbooks and STAR database.
8. The growth rates represent the annual growth rates in passenger-kilometers (cumulative number of kilometers traveled by all passengers). These data come from the Association of European Airlines (AEA). Because the AEA collects data only from its members, which are primarily the established airlines, the growth rates may not reflect the growth that new entrants experienced.
9. For a more detailed discussion of these two sources of competitive advantage, see Michael E. Porter, *Competitive Advantage: Creating and Sustaining Superior Performance* (New York: The Free Press, 1985).
10. Ibid.
11. See *Competing for the Future* by Gary Hammel and C. K. Prahalad (Boston: Harvard Business School Press, 1994) for a more detailed discussion of the concept of core competencies and their critical role in corporate strategy.
12. Kenny Capell, "IKEA, How the Swedish Retailer Became a Global Cult Brand," *Business Week*, November 14, 2005.
13. See K. Kling and I. Goteman, "IKEA CEO Anders Dahlvig on International Growth and IKEA's Unique Corporate Culture and Brand Identity," *Academy of Management Executive*

17 (2003): 31–37; R. Normann and R. Ramirez, "From Value Chain to Value Constellation: Designing Interactive Strategy," *Harvard Business Review* 71 (1993): 65–77; Capell, op. cit.

14. One of the strategic challenges faced by corporations is having to deal with competitors who achieve differentiation with low cost. For example, Japanese auto manufacturers have success-fully demonstrated that there is no necessary trade-off between quality and cost. The example of IKEA also suggests that combining low cost and differentiation strategies is possible when a firm introduces a significant technical or business innovation. However, such cost advantage and differentiation will be sustainable only if there are significant barriers to imitation by competitors.

15. Business segment data come from Thomson Financial's Worldscope.

16. The following works are seminal to transaction cost economics: Ronald Coase, "The Nature of the Firm," *Economica* 4 (1937): 386–405; *Markets and Hierarchies: Analysis and Antitrust Implications* by Oliver Williamson (New York: The Free Press, 1975); David Teece, "Toward an Economic Theory of the Multi-product Firm," *Journal of Economic Behavior and Organization* 3 (1982): 39–63.

17. For a more complete discussion of these issues, see Krishna Palepu and Tarun Khanna, "Building Institutional Infrastructure in Emerging Markets," *Brown Journal of World Affairs*, Winter/Spring 1998, and Tarun Khanna and Krishna Palepu, "Why Focused Strategies May Be Wrong for Emerging Markets," *Harvard Business Review*, July/August 1997.

18. For an empirical study that illustrates this point, see Tarun Khanna and Krishna Palepu, "Is Group Affiliation Profitable in Emerging Markets? An Analysis of Diversified Indian Business Groups," *Journal of Finance* (April 2000): 867–891.

19. See Larry Lang and Rene Stulz, "Tobin's q, diversification, and firm performance," *Journal of Political Economy* 102 (1994): 1248–1280, and Phillip Berger and Eli Ofek, "Diversification's Effect on Firm Value," *Journal of Financial Economics* 37 (1994): 39–65.

20. See Paul Healy, Krishna Palepu, and Richard Ruback, "Which Takeovers Are Profitable: Strategic or Financial?" *Sloan Management Review* 38 (Summer 1997): 45–57.

21. See Katherine Schipper and Abbie Smith, "Effects of Recontracting on Shareholder Wealth: The Case of Voluntary Spinoffs," *Journal of Financial Economics* 12 (December 1983): 437–467; L. Lang, A. Poulsen and R. Stulz, "Asset Sales, Firm Performance, and the Agency Costs of Managerial Discretion," *Journal of Financial Economics* 37 (January 1995): 3–37.

22. "Stelios on Painting the World Orange," *Brand Strategy* (February 2005): 18–19.

23. Ibid.

America Online, Inc.

When it comes to technology companies, the stock market's current mania, it's hard to top America Online, Inc. Technology stocks are hot, up about 50 percent on average this year, but AOL is positively scalding, up about 135 percent. In fact, AOL's stock has soared more than 2,000 percent from its initial public offering, in 1992. The Vienna-based company has 35 times the customers and 20 times the revenue it had five years ago. It's the nation's biggest on-line company and is building a recognized brand.

But look closely and you see that AOL is as much about accounting technology as it is about computer technology. So make sure you understand the numbers before rushing out to buy AOL, which is valued at about $4 billion.

The above report written by Allan Sloan appeared on October 24, 1995, in *Newsweek*'s business section.[1]

Company background

Founded in Vienna, VA, America Online, Inc. (AOL) was a leader in the development of a new mass medium that encompassed online services, the Internet, multimedia, and other interactive technologies. Through its America Online service the company offered members a broad range of features including real-time talk, electronic mail, electronic magazines and newspapers, online classes and shopping, and Internet access. In addition to its online service, AOL's business had expanded during 1995 to include access software for the Internet, production and distribution of original content, interactive marketing and transactions capabilities, and networks to support the transmission of data.

AOL generated revenues principally from consumers through membership fees, as well as from content providers and merchandisers through advertising, commissions on merchandise sales and other transactions, and from other businesses through the sale of network and production services. Through continued investment in the growth of its existing online service, the pursuit of related business opportunities, its ability to provide a full range of interactive services, and its technological flexibility, the company positioned itself to lead the development of the evolving mass medium for interactive services.

Stephen Case and James Kimsey founded America Online's predecessor, Quantum Computer Services, in 1985. Quantum offered its Q-Link service for Commodore computers. In 1989 the service was extended to Apple computers. The company changed its name to America Online in 1991 and went public in 1992. That same year, AOL licensed its on-line technology to Apple for use in eWorld and

Professors Krishna Palepu and Amy Hutton prepared this case. The case is intended solely as the basis for class discussion and is not intended to serve as an endorsement, source of primary data, or illustration of effective or ineffective management. Copyright © 1997 by the President and Fellows of Harvard College. HBS Case 9–196–13.
1. Allan Sloan, "Look Beyond the High-Tech Accounting To Measure America Online's Market Risk," Newsweek, October 24, 1995.

NewtonMail services for which AOL continues to receive a usage-based royalty. In 1993 the company expanded its market with a Windows version of its software and began developing a version for palmtop computers. In 1994 AOL's subscription base surpassed those of CompuServe and Prodigy, two rival online service providers, making AOL the number one consumer online service in the United States. By the end of October 1995, AOL had a subscriber base of more than four million members.

AOL's products

The broad range of features offered by the America Online service was designed to meet the varied needs of its four million members. A key feature of the online service was the ease with which members with related interests could communicate through real-time conferences, e-mail, and bulletin boards. Members used the interactive communications facilities to share information and ideas, exchange advice, and socialize. It was America Online's goal to continue developing and adding new sources of information and content in support of these member activities. The range of features offered by America Online included the following:

- *Online community.* In addition to its e-mail service, AOL promoted real-time online communications by scheduling conferences and discussions on specific topics, offering interactive areas that served as "meeting rooms" for members to participate in lively interactive discussions with other members, and providing public bulletin boards on which members could share information and opinions on subjects of general or specialized interest.

- *Computing.* AOL provided its members access to tens of thousands of public domain and "shareware" software programs, to online help from 300 hardware and software developers, and to online computer shopping and online computer magazines such as *MacWorld*, *PC World,* and *Computer Life*.

- *Education and references.* AOL's online educational services allowed adults and children to learn without leaving their homes. AOL contracted with professional instructors to teach real-time interactive classes in subjects of both general academic interest and adult education (such as creative writing and gourmet cooking). Regular tutoring sessions were offered in English, biology, and math. Education and reference services included the Library of Congress, College Board, CNN, Smithsonian, *Consumer Reports*, and *Compton's Encyclopedia*.

- *News and personal finance.* AOL offered a broad range of information services, including domestic and international news, weather, sports, stock market prices, and personalized portfolio tracking. Members could search news wires for stories of interest, access mutual fund information through Fidelity Online and Morningstar, and execute brokered trades online through PC Financial Network. Subscribers had access to over 70 newspapers, periodicals, and wire services, including *The New York Times, Chicago Tribune, San Jose Mercury News, Time, Scientific American, Investors Business Daily,* and Reuters.

- *Travel and shopping.* AOL members also had access to travel and shopping reference materials and transaction services. Subscribers could send customized greeting cards through Hallmark Corporation, send flowers through 1-800-Flowers, shop for CDs and tapes online at Tower Records, book vacation packages with Preview Vacations, and access account data and travel information and services with American ExpressNet. Additionally, AOL had introduced its own interactive shopping service, 2Market, which featured goods and services from numerous catalogs and retailers.

America Online

■ *Entertainment and children's programming.* AOL provided various clubs and forums for games and sports, multi-player games, and other related content for both adults and children. Specialized content was provided by such organizations as MusicSpace, the Games Channel, Disney Adventures, Comedy Clubs, Nintendo Power Source, Kids Only, Hollywood Online, Warner-Reprise Records, American Association for Retired Persons, MTV, Cooking Club, Environment Club, and Baby Boomers' Forum.

Customer acquisition and retention

AOL's biggest expenditure was the cost of attracting new subscribers. AOL aggressively marketed its online service using both independent marketing efforts, such as direct mail packets with AOL software disks and television and print advertising featuring a toll-free telephone number for ordering the AOL software, as well as co-marketing efforts with computer magazine publishers and personal computer hardware and software producers. These companies bundled the AOL software with their computer products, facilitating easy trial use by their customers. With the AOL software in hand, the customer needed only a personal computer, a telephone line, and a computer modem to gain access to AOL's online service. Accompanying each program disk was a unique registration number and password that could be used to generate a new AOL account. Customers could activate their accounts by providing AOL with their credit card account number. The first ten hours of access by this new account were free, after which AOL automatically billed the customer's credit card account the standard monthly rate until the customer canceled the AOL account.

These types of promotions were expensive, costing more than $40 per new subscriber in 1994. Thus, to retain these new subscribers and increase customer loyalty and satisfaction, AOL invested in specialized retention programs including regularly scheduled online events and conferences, online promotions of upcoming events and new features, and the regular addition of new content, services, and software programs. AOL's goal was to maximize customer subscription life.

Critical to customer retention and usage rates was the content available on AOL. To build and create unique content, AOL participated in numerous joint ventures. During 1995 its alliances grew to include American Express, ABC, Reuters, Shoppers Express, Business Week, Fidelity, Vanguard, and the National Education Association. Also important to AOL were the newest stars of cyberspace, special-interest sites created by entrepreneurs such as Tom and David Gardner, who created Motley Fool and Follywood, two of the most popular sites offered on America Online. These hot special-interest sites kept customers on line, running up metered time and revenues. Traditionally, AOL had kept 80 percent or more of the revenues generated by these sites and had demanded exclusive contracts with the entrepreneurs creating them. However, content providers now had the option of setting up sites on the World Wide Web. While they could not yet collect fees from web browsers, this new distribution channel was changing the balance of power between AOL and its content providers.[2]

Compared to its competitors, AOL's rate structure was the easiest for consumers to understand and anticipate. A monthly fee of $9.95 provided access to all of America Online's services for up to five hours each month. Each additional hour was $2.95 and no additional downloading fees were charged. CompuServe and Prodigy offered the same standard pricing but charged additional fees for premium services

2. Steven Lohr, "On-Line Stars Hear Siren Calls to Free Agency," New York Times, November 25, 1995.

and downloading. Microsoft Network (MSN), the newest entrant into the online services industry, offered a standard monthly plan of up to three hours for $4.95, with each additional hour costing $2.50. Content providers on MSN also applied charges to customers based on usage rates. The additional fees charged by AOL's competitors made it more difficult for their customers to anticipate their monthly spending.

Strategy for future growth

Through a tapestry of alliances and subsidiaries, AOL's goal was to establish a central and defining leadership position in the worldwide market for interactive services. Toward this end, AOL had signed new strategic partnerships with American Express, Business Week Online, and NTN Communications; shipped the 2Market CD-ROM shopping service with an online connection; and completed its acquisitions of Internet software developers BookLink Technologies, Inc., NaviSoft, Inc., and Internet backbone developer Advanced Network & Services (ANS). These deals, along with AOL's growing membership base, its enhanced look and feel, and its ability to program content to appeal to users, uniquely positioned America Online to lead the development of the new interactive services industry. In implementing its strategy, AOL pursued a number of initiatives:

- *Invest in growth of existing service.* AOL planned to continue to invest in the rapid growth of its existing online service. AOL believed it could attract and retain new members by expanding the range of content and services it offered, continuing to improve the engaging multimedia context of its service and building a sense of community online. At the same time, by offering access to a large, growing, and demographically attractive audience, together with software tools and services to develop content and programming for that audience, AOL believed it would continue to appeal to content and service providers.

- *Exploit new business opportunities.* AOL intended to leverage its technology, management skills, and content packaging skills to identify and exploit new business opportunities, such as electronic commerce, entry into international markets, and the "consumerization" of the Internet with its highly graphical interface software and its World Wide Web browser, which used high-speed compression technology to improve access speed and graphic display performance.

- *Provide a full range of interactive services.* Through acquisitions and internal development, AOL had assembled content development, distribution capabilities, access software, and its own communications network to become a full service, vertically integrated provider of interactive services. As a result, AOL believed it was well positioned to influence the evolution of the interactive services market.

- *Maintain technological flexibility.* AOL recognized the need to provide its services over a diverse set of platforms. Its software worked on different types of personal computers and operating systems (including Macintosh, Windows 3.xx, and Windows 95) and supported a variety of different media, including online services, the Internet, and CD-ROM. AOL intended to adapt its products and services as new technologies became available.

While AOL currently generated revenues largely from membership fees, AOL's management believed that these initiatives would allow the company to increase the proportion of its revenues generated from other sources, such as advertising fees, commissions on merchandise sales to consumers, and revenues from the sale of production and network services to other enterprises.

Industry competition and outlook

The online consumer services industry represented $1.1 billion in revenues in 1994 and was expected to grow by 30 percent to $1.4 billion in 1995. Eleven million customers subscribed to commercial online services worldwide and this number was expected to explode in the next five years. Industry leaders AOL, CompuServe, and Prodigy served about 8.5 million of the existing subscribers (4.0 million, 2.8 million, and 1.6 million, respectively). This oligopoly had very successfully acted as middlemen between thousands of content providers and millions of customers. They were the publishers, closely controlling the product and paying content providers, the writers, only modest royalties. However, with the advent of the Internet World Wide Web and the entrance of Microsoft Network, content providers now had alternative distribution channels which offered greater control over their products and potentially higher revenues.

Forbes discussed this topic in its August 28, 1995, issue:

> *Until recently the only way to reach cyberspace browsers was through one of the big three on-line services, America Online, CompuServe and Prodigy. That oligopoly is set to fade fast, and it's not just Microsoft that threatens. It's the whole Internet, the pulsating, undisciplined and rapidly expanding network of World Wide Web computers that contain public data bases.*[3]

While the big three acted as publishers, Microsoft had decided to act more like a bookstore, one in which every author (content provider) was his/her own publisher. Customers of MSN paid $4.95 per month for up to three hours (each additional hour was $2.50). Then each content provider charged whatever it wanted for its material, so much per hour, per page, or per picture. Microsoft kept a 30 percent commission out of the provider's fee and passed along the rest to the content provider. In addition to offering content providers a larger share of the revenues, MSN also offered content providers greater control over their own products. In contrast to the standardized screen displays and icons of the big three, MSN permitted content providers to use any font and format they wished. Thus, while Microsoft still acted as a middleman, it played a very limited and passive role in determining content and fees charged for that content.

Beyond Microsoft lurked the vast potential of the World Wide Web, where the middleman's role was shrunk still further. On the Internet, everyone with a computer was his/her own publisher. Customers would sign up for an Internet on-ramp service, of the sort offered by PST, Netcom, or MCI. Once on the net, the subscriber used browsing software like Netscape or Spyglass to roam the world's databases. While it remained difficult for self-publishers on the Internet to collect fees from browsers who read their pages, that was expected to change quickly as banks, Microsoft, and other intermediaries worked on systems to provide on-line currency.

Many content providers were beginning to take advantage of these alternative distribution channels. For example, *Wired* magazine, unwilling to settle for just 20 percent of the revenues from subscribers spending time on its pages on AOL, created HotWired on the Internet. Andrew Anker, chief technologist at *Wired*, believed that HotWired would soon be more lucrative than the America Online venture and he noted that on the Internet his firm had greater control of its own product. General Electric's NBC decided to switch from AOL to Microsoft Network. "While we had many users visiting us on America Online, we weren't making much revenue," explained Martin Yudkovitz, a senior vice-president at NBC.[4]

---

3. Nikhil Hutheesing, "Who Needs the Middleman?," Forbes, *August 28, 1995.*
4. *Ibid.*

With the migration of proprietary services and content to web sites, the unique offerings of the big three services were declining. However, the online services were still better for interactive communications with full-fledged message boards and live chat. The web, on the other hand, was mainly a publication environment for reading. The question remained, what would be the role of online service providers in the future? Would they become just another Internet access provider with their own look and browsers or could they continue to offer something unique to users?

Some analysts were projecting that the U.S. online services market would grow 30–35 percent annually through the year 2000, and that the Internet market would grow even faster. These analysts expected America Online to retain about a 20 percent market share.[5] On the other hand, Forrester Research of Cambridge, Mass., predicted that the big three, America Online, CompuServe, and Prodigy, would continue to add subscribers only through 1997. After that, Forrester predicted, it would be all downhill for the big three.[6]

AOL's recent performance

For the fourth quarter ended June 30, 1995, America Online announced that its earnings were $0.16, excluding $0.01 merger expenses and $0.02 amortization of goodwill. This was a significant improvement over 1994's fourth-quarter earnings, $0.02, and above analysts' estimate, $0.14. Service revenues surged to $139 million versus analysts' estimate of $132 million, and total revenues rose to $152 million versus $40.4 in the fourth quarter of 1994. For the fiscal year ended June 30, 1995, AOL reported a loss of $33.6 million on revenues of $394 million compared with a profit of $2.5 million on revenues of $116 million a year earlier. New charges recorded for the first time in 1995 included $50.3 million for acquired R&D, $1.7 million amortization of goodwill, and $2.2 million in merger expenses. (See Exhibit 3, America Online's 1995 Abridged Annual Report.)

New subscriber momentum continued to be strong, increasing 233 percent year-over-year and adding 691,000 new net subscribers during the fourth quarter. All major metrics used by analysts to evaluate AOL's franchise and gauge the "health" of its rapidly growing subscriber base also improved during the quarter: projected retention rates rose to 41 months from 39 months; paid usage grew to 2.93 hours from 2.73, and projected lifetime revenues per subscriber increased to $714 from $667. (See Exhibit 2 for the history of America Online's user metrics.) However, analysts were projecting lower gross margins in the future as subscribers continued to transition to higher-speed access and as AOL introduced a heavy-usage pricing plan in response to Microsoft's lower per-hour pricing.

On November 8, 1995, America Online announced its results for the first quarter of fiscal 1996, ended September 30, 1995. Even though revenues rose to $197.9 million from $56 million a year earlier, America Online reported a loss of $10.3 million compared with a profit of $1.5 million a year earlier. America Online took a $16.9 million charge to reflect research and development taking place at Ubique, a company it acquired on September 21, 1995, as well as to pay off other recently acquired assets. It took another charge of $1.7 million for amortization of goodwill. These charges were partially offset by AOL's decision to increase the period over which it amortized subscriber acquisition costs. Effective July 1, 1995, these costs would be amortized

5. A. Pooley, "America Online, Inc.: Company Report," The Chicago Corporation, April 18, 1995.
6. Hutheesing, op. cit.

over 24 months rather than 12–18 months. The effect of the change in accounting esti-mates for the three months ended September 30, 1995, was to decrease the reported loss by $1.95 million. AOL also announced that it added 711,000 subscribers in the first quarter of 1996, bringing its total subscriber base to four million.[7]

America Online's stock price had been on the move since the company's initial public offering (IPO) in March 1992. The stock price appreciated from the IPO price of $2.90 to $7.31, $14.63, and $28.00 at calendar year end 1992, 1993, and 1994, respec-tively. At its current price of $81.63 (dated November 8, 1995), the company's market value was around $4.0 billion. (See Exhibit 1 for the stock price history of America Online, its equity beta, and additional market-based data.)

The controversy surrounding AOL

America Online's stock was one of the most controversial of this period. Some analysts promoted the stock's potential for price appreciation, while others recommended selling the shares short to profit from a decline in price. Bulls saw America Online as part of a revolution in communication, like cellular phones and cable television in the early days. They considered AOL's graphical interface software, its high-speed web browser, and Mr. Case's marketing genius (subscribership had quadrupled to over four million in a little over a year) to be major competitive advantages. Bears, on the other hand, anticipating new entrants competing in the online services industry and a migration of subscribers to the Internet, questioned whether AOL would continue to experience high growth in its subscriber base or be able to retain existing subscribers.

Shortsellers had sold around seven million America Online shares, betting that the stock's price would not go up forever. Shortsellers pointed to the recent hedging activi-ties by Apple Computer to lock in profits on its 5.7 percent stake as an indication that AOL's stock was overvalued. Adding fuel to the shortsellers' fire, corporate insiders at AOL had sold some of their shareholdings. Between March 9 and March 15 of 1995, 17 insiders sold approximately 200,000 shares, including the company founders, President Steven Case (25,000 shares for $2.1 million) and Chairman James Kimsey (40,000 shares for $3.3 million).[8]

Adding to the controversy, some analysts labeled AOL's accounting "aggressive." AOL amortized its software development costs over five years, a long time in the fast-changing, uncertain online services industry, and AOL capitalized subscriber acqui-sition costs when its number one competitor, CompuServe, did not. Furthermore, effective July 1, 1995, AOL extended the amortization period for its subscriber acqui-sition costs from about 15 months to 24 months. Given the uncertainties surrounding AOL's subscriber retention rates and revenue growth as competition emerged in the young industry, analysts questioned the wisdom of AOL's accounting decisions. The big risk AOL faced was that eventually customers could switch online services as frequently as they moved among long-distance carriers.

While America Online expensed the free trial expenses (i.e., those charges incurred from the ten free hours given away in the initial month), it capitalized the marketing costs associated with acquiring a customer, including direct mail, advertising, start-up kits, and bundling costs. As indicated in its annual report, prior to July 1, 1995, the capi-talization had occurred on two schedules depending on the acquisition method. Costs

---

7. *"America Online Posts $10.3 Million Loss But Says Revenue Rose 250% in Quarter,"* The Washington Post, *Nov. 8, 1995.*

8. *As of August 15, 1995 all executive officers and directors as a group continued to own 3,729,547 shares. Steven Case owned 1,036,790 shares and James Kimsey owned 679,616 shares.*

for subscribers acquired through direct marketing programs were amortized over a 12-month period. Costs for subscribers acquired through co-marketing efforts with personal computer producers and magazine publishers were amortized over an 18-month period, as these bundling campaigns had historically shown a longer response time. However, effective July 1, 1995, AOL increased the period over which it amortized subscriber acquisition costs to 24 months for both acquisition methods.

Defending AOL's accounting choices, Lennert Leader, the Chief Financial Officer of America Online, Inc., said that the company was following standard accounting procedures in matching the timing of expenses with the period over which the revenues would be received. He argued that the company's marketing and software development expenses produced customer accounts that last a long time. Thus, he said, it was appropriate to write off the costs over a period of years, even though AOL had spent the cash.[9]

However, some analysts raised red flags about AOL's accounting choices. As noted in an October 24, 1995, *Newsweek* article:

> One of AOL's hidden assets is the brilliant accounting decision it made to treat marketing and research and development costs as capital items rather than expenses... .
>
> AOL charges R&D expenses over a five-year period, a very long time in the online biz. In July, AOL began charging off marketing expenses over two years, up from about 15 months.
>
> Why change to 24 months from 15? Leader said it's because the average life of an AOL account has climbed to 41 months from 25 months in 1992. How many AOL customers have been around for 41 months? Almost none, as Leader concedes. That's understandable, considering that AOL has added virtually all its customers in the past 36 months. Leader says the 41-month average live number comes from projections. Of course, it will take years to find out if he's right... .[10]

Analysts were also concerned about AOL's cash flow situation and the signal sent by the timing of its latest equity offering. The *Newsweek* article continued:

> Accounting is terribly important to AOL. The better the numbers look, the more Wall Street loves it and the easier AOL can sell new shares to raise cash to pay its bills.... On October 10 [AOL] raised about $100 million by selling new shares. AOL sold the stock even though its shares had fallen to $58.37 from about $72 in September, when the sale plans were announced. Most companies would have delayed the offering, waiting for the price to snap back. AOL didn't, prompting cynics to think the company really needed the money... .

Some analysts believed that AOL issued shares when its stock price was low because the company needed the cash immediately. Others argued that AOL was building a war chest needed because deep-pocketed rivals such as Microsoft were about to start an online price war and because information providers increasingly were going directly to the Internet rather than using middlemen such as AOL. Some analysts interpreted CompuServe's recent adoption of more aggressive accounting techniques as a sign that it too was readying for war. Beginning the first quarter of fiscal 1996, CompuServe would capitalize direct response advertising costs associated with customer acquisition activity.[11]

9. Sloan, op. cit.
10. Ibid.
11. Ibid.

While AOL's stock price rebounded to $81.63 by November 8, 1995, there were many questions concerning AOL's future. How would the demand for AOL's services be affected by the entry of Microsoft Network and the growth of the Internet? Would AOL's accounting choices stand the test of time? What if AOL's subscription growth rates slowed or subscriber renewal rates fell? Did AOL have the financial flexibility to face these competitive pressures and accounting risks?

Questions

1. Prior to 1995, why was America Online (AOL) so successful in the commercial online industry relative to its competitors CompuServe and Prodigy?

2. As of 1995, what are the key changes taking place in the commercial online industry? How are they likely to affect AOL's future prospects?

3. Was AOL's policy to capitalize subscriber acquisition costs justified prior to 1995?

4. Given the changes discussed in question 2, do you think AOL should change its accounting policy as of 1995? Is the company's response consistent with your view?

5. What would be the effect on AOL's 1994 and 1995 ending balance sheets if the company had followed the policy of expensing subscriber acquisition outlays instead of capitalizing them? What would be the effect of expensing subscriber acquisition costs on AOL's 1995 income statement?

America Online

EXHIBIT 1 **Stock price history for America Online, Inc.**

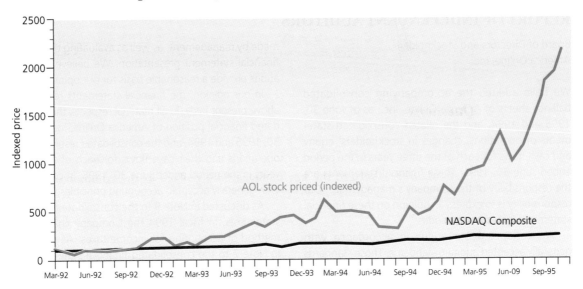

Additional market-based data:

America Online's equity beta	1.4
Moody's AAA corporate debt in November 1995 (%)	7.02
Treasury bills rate in November 1995 (%)	5.35
Government 30-year treasury rates in November 1995 (%)	6.26

Sources: Datastream International, Standard and Poor's Compustat, and *The Wall Street Journal*.

EXHIBIT 2 **America Online, Inc. user metrics to June 30, 1995**

	Dec-93	Mar-94	Jun-94	Sep-94	Dec-94	Mar-95	Jun-95
Paid usage (hours)	1.85	2	2.1	2.27	2.46	2.73	2.93
Projected average months' retention	30	32	32+	34	36	39	41
Projected average lifetime revenue	$443	$496	$496	$551	$612	$667	$714
Internet usage (% time)		1%	3%	4%	5%	6%	9%

Source: Alex Brown & Sons, Inc., August 24, 1995.

EXHIBIT 3   **America Online 1995 abridged annual report**

REPORT OF INDEPENDENT AUDITORS

Board of Directors and Stockholders
America Online, Inc.

We have audited the accompanying consolidated balance sheets of America Online, Inc., as of June 30, 1995 and 1994, and the related consolidated statements of operations, changes in stockholders' equity and cash flows for each of the three years in the period ended June 30, 1995. These financial statements are the responsibility of the Company's management. Our responsibility is to express an opinion on these financial statements based on our audits.

We conducted our audits in accordance with generally accepted auditing standards. Those standards require that we plan and perform the audit to obtain reasonable assurance about whether the financial statements are free of material misstatement. An audit includes examining, on a test basis, evidence supporting the amounts and disclosures in the financial statements. An audit also includes assessing the accounting principles used and significant estimates made by management, as well as evaluating the overall financial statement presentation. We believe that our audits provide a reasonable basis for our opinion.

In our opinion, the financial statements referred to above present fairly, in all material respects, the consolidated financial position of America Online, Inc. at June 30, 1995 and 1994, and the consolidated results of their operations and their cash flows for each of the three years in the period ended June 30, 1995, in conformity with generally accepted accounting principles.

As discussed in Note 9 to the consolidated financial statements, in fiscal 1994 the Company changed its method of accounting for income taxes. As discussed in Note 2 to the consolidated financial statements, in fiscal 1995 the Company changed its method of accounting for short-term investments in certain debt and equity securities.

Ernst & Young LLP
Vienna, Virginia
August 25, 1995

SELECTED CONSOLIDATED FINANCIAL AND OTHER DATA
(in thousands, except per share data)

	Year ended June 30,				
	1995	**1994**	**1993**	**1992**	**1991**
Statements of operations data:					
Online service revenues	$358,498	$100,993	$38,462	$26,226	$19,515
Other revenues	35,792	14,729	13,522	12,527	10,646
Total revenues	394,290	115,722	51,984	38,753	30,161
Income (loss) from operations	(19,294)	4,608	1,925	3,685	1,341
Income (loss) before extraordinary items	(33,647)	2,550	399	2,344	1,100
Net income (loss)[1]	(33,647)	2,550	1,532	3,768	1,761
Income (loss) per common share:					
Income (loss) before extraordinary item	$ (0.99)	$ 0.07	$ 0.01	$ 0.10	$ 0.06
Net income (loss)	$ (0.99)	$ 0.07	$ 0.05	$ 0.17	$ 0.09
Weighted average shares outstanding	33,986	34,208	29,286	22,828	19,304

	As of June 30,				
	1995	**1994**	**1993**	**1992**	**1991**
Balance sheet data:					
Working capital (deficiency)	$ (456)	$47,890	$10,498	$12,363	$ (966)
Total assets	406,464	154,584	39,279	31,144	11,534
Total debt	21,810	9,302	2,959	2,672	1,865
Stockholders' equity (deficiency)	217,944	98,297	23,785	21,611	(8,623)
Other data (at fiscal year end):					
Subscribers	3,005	903	303	182	131

(1) Net loss in the fiscal year ended June 30, 1995, includes charges of $50.3 million for acquired research and development and $2.2 million for merger expenses. See Note 3 of the Notes to Consolidated Financial Statements.

America Online

MANAGEMENT'S DISCUSSION AND ANALYSIS OF FINANCIAL CONDITIONS AND RESULTS OF OPERATIONS

Overview

The Company has experienced a significant increase in revenues over the past three fiscal years. The higher revenues have been principally produced by increases in the Company's subscriber base resulting from growth of the online services market, the introduction of a Windows version of America Online in the middle of fiscal 1993, which greatly increased the available market for the Company's service, as well as the expansion of its services and content. Additionally, revenues have increased as the average monthly revenue per subscriber has risen steadily during the past three years, primarily as a result of an increase in the average monthly paid hours of use per subscriber.

The Company's online service revenues are generated primarily from subscribers paying a monthly member's fee and hourly charges based on usage in excess of the number of hours of usage provided as part of the monthly fee. Through December 31, 1994, the Company's standard monthly membership fee, which includes five hours of service, was $9.95, with a $3.50 hourly fee for usage in excess of five hours per month. Effective January 1, 1995, the hourly fee for usage in excess of five hours per month decreased from $3.50 to $2.95, while the monthly membership fee remained unchanged at $9.95.

The Company's other revenues are generated primarily from providing new media and interactive marketing services, data network services, and multimedia and CD-ROM production services. Additionally, the Company generates revenues related to online transactions and advertising, as well as development and licensing fees.

In fiscal 1995 the Company acquired RCC, NaviSoft, BookLink, ANS, WAIS, Medior and Global Network Navigator, Inc. Additionally, in August 1995, the Company entered into an agreement to acquire Ubique. For additional information relating to these acquisitions, refer to Notes 3 and 13 of the Notes to Consolidated Financial Statements.

The online services market is highly competitive. The Company believes that existing competitors, which include, among others, CompuServe, Prodigy and MSN, are likely to enhance their service offerings. In addition, new competitors have announced plans to enter the online services market, resulting in greater competition for the Company. The competitive environment could require new pricing programs and increased spending on marketing, content procurement and product development; limit the Company's opportunities to enter into and/or renew agreements with content providers and distribution partners; limit the Company's ability to grow its subscriber base; and result in increased attrition in the Company's subscriber base. Any of the foregoing events could result in an increase in costs as a percentage of revenues, and may have a material adverse effect on the Company's financial condition and operating results.

During September 1995, the Company modified the components of subscriber acquisition costs deferred and will be expensing certain subscriber acquisition cost as incurred, effective July 1, 1995. All costs capitalized before this change will continue to be amortized. The effect of this change for the year ended June 30, 1995 (including the amortization of amounts capitalized as of June 30, 1994) would have been to increase marketing costs by approximately $8 million. This change will have a greater impact on the Company's marketing costs in fiscal 1996, as the Company expects to significantly increase subscriber acquisition activity, including those subscriber acquisition expenditures which the Company will be expensing as incurred.

In addition, effective July 1, 1995, the Company changed the period over which it amortizes subscriber acquisition cost from twelve and eighteen months to twenty-four months. Based on the Company's historical average customer life experience, the change in amortization period is being made to more appropriately match subscriber acquisition costs with associated online service revenues. The effect of this change in accounting estimate for the year ended June 30, 1995 would have been to decrease the amount of the amortization of subscriber acquisition costs by approximately $27 million. While this change will thereby positively impact operating margins, the Company expects that any such positive impact will be partially offset by increased investments in marketing and other business activities during fiscal 1996 and the decision, effective July 1, 1995, to expense certain subscriber acquisition costs as incurred.

Results of operations

Fiscal 1995 compared to fiscal 1994

Online service revenues

For fiscal 1995, online service revenues increased from $100,993,000 to $358,498,000, or 255%, over fiscal

1994. This increase was primarily attributable to a 289% increase in revenues from IBM-compatible subscribers and a 196% increase in revenues from Macintosh subscribers as a result of a 273% increase in the number of IBM-compatible subscribers and a 143% increase in the number of Macintosh subscribers. The percentage increase in online service revenues in fiscal 1995 was greater than the percentage increase in subscribers principally due to an increase in the average monthly online service revenue per subscriber, which increased from $15.00 in fiscal 1994 to $17.10 in fiscal 1995.

Other revenues

Other revenues, consisting principally of new media and interactive marketing services, data network services, multimedia and CD-ROM production services, and development and licensing fees, increased from $14,729,000 in fiscal 1994 to $35,792,000 in fiscal 1995. This increase was primarily attributable to data network revenues and multimedia and CD-ROM production service revenues from companies acquired during fiscal 1995.

Cost of revenues

Cost of revenues includes network-related costs, consisting primarily of data and voice communication costs, costs associated with operating the data center and providing customer support, royalties paid to information and service providers and other expenses related to marketing and production services. For fiscal 1995, cost of revenues increased from $69,043,000 to $229,724,000, or 233%, over fiscal 1994, and decreased as a percentage of total revenues from 59.7% to 58.3%.

The increase in cost of revenues was primarily attributable to an increase in data communication costs, customer support costs and royalties paid to information and service providers. Data communication costs increased primarily as a result of the larger customer base and more usage by customers. Customer support costs, which include personnel and telephone costs associated with providing customer support, were higher as a result of the larger customer base and a large number of new subscriber registrations. Royalties paid to information and service providers increased as a result of a larger customer base and more usage and the Company's addition of more service content to broaden the appeal of the America Online service.

The decrease in cost of revenues as a percentage of total revenues is primarily attributable to a decrease in

expenses related to marketing services and personnel related costs as a percentage of total revenues, partially offset by an increase in data communication costs as a percentage of total revenues, primarily resulting from an increase in higher baud speed usage at a higher variable rate as well as lower hourly pricing for online service revenue which became effective January 1, 1995.

Marketing

Marketing expenses include the costs to acquire and retain subscribers and other general marketing expenses. Subscriber acquisition costs are deferred and charged to operations over a twelve or eighteen month period, using the straight-line method, beginning the month after such costs are incurred. For additional information regarding the accounting for deferred subscriber acquisition costs, refer to Note 2 of the Notes to Consolidated Financial Statements. For fiscal 1995, marketing expenses increased from $23,548,000 to $77,064,000, or 227%, over fiscal 1994, and decreased as a percentage of total revenues from 20.3% to 19.5%. The increase in marketing expenses was primarily due to an increase in the number and size of marketing programs to expand the Company's subscriber base. The decrease in marketing expenses as a percentage of total revenues is primarily attributable to a decrease as a percentage of total revenues in personnel related costs.

Product development

Product development costs include research and development expenses, other product development costs and the amortization of software costs. For fiscal 1995, product development expenses increased from $4,961,000 to $12,842,000, or 159%, over fiscal 1994, and decreased as a percentage of total revenues from 4.3% to 3.3%. The increase in product development costs was primarily attributable to an increase in personnel costs related to an increase in the number of technical employees. The decrease in product development costs as a percentage of total revenues was principally a result of the substantial growth in revenues, which more than offset the additional product development costs. Product development costs, before capitalization and amortization, increased by 126% in fiscal 1995.

General and administrative

Fiscal 1995 general and administrative costs increased from $13,562,000 to $41,966,000, or 209%, over

America Online

fiscal 1994, and decreased as a percentage of total revenues from 11.7% to 10.6%. The increase in general and administrative expenses was principally attributable to higher office and personnel expenses related to an increase in the number of employees. The decrease in general and administrative costs as a percentage of total revenues was a result of the substantial growth in revenues, which more than offset the additional general and administrative costs, combined with the semi-variable nature of many of the general and administrative costs.

Acquired research and development

Acquired research and development costs, totaling $50,335,000, relate to in-process research and development purchased pursuant to the Company's acquisition of two early-stage Internet technology companies, BookLink and NaviSoft. The purchased research and development relating to the BookLink and NaviSoft acquisitions was the foundation of the development of the Company's Internet related products.

Amortization of goodwill

Amortization of goodwill relates to the Company's acquisition of ANS, which resulted in approximately $44 million in goodwill. The goodwill related to the ANS acquisition is being amortized on a straight-line basis over a ten-year period.

Other income

Other income consists primarily of investment and rental income net of interest expense. For fiscal 1995, other income increased from $1,774,000 to $3,023,000. This increase was primarily attributable to an increase in interest income generated by higher levels of cash available for investment, partially offset by a decrease in rental income and an increase in interest expense.

Merger expenses

Non-recurring merger expenses totaling $2,207,000 were recognized in fiscal 1995 in connection with the mergers of the Company with RCC, WAIS and Medior.

Provisions for income taxes

The provision for income taxes was $3,832,000 and $15,169,000 in fiscal year 1994 and fiscal 1995, respectively. For additional information regarding income taxes, refer to Note 9 of the Notes to Consolidated Financial Statements.

Net loss

The net loss in fiscal 1995 totaled $33,647,000. The net loss in fiscal 1995 included charges of $50,335,000 for acquired research and development and $2,207,000 for merger expenses.

Liquidity and capital resources

The Company has financed its operations through cash generated from operations, sale of its common stock and funding by third parties for certain product development activities. Net cash provided by operating activities was $2,205,000, $1,884,000 and $15,891,000 for fiscal 1993, fiscal 1994 and fiscal 1995, respectively. Included in operating activities were expenditures for deferred subscriber acquisition costs of $10,685,000, $37,424,000 and $111,761,000 in fiscal 1993, fiscal 1994 and fiscal 1995, respectively. Net cash used in investing activities was $8,915,000, $41,870,000 and $85,725,000 in fiscal 1993, fiscal 1994 and fiscal 1995, respectively. Investing activities included $20,523,000 in fiscal 1995 related to business acquisitions, substantially all of which were related to the acquisition of ANS.

In December 1993 the Company completed a public stock offering of 4,000,000 shares of common stock which generated net cash proceeds of approximately $62.7 million.

In April 1995 the company entered into a joint venture with Bertelsmann to offer interactive online services in Europe. In connection with the agreement, the Company received approximately $54 million through the sale of approximately 5% of its common stock to Bertelsmann.

The Company leases the majority of its equipment under noncancelable operating leases, and as part of its network portfolio strategy is building AOLnet, its data communications network. The buildout of this network requires a substantial investment in telecommunication equipment, which the Company plans to finance principally though leasing. In addition, the Company has guaranteed minimum commitments under certain data and voice communication agreements. The Company's future lease commitments and guaranteed minimums are discussed in Note 6 of the Notes to Consolidated Financial Statements.

The Company uses its working capital to finance ongoing operations and to fund marketing and content programs and the development of its products and services. The Company plans to continue to invest aggressively in acquisition marketing and content programs to expand its subscriber base, as well as in computing and support infrastructure. Additionally, the Company expects to use a portion of its cash for the acquisition and subsequent funding of technologies, products or businesses complementary to the Company's current business. Apart from its agreement to acquire Ubique, as discussed below, the Company has no agreements or understandings to acquire any businesses. The Company anticipates that available cash and cash provided by operating activities will be sufficient to fund its operations for the next fiscal year.

Various legal proceedings have arisen against the Company in the ordinary course of business. In the opinion of management, these proceedings will not have a material effect on the financial position of the Company.

The Company believes that inflation has not had a material effect on its results of operations.

On August 23, 1995, the Company entered into a stock purchase agreement to purchase Ubique, an Israeli company. The Company has agreed to pay approximately $15 million ($1.5 million in cash and $13.5 million in common stock) in the transaction, which is to be accounted for as a purchase. Subject to the results of an in-process valuation, a substantial portion of the purchase price may be allocated to in-process research and development and charged to the Company's operations in the first quarter of fiscal 1996.

CONSOLIDATED STATEMENTS OF OPERATIONS
(Amounts in thousands, except per share data)

	Year ended June 30,		
	1995	1994	1993
Revenues:			
Online service revenues	$358,498	$100,993	$ 38,462
Other revenues	35,792	14,729	13,522
Total revenues	394,290	115,722	51,984
Costs and expenses:			
Cost of revenues	229,724	69,043	28,820
Marketing	77,064	23,548	9,745
Product development	12,842	4,961	2,913
General and administrative	41,966	13,562	8,581
Acquired research and development	50,335	—	—
Amortization of goodwill	1,653	—	—
Total costs and expenses	413,584	111,114	50,059
Income (loss) from operations	(19,294)	4,608	1,925
Other income, net	3,023	1,774	371
Merger expenses	(2,207)	—	—
Income (loss) before provision for income taxes and extraordinary item	(18,478)	6,382	2,296
Provision for income taxes	(15,169)	(3,832)	(1,897)
Income (loss) before extraordinary item	(33,647)	2,550	399
Extraordinary item – tax benefit arising from net operating loss carryforward	—	—	1,133
Net income (loss)	$ (33,647)	$ 2,550	$ 1,532
Earnings (loss) per share:			
Income (loss) before extraordinary item	$ (0.99)	$ 0.07	$ 0.01
Net income (loss)	$ (0.99)	$ 0.07	$ 0.05
Weighted average shares outstanding	33,986	34,208	29,286

America Online

See accompanying notes.

CONSOLIDATED STATEMENTS OF CASH FLOWS
(Amounts in Thousands)

| | Year ended June 30, | | |
	1995	1994	1993
Cash flows from operating activities:			
Net income (loss)	$ (33,647)	$ 2,550	$ 1,532
Adjustments to reconcile net income to net cash provided by operating activities:			
Depreciation and amortization	11,136	2,965	1,957
Amortization of subscriber acquisition costs	60,924	17,922	7,038
Loss/(Gain) on sale of property and equipment	37	5	(39)
Charge for acquired research and development	50,335	—	—
Changes in assets and liabilities:			
Trade accounts receivable	(14,373)	(4,266)	(936)
Other receivables	(9,057)	(681)	(966)
Prepaid expenses and other current assets	(19,641)	(2,867)	(1,494)
Deferred subscriber acquisition costs	(111,761)	(37,424)	(10,685)
Other assets	(8,432)	(2,519)	(89)
Trade accounts payable	60,824	10,204	2,119
Accrued personnel costs	1,846	367	336
Other accrued expenses and liabilities	5,703	9,526	1,492
Deferred revenue	7,190	2,322	1,381
Deferred income taxes	14,763	3,832	759
Deferred rent	44	(52)	(200)
Total adjustments	49,538	(666)	673
Net cash provided by operating activities	15,891	1,884	2,205
Cash flows from investing activities:			
Short-term investments	5,380	(18,947)	(5,105)
Purchase of property and equipment	(57,751)	(17,886)	(2,041)
Product development costs	(13,011)	(5,132)	(1,831)
Sale of property and equipment	180	95	62
Purchase costs of acquired businesses	(20,523)	—	—
Net cash used in investing activities	(85,725)	(41,870)	(8,915)
Cash flows from financing activities:			
Proceeds from issuance of common stock, net	61,253	67,372	609
Principal and accrued interest payments on line of credit and long-term debt	(3,298)	(7,716)	(6,924)
Proceeds from line of credit and issuance of long-term debt	13,741	14,200	7,181
Tax benefit from stock option exercises	—	—	6
Principal payments under capital lease obligations	(375)	(142)	(112)
Net cash provided by financing activities	71,321	73,714	760
Net increase (decrease) in cash and cash equivalents	1,487	33,728	(5,950)
Cash and cash equivalents at beginning of period	43,891	10,163	16,113
Cash and cash equivalents at end of period	$ 45,378	$ 43,891	$ 10,163

(continued)

America Online

CONSOLIDATED STATEMENTS OF CASH FLOWS *(continued)*			
	Year ended June 30,		
	1995	**1994**	**1993**
Supplemental cash flow information			
Cash paid during the period for:			
Interest	1,067	575	193
Income taxes	—	—	15

See accompanying notes.

CONSOLIDATED BALANCE SHEETS
(Amounts in thousands, except per share data)

	June 30,	
	1995	**1994**
ASSETS		
Current assets:		
Cash and cash equivalents	$ 45,378	$ 43,891
Short-term investments	18,672	24,052
Trade accounts receivable	32,176	8,547
Other receivables	11,103	2,036
Prepaid expenses and other current assets	25,527	5,753
Total current assets	132,856	84,279
Property and equipment at cost, net	70,466	20,306
Other assets:		
Product development costs, net	18,914	7,912
Deferred subscriber acquisition costs, net	77,229	26,392
License rights, net	5,537	53
Other assets	11,479	2,800
Deferred income taxes	35,627	12,842
Goodwill, net	54,356	—
	$406,464	$154,584

(continued)

America Online

CONSOLIDATED BALANCE SHEETS *(continued)*

	June 30,	
	1995	**1994**
LIABILITIES AND STOCKHOLDERS' EQUITY		
Current liabilities:		
Trade accounts payable	$ 84,639	$ 15,642
Accrued personnel costs	2,829	896
Other accrued expenses and liabilities	23,509	13,076
Deferred revenue	20,021	4,488
Line of credit	484	1,690
Current portion of long-term debt and capital lease obligations	1,830	597
Total current liabilities	133,312	36,389
Long-term liabilities:		
Notes payable	17,369	5,836
Capital lease obligations	2,127	1,179
Deferred income taxes	35,627	12,842
Deferred rent	85	41
Total liabilities	188,520	56,287
Stockholders' equity:		
Preferred stock, $.01 par value; 5,000,000 shares authorized, none issued	—	—
Common stock, $.01 par value; 100,000,000 shares authorized, 37,554,849 and 30,771,212 shares issued and outstanding at June 30, 1995 and 1994, respectively	375	308
Additional paid-in capital	251,539	98,836
Accumulated deficit	(33,970)	(847)
Total stockholders' equity	217,944	98,297
	$406,464	$154,584

See accompanying notes.

America Online

NOTES TO CONSOLIDATED FINANCIAL STATEMENTS

1. Organization

America Online, Inc. ("the Company") was incorporated in the State of Delaware in May 1985. The Company, based in Vienna, Virginia, is a leading provider of online services, offering its subscribers a wide variety of services, including e-mail, online conferences, entertainment, software, computing support, interactive magazines and newspapers, and online classes, as well as easy and affordable access to services of the Internet. In addition, the Company is a provider of data network services, new media and interactive marketing services, and multimedia and CD-ROM production services.

2. Summary of significant accounting policies

Principles of consolidation

The consolidated financial statements include the accounts of the Company and its subsidiaries. All significant intercompany accounts and transactions have been eliminated. Investments in affiliates owned twenty percent or more and corporate joint ventures are accounted for under the equity method. Other securities in companies owned less than twenty percent are accounted for under the cost method.

Business combinations

Business combinations which have been accounted for under the purchase method of accounting include the results of operations of the acquired business from the date of acquisition. Net assets of the companies acquired are recorded at their fair value to the Company at the date of acquisition.

Other business combinations have been accounted for under the pooling of interests method of accounting. In such cases, the assets, liabilities, and stockholders' equity of the acquired entities were combined with the Company's respective accounts at recorded values. Prior period financial statements have been restated to give effect to the merger unless the effect of the business combination is not material to the financial statements of the Company.

Revenue and cost recognition

Online service revenue is recognized over the period services are provided. Other revenue, consisting principally of marketing, data network and multimedia production services, as well as development and royalty revenues, are recognized as services are rendered. Deferred revenue consists principally of third-party development funding not yet recognized and monthly subscription fees billed in advance.

Property and equipment

Property and equipment are depreciated or amortized using the straight-line method over the estimated useful life of the asset, which ranges from 5 to 40 years, or over the life of the lease.

Property and equipment under capital leases are stated at the lower of the present value of minimum lease payments at the beginning of the lease term or fair value at inception of the lease.

Deferred subscriber acquisition costs

Subscriber acquisition costs are deferred and charged to operations over a twelve or eighteen month period (straight-line method) beginning the month after such costs are incurred. These costs, which relate directly to subscriber solicitations, principally include printing, production and shipping of starter kits and the costs of obtaining qualified prospects by various targeted direct marketing programs (i.e., direct marketing response cards, mailing lists) and from third parties, and are recorded separately from ordinary operating expenses. No indirect costs are included in subscriber acquisition costs. To date, all subscriber acquisition costs have been incurred for the solicitation of specific identifiable prospects. Costs incurred for other than those targeted at specific identifiable prospects for the Company's services, and general marketing, are expensed as incurred.

The Company's services are sold on a monthly subscription basis. Subscriber acquisition costs incurred to obtain new subscribers are recoverable from revenues generated by such subscribers within a short period of time after such costs are incurred.

Effective July 1, 1992, the Company changed, from twelve months to eighteen months, the period over which it amortizes the costs of deferred subscriber acquisition costs relating to marketing activities in which the Company's starter kit is bundled and distributed by a third-party marketing company. The change in accounting estimate was made to more accurately match revenues and expenses. Based on the Company's experience and the distribution channels used in such marketing activities, there is a greater

America Online

time lag between the time the Company incurs the cost for the starter kits and the time the starter kits begin to generate new customers than with direct marketing activities. Also, the period over which new subscribers (and related revenues) are generated is longer than that experienced with the use of traditional independent, direct marketing activities. The effect of this change in accounting estimate for the year ended June 30, 1993 was to increase income before extraordinary item and net income by $264,000 ($.01 per share).

In the first quarter of fiscal 1995 the Company adopted the provisions of Statement of Position ("SOP") 93–7, "Reporting on Advertising Costs," which provides guidance on financial reporting on advertising costs. The adoption of SOP 93–7 had no effect on the Company's financial position or results of operations.

Product development costs

The Company capitalizes cost incurred for the production of computer software used in the sale of its services. Costs capitalized include direct labor and related overhead for software produced by the Company and the costs of software purchased from third parties. All costs in the software development process which are classified as research and development are expensed as incurred until technological feasibility has been established. Once technological feasibility has been established, such costs are capitalized until the software is commercially available. To the extent the Company retains the rights to software development funded by third parties, such costs are capitalized in accordance with the Company's normal accounting policies. Amortization is provided on a product-by-product basis, using the greater of the straight-line method or current year revenue as a percent of total revenue estimates for the related software product not to exceed five years, commencing the month after the date of product release.

Product development costs consist of the following:

	Year ended June 30,	
	1995	1994
	(in thousands)	
Balance, beginning of year	$ 7,912	$3,915
Cost capitalized	13,011	5,132
Cost amortized	(2,009)	(1,135)
Balance, end of year	$18,914	$7,912

The accumulated amortization of product development costs related to the production of computer software totaled $7,894,000, and $5,885,000 at June 30, 1995 and 1994, respectively.

Included in product development costs are research and development costs totaling $3,856,000, $2,126,000, and $1,130,000 and other product development costs totaling $6,977,000, $1,050,000 and $579,000 in the years ended June 30, 1995, 1994 and 1993, respectively.

License rights

The cost of acquired license rights is amortized using the straight-line method over the term of the agreement for such license rights, ranging from one to three years.

Goodwill

Goodwill consists of the excess of cost over the fair value of net assets acquired and certain other intangible assets relating to purchase transactions. Goodwill and intangible assets are amortized over periods ranging from 5–10 years.

Operating lease costs

Rent expense for operating leases is recognized on a straight-line basis over the lease term. The difference between rent expense incurred and rental payments is charged or credited to deferred rent.

Cash, cash equivalents and short-term investments

The Company considers all highly liquid investments with an original maturity of three months or less to be cash equivalents. In fiscal 1995, the Company adopted Statement of Financial Accounting Standards No. 115 ("SFAS 115"), "Accounting for Certain Investments in Debt and Equity Securities." The adoption was not material to the Company's financial position or results of operations. The Company has classified all debt and equity securities as available-for-sale. Available-for-sale securities are carried at fair value, with unrealized gains and losses reported as a separate component of stockholders' equity. Realized gains and losses and declines in value judged to be other-than-temporary on available-for-sale securities are included in other income. Available-for-sale securities at June 30, 1995, consisted of U.S. Treasury Bills and other obligations of U.S. Government agencies totaling $7,579,000 and U.S. corporate debt obligations totaling $11,093,000. At June 20, 1995, the estimated fair value of these securities approximated cost.

Net income (loss) per common share

Net income (loss) per share is calculated by dividing income (loss) before extraordinary item and net income (loss) by the weighted average number of common and, when dilutive, common equivalent shares outstanding during the period.

Reclassification

Certain amounts in prior years' consolidated financial statements have been reclassified to conform to the current year presentation.

3. Business combination

Pooling transactions

On August 19, 1994, Redgate Communications Corporation ("RCC") was merged with and into a subsidiary of the Company. The Company exchanged 1,789,300 shares of common stock for all of the outstanding common and preferred stock and warrants of RCC. Additionally, 401,148 shares of the Company's common stock were reserved for outstanding stock options issued by RCC and assumed by the Company. The merger was accounted for under the pooling of interests method of accounting, and accordingly, the accompanying consolidated financial statements have been restated for all periods prior to the acquisition to include the financial position, results of operations and cash flows of RCC. Effective August 1994, RCC's fiscal year-end has been changed from December 31 to June 30 to conform to the Company's fiscal year-end.

Revenues and net earnings (loss) for the individual entities are as follows:

	Three months ended September 30, 1994 (unaudited)	Year ended June 30, 1994	1993
	(in thousands)		
Total revenues:			
AOL	$50,783	$104,410	$40,019
RCC	3,813	11,312	11,965
Less intercompany sales	(173)	—	—
	$54,423	$115,722	$51,984
Net income (loss):			
AOL	$ 3,018	$ 6,210	$ 4,210
RCC	(42)	(3,660)	(2,678)
Merger expenses	(1,710)	—	—
	$ 1,266	$ 2,550	$ 1,532

In connection with the merger of the Company and RCC, merger expenses of $1,710,000 were recognized during 1995.

During fiscal 1995, Medior, Inc. and Wide Area Information Servers, Inc. were merged into subsidiaries of the Company. The Company issued 1,082,019 shares of its common stock in the transactions. The transactions were accounted for under the pooling of interests method of accounting. Prior year financial statements have not been restated for the transactions because the effect would not be material to the operations of the Company.

Purchase transactions

During fiscal 1995, the Company acquired NaviSoft, Inc. ("NaviSoft"), BookLink Technologies, Inc. ("BookLink"), Advanced Network & Services, Inc. ("ANS") and Global Network Navigator, Inc., in transactions accounted for under the purchase method of accounting. The Company paid a total of $97,669,000, of which $75,697,000 was in stock and $21,972,000 was in cash for the acquisitions. Of the aggregate purchase price, approximately $50,335,000 was allocated to in-process research and development and $55,314,000 was allocated to goodwill and other intangible assets.

The following unaudited pro forma information relating to the BookLink and ANS acquisitions is not necessarily an indication of the combined results that would have occurred had the acquisitions taken place at the beginning of the period, nor is necessarily an indication of the results that may occur in the future. Pro forma information for NaviSoft and Global Network Navigator, Inc. is immaterial to the operations of the consolidated entity. The amount of the aggregate purchase price allocated to in-process research and development for both the NaviSoft and BookLink acquisitions has been excluded from the pro forma information as it is a non-recurring item.

	Year ended June 30,	
	1995	1994
	(in thousands except per share data)	
Revenues	$410,147	$135,785
Income (loss) from operations	23,117	(5,465)
Pro forma income (loss)	11,205	(4,694)
Pro forma income (loss) per share	$ 0.25	$ (0.16)

4. Property and equipment

Property and equipment consist of the following:

	June 30,	
	1995	1994
	(in thousands)	
Computer equipment	$49,167	$12,418
Furniture and fixtures	4,992	1,398
Buildings	13,800	5,648
Land	6,075	2,052
Building improvements	6,284	1,343
Property under capital leases	8,486	2,686
Leasehold improvements	3,059	306
	91,863	25,851
Less accumulated depreciation and amortization	(21,397)	(5,545)
Net property and equipment	$70,466	$20,306

5. License rights

License rights consist of the following:

	June 30,	
	1995	1994
	(in thousands)	
License rights	$ 7,484	$ 954
Less accumulated amortization	(1,947)	(901)
	$ 5,537	$ 53

6. Commitments and contingencies

The Company leases equipment under several long-term capital and operating leases. Future minimum payments under capital leases and noncancelable operating leases with initial terms of one year or more consist of the following:

	Capital leases	Operating leases
Year ending June 30,	(in thousands)	
1996	$1,654	$20,997
1997	1,236	21,264
1998	641	19,450
1999	310	8,711
2000	103	3,511
Thereafter	—	2,636
Total minimum lease payments	3,944	$76,569
Less amount representing interest	(402)	
Present value of net minimum capital lease payments, including current portion of $1,415	$3,542	

The Company's rental expense under operating leases in the years ended June 30, 1995, 1994 and 1993 totaled approximately $10,001,000, $2,889,000, and $2,155,000, respectively.

Communication networks

The Company has guaranteed monthly usage levels of data and voice communications with one of its vendors. The remaining commitments are $113,400,000, $59,000,000, $9,000,000 and $6,750,000 for the years ending June 30, 1996, 1997, 1998 and 1999, respectively. The related expense for the years ended June 30, 1995, 1994 and 1993 was $138,793,000, $40,315,000 and $11,226,000, respectively.

Contingencies

Various legal proceedings have arisen against the Company in the ordinary course of business. In the opinion of management, these proceedings will not have a material effect on the financial position of the Company.

7. Notes payable

Notes payable at June 30, 1995 totaled approximately $18 million and consist primarily of amounts borrowed to finance the purchases of two office buildings. The notes are collateralized by the respective properties. The notes have a variable interest rate equal to 105 basis points above the 30 day London Interbank Offered Rate and a fixed interest rate of 8.48% per annum at June 30, 1995. Aggregate maturities of notes payable for the years ended June 30, 1996, 1997, 1998, 1999, 2000 and thereafterare $415,000, $429,000, $445,000, $462,000, $480,000 and $15,553,000, respectively.

8. Other income

The following table summarizes the components of other income:

	Year ended June 30,		
	1995	1994	1993
	(in thousands)		
Interest income	$3,920	$1,646	$572
Interest expense	(1,054)	(575)	(172)
Other	157	703	(29)
	$3,023	$1,774	$371

9. Income taxes

The provision for income taxes is attributable to:

	Year ended June 30,		
	1995	1994	1993
	(in thousands)		
Income before extraordinary item	$15,169	$3,832	$1,897
Tax benefit arising from net operating loss carryforward	—	—	(1,133)
	$15,169	$3,832	$ 764
Current	$ —	$ —	$ 5
Deferred	15,169	3,832	759
	$15,169	$3,832	$ 764

The provision for income taxes differs from the amount computed by applying the statutory federal income tax rate to income before provision for income taxes and extraordinary item. The sources and tax effects of the differences are as follows:

	Year ended June 30,		
	1995	1994	1993
	(in thousands)		
Income tax at the federal statutory rate of 34%	$ (6,283)	$2,170	$ 781
State income tax, net of federal benefit	1,597	403	200
Losses relating to RCC	—	1,259	916
Nondeductible merger expenses	750	—	—
Nondeductible charge for purchased research and development	17,114	—	—
Loss, for which no tax benefit was derived	1,632	—	—
Other	359	—	—
	$15,169	$3,832	$1,897

Deferred income taxes arise because of differences in the treatment of income and expense items for financial reporting and income tax purposes, primarily relating to deferred subscriber acquisition and product development costs.

As of June 30, 1995, the Company has net operating loss carryforwards of approximately $109 million for tax purposes which will be available, subject to certain annual limitations, to offset future taxable income. If not used, these loss carryforwards will expire between 2001 and 2010. To the extent that net operating loss carryforwards, when realized, relate to stock option deductions, the resulting benefits will be credited to stockholders' equity.

The Company's income tax provision was computed on the federal statutory rate and the average state statutory rates, net of the related federal benefit.

Effective July 1, 1993 the Company changed its method of accounting for income taxes from the deferred method to the liability method required by FASB Statement No. 109, "Accounting for Income Taxes." As permitted under the new rules, prior years' financial statements have not been restated.

No increase to net income resulted from the cumulative effect of adopting Statement No. 109 as of July 1, 1993. The deferred tax asset increased by approximately $5,965,000 as a result of the adoption. Similarly, the deferred tax liability, stockholders' equity and the valuation allowance increased by approximately $3,173,000, $759,000 and $2,033,000, respectively.

Deferred income taxes reflect the net tax effects of temporary differences between the carrying amounts of assets and liabilities for financial reporting purposes and the amounts used for income tax purposes. Significant components of the Company's deferred tax liabilities and assets are as follows:

	Year ended June 30,	
	1995	1994
	(in thousands)	
Deferred tax liabilities:		
Capitalized software costs	$ 7,008	$ 2,962
Deferred member acquisition costs	28,619	9,880
Net deferred tax liabilities	$35,627	$12,842
Deferred tax assets:		
Net operating loss carryforwards	$39,000	$17,510
Total deferred tax assets	39,000	17,510
Valuation allowance for deferred assets	(3,373)	(4,668)
Net deferred tax assets	$35,627	$12,842

13. Subsequent event

On August 23, 1995, the Company entered into a stock purchase agreement to purchase Ubique, Ltd., an Israeli company. The Company has agreed to pay approximately $15 million ($1.5 million in cash and $13.5 million in common stock) in the transaction, which is to be accounted for under the purchase method of accounting. Subject to the results of an in-process valuation, a substantial portion of the purchase price may be allocated to in-process research and development and charged to the Company's operations in the first quarter of fiscal 1996.

America Online

QUARTERLY INFORMATION (unaudited)

| | Quarter ended | | | | |
	September 30	December 31	March 31	June 30	Total
Fiscal 1995[a]					
Online service revenues	$50,056	$69,712	$99,814	$138,916	$358,498
Other revenues	6,880	6,683	9,290	12,939	35,792
Total revenues	56,936	76,395	109,104	151,855	394,290
Income (loss) from operations	4,623	(35,258)	233	11,108	(19,294)
Net income (loss)	1,481	(38,730)	(2,587)	6,189	(33,647)
Net income (loss) per share[b]	$ 0.04	$ (0.20)	$ (0.07)	$ 0.13	$ (0.99)
Fiscal 1994					
Online service revenues	$14,299	$20,292	$28,853	$37,549	$100,993
Other revenues	4,780	4,239	2,836	2,874	14,729
Total revenues	19,079	24,531	31,689	40,423	115,722
Income from operations	531	520	1,931	1,626	4,608
Net income	303	70	1,272	905	2,550
Net income per share[b]	$ 0.01	$ —	$ 0.03	$ 0.02	$ 0.07

a. Historical financial information for amounts previously reported in fiscal 1995 has been adjusted to account for pooling of interest transactions.

b. The sum of per-share earnings (loss) does not equal earnings (loss) per share for the year due to equivalent share calculations which are impacted by the Company's loss in 1995 and by fluctuations in the Company's common stock market prices.

America Online

Overview of Accounting Analysis

The purpose of accounting analysis is to evaluate the degree to which a firm's accounting captures its underlying business reality.[1] By identifying places where there is accounting flexibility, and by evaluating the appropriateness of the firm's accounting policies and estimates, analysts can assess the degree of distortion in a firm's accounting numbers. Another important skill is adjusting a firm's accounting numbers using cash flow information and information from the notes to the financial statements to "undo" any accounting distortions. Sound accounting analysis improves the reliability of conclusions from financial analysis, the next step in financial statement analysis.

THE INSTITUTIONAL FRAMEWORK FOR FINANCIAL REPORTING

There is typically a separation between ownership and management in public corporations. Financial statements serve as the vehicle through which owners keep track of their firms' financial situation. On a periodic basis, firms typically produce four financial reports: (1) an income statement that describes the operating performance during a time period, (2) a balance sheet that states the firm's assets and how they are financed, (3) a cash flow statement (or in some countries, a funds flow statement) that summarizes the cash (or fund) flows of the firm, and (4) a statement of changes in equity that outlines the sources of changes in equity during the period between two consecutive balance sheets. These statements are accompanied by notes that provide additional details on the financial statement line items, as well as by management's narrative discussion of the firm's performance in the Management Report section.[2]

To evaluate effectively the quality of a firm's financial statement data, the analyst needs to first understand the basic features of financial reporting and the institutional framework that governs them, as discussed in the following sections.

Accrual accounting

One of the fundamental features of corporate financial reports is that they are prepared using accrual rather than cash accounting. Unlike cash accounting, accrual accounting distinguishes between the recording of costs and benefits associated with economic activities and the actual payment and receipt of cash. Net profit is the primary periodic performance index under accrual accounting. To compute net profit, the effects of economic transactions are recorded on the basis of *expected,* not necessarily *actual,* cash receipts and payments. Expected cash receipts from the delivery of products or services are recognized as revenues, and expected cash outflows associated with these revenues are recognized as expenses.

While there are many rules and conventions that govern a firm's preparation of financial statements, there are only a few conceptual building blocks that form the foundation of accrual accounting. The following definitions are critical to the income statement, which summarizes a firm's revenues and expenses:[3]

- **Revenues** are economic resources earned during a time period. Revenue recognition is governed by the realization principle, which proposes that revenues should be recognized when (a) the firm has provided all, or substantially all, the goods or services to be delivered to the customer and (b) the customer has paid cash or is expected to pay cash with a reasonable degree of certainty.

- **Expenses** are economic resources used up in a time period. Expense recognition is governed by the matching and the conservatism principles. Under these principles, expenses are (a) costs directly associated with revenues recognized in the same period, or (b) costs associated with benefits that are consumed in this time period, or (c) resources whose future benefits are not reasonably certain.

- **Profit/loss** is the difference between a firm's revenues and expenses in a time period.[4]

The following fundamental relationship is therefore reflected in a firm's income statement:

$$\text{Profit} = \text{Revenues} - \text{Expenses}$$

In contrast, the balance sheet is a summary at one point in time. The principles that define a firm's assets, liabilities, equities, revenues, and expenses are as follows:

- **Assets** are economic resources owned by a firm that are (a) likely to produce future economic benefits and (b) measurable with a reasonable degree of certainty.

- **Liabilities** are economic obligations of a firm arising from benefits received in the past that (a) are required to be met with a reasonable degree of certainty and (b) whose timing is reasonably well defined.

- **Equity** is the difference between a firm's assets and its liabilities.

The definitions of assets, liabilities, and equity lead to the fundamental relationship that governs a firm's balance sheet:

$$\text{Assets} = \text{Liabilities} + \text{Equity}$$

Delegation of reporting to management

While the basic definitions of the elements of a firm's financial statements are simple, their application in practice often involves complex judgments. For example, how should revenues be recognized when a firm sells land to customers and also provides customer financing? If revenue is recognized before cash is collected, how should potential defaults be estimated? Are the outlays associated with research and development activities, whose payoffs are uncertain, assets or expenses when incurred? Are contractual commitments under lease arrangements or post-employment plans liabilities? If so, how should they be valued?

Because corporate managers have intimate knowledge of their firms' businesses, they are entrusted with the primary task of making the appropriate judgments in portraying myriad business transactions using the basic accrual accounting framework. The accounting discretion granted to managers is potentially valuable because it allows them to reflect inside information in reported financial statements. However, since investors view profits as a measure of managers' performance, managers have an incentive to use their accounting discretion to distort reported profits by making biased assumptions. Further, the use of accounting numbers in contracts between the firm and outsiders provides a motivation for management manipulation of accounting numbers.

Earnings management distorts financial accounting data, making them less valuable to external users of financial statements. Therefore, the delegation of financial reporting decisions to managers has both costs and benefits. Accounting rules and auditing are mechanisms designed to reduce the cost and preserve the benefit of delegating financial reporting to corporate managers. The legal system is used to adjudicate disputes between managers, auditors, and investors.

International Financial Reporting Standards

Given that it is difficult for outside investors to determine whether managers have used accounting flexibility to signal their proprietary information or merely to disguise reality, a number of accounting concepts and conventions have evolved to mitigate the problem. For example, in most countries financial statements are prepared using the concept of prudence, where caution is taken to ensure that assets are not recorded at values above their fair values and liabilities are not recorded at values below their fair values. This reduces managers' ability to overstate the value of the net assets that they have acquired or developed. Of course, the prudence concept also limits the information that is available to investors about the potential of the firm's assets, because many firms record their assets at historical exchange prices below the assets' fair values or values in use.

Accounting standards and rules also limit management's ability to misuse accounting judgment by regulating how particular types of transactions are recorded. For example, accounting standards for leases stipulate how firms are to record contractual arrangements to lease resources. Similarly, post-employment benefit standards describe how firms are to record commitments to provide pensions and other post-employment benefits for employees.

More than 70 countries have delegated the task of setting accounting standards to the International Accounting Standards Board (IASB). For example, since 2005 E.U. companies that have their shares traded on a public exchange must prepare their consolidated financial statements in accordance with International Financial Reporting Standards (IFRS) as promulgated by the IASB and endorsed by the European Union. Most E.U. countries, however, also have their own national accounting standard-setting bodies. These bodies may, for example, set accounting standards for private companies and for single entity financial statements of public companies.[5] Another of their tasks is to comment on the IASB's drafts of new or modified standards. There are similar private sector or public sector accounting standard-setting bodies in many other countries. For example, in the United States the Securities and Exchange Commission (SEC) has the legal authority to set accounting standards. Since 1973 the SEC has relied on the Financial Accounting Standards Board (FASB), a private sector accounting body, to undertake this task.

Uniform accounting standards attempt to reduce managers' ability to record similar economic transactions in dissimilar ways either over time or across firms. Thus they create a uniform accounting language and increase the credibility of financial statements by limiting a firm's ability to distort them. Increased uniformity from accounting standards, however, comes at the expense of reduced flexibility for managers to reflect genuine business differences in a firm's accounting decisions. Rigid accounting standards work best for economic transactions whose accounting treatment is not predicated on managers' proprietary information. However, when there is significant business judgment involved in assessing a transaction's economic consequences, rigid standards are likely to be dysfunctional because they prevent managers from using their superior business knowledge. Further, if accounting standards are too rigid, they may induce managers to expend economic resources to restructure business transactions to achieve a desired accounting result.

As a solution to the adverse effects of rigid accounting rules, the IASB often defines standards that are based more on broadly stated principles than on detailed rules. For example, most accountants agree that when a company leases an asset but nevertheless carries substantially all the risk of value loss, the asset is essentially owned by the company and should be recorded as such on the balance sheet. In its standard for leases, the IASB takes this basic principle as a standard and leaves much responsibility to the managers and auditors to decide which leased assets are economically owned by the company. In contrast, the U.S. accounting standard for leases issued by the FASB sets out four numerical criteria that managers and auditors must use to classify leased assets. The U.S. standard thus leaves managers much less room for interpretation than the international standard. However, because the U.S. standard provides explicit guidance, it is also easier for managers to circumvent the intention of the standard, even though they may technically comply with it.

The leasing example illustrates what many see as an important difference in the approaches that the IASB and the FASB are taking to standard-setting. Proponents of the principles-based approach claim that reporting in accordance with principles, instead of technical rules, ensures that the financial statements reflect the economic substance of firms' transactions, instead of their legal form. However, because principles-based standards provide less technical guidance than rules-based standards, they demand more professionalism from auditors in exercising their duties and are more difficult to enforce. Proponents of the rules-based approach therefore claim that using rules-based standards increases the verifiability of the information included in the financial statements, reduces managers' misuse of their reporting discretion, and increases the comparability of financial statements across firms. The FASB, however, is currently turning toward a principles-based approach, which suggests that during the coming years global standard-setting will become more and more principles-based.[6]

External auditing

Broadly defined as a verification of the integrity of the reported financial statements by someone other than the preparer, external auditing ensures that managers use accounting rules and conventions consistently over time, and that their accounting estimates are reasonable. In Europe, all listed companies are required to have their financial statements audited by an independent public accountant. The standards and procedures to be followed by independent auditors are set by various institutions. By means of the Eighth Company Law Directive, the E.U. has set minimum standards for public audits that are performed on companies from its member countries. E.U. countries must have implemented these standards before mid-2008. The standards prescribe, for example, that the external auditor does not provide any nonaudit services to the audited company that may compromise his independence. To maintain independence, the auditor (the person, not the firm) must also not audit the same company for more than five consecutive years. Further, all audits must be carried out in accordance with the International Auditing Standards (ISA), as promulgated by the International Auditing and Assurance Standards Board (IAASB) and endorsed by the E.U. While auditors issue an opinion on published financial statements, it is important to remember that the primary responsibility for the statements still rests with corporate managers.

Auditing improves the quality and credibility of accounting data by limiting a firm's ability to distort financial statements to suit its own purposes. However, as audit failures at companies such as Ahold, Enron, and Parmalat show, auditing is imperfect. Audits cannot review all of a firm's transactions. They can also fail because of lapses in quality, or because of lapses in judgment by auditors who fail to challenge management for fear of losing future business.

Third-party auditing may also reduce the quality of financial reporting because it constrains the kind of accounting rules and conventions that evolve over time. For example, the IASB considers the views of auditors – in addition to other interest groups – in the process of setting IFRS. To illustrate, at least one-third of the IASB board members have a background as practicing auditor. Further, the IASB is advised by the Standards Advisory Committee, which contains several practicing auditors. Finally, the IASB invites auditors to comment on its policies and proposed standards. Auditors are likely to argue against accounting standards that produce numbers that are difficult to audit, even if the proposed rules produce relevant information for investors.

Legal liability

The legal environment in which accounting disputes between managers, auditors, and investors are adjudicated can also have a significant effect on the quality of reported numbers. The threat of lawsuits and resulting penalties have the beneficial effect of improving the accuracy of disclosure. Legal liability regimes vary in strictness across countries. Under strict regimes, such as that found in the U.S., investors can hold managers liable for their investment losses if they prove that the firm's disclosures were misleading, that they relied on the misleading disclosures, and that their losses were caused by the misleading disclosures. Under less strict regimes, such as that found in Germany, investors must additionally prove that managers were (grossly) negligent in their reporting or even had the intent to harm investors.[7]

The potential for significant legal liability might also discourage managers and auditors from supporting accounting proposals requiring risky forecasts – for example, forward-looking disclosures. The U.S. auditing community often expresses this type of concern.

Public enforcement

Several countries adhere to the idea that strong accounting standards, external auditing, and the threat of legal liability do not suffice to ensure that financial statements provide a truthful picture of economic reality. As a final guarantee on reporting quality, these countries have public enforcement bodies that either proactively or on a complaint basis initiate reviews of companies' compliance with accounting standards and take actions to correct noncompliance. In the U.S., the Securities and Exchange Commission (SEC) performs such reviews and frequently disciplines companies for violations of US GAAP. In recent years, several European countries have also set up proactive enforcement agencies that should enforce listed companies' compliance with IFRS. Examples of such agencies are the French AMF (Autorité des Marchés Financiers), the German DPR (Deutsche Prüfstelle für Rechnungslegung), the Italian CONSOB (Commissione Nazionale per le Società e la Borsa), and the U.K. Financial Reporting Review Panel. Because each European country maintains control of domestic enforcement, there is a risk that the enforcement of IFRS exhibits differences in strictness and focus across Europe. To coordinate enforcement activities, however, most European enforcement agencies cooperate in the Committee of European Securities Regulators (CESR). One of the CESR's tasks is to develop mechanisms that lead to consistent enforcement across Europe. For example, the Committee promotes that national enforcement agencies have access to and take notice of each other's enforcement decisions. The coming years will show whether a decentralized system of enforcement can consistently assure that European companies comply with IFRS.

Public enforcement bodies cannot ensure full compliance of all listed companies. In fact, most proactive enforcement bodies conduct their investigations on a sampling basis. For example, the U.K. Financial Reporting Review Panel periodically selects industry sectors on which it focuses its enforcement activities. Within these sectors, the Review Panel then selects individual companies either at random or on the basis of company characteristics such as poor governance. Strict public enforcement can also reduce the quality of financial reporting because, in their attempt to avoid an accounting credibility crisis on public capital markets, enforcement bodies may pressure companies to exercise excessive prudence in their accounting choices.

FACTORS INFLUENCING ACCOUNTING QUALITY

Because the mechanisms that limit managers' ability to distort accounting data themselves add noise, it is not optimal to use accounting regulation to eliminate managerial flexibility completely. Therefore, real-world accounting systems leave considerable room for managers to influence financial statement data. The net result is that information in corporate financial reports is noisy and biased, even in the presence of accounting regulation and external auditing.[8] The objective of accounting analysis is to evaluate the degree to which a firm's accounting captures its underlying business reality and to "undo" any accounting distortions. When potential distortions are large, accounting analysis can add considerable value.[9]

There are three potential sources of noise and bias in accounting data: (1) that introduced by rigidity in accounting rules, (2) random forecast errors, and (3) systematic reporting choices made by corporate managers to achieve specific objectives. Each of these factors is discussed below.

Noise from accounting rules

Accounting rules introduce noise and bias because it is often difficult to restrict management discretion without reducing the information content of accounting data. For example, International Accounting Standard (IAS) 38 issued by the IASB requires firms to recognize assets for development outlays when these are likely to produce future economic benefits, but requires firms to expense the preceding research outlays when they are incurred. Development expenditures are those incurred for the actual design of a new product. In contrast, research expenditures are not directly associated with a product. Clearly, some research expenditures have future value while others do not. However, because IAS 38 does not allow firms to distinguish between the two types of expenditures in the early stages of research, it leads to a systematic distortion of reported accounting numbers. Broadly speaking, the degree of distortion introduced by accounting standards depends on how well uniform accounting standards capture the nature of a firm's transactions.

Forecast errors

Another source of noise in accounting data arises from pure forecast error, because managers cannot predict future consequences of current transactions perfectly. For example, when a firm sells products on credit, accrual accounting requires managers to make a judgment about the probability of collecting payments from customers. If payments are deemed "reasonably certain," the firm treats the transactions as sales, creating trade receivables on its balance sheet. Managers then make an estimate of the proportion of receivables that will not be collected. Because managers do not have perfect foresight, actual defaults are likely to be different from estimated customer defaults, leading to a forecast error. The extent of errors in managers' accounting forecasts depends on a variety of factors, including the complexity of the business transactions, the predictability of the firm's environment, and unforeseen economy-wide changes.

Managers' accounting choices

Corporate managers also introduce noise and bias into accounting data through their own accounting decisions. Managers have a variety of incentives to exercise their accounting discretion to achieve certain objectives:[10]

- *Accounting-based debt covenants.* Managers may make accounting decisions to meet certain contractual obligations in their debt covenants. For example, firms' lending agreements with banks and other debt holders require them to meet covenants related to interest coverage, working capital ratios, and net worth, all defined in terms of accounting numbers. Violation of these constraints may be costly because it allows lenders to demand immediate payment of their loans. Managers of firms close to violating debt covenants have an incentive to select accounting policies and estimates to reduce the probability of covenant violation. The debt covenant motivation for managers' accounting decisions has been analyzed by a number of accounting researchers.[11]

- *Management compensation.* Another motivation for managers' accounting choice comes from the fact that their compensation and job security are often tied to reported profits. For example, many top managers receive bonus compensation if they exceed certain prespecified profit targets. This provides motivation for managers to choose accounting policies and estimates to maximize their expected compensation.[12]

- *Corporate control contests.* In corporate control contests, such as hostile takeovers, competing management groups attempt to win over the firm's shareholders. Accounting numbers are used extensively in debating managers' performance in these contests. Therefore, managers may make accounting decisions to influence investor perceptions in corporate control contests. Also, when takeovers are not necessarily hostile but structured as a share-for-share merger, the acquiring firm may overstate its performance to boost its share price and by this reduce the share exchange ratio.[13]

- *Tax considerations.* Managers may also make reporting choices to trade off between financial reporting and tax considerations. For example, U.S. firms are required to use LIFO inventory accounting for shareholder reporting in order to use it for tax reporting. Under LIFO, when prices are rising, firms report lower profits, thereby reducing tax payments. Some firms may forgo the tax reduction in order to report higher profits in their financial statements. In countries where such a direct link between financial reporting and tax reporting does not exist, tax considerations may still indirectly affect managers' reporting decisions. For example, firms that recognize losses aggressively in their tax statements may support their aggressive tax choices by having the financial reporting treatment of these losses conform to their tax treatment. Having no divergence between the tax treatment and the financial reporting treatment could increase the probability that tax authorities allow the tax treatment.[14]

- *Regulatory considerations.* Since accounting numbers are used by regulators in a variety of contexts, managers of some firms may make accounting decisions to influence regulatory outcomes. Examples of regulatory situations where accounting numbers are used include actions to end or prevent infringements of competition laws, import tariffs to protect domestic industries, and tax policies.[15]

- *Capital market considerations.* Managers may make accounting decisions to influence the perceptions of capital markets. When there are information asymmetries between managers and outsiders, this strategy may succeed in influencing investor perceptions, at least temporarily.[16]

- *Stakeholder considerations.* Managers may also make accounting decisions to influence the perception of important stakeholders in the firm. For example, since labor unions can use healthy profits as a basis for demanding wage increases, managers may make accounting decisions to decrease profit when they are facing union contract negotiations. In countries like Germany, where labor unions are strong, these considerations appear to play an important role in firms' accounting policy. Other important stakeholders that firms may wish to influence through their financial reports include suppliers and customers.

- *Competitive considerations.* The dynamics of competition in an industry might also influence a firm's reporting choices. For example, a firm's segment disclosure decisions may be influenced by its concern that disaggregated disclosure may help competitors in their business decisions. Similarly, firms may not disclose data on their margins by product line for fear of giving away proprietary information. Finally, firms may discourage new entrants by making profit-decreasing accounting choices.

In addition to accounting policy choices and estimates, the level of disclosure is also an important determinant of a firm's accounting quality. Corporate managers can choose disclosure policies that make it more or less costly for external users of financial reports to understand the true economic picture of their businesses. Accounting regulations usually prescribe minimum disclosure requirements, but they do not restrict managers from voluntarily providing additional disclosures. Managers can use various parts of the financial reports, including the Management Report and notes, to describe the company's strategy, its accounting policies, and its current performance. There is wide variation across firms in how managers use their disclosure flexibility.[17]

STEPS IN ACCOUNTING ANALYSIS

In this section we discuss a series of steps that an analyst can follow to evaluate a firm's accounting quality.

Step 1: Identify key accounting policies

As discussed in the chapter on business strategy analysis, a firm's industry characteristics and its own competitive strategy determine its key success factors and risks. One of the goals of financial statement analysis is to evaluate how well these success factors and risks are being managed by the firm. In accounting analysis, therefore, the analyst should identify and evaluate the policies and the estimates the firm uses to measure its critical factors and risks.

Key success factors in the banking industry include interest and credit risk management; in the retail industry, inventory management is a key success factor; and for a manufacturer competing on product quality and innovation, research and development and product defects after the sale are key areas of concern. One of the key success factors in the leasing business is to make accurate forecasts of residual values of the leased equipment at the end of the lease terms. In each of these cases, the analyst has to identify the accounting measures the firm uses to capture these business constructs, the policies that determine how the measures are implemented, and the key estimates embedded in these policies. For example, the accounting measure a bank uses to capture credit risk is its loan loss reserves, and the accounting measure that captures product quality for a manufacturer is its warranty expenses and reserves. For a firm in the equipment leasing industry, one of the most important accounting policies is the way residual values are recorded. Residual values influence the company's reported profits and its asset base. If residual values are overestimated, the firm runs the risk of having to take large write-offs in the future.

Step 2: Assess accounting flexibility

Not all firms have equal flexibility in choosing their key accounting policies and estimates. Some firms' accounting choice is severely constrained by accounting standards and conventions. For example, even though research and development is a key success factor for biotechnology companies, managers have no accounting discretion in reporting on research activities and, in practice, often make no distinction between development and research because the future benefits of development outlays are too difficult to assess. Similarly, even though marketing and brand building are key to the success of consumer goods firms, they are required to expense all their marketing outlays. In contrast, managing credit risk is one of the critical success factors for banks, and bank managers have the freedom to estimate expected defaults on their loans. Similarly, shipbuilding companies can adequately show the profitability status of their long-term projects because they have the flexibility to recognize proportions of the project revenues during the life of the project.

If managers have little flexibility in choosing accounting policies and estimates related to their key success factors (as in the case of biotechnology firms), accounting data are likely to be less informative for understanding the firm's economics. In contrast, if managers have considerable flexibility in choosing the policies and estimates (as in the case of banks), accounting numbers have the potential to be informative, depending upon how managers exercise this flexibility.

Regardless of the degree of accounting flexibility a firm's managers have in measuring their key success factors and risks, they will have some flexibility with respect to several other accounting policies. For example, all firms have to make choices with respect to depreciation policy (straight-line or accelerated methods), inventory accounting policy (LIFO, FIFO, or average cost), policy for amortizing intangible assets other than goodwill (write-off over 20 years or less), and policies regarding the estimation of pension and other post-employment benefits (expected return on plan assets, discount rate for liabilities, and rate of increase in wages and healthcare costs). Since all these policy choices can have a significant impact on the reported performance of a firm, they offer an opportunity for the firm to manage its reported numbers.

Step 3: Evaluate accounting strategy

When managers have accounting flexibility, they can use it either to communicate their firm's economic situation or to hide true performance. Some of the strategy questions one could ask in examining how managers exercise their accounting flexibility include the following:

- How do the firm's accounting policies compare to the norms in the industry? If they are dissimilar, is it because the firm's competitive strategy is unique? For example, consider a firm that reports a lower provision for warranty costs than the industry average. One explanation is that the firm competes on the basis of high quality and has invested considerable resources to reduce the rate of product failure. An alternative explanation is that the firm is merely understating its warranty provision.

- Do managers face strong incentives to use accounting discretion to manage earnings? For example, is the firm close to violating bond covenants? Or are the managers having difficulty meeting accounting-based bonus targets? Does management own a significant amount of shares? Is the firm in the middle of a takeover battle or union negotiations? Managers may also make accounting decisions to reduce tax payments or to influence the perceptions of the firm's competitors.

- Has the firm changed any of its policies or estimates? What is the justification? What is the impact of these changes? For example, if warranty expenses decreased, is it because the firm made significant investments to improve quality?

- Have the company's policies and estimates been realistic in the past? For example, firms may overstate their revenues and understate their expenses during the year by manipulating quarterly or semiannual reports, which are not subject to a full-blown external audit. However, the auditing process at the end of the fiscal year forces such companies to make large year-end adjustments, providing an opportunity for the analyst to assess the quality of the firm's interim reporting. Similarly, firms that depreciate fixed assets too slowly will be forced to take a large write-off later. A history of write-offs may be, therefore, a sign of prior earnings management.

- Does the firm structure any significant business transactions so that it can achieve certain accounting objectives? For example, leasing firms can alter lease terms (the length of the lease or the bargain purchase option at the end of the lease term) so that the transactions qualify as sales-type leases for the lessors. Enron structured acquisitions of joint venture interests and hedging transactions with special purpose entities to avoid having to show joint venture liabilities, and to avoid reporting investment losses in its financial statements.[18] Such behavior may suggest that the firm's managers are willing to expend economic resources merely to achieve an accounting objective.

Step 4: Evaluate the quality of disclosure

Managers can make it more or less easy for an analyst to assess the firm's accounting quality and to use its financial statements to understand business reality. While accounting rules require a certain amount of minimum disclosure, managers have considerable choice in the matter. Disclosure quality, therefore, is an important dimension of a firm's accounting quality.

In assessing a firm's disclosure quality, an analyst could ask the following questions:

- Does the company provide adequate disclosures to assess the firm's business strategy and its economic consequences? For example, some firms use management's narrative report in their financial statements to clearly lay out the firm's industry conditions, its competitive position, and management's plans for the future. Others use the report to puff up the firm's financial performance and gloss over any competitive difficulties the firm might be facing.

- Do the notes to the financial statements adequately explain the key accounting policies and assumptions and their logic? For example, if a firm's revenue and expense recognition policies differ from industry norms, the firm can explain its choices in a note. Similarly, when there are significant changes in a firm's policies, notes can be used to disclose the reasons.

- Does the firm adequately explain its current performance? The Management Report section of the annual report provides an opportunity to help analysts understand the reasons behind a firm's performance changes. Some firms use this section to link financial performance to business conditions. For example, if profit margins went down in a period, was it because of price competition or because of increases in manufacturing costs? If the selling and general administrative expenses went up, was it because the firm is investing in a differentiation strategy, or because unproductive overhead expenses were creeping up?

- If accounting rules and conventions restrict the firm from measuring its key success factors appropriately, does the firm provide adequate additional disclosure to help outsiders understand how these factors are being managed? For example, if a firm invests in product quality and customer service, accounting rules do not allow the management to capitalize these outlays, even when the future benefits are certain. The firm's review of its operations can be used to highlight how these outlays are being managed and their performance consequences. For example, the firm can disclose physical indexes of defect rates and customer satisfaction so that outsiders can assess the progress being made in these areas and the future cash flow consequences of these actions.

- If a firm is in multiple business segments, what is the quality of segment disclosure? Some firms provide excellent discussion of their performance by product segments and geographic segments. Others lump many different businesses into one broad segment. The level of competition in an industry and management's willingness to share desegregated performance data influence a firm's quality of segment disclosure.

- How forthcoming is the management with respect to bad news? A firm's disclosure quality is most clearly revealed by the way management deals with bad news. Does it adequately explain the reasons for poor performance? Does the company clearly articulate its strategy, if any, to address the company's performance problems?

- How good is the firm's investor relations program? Does the firm provide fact books with detailed data on the firm's business and performance? Is the management accessible to analysts?

Step 5: Identify potential red flags

In addition to the above analysis, a common approach to accounting quality analysis is to look for "red flags" pointing to questionable accounting quality. These indicators suggest that the analyst should examine certain items more closely or gather more information on them. Some common red flags are the following:

- *Unexplained changes in accounting, especially when performance is poor.* This may suggest that managers are using their accounting discretion to "dress up" their financial statements.[19]

- *Unexplained transactions that boost profits.* For example, firms might undertake balance sheet transactions, such as asset sales or debt-for-equity swaps, to realize gains in periods when operating performance is poor.[20]

- *Unusual increases in trade receivables in relation to sales increases.* This may suggest that the company is relaxing its credit policies or artificially loading up its distribution channels to record revenues during the current period. If credit policies are relaxed unduly, the firm may face receivable write-offs in subsequent periods as a result of customer defaults. If the firm accelerates shipments to its distributors, it may either face product returns or reduced shipments in subsequent periods.

- *Unusual increases in inventories in relation to sales increases.* If the inventory build-up is due to an increase in finished goods inventory, it could be a sign that demand for the firm's products is slowing down, suggesting that the firm may be forced to cut prices (and hence earn lower margins) or write down its inventory. A build-up in work-in-progress inventory tends to be good news on average, probably signaling that managers expect an increase in sales. If the build-up is in raw materials, it could suggest manufacturing or procurement inefficiencies, leading to an increase in cost of sales (and hence lower margins).[21]

- *An increasing gap between a firm's reported profit and its cash flow from operating activities.* While it is legitimate for accrual accounting numbers to differ from cash flows, there is usually a steady relationship between the two if the company's accounting policies remain the same. Therefore, any *change* in the relationship between reported profits and operating cash flows might indicate subtle changes in the firm's accrual estimates. For example, a firm undertaking large construction contracts might use the percentage-of-completion method to record revenues. While earnings and operating cash flows are likely to differ for such a firm, they should bear a steady relationship to each other. Now suppose the firm increases revenues in a period through an aggressive application of the percentage-of-completion method. Then its earnings will go up, but its cash flow remains unaffected. This change in the firm's accounting quality will be manifested by a *change* in the relationship between the firm's earnings and cash flows.

- *An increasing gap between a firm's reported profit and its tax profit.* Once again, it is quite legitimate for a firm to follow different accounting policies for financial reporting and tax accounting as long as the tax law allows it. However, the relationship between a firm's book and tax accounting is likely to remain constant over time, unless there are significant changes in tax rules or accounting standards. Thus, an *increasing* gap between a firm's reported profit and its tax profit may indicate that financial reporting to shareholders has become more aggressive. For example, warranty expenses are estimated on an accrual basis for financial reporting, but they are recorded on a cash basis for tax reporting. Unless there is a big change in the firm's product quality, these two numbers bear a consistent relationship to each other. Therefore, a change in this relationship can be an indication either that product quality is changing significantly or that financial reporting estimates are changing.

■ *A tendency to use financing mechanisms like research and development partnerships, special purpose entities, and the sale of receivables with recourse.* While these arrangements may have a sound business logic, they can also provide management with an opportunity to understate the firm's liabilities and/or overstate its assets.[22]

■ *Unexpected large asset write-offs.* This may suggest that management is slow to incorporate changing business circumstances into its accounting estimates. Asset write-offs may also be a result of unexpected changes in business circumstances.[23]

■ *Large year-end adjustments.* A firm's annual reports are audited by the external auditors, but its interim financial statements are usually only reviewed. If a firm's management is reluctant to make appropriate accounting estimates (such as provisions for uncollectible receivables) in its interim statements, it could be forced to make adjustments at the end of the year as a result of pressure from its external auditors. A consistent pattern of year-end adjustments, therefore, may indicate aggressive management of interim reporting.[24]

■ *Qualified audit opinions or changes in independent auditors that are not well justified.* These may indicate a firm's aggressive attitude or a tendency to "opinion shop."

■ *Poor internal governance mechanisms.* Internal governance agents, such as independent directors or supervisors, audit committees, and internal auditors, are responsible for assuring the flow of credible information to external parties. When a firm's supervising directors or audit committee lack independence from management or its internal control system has deficiencies, accounting may be of questionable quality.[25] A lack of independence can be the result of, for example, family bonds, economic relationships, or prior working relationships. We discuss the role of governance in more detail in Chapter 13.

■ *Related-party transactions or transactions between related entities.* These transactions may lack the objectivity of the marketplace, and managers' accounting estimates related to these transactions are likely to be more subjective and potentially self-serving.[26]

While the preceding list provides a number of red flags for potentially poor accounting quality, it is important to do further analysis before reaching final conclusions. Each of the red flags has multiple interpretations; some interpretations are based on sound business reasons, and others indicate questionable accounting. It is, therefore, best to use the red flag analysis as a starting point for further probing, not as an end point in itself.[27]

Step 6: Undo accounting distortions

If the accounting analysis suggests that the firm's reported numbers are misleading, analysts should attempt to restate the reported numbers to reduce the distortion to the extent possible. It is, of course, virtually impossible to perfectly undo the distortion using outside information alone. However, some progress can be made in this direction by using the cash flow statement and the notes to the financial statements.

A firm's cash flow statement provides a reconciliation of its performance based on accrual accounting and cash accounting. If the analyst is unsure of the quality of the firm's accrual accounting, the cash flow statement provides an alternative benchmark of its performance. The cash flow statement also provides information on how individual line items in the income statement diverge from the underlying cash flows. For example, if an analyst is concerned that the firm is aggressively capitalizing certain costs that should be expensed, the information in the cash flow statement provides a basis to make the necessary adjustment.

The notes to the financial statements also provide a lot of information that is potentially useful in restating reported accounting numbers. For example, when a firm changes its accounting policies, it provides a note indicating the effect of that change if it is material. Similarly, some firms provide information on the details of accrual estimates such as the provision for doubtful receivables. The tax note usually provides information on the differences between a firm's accounting policies for shareholder reporting and tax reporting. Since tax reporting is often more conservative than shareholder reporting, the information in the tax note can be used to estimate what the earnings reported to shareholders would be under more conservative policies.

In Chapter 4, we show how to make accounting adjustments for some of the most common types of accounting distortions.

ACCOUNTING ANALYSIS PITFALLS

There are several potential pitfalls and common misconceptions in accounting analysis that an analyst should avoid.

Conservative accounting is not "good" accounting

Some firms take the approach that it pays to be conservative in financial reporting and to set aside as much as possible for contingencies. This logic is commonly used to justify the expensing of research and advertising, and the rapid write-down of intangible assets other than goodwill. It is also used to support large loss reserves for insurance companies, for merger expenses, and for restructuring charges.

From the standpoint of a financial statement user, it is important to recognize that conservative accounting is not the same as "good" accounting. Financial statement users want to evaluate how well a firm's accounting captures business reality in an unbiased manner, and conservative accounting can be as misleading as aggressive accounting in this respect.

It is certainly true that it can be difficult to estimate the economic benefits from many intangibles. However, the intangible nature of some assets does not mean that they do not have value. Indeed, for many firms these types of assets are their most valued. For example, Swiss-based pharmaceutical Novartis' two most valued assets are its research capabilities that permit it to generate new drugs, and its sales force that enables it to sell those drugs to doctors. Yet neither is recorded on Novartis' balance sheet. From the investors' point of view, accountants' reluctance to value intangible assets does not diminish their importance. If they are not included in financial statements, investors have to look to alternative sources of information on these assets.

Further, conservative accounting often provides managers with opportunities for reducing the volatility of reported earnings, typically referred to as "earnings smoothing," which may prevent analysts from recognizing poor performance in a timely fashion. Finally, over time investors are likely to figure out which firms are conservative and may discount their management's disclosures and communications.

Not all unusual accounting is questionable

It is easy to confuse unusual accounting with questionable accounting. While unusual accounting choices might make a firm's performance difficult to compare with other firms' performance, such an accounting choice might be justified if the company's business is unusual. For example, firms that follow differentiated strategies or firms that structure their business in an innovative manner to take advantage of particular market situations may make unusual accounting choices to properly reflect their business. Therefore it is important to evaluate a company's accounting choices in the context of its business strategy.

Similarly, it is important not to necessarily attribute all *changes* in a firm's accounting policies and accruals to earnings management motives.[28] Accounting changes might be merely reflecting changed business circumstances. For example, as already discussed, a firm that shows unusual increases in its inventory might be preparing for a new product introduction. Similarly, unusual increases in receivables might merely be due to changes in a firm's sales strategy. Unusual decreases in the allowance for uncollectible receivables might be reflecting a firm's changed customer focus. It is therefore important for an analyst to consider all possible explanations for accounting changes and investigate them using the qualitative information available in a firm's financial statements.

Common accounting standards are not the same as common accounting practices

Listed firms in the E.U. and elsewhere prepare their consolidated financial statements under a common set of accounting standards, IFRS. The adoption of IFRS makes financial statements more comparable across countries and lowers the barriers to cross-border investment analysis. It is important, however, not to confuse the adoption of common accounting *standards* such as IFRS with the introduction of common accounting *practices*.

In this chapter we have discussed some international differences that have remained in place after the adoption of IFRS. For example, although the E.U. sets minimum standards for external auditing, it remains up to the member countries to implement and enforce such rules. Further, IFRS may not be similarly enforced throughout Europe because all European countries have their own public enforcement bodies. Finally, the role of financial reports in communication between managers and investors differs across firms and countries. In Chapter 1 we discussed the reporting differences between private corporations and public corporations. Similar, potentially smaller differences exist between widely held and closely held listed firms. The analyst should therefore carefully consider these aspects of a firm's reporting environment.

VALUE OF ACCOUNTING DATA AND ACCOUNTING ANALYSIS

What is the value of accounting information and accounting analysis? Given the incentives and opportunities for managers to affect their firms' reported accounting numbers, some have argued that accounting data and accounting analysis are not likely to be useful for investors.

Researchers have examined the value of accounting by estimating the return that could be earned by an investor with perfect earnings foresight one year prior to an earnings announcement.[29] The findings show that by buying shares of firms with increased earnings and selling shares of firms with decreased earnings each year, a hypothetical investor could earn an average portfolio return of 37.5 percent in the period 1954 to 1996. This is equivalent to 44 percent of the return that could have been earned if the investor had perfect foresight of the share price itself for one year and bought shares with increased prices and sold shares whose price decreased. Perfect foresight of ROE permits the investor to earn an even higher rate of return – 43 percent – than perfect earnings foresight. This is equivalent to 50 percent of the return that could be earned with perfect share price foresight.

In contrast, cash flow data appear to be considerably less valuable than earnings or ROE information. Perfect foresight of cash flows from operations would permit the hypothetical investor to earn an average annual return of only 9 percent, equivalent to 11 percent of the return that could be earned with perfect foresight of share prices.

Overall, this research suggests that the institutional arrangements and conventions created to mitigate potential misuse of accounting by managers are effective in providing assurance to investors. The research indicates that investors do not view earnings management as so pervasive as to make earnings data unreliable.

A number of research studies have examined whether superior accounting analysis is a valuable activity. By and large, this evidence indicates that there are opportunities for superior analysts to earn positive stock returns. Research findings indicate that companies criticized in the financial press for misleading financial reporting subsequently suffered an average share price drop of 8 percent.[30] Firms where managers appeared to inflate reported earnings prior to an equity issue and subsequently reported poor earnings performance had more negative share price performance after the offer than firms with no apparent earnings management.[31] Finally, U.S. firms subject to SEC investigation for earnings management showed an average share price decline of 9 percent when the earnings management was first announced and continued to have poor share price performance for up to two years.[32]

These findings imply that analysts who are able to identify firms with misleading accounting are able to create value for investors. The findings also indicate that the stock market ultimately sees through earnings management. For all of these cases, earnings management is eventually uncovered and the share price responds negatively to evidence that firms have inflated prior earnings through misleading accounting.

SUMMARY

In summary, accounting analysis is an important step in the process of analyzing corporate financial reports. The purpose of accounting analysis is to evaluate the degree to which a firm's accounting captures the underlying business reality. Sound accounting analysis improves the reliability of conclusions from financial analysis, the next step in financial statement analysis.

There are six key steps in accounting analysis. The analyst begins by identifying the key accounting policies and estimates, given the firm's industry and its business strategy. The second step is to evaluate the degree of flexibility available to managers, given the accounting rules and conventions. Next, the analyst has to evaluate how managers exercise their accounting flexibility and the likely motivations behind managers' accounting strategy. The fourth step involves assessing the depth and quality of a firm's disclosures. The analyst should next identify any red flags needing further investigation. The final accounting analysis step is to restate accounting numbers to remove any noise and bias introduced by the accounting rules and management decisions.

The next chapter discusses how to implement these concepts and shows how to make some of the most common types of adjustments.

DISCUSSION QUESTIONS

1. A finance student states, "I don't understand why anyone pays any attention to accounting earnings numbers, given that a 'clean' number like cash from operations is readily available." Do you agree? Why or why not?

2. Fred argues, "The standards that I like most are the ones that eliminate all management discretion in reporting – that way I get uniform numbers across all companies and don't have to worry about doing accounting analysis." Do you agree? Why or why not?

3. Bill Simon says, "We should get rid of the IASB, IFRS, and E.U. Company Law Directives, since free market forces will make sure that companies report reliable information." Do you agree? Why or why not?

4. Many firms recognize revenues at the point of shipment. This provides an incentive to accelerate revenues by shipping goods at the end of the quarter. Consider two companies, one of which ships its product evenly throughout the quarter, and the second of which ships all its products in the last two weeks of the quarter. Each company's customers pay 30 days after receiving shipment. Using accounting ratios, how can you distinguish these companies?

5. a. If management reports truthfully, what economic events are likely to prompt the following accounting changes?
   - Increase in the estimated life of depreciable assets.
   - Decrease in the allowance for doubtful accounts as a percentage of gross trade receivables.
   - Recognition of revenues at the point of delivery rather than at the point cash is received.
   - Capitalization of a higher proportion of research expenditures costs.

   b. What features of accounting, if any, would make it costly for dishonest managers to make the same changes without any corresponding economic changes?

6. The conservatism (or prudence) principle arises because of concerns about management's incentives to overstate the firm's performance. Joe Banks argues, "We could get rid of conservatism and make accounting numbers more useful if we delegated financial reporting to independent auditors rather than to corporate managers." Do you agree? Why or why not?

7. A fund manager states, "I refuse to buy any company that makes a voluntary accounting change, since it's certainly a case of management trying to hide bad news." Can you think of any alternative interpretation?

NOTES

1. Accounting analysis is sometimes also called quality of earnings analysis. We prefer to use the term accounting analysis because we are discussing a broader concept than merely a firm's earnings quality.

2. At the time of writing there is no globally accepted name for management's narrative discussion of the firm's performance, nor has the IASB set detailed standards on what firms should report in this section. Throughout this book we will refer to this section as the Management Report section and assume that it typically contains at least a Letter to the Shareholders and a review of the firm's financial performance during the fiscal year and its financial position at the end of the year.

3. These definitions paraphrase those of the International Accounting Standards Board, "Framework for the Preparation and Presentation of Financial Statements" (also referred to as the "Conceptual Framework"). Our intent is to present the definitions at a conceptual, not technical, level. For more complete discussion of these and related concepts, see the IASB's Conceptual Framework.

4. Strictly speaking, the comprehensive net income of a firm also includes gains and losses from increases and decreases in equity from nonoperating activities or exceptional items.

5. The E.U. has given its individual member states the option to permit or require private companies to use IFRS for the preparation of their single entity and/or consolidated financial statements. Similarly, member states may permit or require public companies to prepare their single entity financial statements in accordance with IFRS.

6. See "Study Pursuant to Section 108(d) of the Sarbanes-Oxley Act of 2002 on the Adoption by the United States Financial Reporting System of a Principles-Based Accounting System" by the U.S. Securities and Exchange Commission (2003) and "FASB Response to SEC Study on the Adoption of a Principles-Based Accounting System" by the Financial Accounting Standards Board (2004).

7. For a description of international differences in managers' legal liability for the information that they provide in prospectuses, see R. La Porta, F. Lopez-de-Silanes, and A. Shleifer, "What Works in Securities Laws?" *The Journal of Finance* 61 (2006): 1–32.

8. Thus, although accrual accounting is theoretically superior to cash accounting in measuring a firm's periodic performance, the distortions it introduces can make accounting data less valuable to users. If these distortions are large enough, current cash flows may measure a firm's periodic performance better than accounting profits. The relative usefulness of cash flows and accounting profits in measuring performance, therefore, varies from firm to firm. For empirical evidence on this issue, see P. Dechow, "Accounting Earnings and Cash Flows as Measures of Firm Performance: The Role of Accounting Accruals," *Journal of Accounting and Economics* 18 (July 1994): 3–42, and A. Charitou, C. Clubb, and A. Andreou, "The Effect of Earnings Permanence, Growth and Firm Size on the Usefulness of Cash Flows and Earnings in Explaining Security Returns: Empirical Evidence for the UK," *Journal of Business Finance and Accounting* 28 (June/July 2001): 563–594.

9. For example, Abraham Briloff wrote a series of accounting analyses of public companies in *Barron's* over several years. On average, the share prices of the analyzed companies changed by about 8 percent on the day these articles were published, indicating the potential value of performing such analysis. For a more complete discussion of this evidence, see G. Foster, "Briloff and the Capital Market," *Journal of Accounting Research* 17 (Spring 1979): 262–274.

10. For a complete discussion of these motivations, see *Positive Accounting Theory*, by R. Watts and J. Zimmerman (Englewood Cliffs, NJ: Prentice-Hall, 1986). A summary of this research is provided by T. Fields, T. Lys, and L. Vincent in "Empirical Research on Accounting Choice," *Journal of Accounting and Economics* 31 (September 2001): 255–307.

11. The most convincing evidence supporting the covenant hypothesis is reported in a study of the accounting decisions by firms in financial distress: A. Sweeney, "Debt-Covenant Violations and Managers' Accounting Responses," *Journal of Accounting and Economics* 17 (May 1994): 281–308.

12. Studies that examine the bonus hypothesis generally report evidence supporting the view that managers' accounting decisions are influenced by compensation considerations. See, for example, P. Healy, "The Effect of Bonus Schemes on Accounting Decisions," *Journal of Accounting and Economics* 7 (April 1985): 85–107; R. Holthausen, D. Larcker, and R. Sloan,

"Annual Bonus Schemes and the Manipulation of Earnings," *Journal of Accounting and Economics* 19 (February 1995): 29–74; and F. Guidry, A. Leone, and S. Rock, "Earnings-Based Bonus Plans and Earnings Management by Business Unit Managers," *Journal of Accounting and Economics*, 26 (January 1999): 113–142.

13. L. DeAngelo, "Managerial Competition, Information Costs, and Corporate Governance: The Use of Accounting Performance Measures in Proxy Contests," *Journal of Accounting and Economics* 10 (January 1988): 3–36 and M. Erickson and S. Wang, "Earnings Management by Acquiring Firms in Stock for Stock Mergers," *Journal of Accounting and Economics* 27 (1999): 149–176.

14. The trade-off between taxes and financial reporting in the context of managers' accounting decisions is discussed in detail in *Taxes and Business Strategy* by M. Scholes and M. Wolfson (Englewood Cliffs, NJ: Prentice-Hall, 1992). Many empirical studies have examined firms' LIFO/FIFO choices.

15. Several researchers have documented that firms affected by such situations have a motivation to influence regulators' perceptions through accounting decisions. For example, J. Jones documents that firms seeking import protections make profit-decreasing accounting decisions in "Earnings Management During Import Relief Investigations," *Journal of Accounting Research* 29, no. 2 (Autumn 1991): 193–228. Similarly, W. Beekes finds that U.K. water and electricity companies make profit-decreasing accounting choices in years of regulatory price reviews in "Earnings Management in Response to Regulatory Price Review. A Case Study of the Political Cost Hypothesis in the Water and Electricity Sectors in England and Wales," Working paper, Lancaster University, 2003. A number of studies find that banks that are close to minimum capital requirements overstate loan loss provisions, understate loan write-offs, and recognize abnormal realized gains on securities portfolios (see S. Moyer, "Capital Adequacy Ratio Regulations and Accounting Choices in Commercial Banks," *Journal of Accounting and Economics* 12 (1990): 123–154; M. Scholes, G. P. Wilson, and M. Wolfson, "Tax Planning, Regulatory Capital Planning, and Financial Reporting Strategy for Commercial Banks," *Review of Financial Studies* 3 (1990): 625–650; A. Beatty, S. Chamberlain, and J. Magliolo, "Managing Financial Reports of Commercial Banks: The Influence of Taxes, Regulatory Capital and Earnings," *Journal of Accounting Research* 33, no. 2 (1995): 231–261; and J. Collins, D. Shackelford, and J. Wahlen, "Bank Differences in the Coordination of Regulatory Capital, Earnings and Taxes," *Journal of Accounting Research* 33, no. 2 (Autumn 1995): 263–291). Finally, Petroni finds that financially weak property-casualty insurers that risk regulatory attention understate claim loss reserves: K. Petroni, "Optimistic Reporting in the Property Casualty Insurance Industry," *Journal of Accounting and Economics* 15 (December 1992): 485–508.

16. P. Healy and K. Palepu, "The Effect of Firms' Financial Disclosure Strategies on Stock Prices," *Accounting Horizons* 7 (March 1993): 1–11. For a summary of the empirical evidence, see P. Healy and J. Wahlen, "A Review of the Earnings Management Literature and Its Implications for Standard Setting," *Accounting Horizons* 13 (December 1999): 365–384.

17. Financial analysts pay close attention to managers' disclosure strategies; Standard and Poor's publishes scores that rate the disclosure of companies from around the world. For a discussion of these ratings, see, for example, T. Khanna, K. Palepu, and S. Srinivasan, "Disclosure Practices of Foreign Companies Interacting with U.S. Markets," *Journal of Accounting Research* 42 (May 2004): 475–508.

18. See P. Healy and K. Palepu, "The Fall of Enron," *Journal of Economic Perspectives* 17, no. 2 (Spring 2003): 3–26.

19. For detailed analyses of companies that made such changes, see R. Schattke and R. Vergoossen, "Barriers to Interpretation: A Case Study of Philips Electronics NV," *Accounting and Business Research* 27 (1996): 72–84, and K. Palepu, "Anatomy of an Accounting Change," in *Accounting and Management: Field Study Perspectives*, edited by W. Bruns, Jr. and R. Kaplan (Boston: Harvard Business School Press, 1987).

20. Examples of this type of behavior are documented by J. Hand in his study, "Did Firms Undertake Debt-Equity Swaps for an Accounting Paper Profit or True Financial Gain?" *The Accounting Review* 64 (October 1989): 587–623, and by E. Black, K. Sellers, and T. Manley in "Earnings Management Using Asset Sales: An International Study of Countries Allowing Noncurrent Asset Revaluation," *Journal of Business Finance and Accounting* 25 (November/December 1998): 1287–1317.

21. For an empirical analysis of inventory build-ups, see V. Bernard and J. Noel, "Do Inventory Disclosures Predict Sales and Earnings?" *Journal of Accounting, Auditing, and Finance* (Fall 1991).

22. For research on accounting and economic incentives in the formation of R&D partnerships, see A. Beatty, P. Berger, and J. Magliolo, "Motives for Forming Research and Development

Financing Organizations," *Journal of Accounting and Economics* 19 (April 1995): 411–442. An overview of Enron's use of special purpose entities to manage earnings and window-dress its balance is provided by P. Healy and K. Palepu, "The Fall of Enron," *Journal of Economic Perspectives* 17, no. 2 (Spring 2003): 3–26.

23. For an empirical examination of asset write-offs, see J. Elliott and W. Shaw, "Write-offs as Accounting Procedures to Manage Perceptions," *Journal of Accounting Research* 26 (1988): 91–119.

24. R. Mendenhall and W. Nichols report evidence consistent with managers taking advantage of their discretion to postpone reporting bad news until the year-end. See R. Mendenhall and W. Nichols, "Bad News and Differential Market Reactions to Announcements of Earlier-Quarter versus Fourth-Quarter Earnings," *Journal of Accounting Research*, Supplement (1988): 63–86.

25. K. Peasnell, P. Pope, and S. Young report evidence that independent outside directors prevent earnings management. See K. Peasnell, P. Pope, and S. Young, "Board Monitoring and Earnings Management: Do Outside Directors Influence Abnormal Accruals?," *Journal of Business Finance and Accounting* 32 (September 2005): 1311–1346.

26. The role of insider transactions in the collapse of Enron are discussed by P. Healy and K. Palepu, "The Fall of Enron," *Journal of Economic Perspectives* 17, no. 2 (Spring 2003): 3–26.

27. This type of analysis is presented in the context of provisions for bad debts by M. McNichols and P. Wilson in their study, "Evidence of Earnings Management From the Provisions for Bad Debts," *Journal of Accounting Research*, Supplement (1988): 1–31.

28. This point has been made by several accounting researchers. For a summary of research on earnings management, see K. Schipper, "Earnings Management," *Accounting Horizons* (December 1989): 91–102.

29. See J. Chang, "The Decline in Value Relevance of Earnings and Book Values," unpublished dissertation, Harvard University, 1998. Evidence is also reported by J. Francis and K. Schipper, "Have Financial Statements Lost Their Relevance?" *Journal of Accounting Research* 37, no. 2 (Autumn 1999): 319–352; and W. E. Collins, E. Maydew, and I. Weiss, "Changes in the Value-Relevance of Earnings and Book Value over the Past Forty Years," *Journal of Accounting and Economics* 24 (1997): 39–67.

30. See G. Foster, "Briloff and the Capital Market," *Journal of Accounting Research* 17, no. 1 (Spring 1979): 262–274.

31. See S. H. Teoh, I. Welch, and T. J. Wong, "Earnings Management and the Long-Run Market Performance of Initial Public Offerings," *Journal of Finance* 53 (December 1998a): 1935–1974; S. H. Teoh, I. Welch, and T. J. Wong, "Earnings Management and the Post-Issue Underperformance of Seasoned Equity Offerings," *Journal of Financial Economics* 50 (October 1998): 63–99; and S. Teoh, T. Wong, and G. Rao, "Are Accruals During Initial Public Offerings Opportunistic?" *Review of Accounting Studies* 3, no. 1–2 (1998): 175–208.

32. See P. Dechow, R. Sloan, and A. Sweeney, "Causes and Consequences of Earnings Manipulation: An Analysis of Firms Subject to Enforcement Actions by the SEC," *Contemporary Accounting Research* 13, no. 1 (1996): 1–36, and M. D. Beneish, "Detecting GAAP Violation: Implications for Assessing Earnings Management among Firms with Extreme Financial Performance," *Journal of Accounting and Public Policy* 16 (1997): 271–309.

Land Securities Group (A): Choosing cost or fair value on adoption of IFRS

In June 2002 the Council of Ministers of the European Union approved a regulation, proposed by the European Commission in early 2001, to require publicly traded companies on European exchanges to use International Financial Reporting Standards (IFRS) as the basis for presenting their financial statements beginning January 1, 2005.[1] As many European firms were reporting financial statements using the domestic accounting standards for the country in which they were domiciled, the required adoption of IFRS would have far-reaching implications for the financial reporting of many of the 7,000 firms listed on European exchanges. One of these companies was Land Securities Group ("Land Securities"), an investment property firm based in the United Kingdom. Prior to adoption of IFRS, Land Securities was applying U.K. accounting standards, which required investment properties to be reported using the revaluation model. However, adoption of IFRS would require Land Securities to choose between either the cost or fair value models to report its investment properties.

Background

Land Securities was an investment property firm located in the U.K. Investment property firms invest in property to generate rental income and/or long-term capital appreciation.[2] This is distinguished from property used in production or for administrative purposes, as well as from holding property for sale in the ordinary course of business.

The investment property industry in the U.K. was relatively developed, comprising over 50 publicly traded firms ranging from smaller firms such as Cardiff Property and Stewart & Wight (each with approximately £10 million in property) to several large firms, including Land Securities, British Land, and Liberty International (each with

Professor Edward J. Riedl prepared this case. HBS cases are developed solely as the basis for class discussion. Cases are not intended to serve as endorsements, sources of primary data, or illustrations of effective or ineffective management. Copyright © 2004 President and Fellows of Harvard College. HBS Case 9–105–014.

1. *The increased globalization of business over the past several decades has brought a concurrent need for more standardized accounting rules to enhance the comparability of companies across countries. With this intent, the initial body to create international accounting standards was formed in 1973 and continues in its current incarnation as the International Accounting Standards Board, or IASB (akin to the Financial Accounting Standards Board, or FASB, in the U.S.). The IASB includes representatives from a number of countries, such as Canada, France, Japan, the U.K., and the U.S. The objectives of the IASB are to publish accounting standards for the presentation of financial statements and to work generally for the improvement and harmonization of accounting standards. This latter objective has often been referred to as the "convergence" of accounting standards across jurisdictions. To both ends, the primary outputs from the IASB are International Financial Reporting Standards, or IFRS. Note that standards issued by the IASB prior to 2002 are designated as International Accounting Standards, or IAS. However, "IAS" and "IFRS" refer to the same body of international accounting standards.*

2. *Investment property firms are similar to real estate investment trusts (REITs) in the United States, in that both invest in properties. The primary difference relates to the tax treatment: investment property firms generally are required to pay corporate income taxes; however, U.S. REITs generally do not pay taxes (i.e., they are "pass-through entities," wherein the REIT must pay out the bulk of its earnings annually as dividends, which are taxed when received by the owners of the REIT).*

over £4 billion in property).[3] While most of the U.K. firms, including Land Securities, owned properties principally within the U.K., several firms also had substantial property holdings in other countries.

Land Securities was one of the largest investment property companies in the world with over £7.8 billion of investment properties valued on its balance sheet at March 31, 2003 (see Exhibit 1). Land Securities' investment properties fell within two categories: freehold and long leasehold. Freehold is a special right granting the full use of real estate for an indeterminate time. Thus, Land Securities effectively owned its freehold properties, which made up approximately 75% of its investment properties. The remaining were long leaseholds, which are properties held under leases with unexpired terms of generally over 50 years. Land Securities had been profitable and growing since 1990 (see Exhibits 2, 3, and 4).

In 2003, Land Securities had a portfolio of 231 individual investment properties, all of which were located in the U.K. Investment properties may be characterized in a number of ways. Operationally, they may be classified into several categories: offices (such as corporate office buildings); retail (such as shops and stores, including shopping centers); industrial (such as warehouses and manufacturing facilities); leisure (such as hotels); and residential (such as apartment complexes). Investment properties may also be characterized by location, such as urban or suburban, or within particular districts (such as a financial district). Finally, properties may be characterized by various attributes, such as their size (square feet available for rent), use (e.g., a high-technology building), age, the type and number of clients using the space, as well as the nature of the contracts relating to the property (e.g., do the tenants have short-term versus long-term rent agreements). Exhibit 5 shows that Land Securities' portfolio had two primary segments: offices (which made up 42% of the value of its investment properties and were located principally in London) and retail (which made up 50% of the value of its investment properties). Almost one-quarter of rental income was obtained from the 10 largest tenants.

U.K. investment property market: Property values

Over the past 20 years, the U.K. investment property market had experienced substantial upward and downward movements in the values of properties (see Exhibit 6). Following a dramatic increase in property values in the late 1980s was a significant decrease coinciding with the recession in the U.K. of the early 1990s. Values recovered in the late 1990s. Since 2000, the change in property values had been mixed.

Exhibit 7 shows the historical values for the markets in which Land Securities had substantial property interests in 2003. The central London office market recently experienced a downturn, though not as severe as in the early 1990s. However, prospects appeared to be improving; for example, Land Securities' management had recently stated "we now believe that we have reached the low point for asset values in the Central London office market."[4] The retail properties had fared better, not experiencing as sharp a decline in values as in the early 1990s.

---

3. "£" refers to pounds sterling, the currency used in the U.K. The exchange ratio at May 2004 was about US $1.75 to £1.

4. "Preliminary results for the year ended 31 March 2004," Land Securities Group, May 18, 2004, p. 1.

Accounting for investment properties in the U.K.

Prior to adoption of IFRS, Land Securities applied the domestic financial reporting requirements of U.K. accounting standards. One of the key standards was Statement of Standard Accounting Practice 19, *Accounting for Investment Properties* (SSAP 19). SSAP 19 required that investment properties be reported using the revaluation model. Under this model investment properties are not depreciated; rather, they must be revalued each year and listed on the balance sheet at "open market value." SSAP 19 defines "open market value" as "an opinion of the best price at which the sale of an interest in property would have been completed unconditionally for cash consideration on the date of valuation assuming (among other things) that both parties to the transaction had acted knowledgeably, prudently, and without compulsion." SSAP 19 further required that any changes in the value of investment properties be recorded to a revaluation reserve, which is a component of the equity section of the balance sheet (see Exhibit 1).[5] Only decreases in the value of properties that exhaust the revaluation reserve (and thus go below historical cost) are recorded to the income statement as impairment charges. Thus, all of Land Securities' investment properties were reflected on the balance sheet at "open market value," assessed at March 31, 2003 to be £7,824 million.

Under SSAP 19 firms may use either internal or external appraisers to perform the revaluation; however, an external appraisal is required at least once every five years. Internal appraisers typically include directors within the firm, who have the necessary property valuation credentials and experience with the particular type of property to be valued. External appraisers include a number of independent property appraisal firms. Historically, approximately 25% of investment property firms have used internal appraisers to perform the valuation, though this is concentrated within the smaller investment property firms.[6] In either case, appraisers must adhere to the guidance prescribed by the Royal Institute of Chartered Surveyors, which has promulgated valuation standards in the U.K. for over 100 years. Further, auditors must opine on the open market values of properties as part of the investment property firm's audit. Since 1990, Land Securities had employed the external appraiser Knight Frank to revalue its investment property portfolios and PricewaterhouseCoopers to audit them.

Adoption of International Financial Reporting Standards

The required adoption of IFRS effective in 2005 would have a number of effects on European investment property firms, including Land Securities.[7] One of the primary reporting issues related to International Accounting Standard 40, *Investment Property* (IAS 40), which is the international equivalent of SSAP 19. Under IAS 40, Land Securities had to choose either the cost or fair value model and apply the chosen

---

5. Under U.K. generally accepted accounting principles (GAAP), changes in open market value are considered unrealized gains/losses. These are not reported on the income statement; rather, they appear on a supplemental statement referred to as the "Statement of Total Recognized Gains and Losses."

6. Karl Muller and Edward Riedl, "External Monitoring of Property Appraisal Estimates and Information Asymmetry," Journal of Accounting Research 40 (June 2002): 865–881. The above percentage for internal appraisers is from the larger sample referred to in footnote 13 of this paper.

7. While most European companies had to adopt IFRS beginning January 1, 2005, a temporary exception was allowed for (1) companies that traded in the U.S. and used U.S. GAAP, and (2) companies that had issued debt securities but not equity securities. In both cases, those companies had to comply with IFRS by January 1, 2007.

model across all of its investment properties. Under the cost model, investment property is stated on the balance sheet at cost less accumulated depreciation and any impairment losses, and fair value must be disclosed in the footnotes.[8] Under the fair value model, investment property is stated on the balance sheet at fair value, with all changes in fair value reported in the income statement. Fair value is defined in IAS 40 as the amount for which an asset can be exchanged between knowledgeable, willing parties in an arm's-length transaction; thus, it is similar to the U.K.'s "open market value."[9] Similar to SSAP 19, IAS 40 requires that fair value be assessed at the individual property level. In addition, IAS 40 encourages a firm to use an external appraiser in deriving fair value but does not require it. Exhibit 8 provides a summary of the relevant accounting models.

IAS 40 was significant, as it represented the first time the IASB had introduced a fair value accounting model for long-lived nonfinancial assets. When the IASB solicited comments for the exposure draft of IAS 40, there was substantial debate on the merits of applying the fair value model to investment properties (see Exhibit 9).[10] Further, the use of the fair value model contrasted with U.S. GAAP, which generally required nonfinancial assets, including investment properties, to be reported using the cost model. Thus, as reflected in Exhibit 10, Land Securities' choice of cost or fair value had the potential to affect comparability with other large real estate firms, both U.K. and non-U.K. based. Nonetheless, because financial statements require multiple years of presentation for comparative purposes (e.g., two years of balance sheets are typically presented), implementation of IFRS required Land Securities to immediately assess the international standards' impact on its financial reporting.

8. *Impairment losses must be calculated under the requirements of IAS 36, Impairment of Assets. An impairment is a charge to reduce an asset to its fair value. Of note, if certain requirements are met, impairment charges may be reversed under IAS 36. This contrasts with U.S. GAAP, which prohibits reversals of impairments.*
9. *International Accounting Standard 40, Investment Property, 2003 (paragraph 5), International Accounting Standards Board.*
10. *An "exposure draft" is a preliminary version of an accounting standard. As does the FASB in the U.S., the IASB follows a due process in generating accounting standards. This includes obtaining feedback on drafts of standards from various constituents, including accounting firms, trade groups, and companies to be affected by the standard. The IASB may incorporate this feedback into changes in the standard before it is finalized. Exposure drafts are a primary means of obtaining such feedback.*

EXHIBIT 1 **Land Securities Group 2002–2003 balance sheets (£ millions)**

	March 31, 2002		March 31, 2003	
Fixed assets				
Intangible asset – goodwill		38.9		36.7
Tangible assets				
Investment properties				
Freehold	5,715.3		5,759.9	
Leasehold	2,084.7		2,064.0	
Total investment properties		7,800.0		7,823.9
Operating properties[a]		428.9		557.4
Other tangible assets		45.3		41.5
Investment in joint venture, net		188.8		106.8
		8,501.9		8,566.3
Current assets	365.6		441.4	
Creditors falling due within one year	(690.9)		(594.9)	
Net current liabilities		(325.3)		(153.5)
Creditors falling due after more than one year		(2,010.1)		(2,670.7)
Provision for liabilities and charges		(129.9)		(179.0)
Total assets less total liabilities		**6,036.6**		**5,563.1**
Capital and reserves				
Called-up share capital[b]		524.3		76.9
Share premium account		—		13.3
Revaluation reserve		3,376.9		3,038.9
Other reserves[b]		901.3		0.1
Profit and loss account (retained earnings)		1,234.1		2,433.9
Total equity		**6,036.6**		**5,563.1**

a. Operating properties are those managed by Land Securities under contract as part of its "total property outsourcing" strategy. These assets do not satisfy the definition of investment properties and thus must be reported at depreciated cost.

b. Land Securities engaged in a capital restructuring in July 2002 that included a substantial dividend payment to shareholders. This restructuring effectively exchanged one type of common stock shares for another and accounts for the reduction of both "called-up share capital" and "other reserves," as well as much of the increase in "profit and loss account."

Source: Land Securities Group, 2002 and 2003 annual reports.

Land Securities

EXHIBIT 2   **Land Securities Group, 2002–2003 income statements (£ millions)**

	For the year ending March 31, 2002		For the year ending March 31, 2003	
Revenue				
Rental income/other	525.9		519.7	
Total property outsourcing/joint venture	406.2		658.3	
Other income	93.5		61.5	
Total revenue		1,025.6		1,239.5
Expenses				
Rentals	(124.5)		(164.4)	
Direct property or contract expenditures	(249.9)		(399.4)	
Indirect property or contract expenditures	(50.6)		(57.1)	
Depreciation/amortization	(21.0)		(41.9)	
Other	(62.8)		(26.5)	
Total expenses		(508.8)		(689.3)
Operating profit		516.8		550.2
Profit on sale of investment properties		13.4		41.7
Interest and similar charges		(166.7)		(272.3)
Profit on ordinary activities before taxation		363.5		319.6
Taxation		(99.9)		(89.7)
Profit on ordinary activities after taxation		**263.6**		**229.9**
Dividends		(178.4)		(167.4)
Retained profit		**85.2**		**62.5**

Source: Land Securities Group, 2002 and 2003 annual reports.

Land Securities

EXHIBIT 3 Land Securities Group, 1990–2003 summary financial data (£ millions)

	1990	1991	1992	1993	1994	1995	1996	1997	1998	1999	2000	2001[c]	2002[c]	2003[c]
Balance sheet														
Total assets	6,004	4,989	4,712	4,426	5,373	5,482	5,696	6,338	7,091	7,483	7,791	8,509	8,868	9,008
Investment properties:														
Historical cost	2,213	2,478	2,693	2,872	2,981	3,092	3,264	3,411	3,407	3,624	3,871	4,210	4,423	4,785
Revaluation reserve[a]	3,398	2,231	1,608	1,227	2,051	2,078	2,002	2,349	3,029	3,287	3,583	3,696	3,377	3,039
Open market value[a]	5,611	4,709	4,301	4,099	5,032	5,170	5,266	5,760	6,436	6,911	7,454	7,906	7,800	7,824
Income statement														
Revenue	296	360	407	437	449	460	462	471	484	500	528	647	1,026	1,240
Expenses	(172)	(204)	(242)	(267)	(268)	(280)	(290)	(293)	(287)	(284)	(276)	(414)	(762)	(1,010)
Profit on ordinary activities (after tax)	124	156	165	170	181	180	172	178	197	216	252	233	264	230
Cash flow statement														
Operating cash flows[b]	138	228	215	175	185	196	183	195	168	229	247	284	133	109

a. The revaluation reserve (open market value) for investment properties for 1989 was £3,350 (5,211) million.

b. Operating cash flows represent cash flows after interest and taxation. This amount is comparable to cash flows from operations in the U.S.

c. The dramatic increase in revenues and expenses for 2001–2003 reflects the incorporation of "total property outsourcing" into Land Securities' strategy.

Source: Compiled by casewriter from Land Securities Group, 1990–2003 annual reports.

Land Securities

EXHIBIT 4 **Land Securities Group, 1990–2003 profit on ordinary activities (£ millions)**

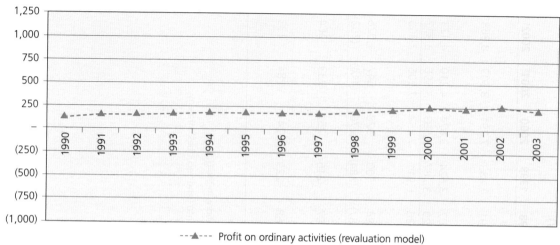

Sources: Compiled by casewriter from Land Securities Group, 1990–2003 annual reports.

EXHIBIT 5 **Land Securities Group, 2003 investment property portfolio**

Investment properties by type

Type	# of properties	Valuation		Rental income		Vacancy rate	Median tenant lease
		£ million	%	£ million	%	%	Years
Offices	69	3,312.5	42	240.4	46	1.9	6.3
Retail:							
Shopping centers	78	2,777.2	36	180.6	35	1.2	9.0
Retail warehouses	43	1,116.8	14	60.1	12	1.2	17.8
Industrial	30	385.9	5	26.0	5	3.5	7.8
Other	11	231.5	3	12.6	2	0.0	12.3
TOTAL	**231**	**7,823.9**	**100**	**519.7**	**100**		

Investment properties by location (all amounts are percent of investment property value)

Type	Central/ Inner London	South East	Midlands	Wales	North	Scotland/ Northern Ireland	TOTAL
Offices	41	1	—	—	—	—	42
Retail:							
Shopping centers	9	4	5	5	7	6	36
Retail warehouses		4	2	1	5	2	14
Industrial	—	5	—	—	—	—	5
Other	1	1	—	—	1	—	3
TOTAL	**51%**	**15%**	**7%**	**6%**	**13%**	**8%**	**100%**

Major tenants

The 10 largest tenants of Land Securities' investment properties account for 23.8% of current rents. The top three are Central Government (9.6%), Allen and Overy (2.8%), and Dresdner Bank (2.2%).

Source: Land Securities Group, 2003 Annual Report.

EXHIBIT 6 **U.K. office property values, 1983–2002**

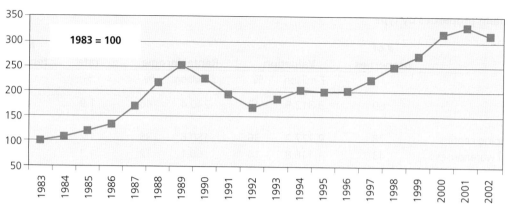

This graph presents an index of property values for U.K. office space for the period 1983–2002. 1983 is the baseline year (value set to 100); subsequent years are set relative to this baseline.

Source: Investment Property Databank, U.K. Key Centres 2003 Report.

EXHIBIT 7 **Property values 1990–2002 for markets in which Land Securities Group has interests**

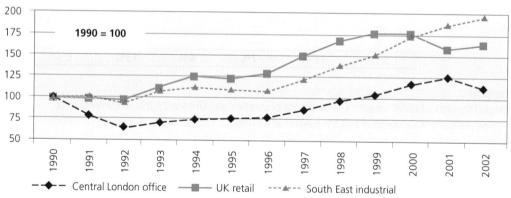

This graph presents an index of property values for the period 1990–2002 for markets in which Land Securities has significant interests in 2003. 1990 is the baseline year (value set to 100); subsequent years are set relative to this baseline.

Source: Investment Property Databank, U.K. Key Centres 2003 Report.

EXHIBIT 8 **Summary of accounting models (as applied in the U.K. for investment properties)**

For purposes of evaluating how these three models are applied to investment properties in the U.K., the term "fair value" is used synonymously with the U.K. term "open market value."

Cost model

The cost model lists investment properties on the balance sheet at cost less accumulated depreciation and any impairment losses. Depreciation is charged to the income statement in the period in which the benefit occurs. Fair values must be disclosed in the footnotes. Any impairment (i.e., evidence that fair value is less than stated cost) requires a reduction in the cost of the investment property to its fair value, with the reduction reflected as an impairment charge on the income statement. In addition, under certain conditions, impairment charges may be reversed under IAS.

Revaluation model

The revaluation model lists investment properties on the balance sheet at their fair value. Under this model, depreciation is not recorded. Increases in fair value are recorded directly to a revaluation reserve that falls under the equity section of the balance sheet. Decreases in fair value are charged directly against any related revaluation reserve. However, if the decrease in fair value exhausts the related revaluation reserve, any remaining decrease is recorded as an impairment charge and included in the income statement.

Fair value model

The fair value model lists investment properties on the balance sheet at their fair value, similar to the revaluation model. However, any changes in fair value are recorded directly to the income statement. No revaluation reserve is used, nor is depreciation recorded.

Source: Compiled by casewriter.

EXHIBIT 9 **Comments on the exposure draft for IAS 40, *Investment Property***

Below are excerpts from comment letters received by the IASB on the exposure draft for IAS 40, Investment Property. The excerpts are responses to the following question: "Do you agree that changes in the fair value of investment properties should be recognized in net profit or loss for the period?"

Investment property industry

Land Securities (U.K.)

In our view, mixing rental income with unrealized holding gains (or losses) would be confusing and such accounting treatment would be a retrograde step and misleading to investors.

Hongkong Land Holdings (Hong Kong)

To reflect fair value changes in the income statement as an operating item increases the volatility of income while not necessarily reflecting the performance of the business. Investment property is a long term business

and the year-on-year change in asset value is not a good yardstick to reflect performance.

Large accounting firms

Ernst and Young

In our view, there are relatively few circumstances ... in which the application of a fair value model with subsequent changes in fair value being recorded in the income statement is appropriate ... we believe that investment properties should be accounted for at either amortized cost or at fair value through equity.

PriceWaterhouseCoopers

Including changes in value in profit (but only for investment properties) creates a curious "mixed model" for the reporting of performance.

Source: Compiled by casewriter from comment letters in *Comment Letters to Exposure Draft E64, Investment Property,* International Accounting Standards Committee, January 2000.

EXHIBIT 10 **Condensed balance sheets and income statements**

Cost model: Vornado Realty Trust (December 31, 2003; $ millions)

Balance sheet		Income statement	
Land	1,504	Revenue	1,503
Buildings	6,244	Expenses:	
Accumulated depreciation	(870)	Operating	(584)
Other assets	2,641	Depreciation	(215)
Total assets	**9,519**	General and administration	(122)
Liabilities (principally debt)	4,520	Interest	(230)
Equity	4,999	Other	(67)
Total liabilities/Equity	**9,519**	**Operating income**	**285**

Footnote excerpt: Real estate is carried at cost, net of accumulated depreciation ... depreciation is provided on a straight-line basis over the assets' estimated useful lives from 7 to 40 years.

Revaluation model: Land Securities Group (March 31, 2003; £ millions)

Balance sheet		Income statement	
Investment properties	7,824	Revenue	1,240
Other assets	1,184	Expenses:	
Total assets	**9,008**	Operating	(621)
Liabilities (principally debt)	3,445	Depreciation	(42)
Revaluation Reserve	3,039	Interest	(272)
Equity	2,524	Other	(75)
Total liabilities/Equity	**9,008**	**Operating income**	**230**

Footnote excerpt: Investment properties are carried at open market values, based on the latest professional valuations. Unrealized capital surpluses and deficits, including those arising on the periodic revaluation of properties, are taken to the revaluation reserve.

Fair value model: Hongkong Land Holdings (December 31, 2003; $ millions)

Balance sheet		Income statement	
Investment properties	5,507	Revenue	384
Other assets	1,083	Expenses:	
Total assets	**6,590**	Decrease in fair value of	
Liabilities (principally debt)	2,950	investment properties	(824)
Equity	3,640	Interest	(65)
Total liabilities/Equity	**6,590**	Cost of sales/Other	(63)
		Operating loss	**(568)**

Footnote excerpt: Investment properties are carried in the balance sheet at fair value, representing open market value determined annually by independent valuers. Changes in fair value are recorded in the consolidated profit and loss account.

Source: Compiled by casewriter from respective 2003 annual reports.

Implementing Accounting Analysis

We learned in Chapter 3 that accounting analysis requires the analyst to adjust a firm's accounting numbers using cash flow information and information from the notes to the financial statements to "undo" any accounting distortions. This entails recasting a firm's financial statements using standard reporting nomenclature and formats. Firms frequently use somewhat different formats and terminology for presenting their financial results. Recasting the financial statements using a standard template, therefore, helps ensure that performance metrics used for financial analysis are calculated using comparable definitions across companies and over time.

Once the financial statements have been standardized, the analyst is ready to identify any distortions in financial statements. The analyst's primary focus should be on those accounting estimates and methods that the firm uses to measure its key success factors and risks. If there are differences in these estimates and/or methods between firms or for the same firm over time, the analyst's job is to assess whether they reflect legitimate business differences and therefore require no adjustment, or whether they reflect differences in managerial judgment or bias and require adjustment. In addition, even if accounting rules are adhered to consistently, accounting distortions can arise because accounting rules themselves do a poor job of capturing firm economics, creating opportunities for the analyst to adjust a firm's financials in a way that presents a more realistic picture of its performance.

This chapter shows how to recast the firm's financial statements into a template that uses standard terminology and classifications, discusses the most common types of accounting distortions that can arise, and shows how to make adjustments to the standardized financial statements to undo these distortions.

A balance sheet approach is used to identify whether there have been any distortions to assets, liabilities, or shareholders' equity. Once any asset and liability misstatements have been identified, the analyst can make adjustments to the balance sheet at the beginning and/or end of the current year, as well as any needed adjustments to revenues and expenses in the latest income statement. This approach ensures that the most recent financial ratios used to evaluate a firm's performance and forecast its future results are based on financial data that appropriately reflect its business economics.

In some instances, information taken from a firm's notes to the financial statements, cash flow statement, and statement of changes in equity enables the analyst to make a precise adjustment for an accounting distortion. However, for many types of accounting adjustments the company does not disclose all of the information needed to perfectly undo the distortion, requiring the analyst to make an approximate adjustment to the financial statements.

RECASTING FINANCIAL STATEMENTS

Firms sometimes use different nomenclature and formats to present their financial results. For example, the asset goodwill can be reported separately using such titles as Goodwill, "Excess of cost over net assets of acquired companies," and "Cost in excess of fair value," or it can be included in the line item Other Intangible Assets. Interest Income can be reported as a subcategory of Revenues, shown lower down the income statement as part of Other Income and Expenses, or it is sometimes reported as Interest Expense, Net of Interest Income.

These differences in financial statement terminology, classifications, and formats can make it difficult to compare performance across firms, and sometimes to compare performance for the same firm over time. The first task for the analyst in accounting analysis is, therefore, to recast the financial statements into a common format. This involves designing a template for the balance sheet, income statement, cash flow statement, and statement of changes in equity that can be used to standardize financial statements for any company.

One particular obstacle that the analyst must overcome in recasting IFRS-based income statements is that the international standards allow firms to classify their operating expenses in two ways: by nature or by function. The classification by nature defines categories with reference to the cause of operating expenses. Firms using this classification typically distinguish between the cost of materials, the cost of personnel, and the cost of non-current assets (depreciation and amortization). In contrast, the classification by function defines categories with reference to the purpose of operating expenses. Under this classification, firms typically differentiate between costs that are incurred for the purpose of producing the products or services sold – labeled Cost of Sales – and costs for overhead activities such as administrative work and marketing – labeled Selling, General and Administrative Expenses (SG&A). Only income statements that are prepared using the latter classification include the line item "Gross Profit," which is defined as the difference between Sales and Cost of Sales and measures the efficiency of a firm's production activities.

Although the classification of expenses by function potentially provides better information about the efficiency and profitability of a firm's operating activities, some analysts prefer the classification of expenses by nature because this classification is less arbitrary and requires less judgment from the firm. The coexistence of two classifications generally will not cause problems as long as the choice for a particular classification is industry-related. For example, firms that operate in the airline industry are more likely to classify their expenses by nature, whereas manufacturing firms are more likely to classify their expenses by function. Firms that operate in similar industries may, however, prefer different classifications.

A further complication may be that firms use similar terminology under different approaches. For example, in 2005 Puma AG reported that its Cost of Sales was 49 percent of Sales, while Adidas-Salomon AG, one of Puma's main competitors, reported that its Cost of Sales was 52 percent of Sales. Because the two firms classified their expenses differently, however, these amounts were not comparable. Puma's nature-based Cost of Sales included the cost of purchased merchandise and materials used in production, whereas Adidas-Salomon's function-based Cost of Sales included similar costs as well as production personnel expenses. Fortunately, the IFRSs require that when firms classify their expenses by function, they should also report a classification of expenses by nature in the notes to the financial statements. Hence, the analyst can always recast Adidas-Salomon's income statement into the format that Puma used.

Tables 4.1, 4.2, 4.3, 4.4, and 4.5 present the format used throughout the book to standardize the income statement, balance sheet, cash flow statement, and statement of changes in equity, respectively.

TABLE 4.1 Standardized income statement format (classification of operating expenses by function)

Standard income statement accounts	Sample line items classified in account
Sales	Revenue(s)
	Turnover
	Membership fees
	Commissions
	Licenses
Cost of Sales (by function)	Cost of merchandise sold
	Cost of products sold
	Cost of revenues
	Cost of services
	Depreciation on manufacturing facilities
SG&A (by function)	General and administrative
	Marketing and sales
	Distribution expenses
	Servicing and maintenance
	Depreciation on selling and administrative facilities
Other Operating Income, Net of Other Operating Expense (by function)	Amortization of intangibles
	Research and development
	Start-up costs
	Special charges
	Gains/Losses on sale of investments/ non-current assets
	Foreign exchange gains/losses
	Asset impairments
	Restructuring charges
Net Interest Expense (Income) Interest Income Interest Expense	Net finance cost
	Interest charge on non-current provisions
	Interest earned
Investment Income	Result from associate companies
	Equity income from associates
	Dividend income
	Rental income
Minority Interest	
Tax Expense	Provision for taxes
Net Profit/Loss	Net income

TABLE 4.2 Standardized income statement format (classification of operating expenses by nature)

Standard income statement accounts	Sample line items classified in account
Sales	Revenue(s)
	Turnover
	Membership fees
	Commissions
	Licenses
Cost of Materials (by nature)	Cost of outsourced work and services received
	Raw materials and work subcontracted
	Cost of components
	Changes in inventories and own work capitalized (correction)
Personnel Expense (by nature)	Salaries and wages
	Social security
	Post-employment/Pension benefits
	Share-based payments
Depreciation and Amortization (by nature)	
Other Operating Income, Net of Other Operating Expense (by nature)	Transport and distribution costs
	Operating lease installments
	Insurance premiums
	Reversal of provisions
	Gains/Losses on sale of investments/non-current assets
	Foreign exchange gains/losses
	Asset impairments
	Restructuring charges
Net Interest Expense (Income)	Net finance cost
Interest Income	Interest charge on non-current provisions
Interest Expense	Interest earned
Investment Income	Result from associate companies
	Equity income from associates
	Dividend income
	Rental income
Minority Interest	
Tax Expense	Provision for taxes
Net Profit/Loss	Net income

TABLE 4.3 Standardized balance sheet format

Standard balance sheet accounts	Sample line items classified in account	Standard balance sheet accounts	Sample line items classified in account
Assets		**Liabilities and equity**	
Cash and Marketable Securities	Cash and cash equivalents Short-term investments Time deposits	*Current Debt*	Current borrowings Notes payable Bank overdrafts Current portion of non-current borrowings Current portion of finance lease obligation
Trade Receivables	Accounts receivable Trade debtors	*Trade Payables*	Accounts payable Trade creditors
Inventories	Inventory Finished goods Raw materials Work-in-progress Stocks	*Other Current Liabilities*	Accrued expenses Amounts due to related parties Income tax liabilities Social security and payroll taxes Dividends payable Current deferred (unearned) revenue Current provisions
Other Current Assets	Prepaid expenses Claims for tax refunds Current assets classified as held for sale Current derivative financial instruments Amounts due from affiliates Amounts due from employees	*Non-Current Debt*	Long-term borrowings/financial liabilities Subordinated debentures Finance lease obligations Convertible debentures Provision for post-employment benefits Provision for decommissioning costs Other non-current provisions
Non-Current Tangible Assets	Property, plant and equipment Land and buildings Non-current assets classified as held for sale	*Deferred Tax Liability*	

TABLE 4.3 Standardized balance sheet format (*continued*)

Standard balance sheet accounts	Sample line items classified in account	Standard balance sheet accounts	Sample line items classified in account
Non-Current Intangible Assets	Goodwill Software/product development costs Deferred financing costs Deferred subscriber acquisition costs Deferred catalog costs Deferred charges Trademarks and licenses	*Other Non-Current Liabilities (non-interest bearing)*	Non-current deferred (unearned) revenues Other non-current liabilities
Deferred Tax Asset		*Minority Interest*	
Other Non-Current Assets	Investments accounted for using the equity method Investments in associates Finance lease receivables Investment property Biological assets Non-current derivative financial instruments	*Preference Shares*	Preference shares Convertible preference shares
		Ordinary Shareholders' Equity	Share capital Share premium Retained earnings Treasury shares/Own shares purchased but not canceled Other reserves

TABLE 4.4 Standardized cash flow statement format

Standard cash flow statement accounts	Sample line items classified in account
Net Profit or Profit minus Taxes Paid	
Non-Operating Gains (Losses)	Gain (loss) on disposal of investments/non-current assets Cumulative effect of accounting changes Gain (loss) on foreign exchange
Non-Current Operating Accruals	Depreciation and amortization Deferred revenues/costs Deferred taxes Impairment of non-current assets Other non-cash charges to operations Equity earnings of affiliates/unconsolidated subs, net of cash received Minority interest Stock bonus awards

Net (Investments in) or Liquidation
    of Operating Working Capital
	Changes in:
	    Trade receivables
	    Other receivables
	    Prepaid expenses
	    Trade payables
	    Accrued expenses (liabilities)
	    Due from affiliates
	    Accounts payable and accrued expenses
	    Refundable/payable income taxes
	    Inventories
	    Provision for doubtful accounts
	    Other current liabilities (excluding current debt)
	    Other current assets

Net (Investment in) or Liquidation of Non-Current Operating Assets	Purchase/disposal of non-current assets Acquisition of research and development Acquisition/sale of business Capital expenditures Acquisition of subsidiaries and equity investments Capitalization of development costs Cost in excess of the fair value of net assets acquired Investment in financing leases
Net Debt (Repayment) or Issuance	Principal payments on debt Borrowings (repayments) under credit facility Issuance (repayment) of long-term debt Net increase (decrease) in short-term borrowings Notes payable
Dividend (Payments)	Cash dividends paid on ordinary shares/preference shares Distributions

TABLE 4.4 Standardized cash flow statement format *(continued)*

Standard cash flow statement accounts	Sample line items classified in account
Net Share (Repurchase) or Issuance	Proceeds from issuance of ordinary shares Issue of ordinary share for services Issue (redemption) of preferred securities Issue of subsidiary equity Purchase (issue) of treasury shares Capital contributions

TABLE 4.5 Standardized statement of changes in equity format

Standard statement of changes in equity accounts	Sample line items classified in account
Beginning-of-Year Shareholders' Equity	
Unrealized Revaluations, Net of Transfers to Income	Effect of change in fair value of available-for-sale securities
Recognized Actuarial Gains/Losses	Actuarial gains/losses on defined benefit schemes
Gains/Losses on Cash Flow Hedges	Change in fair value of derivatives
Foreign Exchange Gains/Losses	Exchange rate differences Foreign currency translation adjustment
Net Profit	Net profit (income) for the period
Capital Distributions/Contributions	Dividends Share issuance Warrants and options exercised Share-based payments Equity settled transactions
Other Changes in Equity	Change in accounting policy
Ending-of-Year Shareholders' Equity	

To create standardized financials for a company, the analyst classifies each line item in that firm's financial statements using the appropriate account name from the templates set out in the tables. This may require using information from the notes to the financial statements to ensure that accounts are classified appropriately. An example, applying the templates to standardize the 2005 financial statements for car manufacturer Volkswagen AG, is shown in the appendix at the end of this chapter.

Once the financials have been standardized, the analyst can evaluate whether accounting adjustments are needed to correct for any distortions in assets, liabilities, or equity.

Extensible Business Reporting Language

An increasing number of firms worldwide prepare and report their financial statements using the Extensible Business Reporting Language (XBRL). These XBRL statements typically complement the traditional financial statements, but in future years XBRL reporting may start to replace the traditional way of financial reporting. XBRL is a language that supports the internet-based communication of financial information. The basic idea underlying this language is that it provides a "tag" for every individual item in a company's financial statements, including the notes, which describes the main characteristics of the item. Tags contain information about, for example, the accounting standards that the company uses to prepare the item as well as the fiscal year and the broader category of items to which the item belongs. The data items including their tags are reported in an XBRL instance document, which the company makes publicly available through the internet. By using the appropriate software that recognizes the tags, an analyst can then extract only the needed information from the instance document and ignore irrelevant items. One advantage of XBRL reporting is therefore that it substantially reduces the time that the analyst needs to collect and summarize financial statement information.

The process of tagging data items is somewhat similar to the process of recasting financial statements. Because companies use accepted taxonomies to categorize their financial statement items, they take over some of the analyst's work of standardizing the financial statements. The IASC Foundation XBRL Team has developed the IFRS GP taxonomy, which classifies all possible data items that may appear in an IFRS-based financial statement and defines the relationships among them. The use of the IFRS GP taxonomy for XBRL reporting by listed European companies may therefore eventually reduce the importance of recasting IFRS-based financial statements.

FIRST-TIME ADOPTION OF IFRS

The widespread use of IFRS to prepare financial statements is a fairly recent phenomenon. By the end of 2004, around 1,000 firms worldwide prepared their financial statements in conformity with IFRS. Since the mandated introduction of IFRS-based reporting in the E.U. in 2005, however, the number of IFRS users has grown explosively to over 8,000 firms. Although the worldwide move to using one common set of accounting rules yields many advantages for the analyst, the switch from local to international accounting rules also complicates the accounting analysis a little.

In the first year that a firm applies IFRS, it is required to provide the current year's IFRS-based financial figures as well as restate prior year's balance sheet and income statement for comparative purposes. This means that the firm traces back every historical event and assumption that is relevant to a particular line item on the opening balance sheet of the prior year, recalculates the impact of these events and assumptions on the items, and essentially produces its first IFRS-based opening balance sheet as if it had applied IFRS all along (though applying current IFRSs). The firm then records all the events during the prior year and the current year in accordance with IFRS. To avoid the misuse of hindsight, when preparing its opening IFRS-based balance sheet the first-time IFRS adopter cannot use information that it received after the balance sheet date.

In their first IFRS-based financial statements firms have to disclose at least the following information to illustrate the effects of IFRS adoption on their financial figures:

■ A description of the sources of differences between equity reported under previous accounting standards and under IFRS as well as the effects of these differences in quantitative terms. The firm must provide such reconciliations for equity in both its opening and its closing comparative balance sheets.

■ A reconciliation of net profit reported under previous accounting standards and under IFRS for the prior year.

Some firms also voluntarily disclose the opening IFRS-based balance sheet of the prior year, improving the analyst's dataset, but they are not required to do so.

Unfortunately, it is practically difficult for a first-time IFRS adopter to trace back every relevant historical event because it may not have collected or stored all the necessary data in the past. Further, the informational benefits of recalculating and restating certain line items may not outweigh the associated costs. For example, firms that consolidate the translated values of subsidiaries' foreign currency-denominated assets on their balance sheets, recognize the cumulative translation difference, which arises because exchange rates fluctuate over the years, as a separate component in equity. When these firms adopt IFRS they would face the tedious task of recalculating all cumulative translation differences on their subsidiaries. Because separately reporting restated cumulative translation differences generates little additional information, however, first-time IFRS adopters can choose to add the cumulative translation differences to equity and reset the line item to zero upon adoption. To facilitate the first-time preparation of an IFRS-based opening balance sheet, the rules on the first-time IFRS application allow more of these exemptions and even prohibit some restatements. At various places throughout this chapter, we address some of these exemptions and prohibitions.

RECOGNITION OF ASSETS

Accountants define assets as resources that a firm owns or controls as a result of past business transactions, and which are expected to produce future economic benefits that can be measured with a reasonable degree of certainty. Assets can take a variety of forms, including cash, marketable securities, receivables from customers, inventories, fixed assets, non-current investments in other companies, and intangibles.

Distortions in asset values generally arise because there is ambiguity about whether:

■ The firm owns or controls the economic resources in question.

■ The economic resources are likely to provide future economic benefits that can be measured with reasonable certainty.

■ The fair value of assets fall below their book values.

■ Fair value estimates are accurate.

Who owns or controls resources?

For most resources used by a firm, ownership or control is relatively straightforward: the firm using the resource owns the asset. However, some types of transactions make it difficult to assess who owns a resource. For example, who owns or controls a resource that has been leased? Is it the lessor or the lessee? Or consider a firm that discounts a customer receivable with a bank. If the bank has recourse against the firm should the customer default, is the real owner of the receivable the bank or the company? Or consider a firm owning 49 percent of another firm's ordinary shares. Does the firm control all of the investment's assets or only the net investment it legally owns?

Accounting rules often leave some discretion to managers and auditors in deciding whether their company owns or controls an asset. Leaving discretion to managers and auditors can be preferred over imposing detailed and mechanical rules if the latter solution causes managers to structure their transactions such that they avoid recognizing an asset. Following this idea, the IASB frequently takes a principles-based approach to setting accounting standards, thereby granting managers greater reporting discretion than under a rules-based approach. For example, the international standard for preparing consolidated financial statements (IAS 27) requires that firm A reports all the assets of firm B on its balance sheet when firm A has the power to govern the financial and operating policies of firm B. This broadly defined principle anticipates situations where firm A owns less than half of firm B's voting shares but has other ways to influence firm B's decisions, such as through board memberships or contractual agreements. Similarly, the international standard on lease accounting (IAS 17) relies on the basic principle that when a lessee carries substantially all the risks of a leased asset, the asset is essentially owned by the lessee and must be reported on its balance sheet. This standard leaves much responsibility to managers and auditors to decide which leased assets are economically owned by the company.

While reporting discretion is necessary to benefit from managers' insider knowledge about the economic substance of their company's transactions, it also permits managers to misrepresent transactions and satisfy their own financial reporting objectives. Accounting analysis, therefore, involves assessing whether a firm's reported assets adequately reflect the key resources that are under its control, and whether adjustments are required to compare its performance with that of competitors. Although firms are generally inclined to understate the assets that they control, thereby inflating the return on capital invested, they may sometimes pretend to control subsidiaries for the sake of inflating asset and revenue growth. For example, in the period from 1999 to 2001, Dutch food retailer Royal Ahold fraudulently reported the assets, liabilities, revenues, and operating profits of jointly controlled joint ventures in its financial statements as if the company fully controlled the joint ventures. The correct accounting treatment would have been to report only half of the joint ventures' assets and liabilities on Ahold's balance sheet and only half of the joint ventures' revenues, expenses, and operating profits in Ahold's income statement. By fully consolidating the joint ventures, Royal Ahold overstated its revenues by a total amount of €27.6 billion and its annual sales growth by an average of 24 percent. Analyzing the accounting of a firm that follows a strategy of growing through acquisitions, such as Ahold, thus would include identifying subsidiaries that are fully consolidated but not fully owned and assessing their impact on the firm's net assets, revenues, and growth figures.

In situations where standard setters or auditors impose rigid and mechanical accounting rules on managers to reduce reporting discretion, accounting analysis is nevertheless also important because these detailed rules permit managers to "groom" transactions to satisfy there own reporting objectives. For example, mechanical U.S. rules on lease accounting permit two lease transactions with essentially the same but slightly different contract terms to be structured so that one is reported as an asset by the lessee, and the other is shown as an asset by the lessor. The analyst may attempt to correct for this distortion by adjusting the way in which the lessee and the lessor report these transactions.

Although a principles-based approach to standard setting may discourage the structuring of transactions, it cannot fully prevent it. In applying broadly defined reporting principles managers and auditors need guidance about, for example, the meaning of "carrying substantially all risks." When standard setters or standard interpretations committees, such as the International Financial Reporting Interpretations Committee (IFRIC), provide such guidance, they are bound to introduce some mechanical rules that auditors and public enforcers may hang on to. For example, the international standard for lease accounting includes several qualitative criteria for assessing whether the lessee is the economic owner of a leased asset. One example of a qualitative lease classification criterion is that leased assets are normally assumed to be owned by the lessee when the lease term covers the major part of the asset's economic useful life. Following the detailed U.S. rules on lease accounting, auditors and public enforcers may themselves attach quantitative values to the term "major part," such as "greater than 75 percent." This practice of quantifying principles-based accounting standards could again encourage managers to structure transactions.

Asset ownership issues also arise indirectly from the application of rules for revenue recognition. Firms are permitted to recognize revenues only when their product has been shipped or their service has been provided to the customer. Revenues are then considered "earned," and the customer has a legal commitment to pay for the product or service. As a result, for the seller, recognition of revenue frequently coincides with "ownership" of a receivable that is shown as an asset on its balance sheet. Accounting analysis that raises questions about whether or not revenues have been earned therefore often affects the valuation of assets.

Ambiguity over whether a company owns an asset creates a number of opportunities for accounting analysis:

- Despite management's best intentions, financial statements sometimes do a poor job of reflecting the firm's economic assets because it is difficult for accounting rules to capture all of the subtleties associated with ownership and control.

- Accounting rules on ownership and control are the result of a trade-off between granting reporting discretion, which opens opportunities for earnings management, and imposing mechanical, rigid reporting criteria, which opens opportunities for the structuring of transactions. Because finding the perfect balance between discretion and rigidity is a virtually impossible task for standard setters, accounting rules cannot always prevent important assets being omitted from the balance sheet even though the firm bears many of the economic risks of ownership.

- There may be legitimate differences in opinion between managers and analysts over residual ownership risks borne by the company, leading to differences in opinion over reporting for these assets.

- Aggressive revenue recognition, which boosts reported earnings, is also likely to affect asset values.

Can economic benefits be measured with reasonable certainty?

It is almost always difficult to accurately forecast the future benefits associated with capital outlays because the world is uncertain. A company does not know whether a competitor will offer a new product or service that makes its own obsolete. It does not know whether the products manufactured at a new plant will be the type that customers want to buy. A company does not know whether changes in oil prices will make the oil drilling equipment that it manufactures less valuable.

Accounting rules deal with these challenges by stipulating which types of resources can be recorded as assets and which cannot. For example, the economic benefits from research and development are generally considered highly uncertain: research projects may never deliver promised new products, the products they generate may not be economically viable, or products may be made obsolete by competitors' research. International rules (IAS 38), therefore, require that research outlays be expensed and development outlays only be capitalized if they meet stringent criteria of technical and economic feasibility (which they rarely do in industries such as the pharmaceutical industry). In contrast, the economic benefits from plant acquisitions are considered less uncertain and are required to be capitalized.

Rules that require the immediate expensing of outlays for some key resources may be good accounting, but they create a challenge for the analyst – namely, they lead to less timely financial statements. For example, if all firms expense R&D, financial statements will reflect differences in R&D success only when new products are commercialized rather than during the development process. The analyst may attempt to correct for this distortion by capitalizing key R&D outlays and adjusting the value of the intangible asset based on R&D updates.[1]

Have fair values of assets declined below book value?

An asset is impaired when its fair value falls below its book value. In most countries accounting rules require that a loss be recorded for permanent asset impairments. International rules (IAS 36) specify that an impairment loss be recognized on a non-current asset when its book value exceeds the greater of its net selling price and the discounted cash flows expected to be generated from future use. If this condition is satisfied, the firm is required to report a loss for the difference between the asset's fair value and its book value.

Of course markets for many non-current operating assets are illiquid and incomplete, making it highly subjective to infer their fair values. Further, if the cash flows of an individual asset cannot be identified, IAS 36 requires that the impairment test be carried out for the smallest possible *group* of assets, called the cash generating unit, that has identifiable cash flows. Consequently, considerable management judgment is involved in defining the boundaries of cash generating units, deciding whether an asset is impaired and determining the value of any impairment loss.

For the analyst, this raises the possibility that asset values are misstated. International accounting rules themselves permit a certain amount of asset overstatement since the test for asset impairment is typically applied to the cash-generating unit. This can create situations where no financial statement loss is reported for an individual asset that is economically impaired but whose impairment is concealed in the group.

Are fair value estimates accurate?

Managers estimate fair values of assets not only for asset impairment testing. One other use of fair value estimates is to adjust the book value of assets when firms use the revaluation method instead of the historical cost method. The international accounting rules for non-current assets (IAS 16) allow firms to record their non-current assets at fair value instead of their historical cost prices. When doing so, firms must regularly assess whether the reported book values deviate too much from the assets' fair values and, if necessary make adjustments. Although revaluation adjustments are recorded in the statement of changes in equity (not in the income statement), revaluations do affect earnings through the depreciation expense because, under this method, depreciation is determined by reference to the assets' fair value.

Fair value estimates are also needed to calculate goodwill in business combinations. Specifically, the amount by which the acquisition cost exceeds the fair value of the acquired net assets is recorded on the balance sheet as goodwill. The international standard for business combinations (IFRS 3) requires that the amount of goodwill is not amortized but regularly tested for impairment. This may create the incentive for managers to understate the fair value of acquired net assets and, consequently, over-state goodwill.

The task of determining fair values is delegated to management, with oversight by the firm's auditors, potentially leaving opportunities for management bias in valuing assets and for legitimate differences in opinion between managers and analysts over asset valuations. In most cases, management bias will lead to overstated assets since managers will prefer not to recognize an impairment or prefer to overstate nonamor-tized goodwill in business combinations. However, managers can also bias asset values downward by "taking a bath," reducing future expenses and increasing future earnings.

In summary, distortions in assets are likely to arise when there is ambiguity about whether the firm owns or controls a resource, when there is a high degree of uncer-tainty about the value of the economic benefits to be derived from the resource, and when there are differences in opinion about the value of asset impairments. Opportunities for accounting adjustments can arise in these situations if:

- accounting rules do not do a good job of capturing the firm's economics, or
- managers use their discretion to distort the firm's performance, or
- there are legitimate differences in opinion between managers and analysts about economic uncertainties facing the firm that are reflected in asset values.

First-time adoption: Fair value as deemed cost

The international rules on the first-time application of IFRS (IFRS 1) suggest one additional use of fair value estimates. When a firm who uses the historical cost method applies IFRS for the first time in its financial statements, it can choose to consider the fair value of its non-current assets, such as property, plant and equipment, and investment property, as the "deemed cost" of its assets. Deemed cost is the assumed cost price of an asset at which it will initially be recorded in the firm's balance sheet. The firm then calculates depreciation on its non-current assets in reference to the deemed cost. First-time IFRS adopters thus have a one-time opportunity to exercise additional discretion over the book values of their non-current assets.

ASSET DISTORTIONS

Asset overstatements are likely to arise when managers have incentives to increase reported earnings. Thus, adjustments to assets also typically require adjustments to the income statement in the form of either increased expenses or reduced revenues. Asset understatements typically arise when managers have incentives to deflate reported earnings. This may occur when the firm is performing exceptionally well and managers decide to store away some of the current strong earnings for a rainy day. Income smoothing, as it has come to be known, can be implemented by overstating current period expenses (and understating the value of assets) during good times. Asset (and expense) understatements can also arise in a particularly bad year, when managers decide to "take a bath" by understating current period earnings to create the appearance of a turnaround in following years.

Accounting rules themselves can also lead to the understatement of assets. In many countries accounting standards require firms to expense outlays for research and advertising because, even though they may create future value for owners, their outcomes are highly uncertain. Also, until recently some acquisitions were accounted for using the pooling method, whereby the acquirer recorded the target's assets at their book value rather than their actual (higher) purchase price. In these cases the analyst may want to make adjustments to the balance sheet and income statement to ensure that they reflect the economic reality of the transactions.

Finally, asset understatements can arise when managers have incentives to understate liabilities. For example, if a firm records lease transactions as operating leases or if it discounts receivables with recourse, neither the assets nor the accompanying obligations are shown on its balance sheet. Yet in some instances this accounting treatment does not reflect the underlying economics of the transactions – the lessee may effectively own the leased assets, and the firm that sells receivables may still bear all of the risks associated with ownership. The analyst may then want to adjust the balance sheet (and also the income statement) for these effects.

Accounting analysis involves judging whether managers have understated or overstated assets (and also earnings) and, if necessary, adjusting the balance sheet and income statement accordingly. The most common items that can lead to overstatement or understatement of assets (and earnings) are the following:

- depreciation and amortization on non-current assets,
- impairment of non-current assets,
- leased assets,
- intangible assets,
- the timing of revenue (and receivables) recognition,
- allowances (e.g., allowances for doubtful accounts or loan losses),
- write-downs of current assets, and
- discounted receivables.

Deferred taxes on adjustments

Most firms use different accounting rules for business reporting and tax reporting. As a consequence, the assets and liabilities that firms report in their financial statements may differ in value from the assets and liabilities that they report in their tax statements. Consider a firm whose property, plant, and equipment have a book value of €300 in its financial statements but a tax base of €100 in its tax statements. Ignoring future investments, the firm will record a total amount of €300 in depreciation in its future financial statements, whereas it can only record an amount of €100 in tax-deductible depreciation in its future tax statements. Because the firm's tax statements are not publicly available, the analyst must estimate the firm's future tax deductions based on the book value of property, plant, and equipment as reported in the financial statements. This book value, however, overstates the firm's future tax deductions by an amount of €200 (€300 – €100). The IFRSs, therefore, require that the firm discloses the amount of overstatement of future tax deductions in its current financial statements. To do this, the firm recognizes a deferred tax liability on its balance sheet. Given a tax rate of 35 percent, the deferred tax liability equals €70 ([€300 – €100] € .35). This liability essentially represents the tax amount that the firm must pay in future years, in excess of the tax expense that the firm will report in its future financial statements. All additions to (reductions in) the deferred tax liability are accompanied by the recognition of a deferred tax expense (income) in the firm's income statement. Assets whose book values in the financial statements are below the tax bases recorded in the tax statements create a deferred tax asset.

When the analyst makes adjustments to the firm's assets or liabilities to undo any distortions, the deferred tax liability (or asset) is also affected. This is because the adjustments do not affect the tax statements and, consequently, change the difference between book values and tax bases. For example, when the analyst reduces the book value of property, plant, and equipment by €50, the deferred tax liability is reduced by an amount of €17.50 (€50 × € .35) to €52.50 ([€250 – €100] × € .35).

The international accounting standard for income taxes (IAS 12) requires that deferred taxes be recognized on any difference between book values and tax bases with the exception of differences related to:

■ nondeductible assets and nontaxable liabilities acquired in transactions other than business combinations, and

■ nondeductible goodwill and nontaxable negative goodwill.

Depreciation and amortization

Because non-current assets such as manufacturing equipment decrease in value over time, accounting rules require that firms systematically depreciate the book values of these assets. The reduction in the book value of the assets must be recognized as depreciation or amortization expense in the income statement. Managers make estimates of asset lives, salvage values, and amortization schedules for depreciable non-current assets. If these estimates are optimistic, non-current assets and earnings will be overstated. This issue is likely to be most pertinent for firms in heavy asset businesses (e.g., airlines, utilities), whose earnings contain large depreciation components. Firms that use tax depreciation estimates of asset lives, salvage values, or amortization rates are likely to amortize assets more rapidly than justifiable given the assets' economic usefulness, leading to non-current asset understatements.

In 2004 Lufthansa, the German national airline, reported that it depreciated its aircraft over 12 years on a straight-line basis, with an estimated residual value of 15 percent of initial cost. These assumptions imply that Lufthansa's annual depreciation expense was, on average, 7.1 percent ([1 – .15]/12) of the initial cost of its aircraft. In contrast, British Airways (BA), the U.K. national carrier, reported that its aircraft depreciation was also estimated using the straight-line method but assuming an average annual depreciation percentage of 4.3 percent of initial cost.

For the analyst these differences raise several questions. Do Lufthansa and BA fly different types of routes, potentially explaining the differences in their depreciation policies? Alternatively, do they have different asset management strategies? For example, does Lufthansa use newer planes to attract more business travelers, to lower maintenance costs, or to lower fuel costs? If there do not appear to be operating differences that explain the differences in the two firms' depreciation rates, the analyst may well decide that it is necessary to adjust the depreciation rates for one or both firms to ensure that their performance is comparable.

The difference in depreciation assumptions for BA and Lufthansa could at least partially reflect Lufthansa's decision to use similar depreciation rates for financial and tax reporting purposes, whereas BA uses different rates for these purposes. To evaluate this explanation, the analyst could examine the airlines' deferred tax liabilities. Recall that the deferred tax liability measures the difference between the book value and the tax base of a firm's net assets. In 2004 Lufthansa's deferred tax liability for depreciation and amortization was €907 million. Based on its tax percentage of 35 percent, this implies that the differences between Lufthansa's tax depreciation (and amortization) and its reported depreciation had accumulated to an amount of €2,591 million (907/.35). This amount is equal to 20.7 percent (2,591/12,492) of accumulated depreciation on Lufthansa's non-current assets, which suggests that, on average, tax depreciation was 20.7 percent greater than reported depreciation. In the same year, BA's deferred tax liability of £1,287 million and accumulated depreciation on its non-current assets of £5,029 million implied that its accumulated differences between tax depreciation and reported depreciation were 85.3 percent ([1,287/.30]/5,029) of accumulated depreciation. Hence, the difference between BA's depreciation rates for financial and tax reporting purposes appears to be substantially greater than the difference between Lufthansa's tax and reported depreciation rates.

To adjust for this effect, the analyst could decrease Lufthansa's depreciation rates to match those of BA's. The following financial statement adjustments would then be required in Lufthansa's financial statements:

1. Increase the book value of the fleet at the beginning of the year to adjust for the relatively high depreciation rates that had been used in the past. The necessary adjustment is equal to the following amount: original minus adjusted depreciation rate × average asset age × initial asset cost. At the beginning of 2004, Lufthansa reported in the notes to its financial statements that its fleet of aircraft had originally cost €15,044 million, and that accumulated depreciation was €8,515 million. This implies that the average age of Lufthansa's fleet was 8.0 years, calculated as follows:

€ (millions unless otherwise noted)

Aircraft cost, 1/1/2004	€15,044	Reported
Depreciable cost	€12,787.4	Cost × (1 − .15)
Accumulated depreciation, 1/1/2004	€8,515	Reported
Accumulated depreciation/Depreciable cost	66.59%	
Depreciable life	12 years	Reported
Average age of aircraft	7.991 years	12 × .6659 years

If Lufthansa used the same life and salvage estimates as BA, the annual depreciation rate would have been 4.3 percent, implying that given the average age of its fleet, accumulated depreciation would have been €5,169 (7.991 × .043 × 15,044) versus the reported €8,515. Consequently, the company's Non-Current Tangible Assets would have increased by €3,346 (8,515 − 5,169).

2. Calculate the offsetting increase in equity (retained earnings) and in the deferred tax liability. Given the 35 percent marginal tax rate, the adjustment to Non-Current

Tangible Assets would have required offsetting adjustments of €1,171 (.35 × 3,346) to the Deferred Tax Liability and €2,175 (.65 × 3,346) to Shareholders' Equity.

3. Reduce the depreciation expense (and increase the book value of the fleet) to reflect the lower depreciation for the current year. Assuming that €306 million net new aircraft purchased in 2004 were acquired throughout the year, and therefore require only half a year of depreciation, the depreciation expense for 2004 (included in Cost of Sales) would have been €653 million {.043 × [15,044 + (306/2)]} versus the €1,076 {(.85/12) × [15,044 + (306/2)]} million reported by the company. Thus Cost of Sales would decline by €423 million.

4. Increase the tax expense, net profit, and the balance sheet values of equity and the deferred tax liability. Given the 35 percent tax rate for 2004, the Tax Expense for the year would increase by €148 million. On the balance sheet, these changes would increase Non-Current Tangible Assets by €423 million, increase Deferred Tax Liability by €148 million, and increase Shareholders' Equity by €275 million.

Note that these changes are designed to show Lufthansa's results as if it had always used the same depreciation assumptions as BA rather than to reflect a change in the assumptions for the current year going forward. This enables the analyst to be able to compare ratios that use assets (e.g., return on assets) for the two companies. By making the adjustments, the analyst substantially improves the comparability of Lufthansa's and BA's financial statements.

In summary, if Lufthansa were using the same depreciation method as BA, its financial statements for the years ended December 31, 2003 and 2004 would have to be modified as follows (references to the above described steps are reported in brackets):

€ (millions)	Adjustments December 31, 2003		Adjustments December 31, 2004	
	Assets	Liabilities	Assets	Liabilities
Balance sheet				
Non-Current Tangible Assets	+3,346 (1)		+3,346 (1) +423 (3)	
Deferred Tax Liability		+1,171 (2)		+1,171 (2) +148 (4)
Shareholders' Equity		+2,175 (2)		+2,175 (2) +275 (4)
Income statement				
Cost of Sales				−423 (3)
Tax Expense				+148 (4)
Net Profit				+275 (4)

Impairment of non-current assets

Deteriorating industry or firm economic conditions can affect the value of non-current assets as well as current assets. When the fair value of an asset falls below its book value, the asset is "impaired." Firms are required to recognize impairments in the values of non-current assets when they arise. However, since second-hand markets for non-current assets are typically illiquid and incomplete, estimates of asset valuations and impairment are inherently subjective. This is particularly true for intangible assets such as goodwill, which is the amount by which the cost of business acquisitions exceeds the fair value of the acquired assets. As a result, managers can use their reporting judgment to delay write-downs on the balance sheet and avoid showing impairment charges in the income statement.[2] This issue is likely to be particularly critical for heavily asset-intensive firms in volatile markets (e.g., airlines) or for firms that follow a strategy of aggressive growth through acquisitions and report substantial amounts of goodwill.[3] Warning signs of impairments in non-current assets include declining non-current asset turnover, declines in return on assets to levels lower than the weighted average cost of capital, write-downs by other firms in the same industry that have also suffered deteriorating asset use, and overpayment for or unsuccessful integration of key acquisitions. Managers may sometimes also have incentives to overstate asset impairment. Overly pessimistic management estimates of non-current asset impairments reduce current period earnings and boost earnings in future periods.

Consider the acquisitions by Germany-based media company EM.TV & Merchandising AG of the Jim Henson Company, creator of The Muppet Show, and Speed Investments Ltd., co-owner of the commercial rights to Formula One motor racing. At the end of the 1990s, EM.TV pursued a strategy of aggressive growth through the acquisitions of TV and marketing rights for well-known cartoon characters, such as the Flintstones, and popular sporting events. After its initial public offering on the Neuer Markt segment of the German Stock Exchange in October 1997, EM.TV's share price soared from €0.35 (split-adjusted) to a high of just above €120 in February 2000. Its high share price helped EM.TV to finance several acquisitions through a secondary stock offering and the issuance of convertible debt. In March and May 2000, respectively, the company made its two largest acquisitions with the intention of expanding its international reputation. The company acquired the Jim Henson Company for €699 million and Speed Investment for €1.55 billion. At the time of the acquisition, Speed Investment's book value of equity was negative and the amount of goodwill that EM.TV recognized on the investment was €2.07 billion. The rationale of capitalizing this amount of goodwill on EM.TV's balance sheet is that it could truly represent the future economic benefits that EM.TV expects to receive from its investment but that are not directly attributable to the investment's recorded assets and liabilities. However, the analyst should consider the possibility that EM.TV has overpaid for its new investments, especially in times where its managers are flush with free cash flow.

At the end of the fiscal year, when EM.TV's share price had already declined to €5.49, the company was forced to admit that it had overpaid for its latest acquisitions. Goodwill impairment charges for the year ending in December 2000 amounted to €340 million for the Jim Henson Company and €600 million for Speed Investment. In its annual report, EM.TV commented that "the salient factor for the write-offs was that, at the time of the acquisitions, the expert valuation was determined by the positive expectations of the capital markets. This was particularly expressed through the use of corresponding multiples." Despite the large write-offs, a considerable amount of goodwill, related to the acquisition of Speed Investment, remained part of EM.TV's assets. This amount of €1.41 billion was equal to 170 percent of EM.TV's book value of equity.

Given the questionable financial health of Speed Investment, did the initial €2.07 billion of goodwill ever represent a true economic asset? Was it reasonable to expect to receive €2.07 billion in future economic benefits from a firm that had not been able to earn profits in the past? If not, was the €600 million write-down adequate? If an analyst decided to record an additional write-down of €1.41 billion in the December 2000 financials, it would be necessary to make the following balance sheet adjustments:

1. Reduce Non-Current Intangible Assets by €1.41 billion.
2. Reduce the Deferred Tax Liability and the Tax Expense for the tax effect of the write-down. Assuming a 50 percent tax rate, this amounts to €705 million.

3. Reduce Shareholders' Equity and Net Profit for the after-tax effect of the write-down (€705 million).

(€ millions)	Adjustment	
	Assets	**Liabilities and Equity**
Balance sheet		
Non-Current Intangible Assets	−1.410 (1)	
Deferred Tax Liability		−0.705 (2)
Shareholders' Equity		−0.705
Income statement		
Other Expenses		+1.410 (3)
Tax Expense		−0.705 (2)
Net Profit		−0.705 (3)

Note that the write-down of depreciable assets at the beginning of the year will require the analyst to also estimate the write-down's impact on depreciation and amortization expense for the year. For EM.TV, since the asset is goodwill, which is not amortized, no such expense adjustment is required.[4]

Leased assets

One of the objectives of the balance sheet is to report the assets for which a firm receives the rewards and bears the risks. These can also be assets the firm does not legally own but leases from another firm. There are two ways in which a firm can record its leased assets. Under the operating method, the firm recognizes the lease payment as an expense in the period in which it occurs, keeping the leased asset off its balance sheet. In contrast, under the finance method, the firm records the asset and an offsetting lease liability on its balance sheet. During the lease period, the firm then recognizes depreciation on the asset as well as interest on the lease liability.

Assessing whether a lease arrangement should be considered a rental contract (and hence recorded using the operating method) or equivalent to a purchase (and hence shown as a finance lease) is subjective. It depends on whether the lessee has effectively accepted most of the risks of ownership, such as obsolescence and physical deterioration. To guide the reporting of lease transactions, the international accounting rules include criteria for distinguishing between the two types. IAS 17 explains that a firm would normally consider a lease transaction equivalent to an asset purchase if any of the following conditions hold: (1) ownership of the asset is transferred to the lessee at the end of the lease term, (2) the lessee has the option to purchase the asset for a bargain price at the end of the lease term, (3) the lease term is for the major part of the asset's expected useful life, (4) the present value of the lease payments is equal to substantially all of the fair value of the asset, and (5) the asset cannot be used by other than the lessee without major modifications. However, because the criteria for reporting leases are broadly defined and inconclusive, they create opportunities for management to circumvent the spirit of the distinction between capital and operating leases, potentially leading to the understatement of lease assets. This is likely to be an important issue for the analysis of heavy asset industries where there are options for leasing (e.g., airlines).[5] Debt rating analysts tend to consider the distinction between operating leases and finance leases as artificial and capitalize the present value of future operating lease payments before analyzing a firm's financial position. An example of how to capitalize operating lease commitments follows.[6]

Finnair, the Finnish airline company, accounts for part of its rented flight equipment using the operating method. These rented resources are therefore excluded from Finnair's balance sheet, making it difficult for an analyst to compare Finnair's financial performance with other airlines that have a different mixture of finance and operating leases. To correct this accounting, the analyst can use the information on noncancelable lease commitments presented in Finnair's lease note to estimate the value of the assets and liabilities that are omitted from the balance sheet. The leased equipment is then depreciated over the life of the lease, and the lease payments are treated as interest and debt repayment.

On December 31, 2004 and 2005, Finnair reports the following minimum future rental payments:

(€ millions)	December 31, 2005	December 31, 2004
Less than 1 year	95.8	80.9
1–2 years	80.5	66.3
2–3 years	78.0	52.6
3–4 years	66.8	50.0
4–5 years	52.9	38.5
More than 5 years	116.9	101.6
Total	490.9	389.9

Because Finnair does not show the present value of its operating lease commitments, the analyst must decide how to allocate the lump sum values of €116.9 and €101.6 over year six and beyond, and estimate a suitable interest rate on the lease debt. It is then possible to compute the present value of the lease payments.

Finnair indicates that its annual interest rate on outstanding interest-bearing debt is 3.6 percent and the lease expense reported in 2005 is €88.5 million. Assume that the annual rental payments in the sixth and seventh years are equal to the rental payment in the fifth year (€38.5 and €52.9) and the remainder of the lump sum values (€24.6 and €11.1) is due in the eighth year. With a discount rate of 3.6 percent, the present values of the minimum rental payments for the years ended December 31, 2004 and 2005 are as follows:

(€ millions)	December 31, 2005	December 31, 2004
Within one year	92.5	78.1
Over one year	339.9	264.5
Total	432.4	342.6

Given this information, the analyst can make the following adjustments to Finnair's beginning and ending balance sheets, and to its income statement for the year ended December 31, 2005:

1. Capitalize the present value of the lease commitments for December 31, 2004, increasing Non-Current Tangible Assets and Non-Current Debt by €342.6.

2. Calculate the value of any change in lease assets and lease liabilities during the year from new lease transactions. On December 31, 2004, Finnair's liability for lease commitments in 2006 and beyond was €264.5. If there had been no changes in these commitments, one year later (on December 31, 2005), they would have been valued at €274.0 (264.5 × 1.036). Yet Finnair's actual lease commitment on December 31, 2005 was €432.4. Further, Finnair's actual lease expense in 2005 was €88.5, instead of the "anticipated" amount of €80.9 (see the table above showing the minimum future rental payments, third column). The unanticipated lease expense reflects an increase

in Finnair's lease commitments of €7.6 ([88.5 − 80.9]) which is paid in the same year as it occurs. In total, these differences indicate that the company increased its leased aircraft capacity by €166.0 ([432.4 − 274.0] + [88.5 − 80.9]). Finnair's Non-Current Tangible Assets and Non-Current Debt therefore increased by €166.0 during 2005.

3. Reflect the change in lease asset value and expense from the depreciation during the year. The depreciation expense for 2005 (included in Cost of Sales) is the depreciation rate (1/8) multiplied by the beginning cost of leased equipment (€342.6) plus depreciation on the increase in leased equipment for 2005 (€166.0), prorated throughout the year. The depreciation expense for 2005 is therefore €53.2 (342.6/8 + .5 × [166.0/8]).

4. Add back the operating lease expense in the income statement, included in Cost of Sales. As previously mentioned, the operating lease expense, which is equal to the lease payment that Finnair made to its lessors, is €88.5. When lease liabilities are recorded on the balance sheet, as under the finance method, the lease payment must be treated as the sum of interest and debt repayment (see next item), instead of being recorded as an expense.

5. Apportion the lease payment between Interest Expense and repayment of Non-Current Debt. The portion of this that is shown as Interest Expense is the interest rate (3.6 percent) multiplied by the beginning lease liability (€342.6) plus interest on the increase in the leased liability for 2005 (€166.0), prorated throughout the year. The interest expense for 2002 is therefore €15.3 (.036 × 342.6 + .5 × .036 × 166.0). The Non-Current Debt repayment portion is then the remainder of the total lease payment, €73.2.

6. Make any needed changes to the Deferred Tax Liability to reflect differences in earnings under the finance and operating lease methods. Finnair's expenses under the finance lease method are €68.5 (€53.2 depreciation expense plus €15.3 interest expense) versus €88.5 under the operating lease method. Finnair will not change its tax books, but for financial reporting purposes it will show higher earnings before tax and thus a higher Tax Expense through deferred taxes. Given its 26 percent tax rate, the Tax Expense will increase by €5.2 (.26 × [88.5 − 68.5]) and the Deferred Tax Liability will increase by the same amount.

In summary, the adjustments to Finnair's financial statements on December 31, 2004 and 2005, are as follows:

€ (millions)	Adjustments December 31, 2004 Assets	Liabilities	Adjustments December 31, 2005 Assets	Liabilities
Balance sheet				
Non-Current Tangible Assets:				
Beginning capitalization	+342.6 (1)		+342.6 (1)	
New leases			+166.0 (2)	
Annual depreciation			−53.2 (3)	
Non-Current Debt:				
Beginning debt		+342.6 (1)		+342.6 (1)
New leases				+166.0 (2)
Debt repayment				−73.2 (5)
Deferred Tax Liability				+5.2 (6)
Shareholders' Equity				+14.8 (6)

(continued)

€ (millions)	Adjustments December 31, 2004		Adjustments December 31, 2005	
	Assets	**Liabilities**	**Assets**	**Liabilities**
Income statement (continued)				
Cost of Sales:				
Lease expense				−88.5 (4)
Depreciation expense				+53.2 (3)
Interest Expense				+15.3 (5)
Tax Expense				+5.2 (6)
Net Profit				+14.8 (6)

These adjustments increase Finnair's fixed assets by 39 percent in 2004 and 54 percent in 2005, reducing the company's asset turnover (sales/assets) from the reported value of 112 percent to 91 percent in 2004, and from 114 percent to 89 percent in 2005. There is also a difference in earnings, since the lease expense is replaced with the depreciation and interest expenses. This leads to an increase in operating earnings (before interest). As a result, the company's return on operating assets for 2005 actually increases from the reported value of 3.4 percent to 5.3 percent.

Intangible assets

Some firms' most important assets are excluded from the balance sheet. Examples include investments in R&D, software development outlays, and brands and membership bases that are created through advertising and promotions. Accounting rules in most countries specifically prohibit the capitalization of research outlays, primarily because it is believed that the benefits associated with such outlays are too uncertain. New products or software may never reach the market due to technological infeasibility or to the introduction of superior products by competitors. Expensing the cost of intangibles has two implications for analysts. First, the omission of intangible assets from the balance sheet inflates measured rates of return on capital (either return on assets or return on equity).[7] For firms with key omitted intangible assets, this has important implications for forecasting long-term performance; unlike firms with no intangibles, competitive forces will not cause their rates of return to fully revert to the cost of capital over time. For example, pharmaceutical firms have shown very high rates of return over many decades, in part because of the impact of R&D accounting. A second effect of expensing outlays for intangibles is that it makes it more difficult for the analyst to assess whether the firm's business model works. Under the matching concept, operating profit is a meaningful indicator of the success of a firm's business model since it compares revenues and the expenses required to generate them. Immediately expensing outlays for intangible assets runs counter to matching and, therefore, makes it more difficult to judge a firm's operating performance. Consistent with this, research shows that investors view R&D and advertising outlays as assets rather than expenses.[8] Understated intangible assets are likely to be important for firms in pharmaceutical, software, branded consumer products, and subscription businesses.

How should the analyst approach the omission of intangibles? One way is to leave the accounting as is, but to recognize that forecasts of long-term rates of return will have to reflect the inherent biases that arise from this accounting method. A second approach is to capitalize intangibles and amortize them over their expected lives.

For example, consider the case of AstraZeneca, one of the largest pharmaceutical companies in the world. AstraZeneca does not capitalize most of its R&D costs because regulatory uncertainties surrounding the development and marketing of new products mean that the recognition criteria for research expenditures are rarely met. What adjustment would be required if the analyst decided to capitalize all of AstraZeneca's R&D and to amortize the intangible asset using the straight-line method over the expected life of R&D investments? Assume for simplicity that R&D spending occurs evenly throughout the year, that only half a year's amortization is taken on the latest year's spending, and that the average expected life of R&D investments is approximately five years. Given R&D outlays for the years 2000 to 2004, the R&D asset at the end of 2004 is $7.9 billion, calculated as follows:

Year	R&D outlay	Proportion capitalized 12/31/04	Asset 12/31/04	Proportion capitalized 12/31/05	Asset 12/31/05
2005	$3.4b			(1 – .2/2)	$3.1b
2004	3.5	(1 – .2/2)	$3.2b	(1 – .2/2 – .2)	2.5
2003	3.0	(1 – .2/2 – .2)	2.1	(1 – .2/2 – .4)	1.5
2002	3.1	(1 – .2/2 – .4)	1.6	(1 – .2/2 – .6)	0.9
2001	2.8	(1 – .2/2 – .6)	0.8	(1 – .2/2 – .8)	0.3
2000	2.9	(1 – .2/2 – .8)	0.3		
Total			$7.9		$8.2

The R&D amortization expense (included in Other Operating Expenses) for 2004 and 2005 are $3.0 billion and $3.1 billion, respectively, and are calculated as follows:

Year	R&D outlay	Proportion amortized 12/31/04	Expense 12/31/04	Proportion amortized 12/31/05	Expense 12/31/05
2005	$3.4b			.2/2	$0.3b
2004	3.5	.2/2	$0.4b	.2	0.7
2003	3.0	.2	0.6	.2	0.6
2002	3.1	.2	0.6	.2	0.6
2001	2.8	.2	0.6	.2	0.6
2000	2.9	.2	0.6	.2/2	0.3
1999	2.5	.2/2	0.3		
Total			$3.0		$3.1

Since AstraZeneca will continue to expense software R&D immediately for tax purposes, the change in reporting method will give rise to a Deferred Tax Liability. Given a marginal tax rate of 30 percent, this liability will equal 30 percent of the value of the Intangible Asset reported, with the balance increasing Shareholders' Equity.

In summary, the adjustments required to capitalize software R&D for AstraZeneca for the years 2004 and 2005 are as follows:

($ billions)	Adjustments Dec. 31, 2004		Adjustments Dec. 31, 2005	
	Assets	**Liabilities**	**Assets**	**Liabilities**
Balance sheet				
Non-Current Intangible Assets	+7.9		+8.2	
Deferred Tax Liability		+2.4		+2.5
Shareholders' Equity		+5.5		+5.7
Income statement				
Other Operating		−3.5		−3.5
Expenses		+3.0		+3.1
Tax Expense		+0.2		+0.1
Net Profit		+0.3		+0.3

Merger accounting

Recent changes in international rules for merger accounting (IFRS 3) require that firms report mergers using the purchase method. Under this method the cost of the merger for the acquirer is the actual value of the consideration paid for the target firm's shares. The identifiable assets and liabilities of the target are then recorded on the acquirer's books at their fair values. If the value of the consideration paid for the target exceeds the fair value of its identifiable assets and liabilities, the excess is reported as goodwill on the acquirer's balance sheet. For example, when company A acquires company B for an amount of €1 billion (paid out in shares) and company B's net assets have a book value of €0.5 billion and a fair value of €0.7 billion, company A would record company B's net assets on its balance sheet for an amount of €0.7 billion and recognize €0.3 billion (1.0 − 0.7) of goodwill. The new rules require goodwill assets to be written off only if they become impaired in the future. However, as recently as 2003 some large acquisitions were reported using the pooling method. Under pooling accounting, the purchase of a target firm's shares is recorded at their historical book value rather than at their market value, so that no goodwill is recorded. Consequently, pooling does not reflect the true economic cost of the acquisition on the acquirer's books, making it more difficult for shareholders to understand the economic performance of the new firm after the merger.[9] For example, in the above example, company A would record company B's net assets on its balance sheet for an amount of €0.5 billion, ignoring the net assets' fair value and the amount of goodwill on the acquisition. This is likely to be a consideration for the analyst in evaluating the performance of serial share-for-share acquirers.[10]

In December 2000 the pharmaceutical companies SmithKline Beecham and Glaxo Wellcome merged their activities to form U.K.-based GlaxoSmithKline. GlaxoSmithKline reported under U.K. Generally Accepted Accounting Principles (U.K. GAAP) and recorded the merger transaction using the pooling method. After the merger, the former shareholders of Glaxo Wellcome held close to 59 percent of GlaxoSmithKline's ordinary shares. Because GlaxoSmithKline's shares were listed on the New York Stock Exchange, the company also had to prepare a reconciliation of its U.K. GAAP statements with U.S. GAAP. The U.S. accounting rules did not, however, consider the transaction a merger of equals but an acquisition of SmithKline Beecham by Glaxo Wellcome. These rules did not permit, therefore, the use of the pooling method to record the transaction.

The additional disclosures that GlaxoSmithKline made as part of its reconciliation to U.S. GAAP provide the analyst with much of the information that is needed to adjust for the distortion from using pooling accounting. Under the terms of the deal, the acquisition price of SmithKline Beecham was £43.9 billion. At the time of the acquisition, the book value of SmithKline Beecham's net assets was £2.7 billion and the fair value adjustments to SmithKline Beecham's net assets amounted up to £25.0 billion. The amount of goodwill thus equaled £16.2 billion (43.9 – 2.7 – 25.0). At the end of the fiscal year 2005, GlaxoSmithKline reported in its first IFRS-based financial statements that its goodwill on the acquisition of SmithKline Beecham had a remaining value of £15.9 billion, while fair value adjustments for acquired product rights were valued at £12.1 billion.

To adjust for the distortion from using pooling accounting, the analyst can restate the acquirer's based financial statements as follows:

1. Revalue the target's assets (and potentially its liabilities) to their fair values.
2. Recognize any goodwill from the transaction, computed as the difference between the purchase price and the fair value of the identifiable net assets of the target.
3. Record the consideration paid by the acquirer – usually acquirer shares – at its fair value.

For Glaxo Wellcome's acquisition of SmithKline Beecham, under pooling accounting, the cost of acquiring SmithKline Beecham is shown at its book value of £2.7 billion, far below the actual purchase price of £43.9 billion. To record the acquisition under the purchase method, the analyst requires information on the fair value of SmithKline Beecham's identifiable assets such as the acquired product rights. If this information were not available, the (second best) solution would be to assign the full £41.2 billion asset adjustment (£43.9 billion less £2.7 billion) to goodwill. This would implicitly assume that the book and fair values of SmithKline Beecham's assets are roughly similar. However, the price paid by Glaxo Wellcome includes a premium for acquired product rights precisely because Glaxo Wellcome expects that some of these products will generate future benefits for shareholders. The U.S. GAAP information helps to assess the fair value of these acquired product rights. The adjustment to the financial statements of the combined firm on December 31, 2005 would therefore be as follows:

	Adjustment	
(£ millions)	Assets	Liabilities and Equity
Balance Sheet		
Non-Current Intangible Assets	+28.0	
Deferred Tax Liability		+3.6
Shareholders' Equity		+24.4

Note that both goodwill (£15.9 billion) and acquired product rights (£12.1 billion) have been classified as Non-Current Intangible Assets. The distinction between goodwill and acquired product rights does, however, affect the adjustment made to the Deferred Tax Liability. Because the international accounting rules for income taxes (IAS 12) prohibit the recognition of deferred taxes on nondeductible goodwill, the Deferred Tax Liability adjustment relates only to the fair value adjustments for acquired product rights (£12.1 billion × 30 percent marginal tax rate).

First-time adoption: Business combinations

The international rules on the first-time application of IFRS require the retrospective application of current IFRSs. Then why didn't GlaxoSmithKline change its way of recording the merger transaction from using the pooling method to using the purchase method? The reason for not doing so is that the international rules on the first-time application of IFRS allow first-time adopters not to restate the accounting for business combinations (mergers and acquisitions) that took place prior to the start of the previous year. Because restating the accounting for previous business combinations can be a complex task that may require previously uncollected information, most first-time adopters have chosen to apply this exemption. Pooling accounting therefore remains to affect several IFRS-based financial statements.

Timing of revenue recognition

Managers typically have the best information on the uncertainties governing revenue recognition – whether a product or service has been provided to customers and whether cash collection is reasonably likely. However, managers may also have incentives to accelerate the recognition of revenues, boosting reported earnings for the period. Trade receivables and earnings will then be overstated. During the 1990s and the early 2000s, aggressive revenue recognition is one of the most popular forms of earnings management cited by the U.S. public enforcer, the SEC.

In November 1999 and January 2000, analysts at the Center for Financial Research and Analysis (CFRA) raised questions about the propriety of revenue recognition for MicroStrategy, a U.S.-based software company. MicroStrategy recognized revenues from the sale of licenses "after execution of a licensing agreement and shipment of the product, provided that no significant Company obligations remain and the resulting receivable is deemed collectible by management."[11] While MicroStrategy prepared its financial statements in accordance with U.S. GAAP, its accounting principle for the recognition of license revenues was also in accordance with the international standard on revenue recognition (IAS 18). CFRA analysts were concerned about MicroStrategy's booking two contracts worth $27 million as quarterly revenues when the contracts were not announced until several days after the quarter's end. If the analysts decided to adjust for these distortions, the following changes would have to be made to MicroStrategy's financial reports:

1. In the quarter that the contracts were booked, Sales and Trade Receivables would both decline by $27 million.

2. Cost of Sales would decline and Inventory would increase to reflect the reduction in sales. The value of the Cost of Sales/Inventory adjustment can be estimated by multiplying the sales adjustment by the ratio of cost of sales to sales. For MicroStrategy, cost of license revenues is only 3 percent of license revenues, indicating that the adjustment would be modest ($0.8m). Also, since MicroStrategy does not have any inventory, the balance sheet adjustment would be to prepaid expenses, which are included in Other Current Assets on the standardized balance sheet.

3. The decline in pretax profit would result in a lower Tax Expense in the company's financial reporting books (but presumably not in its tax books). Consequently, the

Deferred Tax Liability would have to be reduced. MicroStrategy's marginal tax rate was 35 percent, implying that the decline in the Tax Expense and Deferred Tax Liability was $9.2 million [($27 – 0.8) × .35].

The full effect of the adjustment on the quarterly financial statements would therefore be as follows:

($ millions)	Adjustments	
	Assets	**Liabilities and Equity**
Balance sheet		
Trade Receivables	–27.0 (1)	
Other Current Assets	+0.8 (2)	
Deferred Tax Liability		–9.2 (3)
Shareholders' Equity		–17.0 (3)
Income statement		
Sales		–27.0 (1)
Cost of Sales		–0.8 (2)
Tax Expense		–9.2 (3)
Net Profit		–17.0 (3)

Of course, provided the contracts were legitimate transactions, the above adjustments imply that forecasts of the next quarter's revenues should include the $27 million worth of contracts.

In March 2000 MicroStrategy confirmed that the CFRA analysts' suspicions about aggressive revenue recognition were founded. The company announced that it had "recorded revenue on certain contracts in one reporting period where customer signature and delivery had been completed, but where the contract may not have been fully executed by the Company in that reporting period."[12] After reviewing all licensing contracts near the end of the prior three years, MicroStrategy was forced to restate its financial statements to correct for the improprieties. The outcome was that trade receivables for 1999 were reduced from $61.1 million to $37.6 million, leading to a dramatic drop in the company's stock price.

Allowances

Managers make estimates of expected customer defaults on trade receivables and loans. If managers underestimate the value of these allowances, assets and earnings will be overstated. Warning signs of inadequate allowances include growing days receivable, business downturns for a firm's major clients, and growing loan delinquencies. If managers overestimate allowances for doubtful accounts or loan losses, trade receivables and loans will be understated.

Consider the allowances for doubtful accounts reported by Luxemburg-based Metro International S.A. in the years 2002, 2003, and 2004. In these years, Metro International derived most of its revenues from selling advertisements in its international newspaper Metro, which it distributed free in 21 countries. To illustrate the low collection risk on its trade receivables, Metro reported in the notes to its financial statements that its receivables came "from a large number of customers, in different industries and geographical areas, none of which in itself is material in size." On December 31, 2004, Metro reported the following values for its receivables, allowances and write-offs:

($ thousands)	December 31, 2004	December 31, 2003	December 31, 2002
Trade receivables			
Gross accounts receivable	70,817	54,025	39,093
Less allowances for doubtful accounts	−7,073	−5,447	−3,129
Balance at end of year	63,744	48,578	35,964
Allowance for doubtful accounts			
Balance at beginning of year	5,447	3,129	1,882
Provision for bad debts	3,017	3,479	2,267
Write-offs	−1,391	−1,161	−1,020
Balance at end of year	7,073	5,447	3,129

The allowances for doubtful accounts were 10, 10 and 8 percent in 2004, 2003, and 2002, respectively. Metro increased its allowance by 2 percent in 2003, even though the actual amount written off as a percentage of the beginning balance of the allowance decreased from 54 percent to 37 percent. The write-offs in 2004 and 2003 equaled 3 percent of the beginning balances of trade receivables (in both years), which was much less than the 10 percent that Metro added to its allowance. Given the low collection risk on Metro's receivables, Metro could be overstating its allowances. If the analyst decided that allowances were overstated, adjustments would have to be made to Trade Receivables and to Equity for the after-tax cost of the overstated provision for doubtful accounts. For example, if the analyst decided that receivable allowances for Metro in 2004 should be 5 percent rather than 10 percent, the following adjustments would have to be made:

1. Trade Receivables would have to be increased by $3,541 thousand ([.10 − .05] × 70,817).

2. Given the company's marginal tax rate of 28 percent, this would increase Net Profit and Shareholders' Equity by $2,550 thousand ([1 − .28] × 3,541), and increase the Deferred Tax Liability and the Tax Expense by $991 thousand (.28 × 3,541).

The adjustment to the December 31, 2004, financial statements would, therefore, be as follows:

($ thousands)	Adjustments	
	Assets	Liabilities and Equity
Balance sheet		
Trade Receivables	+3,541 (1)	
Deferred Tax Liability		+991 (2)
Shareholders' Equity		+2,550 (2)
Income statement		
Cost of Sales		−3,541 (1)
Tax Expense		+991 (2)
Net Profit		+2,550 (2)

Unfortunately, not all firms that report under IFRS separately disclose the allowances for doubtful accounts (or inventory obsolescence). This makes it sometimes difficult for the analyst to identify the overstatement or understatement of allowances.

Understated allowances are also a point of attention when analyzing the financial statements of loss-making firms. When a firm reports a loss in its tax statements, it does not receive an immediate tax refund but becomes the holder of a claim against the tax authorities, called a tax loss carryforward, which can be offset against future taxable profits. The period over which the firm can exercise this claim differs across tax jurisdictions. The international accounting standard for income taxes (IAS 12) requires that firms record a deferred tax asset for a tax loss carryforward that is probable of being realized. Because changes in this deferred tax asset affect earnings through the tax expense, managers can manage earnings upwards by overstating the probability of realization.

During its first five years of operations, from 2001 to 2005, the Dutch manufacturer of exclusive cars Spyker Cars N.V. had been loss making. In December 2005 and December 2004, when Spyker reported net losses of €1.9 million and €5.0 million, respectively, the company reported the following losses carried forward and deferred tax assets:

(€ millions)	December 31, 2005	December 31,2004
Total loss carried forward	19.822	15.687
× Tax rate	29.6%	34.5%
Calculated deferred tax	5.867	5.412
Allowance	−1.467	−3.058
Recognized deferred tax asset	4.400	2.354

Spyker deducted an allowance from its calculated deferred tax assets because management deemed it not probable that the tax loss carryforwards could be fully realized in future years. The allowance, however, was substantially lower in 2005 than in 2004 because management expected an increase in Spyker's future profitability, justifying a decrease in the allowance from 56.5 percent of the deferred tax asset to 25 percent.

Any increase (decrease) in the deferred tax asset is offset by a decrease (increase) in the tax expense. If the analyst believed that management's optimism in 2005 was unwarranted and decided to increase the allowance to 56.5 percent, it would be necessary to reduce the Deferred Tax Asset, Shareholders' Equity, and Net Profit by €1.848 million ([.565 − .250] × 5.867) and increase the Tax Expense by the same amount.

	Adjustments	
(€ millions)	Assets	Liabilities and Equity
Balance sheet		
Deferred Tax Asset	−1.848	
Shareholders' Equity		−1.848
Income statement		
Tax Expense		+1.848
Net Profit		−1.848

Write-downs of current assets

If current assets become impaired – that is, their book values fall below their realizable values – accounting rules generally require that they be written down to their fair values. Current asset impairments also affect earnings since write-offs are charged directly to earnings. Deferring current asset write-downs is, therefore, one way for managers to boost reported profits.[13] Analysts that cover firms where management of inventories and receivables is a key success factor (e.g., the retail and manufacturing industries) need to be particularly cognizant of this form of earnings management. If managers over-buy or over-produce in the current period, they are likely to have to offer customers discounts to get rid of surplus inventories. In addition, providing customers with credit carries risks of default. Warning signs for delays in current asset write-downs include growing days' inventory and days' receivable, write-downs by competitors, and business downturns for a firm's major customers.

Managers potentially have an incentive to overstate current asset write-downs during years of exceptionally strong performance, or when the firm is financially distressed. By overstating current asset impairments and overstating expenses in the current period, managers can show lower future expenses, boosting earnings in years of sub-par performance or when a turnaround is needed. Overstated current asset write-downs can also arise when managers are less optimistic about the firm's future prospects than the analyst.

Discounted receivables

To improve liquidity a firm may sometimes decide to sell part of its receivables to a financial institution, after which the financial institution services the collection of the receivables. Once the receivables have been sold, the seller must decide whether it accounts for the transaction as a sale or as a received loan collateralized by receivables. Under current international accounting rules (IAS 39 and its implementation guidance), receivables that are discounted with a financial institution are considered "sold" if the "seller" cedes control over the receivables to the financier. Control is surrendered if the receivables are beyond the reach of the seller's creditors should the seller file for bankruptcy, if the financier (and not the seller) has the right to pledge or sell its interest in the receivables, and if the seller has no legal right or commitment to repurchase the receivables. Also, when the seller continues to service the receivables, control is surrendered if the seller has the contractual obligation to transfer any collections to the financier without material delay. The seller can then record the discount transaction as an asset sale. Otherwise it is viewed as a financing transaction that generates a liability for the "seller."

Just because a firm has "sold" receivables for financial reporting purposes does not necessarily mean that it is off the hook for credit risks. Financial institutions that discount receivables often have recourse against the "seller," requiring the seller to continue to estimate bad debt losses and record a recourse liability for the amount of losses that it guarantees. In this event, international accounting rules permit the transaction to be reported as an asset sale only when the seller satisfies the above conditions for surrendering control of the receivables and the financier assumes all risks other than the credit risk. In extreme cases, where there is significant uncertainty about the value of the recourse liability, the analyst has to decide whether to restate the firm's financial statements by returning the "sold" receivables to the balance sheet. This will also increase the firm's liabilities, and it will affect its income statement since any gains and losses on the sale need to be excluded, and interest income on the notes receivables and interest expense on the loan need to be recorded each year.

Sweden-based car manufacturer Volvo regularly discounts a proportion of its customer finance receivables. In 2005 Volvo reported in the notes to its first IFRS-based financial statements that its discounted receivables did not meet the IAS 39 requirements for asset derecognition. In contrast, in Volvo's prior period financial statements, which were prepared in accordance with Swedish GAAP, discounted receivables with similar characteristics were considered "sold" and derecognized from the balance sheet. Because Volvo chose to apply IAS 39 only to the fiscal years starting after January 1, 2005, the receivables that were discounted during 2004 remained off the 2004 balance sheet that Volvo reported in its 2005 financial statements (for comparative purposes), rendering the assets and liabilities for the years 2004 and 2005 not comparable.

In 2004 Volvo reported a contingent liability (off balance) of SEK2,471 million for receivables that had been discounted with recourse. One way for the analyst to make the 2004 balance sheet comparable to the 2005 balance sheet is to reverse the sale and include a liability for the full SEK2,471 million on Volvo's balance sheet. This would require the following adjustments:

1. Volvo's Other Long-Term Assets would be increased by the receivable commitment (SEK2,471 million). In turn, Long-Term Debt would be recorded to reflect the value of the cash advanced to Volvo under the discount transaction. Assuming that Volvo charges its customers an annual interest rate of roughly 9 percent, customers repay the receivables in equal monthly installments over the next four years, and the bank charges a 10 percent interest rate, the receivable loan would be valued at SEK2,428 million. The value of the loan can be calculated as follows. The annual interest rates of 9 and 10 percent correspond with monthly interest rates of 0.721 and 0.797 percent ($1.09^{1/12} - 1$ and $1.1^{1/12} - 1$). The present value of an annuity of SEK1 per month for 48 months is SEK40.45 (SEK39.76) for a monthly interest rate of 0.721 (0.797) percent. Hence, the receivable of SEK2,471 million corresponds with monthly installments of SEK61.09 million (2,471/40.45). Given an annual interest rate of 10 percent and a monthly interest rate of 0.797 percent, these installments have a present value of SEK2,428 million (61.09 × 39.76).

2. The after-tax difference between the face value of the receivables and the loan, which would have been shown as a loss on sale under the reported accounting, needs to be reversed, increasing equity. Given the above assumptions and Volvo's 28 percent marginal tax rate, the adjustment would increase Shareholders' Equity by SEK31 million [43 × (1 – .28)].

3. The impact of the tax deduction from reporting a loss on sale, which would have reduced the Deferred Tax Liability, needs to be reversed. For Volvo, this amount would have resulted in a roughly SEK12 million (43 × .28) increase in the Deferred Tax Liability.

4. During the year ended December 31, 2005, customers are scheduled to make monthly payments on the discounted receivables, reducing the value of notes receivable under the adjusted accounting. For Volvo, these amounted to SEK617.8 million (SEK2,471 million × .25), given the four years duration of the receivables.

5. For 2005, Volvo's income statement would include Interest Income from customer finance receivables of SEK250.2 million {(2,471 × .09) – [(617.8 × .09) × .5]} and Interest Expense from the loan of roughly SEK278 million {(2,471 × .10) – [(617.8 × .10) × .5]} along with any tax effects.[14] The loan would decline by a smaller amount, since SEK27.8 million of the receivable repayments are allocated to covering the higher interest charged on the loan (exactly offsetting the wedge between the Interest Income and the Interest Expense for the year).

6. The value of the loan declines by the value of receivable repayments by customers (SEK617.8 million) net of the portion of the repayment that represents incremental interest charged by the bank relative to the rate Volvo charged its customers (SEK27.8 million, or SEK278 million – SEK250.2 million).

7. The net effect of the income statement adjustments on pretax profit is minus SEK27.8 million in 2005. The Tax Expense would therefore have to be decreased by SEK7.8 million (27.8 × .28) and Net Profit by SEK20.0 million (27.8 × [1 – .28]).

The overall effect of these adjustments on Volvo's financial statements would, therefore, be as follows:

SEK (millions)	Adjustments December 31, 2004		Adjustments December 31, 2005	
	Assets	Liabilities	Assets	Liabilities
Balance sheet				
Other Non-Current Assets	+2,471.0 (1)		+2,471.0 (1)	
			−617.8 (4)	
Non-Current Debt		+2,428.0 (1)		+2,428.0 (1)
				−617.8 (6)
				+27.8 (6)
Deferred Tax Liability		+12.0 (3)		+12.0 (3)
Shareholders' Equity		+31.0 (2)		+31.0 (2)
				−20.0 (7)
Income statement				
Other Operating Income				
Interest Income				+250.2 (5)
Interest Expense				+278.0 (5)
Tax Expense				−7.8 (7)
Net Profit				−20.0 (7)

First-time adoption: Applying the current version of IFRS

Because the IASB regularly revises its set of standards, the international rules on the first-time application of IFRS explicitly mention that a first-time IFRS adopter must apply the rules that are effective at the reporting date, being the fiscal year-end date of the current year. It is possible that a new or revised standard became effective during the year of first-time IFRS adoption. In this situation, a first-time adopter must also apply the new or revised standard to the prior year balance sheet and income statement that it reports for comparative purposes.

The above example provides an illustration of an exception to this general rule. Firms that adopt IFRS for the first time are not allowed to recognize previously derecognized assets in their comparative balance sheets if the assets have been derecognized prior to January 2004. Further, firms that adopted IFRS prior to January 2006, as most European first-time adopters did, were not required to comply with the international accounting rules for financial instruments (IAS 32 and 39), which include the asset derecognition rules, when preparing their first-time IFRS comparative balance sheet. Volvo therefore used different treatments for its discounted receivables in 2004 and 2005. Fortunately, pre-January 2006 adopters of IFRS must disclose the effects of IAS 32 and 39 adoptions on the opening balance sheet of the current year, which helps the analyst to make the necessary adjustments to the comparative statements.

KEY ANALYSIS QUESTIONS

The following are some of the questions an analyst can probe when analyzing whether a firm's assets exhibit distortions:

■ *Depreciation and amortization.* Are the firm's depreciation and amortization rates in line with industry practices? If not, is the firm aggressive or conservative in its estimates of the assets' useful lives? What does the deferred tax liability for depreciation and amortization suggest about the relationship between reported depreciation and tax depreciation?

■ *Asset impairment.* Have industry or firm economic conditions deteriorated such that non-current assets' fair values could have fallen below their book values? Have industry peers recently recognized asset impairments? Does the firm have a history of regular write-downs, suggesting a tendency to delay?

■ *Leased assets.* Does the firm have a material amount of off-balance sheet lease commitments? Is there a large variation in the proportion of operating leases to finance leases across industry peers?

■ *Intangible assets.* Does the firm make material investments in non-current intangible assets, such as research and development, that are omitted from the balance sheet? If so, are these investments likely to yield future economic benefits? Does the immediate expensing of these investments lead to artificially permanent abnormal earnings?

■ *Revenue recognition.* Are trade receivables abnormally high (relative to sales), suggesting aggressive revenue recognition?

■ *Allowances.* Did the firm make unexplained changes in its allowance for doubtful accounts (or loan losses)? Is the size of the allowance in line with industry practices? Did the characteristics of the firm's receivables (e.g., concentration of credit risk) change such that the firm should adjust its allowance? Are the allowances that the firm recognizes systematically smaller or greater than its write-offs? Is it likely that the firm's deferred tax assets for losses carried forward can be realized?

■ *Discounted receivables.* Is the recourse liability sufficiently large to cover the amount of collection losses that the firm guarantees? Is the value of the recourse liability so uncertain that it is better to return the discounted receivables to the balance sheet?

RECOGNITION OF LIABILITIES

Liabilities are defined as economic obligations arising from benefits received in the past, and for which the amount and timing is known with reasonable certainty. Liabilities include obligations to customers that have paid in advance for products or services; commitments to public and private providers of debt financing; obligations to federal and local governments for taxes; commitments to employees for unpaid wages and post-employment benefits; and obligations from court or government fines or environmental clean-up orders.

Distortions in liabilities generally arise because there is ambiguity about whether (1) an obligation has really been incurred and/or (2) the obligation can be measured.

Has an obligation been incurred?

For most liabilities there is little ambiguity about whether an obligation has been incurred. For example, when a firm buys supplies on credit, it has incurred an obligation to the supplier. However, for some transactions it is more difficult to decide whether there is any such obligation. For example, if a firm announces a plan to restructure its business by laying off employees, has it made a commitment that would justify recording a liability? Or, if a software firm receives cash from its customers for a five-year software license, should the firm report the full cash inflow as revenues, or should some of it represent the ongoing commitment to the customer for servicing and supporting the license agreement?

Can the obligation be measured?

Many liabilities specify the amount and timing of obligations precisely. For example, a 20-year €100 million bond issue with an 8 percent coupon payable semiannually specifies that the issuer will pay the holders €100 million in 20 years, and it will pay out interest of €4 million every six months for the duration of the loan. However, for some liabilities it is difficult to estimate the amount of the obligation. For example, a firm that is responsible for an environmental clean-up clearly has incurred an obligation, but the amount is highly uncertain.[15] Similarly, firms that provide post-employment benefits for employees have incurred commitments that depend on uncertain future events, such as employee mortality rates, and on future inflation rates, making valuation of the obligation subjective. Future warranty and insurance claim obligations fall into the same category – the commitment is clear but the amount depends on uncertain future events.

Accounting rules frequently specify when a commitment has been incurred and how to measure the amount of the commitment. However, as discussed earlier, accounting rules are imperfect – they cannot cover all contractual possibilities and reflect all of the complexities of a firm's business relationships. They also require managers to make subjective estimates of future events to value the firm's commitments. Thus the analyst may decide that some important obligations are omitted from the financial statements or, if included, are understated, either because of management bias or because there are legitimate differences in opinion between managers and analysts over future risks and commitments. As a result, analysis of liabilities is usually with an eye to assessing whether the firm's financial commitments and risks are understated and/or its earnings overstated.

LIABILITY DISTORTIONS

Liabilities are likely to be understated when the firm has key commitments that are difficult to value and therefore not considered liabilities for financial reporting purposes. Understatements are also likely to occur when managers have strong incentives to overstate the soundness of the firm's financial position, or to boost reported earnings. By understating leverage, managers present investors with a rosy picture of the firm's financial risks. Earnings management also understates liabilities (namely deferred or unearned revenues) when revenues are recognized upon receipt of cash, even though not all services have been provided.

Accounting analysis involves judging whether managers have understated liabilities and, if necessary, adjusting the balance sheet and income statement accordingly. The most common forms of liability understatement arise when the following conditions exist:

■ unearned revenues are understated through aggressive revenue recognition,

■ provisions are understated,

■ loans from discounted receivables are off-balance sheet,

■ non-current liabilities for leases are off-balance sheet, and/or

■ post-employment obligations, such as pension obligations, are not fully recorded.

Unearned revenues understated

If cash has already been received but the product or service has yet to be provided, a liability (called unearned or deferred revenues) is created. This liability reflects the company's commitment to provide the service or product to the customer and is extinguished once that is accomplished. Firms that recognize revenues prematurely, after the receipt of cash but prior to fulfilling their product or service commitments to customers, understate deferred revenue liabilities and overstate earnings. Firms that bundle service contracts with the sale of a product are particularly prone to deferred revenue liability understatement since separating the price of the product from the price of the service is subjective.

Consider the case of MicroStrategy, the software company discussed earlier, which bundles customer support and software updates with its initial licensing agreements. This raises questions about how much of the contract price should be allocated to the initial license versus the company's future commitments. In March 2000 MicroStrategy conceded that it had incorrectly overstated revenues on contracts that involved significant future customization and consulting by $54.5 million. As a result, it would have to restate its financial statements for 1999 as well as for several earlier years. To undo the distortion to 1999 financials, the following adjustments would have to be made:

1. In the quarter that the contracts were booked by the company, Sales would decline and unearned revenues (included in Other Current Liabilities) would increase by $54.5 million.

2. Cost of Sales would decline and prepaid expenses (inventory for product companies) would increase to reflect the lower sales. As noted earlier, MicroStrategy's cost of license revenues is only 3 percent of license revenues, implying that the adjustment to prepaid expenses (included in Other Current Assets) and Cost of Sales is modest ($1.6 million).

3. The decline in pretax profit would result in a lower Tax Expense in the company's financial reporting books (but presumably not in its tax books). Given MicroStrategy's marginal tax rate of 35 percent, the decline in the Tax Expense as well as in the Deferred Tax Liability is $18.5 million [($54.5 – 1.6) × .35].

The full effect of the adjustment on the quarterly financial statements would, therefore, be as follows:

(€ millions)	Adjustments	
	Assets	Liabilities and Equity
Balance sheet		
Other Current Assets	+1.6 (2)	
Other Current Liabilities		+54.5 (1)
Deferred Tax Liability		−18.5 (3)
Shareholders' Equity		−34.4
Income statement		
Sales		−54.5 (1)
Cost of Sales		−1.6 (2)
Tax Expense		−18.5 (3)
Net Profit		−34.4

MicroStrategy's March 10 announcement that it had overstated revenues prompted the SEC to investigate the company. In the period when it announced its overstatements, MicroStrategy's stock price plummeted 94 percent, compared to the 37 percent drop by the NASDAQ in the same period.

Provisions

Many firms have obligations that are likely to result in a future outflow of cash or other resources but for which the exact amount is hard to establish. Examples of such uncertain liabilities are liabilities that arise from obligations to clean up polluted production sites or to provide warranty coverage for products sold. International accounting rules prescribe that a firm recognizes a provision – or nonfinancial liability – on its balance sheet for such uncertain liabilities when (1) it is probable that the obligation will lead to a future outflow of cash, (2) the firm has no or little discretion to avoid the obligation, and (3) the firm can make a reliable estimate of amount of the obligation. When an uncertain liability does not meet these requirements for recognition, the firm discloses the liability only in the notes to the financial statements, as a "contingent liability." The international rules for the recognition of provisions may result in the understatement of a firm's liabilities. Because of the uncertainty surrounding the obligations, managers have much discretion in deciding whether obligations are probable as well as in estimating the amount of the obligation. Further, the use of a probability threshold below which uncertain liabilities are not recognized may lead to situations in which obligations with a relatively low probability but with a high expected value remain off-balance. An analyst may therefore decide that some of a firm's contingent liabilities are less uncertain than management asserts and undo the distortion by recognizing the liability on-balance as a provision. Additionally, the analyst may be of the opinion that low-probability obligations that nevertheless expose the firm to substantial risks because of their high expected value must also be recognized on the balance sheet.

At the end of the fiscal year 2005, British American Tobacco plc (BAT) – through some of its subsidiaries – was defendant in 3,810 U.S. product liability cases, some of which involved amounts of hundreds of millions of U.S. dollars. The company reported that in several cases that went to trial before the balance sheet date, judges had awarded substantial damages against BAT and that a dozen new cases would come to trial in 2006. Nevertheless, the company chose not to recognize a provision for potential damages because it considered it improbable that individual cases would result in an outflow of resources, even though in the aggregate the cases could have a material effect on the company's cash flow.

Assume that an analyst estimates the present value of future damages and settlements, discounted at BAT's incremental borrowing rate of 7 percent, to be £1 billion. In this particular situation, the analyst could base such an estimate on the historical probability that a tobacco company would lose a product liability case times the average damages awarded. Sometimes a firm's notes on contingent liabilities provide an indication of the size of the liability. For BAT, the following adjustments would have to be made to recognize the liability of £1 billion:

1. At the end of fiscal year 2004, the liability of £1 billion would be recognized as Non-Current Debt. Shareholders' Equity would decline by £0.7 billion (1.0 billion × [1 − .30]) and the Deferred Tax Liability would decline by £0.3 billion (1.0 billion × .30).

2. Because the non-current provision is a discounted liability, the provision increases as interest accrues. In 2005 BAT's income statement would include additional Interest Expense for an amount of £70 million (1.0 billion × .07). Tax Expense and the Deferred Tax Liability would decline by £21 million (70 million × .30) and Net Profit and Shareholders' Equity would decline by £49 million (70 million × [1 − .30]). The additional Interest Expense would result in an increase in Non-Current Debt.

The full effect of the adjustments would be as follows:

£ (millions)	Adjustments December 31, 2004		Adjustments December 31, 2005	
	Assets	Liabilities	Assets	Liabilities
Balance sheet				
Non-Current Debt		+1,000 (1)		+1,000 (1)
				+70 (2)
Deferred Tax Liability		−300 (1)		−300 (1)
				−21 (2)
Shareholders' Equity		−700 (1)		−700 (1)
				−49 (2)
Income statement				
Interest Expense				+70 (2)
Tax Expense				−21 (2)
Net Profit				−49 (2)

Loans from discounted receivables

As discussed earlier, receivables that are discounted with a financial institution are considered "sold" if the "seller" cedes control over the receivables to the financier. Yet if the sale permits the buyer to have recourse against the seller in the event of default, the seller continues to face collection risk. Given the management judgment involved in forecasting default and refinancing costs, as well as the incentives faced by managers to keep debt off the balance sheet, it will be important for the analyst to evaluate the firm's estimates for default as well as the inherent commitments that it has for discounted receivables. Are the firm's estimates reasonable? Is it straightforward to forecast the costs of the default and prepayment risks? If not, does the analyst need to increase the value of the recourse liability? Or, in the extreme, does the analyst need to undo the sale and recognize a loan from the financial institution for the discounted value of the receivables.

Non-current liabilities for leases

As discussed earlier in the chapter, key lease assets and liabilities can be excluded from the balance sheet if the company structures lease transactions to fit the accounting definition of an operating lease. Firms that groom transactions to avoid showing lease assets and obligations will have very different balance sheets from firms with virtually identical economics that either use finance leases or borrow from the bank to actually purchase the equivalent resources. For firms that choose to structure lease transactions to fit the definition of an operating lease, the analyst can restate the leases as finance leases, as discussed in the "Asset distortions" section. This will ensure that the firm's true financial commitments and risks will be reflected on its balance sheet, enabling comparison with peer firms.

Post-employment benefit obligations

Many firms make commitments to provide pension benefits and other post-employment benefits, such as healthcare, to their employees. International accounting rules require managers to estimate and report the present value of the commitments that have been earned by employees over their years of working for the firm. This obligation is offset by any assets that the firm has committed to post-employment plans to fund future plan benefits. If the funds set aside in the post-employment plan are greater (less) than the plan commitments, the plan is overfunded (underfunded). Several important issues arise for analyzing post-employment benefit obligations. First, estimating the obligations themselves is subjective – managers have to make forecasts of future wage and benefit rates, worker attrition rates, the expected lives of retirees, and the discount rate.[16] If these forecasts are too low, the firm's benefit obligations (as well as the annual expenses for benefits reported in the income statement) will be understated.[17] Second, the accounting rules allow that incremental benefit commitments that arise from changes to a plan, and changes in plan funding status that arise from abnormal investment returns on plan assets, are smoothed over time rather than reflected immediately. As a result, for labor-intensive firms that offer attractive post-employment benefits to employees, it is important that the analyst assesses whether reported post-employment plan liabilities reflect the firms' true commitments.

International accounting rules require that firms estimate the value of post-employment commitments, called the post-employment benefit obligation, as the present value of future expected payouts under the plans. The obligation under pension plans is the present value of plan commitments factoring in the impact of future increases in wage rates and salary scales on projected payouts. For other post-employment plans, such as post-employment healthcare or life insurance, the firm's obligation is calculated as the present value of expected future benefits for employees and their beneficiaries.

Each year the firm's post-employment obligations are adjusted to reflect the following factors:

■ *Current service cost.* Defined benefit plans typically provide higher benefits for each additional year of service with the company. For example, a company may promise its employees pension benefits in the amount of 2 percent of their career-average pay for every year worked. The value of incremental benefits earned from another year of service is called the current service cost, and increases the firm's obligation each year.

■ *Interest cost.* The passage of time increases the present value of the firm's obligation. The interest cost recognizes this effect, and it is calculated by multiplying the obligation at the beginning of the year by the discount rate.

■ *Actuarial gains and losses.* Each year the actuarial assumptions used to estimate the firm's commitments are reviewed and, if appropriate, changes are made. The effect of these changes is shown as Actuarial Gains and Losses.

■ *Past service cost.* Occasionally companies may decide to amend their post-employment plans. For example, during recent years some companies have switched from linking pension benefits to employees' career-end pay to linking pension benefits to employees' career-average pay. Because these amendments affect the future payouts under the plans, they also affect the current post-employment benefit obligation. The effect of these amendments is shown as Past Service Cost (or Benefit).

■ *Benefits paid.* The plan commitments are reduced as the plan makes payments to retirees each year.

■ *Other.* The post-employment obligations can change because of changes in foreign exchange rates, plan curtailments, and plan settlements.

For example, in the notes to its financial statements, brewing company Carlsberg provided the following information on its post-employment benefit obligation for the years ended December 31, 2005 and 2004:

DKK (millions)	December 31, 2005	December 31, 2004
Benefit obligation at beginning of year	7,433	7,073
Current service cost	221	210
Interest cost	328	324
Actuarial losses	418	14
Benefits paid	(444)	(498)
Other	109	310
Benefit obligation at end of year	8,065	7,433

Carlsberg's obligation at the end of 2005 was DKK8.1 billion, an 8.5 percent increase over the prior year.

To meet their commitments under post-employment plans, firms make contributions to the plans. These contributions are then invested in equities, debt, and other assets. Plan assets, therefore, are increased each year by new company (and employee) contributions. They are also increased or decreased by the returns generated each year from plan investments. Finally, plan assets decline when the plan pays out benefits to retirees. For the years ended December 31, 2005 and 2004, Carlsberg reported the following assets for post-employment plans:

DKK (millions)	December 31, 2005	December 31, 2004
Fair value of plan assets at beginning of year	5,604	5,735
Actual return on plan assets	592	314
Contributions to plans	203	218
Benefits paid	(358)	(452)
Other	64	(211)
Fair value of plan assets at end of year	6,105	5,604

Carlsberg had expected to earn a return of 5.85 percent on its beginning plan assets in 2005. The company's plan assets increased because they generated an unexpected return of DKK264 million (592 − [.585 × 5,604]) during the year. The difference between Carlsberg's post-employment plan obligations and the plan assets, DKK1.96 billion (8.065 − 6.105), represents the company's unfunded obligation to employees under the plan.

Of course, estimating post-employment obligations is highly subjective. It requires managers to forecast the future payouts under the plans, which in turn involves making projections of employees' service with the firm, retirement ages, and life expectancies, as well as future wage rates. It also requires managers to select an interest rate to estimate the present value of the future benefits. For example, Carlsberg projected that future salaries would grow at 2.4 percent per year, on average. It also assumed that the appropriate discount rate was 4.1 percent. Under the simplified assumption that Carlsberg's retired workforce size remains constant throughout the next 30 years and then gradually decreases to zero over a period of 30 years, a 0.1 percent decrease in the discount rate (or a 0.1 percent increase in salary growth) would increase the post-employment benefit obligation by close to DKK140 million.[18] Given the management judgment involved in making these forecasts and assumptions, analysts should question whether reported obligations adequately reflect the firm's true commitments.

So, given Carlsberg's unfunded post-employment benefit obligation of DKK1.96 billion, it is reasonable that the company reports a liability on its balance sheet for a similar amount. Unfortunately, not all companies follow the same practice. International accounting rules allow that firms smooth out shocks to plan obligations that occur because of actuarial gains or losses. If the value of plan assets increases or decreases unexpectedly in a given year, or there needs to be adjustment in the actuarial assumptions made to estimate the obligation, the financial statement impact can be reflected gradually rather than immediately. For example, consider the post-employment plans of one of Carlsberg's competitors, brewing company Heineken. Even though the actual gap between Heineken's post-employment obligation and plan assets in 2005 is €853 million, this is not the value of the liability recorded on its balance sheet. Heineken provides a separate disclosure that reconciles the actual and the reported obligation:

€ (millions)	December 31, 2005	December 31, 2004
Benefit obligation at end of year	3,121	2,598
Fair value of plan assets at end of year	(2,268)	(1,843)
Funded status	853	755
Unrecognized actuarial loss	(285)	(121)
Recognized liability for post-employment obligations	€568	€634

The unrecognized actuarial loss arises because Heineken's earlier actuarial assumptions about parameters such as future salaries, retirement rates, and assumed rates of return on plan assets have proven to be too optimistic. International rules on post-employment accounting allow companies to choose between fully and immediately recognizing current actuarial gains and losses in the statement of changes in equity (outside the income statement) or recognizing the cumulative actuarial gains and losses over time (in the income statement) rather than right away. In contrast with Carlsberg, Heineken has opted for gradual recognition over time.[19] Consequently, Heineken's reported post-employment liability understates its real commitment by €285 million (2.4 percent of Heineken's total assets).[20]

There is an additional reason why the recognized post-employment liability is not necessarily equal to the unfunded post-employment benefit obligation. International accounting rules require that past service cost be recognized in the income statement on a straight-line basis over the period until the employees become entitled to the additional benefits from the plan amendments (i.e., until the benefits become "vested"). This treatment of past service cost results in the delayed recognition of the effect of pension plan amendments on the post-employment benefit obligation.

What does post-employment accounting imply for financial analysis? It is reasonable for the analyst to raise several questions about a firm's post-employment obligations, particularly for firms in labor-intensive industries.

1. Are the assumptions made by the firm to estimate its post-employment obligations realistic? These include assumptions about the discount rate, which is supposed to represent the current market interest rate for benefits, as well as assumptions about increases in wage and benefit costs. If these assumptions are optimistic, the obligations recorded on the books understate the firm's real economic commitment. As discussed above, the analyst may estimate that a 0.1 percent increase in expected salary growth increases Carlsberg's obligation by DKK140 million and use this information to adjust for any optimism in management's assumptions. For example, if the analyst decided that Carlsberg's forecasts of future salaries were too low and needed to increase by 0.1 percent, the post-employment obligation would have to be increased by DKK140 million, with offsetting declines to equity (for the after-tax effect) and to the deferred tax liability. The adjustment to Carlsberg's 2005 balance sheet, assuming a 28 percent tax rate, would be as follows:

	Adjustment	
DKK (millions)	**Assets**	**Liabilities and Equity**
Balance sheet		
Long-Term Debt		+140
Deferred Tax Liability		−39.2
Shareholders' Equity		−100.8

2. Does the off-balance sheet post-employment obligation need to be brought on the balance sheet? The process of smoothing differences between actual and forecasted parameters for post-employment plans may understate the obligations for post-employment benefits. For some companies this understatement because of cumulative actuarial gains and losses is substantial. As noted above, Heineken reports a liability for post-employment benefits that is €285 million less than the actual unfunded obligations. The analyst can adjust for this distortion by increasing the firm's Long-Term Debt, and making offsetting adjustments to the Deferred Tax Liability (since the change would not affect the company's taxable profit) and Shareholders' Equity. Assuming a 31.5 percent tax rate, the adjustment to Heineken's 2005 balance sheet would be as follows:

	Adjustment	
€ (millions)	**Assets**	**Liabilities and Equity**
Balance sheet		
Long-Term Debt		+285
Deferred Tax Liability		−89.8
Shareholders' Equity		−195.2

3. What effect do post-employment assumptions play in the income statement? The post-employment cost each year comprises (a) service cost, plus (b) interest cost, plus (c) amortization of any past service costs, plus or minus (d) amortization of actuarial gains and losses, minus (e) expected return on plan assets (the expected long-term return multiplied by beginning assets under management). For example, Carlsberg and Heineken show that their post-employment expenses for 2005 and 2004 are as follows:

	Carlsberg		Heineken	
(millions)	2005	2004	2005	2004
Income statement				
Service cost	DKK221	DKK210	€82	€80
Interest cost	328	324	131	132
Expected return on plan assets	(328)	(336)	(112)	(106)
Amortization of past service cost	0	0	0	0
Amortization of cumulative actuarial losses/(gains)	0	0	0	0
Other	0	(42)	(5)	(10)
Net expense	221	156	221	221
Statement of changes in equity				
Recognized net actuarial loss/(gain)	(174)	(22)	0	0

This expense reflects the effect of smoothing actual asset returns and revisions in actuarial assumptions discussed earlier. Conceptually, the post-employment expense should equal the change in the post-employment obligation minus the change in the fair value of plan assets. However, neither Carlsberg nor Heineken fully and immediately recognize the obligations from changes in actuarial assumptions in their income statements. Carlsberg recognizes such changes in the statement of changes in equity, whereas Heineken delays the recognition to future periods. Further, to calculate the post-employment expense companies subtract the expected return on plan assets – instead of the actual return on plan assets – from the interest and service costs. The difference between the expected return and the annual return is added to and treated similarly as the other actuarial gains and losses.

In 2005 Heineken's current period actuarial loss, calculated as the increase in the unrecognized cumulative actuarial losses, was €164 million (disclosed in the notes to the financial statements), while Carlsberg's current period actuarial loss was DKK174 million (recognized in the statement of changes in equity). If the analyst used the current period actuarial losses to undo the earnings effects of smoothing unexpected returns and changes in actuarial assumptions, an additional €164 million and DKK174 million in post-employment expenses, included in personnel expenses, would be required. These adjustments would also lower the firms' tax expenses. The full income statement adjustment would therefore be as follows:

	Adjustment	
(millions)	Carlsberg	Heineken
Income statement		
Personnel Expense	+DKK174	+€164
Tax Expense	−48.7	−51.7
Net Profit	−DKK125.3	−€112.3

If desired, similar adjustments can be made to undo the earnings effects of smoothing past-period service costs (if present).

First-time adoption: Actuarial gains and losses

Rules on the first-time adoption of IFRS allow companies to recognize all cumulative actuarial gains and losses in the opening IFRS balance sheet at the first time of adoption. Immediate recognition of cumulative gains (losses) would result in a decrease (increase) in the on-balance post-employment liability and an offsetting increase (decrease) in opening equity. Firms can choose to do so irrespective of the method they use for recognizing the actuarial gains and losses that occur after the date of the opening IFRS balance sheet. Consequently, the amount of unrecognized cumulative actuarial gains and losses is likely to be small for companies that have recently adopted IFRS.

KEY ANALYSIS QUESTIONS

The following are some of the questions an analyst can probe when analyzing whether a firm's liabilities exhibit distortions:

- *Unearned revenues.* Has the firm recognized revenues for services or products that have yet to be provided?
- *Provisions.* Did the firm disclose contingent liabilities that expose the firm to material risks? If so, can the expected value of such liabilities be estimated and recognized on the balance sheet? Did the firm make unexplained changes in its provisions? Is the size of the provisions in line with industry practices?
- *Post-employment benefits.* Are the assumptions made by the firm to estimate its post-employment obligations realistic? What is the effect of smoothing differences between actual and forecasted parameters for post-employment benefits on the off-balance sheet post-employment obligation? Does the analyst need to adjust long-term debt for the off-balance sheet post-employment obligation?

EQUITY DISTORTIONS

Accounting treats stockholders' equity as a residual claim on the firm's assets, after paying off the other claimholders. Consequently, equity distortions arise primarily from distortions in assets and liabilities. For example, distortions in assets or liabilities that affect earnings also lead to distortions in equity. However, there are forms of equity distortions that would not typically arise in asset and liability analyses. One particular issue is how firms account for contingent claims on their net assets that they sometimes provide to outside stakeholders. Two examples of such contingent claims are employee stock options and conversion options on convertible debentures.

Contingent claims

A stock option gives the holder the right to purchase a certain number of shares at a predetermined price, called the exercise or strike price, for a specified period of time, termed the exercise period. In the 1990s, stock options became the most significant component of compensation for many corporate executives. Proponents of options argue that they provide managers with incentives to maximize shareholder value and make it easier to attract talented managers. Convertible debentures also contain a stock option component. Holders of these debentures have the right to purchase a certain number of shares in exchange for their fixed claim. When deciding on how to account for these contingent claims in a firm's financial statements, the following two factors are important to consider:

- Although providing a contingent claim does not involve a cash outflow for the firm, the claim is by no means costless to the firm's shareholders. The potential exercise of the option dilutes current shareholders' equity and as such imposes an economic cost on the firm's shareholders. To improve current net profit as a measure of the firm's current economic performance the economic cost of contingent claims should therefore be included in the income statement in the same period in which the firm receives the benefits from these claims.

- The contingent claims are valuable to those who receive them. Employees are willing to provide services to the firm in exchange for employee stock options. Convertible debenture holders are willing to charge a lower interest rate to the firm in exchange for the conversion option. If, in future years, the firm wishes to receive similar services or similar low interest rates without providing contingent claims on its net assets, it must be willing to give up other resources. To improve current net profit as a predictor of the firm's future net profit the income statement should therefore include an expense that reflects the value of the contingent claims to the recipients.

These two factors underline the importance of accurately recording the cost of options in a firm's income statement. International rules require firms to report stock options using the fair value method (discussed in IFRS 2). The fair value method requires firms to record an expense for stock option compensation when the options are issued. The value of the options issued is estimated using a recognized valuation model, such as the Black-Scholes model, and is then expensed over the vesting period.[21] Prior to the European adoption of IFRS, the local accounting rules in most European countries permitted firms to report stock options using the intrinsic value method. Under the intrinsic value method, no compensation expense is reported at the grant date for the vast majority of stock options awarded, where the exercise price is equal to the firm's current stock price. If the options are subsequently exercised, there is also no expense recorded, and the new stock that is issued is valued at the exercise price rather than its higher market value.

Although there is no question that Black-Scholes valuations present a more accurate reflection of the economic cost of stock option awards to the firm's shareholders than the zero cost reported under the intrinsic value method, these valuations can be highly sensitive to management's assumptions about its share price characteristics. For example, when using the Black-Scholes model to value options, managers can understate the stock option expense by understating the expected future share price volatility or overstating the expected future dividend yield. One task of the analyst is therefore to assess the adequacy of management's valuation assumptions. Additionally, research suggests that employees attach much lower values than the Black-Scholes values to the nonmarketable options that they receive. This implies that when a firm plans to replace its stock option awards with cash-based forms of compensation, the analyst should assess whether a decrease in the compensation expense can be expected.

International accounting rules also require a firm to separate the debt from the equity component of convertible debentures. To do so, the firm first estimates what the fair value of the debentures would have been if the conversion option had not been attached to the debentures. This fair value is equal to the present value of the future fixed payments on the debentures, discounted at the firm's effective interest rate on nonconvertible debentures. The value of the equity component is then set equal to the proceeds of the debenture issue minus the fair value of the debt component. The economic cost of the conversion option is included in the income statement by calculating the interest expense on the debentures on the basis of the effective interest rate on nonconvertible debentures. Under these rules, firms may have the incentive to understate the effective interest rate on nonconvertible debentures, thereby understating the convertible debentures' equity component and effective interest expense.

Recycling of gains and losses

In accordance with the international accounting rules on the measurement of financial instruments (IAS 39), firms typically record securities held available for sale at fair value and include any (unrealized) fair value gains or losses directly in the statement of changes in equity. In the period in which these instruments are eventually sold, the cumulative unrealized gains and losses are taken from equity and recognized in the income statement. As a result, gains and losses that were previously included in comprehensive income (statement of changes in equity) are "recycled" and reincluded in net profit.

A disadvantage of recycling unrealized gains or losses on financial instruments held available for sale is that the discretionary timing of a firm's securities sales determines in which period gains or losses become realized. This contrasts, for example, with the way in which a firm treats unrealized gains and losses on securities that are held for short-term trading purposes. The difference between securities classified as available for sale and those held for short-term trading is that the former type of securities were originally designated by the firm as long-term investments. Consequently, international accounting rules require that only revaluation gains and losses on securities held for short-term trading be considered as profit from operating activities and directly included in the income statement. The analyst can, however, use the information from the statement of changes in equity to incorporate unrealized gains and losses on financial instruments held available for sale in profits and undo the financial statements from any distortions caused by a firm's discretionary timing of securities sales.

In its statement of changes in equity for the fiscal year 2005, Spain-based Banco Bilbao Vizcaya Argentaria (BBVA) reported that the revaluation gains on its securities held available for sale amounted up to €1,479 million. The amount of revaluation gains transferred from shareholders' equity to the income statement was €429 million. Income tax on the net amount of current unrealized revaluation gains and transfers to the income statement equaled €368 million. The net effect of these amounts resulted in an increase of shareholders' equity by €682 million. To transfer current year's unrealized revaluation gains and losses (net of current realizations) to net income, the following adjustments would have to be made:

€ (millions)	Adjustments
Statement of changes in equity	
Unrealized Revaluations, Net of Transfers to Income	–682
Net Profit	+682
Income statement	
Other Operating Income, Net of Other Operating Expense	+1,050
Tax Expense	+368
Net Profit	+682

These adjustments would increase BBVA's net profit by 16.8 percent and its return on beginning-of-year equity by 6.2 percent.

SUMMARY

To implement accounting analysis, the analyst must first recast the financial statements into a common format so that financial statement terminology and formatting is comparable between firms and across time. A standard template for recasting the financials, presented in this chapter, is used throughout the remainder of the book.

Once the financial statements are standardized, the analyst can determine what accounting distortions exist in the firm's assets, liabilities, and equity. Common distortions that overstate assets include delays in recognizing asset impairments, underestimated allowances, aggressive revenue recognition leading to overstated receivables, and optimistic assumptions on long-term asset depreciation. Asset understatements can arise if managers overstate asset write-offs, use operating leases to keep assets off the balance sheet, or make conservative assumptions for asset depreciation. They can also arise because accounting rules require outlays for key assets (e.g., research outlays and brands) to be immediately expensed.

For liabilities, the primary concern for the analyst is whether the firm understates its real commitments. This can arise from off-balance liabilities (e.g., operating lease obligations), from understated provisions, from questionable management judgment and limitations in accounting rules for estimating post-employment liabilities, and from aggressive revenue recognition that understates unearned revenue obligations. Equity distortions frequently arise when there are distortions in assets and liabilities. However, they can also arise if understated expenses are reported for stock option compensation, or for the issuance of compound financial instruments such as convertible debentures.

Adjustments for distortions can, therefore, arise because accounting standards, although applied appropriately, do not reflect a firm's economic reality. They can also arise if the analyst has a different point of view than management about the estimates and assumptions made in preparing the financial statements. Once distortions have been identified, the analyst can use cash flow statement information and information from the notes to the financial statements to make adjustments to the balance sheet at the beginning and/or end of the current year, as well as any needed adjustments to revenues and expenses in the latest income statement. This ensures that the most recent financial ratios used to evaluate a firm's performance and to forecast its future results are based on financial data that appropriately reflect its business economics.

Several points are worth remembering when undertaking accounting analysis. First, the bulk of the analyst's time and energy should be focused on evaluating and adjusting accounting policies and estimates that describe the firm's key strategic value drivers. Of course this does not mean that management bias is not reflected in other accounting estimates and policies, and the analyst should certainly examine these. But given the importance of evaluating how the firm is managing its key success factors and risks, the bulk of the accounting analysis should be spent examining those policies that describe these factors and risks. Similarly, the analyst should focus on adjustments that have a material effect on the firm's liabilities, equity, or earnings. Immaterial adjustments cost time and energy but are unlikely to affect the analyst's financial and prospective analysis.

It is also important to recognize that many accounting adjustments can only be approximations rather than precise calculations, because much of the information necessary for making precise adjustments is not disclosed. The analyst should, therefore, try to avoid worrying about being overly precise in making accounting adjustments. By making even crude adjustments, it is usually possible to mitigate some of the limitations of accounting standards and problems of management bias in financial reporting.

DISCUSSION QUESTIONS

1. On the companion website to this book there is a spreadsheet containing the financial statements of the Unilever Group. Use the templates shown in Tables 4.1, 4.2, 4.3, and 4.4 to recast Unilever's financial statements.

2. On March 31, 2006, Germany's largest retailer Metro AG reported in its quarterly financial statements that it held inventories for 54 days' sales. The inventories had a book value of €6,345 million. How much excess inventory do you estimate Metro is holding in March 2006 if the firm's optimal Days' Inventories is 45 days? Calculate the inventory impairment charge for Metro if 50 percent of this excess inventory is deemed worthless? Record the changes to Metro's financial statements from adjusting for this impairment.

3. Dutch Food retailer Royal Ahold provides the following information on its finance leases:

   Finance lease liabilities are principally for buildings. Terms range from 10 to 25 years and include renewal options if it is reasonably certain, at the inception of the lease, that they will be exercised. At the time of entering into finance lease agreements, the commitments are recorded at their present value using the interest rate implicit in the lease, if this is practicable to determine; if not the interest rate applicable for long-term borrowings is used.

   The aggregate amounts of minimum lease liabilities to third parties, under non-cancelable finance lease contracts and operating lease contracts for the next five years and thereafter are as follows:

Year ending December 31,	Finance leases	Operating leases
2006	€182	€686
2007	176	641
2008	172	579
2009	168	525
2010	156	489
Thereafter	1,753	4,560
Total	€2,608	€7,480
Interest portion	(1,245)	
Present value of net minimum finance lease payments	€1,362	

What interest rate does Ahold use to capitalize its finance leases? Use this rate to capitalize Ahold's operating leases at December 31, 2005. Record the adjustment to Ahold's balance sheet to reflect the capitalization of operating leases. How would this reporting change affect Ahold's income statement in 2006?

4. What approaches would you use to estimate the value of brands? What assumptions underlie these approaches? As a financial analyst, what would you use to assess whether the brand value of £3.2 billion reported by Cadbury Schweppes in 2005 was a reasonable reflection of the future benefits from these brands? What questions would you raise with the firm's CFO about the firm's brand assets?

5. As the CFO of a company, what indicators would you look at to assess whether your firm's non-current assets were impaired? What approaches could be used, either by management or an independent valuation firm, to assess the value of any asset impairment? As a financial analyst, what indicators would you look at to assess whether a firm's non-current assets were impaired? What questions would you raise with the firm's CFO about any charges taken for asset impairment?

6. Refer to the British American Tobacco example on provisions in this chapter. The cigarette industry is subject to litigation for health hazards posed by its products. In the U.S., the industry has been negotiating a settlement of these claims with state and federal governments. As the CFO for U.K.-based British American Tobacco (BAT), which is affected through its U.S. subsidiaries, what information would you report to investors in the annual report on the firm's litigation risks? How would you assess whether the firm should record a provision for this risk, and if so, how would you assess the value of this provision? As a financial analyst following BAT, what questions would you raise with the CFO over the firm's litigation provision?

7. Refer to the Lufthansa example on asset depreciation estimates in this chapter. What adjustments would be required if Lufthansa's aircraft depreciation was computed using an average life of 25 years and salvage value of 5 percent (instead of the reported values of 12 years and 15 percent)? Show the adjustments to the 2003 and 2004 balance sheets, and to the 2004 income statement.

8. In early 2003 Bristol-Myers Squibb announced that it would have to restate its financial statements as a result of stuffing as much as $3.35 billion worth of products into wholesalers' warehouses from 1999 through 2001. The company's sales and cost of sales during this period were as follows:

(millions)	2001	2000	1999
Net sales	$18,139	$17,695	$16,502
Cost of products sold	$5,454	$4,729	$4,458

The company's marginal tax rate during the three years was 35 percent. What adjustments are required to correct Bristol-Myers Squibb's balance sheet for December 31, 2001? What assumptions underlie your adjustments? How would you expect the adjustments to affect Bristol-Myers Squibb's performance in the coming few years?

NOTES

1. See P. Healy, S. Myers, and C. Howe, "R&D Accounting and the Tradeoff Between Relevance and Objectivity," *Journal of Accounting Research* 40 (June 2002): 677–711, for analysis of the value of capitalizing R&D and then annually assessing impairment.

2. J. Francis, D. Hanna, and L. Vincent find that management is more likely to exercise judgment in its self-interest for goodwill write-offs and restructuring charges than for inventory or PP&E write-offs. See "Causes and Effects of Discretionary Asset Write-Offs," *Journal of Accounting Research* 34, Supplement, 1996.

3. P. Healy, K. Palepu, and R. Ruback find that acquisitions add value for only one-third of the 50 largest acquisitions during the early 1980s, suggesting that acquirers frequently do not recover goodwill. See "Which Takeovers Are Profitable – Strategic or Financial?" *Sloan Management Review*, Summer 1997. Studying a sample of 519 U.K. acquirers between 1983 and 1995, S. Sudarsanam and A. Mahate find in their study "Glamour Acquirers, Method of Payment and Post-acquisition Performance: The UK Evidence," *Journal of Business Finance and Accounting* 30 (January 2003): 299–341, that the risk of not recovering goodwill is especially large for glamour acquirers, who have experienced a large share price run-up prior to the acquisition.

4. In 2000 the international accounting rules required that goodwill was amortized. The adjustments to EM.TV's balance sheet are in conformity with current IFRSs.

5. V. Beattie, K. Edwards, and A. Goodacre show that adjustments to capitalize operating leases have a significant impact on leverage and other key financial ratios of U.K. firms. See "The Impact of Constructive Operating Lease Capitalisation on Key Accounting Ratios," *Accounting and Business Research* 28 (Autumn 1998): 233–254.

6. Some research suggests that the distinction between finance and operating lease obligation is not fully arbitrary. In their study "Recognition Versus Disclosure: An Investigation of the Impact on Equity Risk Using UK Operating Lease Disclosures," *Journal of Business Finance and Accounting* 27 (November/December 2000): 1185–1224, V. Beattie, A. Goodacre, and S. Thomson find that U.K. investors interpret the operating lease obligation as an obligation that increases a firm's equity risk but less so than ordinary debt.

7. P. Healy, S. Myers, and C. Howe, "R&D Accounting and the Tradeoff Between Relevance and Objectivity," *Journal of Accounting Research* 40 (June 2002): 677–711, show that the magnitude of this bias is sizable.

8. See e.g., B. Bublitz and M. Ettredge, "The Information in Discretionary Outlays: Advertising, Research and Development," *The Accounting Review* 64 (1989): 108–124; M. Hirschey and J. Weygandt, "Amortization Policy for Advertising and Research and Development Expenditures," *Journal of Accounting Research* 23 (1985): 326–335; B. Lev and T. Sougiannis, "The Capitalization, Amortization, and Value-Relevance of R&D," *Journal of Accounting and Economics* 21 (1996): 107–138; P. Green, A. Stark, and H. Thomas, "UK Evidence on the Market Valuation of Research and Development Expenditures," *Journal of Business Finance and Accounting* 23 (March 1996): 191–216; D. Aboody and B. Lev, "The Value-Relevance of Intangibles: The Case of Software Capitalization," *Journal of Accounting Research* 36 (1998): 161–191; and M. Ballester, M. Garcia-Ayuso, and J. Livnat, "The Economic Value of the R&D Intangible Asset," *European Accounting Review* 12 (2003): 605–633.

9. U.S. evidence indicates that there are negative stock price effects for acquirers that use pooling. See J. Weber, "Shareholder Wealth Effects of Pooling-of-Interests Accounting: Evidence from the SEC's Restriction on Share Repurchases Following Pooling Transactions," *Journal of Accounting and Economics* 37 (February 2004): 39–57, and A. Martinez-Jarad, "Interaction Between Accounting and Corporate Governance: Evidence from Business Combinations," working paper, Harvard Business School, February 2003.

10. Several studies indicate that some firms were willing to go to considerable lengths, including paying an additional premium, to be able to use the pooling method for recording an acquisition. See J. Robinson and P. Shane, "Acquisition Accounting Method and Bid Premia for Target Firms," *The Accounting Review* 65 (January 1990): 25–49, and T. Lys and L. Vincent, "An Analysis of Value Destruction in AT&T's Acquisition of NCR," *Journal of Financial Economics* 39 (October/November 1995): 353–379.

11. MicroStrategy 1998 10-K, Note 1.

12. Ibid.

13. J. Elliott and D. Hanna find that the market anticipates large write-downs by about one quarter, consistent with managers being reluctant to take write-downs on a timely basis. See "Repeated Accounting Write-Offs and the Information Content of Earnings," *Journal of Accounting Research* 34, Supplement, 1996.

14. The interest expense is only a rough approximation of the amount that would be reported by Volvo, since it does not adjust for the portion of the customer payments that were effectively interest for the bank given the premium rate charged.

15. Mary E. Barth and Maureen McNichols discuss ways for investors to estimate the value of environmental liabilities. See "Estimation and Market Valuation of Environmental Liabilities Relating to Superfund Sites," *Journal of Accounting Research* 32, Supplement, 1994.

16. Defined contribution plans, where companies agree to contribute fixed amounts today to cover future benefits, require very little forecasting to estimate their annual cost since the firm's obligation is limited to its annual obligation to contribute to the employees' pension funds.

17. E. Amir and E. Gordon show that firms with larger post-retirement benefit obligations and more leverage tend to make more aggressive estimates of post-retirement obligation parameters. See "A Firm's Choice of Estimation Parameters: Empirical Evidence from SFAS No. 106," *Journal of Accounting, Auditing and Finance* 11, no. 3, Summer 1996.

18. The annuity of a €1 payout that grows at rate g_a during n_a years and then gradually declines to zero over a period of n_b years can be calculated as follows:

$$\text{Annuity} = \frac{1-\left(\left[1+g_a\right]/\left[1+r\right]\right)^{n_a}}{\left(r-g_a\right)}+\left(\frac{1-\left(\left[1-1/n_b\right]/\left[1+r\right]\right)^{n_b}}{\left(r+1/n_b\right)}\right)\left(\frac{1}{\left(1+r\right)^{n_a}}\right).$$

Given a discount rate (r) of 4.1 percent, g_a equal to 2.4 percent, and n_a and n_b equal to 30 years, the annuity is equal to €26.52. Decreasing the discount rate from 4.1 percent to 4.0 percent increases the annuity by €0.46, or 1.7 percent. 1.7 percent of Carlsberg's post-employment obligation of DKK 8.1 billion is approximately DKK140 million.

19. Gradual recognition implies that if the cumulative actuarial gains and losses exceed an amount of 10 percent of the post-employment benefit obligation (or the fair value of plan assets, if greater), the company amortizes the difference over the average expected remaining working lives of the current workforce.

20. M. Barth finds that investors regard these disclosures in the notes to the financial statements as more useful than the liability reported on the balance sheet. See "Relative Measurement Errors Among Alternative Pension Asset and Liability Measures," *The Accounting Review* 66, no. 3, 1991.

21. The Black-Scholes option pricing model estimates the value of an option as a nonlinear function of the exercise price, the remaining time to expiration, the estimated variance of the underlying stock, and the risk-free interest rate. Studies of the valuation of executive stock options include T. Hemmer, S. Matsunaga, and T. Shevlin, "Optimal Exercise and the Cost of Granting Employee Stock Options with a Reload Provision," *Journal of Accounting Research* 36, no. 2, 1998; C. Cuny and P. Jorion, "Valuing Executive Stock Options with Endogenous Departure," *Journal of Accounting and Economics* 20 (September 1995): 193–206; and S. Huddart, "Employee Stock Options," *Journal of Accounting and Economics* 18 (September 1994): 207–232.

APPENDIX: RECASTING FINANCIAL STATEMENTS INTO STANDARDIZED TEMPLATES

The following tables show the financial statements for Volkswagen AG for the year ended December 31, 2005. The first column in each statement presents the recast financial statement classifications that are used for each line item. Note that the classifications are not applied to subtotal lines such as Total current assets or Net profit. The recast financial statements for Volkswagen are prepared by simply totaling the balances of line items with the same standard classifications. For example, on the recast balance sheet there are two line items classified as Other Current Assets: Prepaid expenses and Other current assets. In Volkswagen's cash flow statement, one line item, the investment in securities, is not classified because we consider this item a change in the bottom line item Cash and Marketable Securities.

Volkswagen reported balance sheet (€ millions)

Classifications	Fiscal year ended December 31	2005
	ASSETS	
Non-Current Intangible Assets	Intangible assets	7,668
Non-Current Tangible Assets	Property, plant and equipment	22,884
Non-Current Tangible Assets	Leasing and rental assets	9,882
Other Non-Current Assets	Investment property	167
Other Non-Current Assets	Investments in Group companies accounted for using the equity method	4,198
Other Non-Current Assets	Other equity investments	336
Other Non-Current Assets	Financial services receivables	24,958
Other Non-Current Assets	Other receivables and financial assets	2,270
Deferred Tax Asset	Deferred tax assets	2,872
	Total non-current assets	**75,235**
Inventories	Inventories	12,643
Trade Receivables	Trade receivables	5,638
Trade Receivables	Financial services receivables	22,412
Other Current Assets	Current tax receivables	317
Other Current Assets	Other receivables and financial assets	4,856
Cash and Marketable Securities	Marketable securities	4,017
Cash and Marketable Securities	Cash and cash equivalents	7,963
	Total current assets	**57,846**
	TOTAL ASSETS	**133,081**
	LIABILITIES AND SHAREHOLDERS' EQUITY	
Preference Shares	Subscribed capital – preference shares	269
Ordinary Shareholders' Equity	Subscribed capital – ordinary shares	824
Ordinary Shareholders' Equity	Capital reserves	4,513
Ordinary Shareholders' Equity	Retained earnings	17,994
	Total shareholders' equity	**23,600**

(continued)

Volkswagen reported balance sheet (€ millions) *(continued)*

Classifications	Fiscal year ended December 31	2005
Non-Current Debt	Non-current financial liabilities	31,014
Other Non-Current Liabilities		
(non-interest-bearing)	Other non-current liabilities	1,591
Deferred Tax Liability	Deferred tax liabilities	1,622
Non-Current Debt	Provisions for pensions	14,003
Other Non-Current Liabilities		
(non-interest-bearing)	Provisions for taxes	2,257
Non-Current Debt	Other non-current provisions	5,638
	Total non-current liabilities	**56,125**
Current Debt	Current financial liabilities	30,992
Trade Payables	Trade payables	8,476
Other Current Liabilities	Current tax payables	150
Other Current Liabilities	Other current liabilities	6,205
Other Current Liabilities	Other current provisions	7,486
	Total current liabilities	**53,309**
	TOTAL LIABILITIES AND SHAREHOLDERS' EQUITY	**133,081**

Volkswagen reported income statement (€ millions)

Classifications	Fiscal year ended December 31	2005
Sales	**Sales revenue**	**95,268**
Cost of Sales	Cost of sales	(82,391)
	Gross profit	**12,877**
SG&A	Distribution expenses	(8,905)
SG&A	Administrative expenses	(2,383)
Other Operating Income	Other operating income	4,552
Other Operating Expenses	Other operating expenses	(3,349)
	Operating profit	**2,792**
Investment Income	Share of profits and losses of Group companies	
	accounted for using the equity method	78
Investment Income	Other expenses from equity investments	(25)
Net Interest Expense (Income)	Interest result	(1,123)
	Profit before tax	**1,722**
Tax Expense	Current tax expense	(876)
Tax Expense	Deferred tax income	274
	Profit after tax	**1,120**
Minority Interest	Minority interest	(0)
	Profit attributable to shareholders of Volkswagen AG	**1,120**

Volkswagen reported cash flow statement (€ millions)

Classifications	Fiscal year ended December 31	2005
	OPERATING ACTIVITIES	
Profit Before Tax	Profit before tax	1,722
	Adjustments for:	
Taxes Paid	Income taxes paid	(354)
Non-Current Operating Accruals	Depreciation and amortization expense	5,614
Non-Current Operating Accruals	Amortization of capitalized development costs	1,438
Non-Current Operating Accruals	Impairment losses on equity investments	6
Non-Current Operating Accruals	Depreciation of leasing and rental assets and investment property	1,596
Non-Current Operating Accruals	Change in provisions	1,351
Non-Operating Gains (Losses)	Loss on disposal of non-current assets	40
Non-Current Operating Accruals	Share of profit or loss of Group companies accounted for using the equity method	294
Non-Operating Gains (Losses)	Other non-cash income/expense	151
Net (Investments in) or Liquidation of Operating Working Capital	Change in inventories	(720)
Net (Investments in) or Liquidation of Operating Working Capital	Change in receivables (excluding financial services)	(757)
Net (Investments in) or Liquidation of Operating Working Capital	Change in liabilities (excluding financial liabilities)	429
	Cash flow from operating activities	10,810
	INVESTING ACTIVITIES	
Net (Investments in) or Liquidation of Non-Current Operating Assets	Acquisition of property, plant and equipment, and intangible assets	(4,434)
Net (Investments in) or Liquidation of Non-Current Operating Assets	Additions to capitalized development costs	(1,432)
Net (Investments in) or Liquidation of Non-Current Operating Assets	Acquisition of subsidiaries and other equity investments	(150)
Net (Investments in) or Liquidation of Non-Current Operating Assets	Disposal of equity investments	166
Net (Investments in) or Liquidation of Non-Current Operating Assets	Loans	(22)
Net (Investments in) or Liquidation of Non-Current Operating Assets	Change in leasing and rental assets and investment property (excluding depreciation)	(2,950)
Net (Investments in) or Liquidation of Non-Current Operating Assets	Change in financial services receivables	(1,948)
Net (Investments in) or Liquidation of Non-Current Operating Assets	Proceeds from disposal of non-current assets (excluding leasing and rental assets and investments property)	304
Net (Investments in) or Liquidation of Non-Current Operating Assets	Change in investments in securities	(820)
	Cash flow from investing activities	(11,286)
		(continued)

Volkswagen reported cash flow statement (€ millions) *(continued)*

Classifications	Fiscal year ended December 31	2005
	FINANCING ACTIVITIES	
Net Share (Repurchase) or Issuance	Capital contributions	66
Dividend (Payments)	Dividends paid	(414)
Net Share (Repurchase) or Issuance	Other changes in equity	13
Net Debt (Repayment) or Issuance	Proceeds from issue of bonds	5,754
Net Debt (Repayment) or Issuance	Repayment of bonds	(9,804)
Net Debt (Repayment) or Issuance	Change in other financial liabilities	3,233
Net Debt (Repayment) or Issuance	Finance lease payments	(3)
Net Debt (Repayment) or Issuance	Change in loans	(639)
	Cash flows from financing activities	(1,794)
Non-Operating Gains (Losses)	Changes in cash and cash and equivalents due to changes in the scope of consolidation	(67)
Non-operating Gains (Losses)	Effect of exchange rate changes on cash and cash equivalents	79
	Net change in cash and cash equivalents	(2,258)
	Cash and cash equivalents at beginning of financial year	10,221
	CASH AND CASH EQUIVALENTS AT YEAR-END	7,963

The standardized financial statements for Volkswagen AG are as follows:

Volkswagen standardized balance sheet (€ millions)

Fiscal year ending December 31,	2005
Assets	
Cash and marketable securities	11,980
Trade receivables	28,050
Inventories	12,643
Other current assets	5,173
Total current assets	**57,846**
Non-current tangible assets	32,766
Non-current intangible assets	7,668
Deferred taxes	2,872
Other non-current assets	31,929
Total non-current assets	**75,235**
Total assets	**133,081**
Liabilities	
Trade payables	8,476
Current debt	30,992
Other current liabilities	13,841
Total current liabilities	**53,309**

continued

Volkswagen standardized balance sheet (€ millions) *(continued)*

Fiscal year ending December 31,	2005
Non-current debt	50,655
Deferred taxes	1,622
Other non-current liabilities (non-interest-bearing)	3,848
Total long-term liabilities	**56,125**
Total liabilities	**109,434**
Minority interest	47
Shareholders' equity	
Preference shares	269
Ordinary shareholders' equity	23,331
Total shareholders' equity	**23,600**
Total liabilities and shareholders' equity	**133,081**

Volkswagen standardized income statement (€ millions)

Fiscal year ending December 31,	2005
Sales	**95,268**
Cost of sales	(82,391)
Gross profit	**12,877**
SG&A	(11,288)
Other operating income, net of other operating expense	1,203
Operating profit	**2,792**
Investment income	53
Net interest expense (income)	(1,123)
Minority interest	0
Profit before tax	**1,722**
Tax expense	(602)
Net profit	**1,120**

Volkswagen standardized cash flow statement (€ millions)

Fiscal year ending December 31,	2005
Profit before tax	**1,722**
Taxes paid	(354)
After-tax net interest expense (income)	730
Non-operating losses (gains)	203
Non-current operating accruals	10,299
Operating cash flow before working capital investments	**12,600**
Net (investments in) or liquidation of operating working capital	(1,048)
Operating cash flow before investment in non-current assets	**11,552**

(continued)

Volkswagen Standardized Cash Flow Statement (€ millions) *(continued)*

Fiscal year ending December 31,	2005
Net (investment in) or liquidation of operating non-current assets	(10,466)
Free cash flow available to debt and equity	**1,086**
After-tax net interest expense (income)	(730)
Net debt (repayment) or issuance	(1,459)
Free cash flow available to equity	**(1,103)**
Dividend (payments)	(414)
Net stock (repurchase) or issuance	79
Net increase (decrease) in cash balance	**(1,438)**

Fiat Group's first-time adoption of IFRS[1]

In June 2002, the Council of the European Union adopted new regulations that required companies listed in the E.U. to prepare their consolidated financial statements in accordance with International Financial Reporting Standards (IFRS). According to the new rules, companies must apply IFRS no later than in the fiscal year starting in 2005. Member states of the E.U. could, however, allow companies that were listed outside the E.U. and prepared their statements in accordance with U.S. Generally Accepted Accounting Principles (U.S. GAAP) to apply IFRS in either 2006 or 2007.

The decision of the European Council also affected Italy-based car manufacturer Fiat, which had its shares traded on the Italian Stock Exchange and reported its financial statements in accordance with Italian accounting standards (henceforth Italian GAAP). The Fiat Group decided not to apply IFRS earlier than required and reported its first IFRS-based annual report in fiscal year 2005.

Business description and financial performance[2]

In 2005 the Italy-based Fiat Group generated its revenues primarily from the production and sales of passenger vehicles, tractors, agricultural equipment, and light commercial vehicles. Its portfolio of passenger car brands included large-volume brands such as Fiat, Alfa Romeo, and Lancia (generating €19.5 billion in revenues), as well as luxury, high-margin brands such as Maserati and Ferrari (generating €1.8 billion in revenues). In addition to these activities, the Fiat Group produced components and production systems, provided administrative and financial services to its group companies, published a daily newspaper (*La Stampa*), and sold advertising space for multimedia customers. Total revenues amounted to €46.5 billion in 2005. The company's pretax profit was €1 billion.

The Fiat Group had its ordinary shares traded on the Italian Stock Exchange and had American Depository Receipts (ADRs) traded on the New York Stock Exchange. About one quarter of the group's ordinary shares were widely held, 45 percent were in the hands of banks and other institutional investors, and 30 percent were held by Fiat's primary shareholder, IFIL investments, which was controlled by the Agnelli family. Through IFIL Investments and several other investment vehicles, the Agnelli family, who were the founders of Fiat, held a substantial voting block in the group. Fiat Group's board of directors consisted of three executive directors and 12 non-executive directors, of which eight were considered "independent" from the company and its major shareholder. The company's chairman of the board of directors was Luca Cordero di Montezemolo, former protégé of Fiat's long-time boss Gianni Agnelli, chief executive officer (CEO) of Fiat's subsidiary Ferrari, and chairman of Italy's employers association Confindustria. Vice-chairman was John Elkann, who was a member of the Agnelli family, and CEO was Sergio Marchionne.

---

1. *Professor Erik Peek prepared this case. The case is intended solely as the basis for class discussion and is not intended to serve as an endorsement, source of primary data, or illustration of effective or ineffective management.*
2. *This section is primarily based on the Fiat Group's 2005 Annual Report and Report on Corporate Governance.*

The first half of the 2000s had not been a successful period for the Fiat Group. Italian GAAP-based revenues had been declining from €57.5 billion in 2000 to €46.7 billion in 2004. Possible causes for the group's underperformance were the economic slowdown in Europe, the group's continued diversification into unrelated industries, and its lack of innovation and development of new car models. In fiscal 2005, however, the company reported a slight increase in (IFRS-based) revenues of 2 percent and its first net profit since 2000, inducing management to designate the year 2005 as a "turning point" for Fiat. In spring 2006, analysts expected the Fiat Group's revenues to grow from €46.5 billion in 2005 to approximately €50.5 billion in 2006 and €52.2 billion in 2007. They also expected the Fiat Group to remain profitable in the next two years. Estimated pretax profits for 2006 and 2007 were €1.2 billion and €1.7 billion, respectively.[3] Exhibit 1 shows the Fiat Group's stock price and accounting performance during the first half of the 2000s as well as its debt ratings in January 2006. In the first half of 2006 the Fiat Group made two Eurobond issues, each for €1 billion.

First-time adoption of IFRS

The general rule

In June 2003, the International Accounting Standards Board (IASB) issued IFRS 1 on firms' first-time adoption of IFRS. The objective of this new standard was to ensure that all firms preparing their financial statements for the first time in accordance with the IFRSs, (1) execute the transition to new reporting principles in a consistent manner and (2) provide sufficient additional disclosures to help the users of their statements understand the effects of the transition. IFRS 1 requires that a first-time adopter applies *retrospectively* the IFRSs that are *effective at the reporting date* of its first IFRS-based statements. Retrospective application of current IFRSs means that the firm recognizes all its assets and liabilities not only as if it has always applied IFRS but also as if the current IFRS version has always been effective and prior IFRS versions have never existed.[4] This illustrates that IFRS 1 aimed especially to improve comparability across first-time adopters, as opposed to improving comparability between first-time adopters and current users of IFRS, whose assets and liabilities are often affected by prior IFRS versions.

As well as the *reporting date* of the first IFRS statements, the *transition date* is important for the application of IFRS 1. The transition date is the beginning of the earliest fiscal year for which the first-time adopter prepares full IFRS-based comparative statements. Every first-time adopter is required to prepare an opening balance sheet at the transition date, although it is not required to publicly disclose this opening balance sheet. The accounting policies that a first-time adopter must use to prepare its opening balance sheet are the same policies that it uses to prepare its first IFRS-based financial statements (including the comparative statements).

Retrospective application of the IFRSs does not imply that on the transition date the first-time adopter can revise the estimates that it made for the same date under previous reporting standards. For example, if a first-time adopter receives information after the transition date that suggests that the economic life of one of its assets is three years instead of the previously assumed two years, the IFRS-based opening balance sheet on the transition date must reflect the "old" economic life assumption

---

3. Source: Reuters consensus estimates.
4. IFRS 1 allows first-time adopters to apply new IFRSs that will become effective on a date after the reporting date but that permit earlier application.

of two years. Hence, IFRS 1 explicitly forbids the first-time adopter modifying its prior financial statements with hindsight.

Exemptions

Retrospective application of current IFRSs may carry costs that exceed the benefits of the information that it produces. The IASB acknowledged the importance of a cost–benefit trade-off and included several exemptions from full retrospective application:

- The international standard on business combinations (IFRS 3) requires firms to recognize their acquisitions of other firms using purchase accounting. Under purchase accounting, a firm separately discloses on its balance sheet the fair value of the acquired assets as well as the excess of the purchase price over this amount (labeled goodwill). Under a few other accounting regimes, such as in the U.K., firms can – or could – record some of their acquisitions using pooling accounting, whereby the acquirer recorded only the historical cost of the acquired assets on its balance sheet. Retrospective application would require a firm to restate all past business combinations that it recorded using the pooling method. IFRS 1 allows first-time adopters not to restate business combinations that occurred prior to the transition date. If a firm nevertheless chooses to restate a business combination that occurred on a date prior to the transition date, it must also restate all other business combinations that occurred after this particular date.

- When a firm records its property, plant and equipment, intangible assets, and investment property at their (depreciated) historical cost, IFRS 1 allows it to assume that these assets' fair values at the transition date are the assets' historical cost. IFRS 1 refers to this assumed value as the assets' "deemed cost." Alternatively, if the firm has revalued any of these assets prior to the adoption of IFRS and the revalued amount is broadly comparable to fair value under IFRS, it can use the revalued amount as deemed cost.

- A first-time adopter may choose to immediately recognize (into equity) the cumulative actuarial gains and losses on all its pension plans. By doing so, the first-time adopter avoids splitting the cumulative gains and losses that have arisen since the inception of the plans into a recognized and an unrecognized portion, which may be a difficult exercise when the firm uses the "corridor approach" for recognizing actuarial gains and losses.[5]

- A firm that consolidates the translated values of subsidiaries' foreign currency-denominated assets on its balance sheet, recognizes the cumulative translation difference, which arises because exchange rates fluctuate over the years, as a separate component in equity. Because separately reporting restated cumulative translation differences generates little additional information, a first-time adopter can choose to add the cumulative translation differences to equity and reset the line item to zero upon adoption.

- International accounting rules require a firm to separate the debt from the equity component of convertible debentures – or similar compound financial instruments

---

5. *Unrecognized actuarial losses arise, for example, when a change in a firm's actuarial assumptions increases its pension obligation, but the resulting change in the obligation is not recognized as a pension expense. Under the "corridor approach," the firm annually compares the cumulative unrecognized actuarial gains and losses to the greater of 10 percent of the pension obligation or 10 percent of the fair value of the pension plan assets. When the cumulative unrecognized actuarial gains and losses exceed their benchmark, the firm amortizes the difference over the remaining working lives of the active employees.*

– and account for these separately. Consequently, the equity component of compound financial instruments may remain on the firm's balance sheet after the debt component is no longer outstanding. IFRS 1 allows a first-time adopter not to separate the debt and equity components of compound financial instruments if the debt component is no longer outstanding on the transition date.

■ A subsidiary that becomes a first-time adopter later than its parent can choose between reporting its assets and liabilities in accordance with IFRS 1 – using its own transition date – or reporting its assets and liabilities in accordance with the reporting principles used by its parent – using its parent's transition date. A parent that becomes a first-time adopter later than its subsidiary must report its subsidiary's assets and liabilities in its consolidated financial statements as they are reported in the subsidiary's financial statements.

■ International rules require firms to report stock options using the fair value method, under which they record an expense for stock option compensation when the options are issued. The value of the options issued is estimated using a recognized option valuation model and is then expensed over the vesting period. A first-time adopter is, however, not required to use this method for options that it issued prior to November 7, 2002 or that vested before the later of (1) the transition date and (2) January 1, 2005.

This list of optional exemptions is nonexhaustive because every time that the IASB issues a new reporting standard, it may decide to exempt a first-time adopter from retrospective application of the new standard. In addition to these optional exemptions, IFRS 1 includes a few mandatory exemptions. For example, a first-time adopter cannot rerecognize assets and liabilities that it derecognized prior to January 1, 2004, under its previous accounting principles.

Required disclosures

According to IFRS 1, a first-time adopter needs to disclose at least the following information in its first-time IFRS-based financial statements:

■ At least one year of comparative information under IFRSs. The comparative information of firms that adopted IFRS before January 1, 2006, such as the Fiat Group and most other listed firms in the E.U., need not comply with the international standards on financial instruments (IAS 32 and IAS 39) and on insurance contracts (IFRS 4). However, these firms must disclose the nature of the adjustments that would make the comparative information comply with these three reporting standards.

■ A reconciliation of equity under IFRS and equity under previous reporting standards at the transition date and at the end of the latest fiscal year prior to the first-time adoption of IFRS.

■ A reconciliation of the profit or loss under IFRS and under previous reporting standards in the latest fiscal year prior to the first-time adoption of IFRS.

■ The additional disclosures required by the international standard on the impairment of assets (IAS 36) if the firm recognized or reversed an impairment loss in its opening IFRS balance sheet.[6]

---

6. *These disclosures are, for example, the amount of impairment, with an indication of the income statement item under which the impairment was categorized; the events that gave rise to the impairment (reversal); the nature of the impaired asset or cash generating unit, and the discount rate used to determine the value in use or the basis for determining the net selling price.*

■ An explanation of the material adjustments made to the cash flow statement.

■ The aggregate adjustments that the firm made to the carrying amounts of the assets for which it uses the fair values as deemed cost.

The Fiat Group's first-time adoption of IFRS

For the Fiat Group the reporting date of its first IFRS statements was December 31, 2005. The company's transition date was January 1, 2004. Despite not being required to do so, the Fiat Group publicized its opening balance sheet for January 1, 2004 on May 11, 2005 in an appendix to the company's interim report for the first quarter of 2005. In addition to the 2004 opening balance sheet, the first-quarter report included an IFRS-based 2004 closing balance sheet, an IFRS-based 2004 income statement, and a reconciliation of IFRS-based and Italian GAAP-based opening and closing equity for fiscal 2004.

Exhibit 3 reports excerpts from appendix 1 to the 2005 financial statements of the Fiat Group. In this appendix, the group outlined the effects of the transition to IFRS on its balance sheet and income statement.

Questions

1. Are there any potential red flags that would make you extra careful when analyzing the Fiat Group's accounting choices?

2. Identify the areas where the Fiat Group had discretion when adopting IFRS for the first time. What are the most critical accounting choices that the Fiat Group made? Do you agree with these choices?

3. Would you characterize the disclosures that the Fiat Group made about the way it adopted IFRS as adequate? If not, what additional information would you need to carefully evaluate the Fiat Group's accounting choices upon first-time adoption of IFRS?

4. Assess, as accurately as possible, the impact that the Fiat Group's most critical accounting choices upon first-time adoption had on its 2004 profit/loss. Was the impact profit-increasing or profit-decreasing? What do you think that the impact was on the company's 2005 profit?

5. Overall, do you think that Italian GAAP profit or IFRS profit was a better reflection of the Fiat Group's performance in 2004?

EXHIBIT 1 Market performance and accounting performance for the Fiat Group

Fiat's stock price and the MSCI World Automobiles Price Index from January 2000 to December 2005

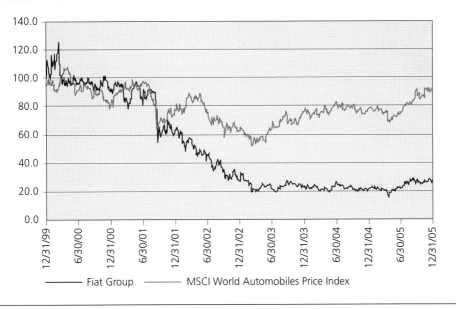

Source: Thomson Datastream.

Fiat's accounting performance from 2000 to 2005

(in € millions)	2005 (IFRS)	2004 (Italian GAAP)	2003 (Italian GAAP)	2002 (Italian GAAP)	2001 (Italian GAAP)	2000 (Italian GAAP)
Consolidated revenues	46,544	46,703	47,271	55,649	58,006	57,555
Operating result	2,215	−833	−510	−762	318	855
Group interest in net result	1,331	−1,586	−1,900	−3,948	−455	644
Group interest in stockholders' equity	8,681	5,099	6,793	7,641	12,170	13,320
Return on equity (in %)	15.3%	−26.7%	−26.3%	−39.9%	−3.5%	5.1%
Cash flow from operations	3,716	−358	−1,947	1,053	2,435	N.A.

Source: Annual reports of the Fiat Group.

Fiat's debt ratings in January 2006

Rating agency	Rating (long-term senior unsecured)	Date of rating	Rating (short-term senior unsecured)	Date of rating
Standard and Poor's	BB–	8/1/2005	B	8/2/2005
Fitch	BB–	1/20/2006	B	1/20/2006
Moody's	Ba3	1/31/2006		

Source: Reuters.

EXHIBIT 2 **Letter from the Chairman and the Chief Executive Officer, December 2005**

2005 marked a turning point for Fiat. We delivered on our commitments, we met all of our targets and we even exceeded a number of them. We had promised that 2004 would be Fiat's final year of net losses – and we achieved net income of over 1.4 billion euros in 2005. We had committed to a drastic cut in net industrial debt – and it was reduced by two-thirds. We had decided to focus on the relaunch of our Automobile activities, and in the last quarter of 2005 Fiat Auto posted a trading profit of 21 million euros after 17 consecutive quarters of losses. This has contributed to restoring Fiat's credibility, not only in Italy, but internationally, as evidenced by the improvement in our debt ratings and our ability to attract a large number of institutional investors in our debt raising activities. Our reputation has also benefited from the launch of new models across all brands that have been received extremely well by the public for their creativity, style, technology, and innovation, qualities that have distinguished the best Fiat cars since the firm was founded.

These breakthroughs, as well as all the other operational and financial improvements highlighted in this annual report, could not have been achieved without the strenuous efforts of the entire Fiat community, each and every one of whose members contributed to the relaunch of the Group with dedication and discipline. To do so, the Fiat people had to endorse fundamental changes in attitude, to assume greater responsibility and accountability, and to show their determination to deliver. We would like to express our sincere thanks to all of them.

During 2005, we also built a strong base for more effective and profitable operations in the future. First of all, we successfully resolved all pending strategic and financial issues: we settled our outstanding matters with General Motors and received a 1.56 billion euro cash payment; the Italenergia Bis transaction led to a 1.8 billion euro reduction in net industrial debt; and finally, conversion of the Mandatory Convertible Facility resulted in a 3 billion euro debt reduction and a sharp improvement in Group equity.

Fiat's business governance structure, especially in Automobiles, was right-sized to match realistic demand and market conditions. In Autos we have put in place a fully market-oriented organization, unbundling the brands: Fiat, Lancia and Alfa Romeo now face the customer on their own, while sharing key functions such as manufacturing, quality and safety.

Everything is driven by the brands and for the brands. Similarly, in Agricultural and Construction Equipment, Case New Holland was reorganized along four brands rather than regions. And we have begun to aggressively streamline processes throughout the organization. The Company will reap the benefits of these structural improvements in 2006 and beyond.

Last year, we made other important decisions that will shape the Group's future, in the form of targeted industrial alliances with major international partners. Seven such agreements were struck in the Automobile Sector – with Pars Industrial Development Foundation (PDIF), PSA-Tofas, Zastava, Suzuki, Ford, Severstal Auto and Tata Motors – while another partnership was established in commercial vehicles and industrial engines, between Iveco and SAIC.

Though much was done in 2005 to set the Company on course towards a real, lasting rebirth of our Group, the process is far from over and much remains to be done. Nonetheless, today's Fiat is a much different company from what it was just a year ago. The Group improved all key financial indicators. Our cash position – about 7 billion euros at 2005 year end – is strong. The financial markets are showing increased confidence in our prospects, as demonstrated by the steady appreciation of the Fiat share price. We have nearly completed the process of making our Internal Control System fully Sarbanes-Oxley compliant, a move that will further enhance confidence in the Group at the international level. The Fiat we are talking about is a Group with a reinvigorated managerial structure, a leaner organization, a solid financial structure and stronger market positions thanks to new products. This new Fiat can achieve new, challenging targets in 2006.

At Group level, we aim to deliver positive cash flow from operations, a trading profit between 1.6 and 1.8 billion euros, and net income of about 700 million euros. While we do not expect market conditions for our operating Sectors to change materially this year, we have set high trading margin targets (trading profit as a percentage of revenues) for all of them: 7% to 7.5% at CNH, 5.5% to 6% at Iveco, and 3.5% to 4% in Components and Production Systems. The Automobile Sector should also turn in a positive performance, with a trading margin of 0.5% to 1%. This result will be supported by the full-year contribution of new models already rolled out. These will be joined in coming months by other new models, as we implement our aggressive product renewal plan calling for the launch of 20 new cars and the restyling of 23 current models between 2005 and 2008.

We made a clean break with the past, while respecting all commitments made to stakeholders. We are clearly within reach of recovering our position as a competitive automotive Group. This is why we are keeping up the pressure that has enabled us to get this far, demanding much from ourselves and from all the men and women of the Fiat community. We have no intention of lessening the momentum that has allowed Fiat to generate a series of steady improvements, quarter after quarter, throughout 2005. We will remain focused on reducing costs in non-essential areas, while continuing to invest in innovation. We will complement our advanced technological resources with better commercial organization and more efficient services. Finally, we will continue to seek new international opportunities, implementing our strategy of targeted alliances with key partners who will help us reduce capital commitments, and share investments and risks.

It is for all these reasons that we feel confident about our future.

Turin, February 28, 2006
Luca Cordero di Montezemolo – Chairman
Sergio Marchionne – Chief Executive Officer

Fiat Group

EXHIBIT 3 Excerpts from Appendix 1 of Fiat's 2005 financial statements: Transition to international financial reporting standards

Following the coming into force of European Regulation No. 1606 dated July 19, 2002, starting from January 1, 2005, the Fiat Group adopted International Financial Reporting Standards (IFRS) issued by the International Accounting Standards Board (IASB).This Appendix provides the IFRS reconciliations of balance sheet data as of January 1 and December 31, 2004, and of income statement data for the year ended December 31, 2004 as required by IFRS 1 – First-time Adoption of IFRS, together with the related explanatory notes. This information has been prepared as part of the Group's conversion to IFRS and in connection with the preparation of its 2005 consolidated financial statements in accordance with IFRS, as adopted by the European Union.

Reconciliations required by IFRS 1

As required by IFRS 1, this note describes the policies adopted in preparing the IFRS opening consolidated balance sheet at January 1, 2004, the main differences in relation to Italian GAAP used to prepare the consolidated financial statements until December 31, 2004, as well as the consequent reconciliations between the figures already published, prepared in accordance with Italian GAAP, and the corresponding figures remeasured in accordance with IFRS. The 2004 restated IFRS consolidated balance sheet and income statement have been prepared in accordance with IFRS 1 – First-time Adoption of IFRS. In particular, the IFRS applicable from January 1, 2005, as published as of December 31, 2004, have been adopted, including the following:

- IAS 39 – Financial Instruments: Recognition and Measurement, in its entirety. In particular, the Group adopted derecognition requirements retrospectively from the date on which financial assets and financial liabilities had been derecognised under Italian GAAP.
- IFRS 2 – Share-based Payment, which was published by the IASB on February 19, 2004 and adopted by the European Commission on February 7, 2005.

First-time adoption of IFRS

General principle

The Group applied the accounting standards in force at December 31, 2004 retrospectively to all periods presented, and to the opening balance sheet except for certain exemptions adopted by the Group in accordance with IFRS 1, as described in the following paragraph. The opening balance sheet at January 1, 2004 reflects the following differences as compared to the consolidated balance sheet prepared at December 31, 2003 in accordance with Italian GAAP:

- All assets and liabilities qualifying for recognition under IFRS, including assets and liabilities that were not recognised under Italian GAAP, have been recognised and measured in accordance with IFRS.
- All assets and liabilities recognised under Italian GAAP that do not qualify for recognition under IFRS have been eliminated; certain balance sheet items have been reclassified in accordance with IFRS.
- The impact of these adjustments is recognised directly in opening equity at the date of transition to IFRS (January 1, 2004).

Optional exemptions adopted by the Group

Business combinations: The Group elected not to apply IFRS 3 – Business Combinations retrospectively to the business combinations that occurred before the date of transition to IFRS.

Employee benefits: The Group elected to recognise all cumulative actuarial gains and losses that existed at January 1, 2004, even though it decided to use the corridor approach for later actuarial gains and losses.

Cumulative translation differences: The cumulative translation differences arising from the consolidation of foreign operations have been set at nil as at January 1, 2004; gains or losses on subsequent disposal of any foreign operation shall only include accumulated translation differences after January 1, 2004.

Description of main differences between Italian GAAP and IFRS

The following paragraphs provide a description of the main differences between Italian GAAP and IFRS that have had effects on Fiat's consolidated balance sheet and income statement. Amounts are shown pre-tax and the related tax effects are separately summarised in the item R. Accounting for deferred income taxes.

A. Development costs

Under Italian GAAP applied research and development costs may alternatively be capitalised or charged to

Fiat Group

operations when incurred. Fiat Group has mainly expensed R&D costs when incurred. IAS 38 – Intangible Assets requires that research costs be expensed, whereas development costs that meet the criteria for capitalisation must be capitalised and then amortised from the start of production over the economic life of the related products.

Under IFRS, the Group has capitalised development costs in the Fiat Auto, Ferrari-Maserati, Agricultural and Construction Equipment, Commercial Vehicle and Components Sectors, using the retrospective approach in compliance with IFRS 1.

The positive impact of 1,876 million euros on the opening IFRS stockholders' equity at January 1, 2004, corresponds to the cumulative amount of qualifying development expenditures incurred in prior years by the Group, net of accumulated amortisation. Consistently, intangible assets show an increase of 2,090 million euros and of 2,499 million euros at January 1, 2004 and at December 31, 2004, respectively.

The 2004 net result was positively impacted by 436 million euros in the year, reflecting the combined effect of the capitalisation of development costs incurred in the period that had been expensed under Italian GAAP, and the amortisation of the amount that had been capitalised in the opening IFRS balance sheet at January 1, 2004. This positive impact has been accounted for in Research and development costs.

In accordance with IAS 36 – Impairment of Assets, development costs capitalised as intangible assets shall be tested for impairment and an impairment loss shall be recognised if the recoverable amount of an asset is less than its carrying amount, as further described in the paragraph I. Impairment of assets.

B. Employee benefits

The Group sponsors funded and unfunded defined benefit pension plans, as well as other long term benefits to employees.

Under Italian GAAP, these benefits, with the exception of the Reserve for Employee Severance Indemnities ("TFR") that is accounted for in compliance with a specific Italian law, are mainly recorded in accordance with IAS 19 – Employee Benefits, applying the corridor approach, which consists of amortising over the remaining service lives of active employees only the portion of net cumulative actuarial gains and losses that exceeds the greater of 10% of either the defined benefit obligation or the fair value of the plan assets, while the portion included in the 10% remains unrecognised.

With the adoption of IFRS, TFR is considered a defined benefit obligation to be accounted for in accordance with IAS 19 and consequently has been recalculated applying the Projected Unit Credit Method. Furthermore, as mentioned in the paragraph "Optional exemptions", the Group elected to recognise all cumulative actuarial gains and losses that existed at January 1, 2004, with a negative impact on opening stockholders' equity at that date of 1,247 million euros.

Consequently pension and other post-employment benefit costs recorded in the 2004 IFRS income statement do not include any amortisation of unrecognised actuarial gains and losses deferred in previous years in the IFRS financial statements under the corridor approach, and recognised in the 2004 income statement under Italian GAAP, resulting in a benefit of 94 million euros.

The Group has elected to use the corridor approach for actuarial gains and losses arising after January 1, 2004.

Furthermore, the Group elected to state the expense related to the reversal of discounting on defined benefit plans without plan assets separately as Financial expenses, with a corresponding increase in Financial expenses of 127 million euros in 2004.

C. Business combinations

As mentioned above, the Group elected not to apply IFRS 3 – Business Combinations retrospectively to business combinations that occurred before the date of transition to IFRS.

As prescribed in IFRS 3, starting from January 1, 2004, the IFRS income statement no longer includes goodwill amortisation charges, resulting in a positive impact on Other operating income and expense of 162 million euros in 2004.

D. Revenue recognition – sales with a buy-back commitment

Under Italian GAAP, the Group recognised revenues from sales of products at the time title passed to the customer, which was generally at the time of shipment. For contracts for vehicle sales with a buy-back commitment at a specified price, a specific reserve for future risks and charges was set aside based on the difference between the guaranteed residual value and the estimated realisable value of vehicles, taking into account the probability that such option would be exercised. This reserve was set up at the time of the initial sale and adjusted periodically over the period of the contract. The costs of refurbishing the vehicles, to be incurred when the buy-back option is exercised, were reasonably estimated and accrued at the time of the initial sale.

Under IAS 18 – Revenue, new vehicle sales with a buy-back commitment do not meet criteria for revenue recognition, because the significant risks and rewards of ownership of the goods are not necessarily transferred to the buyer. Consequently, this kind of contract is treated in a manner similar to an operating lease transaction. More specifically, vehicles sold with a buy-back commitment are accounted for as Inventory if they regard the Fiat Auto business (agreements with normally a short-term buy-back commitment) and as Property, plant and equipment if they regard the Commercial Vehicles business (agreements with normally a long-term buy-back commitment). The difference between the carrying value (corresponding to the manufacturing cost) and the estimated resale value (net of refurbishing costs) at the end of the buy-back period, is depreciated on a straight-line basis over the duration of the contract. The initial sale price received is accounted for as a liability. The difference between the initial sale price and the buy-back price is recognised as rental revenue on a straight-line basis over the duration of the contract.

Opening IFRS stockholders' equity at January 1, 2004 includes a negative impact of 180 million euros mainly representing the portion of the margin accounted for under Italian GAAP on vehicles sold with a buy-back commitment prior to January 1, 2004, that will be recognised under IFRS over the remaining buy-back period, net of the effects due to the adjustments to the provisions for vehicle sales with a buy-back commitment recognised under Italian GAAP.

This accounting treatment results in increases in the tangible assets reported in the balance sheet (1,001 million euros at January 1, 2004 and 1,106 million euros at December 31, 2004), in inventory (608 million euros at January 1, 2004 and 695 million euros at December 31, 2004), in advances from customers (equal to the operating lease rentals prepaid at the date of initial sale and recognised in the item Other payables), as well as in Trade payables, for the amount of the buy-back price, payable to the customer when the vehicle is bought back. In the income statement, a significant impact is generated on revenues (reduced by 1,103 million euros in 2004) and on cost of sales (reduced by 1,090 million euros in 2004), while no significant impact is generated on the net operating result; furthermore, the amount of these impacts in future years will depend on the changes in the volume

and characteristics of these contracts year-over-year. Notwithstanding this, these changes are not expected to have a particularly significant impact on Group reported earnings in the coming years.

E. Revenue recognition – Other

Under Italian GAAP the recognition of disposals is based primarily on legal and contractual form (transfer of legal title).

Under IFRS, when risks and rewards are not substantially transferred to the buyer and the seller maintains a continuous involvement in the operations or assets being sold, the transaction is not recognised as a sale.

Consequently, certain disposal transactions, such as the disposal of the 14% interest in Italenergia Bis and certain minor real estate transactions, have been reversed retrospectively: the related asset has been recognised in the IFRS balance sheet, the initial gain recorded under Italian GAAP has been reversed and the cash received at the moment of the sale has been accounted for as a financial liability.

In particular, in 2001 the Group acquired a 38.6% shareholding in Italenergia S.p.A., now Italenergia Bis S.p.A. ("Italenergia"), a company formed between Fiat, Electricité de France ("EDF") and certain financial investors for the purpose of acquiring control of the Montedison – Edison ("Edison") group through tender offers. Italenergia assumed effective control of Edison at the end of the third quarter of that year and consolidated Edison from October 1, 2001. In 2002 the shareholders of Italenergia entered into agreements which resulted, among other things, in the transfer of a 14% interest in Italenergia from Fiat to other shareholders (with a put option that would require Fiat to repurchase the shares transferred in certain circumstances) and the assignment to Fiat of a put option to sell its shares in Italenergia to EDF in 2005, based on market values at that date, but subject to a contractually agreed minimum price in excess of book value.

Under Italian GAAP, Fiat accounted for its investments in Italenergia under the equity method, based on a 38.6% shareholding through September 30, 2002 and a 24.6% shareholding from October 1, 2002; in addition it recorded a gain of 189 million euros before taxes on the sale of its 14% interest in the investee to other shareholders effective September 30, 2002.

Under IFRS, the transfer of the 14% interest in Italenergia to the other shareholders was not considered to meet the requirements for revenue recognition set out in IAS 18, mainly due to the existence of the put options granted to the transferees and de facto constraints on the transferees' ability to pledge or exchange the transferred assets in the period from the sale through 2005. Accordingly, the gain recorded in 2002 for the sale was reversed, and the results of applying the equity method of accounting to the investment in Italenergia was recomputed to reflect a 38.6% interest in the net results and stockholders' equity of the investee, as adjusted for the differences between Italian GAAP and IFRS applicable to Italenergia.

This adjustment decreased the stockholders' equity at January 1, 2004 and at December 31, 2004 by an amount of 153 million euros and 237 million euros, respectively. Furthermore this adjustment increased the investment for an amount of 291 million euros at January 1, 2004 and of 341 million euros at December 31, 2004 and financial debt for amounts of 572 million euros at January 1, 2004 and of 593 million euros at December 31, 2004, as a consequence of the non-recognition of the transfer of the 14% interest in Italenergia.

F. Scope of consolidation

Under Italian GAAP, the subsidiary B.U.C. – Banca Unione di Credito – as required by law, was excluded from the scope of consolidation as it had dissimilar activities, and was accounted for using the equity method.

IFRS does not permit this kind of exclusion: consequently, B.U.C. is included in the IFRS scope of consolidation. Furthermore, under Italian GAAP investments that are not controlled on a legal basis or a de facto basis determined considering voting rights were excluded from the scope of consolidation.

Under IFRS, in accordance with SIC 12 – Consolidation – Special Purpose Entities, a Special Purpose Entity ("SPE") shall be consolidated when the substance of the relationship between an entity and the SPE indicates that the SPE is controlled by that entity.

This standard has been applied to all receivables securitisation transactions entered into by the Group (see the paragraph Q. Sales of receivables below), to a real estate securitisation transaction entered into in 1998 and to the sale of the Fiat Auto Spare Parts business to "Società di Commercializzazione e Distribuzione Ricambi S.p.A." ("SCDR") in 2001.

In particular, in 1998 the Group entered in a real estate securitisation and, under Italian GAAP, the related revenue was recognised at the date of the legal transfer of the assets involved. In the IFRS balance sheet at January 1, 2004, these assets have been written back at their historical cost, net of revaluations

accounted before the sale, if any. Cash received at the time of the transaction has been accounted for in financial debt for an amount of 188 million euros at January 1, 2004.

The IFRS stockholders' equity at January 1, 2004 was negatively impacted for 105 million euros by the cumulative effect of the reversal of the capital gain on the initial disposal and of the revaluation previously recognised under Italian GAAP, net of the related effect of asset depreciation, as well as the recognition of financial charges on related debt, net of the reversal of rental fees paid, if any. The impact on the 2004 net result is not material.

Furthermore, in 2001 the Group participated with a specialist logistics operator and other financial investors in the formation of "Società di Commercializzazione e Distribuzione Ricambi S.p.A." ("SCDR"), a company whose principal activity is the purchase of spare parts from Fiat Auto for resale to end customers. At that date Fiat Auto and its subsidiaries sold their spare parts inventory to SCDR recording a gain of 300 million euros. The Group's investment in SCDR represents 19% of SCDR's stock capital and was accounted for under the equity method for Italian GAAP.

Under IFRS, SCDR qualifies as a Special Purpose Entity (SPE) as defined by SIC 12 due to the continuing involvement of Fiat Auto in SCDR operations. Consequently, SCDR has been consolidated on a line by line basis in the IFRS consolidated financial statements, with a consequent increase in financial debt of 237 million euros and of 471 million euros at January 1, 2004 and at December 31, 2004, respectively. Opening stockholders' equity at January 1, 2004 was reduced by 266 million euros by the amount corresponding to the unrealised intercompany profit in inventory held by SCDR on that date; this amount did not change significantly at the end of 2004.

G. Property, plant and equipment

Under Italian GAAP and IFRS, assets included in Property, Plant and Equipment were generally recorded at cost, corresponding to the purchase price plus the direct attributable cost of bringing the assets to their working condition.

Under Italian GAAP, Fiat revalued certain Property, Plant and Equipment to amounts in excess of historical cost, as permitted or required by specific laws of the countries in which the assets were located. These revaluations were credited to stockholders' equity and the revalued assets were depreciated over their remaining useful lives.

Furthermore, under Italian GAAP, the land directly related to buildings included in Property, Plant and Equipment was depreciated together with the related building depreciation.

The revaluations and land depreciation are not permitted under IFRS. Therefore IFRS stockholders' equity at January 1, 2004 reflects a negative impact of 164 million euros, related to the effect of the elimination of the asset revaluation recognised in the balance sheet, partially offset by the reversal of the land depreciation charged to prior period income statements.

In the 2004 IFRS income statement, the above-mentioned adjustments had a positive impact of 14 million euros in 2004 due to the reversal of the depreciation of revalued assets, net of adjustments on gains and losses, if any, on disposal of the related assets, and to the reversal of land depreciation.

H. Write-off of deferred costs

Under Italian GAAP, the Group deferred and amortised certain costs (mainly start-up and related charges). IFRS require these to be expensed when incurred.

In addition, costs incurred in connection with share capital increases, which are also deferred and amortised under Italian GAAP, are deducted directly from the proceeds of the increase and debited to stockholders' equity under IFRS.

I. Impairment of assets

Under Italian GAAP, the Group tested its intangible assets with indefinite useful lives (mainly goodwill) for impairment annually by comparing their carrying amount with their recoverable amount in terms of the value in use of the asset itself (or group of assets). In determining the value in use the Group estimated the future cash inflows and outflows of the asset (or group of assets) to be derived from the continuing use of the asset and from its ultimate disposal, and discounted those future cash flows. If the recoverable amount was lower than the carrying value, an impairment loss was recognised for the difference.

With reference to tangible fixed assets, under Italian GAAP the Group accounted for specific write-offs when the asset was no longer to be used. Furthermore, in the presence of impairment indicators, the Group tested tangible fixed assets for impairment using the undiscounted cash flow method in determining the recoverable amount of homogeneous group of assets. If the recoverable amount thus determined was lower than the carrying value, an impairment loss was recognised for the difference.

Under IFRS, intangible assets with indefinite useful lives are tested for impairment annually by a methodology substantially similar to the one required by Italian GAAP. Furthermore, development costs, capitalised under IFRS and expensed under Italian GAAP, are attributed to the related cash generating unit and tested for impairment together with the related tangible assets, applying the discounted cash flow method in determining their recoverable amount.

Consequently, the reconciliation between Italian GAAP and IFRS reflects adjustments due to both impairment losses on development costs previously capitalised for IFRS purposes, and the effect of discounting on the determination of the recoverable amount of tangible fixed assets.

L. Reserves for risks and charges

Differences between Italian GAAP and IFRS refer mainly to the following items:

■ Restructuring reserve: the Group provided restructuring reserves based upon management's best estimate of the costs to be incurred in connection with each of its restructuring programs at the time such programs were formally decided. Under IFRS the requirements to recognise a constructive obligation in the financial statements are more restrictive, and some restructuring reserves recorded under Italian GAAP have been eliminated.

■ Reserve for vehicle sales incentives: under Italian GAAP Fiat Auto accounted for certain incentives at the time at which a legal obligation to pay the incentives arose, which may have been in periods subsequent to that in which the initial sale to the dealer network was made. Under IAS 37 companies are required to make provision not only for legal, but also for constructive, obligations based on an established pattern of past practice. In the context of the IFRS restatement exercise, Fiat has reviewed its practice in the area of vehicle sales incentives and has determined that for certain forms of incentives a constructive obligation exists which should be provided under IFRS at the date of sale.

M. Recognition and measurement of derivatives

Beginning in 2001 the Fiat Group adopted – to the extent that it is consistent and not in contrast with general principles set forth in the Italian law governing financial statements – IAS 39 Financial Instruments: Recognition and Measurement. In particular, taking into account the restrictions under Italian law, the

Fiat Group

Group maintained that IAS 39 was applicable only in part and only in reference to the designation of derivative financial instruments as "hedging" or "nonhedging instruments" and with respect to the symmetrical accounting of the result of the valuation of the hedging instruments and the result attributable to the hedged items ("hedge accounting"). The transactions which, according to the Group's policy for risk management, were able to meet the conditions stated by the accounting principle for hedge accounting treatment, were designated as hedging transactions; the others, although set up for the purpose of managing risk exposure (inasmuch as the Group's policy does not permit speculative transactions), were designated as "trading". The main differences between Italian GAAP and IFRS may be summarised as follows:

- Instruments designated as "hedging instruments" – under Italian GAAP, the instrument was valued symmetrically with the underlying hedged item. Therefore, where the hedged item was not adjusted to fair value in the financial statements, the hedging instrument was also not adjusted. Similarly, where the hedged item had not yet been recorded in the financial statements (hedging of future flows), the valuation of the hedging instrument at fair value was deferred. Under IFRS:

  ❏ In the case of a fair value hedge, the gains or losses from remeasuring the hedging instrument at fair value shall be recognised in the income statement and the gains or losses on the hedged item attributable to the hedge risk shall adjust the carrying amount of the hedged item and be recognised in the income statement. Consequently, no impact arises on net income (except for the ineffective portion of the hedge, if any) and on net equity, while adjustments impact the carrying values of hedging instruments and hedged items.

  ❏ In the case of a cash flow hedge (hedging of future flows), the portion of gains or losses on the hedging instrument that is determined to be an effective hedge shall be recognised directly in equity through the statement of changes in equity; the ineffective portion of the gains or losses shall be recognised in the income statement. Consequently, with reference to the effective portion, only a difference in net equity arises between Italian GAAP and IFRS.

- Instruments designated as "non-hedging instruments" (except for foreign currency derivative instruments) – under Italian GAAP, these instruments were

valued at market value and the differential, if negative compared to the contractual value, was recorded in the income statement, in accordance with the concept of prudence. Under IAS 39 the positive differential should also be recorded. With reference to foreign currency derivative instruments, instead, the accounting treatment adopted under Italian GAAP was in compliance with IAS 39.

In this context, as mentioned in the consolidated financial statements as of December 31, 2003, Fiat was party to a Total Return Equity Swap contract on General Motors shares, in order to hedge the risk implicit in the Exchangeable Bond on General Motors shares. Although this equity swap was entered into for hedging purposes it does not qualify for hedge accounting and accordingly it was defined as a non-hedging instrument. Consequently, the positive fair value of the instrument as of December 31, 2003, amounting to 450 million euros, had not been recorded under Italian GAAP. During 2004 Fiat terminated the contract, realising a gain of 300 million euros.

In the IFRS restatement, the above mentioned positive fair value at December 31, 2003 has been recognized in opening equity, while, following the unwinding of the swap, a negative adjustment of the same amount has been recorded in the 2004 income statement.

N. Treasury stock

In accordance with Italian GAAP, the Group accounted for treasury stock as an asset and recorded related valuation adjustments and gains or losses on disposal in the income statement.

Under IFRS, treasury stock is deducted from stockholders' equity and all movements in treasury stock are recognised in stockholders' equity rather than in the income statement.

O. Stock options

Under Italian GAAP, with reference to share-based payment transactions, no obligations or compensation expenses were recognised.

In accordance with IFRS 2 – Share-based Payment, the full amount fair value of stock options on the date of grant must be expensed. Changes in fair value after the grant date have no impact on the initial measurement. The compensation expense corresponding to the option's fair value is recognised in payroll costs on a straight-line basis over the period from the grant date to the vesting date, with the offsetting credit recognised directly in equity.

The Group applied the transitional provision provided by IFRS 2 and therefore applied this standard to all stock options granted after November 7, 2002 and not yet vested at the effective date of IFRS 2 (January 1, 2005). No compensation expense is required to be recognised for stock options granted prior to November 7, 2002, in accordance with transitional provision of IFRS 2.

P. Adjustments to the valuation of investments in associates

These items represent the effect of the IFRS adjustments on the Group portion of the net equity of associates accounted for using the equity method.

Q. Sales of receivables

The Fiat Group sells a significant part of its finance, trade and tax receivables through either securitisation programs or factoring transactions.

A securitisation transaction entails the sale without recourse of a portfolio of receivables to a securitisation vehicle (special purpose entity). This special purpose entity finances the purchase of the receivables by issuing asset-backed securities (i.e. securities whose repayment and interest flow depend upon the cash flow generated by the portfolio). Asset-backed securities are divided into classes according to their degree of seniority and rating: the most senior classes are placed with investors on the market; the junior class, whose repayment is subordinated to the senior classes, is normally subscribed for by the seller. The residual interest in the receivables retained by the seller is therefore limited to the junior securities it has subscribed for.

Factoring transactions may be with or without recourse on the seller; certain factoring agreements without recourse include deferred purchase price clauses (i.e. the payment of a minority portion of the purchase price is conditional upon the full collection of the receivables), require a first loss guarantee of the seller up to a limited amount or imply a continuing significant exposure to the receivables cash flow.

Under Italian GAAP, all receivables sold through either securitisation or factoring transactions (both with and without recourse) had been derecognised. Furthermore, with specific reference to the securitisation of retail loans and leases originated by the financial services companies, the net present value of the interest flow implicit in the instalments, net of related costs, had been recognised in the income statement.

Under IFRS:

- As mentioned above, SIC 12 – Consolidation – Special Purpose Entities states that an SPE shall be consolidated when the substance of the relationship between the entity and the SPE indicates that the SPE is controlled by that entity; therefore all securitisation transactions have been reversed.

- IAS 39 allows for the derecognition of a financial asset when, and only when, the risks and rewards of the ownership of the assets are substantially transferred: consequently, all portfolios sold with recourse, and the majority of those sold without recourse, have been reinstated in the IFRS balance sheet.

The impact of such adjustments on stockholders' equity and on net income is not material. In particular, it refers mainly to the reversal of the gains arising from the related securitisation transactions on the retail portfolio of receivables of financial service companies, realised under Italian GAAP and not yet realised under IFRS.

With regards to financial structure, the reinstatement in the balance sheet of the receivables and payables involved in these sales transactions causes a significant increase in trade and financial receivables and in financial debt balances, and a worsening in net debt. In particular, in consequence of these reinstatements, trade receivables increase by 3,563 million euros and 2,134 euros at January 1, 2004 and at December 31, 2004, respectively; at the same dates, financial receivables increase by 6,127 million euros and 6,997 euros, and financial debt increased by 10,581 million euros and 10,174 million euros, respectively.

R. Accounting for deferred income taxes

This item includes the combined effect of the net deferred tax effects, after allowance, on the above mentioned IFRS adjustments, as well as other minor differences between Italian GAAP and IFRS on the recognition of tax assets and liabilities.

Fiat Group

Effects of transition to IFRS on the consolidated balance sheet at January 1, 2004

(in € millions)	Italian GAAP	Reclassifi- cations	Adjust- ments	IAS/IFRS	
Intangible assets, of which:	3,724		1,774	5,498	Intangible assets, of which:
Goodwill	2,402			2,402	Goodwill
Other intangible fixed assets	1,322		1,774	3,096	Other intangible fixed assets
Property, plant and equipment, of which:	9,675	(945)	817	9,547	Property, plant and equipment
Property, plant and equipment	8,761	(31)			
Operating leases	914	(914)			
		31		31	Investment property
Financial fixed assets	3,950	70	(121)	3,899	Investment and other financial assets
Financial receivables held as fixed assets	29	(29)			
		914	(50)	864	Leased assets
Deferred tax assets	1,879		266	2,145	Deferred tax assets
Total Non-Current assets	**19,257**	**41**	**2,686**	**21,984**	**Non-current assets**
Net inventories	6,484		1,113	7,597	Inventories
Trade receivables	4,553	(682)	2,678	6,549	Trade receivables
		12,890	7,937	20,827	Receivables from financing activities
Other receivables	3,081	(148)	541	3,474	Other receivables
		407	10	417	Accrued income and prepaid expenses
				2,129	Current financial assets, of which:
		32		32	Current equity investments
		515	260	775	Current securities
		430	892	1,322	Other financial assets
Financial assets not held as fixed assets	120	(120)			
Financial lease contracts receivable	1,797	(1,797)			
Financial receivables	10,750	(10,750)			
Securities	3,789	(3,789)			
Cash	3,211	3,214	420	6,845	Cash and cash equivalents
Total Current assets	**33,785**	**202**	**13,851**	**47,838**	**Current assets**
Trade accruals and deferrals	407	(407)			
Financial accruals and deferrals	386	(386)			
			21	21	Assets held for sale
TOTAL ASSETS	**53,835**	**(550)**	**16,558**	**69,843**	**TOTAL ASSETS**

(continued)

Effects of transition to IFRS on the consolidated balance sheet at January 1, 2004 *(continued)*

(in € millions)	Italian GAAP	Reclassifi- cations	Adjust- ments	IAS/IFRS	
Stockholders' equity	**7,494**	**(934)**		**6,560**	**Stockholders' equity**
				7,455	Provisions, of which:
Reserves for employee severance indemnities	*1,313*	*1,503*	*1,224*	*4,040*	*Employee benefits*
Reserves for risks and charges	*5,168*	*(1,550)*	*(203)*	*3,415*	*Other provisions*
Deferred income tax reserves	211	(211)			
Long-term financial payables	15,418	6,501	14,790	36,709	Debt, of which:
				10,581	*Asset-backed financing*
				26,128	*Other debt*
Total Non-current liabilities	**22,110**	**6,243**			
		568	(223)	345	Other financial liabilities
Trade payables	12,588		(297)	12,291	Trade payables
Others payables	2,742		1,948	4,690	Other payables
Short-term financial payables	6,616	(6,616)			
Total Current liabilities	**21,946**	**(6,048)**			
		211	274	485	Deferred tax liabilities
Trade accruals and deferrals	1,329		(21)	1,308	Accrued expenses and deferred income
Financial accruals and deferrals	956	(956)			
					Liabilities held for sale
TOTAL LIABILITIES AND STOCKHOLDERS' EQUITY	**53,835**	**(550)**	**(934)**	**69,843**	**TOTAL STOCKHOLDERS' EQUITY AND LIABILITIES**

Fiat Group

Effects of transition to IFRS on the consolidated balance sheet at December 31, 2004

(in € millions)	Italian GAAP	Reclassi- fications	Adjust- ments	IAS/IFRS	
Intangible assets, of which:	3,322		2,256	5,578	Intangible assets, of which:
Goodwill	*2,140*		*17*	*2,157*	*Goodwill*
Other intangible fixed assets	*1,182*		*2,239*	*3,421*	*Other intangible fixed assets*
Property, plant and equipment, of which:	9,537	(874)	774	9,437	Property, plant and equipment
Property, plant and equipment	*8,709*	*(46)*			
Operating leases	*828*	*(828)*			
		46		46	Investment property
Financial fixed assets	3,779	86	160	4,025	Investment and other financial assets
Financial receivables held as fixed assets	19	(19)			
		828	(88)	740	Leased assets
Deferred tax assets	2,161		241	2,402	Deferred tax assets
Total Non-Current assets	**18,818**	**67**	**3,343**	**22,228**	**Non-current assets**

(continued)

Effects of transition to IFRS on the consolidated balance sheet at December 31, 2004 *(continued)*

(in € millions)	Italian GAAP	Reclassi-fications	Adjust-ments	IAS/IFRS	
Net inventories	5,972		1,285	7,257	Inventories
Trade receivables	4,777	(755)	1,469	5,491	Trade receivables
		9,662	7,836	17,498	Receivables from financing activities
Other receivables	3,021	(508)	221	2,734	Other receivables
		398	(103)	295	Accrued income and prepaid expenses
				1,237	Current financial assets, of which:
		33		*33*	*Current equity investments*
		135	*218*	*353*	*Current securities*
		599	*252*	*851*	*Other financial assets*
Financial assets not held as fixed assets	117	(117)			
Financial lease contracts receivable	1,727	(1,727)			
Financial receivables	7,151	(7,151)			
Securities	2,126	(2,126)			
Cash	3,164	1,896	707	5,767	Cash and cash equivalents
Total Current assets	**28,055**	**339**	**11,885**	**40,279**	**Current assets**
Trade accruals and deferrals	398	(398)			
Financial accruals and deferrals	3276	(327)			
			15	15	Assets held for sale
TOTAL ASSETS	**47,598**	**(319)**	**15,243**	**62,522**	**TOTAL ASSETS**
Stockholders' equity	**5,757**		**(829)**	**4,928**	**Stockholders' equity**
				7,290	Provisions, of which:
Reserves for employee severance indemnities	*1,286*	*1,432*	*964*	*3,682*	*Employee benefits*
Reserves for risks and charges	*5,185*	*(1,449)*	*(128)*	*3,608*	*Other provisions*
Deferred income tax reserves	197	(197)			
Long-term financial payables	8,933	9,611	13,647	32,191	Debt, of which:
				10,174	*Asset-backed financing*
				22,017	*Other debt*
Total Non-current liabilities	**15,601**	**9,397**			
		629	(426)	203	Other financial liabilities
Trade payables	11,955		(258)	11,697	Trade payables
Others payables	2,565		1,996	4,561	Other payables
Short-term financial payables	9,810	(9,810)			
Total Current liabilities	**24,330**	**(9,181)**			
		197	325	522	Deferred tax liabilities
Trade accruals and deferrals	1,178		(48)	1,130	Accrued expenses and deferred income
Financial accruals and deferrals	732	(732)			
					Liabilities held for sale
TOTAL LIABILITIES AND STOCKHOLDERS' EQUITY	**47,598**	**(319)**	**(829)**	**65,522**	**TOTAL STOCKHOLDERS' EQUITY AND LIABILITIES**

Fiat Group

Effects of transition to IFRS on the income statement for the year ended December 31, 2004

(in € millions)	Italian GAAP	Reclassi- fications	Adjust- ments	IAS/IFRS	
Net revenues	46,703		(1,066)	45,637	Net revenues
Cost of sales	39,623	675	(1,177)	39,121	Cost of sales
Gross operating result	**7,080**				
Overhead	4,629	51	21	4,701	Selling, general and administrative costs
Research and development	1,810	1	(461)	1,350	Research and development costs
Other operating income (expenses)	(619)	346	(142)	(415)	Other income (expenses)
Operating result	**22**	**(381)**	**409**	**50**	**Trading profit**
		154	(4)	150	Gains (losses) on the disposal of equity investments
		496	46	542	Restructuring costs
		(243)		(243)	Other unusual income (expenses)
		(966)	**359**	**(585)**	**Operating result**
		(641)	(538)	(1,179)	Financial income
Result from equity investments	8		127	135	Result from equity investments
Non-operating income (expenses)	(863)	863			
EBIT	**(833)**				
Financial income (expenses)	(744)	744			
Income (loss) before taxes	**(1,577)**		**(52)**	**(1,629)**	**Result before taxes**
Income taxes	(29)		(21)	(50)	Income taxes
Net result of normal operations	**(1,548)**		**(31)**	**(1,579)**	**Net result of normal operations**
Result from discontinued operations					Result from discontinued operations
Net result before minority interest	**(1,548)**		**(31)**	**(1,579)**	**Net result before minority interest**

Fiat Group

Financial Analysis

The goal of financial analysis is to assess the performance of a firm in the context of its stated goals and strategy. There are two principal tools of financial analysis: ratio analysis and cash flow analysis. Ratio analysis involves assessing how various line items in a firm's financial statements relate to one another. Cash flow analysis allows the analyst to examine the firm's liquidity, and how the firm is managing its operating, investment, and financing cash flows.

Financial analysis is used in a variety of contexts. Ratio analysis of a company's present and past performance provides the foundation for making forecasts of future performance. As we will discuss in later chapters, financial forecasting is useful in company valuation, credit evaluation, financial distress prediction, security analysis, mergers and acquisitions analysis, and corporate financial policy analysis.

RATIO ANALYSIS

The value of a firm is determined by its profitability and growth. As shown in Figure 5.1, the firm's growth and profitability are influenced by its product market and financial market strategies. The product market strategy is implemented through the firm's competitive strategy, operating policies, and investment decisions. Financial market strategies are implemented through financing and dividend policies.

Thus the four levers managers can use to achieve their growth and profit targets are (1) operating management, (2) investment management, (3) financing strategy, and (4) dividend policies. The objective of ratio analysis is to evaluate the effectiveness of the firm's policies in each of these areas. Effective ratio analysis involves relating the financial numbers to the underlying business factors in as much detail as possible. While ratio analysis may not give all the answers to an analyst regarding the firm's performance, it will help the analyst frame questions for further probing.

In ratio analysis, the analyst can (1) compare ratios for a firm over several years (a time-series comparison), (2) compare ratios for the firm and other firms in the industry (cross-sectional comparison), and/or (3) compare ratios to some absolute benchmark. In a time-series comparison, the analyst can hold firm-specific factors constant and examine the effectiveness of a firm's strategy over time. Cross-sectional comparison facilitates examining the relative performance of a firm within its industry, holding industry-level factors constant. For most ratios there are no absolute benchmarks. The exceptions are measures of rates of return, which can be compared to the cost of the capital associated with the investment. For example, subject to distortions caused by accounting, the rate of return on equity (ROE) can be compared to the cost of equity capital.

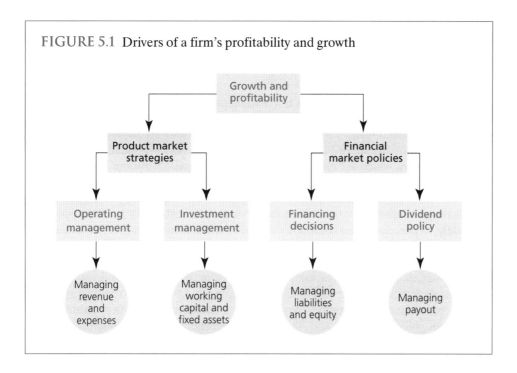

FIGURE 5.1 Drivers of a firm's profitability and growth

In the discussion below, we will illustrate these approaches using the example of Volkswagen AG, a prominent German car manufacturer. We will compare Volkswagen's ratios for the fiscal year ending December 31, 2005, with its own ratios for the fiscal year ending December 31, 2004, and with the ratios for Dr. Ing. h.c.F. Porsche AG, another German car manufacturer, for the fiscal year ending July 31, 2005.[1]

Volkswagen is in the middle of implementing a cost savings program, so analyzing its performance over time allows us to assess how well the program is working in terms of financial performance. Comparison of Volkswagen with Porsche allows us to see the impact of different strategies on financial ratios. While pursuing different competitive strategies, Volkswagen and Porsche also follow different investment and financing strategies. Porsche has low debt and substantial holdings of cash and marketable securities, anticipating a cash-financed acquisition of a 20 percent stake in Volkswagen. Volkswagen uses more debt financing than Porsche and holds less cash and marketable securities. Further, Volkswagen delivers more rental and other financial services to its customers than Porsche. We will illustrate how these differences between the two companies affect their ratios. We will also try to see which strategy is delivering better performance for shareholders.

In order to facilitate replication of the ratio calculations presented below, we present financial statements of both these companies in the appendixes to this chapter. Three versions of these companies' financials are presented in the appendixes. The first version is the one reported by the two companies in their annual reports. The second set of financial statements are presented in the standardized format described in Chapter 4. These "standardized financial statements" put both companies' financials in one standard format to facilitate direct comparison. We also present the two companies' financial statements in a third format in the appendixes. These statements, labeled "Condensed Financial Statements," are essentially a recasting of the standardized financial statements to facilitate the calculation of several ratios discussed in the chapter. We will discuss later in the chapter how this recasting process works.

Background information on Volkswagen and Porsche

Volkswagen

Germany-based Volkswagen AG is a leading car manufacturer, offering a wide variety of car brands, such as Audi, Bentley, Bugatti, Lamborghini, SEAT, Skoda and Volkswagen. During the fiscal year ended December 31, 2005, the company employed approximately 345,000 people worldwide and produced close to 5.2 million cars, of which 4.2 million were sold abroad and 1.0 million in Germany. In 2005 Volkswagen was the market leader in the passenger car markets of western Europe and China. In addition to producing and selling passenger cars, Volkswagen delivered various financial services to its customers. In 2005 approximately 10 percent of the company's revenues came from rental services, dealer and customer financing, leasing, and insurance.

The worldwide market for passenger cars is highly cyclical. In 2004 Volkswagen's earnings performance suffered from the slow economic growth in Germany as well as in the other eurozone countries. At the same time the strong euro harmed the company's exports to its primary markets outside the eurozone, such as the U.S. and Asia. Because most other car manufacturers also had overcapacity, they engaged in price competition, which forced Volkswagen to lower the price premium it had traditionally asked for its products and to focus on cutting production costs. Reducing production costs was difficult, however, for two reasons. First, like several other car manufacturers, Volkswagen's traditional way of achieving economies of scale in production was to let various models share the same production platform (i.e., share a large number of mechanical components). This strategy started to backfire as the company's cheaper brands, such as SEAT and Skoda, cannibalized sales of its premium brands. Second, Volkswagen's personnel costs at its German production plants were extraordinarily high relative to car manufacturers' personnel costs in other countries. The company experienced difficulties in laying off German production workers and cutting German salaries because it faced the opposition of a powerful unionized workforce and its primary shareholder, the State of Lower Saxony. Both its workforce and the State were broadly represented on Volkswagen's Supervisory Board. In addition to the above factors, Volkswagen suffered the consequences of the large investments it had made in Brazil in the 1990s, just before Brazil's economic collapse.

Volkswagen's share price decreased from €51.90 on December 31, 2001 to €35.95 per share on March 31, 2004. Dissatisfied with its earnings performance, Volkswagen launched a cost savings program, called ForMotion, in March 2004. The program focused on cutting product costs, one-time investments and development outlays, and overhead costs and promised to yield €3.1 billion in cost savings in the fiscal year 2005. In 2004 the cost saving program improved Volkswagen's earnings by €1.6 billion.

Porsche

Germany-based Dr. Ing. h.c.F. Porsche AG is a manufacturer of exclusive sports cars and multipurpose SUVs, such as the Porsche 911, the Porsche Boxster, and the Porsche Cayenne. During the fiscal year ending on July 31, 2005, the company employed approximately 12,000 people, primarily in Germany, and produced close to 88,000 cars, of which 14,000 were sold in Germany and 74,000 abroad. Like Volkswagen, Porsche delivered various financial services to its customers. In 2005 approximately 5 percent of the company's revenues came from dealer and customer financing and leasing.

In September 2005 Porsche acquired an 18.5 percent interest in Volkswagen AG, financed by cash, with the intention of becoming Volkswagen's largest single shareholder. Because Porsche and Volkswagen cooperated intensively, for example, in the development and production of the Porsche Cayenne and the Volkswagen Touareg, Porsche's holding in Volkswagen also served to protect Volkswagen from a hostile takeover by any third party. Volkswagen and Porsche were, however, connected in other ways. For example, the Chairman of Volkswagen's Supervisory Board, Ferdinand K. Piëch, was a member of the Piëch family who, together with the Porsche family, owned 50 percent of Porsche.

Porsche's sales were also negatively affected by the slowdown in economic growth in the eurozone, the strong euro, and rising petroleum prices. However, because of the company's focus on the top segment of the passenger car market, it was able to maintain its price premium and stay out of the price wars that were harming Volkswagen's sales. During the first half of the 2000s, Porsche invested heavily in protecting its brand image, for example by unifying the design of Porsche showroom centers, improving after-sales service, increasing the opportunities for vehicle customization, sponsoring major sports events, and building a new Porsche museum. As evidence of its success, in 2005 Porsche's vehicle sales rose by 14 percent. Porsche made its sales primarily within Europe and the U.S. In 2005 sales within Germany accounted for 9.3 percent of total sales. Sales in the rest of Europe and the U.S. accounted for 24.5 and 33.6 percent of total sales, respectively.

Between 1996 and 2005, Porsche had consistently achieved a return on equity above 10 percent. Porsche's strong performance was also reflected in its share price, which had increased by 1,838 percent from €33.75 on July 31, 1995 to €654 on July 31, 2005.

Measuring overall profitability

The starting point for a systematic analysis of a firm's performance is its return on equity (ROE), defined as

$$\text{ROE} = \frac{\text{Net profit}}{\text{Shareholders' equity}}$$

ROE is a comprehensive indicator of a firm's performance because it provides an indication of how well managers are employing the funds invested by the firm's shareholders to generate returns. On average over long periods, large publicly traded firms in Europe generate ROEs in the range of 10 to 12 percent.

In the long run, the value of the firm's equity is determined by the relationship between its ROE and its cost of equity capital.[2] That is, those firms that are expected over the long run to generate ROEs in excess of the cost of equity capital should have market values in excess of book value, and vice versa. (We will return to this point in more detail in Chapter 7 on valuation.)

A comparison of ROE with the cost of capital is useful not only for contemplating the value of the firm but also in considering the path of future profitability. The generation of consistent supernormal profitability will, absent significant barriers to entry, attract competition. For that reason, ROEs tend over time to be driven by competitive forces toward a "normal" level – the cost of equity capital. Thus one can think of the cost of equity capital as establishing a benchmark for the ROE that would be observed in a long-run competitive equilibrium. Deviations from this level arise for two general reasons. One is the industry conditions and competitive strategy that cause a firm to generate supernormal (or subnormal) economic profits, at least over the short run. The second is distortions due to accounting. Table 5.1 shows the ROE based on reported earnings for Volkswagen and Porsche.

Volkswagen's ROE showed an improvement from 2.8 percent to 4.7 percent between 2004 and 2005. This indicates that Volkswagen's strategy of focusing on cost savings and profit improvement is beginning to show positive results. Compared to historical trends of ROE in the economy, Volkswagen's earnings performance can be viewed as being below average. Further, its ROE in 2004 and 2005 is not adequate to cover reasonable estimates of its cost of equity capital. The 1.9 percentage points increase in ROE in 2005 allowed Volkswagen to get closer to both these benchmarks.[3]

Despite the improvement in 2005, Volkswagen's performance was still far behind Porsche's ROE of 26.6 percent. At that performance Porsche was earning excess returns relative to both the historical trends in ROE in the European economy, as well as to its own cost of equity.

Porsche's superior performance relative to Volkswagen is reflected in the difference in the two companies' ratio of market value of equity to book value. As we will discuss in Chapter 7, ROE is a key determinant of a company's market to book ratio. As of December 31, 2005, Volkswagen's market value to book value ratio was 0.7, while the same ratio for Porsche (on July 31, 2005) was 3.4.

Decomposing profitability: Traditional approach

A company's ROE is affected by two factors: how profitably it employs its assets and how big the firm's asset base is relative to shareholders' investment. To understand the effect of these two factors, ROE can be decomposed into return on assets (ROA) and a measure of financial leverage, as follows:

$$ROE = ROA \times Financial\ leverage$$
$$= \frac{Net\ profit}{Assets} \times \frac{Assets}{Shareholders'\ equity}$$

ROA tells us how much profit a company is able to generate for each euro of assets invested. Financial leverage indicates how many euros of assets the firm is able to deploy for each euro invested by its shareholders.

TABLE 5.1 Return on equity for Volkswagen and Porsche

Ratio	Volkswagen 2005	Volkswagen 2004	Porsche 2005
Return on equity	4.7%	2.8%	26.6%

The return on assets itself can be decomposed as a product of two factors:

$$\text{ROA} = \frac{\text{Net profit}}{\text{Sales}} \times \frac{\text{Sales}}{\text{Assets}}$$

The ratio of net profit to sales is called net profit margin or return on sales (ROS); the ratio of sales to assets is known as asset turnover. The profit margin ratio indicates how much the company is able to keep as profits for each euro of sales it makes. Asset turnover indicates how many sales euros the firm is able to generate for each euro of its assets.

Table 5.2 displays the three drivers of ROE for our car manufacturers: net profit margins, asset turnover, and financial leverage. In 2005 Volkswagen's ROE is largely driven by increases in its net profit margin and in its financial leverage. In fact, its asset turnover remained virtually unchanged. Porsche's superior ROE seems to be driven by higher profit margins; Porsche was able to achieve higher ROE than Volkswagen even though it has a lower financial leverage ratio. In other words, Porsche's superior performance is attributable to its superior operating performance, as indicated by its high ROA relative to Volkswagen's ROA. And Volkswagen's inferior operating performance is cushioned by its more aggressive financial management relative to Porsche.

Decomposing profitability: Alternative approach

Even though the above approach is popularly used to decompose a firm's ROE, it has several limitations. In the computation of ROA, the denominator includes the assets claimed by all providers of capital to the firm, but the numerator includes only the earnings available to equity holders. The assets themselves include both operating assets and financial assets such as cash and short-term investments. Further, net profit includes profit from operating activities, as well as interest income and expense, which are consequences of financing decisions. Often it is useful to distinguish between these two sources of performance. Finally, the financial leverage ratio used above does not recognize the fact that a firm's cash and short-term investments are in essence "negative debt" because they can be used to pay down the debt on the company's balance sheet.[4] These issues are addressed by an alternative approach to decomposing ROE discussed below.[5]

Before discussing this alternative ROE decomposition approach, we need to define some terminology used in this section as well as in the rest of this chapter. This terminology is given in Table 5.3.

TABLE 5.2 Traditional decomposition of ROE

Ratio	Volkswagen 2005	Volkswagen 2004	Porsche 2005
Net profit margin (ROS)	1.2%	0.8%	11.8%
× Asset turnover	0.75	0.75	0.73
= Return on assets (ROA)	0.9%	0.6%	8.6%
× Financial leverage	5.32	4.97	3.09
= Return on equity (ROE)	4.7%	2.8%	26.6%

TABLE 5.3 Definitions of accounting items used in ratio analysis

Item	Definition
Net interest expense after tax	(Interest expense – Interest income) × (1 – Tax rate)[a]
Net operating profit after taxes (NOPAT)	Net profit + Net interest expense after tax
Operating working capital	(Current assets – Cash and marketable securities) – (Current liabilities – Current debt and current portion of non-current debt)
Net non-current assets	Total non-current assets – Non-interest-bearing non-current liabilities
Net debt	Total interest-bearing non-current liabilities – Cash and marketable securities
Net assets	Operating working capital + Net non-current assets
Net capital	Net debt + Shareholders' equity

a. The calculation of net interest expense treats interest expense and interest income as absolute values, independent of how these figures are reported in the income statement.

We use the terms defined in Table 5.3 to recast the financial statements of Volkswagen and Porsche. These recast financial statements, which are shown in the appendixes to this chapter, are used to decompose ROE in the following manner:

$$
\begin{aligned}
\text{ROE} &= \frac{\text{NOPAT}}{\text{Equity}} - \frac{\text{Net interest expense after tax}}{\text{Equity}} \\
&= \frac{\text{NOPAT}}{\text{Net assets}} \times \frac{\text{Net assets}}{\text{Equity}} - \frac{\text{Net interest expense after tax}}{\text{Net debt}} \times \frac{\text{Net debt}}{\text{Equity}} \\
&= \frac{\text{NOPAT}}{\text{Net assets}} \left(1 + \frac{\text{Net debt}}{\text{Equity}}\right) - \frac{\text{Net interest expense after tax}}{\text{Net debt}} \times \frac{\text{Net debt}}{\text{Equity}} \\
&= \text{Operating ROA} + (\text{Operating ROA} - \text{Effective interest rate after tax}) \\
&\quad \times \text{Net financial leverage} \\
&= \text{Operating ROA} + (\text{Spread} \times \text{Net financial leverage})
\end{aligned}
$$

Operating ROA is a measure of how profitably a company is able to deploy its operating assets to generate operating profits. This would be a company's ROE if it were financed with all equity. Spread is the incremental economic effect from introducing debt into the capital structure. This economic effect of borrowing is positive as long as the return on operating assets is greater than the cost of borrowing. Firms that do not earn adequate operating returns to pay for interest cost reduce their ROE by borrowing. Both the positive and negative effect is magnified by the extent to which a firm borrows relative to its equity base. The ratio of net debt to equity provides a measure of this net financial leverage. A firm's spread times its net financial leverage, therefore, provides a measure of the financial leverage gain to the shareholders.

Operating ROA can be further decomposed into NOPAT margin and operating asset turnover as follows:

$$
\text{Operating ROA} = \frac{\text{NOPAT}}{\text{Sales}} \times \frac{\text{Sales}}{\text{Net assets}}
$$

NOPAT margin is a measure of how profitable a company's sales are from an operating perspective. Operating asset turnover measures the extent to which a company is able to use its operating assets to generate sales.

Table 5.4 presents the decomposition of ROE for Volkswagen and Porsche. The ratios in this table show that there is a significant difference between Volkswagen's ROA and its operating ROA. In 2005, for example, Volkswagen's ROA was 0.9 percent, while its operating ROA was 2.1 percent.

This difference in ROA and operating ROA is even more remarkable for Porsche: its ROA in 2005 was 8.6 percent whereas the operating ROA was 19.7 percent. Because Porsche had a large amount of non-interest-bearing liabilities, cash and short-term investments, its operating ROA is dramatically larger than its ROA. This shows that, for at least some firms, it is important to adjust the simple ROA to take into account interest expense, interest income, and financial assets.

The appropriate benchmark for evaluating operating ROA is the weighted average cost of debt and equity capital, or WACC. In the long run, the value of the firm's assets is determined by where operating ROA stands relative to this norm. Moreover, over the long run and absent some barrier to competitive forces, operating ROA will tend to be pushed toward the weighted average cost of capital. Since the WACC is lower than the cost of equity capital, operating ROA tends to be pushed to a level lower than that to which ROE tends.

The average operating ROA for large firms in Europe, over long periods of time, is in the range of 8 to 10 percent. Volkswagen's operating ROA in 2004 and 2005 is below this range, indicating that its operating performance is below average. At 19.7 percent, Porsche's operating ROA is far larger than Volkswagen's and also the European industrial average and any reasonable estimates of Porsche's weighted average cost of capital. This dramatic superior operating performance of Porsche would have been obscured by using the simple ROA measure.[6]

Porsche dominates Volkswagen in terms of both operating drivers of ROE – it has a dramatically better NOPAT margin and a higher operating asset turnover. Porsche's higher NOPAT margin is primarily a result of its strategy of focusing on the top segment of the passenger car market and asking premium prices, unlike Volkswagen, which operates in various market segments and is involved in price competition. What is surprising is exclusive car manufacturer Porsche's higher operating asset turnover, given that Volkswagen is supposed to be the firm with the low-cost strategy.

TABLE 5.4 Distinguishing operating and financing components in ROE decomposition

Ratio	Volkswagen 2005	Volkswagen 2004	Porsche 2005
Net operating profit margin	1.9%	1.3%	11.7%
× Net operating asset turnover	1.08	1.07	1.69
= Operating ROA	2.1%	1.4%	19.7%
Spread	1.0%	0.6%	20.5%
× Net financial leverage	2.70	2.51	0.34
= Financial leverage gain	2.6%	1.5%	6.9%
ROE = Operating ROA + Financial leverage gain	4.7%	2.8%	26.6%

Volkswagen's inferior operating asset turnover suggests that the company is unable to utilize its operating assets efficiently enough to compensate for the lower margins on its vehicle sales.

Volkswagen is able to create shareholder value through its financing strategy. In 2004 the spread between Volkswagen's operating ROA and its after-tax interest cost was 0.6 percent; its net debt as a percent of its equity was 251 percent. Both these factors contributed to a net increment of 1.5 percent to its ROE. Thus, while Volkswagen's operating ROA in 2004 was 1.4 percent, its ROE was 2.8 percent. In 2005 Volkswagen's spread increased to 0.9 percent, its net financial leverage went up to 270 percent, leading to a 2.6 percent net increment to ROE due to its debt policy. With an operating ROA of 2.1 percent in that year, its ROE went up to 4.7 percent.

Porsche had a very high spread in 2005, to the tune of 20.5 percent. Note that the financial spread is even greater than the operating ROA because the interest income on Porsche's short-term investments exceeds the interest expense on the company's debt. As a result, even though Porsche had only a modest financial leverage of 34 percent, it had a financial leverage gain of 6.9 percent. This financial leverage gain added to its already higher operating ROA to produce a high ROE of 26.6 percent. In fact, Porsche appears not to have exploited its financial leverage potential fully. With a higher level of leverage, it could have exploited its spread to produce an even higher ROE. In the following year, fiscal year 2006, Porsche did just that. The company used its holdings of cash and marketable securities to finance its acquisition of Volkswagen shares, reducing its cash balance, and issued three new bonds for a total amount of close to €3 billion.

Assessing operating management: Decomposing net profit margins

A firm's net profit margin or return on sales (ROS) shows the profitability of the company's operating activities. Further decomposition of a firm's ROS allows an analyst to assess the efficiency of the firm's operating management. A popular tool used in this analysis is the common-sized income statement in which all the line items are expressed as a ratio of sales revenues. This type of analysis is also referred to as vertical analysis.

Common-sized income statements make it possible to compare trends in income statement relationships over time for the firm, and trends across different firms in the industry. Income statement analysis allows the analyst to ask the following types of questions:

1. Are the company's margins consistent with its stated competitive strategy? For example, a differentiation strategy should usually lead to higher gross margins than a low-cost strategy.

2. Are the company's margins changing? Why? What are the underlying business causes—changes in competition, changes in input costs, or poor overhead cost management?

3. Is the company managing its overhead and administrative costs well? What are the business activities driving these costs? Are these activities necessary?

To illustrate how the income statement analysis can be used, common-sized income statements for Volkswagen and Porsche are shown in Table 5.5. The table also shows some commonly used profitability ratios. We will use the information in Table 5.5 to investigate why Volkswagen had a net profit margin (or return on sales) of 1.2 percent in 2005 and 0.8 percent in 2004, while Porsche had a net margin of 11.8 percent in

TABLE 5.5 Common-sized income statement and profitability ratios

	Volkswagen 2005	Volkswagen 2004	Porsche 2005
Line items as a percent of sales			
Sales	100.0%	100.0%	100.0%
Cost of materials	(65.7%)	(66.5%)	(43.7%)
Personnel expense	(15.4%)	(15.8%)	(14.7%)
Depreciation and amortization	(9.1%)	(9.6%)	(7.8%)
Other operating expense	(6.9%)	(6.2%)	(15.3%)
Net interest expense/income	(1.2%)	(0.8%)	0.2%
Tax expense	(0.6%)	(0.4%)	(7.0%)
Profit from discontinued operations	0.0%	0.0%	0.0%
Net profit	1.2%	0.8%	11.8%
Operating expense by function			
Cost of sales	(86.5%)	(88.2%)	N.A.
Selling, general, and admin. expense	(11.8%)	(11.8%)	N.A.
Other operating income/expense	1.3%	1.8%	N.A.
Key profitability ratios			
Gross profit margin	13.5%	11.8%	N.A.
EBITDA margin	12.0%	11.4%	26.3%
NOPAT margin	1.9%	1.3%	11.7%
Net profit margin	1.2%	0.8%	11.8%

2005. Unfortunately, Volkswagen and Porsche use different formats to present their operating expenses. Volkswagen classifies its expenses by function in the income statement and discloses a classification of its expenses by nature in the notes to the financial statements. Unlike Volkswagen, Porsche only provides a classification of expenses by nature. Consequently, we cannot compare all line items.

Decomposition by function

Although not required to do so by the international accounting rules, some firms classify their operating expensing according to function. The decomposition of operating expenses by function is potentially more informative than the decomposition by nature. This is because the functional decomposition requires the firm to use judgment in dividing total operating expenses into expenses that are directly associated with products sold or services delivered (cost of sales) and expenses that are incurred to manage operations (selling, general, and administrative expense).

The difference between a firm's sales and cost of sales is gross profit. Gross profit margin is an indication of the extent to which revenues exceed direct costs associated with sales, and it is computed as

$$\text{Gross profit margin} = \frac{\text{Sales} - \text{Cost of sales}}{\text{Sales}}$$

Gross margin is influenced by two factors: (1) the price premium that a firm's products or services command in the marketplace and (2) the efficiency of the firm's procurement and production process. The price premium a firm's products or services can command is influenced by the degree of competition and the extent to which its products are unique. The firm's cost of sales can be low when it can purchase its inputs at a lower cost than competitors and/or run its production processes more efficiently. This is generally the case when a firm has a low-cost strategy. Table 5.5 indicates that Volkswagen's gross margin in 2005 increased slightly to 13.5 percent, reflecting increased operational efficiency. This suggests that the company is starting to harvest the benefits of its new cost savings program. In 2004 Volkswagen announced that it expected that the cost savings program would lead to a reduction in production and development costs of close to €1.5 billion annually, or approximately 1.6 percent of 2005 sales. The gross margin improvement of 1.7 percent thus meets, or even slightly exceeds, Volkswagen's initial expectations.

A company's selling, general, and administrative (SG&A) expenses are influenced by the operating activities it has to undertake to implement its competitive strategy. As discussed in Chapter 2, firms with differentiation strategies have to undertake activities to achieve differentiation. A company competing on the basis of quality and rapid introduction of new products is likely to have higher R&D costs relative to a company competing purely on a cost basis. Similarly, a company that attempts to build a brand image, distribute its products through full-service retailers, and provide significant customer service is likely to have higher selling and administration costs relative to a company that sells through warehouse retailers or direct mail and does not provide much customer support.

A company's SG&A expenses are also influenced by the efficiency with which it manages its overhead activities. The control of operating expenses is likely to be especially important for firms competing on the basis of low cost. However, even for differentiators, it is important to assess whether the cost of differentiation is commensurate with the price premium earned in the marketplace. Volkswagen's cost savings program targeted at reducing overhead costs by an amount of €900 million, or close to 1 percent of 2005 sales. The ratio of SG&A expense to sales in Table 5.5 shows how much Volkswagen is spending to generate each sales euro and whether the company is meeting its savings target. Despite its stated goal to manage its profitability better, Volkswagen was not able to improve its cost management in 2005: its SG&A expense as a percent of sales remained constant at 11.8 percent.

Decomposition by nature

The international accounting rules require that all firms reporting under IFRS classify and disclose their operating expenses by nature, either in the income statement or in the notes to the financial statements. Like most firms, Volkswagen and Porsche distinguish four expense categories: (1) cost of materials, (2) personnel expense, (3) depreciation and amortization, and (4) other operating expenses.

Table 5.5 indicates that Volkswagen economized on personnel expense in 2005, despite the difficulties it experienced with laying off personnel or cutting the salaries of its German workforce. The reduction in personnel costs improved the operating margin by 0.4 percent. An advantage of classifying operating expenses by nature is that these expenses can be more easily related to their main driver, such as the number of employees. This helps us to further analyze the development in Volkswagen personnel expenses. In 2005 Volkswagen's average workforce grew by 1.2 percent to 344,000 employees and its personnel cost per employee grew by 2.9 percent to €42,600 per employee. This illustrates that the company neither reduced its workforce nor cut salaries. The main driver behind the improvement in the personnel expense to sales ratio was an increase in employee productivity. Sales per employee increased by 5.8 percent to

€277,000. In 2005 Porsche spent on average €82,000 per employee, which illustrates that the company's focus on the top segments of the car market required a better skilled but more expensive workforce. However, because Porsche was able to maintain its premium pricing strategy and earned €588,000 in sales per employee, its personnel expense to sales ratio was still slightly lower than Volkswagen's.

Volkswagen further reduced its depreciation and amortization expense by 0.5 percent as a result of its savings on capitalized development costs and its cut back on investments in property, plant, and equipment. When we compare Volkswagen's with Porsche's cost of materials, we see that Porsche's cost of materials as a percent of sales is substantially lower. In 2005 the cost of materials per vehicle sold was €32,500 for Porsche in comparison with €12,100 for Volkswagen. However, Porsche earned €74,400 per vehicle sold in comparison with only €18,300 for Volkswagen. This difference in margin is consistent with Porsche's premium pricing strategy.

NOPAT margin and EBITDA margin

Given that Volkswagen and Porsche are pursuing different pricing, merchandising, and service strategies, it is not surprising that they have different cost structures. As a percent of sales, Porsche's cost of materials, personnel expense, and depreciation are lower, and its other operating expense is higher. The question is, when these costs are netted out, which company is performing better? Two ratios provide useful signals here: net operating profit margin (NOPAT margin) and EBITDA margin:

$$\text{NOPAT margin} = \frac{\text{NOPAT}}{\text{Sales}}$$

$$\text{EBITDA margin} = \frac{\text{Earnings before interest, taxes, depreciation and amortization}}{\text{Sales}}$$

NOPAT margin provides a comprehensive indication of the operating performance of a company because it reflects all operating policies and eliminates the effects of debt policy. EBITDA margin provides similar information, except that it excludes depreciation and amortization expense, a significant noncash operating expense. Some analysts prefer to use EBITDA margin because they believe that it focuses on "cash" operating items. While this is to some extent true, it can be potentially misleading for two reasons. EBITDA is not a strictly cash concept because sales, cost of sales, and SG&A expenses often include noncash items. Also, depreciation is a real operating expense, and it reflects to some extent the consumption of resources. Therefore, ignoring it can be misleading.

From Table 5.5 we see that Volkswagen's NOPAT margin and EBITDA margin improved between 2004 and 2005. Even with this improvement, in 2005 the company is able to retain only 1.9 cents in net operating profits for each euro of sales, whereas Porsche is able to retain 11.7 cents. Porsche also has a better EBITDA margin than Volkswagen.

Recall that in Table 5.3 we define NOPAT as net profit plus net interest expense. Therefore, NOPAT is influenced by any nonoperating income (expense) items included in net profit. We can calculate a "recurring" NOPAT margin by eliminating these items. For Volkswagen, recurring NOPAT margin was 1.9 percent in 2005 and 0.8 percent in 2004. The 2004 margin is lower than the NOPAT margin number we discussed above, suggesting that a portion of the company's NOPAT is derived from sources other than its core operations. These sources include an amount of investment income, gains from asset disposals and foreign exchange gains that Volkswagen reported in its financial statements. Recurring NOPAT may be a better benchmark to use when one is extrapolating current performance into the future because it reflects margins from the core business activities of a firm.

Tax expense

Taxes are an important element of firms' total expenses. Through a wide variety of tax planning techniques, firms can attempt to reduce their tax expenses.[7] There are two measures one can use to evaluate a firm's tax expense. One is the ratio of tax expense to sales, and the other is the ratio of tax expense to earnings before taxes (also known as the average tax rate). The firm's tax note provides a detailed account of why its average tax rate differs from the statutory tax rate.

When evaluating a firm's tax planning, the analyst should ask two questions: (1) Are the company's tax policies sustainable, or is the current tax rate influenced by one-time tax credits? (2) Do the firm's tax planning strategies lead to other business costs? For example, if the operations are located in tax havens, how does this affect the company's profit margins and asset utilization? Are the benefits of tax planning strategies (reduced taxes) greater than the increased business costs?

Table 5.5 shows that Volkswagen's tax rate did not change significantly between 2004 and 2005. Volkswagen's taxes as a percent of sales were lower than Porsche's. An important reason for this is that Porsche's pretax profits as a percent of sales were higher. In fact, the average tax rate (ratio of tax expense to pretax profits) for both Volkswagen and Porsche were nearly the same, at 35 percent and 37 percent, respectively.

In summary, we conclude that Volkswagen's small improvement in return on sales is primarily driven by a reduction in its cost of sales. The company was able to reduce its cost of materials as well as its personnel expenses. Porsche is able to earn a superior return on its sales because it follows a premium pricing strategy.

Evaluating investment management: Decomposing asset turnover

Asset turnover is the second driver of a company's return on equity. Since firms invest considerable resources in their assets, using them productively is critical to overall profitability. A detailed analysis of asset turnover allows the analyst to evaluate the effectiveness of a firm's investment management.

There are two primary areas of asset management: (1) working capital management and (2) management of non-current assets. Working capital is defined as the difference between a firm's current assets and current liabilities. However, this definition does not distinguish between operating components (such as trade receivables, inventories, and trade payables) and the financing components (such as cash, marketable securities, and notes payable). An alternative measure that makes this distinction is operating working capital, as defined in Table 5.3:

> Operating working capital = (Current assets – Cash and marketable securities)
> – (Current liabilities – Current debt and current portion of non-current debt)

Working capital management

The components of operating working capital that analysts primarily focus on are trade receivables, inventories, and trade payables. A certain amount of investment in working capital is necessary for the firm to run its normal operations. For example, a firm's credit policies and distribution policies determine its optimal level of trade receivables. The nature of the production process and the need for buffer stocks determine the optimal level of inventories. Finally, trade payables are a routine source of financing for the firm's working capital, and payment practices in an industry determine the normal level of trade payables.

The following ratios are useful in analyzing a firm's working capital management: operating working capital as a percent of sales, operating working capital turnover, trade receivables turnover, inventories turnover, and trade payables turnover. The turnover ratios can also be expressed in number of days of activity that the operating working capital (and its components) can support. The definitions of these ratios are as follows:

$$\text{Operating working capital to sales ratio} = \frac{\text{Operating working capital}}{\text{Sales}}$$

$$\text{Operating working capital turnover} = \frac{\text{Sales}}{\text{Operating working capital}}$$

$$\text{Trade receivables turnover} = \frac{\text{Sales}}{\text{Trade receivables}}$$

$$\text{Inventories turnover} = \frac{\text{Cost of sales}}{\text{Inventories}} \; or \; \frac{\text{Cost of materials}}{\text{Inventories}}$$

$$\text{Trade payables turnover} = \frac{\text{Purchases}}{\text{Trade payables}} \; or \; \frac{\text{Cost of sales}}{\text{Trade payables}} \; or \; \frac{\text{Cost of materials}}{\text{Trade payables}}$$

$$\text{Days' receivables} = \frac{\text{Trade receivables}}{\text{Average sales per day}}$$

$$\text{Days' inventory} = \frac{\text{Inventories}}{\text{Average cost of sales per day}} \; or \; \frac{\text{Inventories}}{\text{Average cost of materials per day}}$$

$$\text{Days' payables} = \frac{\text{Trade payables}}{\text{Average purchases per day}} \; or \; \frac{\text{Trade payables}}{\text{Average cost of sales per day}}$$

$$or \; \frac{\text{Trade payables}}{\text{Average cost of materials per day}}$$

Operating working capital turnover indicates how many euros of sales a firm is able to generate for each euro invested in its operating working capital. Trade receivables turnover, inventories turnover, and trade payables turnover allow the analyst to examine how productively the three principal components of working capital are being used. Days' receivables, days' inventories, and days' payables are another way to evaluate the efficiency of a firm's working capital management.[8]

Non-current assets management

Another area of investment management concerns the utilization of a firm's non-current assets. It is useful to define a firm's investment in non-current assets as follows:

Net non-current assets = (Total non-current assets – Non-interest-bearing non-current liabilities)

Non-current assets generally consist of net property, plant, and equipment (PP&E), intangible assets such as goodwill, and other assets. Non-interest-bearing non-current liabilities include such items as deferred taxes. We define net non-current assets and net working capital in such a way that their sum, net operating assets, is equal to the sum of net debt and equity, or net capital. This is consistent with the way we defined operating ROA earlier in the chapter.

The efficiency with which a firm uses its net non-current assets is measured by the following two ratios: net non-current assets as a percent of sales and net non-current asset turnover. Net non-current asset turnover is defined as:

$$\text{Net non-current asset turnover} = \frac{\text{Sales}}{\text{Net non-current assets}}$$

Property, plant and equipment (PP&E) is the most important non-current asset in a firm's balance sheet. The efficiency with which a firm's PP&E is used is measured by the ratio of PP&E to sales, or by the PP&E turnover ratio:

$$\text{PP\&E turnover} = \frac{\text{Sales}}{\text{Net property, plant and equipment}}$$

The ratios listed above allow the analyst to explore a number of business questions in four general areas:

1. How well does the company manage its inventories? Does the company use modern manufacturing techniques? Does it have good vendor and logistics management systems? If inventories ratios are changing, what is the underlying business reason? Are new products being planned? Is there a mismatch between the demand forecasts and actual sales?

2. How well does the company manage its credit policies? Are these policies consistent with its marketing strategy? Is the company artificially increasing sales by loading the distribution channels?

3. Is the company taking advantage of trade credit? Is it relying too much on trade credit? If so, what are the implicit costs?

4. Are the company's investment in plant and equipment consistent with its competitive strategy? Does the company have a sound policy of acquisitions and divestitures?

Table 5.6 shows the asset turnover ratios for Volkswagen and Porsche. Volkswagen was not able to improve its working capital management between 2004 and 2005, as can be seen from the unchanged operating working capital as a percent of sales and the unchanged operating working capital turnover. Working capital management improved because of an increase in inventories turnover. However, this improvement was fully offset by a reduction in its days' payables and an increase in its days' receivables, which unfavorably impacted the company's working capital management ratios. In addition, Volkswagen's non-current asset utilization slightly improved in 2005: its net non-current asset turnover and PP&E turnover increased. In its annual report, Volkswagen disclosed that it reduced its investments in property, plant and equipment by 20 percent, thereby improving the capital expenditure to sales ratio from 6.8 percent to 5.0 percent.

Porsche achieved better asset utilization ratios in 2005 relative to Volkswagen. Porsche was able to invest a lower amount of money in its operating working capital than Volkswagen by taking better advantage of trade credit from its vendors. Also, because Porsche generated a smaller proportion of its sales from financial services such as customer financing and rental services, it was able to collect its receivables in 43.3 days, in contrast to Volkswagen's 100 receivable days. This is because Volkswagen's and Porsche's financial services receivables had a much longer collection period than their other trade receivables. Volkswagen was able to improve

TABLE 5.6 Asset management ratios

Ratio	Volkswagen 2005	Volkswagen 2004	Porsche 2005
Operating working capital/Sales	23.6%	23.6%	11.4%
Net non-current assets/Sales	69.1%	70.2%	47.9%
PP&E/Sales	33.9%	36.3%	30.9%
Operating working capital turnover	4.2	4.2	8.8
Net non-current asset turnover	1.4	1.4	2.1
PP&E turnover	3.0	2.8	3.2
Trade receivables turnover	3.6	3.7	8.3
Days' receivables	100.0	97.2	43.3
Inventories turnover	5.5	5.1	4.6
Days' inventories	65.8	71.0	78.3
Trade payables turnover	8.4	7.6	7.6
Days' payables	42.7	47.6	47.2

its working capital to sales ratio relative to Porsche's by managing its inventories more efficiently than Porsche. Finally, because Porsche and Volkswagen lease or rent out vehicles to customers, they both had a significant amount of capital tied up in non-current receivables and leased assets, which reduced net non-current asset turnover. The difference between Volkswagen's net non-current asset turnover and Porsche's is explained by the fact that Volkswagen had capitalized a much larger amount of product development costs and held more minority investments than Porsche. Minority investments that are accounted for using the equity method reduce net operating asset turnover because equity income from these unconsolidated subsidiaries is directly included in investment income.

Evaluating financial management: Financial leverage

Financial leverage enables a firm to have an asset base larger than its equity. The firm can augment its equity through borrowing and the creation of other liabilities like trade payables, provisions, and deferred taxes. Financial leverage increases a firm's ROE as long as the cost of the liabilities is less than the return from investing these funds. In this respect it is important to distinguish between interest-bearing liabilities such as notes payable, other forms of current debt and non-current debt that carry an explicit interest charge, and other forms of liabilities. Some of these other forms of liability, such as trade payables or deferred taxes, do not carry any interest charge at all. Other liabilities, such as finance lease obligations or pension obligations, carry an implicit interest charge. Finally, some firms carry large cash balances or investments in marketable securities. These balances reduce a firm's net debt because conceptually the firm can pay down its debt using its cash and short-term investments.

While financial leverage can potentially benefit a firm's shareholders, it can also increase their risk. Unlike equity, liabilities have predefined payment terms, and the firm faces risk of financial distress if it fails to meet these commitments. There are a number of ratios to evaluate the degree of risk arising from a firm's financial leverage.

Current liabilities and short-term liquidity

The following ratios are useful in evaluating the risk related to a firm's current liabilities:

$$\text{Current ratio} = \frac{\text{Current assets}}{\text{Current liabilities}}$$

$$\text{Quick ratio} = \frac{\text{Cash and marketable securities} + \text{Trade receivables (net)}}{\text{Current liabilities}}$$

$$\text{Cash ratio} = \frac{\text{Cash and marketable securities}}{\text{Current liabilities}}$$

$$\text{Operating cash flow ratio} = \frac{\text{Cash flow from operations}}{\text{Current liabilities}}$$

All these ratios attempt to measure the firm's ability to repay its current liabilities. The first three compare a firm's current liabilities with its current assets that can be used to repay those liabilities. The fourth ratio focuses on the ability of the firm's operations to generate the resources needed to repay its current liabilities.

Since both current assets and current liabilities have comparable duration, the current ratio is a key index of a firm's short-term liquidity. Analysts view a current ratio of more than one to be an indication that the firm can cover its current liabilities from the cash realized from its current assets. However, the firm can face a short-term liquidity problem even with a current ratio exceeding one when some of its current assets are not easy to liquidate. Further, firms whose current assets have high turnover rates, such as food retailers, can afford to have current ratios below one. Quick ratio and cash ratio capture the firm's ability to cover its current liabilities from liquid assets. Quick ratio assumes that the firm's trade receivables are liquid. This is true in industries where the creditworthiness of the customers is beyond dispute, or when receivables are collected in a very short period. When these conditions do not prevail, cash ratio, which considers only cash and marketable securities, is a better indication of a firm's ability to cover its current liabilities in an emergency. Operating cash flow is another measure of the firm's ability to cover its current liabilities from cash generated from operations of the firm.

The liquidity ratios for Volkswagen and Porsche are shown in Table 5.7. Volkswagen's liquidity situation in 2004 was comfortable when measured in terms of current ratio or quick ratio. Both these ratios slightly improved in 2005. Porsche also had a comfortable liquidity position, thanks to its large cash balance and a sound operating cash flow. Because Porsche temporarily held cash and marketable securities to finance its pending acquisition of a 20 percent stake in Volkswagen, its current and quick ratios are greater than Volkswagen's.

TABLE 5.7 Liquidity ratios

Ratio	Volkswagen 2005	Volkswagen 2004	Porsche 2005
Current ratio	2.80	2.66	3.08
Quick ratio	2.00	1.82	2.10
Cash ratio	0.66	0.56	1.67
Operating cash flow ratio	0.55	0.60	0.62

Debt and long-term solvency

A company's financial leverage is also influenced by its debt financing policy. There are several potential benefits from debt financing. First, debt is typically cheaper than equity because the firm promises predefined payment terms to debt holders. Second, in most countries, interest on debt financing is tax deductible whereas dividends to shareholders are not tax deductible. Third, debt financing can impose discipline on the firm's management and motivate it to reduce wasteful expenditures. Fourth, it is often easier for management to communicate their proprietary information on the firm's strategies and prospects to private lenders than to public capital markets. Such communication can potentially reduce a firm's cost of capital. For all these reasons, it is optimal for firms to use at least some debt in their capital structure. Too much reliance on debt financing, however, is potentially costly to the firm's shareholders. The firm will face financial distress if it defaults on the interest and principal payments. Debt holders also impose covenants on the firm, restricting the firm's operating, investment, and financing decisions.

The optimal capital structure for a firm is determined primarily by its business risk. A firm's cash flows are highly predictable when there is little competition or there is little threat of technological changes. Such firms have low business risk and hence they can rely heavily on debt financing. In contrast, if a firm's operating cash flows are highly volatile and its capital expenditure needs are unpredictable, it may have to rely primarily on equity financing. Managers' attitude toward risk and financial flexibility also often determine a firm's debt policies.

There are a number of ratios that help the analyst in this area. To evaluate the mix of debt and equity in a firm's capital structure, the following ratios are useful:

$$\text{Liabilities-to-equity ratio} = \frac{\text{Total liabilities}}{\text{Shareholders' equity}}$$

$$\text{Debt-to-equity ratio} = \frac{\text{Current debt} + \text{Non-current debt}}{\text{Shareholders' equity}}$$

$$\text{Net debt-to-equity ratio} = \frac{\text{Current debt} + \text{Non-current debt} - \text{Cash and marketable securities}}{\text{Shareholders' equity}}$$

$$\text{Debt-to-capital ratio} = \frac{\text{Current debt} + \text{Non-current debt}}{\text{Current debt} + \text{Non-current debt} + \text{Shareholders' equity}}$$

$$\text{Net debt-to-net capital ratio} = \frac{\text{Interest bearing liabilities} - \text{Cash and marketable securities}}{\text{Interest bearing liabilities} - \text{Cash and marketable securities} + \text{Shareholders' equity}}$$

The first ratio restates the assets-to-equity ratio (one of the three primary ratios underlying ROE) by subtracting one from it. The second ratio provides an indication of how many euros of debt financing the firm is using for each euro invested by its shareholders. The third ratio uses net debt, which is total debt minus cash and marketable securities, as the measure of a firm's borrowings. The fourth and fifth ratios measure debt as a proportion of total capital. In calculating all the above ratios, it is important to include all interest-bearing obligations, whether the interest charge is explicit or implicit. Recall that examples of line items that carry an implicit interest charge include capital lease obligations and pension obligations. Analysts sometimes include any potential off-balance sheet obligations that a firm may have, such as noncancelable operating leases, in the definition of a firm's debt.

The ease with which a firm can meet its interest payments is an indication of the degree of risk associated with its debt policy. The interest coverage ratio provides a measure of this construct:

$$\text{Interest coverage (earning basis)} = \frac{\text{Net profit} + \text{Interest expense} + \text{Tax expense}}{\text{Interest expense}}$$

$$\text{Interest coverage (cash flow basis)} =$$

$$\frac{\text{Cash flow from operations} + \text{Interest expense} + \text{Taxes paid}}{\text{Interest expense}}$$

One can also calculate coverage ratios that measure a firm's ability to measure all fixed financial obligations, such as interest payments, lease payments, and debt repayments, by appropriately redefining the numerator and denominator in the above ratios. In doing so it is important to remember that while some fixed charge payments, such as interest and lease rentals, are paid with pretax euros, others, such as debt repayments, are made with after-tax euros.

The earnings-based coverage ratio indicates the euros of earnings available for each euro of required interest payment; the cash flow-based coverage ratio indicates the euros of cash generated by operations for each euro of required interest payment. In both these ratios, the denominator is the interest expense. In the numerator we add taxes back because taxes are computed only after interest expense is deducted. A coverage ratio of one implies that the firm is barely covering its interest expense through its operating activities, which is a very risky situation. The larger the coverage ratio, the greater the cushion the firm has to meet interest obligations.

KEY ANALYSIS QUESTIONS

Some of the business questions to ask when the analyst is examining a firm's debt policies are:

■ Does the company have enough debt? Is it exploiting the potential benefits of debt – interest tax shields, management discipline, and easier communication?

■ Does the company have too much debt given its business risk? What type of debt covenant restrictions does the firm face? Is it bearing the costs of too much debt, risking potential financial distress and reduced business flexibility?

■ What is the company doing with the borrowed funds? Investing in working capital? Investing in fixed assets? Are these investments profitable?

■ Is the company borrowing money to pay dividends? If so, what is the justification?

We show debt and coverage ratios for Volkswagen and Porsche in Table 5.8. Volkswagen recorded an increase in its liabilities-to-equity and debt-to-equity ratios. The company's interest coverage remained at comfortable levels. Porsche's debt ratios confirm that it has been following a more conservative debt policy than Volkswagen. Its interest coverage ratios cannot be calculated because Porsche's interest income exceeds its interest expense. Porsche's debt ratios would change slightly but not significantly when one considers the fact that Porsche has off-balance pension obligations for an amount of €135,000 and minimum lease rental obligations with a present value of €78 million.

TABLE 5.8 Debt and coverage ratios

Ratio	Volkswagen 2005	Volkswagen 2004	Porsche 2005
Liabilities-to-equity	4.32	3.97	2.05
Debt-to-equity	3.25	2.96	1.39
Net debt-to-equity	2.70	2.51	0.34
Debt-to-capital	0.76	0.75	0.58
Net debt-to-net capital	0.65	0.61	0.06
Interest coverage (earnings based)	2.53	2.41	not relevant
Interest coverage (cash flow based)	10.95	16.32	not relevant

Ratios of disaggregated data

So far we have discussed how to compute ratios using information in the financial statements. Analysts often probe these ratios further by using disaggregated financial and physical data. For example, for a multibusiness company, one could analyze the information by individual business segments. Such an analysis can reveal potential differences in the performance of each business unit, allowing the analyst to pinpoint areas where a company's strategy is working and where it is not. It is also possible to probe financial ratios further by computing ratios of physical data pertaining to a company's operations. The appropriate physical data to look at varies from industry to industry. As an example in retailing, one could compute productivity statistics such as sales per store, sales per square meter, customer transactions per store, and amount of sales per customer transaction; in the hotel industry, room occupancy rates provide important information; in the cellular telephone industry, acquisition cost per new subscriber and subscriber retention rate are important. These disaggregated ratios are particularly useful for young firms and young industries such as internet firms, where accounting data may not fully capture the business economics due to conservative accounting rules.

Putting it all together: Assessing sustainable growth rate

Analysts often use the concept of sustainable growth as a way to evaluate a firm's ratios in a comprehensive manner. A firm's sustainable growth rate is defined as:

$$\text{Sustainable growth rate} = \text{ROE} \times (1 - \text{Dividend payout ratio})$$

We already discussed the analysis of ROE in the previous four sections. The dividend payout ratio is defined as:

$$\text{Dividend payout ratio} = \frac{\text{Cash dividends paid}}{\text{Net profit}}$$

A firm's dividend payout ratio is a measure of its dividend policy. As we discuss in detail in Chapter 12, firms pay dividends for several reasons. Dividends are a way for the firm to return to its shareholders any cash generated in excess of its operating and investment needs. When there are information asymmetries between a firm's managers and its shareholders, dividend payments can serve as a signal to shareholders about managers' expectation of the firm's future prospects. Firms may also pay dividends to attract a certain type of shareholder base.

Sustainable growth rate is the rate at which a firm can grow while keeping its profitability and financial policies unchanged. A firm's return on equity and its dividend payout policy determine the pool of funds available for growth. Of course the firm can grow at a rate different from its sustainable growth rate if its profitability, payout policy, or financial leverage changes. Therefore, the sustainable growth rate provides a benchmark against which a firm's growth plans can be evaluated. Figure 5.2 shows how a firm's sustainable growth rate can be linked to all the ratios discussed in this chapter. These linkages allow an analyst to examine the drivers of a firm's current sustainable growth rate. If the firm intends to grow at a higher rate than its sustainable growth rate, one could assess which of the ratios are likely to change in the process. This analysis can lead to asking business questions such as these: Where is the change going to take place? Is management expecting profitability to increase? Or asset productivity to improve? Are these expectations realistic? Is the firm planning for these changes? If the profitability is not likely to go up, will the firm increase its financial leverage or cut dividends? What is the likely impact of these financial policy changes?

Table 5.9 shows the sustainable growth rate and its components for Volkswagen and Porsche. Volkswagen had a lower ROE and a higher dividend payout ratio relative to Porsche, leading to a significantly lower sustainable growth rate in both 2005 and 2004. However, Volkswagen improved its sustainable growth rate because of its improved ROE and a decline in its payout ratio.

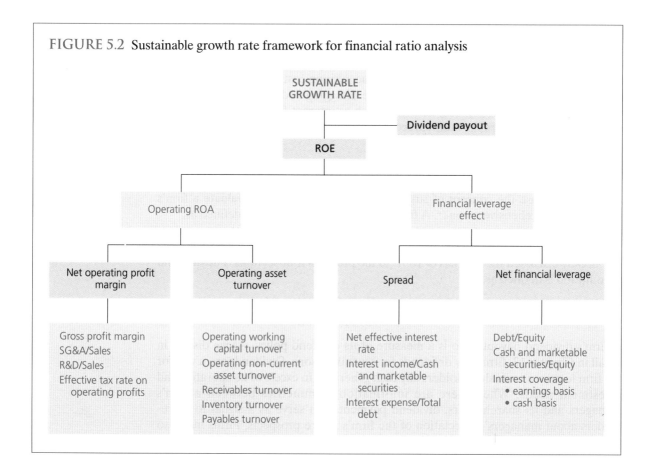

FIGURE 5.2 Sustainable growth rate framework for financial ratio analysis

TABLE 5.9 Sustainable growth rate

Ratio	Volkswagen 2005	Volkswagen 2004	Porsche 2005
ROE	4.7%	2.8%	26.6%
Dividend payout ratio	40.2%	57.1%	11.2%
Sustainable growth rate	2.8%	1.2%	23.6%

Volkswagen's actual growth rates in 2005 in sales, assets, and liabilities were different from its sustainable growth rate in 2004. In 2005 Volkswagen's sales increased by 7.1 percent, net operating assets increased by 5.9 percent, and its net debt grew by 8.8 percent. These differences between Volkswagen's sustainable growth rate and its actual growth rates in sales, net assets, and net debt are reconciled by the fact that Volkswagen increased its net leverage and slightly improved its asset turnover. Volkswagen has the room to grow in future years at about 3 percent without altering its operating and financial policies. In contrast, Porsche has a significantly higher sustainable growth rate of 24 percent, implying that it can grow at a much faster rate than Volkswagen without altering its operating and financial policies.

Historical patterns of ratios for European firms

To provide a benchmark for analysis, Table 5.10 reports historical values of the key ratios discussed in this chapter. These ratios are calculated using financial statement data for our sample of 6,951 publicly listed European companies. The table shows the values of ROE, its key components, and the sustainable growth rate for each of the years 1989 to 2005, and the average for this 17-year period. The data in the table show that the average ROE during this period has been 10.3 percent, average operating ROA has been 8.6 percent, and the average spread between operating ROA and net borrowing costs after tax has been 2.8 percent. The average sustainable growth rate for European companies during this period has been 5.3 percent. Of course an individual company's ratios might depart from these economy-wide averages for a number of reasons, including industry effects, company strategies, and management effectiveness. Nonetheless, the average values in the table serve as useful benchmarks in financial analysis.

CASH FLOW ANALYSIS

The ratio analysis discussion focused on analyzing a firm's income statement (net profit margin analysis) or its balance sheet (asset turnover and financial leverage). The analyst can get further insights into the firm's operating, investing, and financing policies by examining its cash flows. Cash flow analysis also provides an indication of the quality of the information in the firm's income statement and balance sheet. As before, we will illustrate the concepts discussed in this section using Volkswagen's and Porsche's cash flows.

TABLE 5.10 Historical values of key financial ratios

Year	ROE	NOPAT margin	Operating asset turnover	Operating ROA	Spread	Net financial leverage	Sustainable growth rate
1989	18.2%	6.1%	3.10	14.5%	7.1%	0.51	12.4%
1990	15.9%	5.2%	3.02	12.2%	4.4%	0.56	10.5%
1991	11.5%	4.1%	2.93	9.2%	1.1%	0.60	6.5%
1992	9.4%	3.4%	2.90	8.3%	0.4%	0.59	4.6%
1993	9.2%	3.2%	3.02	8.5%	1.0%	0.53	4.3%
1994	12.1%	4.2%	3.08	10.8%	3.4%	0.46	4.3%
1995	13.0%	4.5%	3.12	11.4%	4.3%	0.44	7.5%
1996	11.8%	4.2%	3.10	10.6%	5.2%	0.43	6.5%
1997	14.1%	4.5%	3.12	12.4%	7.2%	0.40	8.5%
1998	12.6%	3.6%	2.98	10.8%	5.5%	0.44	7.2%
1999	11.3%	3.2%	2.79	9.5%	5.4%	0.47	6.3%
2000	8.9%	0.8%	2.55	6.9%	2.6%	0.44	4.6%
2001	4.9%	−0.7%	2.59	3.3%	−1.5%	0.47	1.0%
2002	2.4%	−1.5%	2.70	1.3%	−2.4%	0.46	−1.2%
2003	3.2%	−0.7%	2.77	2.5%	−1.2%	0.44	−0.6%
2004	7.1%	0.6%	2.85	6.1%	1.6%	0.36	3.1%
2005	8.9%	2.0%	2.68	7.8%	4.0%	0.35	4.4%
Average	10.3%	2.7%	2.90	8.6%	2.8%	0.47	5.3%

Source: Financial statement data for all nonfinancial companies publicly listed on one of the seven major European exchanges (Thomson Financial's Worldscope).

Cash flow and funds flow statements

All companies reporting in conformity with IFRSs are required to include a statement of cash flows in their financial statements under IAS 7. In the reported cash flow statement, firms classify their cash flows into three categories: cash flow from operations, cash flow related to investments, and cash flow related to financing activities. Cash flow from operations is the cash generated by the firm from the sale of goods and services after paying for the cost of inputs and operations. Cash flow related to investment activities shows the cash paid for capital expenditures, intercorporate investments, acquisitions, and cash received from the sales of non-current assets. Cash flow related to financing activities shows the cash raised from (or paid to) the firm's shareholders and debt holders.

Firms use two cash flow statement formats: the direct format and the indirect format. The key difference between the two formats is the way they report cash flow from operating activities. In the direct cash flow format, which is used by only a small number of firms in practice, operating cash receipts and disbursements are reported directly. In the indirect format, firms derive their operating cash flows by making adjustments to net profit. Because the indirect format links the cash flow statement with the firm's income statement and balance sheet, many analysts and managers find this format more useful.

Recall from Chapter 3 that net profit differs from operating cash flows because revenues and expenses are measured on an accrual basis. There are two types of accruals embedded in net profit. First, there are current accruals like credit sales and unpaid expenses. Current accruals result in changes in a firm's current assets (such as trade receivables, inventories, and prepaid expenses) and current liabilities (such as trade payables and current provisions). The second type of accruals included in the income statement is non-current accruals such as depreciation, deferred taxes, and equity income from unconsolidated subsidiaries. To derive cash flow from operations from net profit, adjustments have to be made for both these types of accruals. In addition, adjustments have to be made for non-operating gains included in net profit such as profits from asset sales.

As an alternative, some firms report a funds flow statement rather than a cash flow statement of the type described above. Funds flow statements show working capital flows, not cash flows. It is useful for analysts to know how to convert a funds flow statement into a cash flow statement.

Funds flow statements typically provide information on a firm's working capital from operations, defined as net profit adjusted for non-current accruals, and gains from the sale of non-current assets. As discussed above, cash flow from operations essentially involves a third adjustment, the adjustment for current accruals. Thus it is relatively straightforward to convert working capital from operations to cash flow from operations by making the relevant adjustments for current accruals related to operations.

Information on current accruals can be obtained by examining changes in a firm's current assets and current liabilities. Typically, operating accruals represent changes in all the current asset accounts other than cash and cash equivalents, and changes in all the current liabilities other than notes payable and the current portion of non-current debt.[9] Cash from operations can be calculated as follows:

> Working capital from operations
> – Increase (or + decrease) in trade receivables
> – Increase (or + decrease) in inventories
> – Increase (or + decrease) in other current assets excluding cash and cash equivalents
> + Increase (or – decrease) in trade payables
> + Increase (or – decrease) in other current liabilities excluding debt.

Funds flow statements also often do not classify investment and financing flows. In such a case, the analyst has to classify the line items in the funds flow statement into these two categories by evaluating the nature of the business transactions that give rise to the flow represented by the line items.

Analyzing cash flow information

Cash flow analysis can be used to address a variety of questions regarding a firm's cash flow dynamics:

- How strong is the firm's internal cash flow generation? Is the cash flow from operations positive or negative? If it is negative, why? Is it because the company is growing? Is it because its operations are unprofitable? Or is it having difficulty managing its working capital properly?

- Does the company have the ability to meet its short-term financial obligations, such as interest payments, from its operating cash flow? Can it continue to meet these obligations without reducing its operating flexibility?

- How much cash did the company invest in growth? Are these investments consistent with its business strategy? Did the company use internal cash flow to finance growth, or did it rely on external financing?

■ Did the company pay dividends from internal free cash flow, or did it have to rely on external financing? If the company had to fund its dividends from external sources, is the company's dividend policy sustainable?

■ What type of external financing does the company rely on? Equity, current debt, or non-current debt? Is the financing consistent with the company's overall business risk?

■ Does the company have excess cash flow after making capital investments? Is it a long-term trend? What plans does management have to deploy the free cash flow?

While the information in reported cash flow statements can be used to answer the above questions directly in the case of some firms, it may not be easy to do so always for a number of reasons. First, even though IAS 7 provides broad guidelines on the format of a cash flow statement, there is still significant variation across firms in how cash flow data are disclosed. Therefore, to facilitate a systematic analysis and comparison across firms, analysts often recast the information in the cash flow statement using their own cash flow model. Second, firms may choose to include interest expense and interest income in computing their cash flow from operating activities. However, these two items are not strictly related to a firm's operations. Interest expense is a function of financial leverage, and interest income is derived from financial assets rather than operating assets. Therefore it is useful to restate the cash flow statement to take this into account.

Analysts use a number of different approaches to restate the cash flow data. One such model is shown in Table 5.11. This presents cash flow from operations in two stages. The first step computes cash flow from operations before operating working

TABLE 5.11 Cash flow analysis

Line item (€ millions)	Volkswagen 2005	Volkswagen 2004	Porsche 2005
Net profit			779
Profit before taxes minus taxes paid	1,368	1,078	
After-tax net interest expense (income)	730	491	(8)
Non-operating losses (gains)	203	(176)	(32)
Non-current operating accruals	10,299	9,749	553
Operating cash flow before working capital investments	**12,600**	**11,142**	**1,291**
Net (investments in) or liquidation of operating working capital	(1,048)	865	(156)
Operating cash flow before investment in non-current assets	**11,552**	**12,007**	**1,135**
Net (investment in) or liquidation of non-current operating assets	(10,466)	(15,079)	(689)
Free cash flow available to debt and equity	**1,086**	**(3,072)**	**447**
After-tax net interest expense (income)	**(730)**	**(491)**	**8**
Net debt (repayment) or issuance	**(1,459)**	**6,418**	**92**
Free cash flow available to equity	(1,103)	2,855	547
Dividend (payments)	(414)	(457)	(69)
Net share (repurchase) or issuance	79	7	61
Net increase (decrease) in cash balance	**(1,438)**	**2,405**	**539**

capital investments. In computing this cash flow, the model excludes interest expense and interest income. To compute this number starting with a firm's net profit, an analyst adds back three types of items: (1) after-tax net interest expense because this is a financing item that will be considered later, (2) non-operating gains or losses typically arising out of asset disposals or asset write-offs because these items are investment related and will be considered later, and (3) non-current operating accruals such as depreciation and deferred taxes because these are noncash operating charges.

Several factors affect a firm's ability to generate positive cash flow from operations. Healthy firms that are in a steady state should generate more cash from their customers than they spend on operating expenses. In contrast, growing firms – especially those investing cash in research and development, advertising and marketing, or building an organization to sustain future growth – may experience negative operating cash flow. Firms' working capital management also affects whether they generate positive cash flow from operations. Firms in the growing stage typically invest some cash flow in operating working capital items like accounts receivable, inventories, and accounts payable. Net investments in working capital are a function of firms' credit policies (trade receivables), payment policies (trade payables, prepaid expenses, and provisions), and expected growth in sales (inventories). Thus, in interpreting firms' cash flow from operations after working capital, it is important to keep in mind their growth strategy, industry characteristics, and credit policies.

The cash flow analysis model next focuses on cash flows related to long-term investments. These investments take the form of capital expenditures, intercorporate investments, and mergers and acquisitions. Any positive operating cash flow after making operating working capital investments allows the firm to pursue long-term growth opportunities. If the firm's operating cash flows after working capital investments are not sufficient to finance its long-term investments, it has to rely on external financing to fund its growth. Such firms have less flexibility to pursue long-term investments than those that can fund their growth internally. There are both costs and benefits from being able to fund growth internally. The cost is that managers can use the internally generated free cash flow to fund unprofitable investments. Such wasteful capital expenditures are less likely if managers are forced to rely on external capital suppliers. Reliance on external capital markets may make it difficult for managers to undertake long-term risky investments if it is not easy to communicate to the capital markets the benefits from such investments.

Any excess cash flow after these long-term investments is free cash flow that is available for both debt holders and equity holders. Payments to debt holders include interest payments and principal payments. Firms with negative free cash flow have to borrow additional funds to meet their interest and debt repayment obligations, or cut some of their investments in working capital or long-term investments, or issue additional equity. This situation is clearly financially risky for the firm.

Cash flow after payments to debt holders is free cash flow available to equity holders. Payments to equity holders consist of dividend payments and share repurchases. If firms pay dividends despite negative free cash flow to equity holders, they are borrowing money to pay dividends. While this may be feasible in the short term, it is not prudent for a firm to pay dividends to equity holders unless it has a positive free cash flow on a sustained basis. On the other hand, firms that have a large free cash flow after debt payments run the risk of wasting that money on unproductive investments to pursue growth for its own sake. An analyst, therefore, should carefully examine the investment plans of such firms.

The model in Table 5.11 suggests that the analyst should focus on a number of cash flow measures: (1) cash flow from operations before investment in working capital and interest payments, to examine whether or not the firm is able to generate a cash surplus from its operations, (2) cash flow from operations after investment in working capital, to assess how the firm's working capital is being managed and whether or not it has the flexibility to invest in non-current assets for future growth, (3) free cash flow available to debt and equity holders, to assess a firm's ability to meet its interest and principal payments, and (4) free cash flow available to equity holders, to assess the firm's financial ability to sustain its dividend policy and to identify potential agency problems from excess free cash flow. These measures have to be evaluated in the context of the company's business, its growth strategy, and its financial policies. Further, changes in these measures from year to year provide valuable information on the stability of the cash flow dynamics of the firm.

KEY ANALYSIS QUESTIONS

The cash flow model in Table 5.11 can also be used to assess a firm's earnings quality, as discussed in Chapter 3. The reconciliation of a firm's net profit with its cash flow from operations facilitates this exercise. The following are some of the questions an analyst can probe in this respect:

- Are there significant differences between a firm's net profit and its operating cash flow? Is it possible to clearly identify the sources of this difference? Which accounting policies contribute to this difference? Are there any one-time events contributing to this difference?

- Is the relationship between cash flow and net profit changing over time? Why? Is it because of changes in business conditions or because of changes in the firm's accounting policies and estimates?

- What is the time lag between the recognition of revenues and expenses and the receipt and disbursement of cash flows? What type of uncertainties need to be resolved in between?

- Are the changes in receivables, inventories, and payables normal? If not, is there adequate explanation for the changes?

Finally, as we will discuss in Chapter 7, free cash flow available to debt and equity and free cash flow available to equity are critical inputs into the cash flow-based valuation of firms' assets and equity, respectively.

Analysis of Volkswagen's cash flow

Volkswagen and Porsche reported their cash flows using the indirect cash flow statement. Table 5.11 recasts these statements using the approach discussed above so that we can analyze the two companies' cash flow dynamics.

Cash flow analysis presented in Table 5.11 shows Volkswagen had an operating cash flow before working capital investments of €12,600 million in 2005, an improvement from €11,142 million in 2004. The difference between earnings and these cash flows is primarily attributable to the depreciation and amortization charge included in the company's income statement and the increase in non-current provisions.

In 2004 Volkswagen managed to squeeze an additional €865 million from its operating working capital, primarily by stretching investments in other current liabilities. This contrasts with a net operating working capital investment of $1,048 million in 2005. As a result of this increase in working capital, the company had an operating cash flow before long-term investments to the tune of €11,552 million in 2005, a modest decline from the 2004 figure of €12,007 million. As a result, Volkswagen generated more than adequate cash flow from operations in 2005 to meet its total investment in non-current assets. Because of large investments in non-current operating assets, however, in 2004 cash flow from operations fell short of the required amount. Volkswagen thus had €1,086 million of free cash flow available to debt and equity holders in 2005, compared to a deficit of €3,072 million in 2004.

Only in 2004, Volkswagen was a net borrower. As a result, there was considerable free cash flow available to equity holders. The company utilized this free cash flow to pay its regular dividends in 2004. In 2005, however, Volkswagen used its free cash flow available to debt and equity holders to repay a significant amount of debt. As a result, the company's free cash flow to equity holders was negative and Volkswagen had to use its cash balance to make distributions to shareholders. Clearly, Volkswagen's net cash flow worsened significantly in 2005.

Porsche had a strong cash flow situation in 2005. It had €1,291 million in operating cash flow before working capital investments. Because Porsche slightly increased its investments in operating working capital, its cash flow from operations was slightly lower at €1,135 million. Similar to Volkswagen, Porsche was able to fund all its long-term investments in operating assets from its own operating cash flow. As a result, Porsche had €447 million in free cash flow available to debt and equity holders. The company received €8 million in interest (net of taxes) and was a net borrower to the tune of €92 million, leaving it with €547 million in free cash flow available to equity holders. The company distributed almost no cash to its shareholders – €69 million in dividends minus €61 million from share issuances – leaving a cash increase of about €539 million.

SUMMARY

This chapter presents two key tools of financial analysis: ratio analysis and cash flow analysis. Both these tools allow the analyst to examine a firm's performance and its financial condition, given its strategy and goals. Ratio analysis involves assessing the firm's income statement and balance sheet data. Cash flow analysis relies on the firm's cash flow statement.

The starting point for ratio analysis is the company's ROE. The next step is to evaluate the three drivers of ROE, which are net profit margin, asset turnover, and financial leverage. Net profit margin reflects a firm's operating management, asset turnover reflects its investment management, and financial leverage reflects its liability management. Each of these areas can be further probed by examining a number of ratios. For example, common-sized income statement analysis allows a detailed examination of a firm's net margins. Similarly, turnover of key working capital accounts like accounts receivable, inventories, and accounts payable, and turnover of the firm's fixed assets allow further examination of a firm's asset turnover. Finally, short-term liquidity ratios, debt policy ratios, and coverage ratios provide a means of examining a firm's financial leverage.

A firm's sustainable growth rate – the rate at which it can grow without altering its operating, investment, and financing policies – is determined by its ROE and its dividend policy. The concept of sustainable growth provides a way to integrate the ratio analysis and to evaluate whether or not a firm's growth strategy is sustainable. If a firm's plans call for growing at a rate above its current sustainable rate, then the analyst can examine which of the firm's ratios is likely to change in the future.

Cash flow analysis supplements ratio analysis in examining a firm's operating activities, investment management, and financial risks. Firms reporting in conformity with IFRSs are currently required to report a cash flow statement summarizing their operating, investment, and financing cash flows. Since there are wide variations across firms in the way cash flow data are reported, analysts often use a standard format to recast cash flow data. We discussed in this chapter one such cash flow model. This model allows the analyst to assess whether a firm's operations generate cash flow before investments in operating working capital, and how much cash is being invested in the firm's working capital. It also enables the analyst to calculate the firm's free cash flow after making long-term investments, which is an indication of the firm's ability to meet its debt and dividend payments. Finally, the cash flow analysis shows how the firm is financing itself, and whether its financing patterns are too risky.

The insights gained from analyzing a firm's financial ratios and its cash flows are valuable in forecasts of the firm's future prospects.

DISCUSSION QUESTIONS

1. Which of the following types of firms do you expect to have particularly high or low asset turnover? Explain why.
    - A supermarket
    - A pharmaceutical company
    - A jewelry retailer
    - A steel company.

2. Which of the following types of firms do you expect to have high or low sales margins? Why?
    - A supermarket
    - A pharmaceutical company
    - A jewelry retailer
    - A software company.

3. Sven Broker, an analyst with an established brokerage firm, comments: "The critical number I look at for any company is operating cash flow. If cash flows are less than earnings, I consider a company to be a poor performer and a poor investment prospect." Do you agree with this assessment? Why or why not?

4. In 2005 France-based food retailer Groupe Carrefour had a return on equity of 19 percent, whereas France-based Groupe Casino's return was only 6 percent. Use the decomposed ROE framework to provide possible reasons for this difference.

5. Joe Investor asserts, "A company cannot grow faster than its sustainable growth rate." True or false? Explain why.

6. What are the reasons for a firm having lower cash from operations than working capital from operations? What are the possible interpretations of these reasons?

7. ABC Company recognizes revenue at the point of shipment. Management decides to increase sales for the current quarter by filling all customer orders. Explain what impact this decision will have on:

   ■ Days' receivable for the current quarter

   ■ Days' receivable for the next quarter

   ■ Sales growth for the current quarter

   ■ Sales growth for the next quarter

   ■ Return on sales for the current quarter

   ■ Return on sales for the next quarter.

8. What ratios would you use to evaluate operating leverage for a firm?

9. What are the potential benchmarks that you could use to compare a company's financial ratios? What are the pros and cons of these alternatives?

10. In a period of rising prices, how would the following ratios be affected by the accounting decision to select LIFO, rather than FIFO, for inventory valuation?

    ■ Gross margin

    ■ Current ratio

    ■ Asset turnover

    ■ Debt-to-equity ratio

    ■ Average tax rate.

NOTES

1. For Porsche, we will call the fiscal year ending July 2005 as the year 2005, and the fiscal year ending July 2004 as the year 2004.

2. In computing ROE, one can either use the beginning equity, ending equity, or an average of the two. Conceptually, the average equity is appropriate, particularly for rapidly growing companies. However, for most companies, this computational choice makes little difference as long as the analyst is consistent. Therefore, in practice most analysts use ending balances for simplicity. This comment applies to all ratios discussed in this chapter where one of the items in the ratio is a flow variable (items in the income statement or cash flow statement) and the other item is a stock variable (items in the balance sheet). Throughout this chapter we use the beginning balances of the stock variables.

3. We discuss in greater detail in Chapter 8 how to estimate a company's cost of equity capital. The equity beta for both Volkswagen and Porsche was close to one in 2005, and the yield on long-term treasury bonds was approximately 3.5 percent. If one assumes a risk premium of 6 percent, the two firms' cost of equity is 9.5 percent; if the risk premium is assumed to be 8 percent, then their cost of equity is 11.5 percent. Lower assumed risk premium will, of course, lead to lower estimates of equity capital.

4. Strictly speaking, part of a cash balance is needed to run the firm's operations, so only the excess cash balance should be viewed as negative debt. However, firms do not provide information on excess cash, so we subtract all cash balance in our definitions and computations below. An alternative possibility is to subtract only short-term investments and ignore the cash balance completely.

5. See Doron Nissim and Stephen Penman, "Ratio Analysis and Valuation: From Research to Practice," *Review of Accounting Studies* 6 (2001): 109–154, for a more detailed description of this approach.

6. Porsche has a small amount of debt and a cash balance that is almost equal to the size of its debt. Therefore its weighted average cost of capital is likely to be similar to its cost of equity. We will discuss in Chapter 8 how to estimate a company's weighted average cost of capital.

7. See *Taxes and Business Strategy* by Myron Scholes and Mark Wolfson (Englewood Cliffs, NJ: Prentice-Hall, 1992).

8. Average sales (or average cost of sales) is calculated as annual sales (or annual cost of sales) divided by the number of days in the year. There are a number of issues related to the calculation of turnover ratios in practice. First, in calculating all the turnover ratios, the assets used in the calculations can either be beginning of the year values, year-end values or an average of the beginning and ending balances in a year. We use the average values in our calculations. Second, strictly speaking, one should use credit sales to calculate trade receivables turnover and days' receivables. But since it is usually difficult to obtain data on credit sales, total sales are used instead. Similarly, in calculating trade payables turnover or days' payables, cost of sales (or cost of materials) is substituted for purchases for data availability reasons. Third, the ratios for income statements classified by function differ from those for income statements classified by nature. Turnover ratios for the two types of statements are therefore not perfectly comparable.

9. Changes in cash and marketable securities are excluded because this is the amount being explained by the cash flow statement. Changes in current debt and the current portion of non-current debt are excluded because these accounts represent financing flows, not operating flows.

APPENDIX A:
VOLKSWAGEN AG FINANCIAL STATEMENTS

CONSOLIDATED STATEMENTS OF EARNINGS (€ millions)

Fiscal year ended December 31,	2005	2004	2003
Sales revenue	**95,268**	**88,963**	**84,813**
Cost of sales	(82,391)	(78,440)	(74,099)
Gross profit	**12,877**	**10,523**	**10,714**
Distribution expenses	(8,905)	(8,172)	(7,846)
Administrative expenses	(2,383)	(2,316)	(2,274)
Other operating income	4,552	4,461	4,135
Other operating expenses	(3,349)	(2,876)	(3,124)
Operating profit	**2,792**	**1,620**	**1,605**
Share of profits and losses of Group companies accounted for using the equity method	78	255	511
Other expenses from equity investments	(25)	(23)	(32)
Interest result	(1,123)	(753)	(730)
Profit before tax	**1,722**	**1,099**	**1,354**
Current tax expense	(876)	(851)	(623)
Deferred tax income	274	468	272
Profit after tax	**1,120**	**716**	**1,003**
Minority interest	(0)	(39)	(23)
Profit attributable to shareholders of Volkswagen AG	**1,120**	**677**	**980**

Source: 2005 and 2004 Annual Report, Volkswagen AG.

CONSOLIDATED BALANCE SHEETS (€ millions)

Fiscal year ended December 31,	**2005**	**2004**	**2003**
ASSETS			
Intangible assets	7,668	7,490	7,145
Property, plant, and equipment	22,884	23,795	23,852
Leasing and rental assets	9,882	8,484	8,450
Investment property	167	182	456
Investments in Group companies accounted for using the equity method	4,198	4,221	3,339
Other equity investments	336	293	304
Financial services receivables	24,958	22,762	20,840
Other receivables and financial assets	2,270	2,298	1,394
Deferred tax assets	2,872	2,056	1,583
Total non-current assets	**75,235**	**71,581**	**67,363**
Inventories	12,643	11,440	11,670
Trade receivables	5,638	5,357	5,497
Financial services receivables	22,412	21,109	18,525
Current tax receivables	317	469	452
Other receivables and financial assets	4,856	3,862	3,955
Marketable securities	4,017	2,933	3,148
Cash and cash equivalents	7,963	10,221	7,536
Total current assets	**57,846**	**55,391**	**50,783**
TOTAL ASSETS	**133,081**	**126,972**	**118,146**
LIABILITIES AND SHAREHOLDERS' EQUITY			
Subscribed capital – preference shares	269	269	269
Subscribed capital – ordinary shares	820	820	820
Capital reserves	4,513	4,451	4,451
Retained earnings	17,994	18,325	18,219
Total shareholders' equity	**23,600**	**23,865**	**23,759**
Non-current financial liabilities	31,014	32,198	25,936
Other non-current liabilities	1,591	1,355	1,299
Deferred tax liabilities	1,622	2,251	2,154
Provisions for pensions	14,003	10,930	10,618
Provisions for taxes	2,257	2,065	1,378
Other non-current provisions	5,638	5,547	4,885
Total non-current liabilities	**56,125**	**54,346**	**46,270**
Current financial liabilities	30,992	28,885	28,922
Trade payables	8,476	7,434	7,822
Current tax payables	150	57	25
Other current liabilities	6,205	6,303	5,315
Other current provisions	7,486	5,990	5,929
Total current liabilities	**53,309**	**48,669**	**48,013**
TOTAL LIABILITIES AND SHAREHOLDERS' EQUITY	**133,081**	**126,972**	**118,146**

Source: 2005 and 2004 Annual Report, Volkswagen AG.

CONSOLIDATED STATEMENTS OF CASH FLOWS (€ millions)

Fiscal year ended December 31,	2005	2004	2003
OPERATING ACTIVITIES			
Profit before tax	1,722	1,099	1,354
Adjustments for:			
Income taxes paid	(354)	(21)	(987)
Depreciation and amortization expense	5,614	5,648	5,338
Amortization of capitalized development costs	1,438	1,134	1,381
Impairment losses on equity investments	6	62	6
Depreciation of leasing and rental assets and			
investment property	1,596	1,774	1,508
Change in provisions	1,351	1,075	885
Loss on disposal of non-current assets	40	(21)	70
Share of profit or loss of Group companies			
accounted for using the equity method	294	56	(72)
Other non-cash income/expense	151	(177)	(442)
Change in inventories	(720)	178	(1,109)
Change in receivables (excluding financial services)	(757)	(4)	(494)
Change in liabilities (excluding financial liabilities)	429	691	933
Cash flow from operating activities	10,810	11,494	8,371
INVESTING ACTIVITIES			
Acquisition of property, plant and equipment, and			
intangible assets	(4,434)	(5,550)	(6,727)
Additions to capitalized development costs	(1,432)	(1,501)	(1,817)
Acquisition of subsidiaries and other equity investments	(150)	(2,287)	(356)
Disposal of equity investments	166	1,045	0
Loans	(22)	(319)	(67)
Change in leasing and rental assets and investment			
property (excluding depreciation)	(2,950)	(1,942)	(2,963)
Change in financial services receivables	(1,948)	(4,801)	(3,766)
Proceeds from disposal of non-current assets (excluding			
leasing and rental assets and investments property)	304	276	232
Change in investments in securities	(820)	280	229
Cash flow from investing activities	(11,286)	(14,799)	(15,235)
FINANCING ACTIVITIES			
Capital contributions	66	0	0
Dividends paid	(414)	(457)	(539)
Other changes in equity	13	7	(3)
Proceeds from issue of bonds	5,754	13,718	14,850
Repayment of bonds	(9,804)	(5,507)	(3,871)
Change in other financial liabilities	3,233	(1,437)	954
Finance lease payments	(3)	(21)	(27)
Change in loans	(639)	(335)	59
Cash flows from financing activities	(1,794)	5,968	11,423

(continued)

CONSOLIDATED STATEMENTS OF CASH FLOWS (€ millions) *(continued)*

Fiscal year ended December 31,	2005	2004	2003
Changes in cash and cash and equivalents due to changes in the scope of consolidation	(67)	3	77
Effect of exchange rate changes on cash and cash equivalents	79	19	(87)
Net change in cash and cash equivalents	(2,258)	2,685	4,549
Cash and cash equivalents at beginning of financial year	10,221	7,536	2,987
CASH AND CASH EQUIVALENTS AT YEAR-END	7,963	10,221	7,536

Source: 2005 and 2004 Annual Report, Volkswagen AG.

STANDARDIZED STATEMENTS OF EARNINGS (€ millions)

Fiscal year ended December 31,	2005	2004	2003
Sales	**95,268**	**88,963**	**84,813**
Cost of sales	(82,391)	(78,440)	(74,099)
Gross profit	**12,877**	**10,523**	**10,714**
SG&A	(11,288)	(10,488)	(10,120)
Other operating income, net of other operating expense	1,203	1,585	1,011
Other operating income	4,552	4,461	4,135
Other operating expense	(3,349)	(2,876)	(3,124)
Operating profit	**2,792**	**1,620**	**1,605**
Investment income	53	232	479
Net interest expense (income)	(1,123)	(753)	(730)
Interest income	N.A.	N.A.	N.A.
Interest expense	N.A.	N.A.	N.A.
Profit before tax	**1,722**	**1,099**	**1,354**
Tax expense	(602)	(383)	(351)
Profit after tax	**1,120**	**716**	**1,003**
Minority interest	0	(39)	(23)
Net profit	**1,120**	**677**	**980**
Dividends on preference shares	(127)	(117)	(117)
Net profit attributable to ordinary shareholders	**993**	**560**	**863**

Source: Authors' calculations.

STANDARDIZED BALANCE SHEETS (€ millions)

Fiscal year ending December 31,	2005	2004	2003
ASSETS			
Non-current tangible assets	32,766	32,279	32,302
Non-current intangible assets	7,668	7,490	7,145
Deferred taxes – Non-current asset	2,872	2,056	1,583
Other non-current assets	31,929	29,756	26,333
Total non-current assets	**75,235**	**71,581**	**67,363**
Trade receivables	28,050	26,466	24,022
Inventories	12,643	11,440	11,670
Other current assets	5,173	4,331	4,407
Cash and marketable securities	11,980	13,154	10,684
Total current assets	**57,846**	**55,391**	**50,783**
TOTAL ASSETS	**133,081**	**126,972**	**118,146**
LIABILITIES AND SHAREHOLDERS' EQUITY			
Preference shares	269	269	269
Ordinary shareholders' equity	23,331	23,596	23,490
Total shareholders' equity	**23,600**	**23,865**	**23,759**
Minority Interest	**47**	**92**	**104**
Non-current debt	50,655	48,675	41,439
Deferred tax liability	1,622	2,251	2,154
Other non-current liabilities (non interest-bearing)	3,848	3,420	2,677
Total non-current liabilities	**56,125**	**54,346**	**46,270**
Current debt	30,992	28,885	28,922
Trade payables	8,476	7,434	7,822
Other current liabilities	13,841	12,350	11,269
Total current liabilities	**53,309**	**48,669**	**48,013**
TOTAL LIABILITIES AND SHAREHOLDERS' EQUITY	**133,081**	**126,972**	**118,146**

Source: Authors' calculations.

STANDARDIZED STATEMENTS OF CASH FLOWS (€ millions)

Fiscal year ended December 31,	2005	2004	2003
Profit before tax	**1,722**	**1,099**	**1,354**
Taxes paid	(354)	(21)	(987)
After-tax net interest expense (income)	730	491	541
Non-operating losses (gains)	203	(176)	(382)
Non-current operating accruals	10,299	9,749	8,161
Operating cash flow before working capital investments	**12,600**	**10,067**	**8,687**

(continued)

STANDARDIZED STATEMENTS OF CASH FLOWS (€ millions) *(continued)*

Fiscal year ended December 31,	**2005**	**2004**	**2003**
Net (investments in) or liquidation of operating working capital	(1,048)	865	215
Operating cash flow before investment in non-current assets	**11,552**	**12,007**	**8,902**
Net (investment in) or liquidation of non-current operating assets	(10,466)	(15,079)	(15,464)
Free cash flow available to debt and equity	**1,086**	**(3,072)**	**(6,562)**
After-tax net interest expense (income)	(730)	(491)	(541)
Net debt (repayment) or issuance	(1,459)	6,418	11,965
Free cash flow available to equity	**(1,103)**	**2,855**	**4,862**
Dividend (payments)	(414)	(457)	(48,265)
Net share (repurchase) or issuance	79	7	9,232
Net increase (decrease) in cash balance	**(1,438)**	**2,405**	**306,068**

Source: Authors' calculations.

CONDENSED STATEMENTS OF EARNINGS (€ millions)

Fiscal year ended December 31,	**2005**	**2004**	**2003**
Sales	95,268	88,963	84,813
Net operating profit after tax	1,850	1,168	1,521
Net profit	1,120	677	980
+ Net interest expense after tax	730	491	541
= Net operating profit after tax	**1,850**	**1,168**	**1,521**
– Net interest expense after tax	**730**	**491**	**541**
= Net interest expense (income)	1,123	753	730
× (1 – Tax expense/Profit before tax)	0.6504	0.6515	0.7408
= Net interest expense after tax	**730**	**491**	**541**
= Net profit	**1,120**	**677**	**980**
– Dividends on preference shares	127	117	117
= Net profit attributable to ordinary shareholders	**993**	**560**	**863**

Source: Authors' calculations.

CONDENSED BALANCE SHEETS (€ millions)

Fiscal year ended December 31,	2005	2004	2003
Net working capital			
Trade receivables	28,050	26,466	24,022
+ Inventories	12,643	11,440	11,670
+ Other current assets	5,173	4,331	4,407
– Trade payables	8,476	7,434	7,822
– Other current liabilities	13,841	12,350	11,269
= Net working capital	**23,549**	**22,453**	**21,008**
+ Net non-current assets			
Non-current tangible assets	32,766	32,279	32,302
+ Non-current intangible assets	7,668	7,490	7,145
+ Other non-current assets	31,929	29,756	26,333
– Minority interest	47	92	104
– Deferred taxes	(1,250)	195	571
– Other non-current liabilities (non-interest-bearing)	3,848	3,420	2,677
= Net non-current assets	**64,080**	**60,271**	**57,543**
= Total assets	**87,629**	**82,724**	**78,551**
Net debt			
Current debt	30,992	28,885	28,922
+ Non-current debt	45,017	43,128	36,554
– Cash	11,980	13,154	10,684
= Net debt	**64,029**	**58,859**	**54,792**
+ Preference shares	**269**	**269**	**269**
+ Ordinary shareholders' equity	**23,331**	**23,596**	**23,490**
= Total net capital	**87,629**	**82,724**	**78,551**

Source: Authors' calculations.

APPENDIX B:
DR. ING. H.C.F. PORSCHE AG
FINANCIAL STATEMENTS

CONSOLIDATED STATEMENTS OF EARNINGS (€ millions)

Fiscal year ended July 31,	2005	2004
Sales revenue	6,574	6,148
Changes in inventories and own work capitalized	74	189
Total operating performance	**6,648**	**6,337**
Other operating income	207	211
Cost of materials	(2,950)	(2,875)
Personnel expenses	(965)	(950)
Amortization and depreciation	(510)	(382)
Other operating expenses	(1,211)	(1,221)
Earnings before financial income	**1,219**	**1,121**
Income from equity investments	0	1
Other interest and similar income	172	130
Interest and similar expenses	(158)	(111)
Other financial result	5	(4)
Profit from ordinary activities	**1,238**	**1,137**
Income taxes	(459)	(447)
Profit after tax	**779**	**690**
Minority interest	(4)	(4)
Net profit	**775**	**686**

Source: 2005 Annual Report, Dr. Ing. h.c.F. Porsche AG.

CONSOLIDATED BALANCE SHEETS (€ millions)

Fiscal year ended July 31,	2005	2004
ASSETS		
Intangible assets	294	327
Property, plant, and equipment	1,141	1,108
Financial assets	27	22
Receivables from financial services	1,183	923
Leased assets	967	922
Total non-current assets	**3,612**	**3,303**

(continued)

CONSOLIDATED BALANCE SHEETS (€ millions) *(continued)*

Fiscal year ended July 31,	2005	2004
Inventories	572	626
Trade receivables	308	311
Receivables from financial services	384	480
Other receivables and assets	1,005	1,153
Securities	1,871	1,611
Cash and cash equivalents	1,755	1,459
Total current assets	**5,895**	**5,638**
Deferred tax assets	**185**	**57**
Prepaid expenses	**19**	**17**
TOTAL ASSETS	**9,710**	**9,014**
LIABILITIES AND SHAREHOLDERS' EQUITY		
Subscribed capital – preference shares	23	23
Subscribed capital – ordinary shares	23	23
Capital reserves	122	122
Revenue reserves	3,234	2,746
Translation differences	11	1
Capital allocable to shareholders	**3,412**	**2,914**
Minority interests	**8**	**6**
Pension provisions	596	551
Tax provisions	164	364
Other current provisions	842	791
Other non-current provisions	685	554
Total provisions	**2,287**	**2,260**
Deferred tax liabilities	**180**	**207**
Financial liabilities	3,092	2,947
Trade payables	443	377
Other liabilities	235	256
Deferred income	52	47
Total liabilities	**3,823**	**3,627**
TOTAL LIABILITIES AND SHAREHOLDERS' EQUITY	**9,710**	**9,014**

Source: 2005 Annual Report, Dr. Ing. h.c.F. Porsche AG.

CONSOLIDATED STATEMENTS OF CASH FLOWS (€ millions)

Fiscal year ended July 31,	2005	2004
OPERATING ACTIVITIES		
Net profit	779	690
Adjustments for:		
Amortization and depreciation	510	382
Change in pension provision	46	49
Changes in other provisions	(3)	391
Other noncash expense/income	62	50
Gain/loss from disposal of non-current assets	(62)	(43)
Change in inventories, trade receivables and other assets	(216)	(73)
Change in trade payables and other liabilities		
(without other provisions)	60	(141)
Cash flow from operating activities	1,175	1,304
INVESTING ACTIVITIES		
Cash received from the disposal of non-current assets	412	368
Cash received from the disposal of equity investments	0	8
Cash paid for investments in non-current assets	(914)	(961)
Cash paid for the acquisition of consolidated entities	0	(76)
Receivables from financial services	(186)	(380)
Change in investments in securities	(243)	(827)
Cash flow from investing activities	(931)	(1,868)
FINANCING ACTIVITIES		
Cash payments to shareholders	(69)	(59)
Capital contributions	6	9
Cash received from the issue of loans/cash repayment		
of loans	55	(28)
Cash received from the issue of bonds	0	632
Cash received from the other financial liabilities	92	322
Cash flows from financing activities	84	876
Exchange-rate related changes in cash and cash equivalents	(32)	7
Net change in cash and cash equivalents	296	319
Cash and cash equivalents at beginning of financial year	1,459	1,140
CASH AND CASH EQUIVALENTS AT YEAR-END	1,755	1,459

Source: 2005 Annual Report, Dr. Ing. h.c.F. Porsche AG.

STANDARDIZED STATEMENTS OF EARNINGS (€ millions)

Fiscal year ended July 31,	2005	2004
Sales	**6,574**	**6,148**
Cost of materials	(2,876)	(2,686)
Personnel expense	(965)	(950)
Depreciation and amortization	(510)	(382)
Other operating income, net of other operating expense	(1,004)	(1,010)
Other operating income	207	211
Other operating expense	(1,211)	(1,221)
Operating profit	**1,219**	**1,121**
Investment income	5	(3)
Net interest expense (income)	13	20
Interest income	N.A.	N.A.
Interest expense	N.A.	N.A.
Profit before tax	**1,238**	**1,137**
Tax expense	(459)	(447)
Profit after tax	**779**	**690**
Minority interest	(4)	(4)
Net profit	**779**	**690**
Dividends on preference shares	(44)	(35)
Net profit attributable to ordinary shareholders	**732**	**651**

Source: Authors' calculations.

STANDARDIZED BALANCE SHEETS (€ millions)

Fiscal year ending July 31,	2005	2004
ASSETS		
Non-current tangible assets	2,108	2,031
Non-current intangible assets	294	327
Deferred tax asset	185	57
Other non-current assets	1,210	945
Total non-current assets	**3,797**	**3,360**
Trade receivables	692	790
Inventories	572	626
Other current assets	1,024	1,169
Cash and marketable securities	3,626	3,069
Total current assets	**5,914**	**5,654**
TOTAL ASSETS	**9,710**	**9,014**

(continued)

STANDARDIZED BALANCE SHEETS (€ millions) (continued)

Fiscal year ending July 31,	2005	2004
LIABILITIES AND SHAREHOLDERS' EQUITY		
Preference shares	23	23
Ordinary shareholders' equity	3,389	2,892
Total shareholders' equity	**3,412**	**2,914**
Minority interest	**8**	**6**
Non-current debt	4,373	4,052
Deferred tax liability	180	207
Other non-current liabilities (non interest-bearing)	0	0
Total non-current liabilities	**4,553**	**4,258**
Current debt	0	0
Trade payables	443	377
Other current liabilities	1,293	1,458
Total current liabilities	**1,736**	**1,835**
TOTAL LIABILITIES AND SHAREHOLDERS' EQUITY	**9,710**	**9,014**

Source: Authors' calculations.

STANDARDIZED STATEMENTS OF CASH FLOWS (€ millions)

Fiscal year ended July 31,	2005	2004
Net profit	**779**	**690**
After-tax net interest expense (income)	(8)	(12)
Non-operating losses (gains)	(32)	14
Non-current operating accruals	553	822
Operating cash flow before working capital investments	**1,291**	**1,514**
Net (investments in) or liquidation of operating working capital	(156)	(215)
Operating cash flow before investment in non-current assets	**1,135**	**1,299**
Net (investment in) or liquidation of non-current operating assets	(689)	(1,042)
Free cash flow available to debt and equity	**447**	**257**
After-tax net interest expense (income)	8	12
Net debt (repayment) or issuance	92	954
Free cash flow available to equity	**547**	**1,223**
Dividend (payments)	(69)	(59)
Net share (repurchase) or issuance	61	(19)
Net increase (decrease) in cash balance	**539**	**1,145**

Source: Authors' calculations.

CONDENSED STATEMENTS OF EARNINGS (€ millions)

Fiscal year ended July 31,	2005	2004
Sales	6,574	6,148
Net operating profit after tax	767	674
Net profit	775	686
+ Net interest expense after tax	(8)	(12)
= **Net operating profit after tax**	**767**	**674**
− **Net interest expense after tax**	(8)	(12)
= Net interest expense (income)	(13)	(20)
× (1 − Tax expense/Income before taxes)	0.6292	0.6069
= **Net interest expense after tax**	**(8)**	**(12)**
= **Net profit**	775	686
− Dividends on preference shares	44	35
= **Net profit attributable to ordinary shareholders**	**732**	**651**

Source: Authors' calculations.

CONDENSED BALANCE SHEETS (€ millions)

Fiscal Year Ended July 31,	2005	2004
Net working capital		
Trade receivables	692	790
+ Inventories	572	626
+ Other current assets	1,024	1,169
− Trade payables	443	377
− Other current liabilities	1,293	1,458
= **Net working capital**	**551**	**750**
+ Net non-current assets		
Non-current tangible assets	2,108	2,031
+ Non-current intangible assets	294	327
+ Other non-current assets	1,210	945
− Minority interest	8	6
− Deferred taxes	(4)	150
− Other non-current liabilities (non-interest-bearing)	0	0
= **Net non-current assets**	**3,608**	**3,147**
= **Total assets**	**4,159**	**3,897**

(continued)

CONDENSED BALANCE SHEETS (€ millions) *(continued)*

Fiscal Year Ended July 31,	2005	2004
Net debt		
Current debt	0	0
+ Non-current debt	4,373	4,052
– Cash	3,626	3,069
= Net debt	**747**	**982**
+ Preference shares	**23**	**23**
+ Ordinary shareholders' equity	**3,389**	**2,892**
= Total net capital	**4,159**	**3,897**

Source: Authors' calculations.

Carrefour S.A.[1]

Analyst Chrystelle Moreau of Leblanc Investissements, a small Paris-based investment firm, glanced through the annual report of Groupe Carrefour for the fiscal year 2005 that she had just received. The past year had been a turbulent year for Carrefour's shareholders and the analyst wondered what had caused the turbulence and whether a turnaround could be expected. In February 2005, Daniel Bernard had stepped down as Carrefour's President and Chief Executive Officer (CEO). Bernard had been succeeded as CEO by Jose Luis Duran, Carrefour's former Chief Financial Officer. Luc Vandevelde – protégé of Carrefour's principal shareholder, the Halley family, and former CEO of Promodès and Marks and Spencer – had become President of the company's Supervisory Board.[2] Following the departure of Daniel Bernard, three other members of the Management Board had also resigned from their positions.

When publicly announcing Bernard's resignation, the company's Board acknowledged Bernard's achievements by reporting that:

> … in 13 years Carrefour has gone from the number 1 in the French market to a strong world number 2 in retail and an uncontested European number 1 that masters the four formats of modern commerce. In Asia, Latin America as in Europe, the group has become the leading player. Over this time, revenue has grown more than four-fold and net profit, at end 2003, has increased eight-fold corresponding to a 19 percent annual growth rate. Over this period, the share price has been multiplied by 4, one of the three best world-wide performances of the sector and the 11th of the CAC40.

Yet rumors suggested that Carrefour's largest shareholder had become unhappy with Daniel Bernard's performance and Carrefour's share price responded positively to the announcement of Bernard's resignation.[3]

During the 1990s, Carrefour had been one of Moreau's favorite shares. The company had created a great reputation for its broad assortment and low prices, and had shown an outstanding share price performance. During the first half of the 2000s, however, Carrefour's share price had fallen from about €80 to €40, despite the fact that the company had consistently earned returns on equity in excess of 17 percent. At the beginning of 2005, investors speculated that Carrefour would be taken over by its U.S. rival Wal-Mart. Moreau's investment firm had not sold its Carrefour holdings following Carrefour's merger with Promodès in 1999 and, consequently, had incurred substantial losses on its investment. Moreau was preparing herself for Carrefour's upcoming shareholders' meeting. In particular, she wanted to get a better understanding of what had caused Carrefour's share price decline during the past years as well as the company's current financial position, before voting on any proposals that Carrefour's new management would make during the meeting.

---

1. Professor Erik Peek prepared this case. The case is intended solely as the basis for class discussion and is not intended to serve as an endorsement, source of primary data, or illustration of effective or ineffective management.
2. Concurrent with Carrefour's management change, the company switched from having a one-tier board structure to having a two-tier board structure. That is, the company split its Board of Directors into a Management Board and a Supervisory Board.
3. See "Changing shopkeepers," The Economist, February 3, 2005.

Company background

France-based food retailer Carrefour was established in 1959 by the Fournier and Defforey families and opened it first hypermarket in Sainte-Geneviève-de-Bois in 1963. The hypermarket concept was the store concept that Carrefour would eventually become most famous for. The typical characteristic of such hypermarkets is that they offer a wide assortment of food as well as nonfood products at economic prices and are of a much greater size than the traditional supermarkets. Specifically, the size of hypermarkets can range from 5,000 to 20,000 square meters. In comparison, Carrefour's regular supermarkets, which operate under the names Champion, GB, Globi, GS, and Gima, have an average size of between 1,000 and 2,000 square meters.

In 1979 Carrefour opened its first hard discount stores under the "Ed" banner in France and under the "Dia" banner in Spain. The hard discount stores sell a much smaller variety of products than the hypermarkets (on average 800 products versus 20,000 to 80,000) on a much smaller store space (between 200 and 800 square meters) at discount prices. Some of the discount products are sold under own brand names, such as the Dia brand name. In 1985 Carrefour also started to sell products under its own brand name in its other, non-discount stores.

During the 1970s and 1980s, Carrefour expanded across the oceans and established hypermarkets in, for example, Brazil (1975), Argentina (1982), and Taiwan (1989). The international and intercontinental expansion of Carrefour took off especially in the 1990s when Carrefour opened a large number of hypermarkets in southern Europe (Greece, Italy, and Turkey), eastern Europe (Poland), Asia (China, Hong Kong, Korea, Malaysia, Singapore, and Thailand), and Latin America (Mexico, Chile, and Colombia). Exhibit 1 provides information about Carrefour's operations by geographic segment and by store format. The exhibit also illustrates that intercontinental expansion primarily occurred through the opening of hypermarkets. Most of Carrefour's smaller supermarkets were located throughout Europe.

In addition to its traditional food and nonfood retailing activities, the company soon offered traveling, financial, and insurance services to its customers in Brazil, France, and Spain. For example, Carrefour has its own payment card, the "Pass" card, which it introduced in the early 1980s. In the beginning, the Pass card offered customers priority at store check-outs and allowed them to pay their bills in installments. Later, the card became linked to a Visa credit card and customers could borrow money for out-of-store purchases. By the end of 2005, Carrefour's financial services unit had €3.5 billion in credit outstanding throughout the world.

One of the key events in Carrefour's history took place in 1999, when it merged with Promodès, a large French food retailer that owned the Champion supermarket chain. At the time of the merger, Carrefour and Promodès were, respectively, the sixth and ninth largest retailers in the world and held market shares of around 18 and 12 percent in France. After the merger, the combined company, which continued under the name Carrefour, became Europe's largest retailer, the world's second largest retailer, and the world's most international supermarket chain. An important trigger for the merger was that in the late 1990s, U.S.-based Wal-Mart, the world's largest retailer, was expanding its operations to Europe and posed a potential threat to the French retailer's strong position in their home market. As a result of the merger, the Halley family, who had founded Promodès and had always been its controlling shareholder, became the principal shareholder of Carrefour, holding a 13 percent stake in Carrefour by the end of 2005.

The integration of the operations of Promodès and Carrefour went slowly and the merger of the two retailers was the start of a difficult period. Immediately following the merger, Carrefour acquired a few other supermarket chains, such as Norte in

Argentina, GS in Italy, and GB in Belgium, emphasizing its desire to aggressively expand its operations and become the leading international retailer. However, over the years, competition in the food retailing industry substantially increased and all retailers came under pressure to cut prices. The need to lower prices became even stronger when the European economy slowed down in 2001. Carrefour's sales growth in its home market suffered from the competition of France-based Leclerc and Auchan, which focused their strategy on cutting prices and gaining market share. Although Carrefour did join its French rivals in cutting prices, the company aimed much more at improving its margins than increasing sales volumes. Only in 2003, when Carrefour's sales growth in France approached zero, did the company start to put more emphasis on competing on price, gaining market share, and stimulating customer loyalty. In April 2004, Carrefour launched a new customer loyalty program. The customer loyalty card helped the company to create a database that registers the purchasing habits of its customers and helps it respond more promptly to changes in customer preferences. By that time, Carrefour's sales growth in its home market had come to a halt and the company started to lose market share. Analysts worried that this could hinder Carrefour's international expansion. One analyst stated:[4]

> We are seeing that there is a lack of growth and a decline in the market share in the main businesses, which are the hypermarkets in France. Without the contribution of the hypermarkets in France, we don't have enough resources to fuel the growth outside France.

Carrefour had been listed on the Paris Stock Exchange (Euronext) since 1970. The company's stock price performance during the first half of the 2000s is summarized in Exhibit 2.

Carrefour after its management change

After having replaced Daniel Bernard, Jose Luis Duran announced in Carrefour's 2004 Annual Report that one of his primary goals was to make Carrefour a growth company. He commented on his plans as follows:

> In 2004, the growth in our sales, neglecting the effects of exchange rates, was about 4%, of which 3% were attributable to the increase in sales floor area and 1% to growth on a like for like basis. In the future, we must record a growth in sales as close as possible to double digits. To do this, the contribution from new openings should be on the order of 3% to 5%, from like for like sales of 1% to 3% and from tactical acquisitions of 1% to 2%.

Although his focus was to improve growth, the new CEO planned to put an end to Carrefour's over-aggressive expansion abroad and its incoherent pricing strategy in France.[5] Carrefour's new strategy was to withdraw from poorly performing markets and increase its capital expenditures in successful markets. In addition, the company intended to focus less on margins, but more on increasing sales volume and cost savings. In its home market, the company hoped to regain market share from its French competitors, Leclerc and Auchan, as well as from deep-discounters such as Aldi and Lidl. To regain price competitiveness, Carrefour frequently surveyed its hypermarket customers and quickly adjusted its prices on the basis of the survey

4. See "Sign of the Times for Carrefour," BBC News website, February 3, 2005.
5. See "Carrefour at Crossroads," The Economist, October 20, 2005.

outcomes. Finally, Carrefour planned to broaden its product assortment and lengthen the opening hours of its stores. To achieve the latter goal, Carrefour needed to increase its staff.

For 2006, Carrefour expected to open about 1.5 million square meters of new store space (worldwide), of which 425,000 square meters was to be through acquisitions, and achieve sales growth above its growth rate in 2005. In 2005, Carrefour had spent €1.8 billion on store openings and enlargements. Total capital expenditure would increase from €2.5 billion in 2004 and €3.1 billion in 2005 to €10 billion in the 2006–2008 period. The company would, however, remain engaged in price wars in many of its markets, including France, albeit possibly to a lesser extent. Carrefour's leading positions in China and Europe would also remain under attack from U.S. retailer Wal-Mart. One way in which it could relieve some of the pressure on its margins was to negotiate with its suppliers on pricing. In 2004 and 2005, Carrefour had managed to come to an agreement with its key suppliers of branded consumer goods that they would cut or only moderately increase their prices. However, suppliers were planning to raise their prices by 4–6 percent in 2006. In addition, the new French Dutreil law that took effect on January 1, 2006, ruled that supplier discounts in excess of 20 percent must be passed on to retailers' customers in the form of lower prices. Given these developments, Carrefour's price cuts in 2006 would likely focus on its private labels. In 2005, Carrefour had relaunched its private labels on prominent display and the company expected its Carrefour product range to include 11,000 products by the end of 2006.

Tesco

In 2005 one of Carrefour's European industry peers was U.K.-based Tesco, the world's third largest retailer, after Carrefour and Wal-Mart. The company had been founded in 1919 and had become the leading retailer in its domestic market in 1995.

The strategies of Carrefour and Tesco exhibited some similarities. Particularly, both retailers strived for international expansion and reserved a substantial amount of store space for nonfood products. Tesco's operations were less international than Carrefour's. In 2005, 70 percent of Carrefour's store space was outside France, whereas 56 percent of Tesco's store space was located outside the U.K. Tesco operated primarily in eastern Europe (Czech Republic, Hungary, Poland, and Slovakia) and Asia (e.g., China, Japan, South Korea, and Thailand).

The company had four different store formats, which all operated under the Tesco banner. Tesco Express and Metro stores were the smallest type of stores (with up to 5,000 square meters) and focused on selling food products. Tesco's Superstores occupied between 7,000 and 16,000 square meters and offered both food and nonfood products. Since 1997, Tesco also operated Extra stores, which offered a wide range of food and nonfood lines, including electrical equipment, clothing, and health and pharmaceutical products. These stores had store spaces of approximately 20,000 square meters. Tesco's Superstores and Extra stores were thus comparable, at least in size and assortment, to Carrefour's Hypermarkets. Illustrative of the similarity between the two retailer's operations is that in September 2005 the companies swapped stores. Tesco received 15 Carrefour stores in the Czech Republic and Slovakia in return for six Tesco stores in Taiwan.

Although Tesco seemed to follow the example of Carrefour in terms of the international expansion and the adoption of a multiformat approach, the U.K. retailer had set an example for creating customer loyalty in the 1990s. The problem of a declining market share that Carrefour experienced in its domestic market in 2005 was fairly similar to the problem that Tesco had experienced in the early 1990s. In those years, Tesco suffered from slowing sales growth and lower margins, primarily because it was stuck between two strategies: the strategy of deep-discounters such as Asda and the strategy of high-quality retailers such as Sainsbury's. In response to the problems, Tesco lowered its prices, introduced its private brand label, which became highly successful, expanded its nonfood operations, and introduced a loyalty card that helped the retailer to observe the shopping patterns of its customers. These actions boosted Tesco's sales growth and profits and helped the company to become the market leader in the U.K.

In 2005 Tesco's sales of nonfood products grew twice as fast as its sales of food products. Like Carrefour, Tesco offered financial services, such as banking and insurance services, to its customers. Unlike Carrefour, Tesco operated a very successful online grocery store in the U.K., which had 170,000 registered customers. In the fiscal year ending on February 25, 2006, Tesco's return on equity of 16.7 percent was comparable to Carrefour's ROE in 2005 of 17.1 percent. Exhibit 5 shows a summary of Tesco's financial performance in 2005. Tesco's market performance in the first half of the 2000s had been significantly better than Carrefour's. Between January 1, 2000 and February 25, 2006, Tesco's share price increased by 82 percent. This total return corresponded to an average annual return of slightly above 10 percent.

Concurrent with the presentation of its results for fiscal 2005, Tesco announced that it planned to sell and lease back close to £5 billion of property over the next five years. During 2005, the company had already sold and leased back close to £0.4 billion of property. Approximately £1.5 billion of the proceeds from these sale and leaseback transactions would be used to return cash to Tesco's shareholders and reduce the company's investment base.

Carrefour

EXHIBIT 1 Carrefour's operations by geographic segment and store format

	Fiscal year	France	Rest of Europe	Latin America	Asia	Hyper-market	Super-market	Hard discount	Other
Net sales (in € millions)	2005	35,577	27,102	5,075	5,744	43,802	13,239	6,441	11,015
	2004	35,723	27,123	4,721	5,101	42,147	13,080	5,813	11,627
	2003	35,704	25,527	4,619	4,637	41,587	12,688	4,934	11,278
	2002	35,101	23,608	5,382	4,639	40,551	12,371	5,498	10,310
	2001	34,335	22,144	8,440	4,567	40,997	13,897	4,864	9,728
Earnings before interest and taxes (in € millions)	2005	1,713	1,145	133	185				
	2004	1,965	1,070	50	149				
	2003	2,144	952	13	143				
	2002	2,065	796	23	141				
	2001	1,905	733	53	134				
Capital expenditures (in € millions)	2005	791	1,192	248	381				
	2004	874	1,008	231	336				
	2003	818	1,169	295	436				
	2002	609	1,224	276	355				
	2001	776	1,438	370	318				
Sales area of consolidated stores (in square meters, thousands)	2005	3,245	4,596	1,621	1,618	7,087	2,319	1,674	
	2004	3,056	4,265	1,854	1,496	6,885	2,321	1,466	
	2003	2,919	3,994	1,902	1,228	6,510	2,277	1,255	
	2002	2,781	4,142	1,792	1,051	6,180	2,132	1,093	
	2001	2,716	3,752	1,783	899	5,674	2,177	997	

Carrefour

EXHIBIT 2 **Carrefour's stock price and the MSCI World Retailing Price Index from December 1995 to February 2006 (price on December 29, 1995 = 100)**

Source: Thomson Datastream.

EXHIBIT 3 Carrefour's consolidated income statements, balance sheets, and cash flow statements, 2001 to 2005 (in € millions)

Consolidated income statements

	2005 IFRS	2004 Restated to IFRSª	2004 French GAAP	2003 French GAAP	2002 French GAAP	2001 French GAAP
Net sales	74,496.8	72,668.0	72,668.0	70,486.2	68,728.8	69,486.1
Other income	1,011.3	1,038.6	0.0	0.0	0.0	0.0
Total income	**75,508.1**	**73,706.6**	**72,668.0**	**70,486.2**	**68,728.8**	**69,486.1**
Cost of sales	(58,626.5)	(57,052.8)	(56,554.2)	(54,630.4)	(53,182.1)	(53,875.0)
Gross margin from current operations	**16,881.6**	**16,653.8**	**16,113.8**	**15,855.8**	**15,546.7**	**15,611.1**
Sales, general, and administrative expenses	(12,232.7)	(11,888.2)	(11,792.9)	(11,478.4)	(11,419.2)	(11,728.7)
Other income and expenses	0.0	0.0	596.2	493.6	547.5	645.2
Depreciation, amortization, and provisions	(1,474.2)	(1,652.3)	(1,683.4)	(1,619.6)	(1,649.6)	(1,702.0)
Activity contribution	**3,174.7**	**3,113.3**	**3,233.8**	**3,251.4**	**3,025.4**	**2,825.6**
Nonrecurring income	264.6	229.5	0.0	0.0	0.0	0.0
Nonrecurring expenses	(285.0)	(305.5)	0.0	0.0	0.0	0.0
EBIT	**3,154.2**	**3,037.3**	**3,233.8**	**3,233.8**	**3,233.8**	**3,233.8**
Interest income, of which	(454.6)	(484.5)	(424.1)	(463.7)	(526.9)	(646.2)
Net debt expense	(395.9)	(401.9)	(493.8)	(548.3)	(669.5)	(778.6)
Other financial income and expenses	(58.7)	(82.6)	69.7	84.6	142.6	132.4
Earnings before taxes	**2,699.6**	**2,552.8**	**2,809.7**	**2,787.7**	**2,498.5**	**2,179.4**
Income tax	(793.9)	(762.7)	(836.4)	(846.2)	(736.4)	(585.7)
Net income from recurring operations of consolidated companies	**1,905.7**	**1,790.2**	**1,905.7**	**1,941.5**	**1,762.1**	**1,593.7**
Net income from companies consolidated by the equity method	50.6	40.7	101.4	107.2	107.4	127.0
Net income before from recurring operations	**1,956.3**	**1,830.9**	**2,074.7**	**2,048.7**	**1,869.5**	**1,720.7**
Goodwill amortization	0.0	0.0	(319.3)	(318.0)	(309.7)	(368.5)
Nonrecurring income	0.0	0.0	(246.2)	9.1	(14.9)	59.2
Net income from discontinued operations	(374.2)	(85.5)	0.0	0.0	0.0	0.0
Minority interest	(146.1)	(154.2)	(122.4)	(110.7)	(170.8)	(145.6)
Total net income, Group share	**1,436.0**	**1,591.1**	**1,386.8**	**1,629.1**	**1,374.1**	**1,265.8**
Net earnings per share (€)	2.05	2.28	1.99	2.27	1.93	1.78
Net earnings per share (€) – diluted	2.05	2.28	1.99	2.24	1.87	1.72
Weighted average shares outstanding	699,470	697,161	697,161	716,142.4	711,164.0	711,147.1
Weighted average shares outstanding, diluted	699,471	697,161	697,161	728,070.1	734,303.5	734,295.7
Pro forma: Labor costs	(7,115.1)	(6,579.5)	(6,877.2)	(6,519.9)	(6,308.8)	(6,447.7)

a. In 2005, Carrefour changed its depreciation period for buildings (from 20 years to 40 years). The column "2004 Restated to IFRS" reports IFRS-based income statement figures after restating buildings depreciation. The income statement figures in column "2004 French GAAP" are based on the original buildings depreciation period of 20 years.

Consolidated balance sheets

	2005 IFRS	2004 Restated to IFRS	2004 French GAAP	2003 French GAAP	2002 French GAAP	2001 French GAAP
Goodwill	10,235.0	9,329.0	8,851.0	9,131.5	9,302.0	9,813.9
Other intangible assets	862.0	730.0	1,046.0	1,066.3	998.5	987.7
Tangible fixed assets	13,401.0	12,617.0	12,897.0	12,255.0	12,384.5	13,630.7
Financial assets	1,175.0	1,141.0	1,014.0	825.2	889.9	996.5
Investment in companies accounted for by the equity method	467.0	247.0	551.0	630.5	607.0	542.7
Deferred tax assets	1,029.0	1,066.0	1,049.0	633.4	576.3	589.1
Investment properties	463.0	481.0	0.0	0.0	0.0	0.0
Consumer credit from financial companies	1,398.0	1,594.0	0.0	0.0	0.0	0.0
Non-current assets	**29,030.0**	**27,205.0**	**25,406.0**	**24,541.9**	**24,758.2**	**26,560.6**
Inventories	6,110.0	5,621.0	6,243.0	5,690.7	5,722.8	5,909.4
Commercial receivables	3,451.0	3,147.0	3,059.0	3,182.2	3,154.6	2,945.6
Consumer credit from financial companies short-term	2,357.0	1,627.0	0.0	0.0	0.0	0.0
Tax receivables	598.0	423.0	411.0	764.4	607.5	542.9
Other assets	813.0	900.0	928.0	1,463.7	1,652.7	2,715.0
Cash and cash equivalents	3,733.0	3,203.0	2,930.0	3,420.4	3,028.5	4,796.9
Assets held for sale	158.0	0.0	0.0	0.0	0.0	0.0
Non-current assets	**17,220.0**	**14,921.0**	**13,571.0**	**14,521.4**	**14,166.1**	**16,909.8**
Total assets	**46,250.0**	**42,126.0**	**38,977.0**	**39,063.3**	**38,924.3**	**43,470.4**
Shareholders' equity, group share	8,385.0	6,947.0	7,549.0	7,089.3	6,623.3	7,377.4
Shareholders' equity, minority interest	1,001.0	929.0	780.0	891.0	922.7	1,294.0
Shareholders' equity	**9,386.0**	**7,876.0**	**8,329.0**	**7,980.3**	**7,546.0**	**8,671.4**
Borrowings	7,628.0	7,340.0	7,126.7	7,231.4	8,330.6	10,304.1
Provisions	2,325.0	1,954.0	1,274.0	1,165.1	1,157.5	1,310.1
Deferred tax liabilities	226.0	353.0	471.0	483.8	516.8	716.4
Consumer credit refinancing	264.0	255.0	0.0	0.0	0.0	0.0
Non-current liabilities	**10,443.0**	**9,902.0**	**8,871.7**	**8,880.3**	**10,004.9**	**12,330.6**
Borrowings – under 1 year	2,895.0	2,632.0	2,597.3	4,080.9	3,718.6	3,167.2
Trade payables	16,025.0	14,721.0	14,362.0	13,660.4	13,278.2	12,996.7
Consumer credit refinancing short-term	3,199.0	2,654.0	0.0	0.0	0.0	0.0
Tax payables	1,241.0	1,388.0	1,368.0	0.0	0.0	0.0
Other liabilities	3,022.0	2,952.0	3,448.0	4,461.4	4,376.6	6,304.5
Liabilities held for sale	38.0	0.0	0.0	0.0	0.0	0.0
Current liabilities	**26,420.0**	**24,347.0**	**21,775.3**	**22,202.7**	**21,373.4**	**22,468.4**
Total liabilities and shareholders' equity	**46,250.0**	**42,126.0**	**38,977.0**	**39,063.3**	**38,924.3**	**43,470.4**

Carrefour

Consolidated cash flow statements

	2005 IFRS	2004 Restated to IFRS	2004 French GAAP	2003 French GAAP	2002 French GAAP	2001 French GAAP
Net income			1,509.1	1,737.6	1,539.4	1438.5
Income before tax	2,700.0	2,553.0				
Tax	(757.0)	(830.0)				
Provision for amortization	1,564.0	1,939.0	2,102.2	2,066.0	1,950.0	2,537.8
Capital gains and losses on sales of assets	(160.0)	(56.0)	(69.9)	(190.5)	(266.1)	(1,106.5)
Changes in provisions	300.0	(127.0)	(87.0)	(118.4)	(119.0)	(82.2)
Dividends on companies accounted for by the equity method	6.0	(47.0)	(48.0)	(63.2)	(78.5)	(87.4)
Impact of discontinued activities	(71.0)	0.0	0.0	0.0	0.0	0.0
Cash flow from operations	**3,582.0**	**3,432.0**	**3,406.4**	**3,431.6**	**3,025.8**	**2,700.3**
Change in working capital	175.0	875.0	841.2	323.0	(149.0)	837.9
Impact of discontinued activities	19.0	0.0	0.0	0.0	0.0	0.0
Change in cash flow from operating activities (excluding financial companies)	**3,775.0**	**4,307.0**	**4,247.6**	**3,754.5**	**2,876.8**	**3,538.2**
Acquisition of tangible and intangible fixed assets	(3,026.0)	(2,570.0)	(2,563.7)	(2,717.3)	(2,423.0)	(3,397.8)
Acquisition of financial assets	(51.0)	(123.0)				
Acquisition of subsidiaries	(775.0)	(315.0)	(438.6)	(349.9)	(582.0)	(951.3)
Disposals of subsidiaries	565.0	19.0				
Disposals of fixed assets	707.0	546.0	545.8	883.2	704.7	1,952.4
Disposals of investments	26.0	375.0	394.3	302.7	245.5	1,705.6
Other uses	(126.0)	(80.0)	(84.4)	(84.9)	(1,108.9)	(314.5)
Impact of discontinued activities	63.0	0.0	0.0	0.0	0.0	0.0
Net cash from investing activities	**(2,617.0)**	**(2,148.0)**	**(2,146.6)**	**(1,966.1)**	**(3,163.7)**	**(1,005. 6)**
Proceeds on issue of shares	88.0	(368.0)	(367.6)	17.3	300.4	183.7
Dividends paid by Carrefour (parent company)	(656.0)	(525.0)	(608.9)	(522.5)	(475.5)	(424.6)
Dividends paid by consolidated companies to minority interests	(102.0)	(152.0)				
Change in borrowings	128.0	(1,596.0)	(1,588.0)	(737.0)	(1,422.1)	(477.2)
Net cash from financing activities	**(542.0)**	**(2,641.0)**	**(2,564.5)**	**(1,242.2)**	**(1,597.3)**	**(718.0)**
Impact of currency fluctuations	(59.0)	(27.0)	(26.6)	(154.5)	115.7	41.3
Net change in cash and cash equivalents	**531.0**	**(514.0)**	**(490.1)**	**391.8**	**(1,768.4)**	**1,855.9**
Cash and cash equivalents at beginning of year	3,202.0	3,717.0	3,420.6	3,028.6	4,797.0	2,941.1
Cash and cash equivalents at end of year	**3,733.0**	**3,202.0**	**2,930.4**	**3,420.5**	**3,028.6**	**4,797.0**

Carrefour

EXHIBIT 4 **Excerpts from Carrefour's Annual Report for the fiscal year ending December 31, 2005**

A. Interview with the Chairman of the Management Board

José Luis Duran, with the publication of the 2005 Annual Report, what is your overall assessment of the year 2005?

2005 represents a crucial turning point in the Carrefour group's strategy. We confronted this crucial period against a difficult background of intensified competition, weaker consumer spending in Europe and a rapidly changing regulatory environment in France. In the light of this situation, we not only rethought our economic model and our strategy, but above all our ambitions. By tracing out the most direct route from the existing situation to our objectives, we dared to break a number of taboos. In particular, we broke with a policy of short-term results, which favoured margin growth to the detriment of growth in sales and long-term results. Our objective is to be among the three leading players in the retail distribution sector in each of our markets. And the first results are already in:

- We have found the way back to growth, with the opening of more than a million square meters of new sales floor area through organic growth, in addition to 425,000 square meters from tactical acquisitions, whilst the average pace of growth over the last five years never exceeded one million square meters.

- Our sales increased by 6.1% on a like-for-like basis and by 4.3% worldwide at constant exchange rates, and by 28% in Latin America, 20.5% in Asia, 6.1% in Europe (excluding France) and 1.2% in France.

- We have recaptured market share in grocery retailing as a result of our determined pricing policy, particularly in France. In this market, our entire range of banners gained market share of 0.6 points in grocery retailing in 2005 and, as a result of their pricing offensive, Carrefour hypermarkets in France increased their market share by 0.3 points. This shows the exceptional vitality of the hypermarket format when we offer customers the best product range at the best price.

Thanks to the efforts made in 2005, the Carrefour Group has built a firm foundation for stronger and more sustainable growth in 2006. That is also why we withdrew from four countries (Japan, Mexico, the Czech Republic and Slovakia) and why we disposed of two of our activities (catering outlets in France and the cash & carry business in Spain) where the Group was no longer in a position to maintain its leadership position. From now on, we are concentrating all our resources on our strategic assets (i.e. those that show a potential for profitability and strong growth). Today, the course is clear for us and our teams.

What is your outlook for 2006–2008?

The strategy begun in 2005 is a fundamental strategy designed for the medium term (through to 2008), and we are pursuing it with determination. We are controlling costs in all regions. Our average net debt is improving, in spite of rising investments and dividends. Our financial expenses are down by 6%. Our net income per share from recurring operations is stable overall and our healthy net cash flow ensures that we have the resources we need to carry out our strategic plan. Although I remain cautious, I am optimistic: the Group has a high potential for growth. Over the 2006–2008 period, we will open on average twice as many hypermarkets throughout the world as between 2001 and 2004. In fact, we plan to add 1.5 million square meters annually through organic growth and we will take advantage of the best opportunities for tactical acquisitions. Naturally, we will pay scrupulous attention to the allocation of capital and to the profitability of all these investments.

How do you intend to build loyalty among your customers?

Our customers are at the heart of the Carrefour Group's strategy. The best proof that we have regained the trust of our customers is an increase in sales and in our grocery market share in France. The new pricing strategy in France that I have already mentioned was a necessary prerequisite, and we plan to maintain our competitiveness in 2006. And we are going even further, by strengthening our initiatives in the area of customer relations. To that end, we still need to increase our understanding of current trends in our customers' purchasing behaviours, customs and lifestyles. This can be accomplished by making better use of our databases. On the basis of this improved understanding of the attitudes of our customers and by more clearly anticipating their expectations, we can adapt our product range accordingly by implementing a more targeted price strategy and by further developing our product mix and services. In 2005, we launched some major strategic programmes to prepare for these changes. This involves an in-depth change in our approach to developing goods and services.

What are the priorities and time frames for these projects?

These programmes will be implemented over the entire duration of the plan. They naturally imply a profound change in our management methods and tools. In practice, this project must enable us to win market share in all sectors, and not only in the grocery and fresh produce sector where we are already the leader, but in non-food segments as well. All our teams are mobilized to offer the best range of products and services. Market testing carried out in Spain in 2005, with small Carrefour hypermarkets and the MaxiDia stores, shows that we are continually getting closer to our customers and their expectations and that innovation in this sphere tends to pay off.

How is this strategy put into practice by employees?

A strategy can only succeed if the idea is transformed into action, and then the action is transformed into results. The best guarantee of the successful implementation of our strategy is therefore the exceptional know-how and energy of our 436,000 employees. Their daily commitment to customer service is without a doubt our best asset. A number of teams participated directly in the preparation of the strategic plan through participating in task forces that brought together people from all store formats and all geographical areas, possessing the full range of functional and operational skills. It is this direct upstream involvement that facilitates implementation and guarantees that these programmes can be made fully operational. Based on the success of these task forces, we decided to modify the organization of the Group by simplifying our structures and reinforcing the teams in direct contact with the customer. This simplification and the reallocation of resources have allowed us to strengthen our in-store teams. In France, we recruited and trained some 15,000 employees, which puts the Carrefour Group, once again, at the top of the list of national recruiters.

What are your priorities in terms of sustainable development?

Our customers also think and act as citizens. We have fully incorporated sustainable development into our new strategy. All of the Group's employees are developing projects that respond in concrete terms to the concerns and expectations of the populations that we serve throughout the world, in areas such as food safety, nutrition and social responsibility. For instance, in Colombia, Carrefour was one of the main industry leaders involved in the production and sale of substitute products to replace the cultivation of crops for illicit use. For its efforts in this area, Carrefour Colombia was awarded the United Nations Vienna prize. In Thailand, Carrefour has initiated an aquaculture project at Baan Nam Kem to help the fishermen of southern Thailand reconstruct the aquaculture facilities destroyed by the tsunami of December 2004. At a time when the overexploitation of marine resources is becoming a cause for alarm, the Carrefour Group is marketing four frozen fish items in France and Belgium under its own brand name which are the product of responsible, environmentally friendly fishing practices. These are just a few examples that illustrate our commitment to sustainable development.

In conclusion, would you say that the Carrefour Group is once again a growth company?

Trust cannot be imposed; it must be earned. Carrefour is an extraordinarily modern and proactive retail distribution enterprise turned resolutely towards the future; it is the second largest such enterprise in the world, and certainly the most international in scope. I believe in our teams' ability to make the Carrefour Group a lasting vehicle for international growth, and I am totally committed to that objective, as is the entire management team.

B. Excerpts from the notes to the consolidated financial statements

Note 1: Accounting principles

Under the terms of European regulation 1606/2002 of July 19, 2002 on international standards, the Carrefour Group's consolidated financial statements for the fiscal year 2005 have been drawn up for the first time in accordance with IFRS international accounting standards applicable as from January 1, 2005, as approved by the European Union. The consolidated financial statements have been drawn up on the basis of historic cost, with the exception of certain assets and liabilities subject to IFRS standards. The asset and liability categories concerned are described, where applicable, in the corresponding notes below. Non-current assets and groups of assets held for sale are valued at their book value or the fair value minus sale costs, whichever is the lower.

The main estimates made by management when preparing the financial statements concern the valuations and useful lives of current and non-current operating assets and goodwill, the amount of provisions for risks and other provisions relating to the business, as well as assumptions made for the calculation of retirement pension commitments or deferred taxes. Details of the main assumptions retained by the Group are provided in each of the paragraphs in the Appendix devoted to the financial statements. The specific rules for initial adoption, as defined in IFRS1 "Initial adoption of international financial information standards", have been applied. We have opted to present the income statement by type. The other options selected, where applicable, are indicated in the following sections. IAS 32 and IAS 39 relating to financial instruments have been applied as from January 1, 2005. IFRS 5 relating to non-current assets held for sale and discontinued operations was applied as of January 1, 2004.

Change in estimate

In 2005, the Group decided to make a change in estimate as to the duration of the depreciation of its buildings, increasing it from 20 to 40 years. The change in estimate, reflected in a change in the duration of depreciation retroactive to January 1, 2005, can be justified by the fact that the contribution values of the stores, as determined by expert assessors within the context of the project for the creation of the European property company, Carrefour Property, in 2005, have proved that buildings still have significant market value after 20 years. Following the creation of Carrefour Property, the Group decided to engage in an overall review of the useful economic life of its assets. AFREXIM (association of property experts) has thus conducted a sectoral study of the economic life span of a building. The property expert's report concluded in 2005 that the economic life span of a building within the Group is 40 years. An income statement and balance sheet restated under this change in estimate were communicated for the purpose of comparison with 2004 in December 2004. This information was prepared on the basis of the "published" IFRS financial statements drawn up on December 31, 2004.

Groups of companies

The Group has chosen the option offered by IFRS 1, which does not restate company groupings prior to January 1, 2004 in accordance with IFRS 3. As from January 1, 2004, all company groupings are entered in the accounts by the acquisition method. The difference between the acquisition cost, which includes expenses directly attributable to the acquisition, and the fair value of assets, net of liabilities and any liabilities accepted as part of the business composition, is shown as goodwill. Negative goodwill resulting from the acquisition is immediately entered in the income statement. For companies acquired during the course of the fiscal year and increases in investments, only the income for the period after the acquisition date is shown in the consolidated income statement. For companies disposed of during the course of the fiscal year and dilutions, only the income for the period prior to the disposal date is shown in the consolidated income statement.

Conversion rate for foreign companies

In accordance with the option offered under IFRS 1, the Group has chosen to restate the translation adjustments accumulated at January 1, 2004 under "consolidated reserves". This option has no impact on the Group's total shareholders' equity; it involves a reclassification within shareholders' equity from the entry "Translation adjustments" to the entry "Other reserves" totaling 3,236 million euros.

Fixed assets

2 – Goodwill

In accordance with IFRS 3, goodwill has not been amortized since January 1, 2004. Instead, goodwill is subject to an impairment test during the second half of each year. IAS 36, "Depreciation of assets", states that this impairment test should be conducted either at the level of each Cash Flow Generating Unit (CFGU) to which goodwill has been allocated or at business group level within a business sector or geographic sector in which the return on investment of acquisitions is evaluated. The level of analysis at which Carrefour evaluates the current value of goodwill generally corresponds to countries or to operations by country.

The need to record a loss in value is evaluated by comparing the book value of CFGU or CFGU group assets and liabilities and their recoverable value. The recoverable value is the market value or useful value, whichever is the higher. The useful value is estimated by discounting future cash flows over a period of 4 years with determination of a final value calculated on the basis of the discounting of the fourth year figures at the perpetual rate of growth to infinity and the use of a discount rate specific to each country. The specific discounting rate for each country takes into consideration the specific risk to a country determined by a grid containing the five weighted indicators below: monetary risk; political and regulatory situation; competition; Carrefour's experience curve in the country; potential for growth in the market.

These discounting rates are validated by the Group's Management Committee and were between 5.7% and 11.6% for the fiscal year 2005, depending on the country. The market value is assessed with regard to recent transactions or professional practices.

3 – Intangible fixed assets

Other intangible fixed assets basically correspond to software programs that are depreciated over between one and five years.

4 – Tangible fixed assets

In accordance with IAS 16 "Tangible fixed assets", land, buildings and equipment, fixtures and fittings are evaluated at their cost price at acquisition or the cost of sales, less depreciation and loss in value. [...] Tangible fixed assets are depreciated on a straight line basis according to the following average useful lives:

- Construction: buildings 40 years, grounds 10 years, car parks $6^2/_3$ years
- Equipment, fixtures and fittings and installations $6^2/_3$ years to 8 years
- Other fixed assets 4 to 10 years

Customer receivables outstanding: Refinancing to financial service companies

Customer receivables due to financial service companies refer primarily to consumer credit granted to customers of companies within the Group's scope of consolidation. These loans, together with the amounts outstanding from refinancing that back them, are considered to be assets and liabilities, held until their maturity date and are classified on the basis of their maturity date as current or non-current assets and liabilities.

Employee benefits

The Group's employees enjoy short-term benefits (paid leave, sick leave, profit-sharing), long-term benefits (long-service medals, seniority bonus etc.) and post-employment advantages on the basis of specific contributions/benefits (retirement benefit).

b – Schemes with defined benefits and long-term advantages

The Carrefour Group makes provision for the various defined benefit schemes dependent on the accumulated years of service within the Group that are not totally pre-financed. This commitment is calculated annually on the basis of the method of projected units of credit, on an actuarial basis, taking into consideration factors such as salary increases, age of departure, mortality, personnel rotation and discount rates. The Group has decided to apply the "corridor" method, whereby the effect of variations in actuarial terms is not recognized on the income statement, as long as the former remain within a range of 10%. Thus actuarial differences exceeding 10% between the value of the commitment and the value of the hedging assets – whichever is the higher – on the income statement are spread over the expected average working life of employees benefiting from this scheme.

In accordance with the option offered by IFRS 1, the Group has chosen to record all its actuarial losses and gains in its pension commitments that have not yet been recognized in the French financial statements at December 31, 2003, directly, corresponding to shareholders' equity at January 1, 2004.

c – Share-based compensation

In accordance with the option offered by IFRS 1, the Group has decided to limit the application of IFRS 2 to stock option plans paid in shares, allocated after November 7, 2002, the rights to which had not yet been acquired at January 1, 2004. This application had no effect on total shareholders' equity at January 1, 2004. Three plans granted between 2003 and 2005 fall within the scope of IFRS2 "Share-based compensation". These are subscription or purchase options reserved for employees with no special acquisition conditions, aside from effective presence at the end of the period of the vesting period.

The benefits granted that are remunerated by these schemes are posted as expenses, which corresponds to an increase in shareholders' equity over the vesting period. The accounting expense for each period corresponds to the fair value of the assets and services received on the basis of the "Black & Scholes" formula on the date on which these were granted and spread over the vesting period.

The restricted stock plans granted by the Group are recognized as an expense spread over the period of acquisition of the rights. The plans granted in 2004 and 2005 are dependent on the achievement of non-market objectives; since, however, it is thought to be unlikely that these objectives will be achieved, no expense has been recognized for the allocation of free shares in 2005. Details of share allocation plans are provided in the management report.

Financial debt and financial instruments

d – Derecognition of financial assets

In December 2002, the Group contracted into a programme for securitizing receivables. This programme only partially transfers the risks and advantages of the variation in value discounted by future cash flows from receivables. As a result, part of these securitized receivables have been recognized as financial debt.

Other revenues

Other revenues (financial and travel services, rental income, franchise fees etc.) are recorded on a separate line called "other revenues" and recorded underneath the "net sales" line in the income statement. Some expenses, such as the cost of payments made by customers in several installments and of loyalty schemes not funded by suppliers, are recorded net of other revenues. This entry includes fees received by finance companies from debit cards, traditional credit applications or revolving credit applications. Fees are spread across the duration of the contract.

Note 4: Net sales

(€ millions)	31/12/2005	31/12/2004 published restated Dep/40 yrs	%Var	31/12/2004 IFRS
Sales	74,496.8	72,668.0	2.5%	70,284.2

At constant exchange rates, net sales would have been 73,325 million euros. The impact of exchange rate fluctuations represented 1,172 million euros at December 31, 2005, of which 655 million euros in the Latin America region, 339 million euros in the Europe region (mainly Turkey and Poland) and 178 million euros in the Asia region. Excluding the sale of Japan, the Czech Republic, Slovakia, Mexico, Prodirest, supermarkets in Brazil and in Spain, and PuntoCash, sales

would have risen by 6% at current exchange rates and 4.3% at constant exchange rates.

Note 12: Net income from discontinued operations

(€ millions)	31/12/2005	31/12/2004 published restated Dep/40 yrs	31/12/2004 IFRS
Discontinued operations, group share	(371.5)	(84.8)	(154.9)
Discontinued operations, minority share	(2.7)	(0.7)	11.6
Total	(374.2)	(85.5)	(143.3)

In December 2005, net income from discontinued operations were accounted for by:

- the impact of the sale of Japan for 1 million euros, a provision for depreciation of 90 million euros having been recorded at December 31, 2004;

- the impact of the sale of Mexico for (29) million euros, corresponding for the most part to capital losses, since income for the period was not significant;

- net income for the period and net income from the sale of the food service activity in France, amounting to (22) million euros;

- losses for the year in the Czech Republic and Slovakia amounting to (63) million euros;

- losses for the year from Cash & Carry in Spain (Puntocash) amounting to (2) million euros;

- the impact of the closure of the Brazilian supermarkets in 2005 amounting to (196) million euros;

- the impact of the closure of the Spanish supermarkets in 2005 amounting to (63) million euros.

In December 2004, net income from discontinued operations resulted from (published financial statements):

- latent losses of 90 million euros in Japan,

- gains from the disposal of securities (Modelo Continente, Optique in the Czech Republic), amounting to 10.6 million euros,

- other items for a net expense of 5.4 million euros.

Note 14: Intangible fixed assets

(€ millions)	31/12/2005	31/12/2004 published
Net goodwill	10,235	9,329
Other net intangible fixed assets	657	623
Intangible fixed assets in progress	205	106
Net intangible fixed assets	11,097	10,059

(€ millions)	Net goodwill end 2004 IFRS	Acquisitions 2005	Impairments 2005	Foreign currency translation adjustments 2005	Net goodwill end 2005
France	3,340	281			3,621
Italy	2,971	140			3,111
Belgium	925	3			928
Spain	1,213	9	(4)		1,218
Brazil	273	53	(92)	85	319
Argentina	184			25	209
Other countries	423	390		17	830
Total	9,329	876	(96)	127	10,235

At December 31, 2005, goodwill in France consisted of Comptoirs Modernes and Euromarché, in Italy GS, in Belgium GB, in Spain Continente and the buyback of the shares of minority shareholders in Centros Comerciales Carrefour, in Brazil the Sonae stores and in Argentina Norte.

The main acquisitions in the year were Hyparlo and Pennymarket in France, the buyback of 2% of GS Spa in Italy, the acquisition of 10 Sonae hypermarkets in Brazil and for the "other countries" of the Group Hypernova (Poland), Gima and Endi (Turkey). An impairment was recorded in Brazil for the supermarkets sold off in 2005.

Change to intangible fixed assets

(€ millions)	Gross	Depreciation	Net
At January 1, 2005	13,719	(3,660)	10,059
Acquisitions	428	(251)	177
Disposals	(21)		(21)
Foreign currency adjustments	103	51	154
Changes in consolidation scope and transfer	867	(140)	727
At December 31, 2005	15,097	(4,000)	11,097

Note 15: Tangible fixed assets

(€ millions)	31/12/2005	31/12/04 published restated Dep/40yrs	31/12/2004 published
Land	3,110	3,117	3,117
Buildings	8,031	7,330	7,330
Equipment, fixtures & fittings and installations	12,064	10,987	10,987
Other fixed assets	1,108	1,077	1,077
Fixed assets in progress	1,055	844	844
Leased land	144	145	145
Leased buildings	1,268	1,217	1,217
Leased equipment, fixtures & fittings and installations	134	99	99
Other leased fixed assets	32	1	1
Gross tangible fixed assets	26,947	24,816	24,816
Depreciation	(12,319)	(10,974)	(11,132)
Depreciation of leased fixed assets	(944)	(843)	(843)
Impairment	(283)	(223)	(223)
Net tangible fixed assets	13,401	12,775	12,617

The Carrefour Group has carried out a review of all its property leasing agreements. Agreements considered to be as financial leasing agreements have been recapitalized in the opening balance, whereas other agreements have been considered as operating lease agreements.

Leased fixed assets (€ millions)	Total	Less than 1 year	1 to 5 years	More than 5 years
Financing lease agreements				
Minimum rents to be paid	805	52	196	557
Discounted value	372	34	123	215
Total sub-leasing income receivable	13			
Minimum rents paid during the year	171	NA	NA	NA
Conditional rents	NA	NA	NA	NA
Sub-leasing income	3			
Simple lease agreements				
Minimum rents to pay	5,202	751	1,780	2,670
Total minimum income to be received from sub-leasing	77	NA	NA	NA
Minimum rents paid during the year	860	NA	NA	NA
Conditional rents	31	NA	NA	NA

Note 20: Commercial receivables

(€ millions)	31/12/2005	31/12/2004 published
Trade receivables	1,246	1,236
Depreciation on bad debts	(143)	(150)
Net receivables from customers	1,103	1,137
Supplier receivables	2,348	2,011
Total	3,451	3,147

Trade receivables are primarily those due from Group franchisees. Supplier receivables correspond to rebates owed by the Group's suppliers.

Carrefour

Note 26: Borrowings

Breakdown of debt (€ millions)	31/12/2005	31/12/2004 published (2)
Bonds	7,737	7,280
Derivatives – liabilities	294	
Other borrowings	1,329	1,459
Other LT debts	188	186
Commercial paper	520	577
Leasing	455	470
Total borrowings (1)	10,523	9,972
Total restatement of borrowings	10,497	9,972

(1) Amount of borrowing restated to include the derivatives shown as assets in the balance sheet.
(2) IAS 32 and IAS 39 relating to financial instruments were applied as from January 1, 2005. Only the financial statements to December 31, 2005 are affected by the application of these standards, which explains why the fair value of the derivatives in the balance sheet was zero at December 31, 2004.

Based on equivalent accounting principles (by applying IAS 32 and IAS 39 to the 2004 financial statements), the Group's net debt would have been 7,546 million euros at the end of 2004.

At December 31, 2005, the Group had no bank covenants.

Carrefour

Main adjustments

Main adjustments to the income statement at December 31, 2004, drawn up in accordance with French standards, with the income statement at December 31, 2004 drawn up in accordance with IFRS

(€ millions)	Adjustments	Ending of goodwill amortization	Financial leasing (IAS 17)	Employee benefits (IAS 19)	Valuation of inventories (IAS 2)	Stock options (IFRS 2)	Other adjustments	Reclassifications
Net sales								1,038.6
Other income								1,038.6
Cost of sales	(84.2)				(84.2)			(414.4)
Gross margin from current operations	**(84.2)**				**(84.2)**			**624.2**
Sales, general and administrative expenses	(6.3)		18.5	(9.0)	(0.5)		(15.3)	(89.0)
Other income and expenses	13.8			13.8				(610.0)
Depreciation, amortization and provisions	0.4		(11.2)				11.6	30.7
Activity contribution	**(76.3)**		**7.3**	**4.8**	**(84.7)**	**(30.6)**	**(11.0)**	**(44.1)**
Non-recurring income and expenses	(37.9)		0.0	0.0	0.0	(30.6)	(7.3)	(38.1)
EBIT	**(114.2)**		**7.3**	**4.8**	**(84.7)**	**(30.6)**	**(11.0)**	**(82.2)**
Interest income	(48.7)		(14.1)	(32.7)	(0.6)		(1.3)	(11.7)
Income before tax	**(162.9)**		**(6.8)**	**(27.9)**	**(85.3)**	**(30.6)**	**(12.3)**	**(93.9)**
Income tax	39.8		1.9	2.8	25.2	10.7	(0.8)	(33.9)
Share of net income of accounted for by the equity method								(60.7)
Net income from recurring operations	**(123.1)**		**(4.9)**	**(25.1)**	**(60.1)**	**(19.9)**	**(13.1)**	**(120.7)**
Net income from recurring operations, Group share	(109.7)		(3.9)	(25.1)	(55.1)	(19.9)	(5.7)	(195.4)
Goodwill amortization	319.3	319.3						
Non-recurring income								246.2
Impact of discontinued operations, group share	(5.8)						(5.8)	(79.0)
Total net income, Group share	**203.8**	**319.3**	**(3.9)**	**(25.1)**	**(55.1)**	**(19.9)**	**(11.5)**	**0.0**

Carrefour

Carrefour

Main adjustments to the balance sheet at December 31, 2004, drawn up in accordance with French standards, with the balance sheet at December 31, 2004 drawn up in accordance with IFRS

(€ millions)	Consolidation of finance companies (IAS 27)	Ending of goodwill amortization	Employee benefits (IAS 19)	Financial leasing (IAS 17)	Inventories (IAS 2)	Preopening costs and rebates	Deferred tax (IAS 12)	Other adjustments	Total adjustments	Reclassifications
Goodwill		319							319	159
Other intangible fixed assets								(10)	(10)	(306)
Tangible fixed assets	3			226				(36)	193	(473)
Financial assets	19			(3)			2		18	109
Investments in companies accounted for by the equity method	(304)								(304)	0
Deferred tax assets				(16)			(96)		(112)	131
Investment properties									0	481
Consumer credit from financial companies	1,594								1,594	0
Non-current assets	**1,312**	**319**		**207**			**(94)**	**(46)**	**1,698**	**(58)**
Inventories					(635)				(635)	13
Commercial receivables									0	89
Consumer credit from financial companies – short-term	1,617								1,617	10
Tax receivables									0	12
Other assets	57					(26)			31	(59)
Cash and equivalents	306								306	(34)
Current assets	**1,980**				**(635)**	**(26)**			**1,319**	**31**
Total assets	**3,292**	**319**		**207**	**(635)**	**(26)**	**(94)**	**(46)**	**3,017**	**132**
Shareholders' equity, Group share	2	319	(318)	(37)	(418)	(22)			(602)	0
Shareholders' equity, non-Group share	209		(2)	(6)	(36)	(4)			149	0
Shareholders' equity	**211**	**319**	**(320)**	**(43)**	**(454)**	**(26)**	**(94)**	**(46)**	**(453)**	**0**
Borrowings									0	7,340
Provisions	81		531						612	148
Deferred tax liabilities					(181)				(181)	(17)
Bank loan refinancing	255								255	70
Non-current liabilities	**336**		**531**		**(181)**				**686**	**7,471**
Borrowings – less than 1 year				245					245	(7,337)
Trade payables									0	359
Consumer credit from financial companies – short-term	2,654								2,654	0
Tax payables									0	20
Other liabilities	91		(211)	5					(115)	(380)
Current liabilities	**2,745**		**(211)**	**250**					**2,784**	**(7,338)**
Total liabilities and shareholders' equity	**3,292**	**319**		**207**	**(635)**	**(26)**	**(94)**	**(46)**	**3,017**	**132**

EXHIBIT 5 **Summary of Tesco's IFRS-based accounting performance in the fiscal years ending February 26, 2005 and February 25, 2006**[a]

	2006 (IFRS)	2005 (IFRS)
Sales	100.0%	100.0%
Cost of materials / Sales	(75.1%)	(74.6%)
Personnel expenses / Sales	(10.8%)	(10.9%)
Depreciation and amortization / Sales	(2.1%)	(2.2%)
Other operating income / Sales	0.2%	0.1%
Other operating expenses / Sales	(6.4%)	(6.7%)
Net interest expense or income / Sales	(0.3%)	(0.4%)
Investment income / Sales	0.2%	0.2%
Tax expense / Sales	(1.6%)	(1.6%)
Net profit margin	**4.0%**	**4.0%**
Net interest expense after tax / Sales	0.2%	0.2%
Net operating profit margin	4.2%	4.2%
× Net operating asset turnover	2.69	2.56
= Operating ROA	11.3%	10.9%
Spread	9.6%	8.8%
× Financial leverage	0.56	0.54
= Financial leverage gain	5.4%	4.8%
ROE = Operating ROA + Financial leverage gain	**16.7%**	**15.6%**
Operating working capital / Sales	(8.3%)	(9.2%)
Net long-term assets / Sales	45.5%	48.3%
PP&E / Sales	40.3%	42.9%
Operating working capital turnover	(12.0)	(10.9)
Net long-term asset turnover	2.2	2.1
PP&E turnover	2.5	2.3
Accounts receivable turnover	44.2	44.0
Inventory turnover	20.2	19.3
Accounts payable turnover	3.2	2.9
Days' accounts receivable	8.1	8.2
Days' inventory	17.8	18.6
Days' accounts payable	113.9	122.6

a. The ratios in this table are based on balance sheet items' ending balances. The results for the year ended 25 February 2006 include 52 weeks for the U.K. and Ireland and 14 months for the majority of the remaining International Business.

Carrefour

6

Prospective Analysis: Forecasting

Most financial statement analysis tasks are undertaken with a forward-looking decision in mind – and, much of the time, it is useful to summarize the view developed in the analysis with an explicit forecast. Managers need forecasts for planning and to provide performance targets; analysts need forecasts to help communicate their views of the firm's prospects to investors; bankers and debt market participants need forecasts to assess the likelihood of loan repayment. Moreover, there are a variety of contexts (including but not limited to security analysis) where the forecast is usefully summarized in the form of an estimate of the firm's value – an estimate that, after all, can be viewed as the best attempt to reflect in a single summary statistic the manager's or analyst's view of the firm's prospects.

Prospective analysis includes two tasks – forecasting and valuation – that together represent approaches to explicitly summarizing the analyst's forward-looking views. In this chapter we focus on forecasting, while valuation is the topic of the next two chapters. The key concepts discussed in this chapter are illustrated using analysts' forecasts for Porsche.

RELATION OF FORECASTING TO OTHER ANALYSES

Forecasting is not so much a separate analysis as it is a way of summarizing what has been learned through business strategy analysis, accounting analysis, and financial analysis. For example, a projection of the future performance of Porsche as of early fiscal year 2006 must be grounded ultimately in an understanding of questions such as these:

- *From business strategy analysis.* How long will Porsche's strategy and competitive advantage yield the type of spectacular performance it reported in prior years? At what rate can the company grow both in the short term and in the long term without sacrificing its superior margins? Will competition put pressure on Porsche's margins?

- *From accounting analysis.* Are there any aspects of Porsche's accounting that suggest past earnings and assets are overstated, or expenses or liabilities are understated? If so, what are the implications for future accounting statements?

- *From financial analysis.* What are the sources of Porsche's superior performance? Is it sustainable?

The upshot is that a forecast can be no better than the business strategy analysis, accounting analysis, and financial analysis underlying it. However, there are certain techniques and knowledge that can help a manager or analyst to structure the best possible forecast, conditional on what has been learned in the previous steps. Below we summarize an approach to structuring the forecast, offer information useful in getting started, and give detailed steps to forecast earnings, balance sheet data, and cash flows.

THE TECHNIQUES OF FORECASTING

The overall structure of the forecast

The best way to forecast future performance is to do it comprehensively – producing not only an earnings forecast, but a forecast of cash flows and the balance sheet as well. A comprehensive approach is useful, even in cases where one might be interested primarily in a single facet of performance, because it guards against unrealistic implicit assumptions. For example, if an analyst forecasts growth in sales and earnings for several years without explicit consideration of the required increases in working capital and plant assets and the associated financing, the forecast might possibly imbed unreasonable assumptions about asset turnover, leverage, or equity capital infusions.

A comprehensive approach involves many forecasts, but in most cases they are all linked to the behavior of a few key "drivers." The drivers vary according to the type of business involved, but for businesses outside the financial services sector, the sales forecast is nearly always one of the key drivers; profit margin is another. When asset turnover is expected to remain stable – often a realistic assumption – working capital accounts and investment in plant should track the growth in sales closely. Most major expenses also track sales, subject to expected shifts in profit margins. By linking forecasts of such amounts to the sales forecast, one can avoid internal inconsistencies and unrealistic implicit assumptions.

In some contexts the manager or analyst is interested ultimately in a forecast of cash flows, not earnings per se. Nevertheless, even forecasts of cash flows tend to be grounded in practice on forecasts of accounting numbers, including sales, earnings, assets, and liabilities. Of course it would be possible in principle to move *directly* to forecasts of cash flows – inflows from customers, outflows to suppliers and laborers, and so forth – and in some businesses this is a convenient way to proceed. In most cases, however, the growth prospects, profitability, and investment and financing needs of the firm are more readily framed in terms of accrual-based sales, operating earnings, assets, and liabilities. These amounts can then be converted to cash flow measures by adjusting for the effects of noncash expenses and expenditures for working capital and plant.

The most practical approach to forecasting a company's financial statements is to focus on projecting "condensed" financial statements, as used in the ratio analysis in Chapter 5, rather than attempting to project detailed financial statements that the company reports. There are several reasons for this recommendation. First, this approach involves making a relatively small set of assumptions about the future of the firm, so the analyst will have more ability to think about each of the assumptions carefully. A detailed line item forecast is likely to be very tedious, and an analyst may not have a good basis to make all the assumptions necessary for such forecasts. Further, for most purposes condensed financial statements are all that are needed for analysis and decision making. We therefore approach the task of financial forecasting with this framework.

Recall that the condensed income statement that we used in Chapter 5 consists of the following elements: sales, net operating profits after tax (NOPAT), net interest expense after tax, taxes, and net profit. The condensed balance sheet consists of: net operating working capital, net non-current assets, net debt, and equity. Also recall that we start with a balance sheet at the beginning of the forecasting period. Assumptions about how we use the beginning balance sheet and run the firm's operations will lead to the income statement for the forecasting period; assumptions about investment in working capital and non-current assets, and how we finance these assets, results in a balance sheet at the end of the forecasting period.

To forecast the condensed income statement, one needs to begin with an assumption about next-period sales. Beyond that, assumptions about NOPAT margin, interest rate on beginning debt, and tax rate are all that are needed to prepare the condensed income statement for the period.

To forecast the condensed balance sheet for the end of the period (or the equivalent, the beginning of the next period), we need to make the following additional assumptions: the ratio of operating working capital to the sales to estimate the level of working capital needed to support those sales; the ratio of net operating non-current assets to the following year's sales to calculate the expected level of net operating non-current assets; and the ratio of net debt to capital to estimate the levels of debt and equity needed to finance the estimated amount of assets in the balance sheet.

Once we have the condensed income statement and balance sheet, it is relatively straightforward to compute the condensed cash flow statement, including cash flow from operations before working capital investments, cash flow from operations after working capital investments, free cash flow available to debt and equity, and free cash flow available to equity.

Below we discuss how best to make the necessary assumptions to forecast the condensed income statement, balance sheet, and cash flow statements.

Getting started: Points of departure

Every forecast has, at least implicitly, an initial "benchmark" or point of departure – some notion of how a particular amount, such as sales or earnings, would be expected to behave in the absence of detailed information. For example, in starting to contemplate fiscal 2006 profitability for Porsche, one must begin somewhere. A possibility is to begin with the 2005 performance. Another starting point might be 2005 performance adjusted for recent trends. A third possibility that might seem reasonable – but one that generally turns out not to be very useful – is the average performance over several prior years.

By the time one has completed a business strategy analysis, an accounting analysis, and a detailed financial analysis, the resulting forecast might differ significantly from the original point of departure. Nevertheless, simply for purposes of having a starting point that can help anchor the detailed analysis, it is useful to know how certain key financial statistics behave "on average."

In the case of some key statistics, such as earnings, a point of departure based only on prior behavior of the number is more powerful than one might expect. Research demonstrates that some such benchmarks for earnings are not much less accurate than the forecasts of professional security analysts, who have access to a rich information set. (We return to this point in more detail later.) Thus the benchmark is often not only a good starting point but also close to the amount forecast after detailed analysis. Large departures from the benchmark could be justified only in cases where the firm's situation is demonstrably unusual.

Reasonable points of departure for forecasts of key accounting numbers can be based on the evidence summarized below. Such evidence may also be useful for checking the reasonableness of a completed forecast.

The behavior of sales growth

Sales growth rates tend to be "mean-reverting": firms with above-average or below-average rates of sales growth tend to revert over time to a "normal" level (historically in the range of 6 to 9 percent for European firms) within three to ten years. Figure 6.1 documents this effect for 1989 through 2005 for all the publicly traded European (nonfinancial) firms covered by Thomson Financial's Worldscope database. All firms are ranked in terms of their sales growth in 1989 (year 1) and formed into five portfolios based on the relative ranking of their sales growth in that year. Firms in portfolio 1 have the top 20 percent of rankings in terms of their sales growth in 1989, and those in portfolio 2 fall into the next 20 percent; those in portfolio 5 have the bottom 20 percent sales growth ranks. The sales growth rates of firms in each of these five portfolios are traced from 1989 through the subsequent nine years (years 2 to 10). The same experiment is repeated with every year between 1990 and 1996 as the base year (year 1). The results are averaged over the eight experiments and the resulting sales growth rates of each of the five portfolios for years 1 through 10 are plotted in the figure.

The figure shows that the group of firms with the highest growth initially – sales growth rates of just over 50 percent – experience a decline to about 14 percent growth rate within two years and are never above 14 percent in the next seven years. Those with the lowest initial sales growth rates, minus 15 percent, experience an increase to about a 11 percent growth rate by year 6, and average about 8 percent annual growth in years 7 through 10. One explanation for the pattern of sales growth seen in Figure 6.1 is that as industries and companies mature, their growth rate slows down due to demand saturation and intraindustry competition. Therefore, even when a firm is growing rapidly at present, it is generally unrealistic to extrapolate the current high growth indefinitely. Of course, how quickly a firm's growth rate reverts to the average depends on the characteristics of its industry and its own competitive position within an industry.

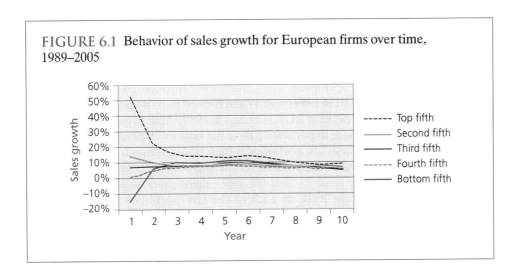

FIGURE 6.1 Behavior of sales growth for European firms over time, 1989–2005

The behavior of earnings

Earnings have been shown on average to follow a process that can be approximated by a "random walk" or "random walk with drift." Thus the prior year's earnings figure is a good starting point in considering future earnings potential. As will be explained, it is reasonable to adjust this simple benchmark for the earnings changes of the most recent quarter (that is, changes relative to the comparable quarter of the prior year after controlling for the long-run trend in the series). Even a simple random walk forecast – one that predicts next year's earnings will be equal to last year's earnings – is surprisingly useful. One study documents that professional analysts' year-ahead forecasts are only 22 percent more accurate, on average, than a simple random walk forecast.[1] Thus a final earnings forecast will *usually* not differ dramatically from a random walk benchmark.

The implication of the evidence is that, in beginning to contemplate future earnings possibilities, a useful number to start with is last year's earnings; the average level of earnings over several prior years is not useful. Long-term trends in earnings tend to be sustained on average, and so they are also worthy of consideration. If quarterly or semiannual data are also included, then some consideration should usually be given to any departures from the long-run trend that occurred in the most recent quarter or half year. For most firms, these most recent changes tend to be partially repeated in subsequent quarters or half years.[2]

The behavior of returns on equity

Given that prior earnings serves as a useful benchmark for future earnings, one might expect the same to be true of rates of return on investment, like ROE. That, however, is not the case for two reasons. First, even though the *average* firm tends to sustain the current earnings level, this is not true of firms with unusual levels of ROE. Firms with abnormally high (low) ROE tend to experience earnings declines (increases).[3]

Second, firms with higher ROEs tend to expand their investment bases more quickly than others, which causes the denominator of the ROE to increase. Of course, if firms could earn returns on the new investments that match the returns on the old ones, then the level of ROE would be maintained. However, firms have difficulty pulling that off. Firms with higher ROEs tend to find that, as time goes by, their earnings growth does not keep pace with growth in their investment base, and ROE ultimately falls.

The resulting behavior of ROE and other measures of return on investment is characterized as "mean-reverting": firms with above-average or below-average rates of return tend to revert over time to a "normal" level (for ROE, historically in the range of 10 to 12 percent for European firms) within no more than ten years.[4] Figure 6.2 documents this effect for European firms from 1989 through 2005. All firms are ranked in terms of their ROE in 1989 (year 1) and formed into five portfolios. Firms in portfolio 1 have the top 20 percent ROE rankings in 1989, those in portfolio 2 fall into the next 20 percent, and those in portfolio 5 have the bottom 20 percent. The average ROE of firms in each of these five portfolios is then traced through nine subsequent years (years 2 to 10). The same experiment is repeated with every year between 1990 and 1996 as the base year (year 1), and the subsequent years as years +2 to +10. Figure 6.2 plots the average ROE of each of the five portfolios in years 1 to 10 averaged across these eight experiments.

Though the five portfolios start out in year 1 with a wide range of ROEs (−24 percent to +44 percent), by year 10 the pattern of mean-reversion is clear. The most

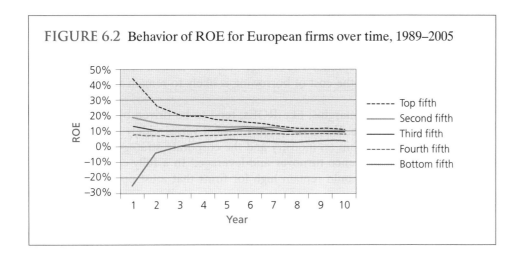

FIGURE 6.2 Behavior of ROE for European firms over time, 1989–2005

profitable group of firms initially – with average ROEs of 44 percent – experience a decline to 21 percent within three years. By year 10 this group of firms has an ROE of 11 percent. Those with the lowest initial ROEs (–24 percent) experience a dramatic increase in ROE and then level off at 3 percent in year 10.

The pattern in Figure 6.2 is not a coincidence; it is exactly what the economics of competition would predict. The tendency of high ROEs to fall is a reflection of high profitability attracting competition; the tendency of low ROEs to rise reflects the mobility of capital away from unproductive ventures toward more profitable ones.

Despite the general tendencies documented in Figure 6.2, there are some firms whose ROEs may remain above or below normal levels for long periods of time. In some cases the phenomenon reflects the strength of a sustainable competitive advantage (e.g., Wal-Mart), but in other cases it is purely an artifact of conservative accounting methods. A good example of the latter phenomenon is pharmaceutical firms, whose major economic asset, the intangible value of research and development, is not recorded on the balance sheet and is therefore excluded from the denominator of ROE. For those firms, one could reasonably expect high ROEs – in excess of 20 percent – over the long run, even in the face of strong competitive forces.

The behavior of components of ROE

The behavior of rates of return on equity can be analyzed further by looking at the behavior of its key components. Recall from Chapter 5 that ROEs and profit margins are linked as follows:

$$\text{ROE} = \text{Operating ROA} + (\text{Operating ROA} - \text{Net interest rate after tax})$$
$$\times \text{Net financial leverage}$$
$$= (\text{NOPAT margin} \times \text{Operating asset turnover}) +$$
$$(\text{Spread} \times \text{Net financial leverage})$$

The time-series behavior of the components of ROE for European companies for 1989 through 2005 are shown in a series of figures in the appendix to this chapter. Some major conclusions can be drawn from these figures: (1) Operating asset turnover tends to be rather stable, in part because it is so much a function of the technology of the industry. The only exception to this is the set of firms with very high asset turnover, which tends to decline somewhat over time before stabilizing. (2) Net financial leverage also tends to be stable, simply because management policies on capital structure aren't often changed. (3)NOPAT margin and spread stand out as the most variable component of ROE; if the forces of competition drive abnormal ROEs toward more normal levels, the change is most likely to arrive in the form of changes in profit margins and the spread. The change in spread is itself driven by changes in NOPAT margin, because the cost of borrowing is likely to remain stable if leverage remains stable.

To summarize, profit margins, like ROEs, tend to be driven by competition to "normal" levels over time. What constitutes normal varies widely according to the technology employed within an industry and the corporate strategy pursued by the firm, both of which influence turnover and leverage.[5] In a fully competitive equilibrium, profit margins should remain high for firms that must operate with a low turnover, and vice versa.

The above discussion of rates of return and margins implies that a reasonable point of departure for forecasting such a statistic should consider more than just the most recent observation. One should also consider whether that rate or margin is above or below a normal level. If so, then absent detailed information to the contrary, one would expect some movement over time to that norm. Of course this central tendency might be overcome in some cases – for example, where the firm has erected barriers to competition that can protect margins, even for extended periods. The lesson from the evidence, however, is that such cases are unusual.

In contrast to rates of return and margins, it is reasonable to assume that asset turnover, financial leverage, and net interest rate remain relatively constant over time. Unless there is an explicit change in technology or financial policy being contemplated for future periods, a reasonable point of departure for assumptions for these variables is the current period level. The only exceptions to this appear to be firms with either very high asset turnover that experience some decline in this ratio before stabilizing, or those firms with very low (usually negative) net debt to capital that appear to increase leverage before stabilizing.

As we proceed with the steps involved in producing a detailed forecast, the reader will note that we draw on the above knowledge of the behavior of accounting numbers to some extent. However, it is important to keep in mind that a knowledge of *average* behavior will not fit all firms well. The art of financial statements analysis requires not only knowing what the "normal" patterns are but also having expertise in identifying those firms that will *not* follow the norm.

MAKING FORECASTS

Here we summarize steps that could be followed in producing a comprehensive forecast. The discussion assumes that the firm being analyzed is among the vast majority for which the forecast would reasonably be anchored by a sales forecast. We use the example of Porsche, the car manufacturer discussed in Chapter 5, to illustrate the mechanics of forecasting. In Chapter 5 we analyzed the performance of Porsche during the fiscal year ending July 31, 2005. We begin our forecasting exercise using this as the point of departure.

Table 6.1 shows the forecasting assumptions for fiscal years 2006 to 2010. Table 6.2 shows the forecasted income statements for these same fiscal years, and beginning of the year balance sheets for fiscal years 2006 to 2010 (that for fiscal 2005 is the actual balance sheet reported by the company for the year ending July 31, 2005). We discuss below the logic behind the forecasting assumptions.

TABLE 6.1 Forecasting assumptions for Porsche

For fiscal year	2006	2007	2008	2009	2010	2011	2012	2013	2014	2015
Sales growth	4.7%	0.9%	10.7%	22.9%	9.3%	7.5%	7.5%	7.5%	7.5%	7.5%
NOPAT margin	11.5%	11.0%	10.5%	10.0%	9.5%	9.0%	8.5%	8.0%	7.5%	7.0%
After-tax net interest rate	–0.9%	–0.9%	–0.9%	–0.9%	–0.9%	–0.9%	–0.9%	–0.9%	–0.9%	–0.9%
Beginning net working capital to sales ratio	8.0%	8.0%	8.0%	8.0%	8.0%	8.0%	8.0%	8.0%	8.0%	8.0%
Beginning net non-current assets to sales ratio	52.4%	52.4%	52.4%	52.4%	52.4%	52.4%	52.4%	52.4%	52.4%	52.4%
Beginning net debt to capital ratio	18.0%	18.0%	18.0%	18.0%	18.0%	18.0%	18.0%	18.0%	18.0%	18.0%

Note: In addition to these assumptions, we also assume that sales will continue to grow at 7.5 percent in 2016 and all the balance sheet ratios remain constant, to compute the beginning balance sheet for 2016 and cash flows for 2015.

One year ahead forecasts

As mentioned above, we have the actual balance sheet for the beginning of the year in fiscal 2006, so there is no need to forecast this. In general, making a short-term income statement forecast, such as a one year ahead forecast, is often a straightforward extrapolation of recent performance. This is a particularly valid approach for an established company for several reasons. First, an established company is unlikely to effect major changes in its operating and financing policies in the short term, unless it is in the middle of a restructuring program. Second, the beginning of the year balance sheet for any given year will put constraints on operating activities during that fiscal year. For example, inventories at the beginning of the year will determine to some extent the sales activities during the year; plant and equipment in operation at the beginning of the year also determine to some extent the level of production and sales achievable during the year. To put it another way, because our discussion above shows that asset turnover for a company does not usually change significantly over time, sales in any period are to some extent constrained by the beginning of the period assets in place in the company's balance sheet. Of course it is possible to achieve some flexibility in this regard if there are explicit plans to either expand assets significantly during the year (for example, through new production facilities in the case of Porsche), or through a change in the asset utilization (for example, a change in production efficiency in the case of Porsche).

When constructing an estimate of future sales it is helpful to start with identifying the firm's primary sales drivers. For example, we could first predict future changes in unit sales for each of Porsche's car models separately and then derive a total sales estimate from the unit sales forecasts and the models' individual contributions to sales.

With this framework in mind, our assumptions for Porsche for fiscal 2006 are the following. We assume that sales will grow at 4.7 percent. This sales growth rate is based on the following assumptions about unit sales:

■ Porsche is expected to sell 34,000 units of its Porsche 911 model. The 911 model, which contributes an estimated €90,000 per unit to total sales, is Porsche's fastest growing model with an expected growth rate of 22 percent.

- Unit sales of the Porsche Boxster/Cayman model, with an average sales contribution per unit of €48,000, is expected to grow at a rate of 11 percent from 18,000 to 20,000 units.

- Because Porsche's currently most successful model, the Porsche Cayenne, has reached its fourth year of production, this model's unit sales will decline by 13 percent from 41,300 to 36,000 units. This model contributes on average €60,000 per unit to sales.

- The production of the Porsche Carrera GT, Porsche's most expensive model with an estimated contribution to sales of €290,000 thousand per unit, stops in April 2006. Porsche is expected to sell only 500 units of this model in 2006, which corresponds to a decline of 24 percent.

- Sales from other activities, such as the sale of spare parts and financial services, will increase by 4 percent from an estimated €536 million to €557 million.

These assumptions lead to an expected sales level in fiscal 2006 of €6,882 million. The estimated number of units that will be sold in 2006 is 90,500, which is in line with management's prediction that unit sales in 2006 will be more than 90,000. The implied ratio of beginning net working capital to sales is 8.0 percent, and the beginning non-current assets to sales ratio is 52.4 percent, or a total of net operating assets to sales ratio of 60.4 percent. This is in line with the company's net operating assets to sales ratio for the previous year, which was 59.3 percent.

Notice that a beginning of year balance sheet at the start of the forecasting horizon is a given. Therefore, we are starting with a given level of assets to work with. So we can either make an assumption about sales growth rate and check the implied ratio of beginning net assets to sales for reasonableness, or make an assumption of the beginning net assets to sales ratio for the year, and check for the reasonableness of the implied sales growth rate. In other words, we are free to make only one of the two assumptions – either sales growth or net asset turnover. In subsequent years in the forecast horizon, we relax this constraint because we can build up both a desired beginning balance sheet and income statement for the following years.

Another assumption we make for Porsche for fiscal 2006 is that its NOPAT margin will be 11.5 percent, slightly lower than the extraordinarily high margin the company achieved in the previous year (11.7 percent). Notice that the time-series trends in NOPAT margins discussed earlier suggest that companies with very high margins tend to experience a gradual decline in margins over time. Our assumption for fiscal 2006 begins to reflect this trend.

The third assumption we make to forecast Porsche's income statement for fiscal 2006 relates to the after-tax cost of debt. We know the company's beginning level of debt and its beginning debt to capital ratio for fiscal 2006, based on the company's actual balance sheet at that time. These ratios are somewhat similar to the ratios at the beginning of the previous fiscal year. Therefore, it is reasonable to assume that the company's interest rate on its debt will be somewhat similar to the effective interest during the previous year, which was about –1.4 percent (interest income). With an assumed tax rate of 37 percent, the after-tax interest rate is –0.9 percent.

These assumptions together lead to a projected €798.2 million net profit in fiscal year 2006 compared with a reported net profit of €775.5 million in fiscal 2005.

Forecasts for years two to ten

In making longer-term forecasts, such as for years two to ten, we can rely on the time-series behavior of various performance ratios we discussed earlier in the chapter.

Based on Porsche's announced investment plans for the coming years, however, we can estimate sales growth for the fiscal years 2007 through 2010 in detail. We make the following assumptions:

- Between 2007 and 2010, unit sales of Porsche's 911 and Boxster/Cayman models continues to grow at a rate of 10 percent per year, while unit sales of Porsche's Cayenne model continues to decline at a rate of 10 percent. We assume that these models' contribution to sales per unit remains constant.

- In 2008, Porsche will start with the production of the Porsche Panamera model. We estimate that Porsche will sell 5,000 units of the Panamera model in 2008, 20,000 units in 2009, and 25,000 units in 2010. The estimated contribution of this model to sales is €95,000 per unit.

- Sales from other activities, such as the sale of spare parts and financial services, will increase by 4 percent per year.

These assumptions lead to expected sales growth rates of 0.9, 10.7, 22.9, and 9.3 percent in fiscal 2007, 2008, 2009, and 2010, respectively. Beyond 2010, we assume that the sales growth rate will stabilize at 7.5 percent per year, which is close to the European historical average sales growth rate.

We assume a pattern of declining NOPAT margins over time, consistent with the time-series trend we documented earlier in the chapter for firms with initially high NOPAT. While Porsche clearly has a great deal of competitive advantage over its rivals, it is prudent to assume, given the history of European firms, that this advantage will decline over time. So we assume that the company's NOPAT margin will decline by half a percentage point per year, from 11.5 percent in 2006 to 7.0 percent in 2015. At that point we will assume that the NOPAT margin will have reached steady state and will remain at that level in subsequent years.

Because asset turnover generally shows a flat time-series trend, we will assume that the ratio of beginning operating working capital to sales and beginning non-current assets to sales will remain unchanged during the entire forecasting period. Thus we assume that the beginning operating working capital to sales ratio will remain at 8.0 percent from 2006 to 2015 and beyond; we also assume that the beginning non-current assets to sales ratio will remain at 52.4 percent throughout this period.

We make a similar assumption for the company's capital structure policy. The company has a relatively conservative financing policy with 18.0 percent net debt to net capital ratio at the beginning of 2006. We assume that it will remain at this level during the entire forecasting period.[6] This assumption of a constant capital structure policy is consistent with the general pattern observed in historical data discussed earlier in the chapter. Since we hold the capital structure constant, we can assume that the company's borrowing rate remains unchanged, at –1.4 percent before tax, or –0.9 percent after tax.

With these assumptions it is a straightforward task to derive the forecasted income statements for fiscal years 2006 to 2015, and beginning balance sheets for years 2007 to 2015, as shown in Table 6.2. Under these forecasts Porsche's sales will grow to €14.8 billion by 2015. By the beginning of 2015, Porsche will have a net asset base of €9.0 billion. Its return on beginning equity will be at 23.4 percent in 2006. It will gradually decline from this high level to 14.3 percent in 2015, a level closer to its cost of equity.

Cash flow forecasts

Once we have forecasted income statements and balance sheets, deriving cash flows for the years 2006 to 2015 is straightforward. Note that we need to forecast the beginning balance sheet for 2016 to compute the cash flows for 2015. This balance sheet is not

TABLE 6.2 Forecasted financial statements for Porsche

Fiscal year	2006	2007	2008	2009	2010	2011	2012	2013	2014	2015
Beginning balance sheet (€ millions)										
Beginning net working capital	551.1	556.1	615.6	756.5	826.9	888.9	955.6	1,027.3	1,104.3	1,187.1
+ Beginning net non-current assets	3,608.1	3,640.6	4,030.1	4,953.1	5,413.7	5,819.7	6,256.2	6,725.4	7,229.8	7,772.0
= Net operating assets	**4,159.3**	**4,196.7**	**4,645.7**	**5,709.6**	**6,240.6**	**6,708.6**	**7,211.8**	**7,752.7**	**8,334.1**	**8,959.2**
Net debt	747.1	753.8	834.5	1,025.6	1,121.0	1,205.1	1,295.4	1,392.6	1,497.0	1,609.3
+ Shareholders' equity	3,412.1	3,442.8	3,811.2	4,684.0	5,119.6	5,503.6	5,916.4	6,360.1	6,837.1	7,349.9
= Net capital	**4,159.3**	**4,196.7**	**4,645.7**	**5,709.6**	**6,240.6**	**6,708.6**	**7,211.8**	**7,752.7**	**8,334.1**	**8,959.2**
Income statement (€ millions)										
Sales	6,882.0	6,943.9	7,686.9	9,447.2	10,325.8	11,100.3	11,932.8	12,827.8	13,789.8	14,824.1
Net operating profits after tax	791.4	763.8	807.1	944.7	981.0	999.0	1,014.3	1,026.2	1,034.2	1,037.7
– Net interest expense after tax	–6.7	–6.8	–7.5	–9.2	–10.1	–10.8	–11.7	–12.5	–13.5	–14.5
= Net profit	**798.2**	**770.6**	**814.6**	**954.0**	**991.1**	**1,009.9**	**1,025.9**	**1,038.8**	**1,047.7**	**1,052.2**
Operating ROA	19.0%	18.2%	17.4%	16.5%	15.7%	14.9%	14.1%	13.2%	12.4%	11.6%
ROE	23.4%	22.4%	21.4%	20.4%	19.4%	18.3%	17.3%	16.3%	15.3%	14.3%
BV of assets growth rate	6.7%	0.9%	10.7%	22.9%	9.3%	7.5%	7.5%	7.5%	7.5%	7.5%
BV of equity growth rate	17.1%	0.9%	10.7%	22.9%	9.3%	7.5%	7.5%	7.5%	7.5%	7.5%
Net operating asset turnover	1.7	1.7	1.7	1.7	1.7	1.7	1.7	1.7	1.7	1.7
Free cash flow to capital	754.0	314.8	–256.7	413.7	512.9	495.9	473.4	444.8	409.2	365.7
Free cash flow to equity	767.4	402.2	–58.1	518.3	607.1	597.1	582.2	561.7	534.9	500.9

Note: We do not show the beginning balance sheet forecasted for 2016 here, but it is implicit in the calculation of cash flows for 2015. As stated in Table 6.1, we assume that sales continue to grow in 2016 and that all the balance sheet ratios continue to be the same, to derive the beginning balance sheet for 2016.

shown in Table 6.2. For the purpose of illustration, we assume that all the sales growth and all the balance sheet ratios remain the same in 2016 as in 2015. Based on this we project a beginning balance sheet for 2016 and compute the cash flows for 2015. Cash flow to capital is equal to NOPAT minus increases in net working capital and net non-current assets. Cash flow to equity is cash flow to capital minus net interest after tax plus increase in net debt. These two sets of forecasted cash flows are shown in Table 6.2.

SENSITIVITY ANALYSIS

The projections discussed thus far represent nothing more than a "best guess." Managers and analysts are typically interested in a broader range of possibilities. For example, in considering the likelihood that short-term financing will be necessary, it would be wise to produce projections based on a more pessimistic view of profit margins and asset turnover. Alternatively, an analyst estimating the value of Porsche should consider the sensitivity of the estimate to the key assumptions about sales growth, profit margins, and asset utilization. What if Porsche is able to retain its competitive advantage better than assumed in the above forecasts? What if Porsche is unable to maintain its high profit margins assumed?

There is no limit to the number of possible scenarios that can be considered. One systematic approach to sensitivity analysis is to start with the key assumptions under-lying a set of forecasts and then examine the sensitivity to the assumptions with greatest uncertainty in a given situation. For example, if a company has experienced a variable pattern of gross margins in the past, it is important to make projections using a range of margins. Alternatively, if a company has announced a significant change in its expansion strategy, asset utilization assumptions might be more uncertain. In determining where to invest one's time in performing sensitivity analysis, it is therefore important to consider historical patterns of performance, changes in industry conditions, and changes in a company's competitive strategy.

Seasonality and interim forecasts

Thus far we have concerned ourselves with annual forecasts. However, traditionally for security analysts in the U.S. and increasingly for security analysts in Europe, fore-casting is very much a quarterly game. Forecasting quarter by quarter raises a new set of questions. How important is seasonality? What is a useful point of departure – the most recent quarter's performance? The comparable quarter of the prior year? Some combination of the two? How should quarterly data be used in producing an annual forecast? Does the item-by-item approach to forecasting used for annual data apply equally well to quarterly data? Full consideration of these questions lies outside the scope of this chapter, but we can begin to answer some of them.

Seasonality is a more important phenomenon in sales and earnings behavior than one might guess. It is present for more than just the retail sector firms that benefit from holiday sales. Seasonality also results from weather-related phenomena (e.g., for electric and gas utilities, construction firms, and motorcycle manufacturers), new product introduction patterns (e.g., for the automobile industry), and other factors. Analysis of the time-series behavior of earnings for U.S. firms suggests that at least some seasonality is present in nearly every major industry.

The implication for forecasting is that one cannot focus only on performance of the most recent quarter as a point of departure. In fact the evidence suggests that, in forecasting earnings, if one had to choose only one quarter's performance as a point of departure, it would be the comparable quarter of the prior year, not the most recent quarter. Note how this finding is consistent with the reports of analysts or the financial press; when they discuss a quarterly earnings announcement, it is nearly always evaluated relative to the performance of the comparable quarter of the prior year, not the most recent quarter.

Research has produced models that forecast sales, earnings, or EPS based solely on prior quarters' observations. Such models are not used by many analysts, because analysts have access to much more information than such simple models contain. However, the models are useful for helping those unfamiliar with the behavior of earnings data to understand how it tends to evolve through time. Such an understanding can provide useful general background, a point of departure in forecasting that can be adjusted to reflect details not revealed in the history of earnings, or a "reasonableness" check on a detailed forecast.

Using Q_t to denote earnings (or EPS) for quarter t, and $E(Q_t)$ as its expected value, one model of the earnings process that fits well across a variety of industries is the so-called Foster model:[7]

$$E(Q_t) = Q_{t-4} + \delta + \phi\,(Q_{t-1} - Q_{t-5})$$

Foster shows that a model of the same form also works well with sales data.

The form of the Foster model confirms the importance of seasonality because it shows that the starting point for a forecast for quarter t is the earnings four quarters ago, Q_{t-4}. It states that, when constrained to using only prior earnings data, a reasonable forecast of earnings for quarter t includes the following elements:

- the earnings of the comparable quarter of the prior year (Q_{t-4});
- a long-run trend in year-to-year quarterly earnings increases (δ); and
- a fraction (ϕ) of the year-to-year increase in quarterly earnings experienced most recently ($Q_{t-1} - Q_{t-5}$).

The parameters δ and ϕ can easily be estimated for a given firm with a simple linear regression model available in most spreadsheet software.[8] For most firms the parameter ϕ tends to be in the range of .25 to .50, indicating that 25 to 50 percent of an increase in quarterly earnings tends to persist in the form of another increase in the subsequent quarter. The parameter δ reflects in part the average year-to-year change in quarterly earnings over past years, and it varies considerably from firm to firm.

Research indicates that the Foster model produces one-quarter-ahead forecasts that are off, on average, by $.30 to $.35 per share.[9] Such a degree of accuracy stacks up surprisingly well with that of security analysts, who obviously have access to much information ignored in the model. As one would expect, most of the evidence supports analysts being more accurate, but the models are good enough to be "in the ball park" in most circumstances. While it would certainly be unwise to rely completely on such a naïve model, an understanding of the typical earnings behavior reflected by the model is useful.

SUMMARY

Forecasting represents the first step of prospective analysis and serves to summarize the forward-looking view that emanates from business strategy analysis, accounting analysis, and financial analysis. Although not every financial statement analysis is accompanied by such an explicit summarization of a view of the future, forecasting is still a key tool for managers, consultants, security analysts, investment bankers, commercial bankers and other credit analysts, and others.

The best approach to forecasting future performance is to do it comprehensively – producing not only an earnings forecast but a forecast of cash flows and the balance sheet as well. Such a comprehensive approach provides a guard against internal inconsistencies and unrealistic implicit assumptions. The approach described here involves line-by-line analysis, so as to recognize that different items on the income statement and balance sheet are influenced by different drivers. Nevertheless, it remains the case that a few key projections – such as sales growth and profit margin – usually drive most of the projected numbers.

The forecasting process should be embedded in an understanding of how various financial statistics tend to behave on average, and what might cause a firm to deviate from that average. Absent detailed information to the contrary, one would expect sales and earnings numbers to persist at their current levels, adjusted for overall trends of recent years. However, rates of return on investment (ROEs) tend, over several years, to move from abnormal to normal levels – close to the cost of equity capital – as the forces of competition come into play. Profit margins also tend to shift to normal levels, but for this statistic "normal" varies widely across firms and industries, depending on the levels of asset turnover and leverage. Some firms are capable of creating barriers to entry that enable them to fight these tendencies toward normal returns, even for many years, but such firms are the unusual cases.

For some purposes, including short-term planning and security analysis, forecasts for quarterly periods are desirable. One important feature of quarterly data is seasonality; at least some seasonality exists in the sales and earnings data of nearly every industry. An understanding of a firm's within-year peaks and valleys is a necessary ingredient of a good forecast of performance on a quarterly basis.

There are a variety of contexts (including but not limited to security analysis) where the forecast is usefully summarized in the form of an estimate of the firm's value – an estimate that, after all, can be viewed as the best attempt to reflect in a single summary statistic the manager's or analyst's view of the firm's prospects. That process of converting a forecast into a value estimate is labeled valuation. It is to that topic that we turn in the next chapter.

DISCUSSION QUESTIONS

1. GlaxoSmithKline is one of the largest pharmaceutical firms in the world, and over an extended period of time in the recent past it consistently earned higher ROEs than the pharmaceutical industry as a whole. As a pharmaceutical analyst, what factors would you consider to be important in making projections of future ROEs for GlaxoSmithKline? In particular, what factors would lead you to expect GlaxoSmithKline to continue to be a superior performer in its industry, and what factors would lead you to expect GlaxoSmithKline's future performance to revert to that of the industry as a whole?

2. An analyst claims, "It is not worth my time to develop detailed forecasts of sales growth, profit margins, etcetera, to make earnings projections. I can be almost as accurate, at virtually no cost, using the random walk model to forecast earnings." What is the random walk model? Do you agree or disagree with the analyst's forecast strategy? Why or why not?

3. Which of the following types of businesses do you expect to show a high degree of seasonality in quarterly earnings? Explain why.

   ■ a supermarket

   ■ a pharmaceutical company

   ■ a software company

   ■ an auto manufacturer

   ■ a clothing retailer.

4. What factors are likely to drive a firm's outlays for new capital (such as plant, property, and equipment) and for working capital (such as receivables and inventory)? What ratios would you use to help generate forecasts of these outlays?

5. How would the following events (reported this year) affect your forecasts of a firm's future net profit?

   ■ an asset write-down

   ■ a merger or acquisition

   ■ the sale of a major division

   ■ the initiation of dividend payments.

6. Consider the following two earnings forecasting models:

$$\text{Model 1: } E_t \ (EPS_{t+1}) = EPS_t$$

$$\text{Model 2: } E_t \ (EPS_{t+1}) = \frac{1}{5} \sum_{t=1}^{5} EPS_t$$

   $E_t(EPS)$ is the expected forecast of earnings per share for year $t+1$, given information available at t. Model 1 is usually called a random walk model for earnings, whereas Model 2 is called a mean-reverting model. The earnings per share for Telefónica for the period 2000 to 2004 are as follows:

Year	1	2	3	4	5
EPS	€0.61	€0.43	€(1.08)	€0.40	€0.58

   a. What would be the year 6 forecast for earnings per share for each model?

   b. Actual earnings per share for Telefónica in 6 were €0.91. Given this information, what would be the year 7 forecast for earnings per share for each model? Why do the two models generate quite different forecasts? Which do you think would better describe earnings per share patterns? Why?

7. An investment banker states, "It is not worth my while to worry about detailed long-term forecasts. Instead, I use the following approach when forecasting cash flows beyond three years. I assume that sales grow at the rate of inflation, capital expenditures are equal to depreciation, and that net profit margins and working capital to sales ratios stay constant." What pattern of return on equity is implied by these assumptions? Is this reasonable?

NOTES

1. See Patricia O'Brien, "Analysts' Forecasts as Earnings Expectations," *Journal of Accounting and Economics* (January 1988): 53–83.
2. See George Foster, "Quarterly Accounting Data: Time Series Properties and Predictive Ability Results," *The Accounting Review* (January 1977): 1–21.
3. See Robert Freeman, James Ohlson, and Stephen Penman, "Book Rate-of-Return and Prediction of Earnings Changes: An Empirical Investigation," *Journal of Accounting Research* (Autumn 1982): 639–653.
4. See Stephen H. Penman, "An Evaluation of Accounting Rate-of-Return," *Journal of Accounting, Auditing, and Finance* (Spring 1991): 233–256; Eugene Fama and Kenneth French, "Size and Book-to-Market Factors in Earnings and Returns," *Journal of Finance* (March 1995): 131–156; and Victor Bernard, "Accounting-Based Valuation Methods: Evidence on the Market-to-Book Anomaly and Implications for Financial Statements Analysis," University of Michigan, working paper (1994). Ignoring the effects of accounting artifacts, ROEs should be driven in a competitive equilibrium to a level approximating the cost of equity capital.
5. A "normal" profit margin is that which, when multiplied by the turnover achievable within an industry and with a viable corporate strategy, yields a return on investment that just covers the cost of capital. However, as mentioned above, accounting artifacts can cause returns on investment to deviate from the cost of capital for long periods, even in a competitive equilibrium.
6. To simplify our analysis, we ignore the fact that at the end of fiscal 2005 investors may have been aware of the fact that Porsche was about to issue new bonds for an amount of €3.0 billion and acquire a 20 percent stake in Volkswagen for the same amount. If we wanted to take the pending bond issue and acquisition into account, it would be easier to value the firm's operating activities separately from its investment in Volkswagen. Consequently, we would assume that net debt and net non-current assets would increase by €3.0 billion as a result of the acquisition and bond issue. Taking the investment in Volkswagen "off balance" to value it separately would decrease net non-current assets and equity by €3.0 billion. The net effect of these adjustments on the beginning non-current assets to sales ratio for 2007 would be zero. The adjustments would increase the beginning net debt to net capital ratio in 2007 from 18.0 percent to 89.5 percent. Under the assumption that Porsche's effective interest rate on new debt is 5.0 percent (before tax), Porsche's net interest rate after tax would increase from –0.9 percent to approximately 2.7 percent.
7. See Foster, op. cit. A somewhat more accurate model is furnished by Brown and Rozeff, but it requires interactive statistical techniques for estimation – Lawrence D. Brown and Michael Rozeff, "Univariate Time Series Models of Quarterly Accounting Earnings per Share," *Journal of Accounting Research* (Spring 1979): 179–189.
8. To estimate the model, we write in terms of realized earnings (as opposed to expected earnings) and move Q_{t-4} to the left-hand side:

$$Q_t - Q_{t-4} = \delta + \phi(Q_{t-1} - Q_{t-5}) + e_t$$

We now have a regression where $(Q_t - Q_{t-4})$ is the dependent variable, and its lagged value – $(Q_{t-1} - Q_{t-5})$ – is the independent variable. Thus, to estimate the equation, prior earnings data must first be expressed in terms of year-to-year changes; the change for one quarter is then regressed against the change for the most recent quarter. The intercept provides an estimate of δ, and the slope is an estimate of ϕ. The equation is typically estimated using 24 to 40 quarters of prior earnings data.
9. See O'Brien, op. cit.

APPENDIX: THE BEHAVIOR OF COMPONENTS OF ROE

In Figure 6.2 we show that ROEs tend to be mean-reverting. In this appendix we show the behavior of the key components of ROE – operating ROA, operating margin, operating asset turnover, spread, and net financial leverage. These ratios are computed using the same portfolio approach described in the chapter, based on the data for all European firms for the time period 1989 through 2005.

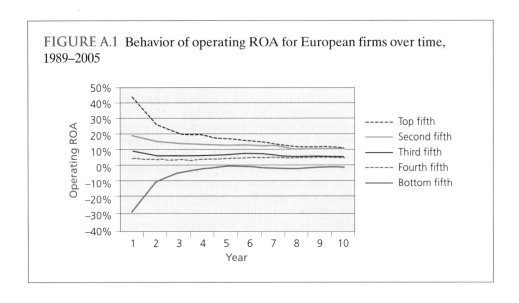

FIGURE A.1 Behavior of operating ROA for European firms over time, 1989–2005

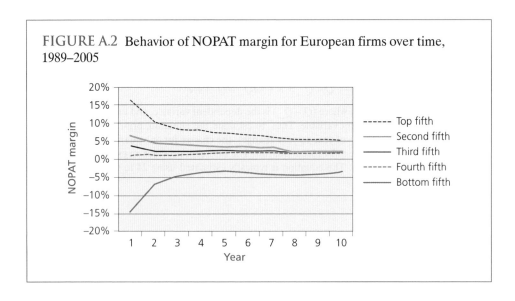

FIGURE A.2 Behavior of NOPAT margin for European firms over time, 1989–2005

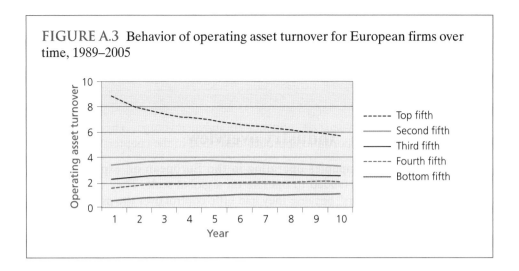

FIGURE A.3 Behavior of operating asset turnover for European firms over time, 1989–2005

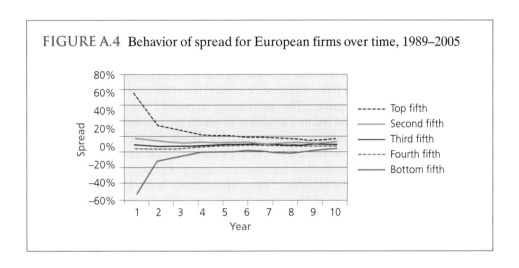

FIGURE A.4 Behavior of spread for European firms over time, 1989–2005

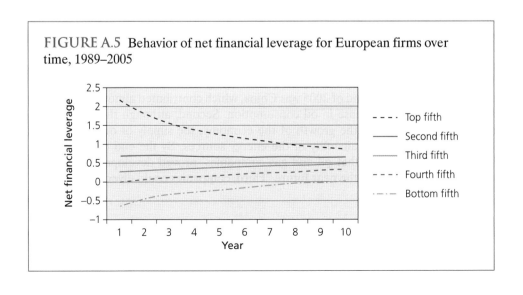

FIGURE A.5 Behavior of net financial leverage for European firms over time, 1989–2005

Forecasting earnings and earnings growth in the European oil and gas industry[1]

Industry overview

In 2005 the largest companies operating in the European oil exploration and production industry all tended to operate on a global scale. They were typically categorized as "price takers" because they had little control over the prices that they could ask from their customers. One reason for this small influence on prices was that the 11 oil-producing developing countries that coordinated their production activities through the OPEC organization had a strong influence on the worldwide oil supply and crude oil prices. Although the OPEC countries possessed close to 75 percent of the worldwide proved oil reserves, they supplied only 40 percent of the worldwide oil production to stabilize prices at higher levels. National taxes also influenced local prices and demand for oil. For example, in Europe fuel prices were, on average, four times as large as fuel prices in the U.S., tempering the demand in Europe.

During the first half of the 2000s, crude oil prices soared to record levels. While at the end of 1999 the price for a barrel of crude oil was close to $25, the crude oil price was above $55 by the end of 2005. There were several potential reasons for this strong increase in the crude oil price.[2] The increasing demand for oil from emerging economies such as China had led to a situation in which the amount of oil demanded had approached the maximum production capacity. While the OPEC countries had increased their production to record levels, they had invested insufficiently in new capacity and were unable to further increase oil supply. Oil supply had also come under pressure because of the close to 12 percent reduction in the U.S. oil production capacity after the devastations of Hurricane Katrina in 2005. Further, oil prices were strongly affected by speculative trading in the commodity markets in response to the crisis in the Middle East and the political instability in oil-producing African countries. Exhibit 1 shows the crude oil price between January 2000 and December 2005 as well as the prices of oil futures at the end of 2005.

Because oil and gas companies were price takers, their success critically depended on (1) their ability to grow and (2) the efficiency of their exploration and production activities. Although the growth of the energy markets typically followed the growth in gross domestic product, oil and gas companies could grow at a faster or slower rate than the economy average for the following reasons. First, some companies were able to open up new markets, primarily in the emerging countries. The most important emerging market at the end of 2005 was China, which contributed almost one-third to the total worldwide increase in oil consumption. Second, although the demand for energy tended to follow the growth of the economy, the supply of oil and gas was limited by the natural availability of the energy sources. By the end of 2005, many industry analysts feared that oil and gas companies' proved developed oil and gas reserves would reduce in the near future. Third, companies could diversify into other

---

1. Professor Erik Peek prepared this case. The case is intended solely as the basis for class discussion and is not intended to serve as an endorsement, source of primary data, or illustration of effective or ineffective management.
2. See "The Structure of the Oil Market and Causes of High Prices" by Pelin Berkmen, Sam Ouliaris, and Hossein Samiei, International Monetary Fund, 2005.

segments of the energy market. For example oil and natural gas companies produced or started to produce coal, nuclear energy, or hydroelectric energy.

The increasing oil price tended to have a positive impact on oil and gas companies' profits in the first half of the 2000s. Nonetheless, various other developments put pressure on the companies' profit margins. First, because oil was traded in US dollars, the weak dollar implied that it was expensive for oil companies to buy resources in other currencies. Second, steel prices were also rising, making oil and gas companies' capital investments more expensive. Third, and most importantly, during the first half of the 2000s exploration costs per barrel of oil equivalent (BOE) had risen sharply.[3]

Oil and gas companies that had operations in developing countries were also subject to a substantial degree of country risk. Many companies were extending their operations to developing countries in, for example, West Africa or around the Caspian Sea, because they were running out of reserves in the developed countries. Operations in such developing countries could, however, be disrupted by political crises, acts of war, and expropriation or nationalization of reserves and production facilities by governments. For example, in 2006 Bolivia announced plans to nationalize its oil and gas fields, which were then owned by several international oil and gas producers.

Oil and gas companies' accounting and disclosure

As argued, because oil and gas companies are price takers, their future profitability depends primarily on (1) the quantity and quality of their current oil and gas reserves, (2) their ability to efficiently extract and produce oil and gas, and (3) their ability to replace extracted reserves. Some inherent characteristics of oil and gas companies' exploration and development activities, however, make accounting for these activities a difficult exercise. Particularly, because the future economic benefits of current exploration and development expenditures are hard to establish, deciding on which expenditures must be capitalized as assets and which expenditures must be categorized as "unsuccessful" and immediately written-off can be problematic.

Most oil and gas companies use the "successful efforts method" of accounting for exploration and development activities. Under this method, the key financial reporting estimate is for proved oil and gas reserves. Accounting standards consider oil and gas reserves to be proved when the company has government and regulatory approval for the extraction of reserves and is able to bring the reserves quickly to the market in a commercially viable manner. Companies make these estimates using geological information about each reservoir, reservoir production histories, and reservoir pressure histories. The distinction between proved and unproved reserves is important because only exploration expenditures that are associated with proved reserves are capitalized as assets. Specifically, under the successful efforts method, companies capitalize their exploration expenditures for a short period, after which they choose between continued capitalization and immediate amortization based on whether the exploration has successfully led to the booking of proved reserves. In addition, oil companies' depreciation, depletion, and amortization of production plants are typically calculated using the unit-of-production method, where the expected production capacity is derived from the proved reserves. The following paragraphs from British Petroleum's (BP's) 2005 Annual Report describe how BP

---

3. See *"Oil Companies' Profits: Not Exactly What They Seem to Be,"* The Economist, *October 28, 2004.*

accounts for exploration and development expenditures and illustrates the basic idea underlying the successful efforts method:

> *Exploration and property leasehold acquisition costs are capitalized within intangible fixed assets and amortized on a straight-line basis over the estimated period of exploration. Each property is reviewed on an annual basis to confirm that drilling activity is planned and it is not impaired. If no future activity is planned, the remaining balance of the licence and property acquisition costs is written off. Upon determination of economically recoverable reserves ("proved reserves" or "commercial reserves"), amortization ceases and the remaining costs are aggregated with exploration expenditure and held on a field-by-field basis as proved properties awaiting approval within other intangible assets. When development is approved internally, the relevant expenditure is transferred to property, plant and equipment.*
>
> *Geological and geophysical exploration costs are charged against income as incurred. Costs directly associated with an exploration well are capitalized as an intangible asset until the drilling of the well is complete and the results have been evaluated. These costs include employee remuneration, materials and fuel used, rig costs, delay rentals and payments made to contractors. If hydrocarbons are not found, the exploration expenditure is written off as a dry hole. If hydrocarbons are found and, subject to further appraisal activity, which may include the drilling of further wells (exploration or exploratory-type stratigraphic test wells), are likely to be capable of commercial development, the costs continue to be carried as an asset. All such carried costs are subject to technical, commercial and management review at least once a year to confirm the continued intent to develop or otherwise extract value from the discovery. When this is no longer the case, the costs are written off. When proved reserves of oil and natural gas are determined and development is sanctioned, the relevant expenditure is transferred to property, plant and equipment.*
>
> *Expenditure on the construction, installation or completion of infrastructure facilities such as platforms, pipelines and the drilling of development wells, including unsuccessful development or delineation wells, is capitalized within property, plant and equipment.*

The method that BP uses to account for its exploration and development expenditures is similar to the method used by many other oil and gas companies, including Repsol YPF and Royal Dutch Shell. Most oil and gas companies also provide supplemental disclosures about their oil and gas reserves. These disclosures typically show (1) the exploration and development costs that the company incurred during the year, (2) the exploration and development costs that the company capitalized over the years, (3) the results of the company's oil and gas exploration and development activities, and (4) the movements in the company's proved and unproved oil and gas reserves during the year. Exhibit 2 summarizes the supplemental information that BP, Repsol YPF, and Royal Dutch Shell provided in annual reports for the fiscal year ended on December 31, 2005.

A description of three European oil and gas companies

Following are the descriptions of three European companies that operated in the oil and gas industry in 2005: British Petroleum, Repsol YPF, and Royal Dutch Shell.

British Petroleum

At the end of the second half of the 2000s, British Petroleum (BP) was the world's largest oil and gas company in terms of revenues. The company operated in more than 100 countries, in which it employed approximately 96,000 people. Between 2001 and 2005, BP's return on assets gradually increased from 5 percent to 12 percent. In that period – between December 31, 2000 and December 31, 2005 – BP's share price increased by 14.6 percent, yielding an average annual return of 2.8 percent. By the end of 2005, BP's market value was £127.9 billion.

BP's shares were widely held. In 2005, the company's largest shareholder owned less than 4 percent of BP's ordinary shares outstanding. Like many other oil and gas companies, BP had excess cash that it returned to its shareholders through share repurchases and dividends. In 2005, the company repurchased ordinary shares for an amount of £6.7 billion and paid out £4.0 billion in dividends. BP was a financially healthy company. Standard and Poor's had rated BP's public debt at AA.

Although BP's primary activities were the exploration, development, and production of oil and natural gas, the company also operated in other product segments. However, in 2005 less than 10 percent of the company's revenues and less than 5 percent of its net profits came from the marketing and trading of liquefied natural gas, solar energy, and renewables. BP's primary geographical segment was Europe, where it generated 43 percent of its revenues, followed by the U.S. (40 percent of its revenues).

Fiscal year 2005 had been a year of contrasts for BP. Whereas the company's profitability improved because of rising oil prices, its performance was negatively affected by several events that impaired production and distribution: an explosion at the company's Texas City refinery, the Asian tsunami, and hurricanes in the Gulf of Mexico. BP's income statement for fiscal 2005 included a charge of $700 million for fatality and personal injury claims resulting from the explosion at the Texas City refinery. The company reported that the Texas City incident and extreme weather conditions had resulted in an approximate total loss of $2 billion because of forgone production and repair costs.

BP's capital expenditures in the exploration and production segment totaled $10.1 billion in 2005.[4] The company's proved developed and undeveloped reserves increased by 1 billion barrels of oil equivalent (BOE) because of discoveries and improvements in recovery techniques. BP's daily production in 2005 was approximately 4 million BOEs.

Repsol YPF

Of the three described European oil and gas companies – BP, Royal Dutch Shell and Repsol YPF – Repsol was a smallest, although the company was one of the ten largest oil producers in the world. In 2005, the company operated in more than 20 countries, primarily in Europe and Latin America, employing approximately 36,000 people. Between 2001 and 2005, Repsol's return on assets gradually increased from 4.5 to 8.5 percent. During these years, the company's share price had increased by an average of 7.7 percent, to reach a market value of €30.1 billion on December 31, 2005. Repsol had a few large shareholders, who were primarily banks and pension funds. These shareholders held in total close to 45 percent of the company's ordinary share capital. Repsol's dividends totaled €732 million in 2005. In that year the company had not repurchased ordinary shares, but it had announced plans to do so in the near future.

---

4. *Note that BP's reporting currency was US dollars, whereas the company's shares were traded in British pounds.*

Excess cash was also used to reduce the company's net debt and improve its financial strength. In 2005, Standard and Poor's rated Repsol's public debt at BB.

Repsol's operating activities were strongly focused on exploring for, producing, and retailing oil and natural gas. The company generated a small fraction of its revenues – less than 5 percent – from electricity generation. In addition, Repsol was active in researching and testing bio-fuels. The company had most of its operations located in Europe and Latin America and was less geographically diversified than BP and Royal Dutch Shell. Its primary markets were Spain and Argentina, Bolivia, and Brazil, where it made 44 percent (Spain) and 16 percent (ABB) of its sales, respectively.

Fiscal year 2005 had been one Repsol's most successful years in its history. The company's profitability had benefited from the economic growth in its primary markets, the rising oil prices, and improved refining margins. At the end of 2005, however, Repsol announced that it had downwardly revised its estimates of proved reserves. In particular, estimated reserves were adjusted by 659 million BOEs in Bolivia, 509 million BOEs in Argentina, and 86 million BOEs in the rest of the world. The adjustments to the Bolivian reserves were primarily made because of the political uncertainty in that country. However, adjustments in the other countries were the result of "a better knowledge of the field data." Repsol's daily production in 2005 was approximately 1.1 million BOEs.

For the years 2005–2009, Repsol's management targeted double-digit growth. In 2005, the company made capital expenditures of €1.9 billion in the exploration and production segment and was expanding its operations to other geographical areas, such as North Africa, Russia, and Central Asia. In its 2005 Annual Report, the company identified as one of its most important tasks for the near future to increase its reserves replacement rate.

Royal Dutch Shell

By the beginning of 2006, Royal Dutch Shell Plc was the world's third largest energy and petrochemical group. The company employed more than 110,000 people in 140 countries. Prior to 2005, Royal Dutch Shell was the umbrella name for a group of operating companies that were owned by two exchange-listed companies with separate management boards: Netherlands-based Royal Dutch Petroleum Company and U.K.-based Shell Transport and Trading Company. Royal Dutch held a 60 percent stake in the operating companies, while Shell Transport and Trading held a 40 percent stake. Because the complex ownership structure inhibited effective decision making and governance, however, in July 2005 the two exchange-listed companies unified under a single parent company – Royal Dutch Shell Plc. The shares of Royal Dutch Shell were widely held. The company's largest shareholder held less than 7 percent of the company's ordinary share capital.

Royal Dutch Shell's core activities were the production, development, and retailing of oil and natural gas. Almost 90 percent of its revenues came from these activities; the remainder came from the production of petrochemical products. Forty percent of Royal Dutch Shell's revenues in 2005 came from its European operations, 33 percent of its revenues came from its U.S. operations, and 20 percent of its sales was made in non-European countries from the eastern hemisphere.

In the period from 2000 to 2002, the Royal Dutch Shell group reported gradually declining returns on its assets of between 20 percent and 14 percent. Both exchange-listed holding companies experienced share price declines of about 30 and 20 percent, respectively, reaching a combined market capitalization of €148.6 billion. In 2003, Royal Dutch Shell's return on assets increased to 17 percent but its (combined) market value remained almost unchanged.

On January 9, 2004, Royal Dutch Shell surprised investors with the announcement that its proved oil and gas reserves were about 20 percent smaller than it had previously disclosed. Specifically, the company reclassified 2.7 billion barrels of oil and natural gas liquids as well as 7.2 trillion standard cubic feet of natural gas as "probable but not proved." The estimated value of the reclassified reserves was close to €6 billion. The market value of Royal Dutch Shell decreased by 7.5 percent, or €10.6 billion, in response to the announcement. In February and March, two exchange regulators, the U.S. Securities and Exchange Commission (SEC) and the U.K. Financial Services Authority (FSA), started their investigations into the matter. On April 30, 2004, the company's market value had decreased by 8.9 percent (adjusted for changes in the FTSE All-World Oil & Gas Price Index), or €12.6 billion since the day before the announcement. By that time, rating agency Standard and Poor's had also downgraded Royal Dutch Shell's debt from AAA to AA.

To restore credibility after the restatements of its oil and gas reserves, Royal Dutch Shell undertook several steps. The company improved its internal control systems, replaced some of its directors, abandoned its practice of evaluating business unit's performance and calculating managers' bonuses based on reserve bookings, and unified Royal Dutch Petroleum and Shell Transport and Trading under a single parent company. On April 29, 2004, Royal Dutch Shell also announced that it would immediately relaunch its share repurchase program. The company would return close to €1.4 billion to its shareholders in 2004 and €3.6 billion in 2005.

In 2005, Royal Dutch Shell reported a return on assets of 11.5 percent. In that year, the company's share price increased by close to 17 percent, to reach a market value of €176 billion. Royal Dutch Shell's capital expenditures in the exploration and production segments were $10.8 billion in 2005, when its daily oil and gas production level had declined from 3.7 million to 3.4 million BOEs.

Questions

1. What are the European oil and gas companies' drivers of profitability? What are their key risks?

2. Using the supplemental information summarized in Exhibit 2, analysts can produce several ratios that provide insight into the efficiency of the companies' exploration, development, and production activities as well as their growth opportunities. Develop a set of ratios that provide such insights. How efficient are the three oil and gas companies in exploration and production?

3. Exhibit 3 summarizes analysts' one-year-horizon (2006), two-year-horizon (2007), and three-year-horizon (2008) forecasts of sales growth and profit margins. For each of the three oil and gas companies, provide arguments justifying the most pessimistic scenarios as well as arguments justifying the most optimistic scenarios.

4. Given your answers to the previous questions, what are your forecasts of the oil and gas companies' net profits for fiscal year 2006? What are your expectations about each of the companies' long-term earnings growth (i.e., growth in 2007 and 2008)?

Forecasting earnings and earnings growth in the European oil and gas industry

EXHIBIT 1 **Crude Brent oil prices**

Crude Brent oil price from December 1999 to December 2005

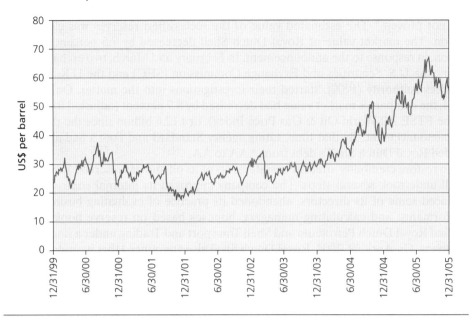

Source: Thomson Datastream.

Crude Brent oil futures prices on December 31, 2005

Crude Brent oil futures for delivery in	Price in US$ per barrel
December 2006	62.27
December 2007	62.05
December 2008	60.47
December 2009	59.01
December 2010	57.97
December 2011	57.45

Source: Thomson Datastream.

Forecasting earnings and earnings growth in the European oil and gas industry

EXHIBIT 2 Supplementary information about BP's, Repsol YPF's, and Royal Dutch Shell's oil and natural gas reserves

	British Petroleum (in US$ millions)		Repsol YPF (in € millions)		Royal Dutch Shell (in US$ millions)	
	2005	2004	2005	2004	2005	2004
Gross capitalized costs of oil and natural gas exploration and development						
Proved properties	109,223	102,819	26,066	22,099	102,373	99,090
Unproved properties	4,661	4,311	1,217	728	4,382	4,307
Auxiliary equipment and facilities	N.A.	N.A.	1,756	1,149	3,988	3,868
Accumulated depreciation and impairment losses	(57,907)	(53,671)	(17,025)	(13,943)	(62,592)	(59,307)
Net capitalized costs	55,977	53,459	11,954	10,033	48,151	47,958
Costs of oil and natural gas exploration and development incurred during the year						
Acquisition of properties						
Proved	0	0	166	209	37	19
Unproved	63	78	650	118	262	2
Exploration and appraisal costs	1,266	1,039	1,417	1,164	413	317
Development costs	7,678	7,270	9,159	8,414	1,448	1,013
Total costs	9,007	8,387	11,392	9,905	2,159	1,351
Results of oil and natural gas exploration, development, and production activities						
Sales and other operating revenues						
To third parties	12,695	9,472	2,359	1,861	10,936	9,400
To group companies	29,119	22,264	4,398	3,961	31,579	24,807
Other income	N.A.	N.A.	731	399	N.A.	N.A.
Total sales	41,814	31,736	7,488	6,221	42,515	34,207
Exploration expenditure	(684)	(637)	(275)	(309)	(1,158)	(1,102)
Production costs	(4,391)	(3,577)				
Production taxes	(2,999)	(2,087)				
Production costs (including taxes)			(2,356)	(1,895)	(7,349)	(6,497)
Other operating costs	(6,857)	(3,764)	(404)	(287)	(1,639)	(1,983)
Depreciation, depletion and amortization	(5,628)	(5,157)	(1,280)	(1,239)	(8,381)	(7,797)
Impairment and (gains) losses on sale of business and fixed assets	893	(469)	N.A.	N.A.	N.A.	N.A.
Profit before taxation	22,148	16,045	3,173	2,491	23,988	16,828
Taxes	(7,950)	(5,327)	(1,960)	(1,376)	(14,523)	(9,769)
Results of operations	14,198	10,718	1,213	1,115	9,465	7,059

(continued)

Forecasting earnings and earnings growth in the European oil and gas industry

EXHIBIT 2 **Supplementary information about BP's, Repsol YPF's, and Royal Dutch Shell's oil and natural gas reserves** *(continued)*

	British Petroleum (in US$ millions)		Repsol YPF (in € millions)		Royal Dutch Shell (in US$ millions)	
	2005	2004	2005	2004	2005	2004
Proved developed and undeveloped reserves of crude oil and natural gas liquids (in million barrels)						
Reserves at the beginning of the year						
Developed reserves	6,084	5,872	1,311	1,412	3,234	3,858
Undeveloped reserves	4,646	4,444	373	469	1,654	1,955
Total reserves	10,730	10,316	1,683	1,882	4,888	5,813
Revision of previous estimates	107	517	(370)	(42)	92	(195)
Increase due to improvements in recovery techniques	335	210	7	19	6	50
Extensions and discoveries	220	371	17	26	380	110
Purchases of reserves-in-place	2	252	38	11	14	0
Sales of reserves-in-place	(75)	(37)	(14)	(5)	(15)	(95)
Production	(912)	(899)	(194)	(208)	(729)	(795)
Reserves at the end of the year						
Developed reserves	5,532	6,084	875	1,311	2,898	3,234
Undeveloped reserves	4,875	4,646	291	373	1,738	1,654
Total reserves	10,407	10,730	1,167	1,683	4,636	4,888
Proved developed and undeveloped reserves of natural gas (in billion cubic feet)						
Reserves at the beginning of the year						
Developed reserves	21,004	22,698	12,077	10,182	21,352	20,869
Undeveloped reserves	24,546	23,831	6,130	9,759	19,215	20,690
Total reserves	45,550	46,529	18,207	19,942	40,567	41,559
Revision of previous estimates	2,046	(2,189)	(4,960)	(1,014)	(612)	(113)
Increase due to improvements in recovery techniques	2,017	1,173	0	2	2	58
Extensions and discoveries	567	3,876	129	523	2,577	2,970
Purchases of reserves-in-place	68	5	34	29	135	9
Sales of reserves-in-place	(1,491)	(643)	(27)	(45)	(21)	(708)
Production	(3,148)	(3,201)	(1,247)	(1,230)	(3,032)	(3,208)
Reserves at the end of the year						
Developed reserves	20,750	21,004	7,160	12,077	20,999	21,352
Undeveloped reserves	24,859	24,546	4,977	6,130	18,617	19,215
Total reserves	45,609	45,550	12,137	18,207	39,616	40,567
Conversion rate: × billion cubic feet of gas = 1 million barrel of oil equivalents	5.80	5.80	5.80	5.80	5.80	5.80

Source: Annual Reports for the fiscal year ended on December 31, 2005 of British Petroleum, Repsol YPF, and Royal Dutch Shell.

Forecasting earnings and earnings growth in the European oil and gas industry

EXHIBIT 3 **Analysts' forecasts for fiscal years 2006, 2007, and 2008 at the beginning of 2006**

Forecasts of sales growth

Fiscal year 2006 relative to fiscal year 2005	Most pessimistic forecast	Consensus forecast	Most optimistic forecast
British Petroleum	3.0%	19.5%	47.3%
Repsol YPF	−7.8%	9.6%	28.6%
Royal Dutch Shell	−5.1%	6.5%	18.2%

Fiscal year 2007 relative to fiscal year 2005	Most pessimistic forecast	Consensus forecast	Most optimistic forecast
British Petroleum	−5.4%	17.2%	41.9%
Repsol YPF	−8.5%	7.3%	15.4%
Royal Dutch Shell	−14.0%	0.4%	11.7%

Fiscal year 2008 relative to fiscal year 2005	Most pessimistic forecast	Consensus forecast	Most optimistic forecast
British Petroleum	−9.8%	9.2%	25.6%
Repsol YPF	0.4%	5.5%	13.1%
Royal Dutch Shell	−17.2%	−4.7%	10.0%

Forecasts of net profit margins

Fiscal year 2006 relative to fiscal year 2005	Most pessimistic forecast	Consensus forecast	Most optimistic forecast
British Petroleum	6.7%	7.8%	8.8%
Repsol YPF	5.7%	6.5%	7.2%
Royal Dutch Shell	6.5%	7.6%	8.8%

Fiscal year 2007 relative to fiscal year 2005	Most pessimistic forecast	Consensus forecast	Most optimistic forecast
British Petroleum	6.5%	7.9%	8.9%
Repsol YPF	5.5%	6.3%	7.0%
Royal Dutch Shell	6.6%	7.4%	8.2%

Fiscal year 2008 relative to fiscal year 2005	Most pessimistic forecast	Consensus forecast	Most optimistic forecast
British Petroleum	7.2%	8.2%	9.0%
Repsol YPF	5.7%	6.2%	6.9%
Royal Dutch Shell	6.6%	7.3%	8.8%

Source: Reuters Estimates.

Forecasting earnings and earnings growth in the European oil and gas industry

EXHIBIT 4 **Financial statements of British Petroleum, Royal Dutch Shell, and Repsol YPF for the fiscal year ended December 31, 2005**

CONSOLIDATED INCOME STATEMENTS – BRITISH PETROLEUM ($ millions)

Fiscal year ended December 31,	2005	2004
Sales and other operating revenues	**249,465**	**199,876**
Earnings from jointly controlled entities – after interest and tax	3,083	1,818
Earnings from associates – after interest and tax	460	462
Interest and other revenues	613	615
Total revenues	**253,621**	**202,771**
Gains on sale of businesses and fixed assets	1,538	1,685
Total revenues and other income	**255,159**	**204,456**
Purchases	(172,699)	(135,907)
Production and manufacturing expenses	(21,092)	(17,330)
Production and similar taxes	(3,010)	(2,149)
Depreciation, depletion and amortization	(8,771)	(8,529)
Impairment and losses on sale of businesses and fixed assets	(468)	(1,390)
Exploration expense	(684)	(637)
Distribution and administration expenses	(13,706)	(12,768)
Fair value (gain) loss on embedded derivatives	(2,047)	0
Profit before interest and taxation from continuing operations	**32,682**	**25,746**
Finance costs	(616)	(440)
Other finance expense	(145)	(340)
Profit before taxation from continuing operations	**31,921**	**24,966**
Taxation	(9,473)	(7,082)
Profit from continuing operations	**22,448**	**17,884**
Profit (loss) from Innovene operations	184	(622)
Minority interest	(291)	(187)
Profit for the year	**22,341**	**17,075**

CONSOLIDATED BALANCE SHEETS – BRITISH PETROLEUM ($ millions)

Fiscal year ended December 31,	2005	2004
Property, plant, and equipment	85,947	93,092
Goodwill	10,371	10,857
Intangible assets	4,772	4,205
Investments in jointly controlled entities	13,556	14,556
Investments in associates	6,217	5,486
Other investments	967	394
Fixed assets	**121,830**	**128,590**
Loans	821	811
Other receivables	770	429
Derivative financial instruments	3,652	898
Prepayments and accrued income	1,269	354
Defined benefit pension plan surplus	3,282	2,105
Total non-current assets	**131,624**	**133,187**
Loans	132	193
Inventories	19,760	15,645
Trade and other receivables	40,902	37,099
Derivative financial instruments	9,726	5,317
Prepayments and accrued income	1,598	1,671
Current tax receivable	212	159
Cash and cash equivalents	2,960	1,359
Total current assets	**75,290**	**61,443**
TOTAL ASSETS	**206,914**	**194,630**
Trade and other payables	42,136	38,540
Derivative financial instruments	9,083	5,074
Accruals and deferred income	5,970	4,482
Finance debt	8,932	10,184
Current tax payable	4,274	4,131
Provisions	1,102	715
Total current liabilities	**71,497**	**63,126**
Other payables	1,935	3,581
Derivative financial instruments	3,696	158
Accruals and deferred income	3,164	699
Finance debt	10,230	12,907
Deferred tax liabilities	16,443	16,701
Provisions	9,954	8,884
Defined benefit pension plan and other post-retirement benefit plan deficits	9,230	10,339
Total non-current liabilities	**54,652**	**53,269**
Share capital	5,185	5,403
Reserves	74,791	71,489
BP shareholders' equity	79,976	76,892
Minority interest	789	1,343
TOTAL LIABILITIES AND SHAREHOLDERS' EQUITY	**206,914**	**194,630**

Forecasting earnings and earnings growth in the European oil and gas industry

CONSOLIDATED INCOME STATEMENTS – REPSOL YPF (€ millions)

Fiscal year ended December 31,	2005	2004
Sales	48,024	38,273
Other income	3,021	2,019
Material used	(32,512)	(24,920)
Staff costs	(1,542)	(1,330)
Depreciation and amortization charge	(2,450)	(2,368)
Other expenses	(8,380)	(6,988)
Profit from continuing operations before finance costs	6,161	4,686
Finance costs	(722)	(624)
Income tax	(2,332)	(1,627)
Share of results of companies accounted for using the equity method	117	131
Profit for the year	3,224	2,566
Minority interests	(104)	(152)
Net income	3,120	2,414

CONSOLIDATED BALANCE SHEETS – REPSOL YPF (€ millions)

Fiscal year ended December 31,	2005	2004
Property, plant, and equipment	23,304	20,303
Investment property	54	52
Goodwill	3,773	3,204
Other intangible assets	1,003	693
Available-for-sale financial assets	1	83
Investments accounted for using the equity method	399	449
Financial assets	1,746	2,030
Deferred tax assets	1,197	1,099
Total non-current assets	31,477	27,913
Inventories	3,730	2,638
Trade and other receivables	6,841	5,277
Income tax receivables	586	270
Current financial assets	501	267
Cash and cash equivalents	2,647	3,328
Total current assets	14,305	11,780
TOTAL ASSETS	45,782	39,693
Equity attributable to shareholders of the Parent	16,262	12,806
Minority interests	528	424
Total equity	16,790	13,230
Preference shares	3,485	3,386
Non-current bank borrowings and other financial liabilities	6,236	7,333
Deferred tax liabilities	3,380	2,960
Non-current provisions for contingencies and expenses	2,878	1,996
Other non-current liabilities	1,704	1,618
Total non-current liabilities	17,683	17,293

(continued)

CONSOLIDATED BALANCE SHEETS – REPSOL YPF (€ millions) *(continued)*

Fiscal year ended December 31,	**2005**	**2004**
Current bank borrowings and other financial liabilities	2,701	3,142
Trade and other payables	7,783	5,550
Income tax payable	635	445
Current provisions for contingencies and expenses	190	33
Total current liabilities	11,309	9,170
TOTAL EQUITY AND LIABILITIES	45,782	39,693

CONSOLIDATED INCOME STATEMENTS – ROYAL DUTCH SHELL ($ millions)

Fiscal year ended December 31,	**2005**	**2004**
Revenue	306,731	266,386
Cost of sales	(252,622)	(223,259)
Gross profit	54,109	43,127
Selling, distribution and administrative expenses	(15,482)	(15,098)
Exploration	(1,286)	(1,809)
Share of profit of equity accounted investments	7,123	5,015
Interest and other income	1,171	1,483
Interest expense	(1,068)	(1,059)
Income before taxation	44,567	31,659
Taxation	17,999	12,168
Income from continuing operations	26,568	19,491
Income/(loss) from discontinued operations	(307)	(234)
Income attributable to minority interest	(950)	(717)
Income for the period	25,311	18,540

CONSOLIDATED BALANCE SHEETS – ROYAL DUTCH SHELL ($ millions)

Fiscal year ended December 31,	**2005**	**2004**
Intangible assets	4,350	4,528
Property, plant and equipment	87,558	87,918
Investments:		
Equity accounted investments	16,905	19,190
Financial assets	3,672	2,700
Deferred tax	2,562	2,789
Prepaid pension costs	2,486	2,479
Other	4,091	5,793
Total non-current assets	121,624	125,397
Inventories	19,776	15,375
Accounts receivable	66,386	37,473
Cash and cash equivalents	11,730	9,201
Total current assets	97,892	62,049
TOTAL ASSETS	219,516	187,446

(continued)

Forecasting earnings and earnings growth in the European oil and gas industry

CONSOLIDATED BALANCE SHEETS – ROYAL DUTCH SHELL ($ millions) *(continued)*

Fiscal year ended December 31,	2005	2004
Debt	7,578	8,858
Deferred tax	10,763	12,930
Retirement benefit obligations	5,807	6,795
Other provisions	7,385	6,828
Other	5,095	5,800
Total non-current liabilities	36,628	41,211
Debt	5,338	5,734
Accounts payable and accrued liabilities	69,013	37,909
Taxes payable	8,782	9,058
Retirement benefit obligations	282	339
Other provisions	1,549	1,812
Total current liabilities	84,964	54,852
Ordinary share capital	571	584
Preference share capital	0	20
Treasury shares	(3,809)	(4,187)
Other reserves	3,584	8,865
Retained earnings	90,578	80,788
Minority interest	7,000	5,313
Total equity	97,924	91,383
TOTAL LIABILITIES AND SHAREHOLDERS' EQUITY	219,516	187,446

Prospective Analysis: Valuation Theory and Concepts

The previous chapter introduced forecasting, the first stage of prospective analysis. In this and the following chapter we describe the second and final stage of prospective analysis, valuation. This chapter focuses on valuation theory and concepts, and the following chapter discusses implementation issues using the real-life example of Porsche.

Valuation is the process of converting a forecast into an estimate of the value of the firm or some component of the firm. At some level, nearly every business decision involves valuation (at least implicitly). Within the firm, capital budgeting involves consideration of how a particular project will affect firm value. Strategic planning focuses on how value is influenced by larger sets of actions. Outside the firm, security analysts conduct valuation to support their buy/sell decisions, and potential acquirers (often with the assistance of their investment bankers) estimate the value of target firms and the synergies they might offer. Valuation is necessary to price an initial public offering and to inform parties to sales, estate settlements, and divisions of property involving ongoing business concerns. Even credit analysts, who typically do not explicitly estimate firm value, must at least implicitly consider the value of the firm's equity "cushion" if they are to maintain a complete view of the risk associated with lending activity.

In practice, a wide variety of valuation approaches are employed. For example, in evaluating the fairness of a takeover bid, investment bankers commonly use five to ten different methods of valuation. Among the available methods are the following:

- *Discounted dividends.* This approach expresses the value of the firm's equity as the present value of forecasted future dividends.

- *Discounted abnormal earnings.* Under this approach the value of the firm's equity is expressed as the sum of its book value and discounted forecasts of abnormal earnings.

- *Discounted abnormal earnings growth.* This approach defines the value of the firm's equity as the sum of its capitalized next-period earnings forecast and discounted forecasts of abnormal earnings growth beyond the next period.

- *Valuation based on price multiples.* Under this approach a current measure of performance or single forecast of performance is converted into a value through application of some price multiple for other presumably comparable firms. For example, firm value can be estimated by applying a price-to-earnings ratio to a forecast of the firm's earnings for the coming year. Other commonly used multiples include price-to-book ratios and price-to-sales ratios.

■ *Discounted cash flow (DCF) analysis.* This approach involves the production of detailed, multiple-year forecasts of cash flows. The forecasts are then discounted at the firm's estimated cost of capital to arrive at an estimated present value.

All of the above approaches can be structured in two ways. The first is to directly value the equity of the firm, since this is usually the variable the analyst is directly interested in estimating. The second is to value the assets of the firm, that is, the claims of equity and net debt, and then to deduct the value of net debt to arrive at the final equity estimate. Theoretically, both approaches should generate the same values. However, as we will see in the following chapter, there are implementation issues in reconciling the approaches. In this chapter we illustrate valuation using an all-equity firm to simplify the discussion. Where appropriate we discuss the theoretical issues in valuing the firm's assets.

From a theoretical perspective, shareholder value is the present value of future dividend payoffs. This definition can be implemented by forecasting and discounting future dividends directly. Alternatively, it can be framed by recasting dividends in terms of earnings and book values, in terms of earnings and earnings growth, or in terms of free cash flows to shareholders. These methods are developed throughout the chapter, and their pros and cons discussed.

Valuation using multiples is also discussed. Multiples are a popular method of valuation because, unlike the discounted dividend, discounted abnormal earnings (growth), and discounted cash flow methods, they do not require analysts to make multiyear forecasts. However, the identification of comparable firms is a serious challenge in implementing the multiples approach. The chapter discusses how the discounted abnormal earnings valuation approach can be recast to generate firm-specific estimates of two popular multiples – value-to-book and value-earnings ratios. Value-to-book multiples are shown to be a function of future abnormal ROEs, book value growth, and the firm's cost of equity. Value-earnings multiples are driven by the same factors and also the current ROE. The chapter further discusses the relationship between the discounted abnormal earnings growth valuation approach and value-earnings multiples.

DEFINING VALUE FOR SHAREHOLDERS

How should shareholders think about the value of their equity claims on a firm? Finance theory holds that the value of any financial claim is simply the present value of the cash payoffs that its claimholders receive. Since shareholders receive cash payoffs from a company in the form of dividends, the value of their equity is the present value of future dividends (including any liquidating dividend).[1]

Equity value = PV of expected future dividends

If we denote the expected future dividend for a given year as *DIV* and r_e as the cost of equity capital (the relevant discount rate), the equity value is as follows:

$$\text{Equity value} = \frac{DIV_1}{(1+r_e)} + \frac{DIV_2}{(1+r_e)^2} + \frac{DIV_3}{(1+r_e)^3} + \dots$$

Notice that the valuation formula views a firm as having an indefinite life. But in reality firms can go bankrupt or get taken over. In these situations shareholders effectively receive a terminating dividend on their shares.

If a firm had a constant dividend growth rate (g^d) indefinitely, its value would simplify to the following formula:

$$\text{Equity value} = \frac{DIV_1}{r_e - g^d}$$

To better understand how the discounted dividend approach works, consider the following example. At the beginning of year 1, Down Under Company raises €60 million of equity and uses the proceeds to buy a fixed asset. Operating profits before depreciation (all received in cash) and dividends for the company are expected to be €40 million in year 1, €50 million in year 2, and €60 million in year 3, at which point the company terminates. The firm pays no taxes. If the cost of equity capital for this firm is 10 percent, the value of the firm's equity is computed as follows:

Year	Dividend	PV factor	PV of dividend
1	€40m	0.9091	€36.4m
2	50	0.8264	41.3
3	60	0.7513	45.1
Equity value			€122.8m

The above valuation formula is called the dividend discount model. It forms the basis for most of the popular theoretical approaches for equity valuation. The remainder of the chapter discusses how this model can be recast to generate the discounted abnormal earnings, discounted abnormal earnings growth, discounted cash flow, and price multiple models of value.

THE DISCOUNTED ABNORMAL EARNINGS VALUATION METHOD

As discussed in Chapter 3, there is a link between dividends and earnings. If all equity effects (other than capital transactions) flow through the income statement,[2] the expected book value of equity for existing shareholders at the end of year 1 (BVE_1) is simply the book value at the beginning of the year (BVE_0) plus expected net profit (NP_1) less expected dividends (DIV_1).[3] This relation can be rewritten as follows:

$$DIV_1 = NP_1 + BVE_0 - BVE_1$$

By substituting this identity for dividends into the dividend discount formula and rearranging the terms, equity value can be rewritten as follows:[4]

Equity value = Book value of equity + PV of expected future abnormal earnings

Abnormal earnings are net profit adjusted for a capital charge computed as the discount rate multiplied by the beginning book value of equity. Abnormal earnings therefore make an adjustment to reflect the fact that accountants do not recognize any opportunity cost for equity funds used. Thus, the discounted abnormal earnings valuation formula is

$$\text{Equity value} = BVE_0 + \frac{NP_1 - r_e \cdot BVE_0}{(1+r_e)} + \frac{NP_2 - r_e \cdot BVE_1}{(1+r_e)^2} + \frac{NP_3 - r_e \cdot BVE_2}{(1+r_e)^3} + \dots$$

As noted earlier, equity values can also be estimated by valuing the firm's assets and then deducting its net debt. Under the earnings-based approach, this implies that the value of the assets is

$$\text{Asset value} = BVA_0 + \frac{NOPAT_1 - WACC \cdot BVA_0}{(1 + WACC)} + \frac{NOPAT_2 - WACC \cdot BVA_1}{(1 + WACC)^2} + \dots$$

BVA is the book value of the firm's assets, NOPAT is net operating profit (before interest) after tax, and WACC is the firm's weighted-average cost of debt and equity. From this asset value the analyst can deduct the market value of net debt to generate an estimate of the value of equity.

The earnings-based formulation has intuitive appeal. It implies that if a firm can earn only a normal rate of return on its book value, then investors should be willing to pay no more than book value for its shares. Investors should pay more or less than book value if earnings are above or below this normal level. Thus the deviation of a firm's market value from book value depends on its ability to generate "abnormal earnings." The formulation also implies that a firm's equity value reflects the cost of its existing net assets (that is, its book equity) plus the net present value of future growth options (represented by cumulative abnormal earnings).

To illustrate the earnings-based valuation approach, let's return to the Down Under Company example. Since the company is an all-equity firm, the value of the firm's equity and its assets (debt plus equity) are the same. If the company depreciates its fixed assets using the straight-line method, its beginning book equity, earnings, abnormal earnings, and valuation will be as follows:

Year	Beginning book value	Earnings	Abnormal earnings	PV factor	PV of abnormal earnings
1	€60m	€20m	€14m	0.9091	€12.7m
2	40	30	26	0.8264	21.5
3	20	40	38	0.7513	28.6
Cumulative PV of abnormal earnings					62.8
+ Beginning book value					60.0
= Equity value					€122.8m

This equity valuation of €122.8 million is identical to the value estimated when the expected future dividends are discounted directly.

KEY ANALYSIS QUESTIONS

Valuation of equity (debt plus equity) under the discounted abnormal earnings method requires the analyst to answer the following questions:

■ What are expected future net profit (NOPAT) and book values of equity (assets) over a finite forecast horizon (usually five to ten years)?

■ What are expected future abnormal earnings (NOPAT), after deducting a capital charge from forecasts of net profit (NOPAT)? The capital charge is the firm's cost of equity (WACC) multiplied by beginning book equity (assets).

- What is expected future abnormal net profit (NOPAT) beyond the final year of the forecast horizon (called the "terminal year") based on some simplifying assumption?

- What is the present value of abnormal earnings (NOPAT) discounted at the cost of equity capital (WACC)?

- What is the estimated value of equity, computed by adding the current book value of equity (assets) to the cumulated present value of future abnormal earnings (NOPAT)? Are there nonoperating assets held by the firm that have been ignored in the previous abnormal earnings (NOPAT) forecasts (e.g., marketable securities or real estate held for sale)? If so, their values should be included in the equity estimate.

Research has shown that abnormal earnings estimates of value outperform traditional multiples, such as price-earnings ratios, price-to-book ratios, and dividend yields, for predicting future share price movements.[5] Firms with high abnormal earnings model estimates of value relative to current price show positive abnormal future stock returns, whereas firms with low estimated value-to-price ratios have negative abnormal share price performance.

Accounting methods and discounted abnormal earnings

It may seem odd that firm value can be expressed as a function of accounting numbers. After all, accounting methods per se should have no influence on firm value (except as those choices influence the analyst's view of future real performance). Yet the valuation approach used here is based on numbers – earnings and book value – that vary with accounting method choices. How then can the valuation approach deliver correct estimates?

It turns out that because accounting choices affect *both* earnings *and* book value, and because of the self-correcting nature of double-entry bookkeeping (all "distortions" of accounting must ultimately reverse), estimated values based on the discounted abnormal earnings method will not be affected by accounting choices per se. For example, assume that Down Under Company's managers choose to be conservative and expense some unusual costs that could have been capitalized as inventory at year 1, causing earnings and ending book value to be lower by €10 million. This inventory is then sold in year 2. For the time being, let's say the accounting choice has no influence on the analyst's view of the firm's real performance.

Managers' choice reduces abnormal earnings in year 1 and book value at the beginning of year 2 by €10 million. However, future earnings will be higher, for two reasons. First, future earnings will be higher (by €10 million) when the inventory is sold in year 2 at a lower cost of sales. Second, the benchmark for normal earnings (based on book value of equity) will be lower by €10 million. The €10 million decline in abnormal earnings in year 1 is perfectly offset (on a present value basis) by the €11 million higher abnormal earnings in year 2. As a result, the value of Down Under Company under conservative reporting is identical to the value under the earlier accounting method (€122.8 million).

Year	Beginning book value	Earnings	Abnormal earnings	PV factor	PV of abnormal earnings
1	€60m	€10m	€4m	0.9091	€3.6m
2	30	40	37	0.8264	30.6
3	20	40	38	0.7513	28.6
Cumulative PV of abnormal earnings					62.8
+ Beginning book value					60.0
= Equity value					€122.8m

Provided the analyst is aware of biases in accounting data as a result of the use of aggressive or conservative accounting choices by management, abnormal earnings-based valuations are unaffected by the variation in accounting decisions. This implies that strategic and accounting analyses are critical precursors to abnormal earnings valuation. The strategic and accounting analysis tools help the analyst to identify whether abnormal earnings arise from sustainable competitive advantage or from unsustainable accounting manipulations. For example, consider the implications of failing to understand the reasons for a decline in earnings from a change in inventory policy for Down Under Company. If the analyst mistakenly interpreted the decline as indicating that the firm was having difficulty moving its inventory, rather than that it had used conservative accounting, she might reduce expectations of future earnings. The estimated value of the firm would then be lower than that reported in our example. To avoid such mistakes, the analyst would be wise to go through all steps of the accounting analysis, including step 6 (undo accounting distortions), and then perform the financial and prospective analyses using the restated financial statements.

THE DISCOUNTED ABNORMAL EARNINGS GROWTH VALUATION METHOD

As discussed above, abnormal earnings are the amount of earnings that a firm generates in excess of the opportunity cost for equity funds used. The annual change in abnormal earnings is generally referred to as abnormal earnings growth and can be rewritten as follows:

$$\text{Abnormal earnings growth} = (NP_{t+1} - r_e \cdot BVE_t) - (NP_t - r_e \cdot BVE_{t-1})$$
$$= (NP_{t+1} - r_e \cdot [NP_t + BVE_{t-1} - DIV_t]) - (NP_t - r_e \cdot BVE_{t-1})$$
$$= NP_{t+1} + r_e \cdot DIV_t - (1 + r_e) \cdot NP_t$$
$$= \Delta NP_{t+1} - r_e \cdot (NP_t - DIV_t)$$

This formula shows that abnormal earnings growth is actual earnings growth benchmarked against the product of retained prior period earnings and a normal rate of return. When abnormal earnings growth is zero, the firm functions like a savings account. In this particular case, an investor is indifferent between reinvesting earnings in the firm and receiving all earnings in dividends.

The discounted dividend model can also be recast to generate a valuation model that defines equity value as the sum of capitalized next-period earnings and the discounted value of abnormal earnings growth beyond the next period. The discounted abnormal earnings growth valuation formula is:[6]

$$\text{Equity value} = \frac{NP_1}{r_e} + \frac{1}{r_e}\left[\frac{NP_2 + r_e DIV_1 - (1+r_e)NP_1}{(1+r_e)} + \frac{NP_3 + r_e DIV_2 - (1+r_e)NP_2}{(1+r_e)^2} + \ldots\right]$$

This approach, under which valuation starts with capitalizing next-period earnings, has practical appeal because investment analysts spend much time and effort on estimating near-term earnings as the starting point of their analysis. The valuation formula shows that differences between equity value and capitalized next-period earnings are explained by abnormal changes in earnings – or changes in abnormal earnings – beyond the next period.

Notice that this formula also views the firm as having an indefinite life. However, the formula can be easily used for the valuation of a finite-life investment by extending the investment's life by one year and setting earnings and dividends equal to zero in the last year. For example, consider the earnings and dividends of the Down Under Company during its three years of existence. Capitalized year 1 earnings are equal to €200.0 million (20.0/.1). Abnormal earnings growth equals €12.0 million in year 2 (30.0 + 40.0 × .1 − 20.0 × 1.1) and €12.0 million in year 3 (40.0 + 50.0 × .1 − 30.0 × 1.1). In year 4, when earnings and dividends are zero, abnormal earnings growth is −€38.0 million (0.0 + 60.0 × .1 − 40.0 × 1.1). The total value of the firm's equity is computed as follows:

Year	Earnings	Dividends	Abnormal earnings growth	PV factor	PV of abnormal earnings growth
1	€20m	€40m			
2	30	50	€12m	0.9091	10.91
3	40	60	12	0.8264	9.92
4	0	0	−38	0.7513	−28.55
Cumulative PV of abnormal earnings growth					−7.72
+ Earnings in year 1					20.00
=					€12.28m
× 1/r_e					10.00
= Equity value					€122.8m

Like the abnormal earnings method, the value estimate from the abnormal earnings growth model is not affected by the firm's accounting choices. For example, recall the situation where the Down Under Company reports conservatively and expenses unusual costs that could have been capitalized in year 1, thereby reducing earnings by €10.0 million. Under conservative accounting, the value of capitalized year 1 earnings decreases from €200.0 million to €100.0 million. This reduction, however, is exactly offset by an increase in the discounted value of abnormal earnings growth, as shown in the following table:

Year	Earnings	Dividends	Abnormal earnings growth	PV factor	PV of abnormal earnings growth
1	€10m	€40m			
2	40	50	€33m	0.9091	30.00
3	40	60	1	0.8264	0.83
4	0	0	−38	0.7513	−28.55
Cumulative PV of abnormal earnings growth					2.28
+ Earnings in year 1					10.00
=					€12.28m
× 1/r_e					10.00
= Equity value					€122.8m

This value is again identical to the value estimated under the discounted dividends and abnormal earnings approaches.

VALUATION USING PRICE MULTIPLES

Valuations based on price multiples are widely used by analysts. The primary reason for their popularity is their simplicity. Unlike the discounted abnormal earnings (growth), discounted dividend, and discounted cash flow methods, they do not require detailed multiple-year forecasts about a variety of parameters, including growth, profitability, and cost of capital.

Valuation using multiples involves the following three steps:

1. Select a measure of performance or value (e.g., earnings, sales, cash flows, book equity, book assets) as the basis for multiple calculations.

2. Estimate price multiples for comparable firms using the measure of performance or value.

3. Apply the comparable firm multiple to the performance or value measure of the firm being analyzed.

Under this approach, the analyst relies on the market to undertake the difficult task of considering the short- and long-term prospects for growth and profitability and their implications for the values of the comparable firms. Then the analyst *assumes* that the pricing of those other firms is applicable to the firm at hand.

On the surface, using multiples seems straightforward. Unfortunately, in practice it is not as simple as it would appear. Identification of "comparable" firms is often quite difficult. There are also some choices to be made concerning how multiples will be calculated. Finally, explaining why multiples vary across firms, and how applicable another firm's multiple is to the one at hand, requires a sound understanding of the determinants of each multiple.

Selecting comparable firms

Ideally, price multiples used in a comparable firm analysis are those for firms with similar operating and financial characteristics. Firms within the same industry are the most obvious candidates. But even within narrowly defined industries, it is often difficult to find multiples for similar firms. Many firms are in multiple industries, making it difficult to identify representative benchmarks. In addition, firms within the same industry frequently have different strategies, growth opportunities, and profitability, creating comparability problems.

One way of dealing with these issues is to average across *all* firms in the industry. The analyst implicitly hopes that the various sources of noncomparability cancel each other out, so that the firm being valued is comparable to a "typical" industry member. Another approach is to focus on only those firms within the industry that are most similar.

For example, consider using multiples to value Volkswagen. Reuters classifies the company in the Automobile Manufacturers industry, and reported that Volkswagen's primary competitors, with equity values above €10 billion, could be narrowed to the following firms: BMW, DaimlerChrysler, Fiat, Ford Motor, General Motors, Honda, Hyundai, Nissan, Peugeot, Renault, and Toyota. The average price-earnings ratio for these direct competitors was 8.9 and the average price-to-book ratio was 1.3.

A potential problem of choosing comparable firms from different countries is that a variety of factors that influence multiples may differ across countries. For example, the cost of equity, which is inversely related to the price-earnings multiple, is affected by the risk-free interest rate. Consequently, international differences in risk-free interest rates lead to international differences in price-earnings multiples. In addition, international differences in accounting standards may lead to systematic international differences in net profits, which is the denominator in price-earnings multiples. The most obvious way to get around this problem is to choose comparable firms from one country. This is, however, often not feasible in smaller equity markets. The alternative solution is to explicitly take into account the country factors that affect multiples. For example, when using the multiples of the above group of competitors, it is important to realize that at the time that the multiples were calculated, risk-free interest rates in the European (Monetary) Union were higher than the risk-free interest rate in Japan (domicile of Honda, Nissan, and Toyota) and lower than the risk-free interest rate in the U.S. (domicile of Ford Motor and General Motors). This may have caused price-earnings multiples to be relatively high in Japan and relatively low in the U.S.

Multiples for firms with poor performance

Price multiples can be affected when the denominator variable is performing poorly. This is especially common when the denominator is a flow measure, such as earnings or cashflows. For example, General Motors had negative earnings in 2005, making the price-earnings ratio negative.

What are analysts' options for handling the problems for multiples created by transitory shocks to the denominator? One option is to simply exclude firms with large transitory effects from the set of comparable firms. If General Motors is excluded from Volkswagen's peer set, the average industry price-earnings ratio increases from 8.9 to 10.0. This change in the industry average shows the sensitivity of price-earnings multiples to transitory shocks.

As an alternative to excluding some firms from the industry comparison group, if the poor performance is due to a transitory shock such as a write-off or special item, the effect can be excluded from computation of the multiple. Finally, the analyst can use a denominator that is a forecast of future performance rather than a past measure. Multiples based on forecasts are termed *leading* multiples, whereas those based on historical data are called *trailing* multiples. Leading multiples are less likely to include one-time gains and losses in the denominator, simply because such items are difficult to anticipate. The average leading price-earnings ratio for Volkswagen's direct competitors was 13.7.

Adjusting multiples for leverage

Price multiples should be calculated in a way that preserves consistency between the numerator and denominator. Consistency is an issue for those ratios where the denominator reflects performance *before* servicing debt. Examples include the price-to-sales multiple and any multiple of operating earnings or operating cash flows. When calculating these multiples, the numerator should include not just the market value of equity but the value of debt as well.

Determinants of value-to-book and value-earnings multiples

Even across relatively closely related firms, price multiples can vary considerably. Careful analysis of this variation requires consideration of factors that might explain why one firm's multiples should be higher than those of benchmark firms. We therefore return to the abnormal earnings valuation method and show how it provides insights into differences in value-to-book and value-to-earnings multiples across firms

If the abnormal earnings formula is scaled by book value, the left-hand side becomes the equity value-to-book ratio as opposed to the equity value itself. The right-hand side variables are now earnings deflated by book value, or our old friend return on equity (ROE), discussed in Chapter 5.[7] The valuation formula becomes:

$$\text{Equity value-to-book ratio} = 1 + \frac{ROE_1 - r_e}{(1+r_e)} + \frac{(ROE_2 - r_e)(1 + gbve_1)}{(1+r_e)^2}$$

$$+ \frac{(ROE_3 - r_e)(1 + gbve_1)(1 + gbve_2)}{(1+r_e)^3} + \ldots$$

where $gbve_t$ = growth in book value (*BVE*) from year *t*–1 to year *t* or:

$$\frac{BVE_t - BVE_{t-1}}{BVE_{t-1}}$$

The formulation implies that a firm's equity value-to-book ratio is a function of three factors: its future abnormal ROEs, its growth in book equity, and its cost of equity capital. Abnormal ROE is defined as ROE less the cost of equity capital ($ROE - r_e$). Firms with positive abnormal ROE are able to invest their net assets to create value for shareholders and have price-to-book ratios greater than one. Firms that are unable to generate returns greater than the cost of capital have ratios below one.

The magnitude of a firm's value-to-book multiple also depends on the amount of growth in book value. Firms can grow their equity base by issuing new equity or by reinvesting profits. If this new equity is invested in positive valued projects for shareholders – that is, projects with ROEs that exceed the cost of capital – the firm will boost its equity value-to-book multiple. Of course for firms with ROEs that are less than the cost of capital, equity growth further lowers the multiple.

The valuation task can now be framed in terms of two key questions about the firm's "value drivers":

- How much greater (or smaller) than normal will the firm's ROE be?
- How quickly will the firm's investment base (book value) grow?

If desired, the equation can be rewritten so that future ROEs are expressed as the product of their components: profit margins, sales turnover, and leverage. Thus the approach permits us to build directly on projections of the same accounting numbers utilized in financial analysis (see Chapter 5) without the need to convert projections of those numbers into cash flows. Yet in the end, the estimate of value should be the same as that from the dividend discount model.[8]

It is also possible to structure the multiple valuation as the debt plus equity value-to-book assets ratio by scaling the abnormal NOPAT formula by book value of net operating assets. The valuation formula then becomes:

$$\text{Debt plus equity value-to-book ratio} = 1 + \frac{ROA_1 - WACC}{(1+WACC)} + \frac{(ROA_2 - WACC)(1+gbva_1)}{(1+WACC)^2}$$

$$+ \frac{(ROA_3 - WACC)(1+gbva_1)(1+gbva_2)}{(1+WACC)^3} + \ldots$$

where ROA = operating return on assets = NOPAT/(Operating working capital + Net non-current assets)

$WACC$ = weighted average cost of debt and equity

$gbva_t$ = growth in book value of assets (BVA) from year t-1 to year t or

$$\frac{BVA_t - BVA_{t-1}}{BVA_{t-1}}$$

The value of a firm's debt and equity to net operating assets multiple therefore depends on its ability to generate asset returns that exceed its WACC, and on its ability to grow its asset base. The value of equity under this approach is then the estimated multiple times the current book value of assets less the market value of debt.

Returning to the Down Under Company example, the implied equity value-to-book multiple can be estimated as follows:

	Year 1	Year 2	Year 3
Beginning book value	€60m	€40m	€20m
Earnings	€20m	€30m	€40m
ROE	0.33	0.75	2.00
– Cost of capital	0.10	0.10	0.10
= Abnormal ROE	0.23	0.65	1.90
× (1+ cumulative book value growth)	1.00	0.67	0.33
= Abnormal ROE scaled by book value growth	0.23	0.43	0.63
× PV factor	0.909	0.826	0.751
= PV of abnormal ROE scaled by book value growth	0.212	0.358	0.476
Cumulative PV of abnormal ROE scaled by book value growth	1.046		
+ 1.00	1.006		
= Equity value-to-book multiple	2.046		

The equity value-to-book multiple for Down Under is therefore 2.046, and the implied equity value is €122.8 (€60 times 2.046), once again identical to the dividend discount model value. Recall that Down Under is an all-equity firm, so that the abnormal ROE and abnormal ROA structures for valuing the firm are the same.

The equity value-to-book formulation can also be used to construct the equity value-earnings multiple as follows:

$$\text{Equity value-to-earnings ratio} = \text{Equity value-to-book multiple} \times \frac{\text{Book value of equity}}{\text{Earnings}}$$

$$= \frac{\text{Equity value-to-book multiple}}{\text{ROE}}$$

In other words, the same factors that drive a firm's equity value-to-book multiple also explain its equity value-earnings multiple. The key difference between the two multiples is that the value-earnings multiple is affected by the firm's current level of ROE performance, whereas the value-to-book multiple is not. Firms with low current ROEs therefore have very high value-earnings multiples and vice versa. If a firm has a zero or negative ROE, its PE multiple is not defined. Value-earnings multiples are therefore more volatile than value-to-book multiples.

The following data for a subset of firms in the Automobile Manufacturers industry illustrate the relation between ROE, the price-to-book ratio, and the price-earnings ratio:

Company	ROE	Price-to-book ratio	Price-earnings ratio
Ford Motor	17.30%	0.97	5.61
DaimlerChrysler	7.81%	1.04	13.35
Toyota Motor	12.99%	1.96	15.05
Renault	17.54%	1.25	7.13

Both the price-to-book and price-earnings ratios are high for Toyota. Investors therefore expect that in the future Toyota will generate higher ROEs than its current level (13.0 percent). In contrast, Renault has a price-to-book ratio greater than one (1.25) but a low price-earnings ratio (7.13). This indicates that investors expect that Renault will continue to generate positive abnormal ROEs but that the current level of ROE (17.5 percent) is not sustainable. DaimlerChrysler has a price-to-book ratio of 1.04, indicating that investors expect it to earn about normal ROEs. However it has a high price-earnings multiple (13.35), suggesting that the current low ROE (7.8 percent) is considered temporary. Finally, Ford has a relatively low price-to-book ratio, 0.97, and a low price-earnings multiple. Investors apparently do not expect Ford to sustain its good performance.

The effect of future growth in net profit on the price-earnings multiple can also be seen from the model that arises when we scale the abnormal earnings growth valuation formula by next-period net profit. The valuation formula then becomes:

Leading equity value-to-earnings ratio =

$$\frac{1}{r_e} + \frac{1}{r_e} \left[\frac{gnp_2 + (p_1 - 1)r_e}{(1+r_e)} + \frac{(1+gnp_2)\big[gni_3 + (p_2 - 1)r_e\big]}{(1+r_e)^2} + \ldots \right]$$

where p_t = dividend payout ratio in year t
gnp_t = growth in net profit (NP) from year $t-1$ to year t or

$$\frac{NI_t - NI_{t-1}}{NI_{t-1}}$$

In this formula, future earnings growth rates and dividend payouts are the basis for estimating price-earnings multiples.[9] Consider the earnings growth rates and dividend payout ratios of the Down Under Company. The earnings growth rates (gnp_t) are 50,

33, and −100 percent in years 2, 3, and 4, respectively. Dividend payouts are 200 percent, 167 percent, and 150 percent in years 1, 2, and 3, respectively. Substituting these percentages in the leading price-earnings formula yields:

Leading equity value-to-earnings ratio =

$$\frac{1}{r_e}+\frac{1}{r_e}\left[\frac{gnp_2+(p_1-1)r_e}{(1+r_e)}+\frac{(1+gnp_2)\left[gnp_3+(p_2-1)r_e\right]}{(1+r_e)^2}+\frac{(1+gnp_2)(1+gnp_3)\left[gnp_4+(p_3-1)r_e\right]}{(1+r_e)^3}\right]=$$

$$\frac{1}{.1}+\frac{1}{.1}\times\left[\frac{.5+.1}{1.1}+\frac{1.5\times[.33+.067]}{1.1^2}+\frac{1.5\times1.33\times[-1+.05]}{1.1^3}\right]=6.14$$

The price-earnings multiple of 6.14 is consistent with a value of equity of €122.8 (6.14 × €20).

KEY ANALYSIS QUESTIONS

To value a firm using multiples, an analyst has to assess the quality of the variable used as the multiple basis, and to determine the appropriate peer firms to include in the benchmark multiple. Analysts are therefore likely to be interested in answering the following questions:

- What is the expected future growth in the variable to be used as the basis for the multiple? For example, if the variable is earnings, has the firm made conservative or aggressive accounting choices that are likely to unwind in the coming years? If the multiple is book value, what is the sustainability of the firm's growth and ROE? What are the dynamics of the firm's industry and product market? Is it a market leader in a high growth industry, or is it in a mature industry with fewer growth prospects? How is the firm's future performance likely to be affected by competition or potential new entry to the industry?

- Which are the most suitable peer companies to include in the benchmark multiple computation? Have these firms had comparable growth (earnings or book values), profitability, and quality of earnings as the firm being analyzed? Do they have the same risk characteristics?

SHORTCUT FORMS OF EARNINGS-BASED VALUATION

The discounted abnormal earnings valuation formula can be simplified by making assumptions about the relation between a firm's current and future abnormal earnings. Similarly, the equity value-to-book formula can be simplified by making assumptions about long-term ROEs and growth.

Relation between current and future abnormal earnings

Several assumptions about the relation between current and future abnormal earnings are popular for simplifying the abnormal earnings model and the abnormal earnings growth model. First, abnormal earnings are assumed to follow a random walk. The random walk model for abnormal earnings implies that an analyst's best guess about future expected abnormal earnings are current abnormal earnings. The model assumes that past shocks to abnormal earnings persist forever, but that future shocks are random or unpredictable. The random walk model can be written as follows:

$$\text{Forecasted } AE_1 = AE_0$$

Forecasted AE_1 is the forecast of next year's abnormal earnings and AE_0 is current period abnormal earnings. Under the model, forecasted abnormal earnings for two years ahead are simply abnormal earnings in year one, or once again current abnormal earnings. In other words, the best guess of abnormal earnings in any future year is just current abnormal earnings.[10]

How does the above assumption about future abnormal earnings simplify the discounted abnormal earnings valuation model? If abnormal earnings follow a random walk, all future forecasts of abnormal earnings are simply current abnormal earnings. It is then possible to rewrite value as follows:

$$\text{Equity value} = BVE_0 + \frac{AE_0}{r_e}$$

Equity value is the book value of equity at the end of the year plus current abnormal earnings divided by the cost of capital.

A logical consequence of the above assumption is also that future abnormal earnings growth equals zero. When abnormal earnings growth in any future year is zero, the abnormal earnings growth valuation model can be rewritten as follows:

$$\text{Equity value} = \frac{NP_1}{r_e}$$

Equity value is then set equal to the capitalized value of next-period net profit.

In reality of course, shocks to abnormal earnings are unlikely to persist forever. Firms that have positive shocks are likely to attract competitors that will reduce opportunities for future abnormal performance. Firms with negative abnormal earnings shocks are likely to fail or to be acquired by other firms that can manage their resources more effectively. The persistence of abnormal performance will therefore depend on strategic factors such as barriers to entry and switching costs, discussed in Chapter 2. To reflect this, analysts frequently assume that current shocks to abnormal earnings decay over time. Under this assumption, abnormal earnings are said to follow an autoregressive model. Forecasted abnormal earnings are then:

$$\text{Forecasted } AE_1 = \beta AE_0$$

β is a parameter that captures the speed with which abnormal earnings decay over time. If there is no decay, β is one and abnormal earnings follow a random walk. If β is zero, abnormal earnings decay completely within one year. Estimates of β using actual company data indicate that for a typical U.S. firm, β is approximately 0.6. However, it varies by industry, and is smaller for firms with large accruals and one-time accounting charges.[11]

The autoregressive model implies that equity values can again be written as a function of current abnormal earnings and book values:[12]

$$\text{Equity value} = BVE_0 + \frac{\beta AE_0}{1 + r_e - \beta}$$

This formulation implies that equity values are simply the sum of current book value plus current abnormal earnings weighted by the cost of equity capital and persistence in abnormal earnings.

Under the assumption that abnormal earnings follow an autoregressive model, abnormal earnings growth, or the change in abnormal earnings, in year 1 can be rewritten as $(\beta - 1)AE_0$ and the abnormal earnings growth model simplifies to:

$$\text{Equity value} = \frac{NP_1}{r_e} + \frac{1}{r_e}\left[\frac{(\beta-1)AE_1}{1+r_e-\beta}\right]$$

This formula illustrates that equity values can be expressed as the sum of capitalized next-period earnings plus next-period abnormal earnings weighted by the cost of equity capital and persistence in abnormal earnings.

An advantage of the abnormal earnings growth model over the abnormal earnings model is that the former model can be simplified by making assumptions about the change in abnormal earnings. This can be useful in situations where the analyst believes, for example, that a firm has a sustainable competitive advantage but expects that the growth in abnormal earnings will gradually decay over time. Under the assumption that:

$$\text{Forecasted } (AE_2 - AE_1) = \beta\,(AE_1 - AE_0)$$

the abnormal earnings growth model simplifies to:

$$\text{Equity value} = \frac{NP_1}{r_e} + \frac{1}{r_e}\left[\frac{\beta\,(AE_1 - AE_0)}{1+r_e-\beta}\right]$$

ROE and growth simplifications

It is also possible to make simplifications about long-term ROEs and equity growth to reduce forecast horizons for estimating the equity value-to-book multiple. Firms' long-term ROEs are affected by such factors as barriers to entry in their industries, change in production or delivery technologies, and quality of management. As discussed in Chapter 6, these factors tend to force abnormal ROEs to decay over time. One way to model this decay is to assume that ROEs follow a mean-reverting process. Forecasted ROE in one period's time then takes the following form:

$$\text{Forecasted } ROE_1 = ROE_0 + \beta(ROE_0 - \overline{ROE})$$

$\overline{ROE}$ is the steady state ROE (either the firm's cost of capital or the long-term industry ROE) and β is a "speed of adjustment factor" that reflects how quickly it takes the ROE to revert to its steady state.[13]

Growth rates are affected by several factors. First, the size of the firm is important. Small firms can sustain very high growth rates for an extended period, whereas large firms find it more difficult to do so. Second, firms with high rates of growth are likely to attract competitors, which reduces their growth rates. As discussed in Chapter 6, book value growth rates for real firms exhibit considerable reversion to the mean.

The long-term patterns in ROE and book equity growth rates imply that for most companies there is limited value in making forecasts for valuation beyond a relatively short horizon – three to five years. Powerful economic forces tend to lead firms with superior or inferior performance early in the forecast horizon to revert to a level that is comparable to that of other firms in the industry or the economy. For a firm in steady state, that is, expected to have a stable ROE and book equity growth rate (*gbve*), the value-to-book multiple formula simplifies to the following:

$$\text{Equity value-to-book multiple} = 1 + \frac{ROE_0 - r_e}{r_e - gbve}$$

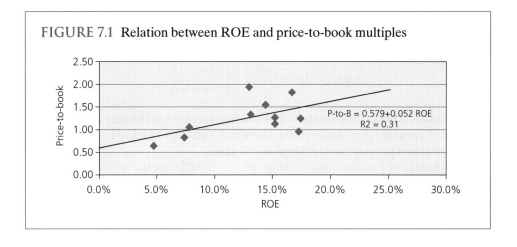

FIGURE 7.1 Relation between ROE and price-to-book multiples

Consistent with this simplified model, there is a strong relation between price-to-book ratios and current ROEs. Figure 7.1 shows the relation between these variables for firms in the Automobile Manufacturers industry we discussed earlier. The correlation between the two variables is 0.56.

Of course, analysts can make a variety of simplifying assumptions about a firm's ROE and growth. For example, they can assume that they decay slowly or rapidly to the cost of capital and the growth rate for the economy. They can assume that the rates decay to the industry or economy average ROEs and book value growth rates. The valuation formula can easily be modified to accommodate these assumptions

THE DISCOUNTED CASH FLOW MODEL

The final valuation method discussed here is the discounted cash flow approach. This is the valuation method taught in most finance classes. Like the abnormal earnings and abnormal earnings growth approaches, it is derived from the dividend discount model. It is based on the insight that dividends can be recast as free cash flows[14] – that is:

$$\text{Dividends} = \text{Operating cash flow} - \text{Capital outlays} + \text{Net cash flows from debt owners}$$

As discussed in Chapter 5, operating cash flows to equity holders are simply net profit plus depreciation less changes in working capital accruals. Capital outlays are capital expenditures less asset sales. Finally, net cash flows from debt owners are issues of new debt less retirements less the after-tax cost of interest. By rearranging these terms, the free cash flows to equity can be written as follows:

$$\text{Dividends} = \text{Free cash flows to equity} = NP - \Delta BVA + \Delta BVND$$

where NP is net profit, ΔBVA is the change in book value of operating net assets (including changes in working capital plus capital expenditures less depreciation expense), and $\Delta BVND$ is the change in book value of net debt (interest-bearing debt less excess cash).

The dividend discount model can therefore be written as the present value of free cash flows to equity. Under this formulation firm value is estimated as follows:

Equity value = PV of free cash flows to equity claim holders

$$= \frac{NP_1 - \Delta BVA_1 + \Delta BVND_1}{(1+r_e)} + \frac{NP_2 - \Delta BVA_2 + \Delta BVND_2}{(1+r_e)^2} + \dots$$

Alternatively, the free cash flow formulation can be structured by estimating the value of claims to net debt and equity and then deducting the market value of net debt. This approach is more widely used in practice because it does not require explicit forecasts of changes in debt balances.[15] The value of debt plus equity is then:

Debt plus equity value = PV of free cash flows to net debt and equity claim holders

$$= \frac{NOPAT_1 - \Delta BVA_1}{(1+WACC)} + \frac{NOPAT_2 - \Delta BVA_2}{(1+WACC)^2} + \dots$$

Valuation under the discounted cash flow method therefore involves the following three steps:

1. Forecast free cash flows available to equity holders (or to debt and equity holders) over a finite forecast horizon (usually 5 to 10 years).

2. Forecast free cash flows beyond the terminal year based on some simplifying assumption.

3. Discount free cash flows to equity holders (debt plus equity holders) at the cost of equity (weighted average cost of capital). The discounted amount represents the estimated value of free cash flows available to equity (debt and equity holders as a group).

Returning to the Down Under Company example, there is no debt, so that the free cash flows to owners are simply the operating profits before depreciation. Since Down Under is an all-equity firm, its WACC is the cost of equity (10 percent), and the present value of the free cash flows is as follows:

Year	Free cash flows	PV factor	PV of free cash flows
1	€40m	0.9091	€36.4m
2	50	0.8264	41.3
3	60	0.7513	45.1
Equity value			€122.8m

COMPARING VALUATION METHODS

We have discussed four methods of valuation derived from the dividend discount model: discounted dividends, discounted abnormal earnings (or abnormal ROEs), discounted abnormal earnings growth, and discounted cash flows. What are the pluses and minuses of these approaches? Since the methods are all derived from the same underlying model, no one version can be considered superior to the others. As long as analysts make the same assumptions about firm fundamentals, value estimates under all four methods will be identical.

However, there are several important differences between the models that are worth noting:

- they focus the analyst's task on different issues;
- they require different levels of structure for valuation analysis; and
- they have different implications for the estimation of terminal values.

Focus on different issues

The methods frame the valuation task differently and can in practice focus the analyst's attention on different issues. The earnings-based approaches frame the issues in terms of accounting data such as earnings and book values. Analysts spend considerable time analyzing historical income statements and balance sheets, and their primary forecasts are typically for these variables.

Defining values in terms of ROEs has the added advantage that it focuses analysts' attention on ROE, the same key measure of performance that is decomposed in a standard financial analysis. Further, because ROEs control for firm scale, it is likely to be easier for analysts to evaluate the reasonableness of their forecasts by benchmarking them with ROEs of other firms in the industry and the economy. This type of benchmarking is more challenging for free cash flows and abnormal earnings.

Differences in required structure

The methods differ in the amount of analysis and structure required for valuation. The discounted abnormal earnings and ROE methods require analysts to construct both pro forma income statements and balance sheets to forecast future earnings and book values. In contrast, the discounted abnormal earnings growth model requires analysts to forecast future earnings and dividends. The discounted cash flow method requires analysts to forecast income statements and changes in working capital and long-term assets to generate free cash flows. Finally, the discounted dividend method requires analysts to forecast dividends.

The discounted abnormal earnings (growth), ROE, and free cash flow models all require more structure for analysis than the discounted dividend approach. They therefore help analysts to avoid structural inconsistencies in their forecasts of future dividends by specifically allowing for firms' future performance and investment opportunities. Similarly, the discounted abnormal earnings/ROE method requires more structure and work than the discounted cash flow method and the discounted abnormal earnings growth method to build full pro forma balance sheets. This permits analysts to avoid inconsistencies in the firm's financial structure.

Differences in terminal value implications

A third difference between the methods is in the effort required for estimating terminal values. Terminal value estimates for the abnormal earnings, abnormal earnings growth, and ROE methods tend to represent a much smaller fraction of total value than under the discounted cash flow or dividend methods. On the surface, this would appear to mitigate concerns about the aspect of valuation that leaves the analyst most uncomfortable. Is this apparent advantage real? As explained below, the answer turns on how well value is already reflected in the accountant's book value.

The abnormal earnings and abnormal earnings growth valuations do not eliminate the discounted cash flow terminal value problem, but they do reframe it. Discounted cash flow terminal values include the present value of *all* expected cash flows beyond the forecast horizon. Under abnormal earnings valuation, that value is broken into two parts: the present values of *normal* earnings and *abnormal* earnings beyond the terminal year. The terminal value in the abnormal earnings technique includes only the *abnormal* earnings. The present value of *normal* earnings is already reflected in the original book value or growth in book value over the forecast horizon. Similarly, under the abnormal earnings growth approach the present value of near-term abnormal earnings is already reflected in next-period earnings or the growth in earnings over the forecast horizon. The terminal value includes only the *changes in abnormal* earnings that are expected to occur in the years beyond the terminal year.

The abnormal earnings and abnormal earnings growth approaches, then, recognize that current book value and/or earnings over the forecast horizon already reflect many of the cash flows expected to arrive after the forecast horizon. The approaches build directly on accrual accounting. For example, under accrual accounting book equity can be thought of as the minimum recoverable future benefits attributable to the firm's net assets. In addition, revenues are typically realized when earned, not when cash is received. The discounted cash flow approach, on the other hand, "unravels" all of the accruals, spreads the resulting cash flows over longer horizons, and then reconstructs its own "accruals" in the form of discounted expectations of future cash flows. The essential difference between the two approaches is that abnormal earnings (growth) valuation recognizes that the accrual process may already have performed a portion of the valuation task, whereas the discounted cash flow approach ultimately moves back to the primitive cash flows underlying the accruals.

The usefulness of the accounting-based perspective thus hinges on how well the accrual process reflects future cash flows. The approach is most convenient when the accrual process is "unbiased," so that earnings can be abnormal only as the result of economic rents and not as a product of accounting itself.[16] The forecast horizon then extends to the point where the firm is expected to approach a competitive equilibrium and earn only normal earnings on its projects. Subsequent abnormal earnings would be zero, and the terminal value at that point would be zero. In this extreme case, *all* of the firm's value is reflected in the book value and earnings projected over the forecast horizon.

Of course accounting rarely works so well. For example, in most countries research and development costs are expensed, and book values fail to reflect any research and development assets. As a result, firms that spend heavily on research and development – such as pharmaceuticals – tend on average to generate abnormally high earnings even in the face of stiff competition. Purely as an artifact of research and development accounting, abnormal earnings would be expected to remain positive indefinitely for such firms, and, under the abnormal earnings approach, the terminal value could represent a substantial fraction of total value.

If desired, the analyst can alter the accounting approach used by the firm in his or her own projections. "Better" accounting would be viewed as that which reflects a larger fraction of the firm's value in book values and earnings over the forecast horizon.[17] This same view underlies analysts' attempts to "normalize" earnings; the adjusted numbers are intended to provide better indications of value, even though they reflect performance only over a short horizon.

Research has focused on the performance of abnormal earnings-based valuation relative to discounted cash flow and discounted dividend methods. The findings indicate that over relatively short forecast horizons (ten years or less), valuation estimates using the abnormal earnings approach generate more precise estimates of value than either the discounted dividend or discounted cash flow models. This advantage for the abnormal earnings-based approach persists for firms with conservative or aggressive accounting, indicating that accrual accounting does a reasonably good job of reflecting future cash flows.[18] The performance of the abnormal earnings growth valuation model has not yet been extensively studied. However, the model's close relationship to the abnormal earnings model makes it subject to many of the same practical advantages.

KEY ANALYSIS QUESTIONS

The above discussion on the trade-offs between different methods of valuing a company raises several questions for analysts about how to compare methods and to consider which is likely to be most reliable for their analysis:

- What are the key performance parameters that the analyst forecasts? Is more attention given to forecasting accounting variables, such as earnings and book values, or to forecasting cash flow variables?

- Has the analyst linked forecasted income statements and balance sheets? If not, is there any inconsistency between the two statements, or in the implications of the assumptions for future performance? If so, what is the source of this inconsistency and does it affect discounted earnings-based and discounted cash flow methods similarly?

- How well does the firm's accounting capture its underlying assets and obligations? Does it do a good enough job that we can rely on book values as the basis for long-term forecasts? Alternatively, does the firm rely heavily on off-balance sheet assets, such as R&D, which make book values a poor lower bound on long-term performance?

- Has the analyst made very different assumptions about long-term performance in the terminal value computations under the different valuation methods? If so, which set of assumptions is more plausible given the firm's industry and its competitive positioning?

SUMMARY

Valuation is the process by which forecasts of performance are converted into estimates of price. A variety of valuation techniques are employed in practice, and there is no single method that clearly dominates others. In fact, since each technique involves different advantages and disadvantages, there are gains to considering several approaches simultaneously.

For shareholders, a firm's equity value is the present value of future dividends. This chapter described four valuation techniques directly based on this dividend discount definition of value: discounted dividends, discounted abnormal earnings/ROEs, discounted abnormal earnings growth, and discounted free cash flows. The discounted dividend method attempts to forecast dividends directly. The abnormal earnings approach expresses the value of a firm's equity as book value plus discounted expectations of future abnormal earnings. The abnormal earnings growth approach defines equity value as capitalized next-period earnings plus the present value of future changes in abnormal earnings. Finally, the discounted cash flow method represents a firm's equity value by expected future free cash flows discounted at the cost of capital.

Although these four methods were derived from the same dividend discount model, they frame the valuation task differently. In practice they focus the analyst's attention on different issues and require different levels of structure in developing forecasts of the underlying primitive, future dividends.

Price multiple valuation methods were also discussed. Under these approaches, analysts estimate ratios of current price to historical or forecasted measures of performance for comparable firms. The benchmarks are then used to value the performance of the firm being analyzed. Multiples have traditionally been popular, primarily because they do not require analysts to make multiyear forecasts of performance. However, it can be difficult to identify comparable firms to use as benchmarks. Even across highly related firms, there are differences in performance that are likely to affect their multiples.

The chapter discussed the relation between two popular multiples, value-to-book and value-earnings ratios, and the discounted abnormal earnings valuation. The resulting formulations indicate that value-to-book multiples are a function of future abnormal ROEs, book value growth, and the firm's cost of equity. The value-earnings multiple is a function of the same factors and also the current ROE.

DISCUSSION QUESTIONS

1. Jonas Borg, an analyst at EMH Securities, states: "I don't know why anyone would ever try to value earnings. Obviously, the market knows that earnings can be manipulated and only values cash flows." Discuss.

2. Explain why terminal values in accounting-based valuation are significantly less than those for DCF valuation.

3. Manufactured Earnings is a "darling" of European analysts. Its current market price is €15 per share, and its book value is €5 per share. Analysts forecast that the firm's book value will grow by 10 percent per year indefinitely, and the cost of equity is 15 percent. Given these facts, what is the market's expectation of the firm's long-term average ROE?

4. Given the information in question 3, what will be Manufactured Earnings' share price if the market revises its expectations of long-term average ROE to 20 percent?

5. Analysts reassess Manufactured Earnings' future performance as follows: growth in book value increases to 12 percent per year, but the ROE of the incremental book value is only 15 percent. What is the impact on the market-to-book ratio?

6. How can a company with a high ROE have a low PE ratio?

7. What types of companies have:
    a. A high PE and a low market-to-book ratio?
    b. A high PE ratio and a high market-to-book ratio?
    c. A low PE and a high market-to-book ratio?
    d. A low PE and a low market-to-book ratio?

8. Free cash flows (FCF) used in DCF valuations discussed in the chapter are defined as follows:

$$\text{FCF to debt and equity} = \text{Earnings before interest and taxes} \times (1 - \text{tax rate}) +$$
$$\text{Depreciation and deferred taxes} - \text{Capital}$$
$$\text{expenditures} -/+ \text{Increase/decrease in working capital}$$

$$\text{FCF to equity} = \text{Net profit} + \text{Depreciation and deferred taxes} - \text{Capital}$$
$$\text{expenditures} -/+ \text{Increase/decrease in working capital}$$
$$+/- \text{Increase/decrease in debt}$$

Which of the following items affect free cash flows to debt and equity holders? Which affect free cash flows to equity alone? Explain why and how.

- An increase in trade receivables
- A decrease in gross margins
- An increase in property, plant, and equipment
- An increase in inventories
- Interest expense
- An increase in prepaid expenses
- An increase in notes payable to the bank.

9. Starite Company is valued at €20 per share. Analysts expect that it will generate free cash flows to equity of €4 per share for the foreseeable future. What is the firm's implied cost of equity capital?

10. Janet Stringer argues that "the DCF valuation method has increased managers' focus on short-term rather than long-term performance, since the discounting process places much heavier weight on short-term cash flows than long-term ones." Comment.

NOTES

1. From a theoretical perspective, it is preferred to express equity *per share* as a function of dividends *per share*. This is because only the discounted dividends *per share* model accurately accounts for the wealth transfer from new shareholders to the current shareholders that occurs when a firm offers shares to new shareholders in future years at a price that is not equal to the prevailing market price. To simplify the discussion of the other valuation models, however, we describe all models on a "total equity value basis," thereby implicitly assuming that future capital transactions do not affect the firm's current equity value per share – i.e., are value neutral.
2. The incorporation of all nonowner changes in equity into profit is called clean surplus accounting. It is analogous to "recognized income and expense," the concept defined in IAS 1.
3. Changes in book value also include new capital contributions. However the dividend discount model assumes that new capital is issued at fair value. As a result, any incremental book value from capital issues is exactly offset by the discounted value of future dividends to new shareholders. Capital transactions therefore do not affect firm valuation.
4. The appendix to this chapter provides a simple proof of the earnings-based valuation formula.
5. See C. Lee and J. Myers, "What is the Intrinsic Value of the Dow?" *The Journal of Finance* 54 (October 1999): 1693–1741.
6. The abnormal earnings growth model and its properties are extensively discussed in the following articles: J. A. Ohlson and B. E. Juettner-Nauroth, "Expected EPS and EPS Growth as Determinants of Value," *Review of Accounting Studies* (2005): 349–365; J. A. Ohlson, "On Accounting-Based Valuation Formulae," *Review of Accounting Studies* (2005): 323–347; S. H. Penman, "Discussion of 'On Accounting-Based Valuation Formulae' and 'Expected EPS and EPS Growth as Determinants of Value'," *Review of Accounting Studies* (2005): 367–378.

7. There is an important difference between the way ROE is defined in the value-to-book formulation and the way it is defined in Chapter 5. The valuation formula defines ROE as return on beginning equity, whereas in our ratio discussion we used return on ending or return on average equity.

8. It may seem surprising that one can estimate value with no explicit attention to two of the cash flow streams considered in DCF analysis – investments in working capital and capital expenditures. The accounting-based technique recognizes that these investments cannot possibly contribute to value without impacting abnormal earnings, and that therefore only their earnings impacts need be considered. For example, the benefit of an increase in inventory turnover surfaces in terms of its impact on ROE (and thus, abnormal earnings), without the need to consider explicitly the cash flow impacts involved.

9. This model must no be confused with the PEG ratio. The PEG ratio, which is defined as the price-earnings ratio divided by the short-term earnings growth rate, is a rule-of-thumb used by some analysts to determine whether a share is overpriced. The rule suggests that shares whose PEG ratio is above one are overpriced. Valuation using the PEG ratio has, however, no clear theoretical basis.

10. It is also possible to include a drift term in the model, allowing earnings to grow by a constant amount, or at a constant rate each period.

11. See P. M. Dechow, A. P. Hutton, and R. G. Sloan, "An Empirical Assessment of the Residual Income Valuation Model," *Journal of Accounting and Economics* 23 (January 1999).

12. This formulation is a variant of a model proposed by James Ohlson, "Earnings, Book Values, and Dividends in Security Valuation," *Contemporary Accounting Research* 11 (Spring 1995). Ohlson includes in his forecasts of future abnormal earnings a variable that reflects relevant information other than current abnormal earnings. This variable then also appears in the equity valuation formula. Empirical research by Dechow, Hutton, and Sloan, "An Empirical Assessment of the Residual Income Valuation Model," *Journal of Accounting and Economics* 23 (January 1999), indicates that financial analysts' forecasts of abnormal earnings do reflect considerable information other than current abnormal earnings, and that this information is useful for valuation.

13. This specification is similar to the model for dividends developed by J. Lintner, "Distribution of Incomes of Corporations Among Dividends, Retained Earnings, and Taxes," *American Economic Review* 46 (May 1956): 97–113.

14. In practice, firms do not have to pay out all of their free cash flows as dividends; they can retain surplus cash in the business. The conditions under which a firm's dividend decision affects its value are discussed by M. H. Miller and F. Modigliani in "Dividend Policy, Growth and the Valuation of Shares," *Journal of Business* 34 (October 1961): 411–433.

15. A good forecast, however, would be grounded in an understanding of these changes as well as all other key elements of the firm's financial picture. The changes in financing cash flows are particularly critical for firms that anticipate changing their capital structure.

16. Unbiased accounting is that which, in a competitive equilibrium, produces an expected ROE equal to the cost of capital. The actual ROE thus reveals the presence of economic rents. Market value accounting is a special case of unbiased accounting that produces an expected ROE equal to the cost of capital, even when the firm is *not* in a competitive equilibrium. That is, market value accounting reflects the present value of future economic rents in book value, driving the expected ROEs to a normal level. For a discussion of unbiased and biased accounting, see G. Feltham and J. Ohlson, "Valuation and Clean Surplus Accounting for Operating and Financial Activities," *Contemporary Accounting Research* 11, No. 2 (Spring 1995): 689–731.

17. In Bennett Stewart's book on EVA valuation, *The Quest for Value* (New York: HarperBusiness, 1999), he recommends a number of accounting adjustments, including the capitalization of research and development.

18. S. Penman and T. Sougiannis, "A Comparison of Dividend, Cash Flow, and Earnings Approaches to Equity Valuation," *Contemporary Accounting Research* (Fall 1998): 343–383, compares the valuation methods using actual realizations of earnings, cash flows, and dividends to estimate prices. J. Francis, P. Olsson, and D. Oswald, "Comparing Accuracy and Explainability of Dividend, Free Cash Flow and Abnormal Earnings Equity Valuation Models," *Journal of Accounting Research* 38 (Spring 2000): 45–70, estimates values using *Value Line* forecasts.

APPENDIX: RECONCILING THE DISCOUNTED DIVIDENDS, DISCOUNTED ABNORMAL EARNINGS, AND DISCOUNTED ABNORMAL EARNINGS GROWTH MODELS

To derive the abnormal earnings model from the dividend discount model, consider the following two-period valuation:

$$\text{Equity value} = \frac{DIV_1}{(1+r_e)} + \frac{DIV_2}{(1+r_e)^2}$$

With clean surplus accounting, dividends (DIV) can be expressed as a function of net profit (NP) and the book value of equity (BVE):

$$DIV_t = NP_t + BVE_{t-1} - BVE_t$$

Substituting this expression into the dividend discount model yields the following:

$$\text{Equity value} = \frac{NP_1 + BVE_0 - BVE_1}{(1+r_e)} + \frac{NP_2 + BVE_1 - BVE_2}{(1+r_e)^2}$$

This can be rewritten as follows:

$$\text{Equity value} = \frac{NP_1 - r_e BVE_0 + (1+r_e)BVE_0 - BVE_1}{(1+r_e)}$$

$$+ \frac{NP_2 - r_e BVE_1 + (1+r_e)BVE_1 - BVE_2}{(1+r_e)^2}$$

$$= BVE_0 + \frac{NP_1 - r_e BVE_0}{(1+r_e)} + \frac{NP_2 - r_e BVE_1}{(1+r_e)^2} - \frac{BVE_2}{(1+r_e)^2}$$

The value of equity is therefore the current book value plus the present value of future abnormal earnings. As the forecast horizon expands, the final term (the present value of liquidating book value) becomes inconsequential under the assumption that the long-term growth in the book value of equity is less than the cost of equity. A simple and appealing condition under which this assumption holds is when the firm has a constant dividend payout ratio.[1]

To derive the abnormal earnings growth model from the dividend discount model consider the same two-period dividend model and express dividends in the second (and final) period as a function of net profit and first-period dividends:

$$DIV_2 = NP_2 + NP_1 - DIV_1$$

Substituting this expression into the dividend discount model yields the following:

$$\text{Equity value} = \frac{NP_1 + DIV_1 - NP_1}{(1+r_e)} + \frac{NP_1 + NP_2 - DIV_1}{(1+r_e)^2}$$

---

1. *R. P. Brief, J. O'Hanlon, and K. V. Peasnell explain under which conditions the equality between the discounted abnormal earnings (growth) model and the discounted dividends model holds in the following study: "Error in Constant Growth Accounting Valuation Models," New York University and Lancaster University, working paper, 2005.*

This can be rewritten as follows:

$$\text{Equity value} = \frac{NP_1}{(1+r_e)} + \frac{NP_1}{(1+r_e)^2} - \frac{(NP_1 - DIV_1)(1+r_e)}{(1+r_e)^2}$$

$$+ \frac{(NP_2 - DIV_1)}{(1+r_e)^2}$$

$$= \frac{NP_1}{(1+r_e)} + \frac{NP_1}{(1+r_e)^2} + \frac{NP_2 + r_e DIV_1 - (1+r_e)NP_1}{(1+r_e)^2}$$

The value of equity is therefore the capitalized value of first-period earnings plus the present value of second-period abnormal earnings growth. Note that in contrast to the abnormal earnings model, the abnormal earnings growth model does not assume clean surplus accounting.

Puma AG Rudolf Dassler Sport[1]

During the second half of the 1990s and the first half of the 2000s one of the success stories of the Deutsche Börse, the German stock exchange, was athletic shoe and apparel manufacturer Puma AG Rudolf Dassler Sport. Between its initial public offering in 1986 and 1993, Puma AG had been making losses. After 1993, however, the company managed to successfully restructure its operations, started to report profits again, and became one of the most profitable investments on the German exchange. Investors who had been wise enough to invest in Puma's shares at the beginning of 1994 earned an average annual return on their investment of 33 percent during the next 12 years.

Puma AG[2]

The history of Puma AG started in 1924 when the two brothers Rudolf Dassler and Adolf Dassler founded the "Gebrüder Dassler Shuhfabrik" (Dassler Brothers Shoe Company) in Herzogenaurach, Germany. After a difference of opinion with his brother, Rudolf Dassler left the family business and founded the "Puma Shuhfabrik Rudolph Dassler" in 1948. Adolf Dassler also started his own sports shoe company under the name Adidas, which would become one of Puma's principal competitors.

During the first four decades of operations, Puma grew to become one of the world's premier athletic shoe and apparel manufacturers. Various famous athletes achieved their successes in Puma sports shoes. In football, Pelé wore Puma shoes while winning the World Cup with the Brazilian national team in 1958, 1962, and 1970. In tennis, Boris Becker won Wimbledon wearing Puma shoes in 1985. In athletics, Jim Hines was the first man to finish the 100 meters sprint within 10 seconds, wearing Puma shoes, in 1968.

In the early 1990s Puma's European market share came under increasing pressure when U.S.-based athletic shoe manufacturers Nike and Reebok penetrated the European market for athletic shoes and apparel. Puma lost its position as the second largest European athletic shoe seller and became fourth largest, after Adidas, Nike and Reebok. By that time Puma had already suffered a series of losses and had accumulated a substantial amount of debt. Primary reasons for its losses were that the company's marketing activities were unfocused, the company failed to innovate, its production costs were too high, and its product range was too broad.[3] Puma's weak financial health also made it difficult for the company to compete in marketing with its two U.S. competitors. The company especially failed to compete successfully outside its primary segments, soccer and track and field, in growth segments such as basketball.

The year 1993, however, became Puma's turnaround year. In an attempt to reverse the situation, Puma appointed the then 30-year-old Jochen Zeitz as the company's Chief Executive Officer (CEO). Under the leadership of Zeitz the company began to

---

1. Professor Erik Peek prepared this case. The case is intended solely as the basis for class discussion and is not intended to serve as an endorsement, source of primary data, or illustration of effective or ineffective management.
2. Material in this section is drawn from Puma's 2005 Annual Report and its corporate website.
3. See "Where Nike and Reebok Have Plenty of Running Room," Business Week, March 11, 1991.

implement a long-term worldwide restructuring program. To improve transparency toward its investors, Puma also started to report its financial statements in accordance with International Accounting Standards (IAS), thereby being one of the first companies worldwide to adopt these standards.

Puma's long-term business plan

Puma's worldwide business plan consisted of four different phases. The first phase of restructuring started in fiscal 1993 and ended in fiscal 1997. During this phase, the company restructured its worldwide organization, closed inefficient production plants, and streamlined its product range to increase profitability and reduce indebtedness. The restructuring led to the first success of CEO Jochen Zeitz in 1994, when Puma reported its first net profit since its initial public offering on the German stock exchange in 1986.

The second phase of the plan was aimed at reinforcing Puma's brand image. In this phase Puma invested extensively in marketing and product development, effectively increasing its marketing and R&D outlays by 2–4 percent and 10–15 percent, respectively. The brand image that Puma built was that of one of the most desirable "Sportlifestyle" brands, a brand with distinctive designs that combined style and function. Some steps that Puma took to create this image were to (1) enter into contracts with major designers such as Jill Sander, Marc Jacobs, and Philippe Starck, (2) reduce the number of shops selling its products, (3) start targeted marketing campaigns, for example, by using product placements in movies and TV shows, (4) connect to its customers through famous spokespersons such as tennis player Serena Williams and athlete Wilson Kipketer, and (5) engage in co-branding arrangements with, for example, Porsche.[4]

The third phase, which followed the second phase in 2002, had the objectives to further strengthen Puma's brand image, consistently achieve double-digit sales growth, and reach a sales level of €2 billion by the end of 2006. To improve sales growth Puma invested in product innovation and started to develop its own retail business. In 2002, Puma opened concept retail stores in Frankfurt, London, Rome, Milan, Melbourne, Tokyo, Boston, and Seattle. In 2003, further stores were opened in the cities of Amsterdam, Stockholm, Sydney, Osaka, Philadelphia, and Las Vegas. Puma targeted generating 10 percent of its corporate sales from retail. The company achieved this target in fiscal 2004.

Puma launched the fourth phase of its business plan in 2006. This phase focused on the expansion of Puma to achieve a target sales level of €3.5 billion. Puma planned to expand its product categories in existing business segments as well as in previously unexplored segments. For example, in March 2006 Puma licensed the Japan-based Charmant Group to sell Puma branded eyewear. The management of Puma believed such an expansion into fashion to be a necessary step in creating a company that was truly "Sportlifestyle" based.

Puma realized its geographic expansion plans, in particular by acquiring firms in so-called license markets, where in prior years independent distributors sold Puma branded products under license. Target firms were very often the licensees of these markets. For example, in 2005 Puma agreed to acquire the Argentinean licensee Unisol, the Japanese licensee for apparel Hit Union, and Hong-Kong-based Swire Pacific, which was the company's licensee in Hong Kong and China.

Puma

---

4. See "Stay Cool: Apple Shines and Puma Sprints Ahead as the Two Brands Capture the 'cool factor'," Marketing Management, September/October 2005.

Puma also planned to expand its non-Puma brands. One of Puma's primary non-Puma brands was the Tretorn brand, which Puma had purchased in 2001. To expand its non-Puma brands, Puma repositioned the Tretorn brand by expanding the brand's product range. In addition to the repositioning of the Tretorn brand, Puma had plans to acquire more non-Puma brands in subsequent years.

Sales and production

Puma made use of two different approaches to selling its products. One approach was to let Puma subsidiaries distribute Puma branded products to its customers. The other approach was to license independent companies to produce and distribute Puma branded products. Under a licensing contract, the licensee typically provides a minimum guarantee of sales, either paid in advance or in installments. Further, the licensor typically charges the licensee additional royalties based on the number of products sold. In the early 1990s, the sports licensing business was highly competitive and several licensing companies went bankrupt. By 2006, however, the licensing industry had gone through a process of consolidation and licensees had become financially healthier.

Puma outsourced much of its production to independent factories, mostly located in low-wage countries. In 2004, 81 percent of Puma's production came from the Far East/Asia. The remainder was produced in Europe and America. The companies to which Puma sourced its production were by no means small, powerless production companies. For example, one of Puma's suppliers was Hong-Kong-based Yue Yuen. This supplier employed 252,000 people, had production plants in China, Vietnam, and Indonesia with, in total, 3.4 million square meters of floor space, and produced 167.2 million pairs of shoes per year for most of the larger athletic shoe sellers.

The development and design of new products took place in Puma's product development centers in Herzogenaurauch, London, Taiwan, and Boston. Puma invested an increasing amount of money and resources in product development. Between 2000 and 2005, product development expenses had increased from €18.2 million to €42 million. In percentage terms this increase in product development outlays was, however, smaller than the increase in Puma's consolidated sales.

Puma's financial performance

Exhibit 1 summarizes Puma's financial performance between 1993 and 2005. During these years Puma reported its financial statements in accordance with International Accounting Standards (IAS/IFRS). Hence, all reported figures were prepared under one set of standards. The exhibit shows that Puma increased its consolidated sales from €210 million in 1993 to close to €1.8 billion in 2005. The company remained profitable in each year after 1993, although operating asset turnover and NOPAT margins came under pressure during the implementation of the second phase of Puma's long-term business plan between 1998 and 2002. While accessories made up 4 percent of sales in 1993, the segment generated 11 percent of consolidated sales in 2005, which illustrates Puma's change in strategy.

Questions

1. Puma's profit margin decreased from 16.8 to 16.1 percent in 2005. Consensus earnings forecasts for fiscal 2006 (see Exhibit 1) indicate that analysts expect a further decline in Puma's profit margin to 11.1 percent. On which factors do Puma's future profit

margins critically depend? Do you expect these factors to change over the coming years? Do you agree with analysts' assessment of Puma's next year's profitability?

2. Assume that investors had perfect foresight of one-year-ahead earnings at the end of each fiscal year between 1993 and 2004. Which long-term growth rate assumptions are consistent with the observed end-of-year share prices between 1993 and 2004? When are investors typically positive about long-term growth in earnings?

3. Given your expectations about one-year-ahead earnings and long-term earnings growth, what is your assessment of the value of Puma's shares at the end of fiscal 2005?

Puma

Puma

EXHIBIT 1   **Puma's historical and expected performance, 1993–2007**

(€ millions)	2007E	2006E	2005	2004	2003	2002	2001	2000	1999	1998	1997	1996	1995	1994	1993
Brand sales			2,387.0	2,016.6	1,691.5	1,380.0	1,011.7	831.1	714.9	647.4	622.5	594.0	577.2	554.2	541.3
Percentage growth in brand sales			18.4%	19.2%	22.6%	36.4%	21.7%	16.3%	10.4%	4.0%	4.8%	2.9%	4.2%	2.4%	
Consolidated sales	2,747.0	2,386.0	1,777.5	1,530.3	1,274.0	909.8	598.1	462.4	372.7	302.5	279.7	250.5	211.5	199.5	210.0
Percentage growth in consolidated sales	15.1%	34.2%	16.2%	20.1%	40.0%	52.1%	29.3%	24.1%	23.2%	8.2%	11.7%	18.4%	6.0%	-5.0%	
Footwear			1,175.0	1,011.4	859.3	613.0	384.1	270.9	209.0	202.5	193.8	176.2	154.4	143.5	141.9
Apparel			473.9	416.0	337.0	238.5	169.5	163.5	139.0	85.8	73.1	64.4	50.3	49.9	59.8
Accessories			128.6	102.9	77.7	58.3	44.5	28.0	24.7	14.2	12.9	9.9	6.8	6.2	8.4
Gross profit	1,395.5	1,214.5	929.8	794.0	620.0	396.9	250.6	176.4	141.7	108.2	102.3	94.0	79.0	69.5	62.8
Profit from operations	463.0	378.0	397.7	360.0	263.2	125.0	59.0	22.8	16.3	4.7	36.3	33.3	31.0	23.1	-26.1
Earnings before taxes	474.0	388.0	404.1	365.7	264.1	124.4	57.4	21.2	14.4	3.4	37.4	33.2	26.5	17.3	-35.4
Net earnings	322.0	265.0	285.8	257.3	179.3	84.9	39.7	17.6	9.5	4.0	34.6	42.8	24.6	14.9	-36.9
Dividends			31.9	16.1	11.2	8.8	4.6	1.6	1.6	1.6	1.6	1.6	0.0	0.0	0.0
Royalty and commission income			55.7	43.7	40.4	44.9	37.2	28.9	23.9	24.5	25.9	25.5	26.0	27.1	21.4
Marketing and retail expenses			272.0	214.6	163.9	125.1	86.9	67.0	61.0	47.9	29.0	N.A.	N.A.	N.A.	N.A.
Product development and design expenses			42.0	36.9	29.9	24.2	19.9	18.2	15.2	15.2	7.3	N.A.	N.A.	N.A.	N.A.
Personnel expenses			199.4	157.5	126.6	103.0	81.1	64.4	51.5	41.3	35.2	N.A.	N.A.	N.A.	N.A.
End-of-year order backlog			1,069.0	822.6	722.0	531.1	360.1	232.1	187.2	133.5	130.8	111.4	90.9	94.4	85.2

continued

(€ millions)	2007E	2006E	2005	2004	2003	2002	2001	2000	1999	1998	1997	1996	1995	1994	1993
Operating working capital			234.6	65.9	92.0	73.4	109.1	78.2	64.1	50.1	70.0	21.2	17.8	6.6	34.1
Net non-current assets			217.4	129.7	131.3	100.0	87.9	64.0	60.5	45.4	18.3	24.9	24.0	26.5	32.1
Net assets			452.0	195.6	223.3	173.4	197.0	142.2	124.7	95.5	88.3	46.2	41.7	33.1	66.2
Equity			870.9	535.8	383.0	252.2	176.7	131.3	112.2	97.7	96.7	61.6	-13.6	-38.1	-53.0
Net debt			-419.0	-340.3	-159.7	-78.8	20.3	10.9	12.5	6.2	-8.4	-15.5	55.3	71.3	119.2
Profit margin	11.7%	11.1%	16.1%	16.8%	14.1%	9.3%	6.6%	3.8%	2.5%	1.3%	12.4%	17.1%	11.6%	7.5%	-17.6%
ROE (end-of-year equity)			32.8%	48.0%	46.8%	33.7%	22.5%	13.4%	8.5%	4.1%	35.8%	69.4%	N.A.	N.A.	N.A.
ROE (beginning-of-year equity)		30.4%	53.3%	67.2%	71.1%	48.0%	30.2%	15.7%	9.7%	4.1%	56.1%	N.A.	N.A.	N.A.	N.A.
NOPAT			281.3	253.3	178.7	85.3	40.8	18.9	10.6	3.8	33.6	42.9	28.8	19.9	-27.2
NOPAT margin			15.8%	16.6%	14.0%	9.4%	6.8%	4.1%	2.8%	1.3%	12.0%	17.1%	13.6%	10.0%	-13.0%
Operating asset turnover			3.9	7.8	5.7	5.2	3.0	3.3	3.0	3.2	3.2	5.4	5.1	6.0	3.2
Operating ROA			62.2%	129.5%	80.0%	49.2%	20.7%	13.3%	8.5%	4.0%	38.0%	93.0%	69.0%	60.1%	-41.1%
Net financial leverage			-0.48	-0.64	-0.42	-0.31	0.11	0.08	0.11	0.06	-0.09	-0.25	N.A.	N.A.	N.A.
Spread			61.1%	128.3%	79.6%	49.7%	13.3%	-1.1%	-6.1%	-21.9%	25.2%	93.7%	N.A.	N.A.	N.A.
Financial leverage effect			-29.4%	-81.5%	-33.2%	-15.5%	1.5%	-0.1%	-0.7%	-1.4%	-2.2%	-23.5%	N.A.	N.A.	N.A.
Weighted average shares outstanding	15,672	15,898	16,066	16,025	15,932	15,611	15,392	15,390	15,390	15,390	15,390	15,390	14,000	14,000	14,000
Net earnings per share	20.55	16.67	17.79	16.06	11.25	5.44	2.58	1.14	0.62	0.26	2.25	2.78	1.76	1.06	-2.64
End-of-year equity per share			54.21	33.44	24.04	16.16	11.48	8.53	7.29	6.35	6.28	4.00	-0.97	-2.72	-3.79
End-of-year share price			246.70	202.30	140.00	65.03	34.05	12.70	17.20	11.25	18.61	26.69	18.41	14.93	7.75

Source: Puma's annual reports and corporate website.

Puma

EXHIBIT 2 Management's outlook for fiscal year 2006

Outlook

For the year 2006 PUMA again expects a very successful year. The Soccer World Cup offers PUMA an ideal platform for heightening the brand presence while also impressively highlighting its product capabilities. With a total of 12 teams and numerous individual players, PUMA has the largest World Cup portfolio and is therefore the leading outfitter of this tournament. In addition to the three-time World Champion, Italy, eleven more teams will contribute to a strengthening of the brand presence. Through the use of new technologies, innovative designs and creative concepts as well as the biggest advertising campaign in the company's history, PUMA will set strong accents at the Soccer World Cup with the aim to further consolidate its position as one of the leading soccer brands worldwide.

Further expansion of the global economy in 2006

According to a report of the "Kiel Institute for the World Economy" (Institut für Weltwirtschaft an der Universität Kiel) under the present general political and economic conditions and assuming that oil prices and exchange rates will remain largely constant, global economic expansion will continue in the year 2006, although at a somewhat slower pace than in the first half of 2005. In the oil-importing industrial and emerging nations, the oil price will continue to have a dampening effect for some time. However, the world economy should remain highly dynamic since the stimulating factors will also remain effective.

Overall economic demand could expand more gradually in the USA. Private consumption is expected to flatten out, since the stabilization of real estate prices tends to encourage saving. In Japan, where the adjustment processes could bear fruit in the corporate and banking sector, the overall economy should continue on an upward course. Due to growing demand, a slight economic recovery is expected in the Euro zone. In particular, the progress in the restructuring of the corporate sector will result in a more pronounced increase in investment activity. The mood in the overall economy is expected to remain cautious, however.

The world economic forecasts should also make themselves felt in the sporting goods sector since global economic development can significantly influence general consumer behaviour. Particularly in the year of the World Soccer Championships, an upswing in the sporting goods industry is to be expected in Europe.

In the 2006 Word Soccer Championships year, PUMA will present new product innovations in typical PUMA style. The products will have an authentic brand design, high functionality and unmistakable marketing. The year 2006 will also see the largest marketing campaign in the company's history.

The aim is to achieve a high market presence through the soccer products and the global marketing campaigns, and therefore to strengthen the brand image even further.

Management raises sales forecast to new record-high for the first year of Phase IV

Due to a significant improvement in the orders position for the EMEA region, a stronger than expected orders volume in America and the accelerated integration of six license markets into the group, as early as at the beginning of the year, management raised the original sales target for the first year of Phase IV. On a currency neutral basis, a growth of approximately 30% on consolidated sales, and thus a new record high of approximately €2.3 billion is expected.

Sales increases in all regions

The planned sales growth will extend throughout all regions. Due to the takeovers of individual license markets, the regional distribution of sales will improve as planned. The share of Asia/Pacific should grow from 11% to 20% of consolidated sales. America will continue to yield 27%, while the EMEA region is expected to decline from 62% to approximately 53% according to plan.

Operating profit raised to €350 million

As already announced in the publication of Phase IV measures, the regional change will impact the average gross profit margin. Overall, the gross profit margin in 2006 is expected to fluctuate within the range of 50% and 51%. The takeover of six license markets into the consolidated business will lead to a corresponding reduction in royalty and commission income. Selling, general and administrative expenses will be impacted in particular by disproportionately high marketing expenses for the World Cup and other PUMA campaigns, as well as by planned expansion of the group's retail operations and higher expenses for product development, design and distribution. Overall, however, due to the higher sales expectations, operating expenses will rise to only approximately 35% of sales, compared to the expected 37%. The operating margin is expected to decrease to approximately 15% as a result of brand-building investments in 2006 and conversion of the license businesses into consolidated business. Based on the very positive orders position and the rapid implementation of Phase IV measures, management now expects operating profit of at least €350 million, compared to the original expectation of between €300 million and €330 million. The tax rate is expected to be in the 31%–33% range.

Despite the planned strategic expenditure, consolidated earnings are expected to fall only 10%–15% below the previous year's level, compared to the announced level of 20%. Thus, in absolute figures consolidated earnings are expected to significantly exceed the original expectations.

Expansion of the consolidation group in 2006

Beginning in financial year 2006, the consolidated group will be expanded by companies in Japan, Taiwan, China, Hong Kong, Argentina and Canada. The effects on the net assets, financial position, and results of operations are presented in the Notes. The structuring of contracts with some joint venture companies is such that a disclosure of minority interests is not required since, in economic terms, these companies are fully allocable to PUMA as of January 1, 2006.

Capital expenditures

The investment planning for 2006 provides for capital expenditure of between €130 million and €150 million.

Investments in intangible assets will be necessary, primarily for continued expansion of the group's own retail operations. Capital expenditure of approximately €70 million for the acquisition of new subsidiaries and joint venture companies is included in this calculation.

The targeted investments at the start of Phase IV of the long-term corporate development will lead to introduction of the steps required to strengthen PUMA's position as one of the three leading companies in the sporting goods industry, with the long-term objective of becoming the most desirable Sportlifestyle company.

Management is optimistic

Management is optimistic that the PUMA brand will take yet another large and successful leap in international competition in the year of the Soccer World Cup and during the first year of Phase IV. New sales records are expected for the year 2006. The high level of planned investment activity and an associated increase in the cost ratio at the start of Phase IV should impact profits to a significantly lesser extent than originally expected. Therefore, the operating profit in the current year is expected to be at the high level of €350 million, despite the large amount of investments planned. Beginning from 2007, the cost ratio is expected to decline, and management is confident that yet another record high result can be achieved in addition to continuing record sales. This positive development should lead to at least full exploitation of the calculated sales potential of €3.5 billion in Phase IV of the long-term oriented business plan.

Herzogenaurach, January 25, 2006
The Board of Management

EXHIBIT 3 **Puma AG Rudolf Dassler Sport: Selected notes to the financial statements**

1. General remarks

Under the "PUMA" brand name, PUMA Aktiengesellschaft Rudolf Dassler Sport (hereinafter "PUMA AG") and its subsidiaries are engaged in the development and sales of a broad range of sport and sportlifestyle articles that includes footwear, apparel and accessories. The company is a joint stock company under German law and has its registered head office in Herzogenaurach, Federal Republic of Germany; its responsible court of registration is at Fürth (Bavaria, Germany).

The consolidated financial statements of PUMA AG and its subsidiaries (hereinafter the "Company" or "PUMA"), were prepared in accordance with the "International Financial Reporting Standards (IFRS)" issued by the International Accounting Standards Board (IASB) and the supplementary provisions to be applied in accordance with Section 315a (1) of the German Commercial Code (HGB). All IASB standards and interpretations as adopted by the EU that are obligatory for financial years as from January 1, 2005 have been applied. In August 2005, the IASB published IFRS 7 "Financial Instruments: Disclosures"; this standard will lead to a fundamental change in disclosing requirements concerning financial instruments. In accordance with IFRS 7, companies are required to provide more detailed information on the type and extent of risks associated with financial instruments, in addition to the disclosure requirements relating to the reporting, disclosure and valuation requirements for financial instruments that are already in place. The standard will come into force on January 1, 2007 and is not applied prior to that date.

The consolidated financial statements of PUMA AG are prepared in euro currency (EUR or €). Disclosures in million euros may lead to rounding-off differences since the calculation of individual items is based on figures presented in thousands.

In accordance with IFRS 2, the figures from 2004 were correspondingly restated. In addition, a claim for a tax return in the USA leads to an adjustment of the previous year's figures. The adjustments were explained in the respective disclosures in the notes to the consolidated financial statements ("Notes") where necessary.

Also, in 2005, other operating income was directly netted with the respective administration and general expenses. The previous year's figure was adjusted accordingly.

2. Significant accounting and valuation principles [selection]

Recognition of sales

Sales are recognized and included in profits at the time of the passage of risks. Sales are disclosed net of returned purchases, discounts, rebates, and sales-dependent advertising costs.

Royalty and commission income

Royalty income is treated as income in accordance with the statements to be presented by the licensees. In certain cases, values must be assessed in order to permit accounting on an accrual basis. Commission income is invoiced to the extent that the underlying purchase transaction is deemed realized.

Advertising and promotion expenses

The company recognizes advertising expenses at the time of origin. Generally, promotion expenditure is spread over the contract term as an expense on an accrual basis.

Product development

The company is continuously engaged in developing new products in order to comply with market requirements or market changes. The costs are recorded as an expense at the date of origin; they are not capitalized since the criteria specified in IAS 38 are not fulfilled.

3. Corporate acquisitions

The corporate acquisitions described under "Consolidated Group" had no significant impact on the company's results of operations in 2005.

The goodwill acquired in the financial year is as follows:

(€ millions)	2005
Total purchase prices – of which paid (€17.9 million)	35.6
Fair value of acquired net assets	11.0
Goodwill	24.6

Transactions from acquisition impacted the net assets and financial position in fiscal year 2005 as follows:

(€ millions)	2005
Inventories	11.1
Receivables	30.2
Goodwill	24.6
Other assets	22.1
Bank debt	−14.8
Other liabilities	−38.1
Purchase price	35.6

€18 million from the total purchase price amounting to €36 million were already paid in 2005. The remaining amount of €18 million is classified as liabilities from acquisitions. The liabilities from acquisitions include the amount of €7 million, which is due within one year, and €11 million due in 5 years.

The position "Other assets" includes prepayments from acquisitions amounting to €10 million (please see paragraph 7 of these Notes).

5. Inventories

Inventories are divided into the following main categories:

(€ millions)	2005	2004
Raw materials and supplies	0.5	0.5
Finished goods and merchandise		
Footwear	114.2	106.9
Apparel	86.5	71.9
Accessories/Others	19.5	18.2
Goods in transit	76.1	54.1
Inventories, gross	296.8	251.6
Value adjustments	−58.5	−50.5
Inventories, net	238.3	201.1

Of the total amount of reported inventories, the amount of €64 million (previous year: €58 million) is stated at net realizable value.

6. Trade receivables

(€ millions)	2005	2004
Trade receivables, gross	303.3	188.2
Value adjustments	−25.8	−20.1
Trade receivables, net	277.5	168.1

Advance payments on acquisitions relate to majority shares acquired in companies in Taiwan and China/Hong Kong in 2006. The item is reclassified to shares in affiliated companies upon transfer of the shares and eliminated within the scope of consolidation.

Other current assets are due within one year. The fair value represents the book value. As of tax reclaims

relating to the management incentive program the last year's figures were restated amounting to €13 million.

25. Management of the currency risk

The company is exposed to currency risks which result from an imbalance in the global cashflow. This imbalance is largely due to the high level of sourcing on a US Dollar basis in the Far East. Sales are invoiced in other currencies to a great extent; in addition, the company earns royalty income mainly in Japanese YEN (JPY) and USD. The resulting assets and liabilities are subject to exchange-rate fluctuations from the date of their origin up to realization.

The PUMA Group uses derivative and primary hedging instruments to minimize the currency risk arising from currency fluctuations. Derivative transactions are concluded if a hedging requirement arises from future transactions or after netting existing foreign currency receivables and liabilities. In accordance with the Group's treasury principles, no derivative financial instruments are held for trading purposes. As a general rule, derivatives are combined with the associated underlying transactions to valuation units (hedge accounting) and, to this extent do not impact the net income/net loss for the year.

The company hedges its net demand or net surplus of the respective currencies on a rolling basis 24 months in advance, thus hedging the planning period for the years 2006 and 2007 against currency fluctuations.

The net demand or net surplus results from the demand for a certain currency, net of expected income in the same currency. Forward exchange deals are used to hedge exchange rate risks.

For accounting purposes, hedging transactions are clearly linked to certain parts of the overall risk position. As of the balance sheet date, forward exchange deals related almost exclusively to the purchase of USD and EUR, and the sale of JPY and USD concluded with international renowned financial institutions only. The credit risk is therefore assessed as being very low or unlikely. At present, the terms of the derivatives are up to 24 months. The contracts are used exclusively to hedge contracts already concluded, or where conclusion is expected.

The nominal amounts and market values of open rate-hedging transactions, largely related to cashflow hedging, are structured as follows:

(€ millions)	Nominal amount 2005	Nominal amount 2004	Market value 2005	Market value 2004
Total forward exchange transactions	616.1	724.6	27.6	−59.6

Puma

The nominal amount corresponds to the amounts of the respective hedging transactions as agreed upon between the parties involved. The market value is the amount at which the financial instrument would be traded between interested parties on the balance sheet date. As a general rule, the market values are determined on the basis of the market values communicated by the respective banks. The market value is reported under Other Financial Assets or Other Liabilities in accordance with IAS 39, and offset against equity with neutral effects on profits in as much as the hedging transaction relates to future transactions.

The underlying and hedging transactions will probably impact the revenue results within the next 24 months. In the financial year, the amount of €22 million was reclassified from equity as inventory acquisition costs (IAS 32.59). Management does not expect any adverse influences on the Group's financial position from the use of derivative financial instruments.

29. Other financial obligations

The company's other financial obligations relate to license, promotion and advertising contracts. In addition, the company leases and rents offices, warehouses, facilities, a car park and also sales premises for its own retail business. The residual term of the lease contract for the logistics centre in Germany (operative leasing) is 6 years. The term of rental contracts concerning the retail business is between 5 and 15 years. The terms of all other rental and lease contracts are between 1 and 5 years.

As of the balance sheet date, the company's financial obligations were as follows:

(€ millions)	2005	2004
From license, promotion and advertising contracts:		
2006 (2005)	47.4	33.4
2007–2010 (2006–2009)	170.5	53.4
From rental and lease contracts:		
2006 (2007)	46.6	29.5
2007–2010 (2006–2009)	153.3	90.8
As from 2001 (as from 2010)	81.3	48.4

32. Events after the balance sheet date

In the context of its long-term corporate development plan (Phase IV) published in July 2005, PUMA will acquire the majority share or 100% respectively, in the following companies in January 2006. These companies will then be responsible for the sales & marketing of PUMA products in the respective countries with immediate effect. In accordance with the agreements concluded with minority shareholders with a view to acquisition after expiry of the term of the agreement, the companies in Japan and Taiwan are to be allocated to the PUMA Group at 100% in economic terms with effect from January 1, 2006. The other companies are purely joint ventures which are recognized through taking the respective minority interest into account. The following companies were founded – or a majority interest was acquired – and they were included in consolidation with effect from January 1, 2006.

Asia Pacific	America
PUMA Apparel Japan K.K., Japan	Unisol S.A., Argentina
PUMA Taiwan Sports Ltd., Taiwan	ATA Inc., Canada
Liberty China Holding Ltd., British Virgin Islands	
Liberty Sports Marketing Ltd., Hong Kong	
Liberty Shanghai Ltd., China	

The change in the consolidated group is expected to impact net assets and the financial position as of the time of initial consolidation (January 1, 2006) as follows.

(€ millions)	Asia/Pacific	America	Total
Total purchase price	73.6	42.4	115.9
Fair value of the net assets acquired	25.5	20.9	46.4
Goodwill	48.0	21.5	69.5

€10 million from the total purchase price amounting to €116 million were already paid in 2005 (please see paragraph 7 of these Notes).

Prospective Analysis: Valuation Implementation

To move from the valuation theory discussed in the previous chapter to the actual task of valuing a company, one has to deal with a number of issues. First, the analyst needs to make forecasts of financial performance stated in terms of abnormal earnings and book values, or free cash flows over the life of the firm. As a practical matter, the forecasting task is often divided into two subcomponents – detailed forecasts over a finite number of years and a forecast of "terminal value," which represents a summary forecast of performance beyond the period of detailed forecasts. Second, the analyst needs to estimate the cost of capital to discount these forecasts. We discuss these issues in this chapter, and provide guidance on how to deal with them.

DETAILED FORECASTS OF PERFORMANCE

The horizon over which detailed forecasts are to be made is itself a choice variable. We will discuss later in this chapter how the analyst might make this choice. Once it is made, the next step is to consider the set of assumptions regarding a firm's performance that are needed to arrive at the forecasts. We described in Chapter 6 the general framework of financial forecasting. Since valuation involves forecasting over a long time horizon, it is not practical to forecast all the line items in a company's financial statements. Instead, the analyst has to focus on the key elements of a firm's performance.

The key to sound forecasts, of course, is that the underlying assumptions are grounded in a company's business reality. Strategy analysis provides a critical understanding of a company's value proposition, and whether current performance is likely to be sustainable in future. Accounting analysis and ratio analysis provide a deep understanding of a company's current performance, and whether the ratios themselves are reliable indicators of performance. It is, therefore, important to see the valuation forecasts as a continuation of the earlier steps in business analysis rather than as a discreet exercise unconnected from the rest of the analysis.

Recall that we used car manufacturers Volkswagen and Porsche to illustrate ratio analysis and financial forecasting in Chapters 5 and 6. Specifically, we forecasted in Chapter 6 Porsche's condensed income statement, beginning balance sheet, and free cash flows for a period of ten years starting in fiscal year 2006 (year beginning in August 2005). We will use these same forecasting assumptions and financial forecasts, which are shown in Tables 6.1 and 6.2, as a starting point to value Porsche as of

August 1, 2005. A spreadsheet containing Porsche's actual and forecasted financial statements as well as the valuation described in this chapter is available on the companion website of this book.

The key forecasts required to use the formulas discussed in Chapter 7 for valuing a firm's equity are: abnormal earnings, abnormal ROE, abnormal earnings growth, and free cash flows to equity. If one is valuing a firm's assets, the corresponding variables of interest are abnormal NOPAT, abnormal operating ROA, abnormal NOPAT growth, and free cash flows to debt and equity. To calculate abnormal earnings and abnormal returns, we can begin with the forecasts in Table 6.2 for Porsche, but we also need estimates of its cost of capital. So let us begin our discussion with a framework for estimating a firm's cost of capital. Then we will try to convert the financial forecasts in Table 6.2 into estimates of value.

COMPUTING A DISCOUNT RATE

To value a company's assets, the analyst discounts abnormal NOPAT (growth), abnormal operating ROA, or cash flows available to both debt and equity holders. The proper discount rate to use is therefore the weighted average cost of capital (WACC). The WACC is calculated by weighting the costs of debt and equity capital according to their respective market values:

$$\text{WACC} = \frac{V_d}{V_d + V_e} r_d (1 - T) + \frac{V_e}{V_d + V_e} r_e$$

where V_d = the market value of debt and V_e = the market value of equity
r_d = the cost of debt capital
r_e = the cost of equity capital
T = the tax rate reflecting the marginal tax benefit of interest

Weighting the costs of debt and equity

The weights assigned to debt and equity represent their respective fractions of total capital provided, measured in terms of market values. Computing a market value for debt should not be difficult. It is reasonable to use book values if interest rates have not changed significantly since the time the debt was issued. Otherwise, the value of the debt can be estimated by discounting the future payouts at current market rates of interest applicable to the firm.

What is included in debt? Should short-term as well as long-term debt be included? Should payables and accruals be included? The answer is revealed by considering how we calculated free cash flows. Free cash flows are the returns to the providers of the capital to which the WACC applies. The cash flows are those available *before* servicing short-term and long-term debt – indicating that both short-term and long-term debt should be considered a part of capital when computing the WACC. Servicing of other liabilities, such as accounts payable or accruals, should already have been considered as we computed free cash flows. Thus internal consistency requires that operating liabilities should not be considered a part of capital when computing the WACC.

The tricky problem we face is assigning a market value to equity. That is the very amount we are trying to estimate in the first place! How can the analyst possibly assign a market value to equity at this intermediate stage, given that the estimate will not be known until all steps in the DCF analysis are completed?

One common approach to the problem is to insert at this point "target" ratios of debt to capital $[V_d/(V_d+V_e)]$ and equity to capital $[V_e/(V_d+V_e)]$. For example, one might expect that a firm will, over the long run, maintain a capital structure that is 40 percent debt and 60 percent equity. The long-run focus is reasonable because we are discounting cash flows over a long horizon.

Another way around the problem is to start with book value of equity as a weight for purposes of calculating an initial estimate of the WACC, which in turn can be used in the discounting process to generate an initial estimate of the value of equity. That initial estimate can then be used in place of the guess to arrive at a new WACC, and a second estimate of the value of equity can be produced. This process can be repeated until the value used to calculate the WACC and the final estimated value converge.

Estimating the cost of debt

The cost of debt (r_d) is the interest rate on the debt. If the assumed capital structure in future periods is the same as the historical structure, then current interest rate on debt will be a good proxy for this. However, if the analyst assumes a change in capital structure, then it is important to estimate the expected interest rate given the new level of debt ratio. One approach to this would be to estimate the expected credit rating of the company at the new level of debt and use the appropriate interest rates for that credit category.

The cost of debt should be expressed on a net-of-tax basis because it is after-tax cash flows that are being discounted. In most settings the market rate of interest can be converted to a net-of-tax basis by multiplying it by one minus the marginal corporate tax rate.

Estimating the cost of equity

Estimating the cost of equity (r_e) can be difficult, and a full discussion of the topic lies beyond the scope of this chapter. In any case, even an extended discussion would not supply answers to all the questions that might be raised in this area because the field of finance is in a state of flux over what constitutes an appropriate measure of the cost of equity.

One possibility is to use the capital asset pricing model (CAPM), which expresses the cost of equity as the sum of a required return on riskless assets plus a premium for systematic risk:

$$r_e = r_f + \beta[E(r_m) - r_f]$$

where r_f is the riskless rate;
$[E(r_m) - r_f]$ is the risk premium expected for the market as a whole, expressed as the excess of the expected return on the market index over the riskless rate;
and β is the systematic risk of the equity.

To compute r_e, one must estimate three parameters: the riskless rate, r_f, the market risk premium $[E(r_m) - r_f]$, and systematic risk, β. Systematic risk (β) reflects the sensitivity of the firm's value to economy-wide market movements.[1] For r_f, analysts often use the rate on intermediate-term government bonds, based on the observation that it is cash flows beyond the short term that are being discounted.[2] When r_f is measured in that way, then average worldwide common stock returns (based on the returns to a 16-country, common-currency equity index) have exceeded that rate by 4.9 percent over the 1900–2002 period.[3] This excess return constitutes an estimate of the market risk premium $[E(r_m) - r_f]$. Based on the risk premium's historical means and variances between 1900 and 2002, one study reports that plausible estimates of future market risk premiums for the "world market", the U.K., and the U.S. are somewhere around 5.0, 5.5, and 5.5 percent, respectively. However, it is important to realize that the market risk premium has varied substantially across countries and will likely continue to do so, albeit to a lesser degree when worldwide stock markets will further integrate and worldwide disclosure and securities regulation will be further harmonized.[4] In addition, while the historical risk premium has been calculated over a long time period, the premium is likely to change over time because of, for example, the changing risk preferences of investors.

Although the above CAPM is often used to estimate the cost of capital, the evidence indicates that the model is incomplete. Assuming stocks are priced competitively, stock returns should be expected just to compensate investors for the cost of their capital. Thus long-run average returns should be close to the cost of capital and should (according to the CAPM) vary across stocks according to their systematic risk. However, factors beyond just systematic risk seem to play some role in explaining variation in long-run average returns. The most important such factor is labeled the "size effect": smaller firms (as measured by market capitalization) tend to generate higher returns in subsequent periods. Why this is so is unclear. It could mean either that smaller firms are riskier than indicated by the CAPM or that they are underpriced at the point their market capitalization is measured, or some combination of both.

Average stock returns for European firms (from the 12 European countries described in Chapter 1) varied across size deciles from 1989 to 2005 as shown in Table 8.1. The table shows that, historically, investors in firms in the top two deciles of the size distribution have realized returns of only 8.9 to 9.1 percent. In contrast, firms in the smallest two size deciles have realized significantly higher returns, ranging from 12.8 to 19.4 percent. Note, however, that if we use firm size as an indicator of the cost

TABLE 8.1 European firms' stock returns and firm size

Size deciles	Market value of largest company in decile, in 2005 (€ millions)	Average annual stock return 1989–2005 (%)	Fraction of total market capitalization represented by decile (in 2005, %)
1-small	5.7	19.4%	0.02
2	13.1	12.8%	0.07
3	24.4	10.3%	0.13
4	43.5	7.7%	0.24
5	77.4	8.5%	0.43
6	135.9	7.8%	0.76
7	254.4	8.6%	1.37
8	583.4	8.8%	2.84
9	1,846.5	9.1%	7.77
10-large	154,408.1	8.9%	86.37

Source: Thomson Datastream. Annual stock returns are based on compounded monthly returns. The returns come from all European companies that were listed on one of the seven major European stock exchanges between 1989 and 2005 (see Chapter 1 for details).

of capital, we are implicitly assuming that large size is indicative of lower risk. Yet finance theorists have not developed a well-accepted explanation for why that should be the case.

One method for combining the cost of capital estimates is based on the CAPM and the "size effect." The approach calls for adjustment of the CAPM-based cost of capital, based on the difference between the average return on the market index used in the CAPM and the average return on firms of size comparable to the firm being evaluated. The resulting cost of capital is

$$r_e = r_f + \beta[E(r_m) - r_f] + r_{SIZE}$$

In light of the continuing debate on how to measure the cost of capital, it is not surprising that managers and analysts often consider a range of estimates. In particular, there has been considerable debate in recent times about whether or not the historical risk premium of 5 percent is valid today. Many analysts argue that a variety of changes in the world economy make the historical risk premium an invalid basis for forecasting the expected risk premium going forward. Some academic research has provided evidence that suggests that the expected risk premium in the U.S. stock market in recent years has declined substantially, to the range of 3 to 4 percent.[5] Since this debate is still unresolved, it is prudent for analysts to use a range of risk premium estimates in computing a firm's cost of capital.

Adjusting cost equity for changes in leverage

Both cost of debt and cost of equity change as a function of a firm's leverage. As the leverage increases, debt and equity become more risky so they become more costly. If an analyst is contemplating changing capital structure during the forecasting time period relative to the historical capital structure of the firm, or changing the capital structure over time during the forecasting period, it is important to re-estimate the cost of debt and equity to take these changes into account. We describe below a simple approach to this task.

We begin with the observation that the beta of a firm's assets is equal to the weighted average of its debt and equity betas, weighted by the proportion of debt and equity in its capital structure. A firm's equity beta can be estimated directly using its stock returns and the capital asset pricing model. Its debt beta can be inferred from the capital asset pricing model if we have information on the current interest rate and risk-free rate. From these estimated equity and debt betas at the current capital structure, we can infer the firm's asset beta.

When the firm's capital structure changes, its equity and debt betas will change, but its asset beta remains the same. We can take advantage of this fact to estimate the expected equity beta for the new capital structure. We first have to get an estimate of the interest rate on debt at the new capital structure level. Once we have this information, we can estimate the implied debt beta using the capital asset pricing model and the risk-free rate. Now we can estimate the equity beta for the new capital structure using the identity that the new equity beta and the new debt beta, weighted by the new capital structure weights, have to add up to the asset beta estimated earlier.

Estimating Porsche's cost of capital

To estimate the cost of capital for Porsche, we start with the assumption that its after-tax cost of debt is –0.9 percent, based on the ratio of the net interest expense after tax to beginning net debt in fiscal 2005. With an assumed tax rate of 37 percent, this translates into a pre-tax cost of debt of –1.4 percent (recall that Porsche earned net interest income on its net debt, hence the negative sign). The company's equity beta estimated in August 2006 was 1.03.[6] The ten-year government bond rate in Germany at that time was 3.25 percent. Using the historical risk premium for equities of 4.9 percent, we can calculate its cost of equity to be 8.3 percent. Clearly this estimate is only a starting point, and the analyst can change the estimate by changing the assumed market risk premium or by adjusting for the size effect.

Porsche's equity market value in August 2006 was €11,445 million; its net book debt was €747.1 million. Using these numbers we can calculate the "market value" weights of debt and equity in the company's capital structure as 2 percent and 98 percent respectively. Based on these weights and the above estimates of costs of equity and debt, our estimate of Porsche's weighted average cost of capital (WACC) in August 2006 is 7.7 percent (which is close to the cost of equity because the company uses so little debt).

Since we keep the capital structure of Porsche constant throughout the forecasting period, we will use these estimates of cost of equity and cost of capital.

Making performance forecasts for valuing Porsche

Recall that we made income statement, balance sheet, and cash flow forecasts for Porsche for fiscal years 2006 to 2015 in Chapter 6 (Tables 6.1 and 6.2). Tables 8.2 and 8.3 present these same forecasts. Table 8.4 shows the performance forecasts implied by these financial statement forecasts for the ten-year period 2006 to 2015. Eight performance forecasts, which can be used as input into the valuation exercise, are shown in the table. Abnormal earnings, abnormal ROE, abnormal earnings growth, and free cash flows to equity are inputs to value Porsche's equity. Abnormal NOPAT, abnormal operating ROA, abnormal NOPAT growth, and free cash flows to debt and equity holders are three alternative inputs to value Porsche's assets.

The calculations of performance forecasts in Table 8.4 use the following definitions: (1) abnormal earnings is net profit less shareholders' equity at the beginning

TABLE 8.2 Forecasting assumptions for Porsche

For fiscal year	2006	2007	2008	2009	2010	2011	2012	2013	2014	2015
Sales growth	4.7%	0.9%	10.7%	22.9%	9.3%	7.5%	7.5%	7.5%	7.5%	7.5%
NOPAT margin	11.5%	11.0%	10.5%	10.0%	9.5%	9.0%	8.5%	8.0%	7.5%	7.0%
After-tax net interest rate	–0.9%	–0.9%	–0.9%	–0.9%	–0.9%	–0.9%	–0.9%	–0.9%	–0.9%	–0.9%
Beginning net working capital to sales ratio	8.0%	8.0%	8.0%	8.0%	8.0%	8.0%	8.0%	8.0%	8.0%	8.0%
Beginning net non-current assets to sales ratio	52.4%	52.4%	52.4%	52.4%	52.4%	52.4%	52.4%	52.4%	52.4%	52.4%
Beginning net debt to capital ratio	18.0%	18.0%	18.0%	18.0%	18.0%	18.0%	18.0%	18.0%	18.0%	18.0%

TABLE 8.3 Forecasted financial statements for Porsche

Fiscal year	2006	2007	2008	2009	2010	2011	2012	2013	2014	2015
Beginning balance sheet (€ millions)										
Beginning net working capital	551.1	556.1	615.6	756.5	826.9	888.9	955.6	1,027.3	1,104.3	1,187.1
+ Beginning net non-current assets	3,608.1	3,640.6	4,030.1	4,953.1	5,413.7	5,819.7	6,256.2	6,725.4	7,229.8	7,772.0
= Net operating assets	**4,159.3**	**4,196.7**	**4,645.7**	**5,709.6**	**6,240.6**	**6,708.6**	**7,211.8**	**7,752.7**	**8,334.1**	**8,959.2**
Net debt	747.1	753.8	834.5	1,025.6	1,121.0	1,205.1	1,295.4	1,392.6	1,497.0	1,609.3
+ Shareholders' equity	3,412.1	3,442.8	3,811.2	4,684.0	5,119.6	5,503.6	5,916.4	6,360.1	6,837.1	7,349.9
= Net capital	**4,159.3**	**4,196.7**	**4,645.7**	**5,709.6**	**6,240.6**	**6,708.6**	**7,211.8**	**7,752.7**	**8,334.1**	**8,959.2**
Income statement (€ millions)										
Sales	6,882.0	6,943.9	7,686.9	9,447.2	10,325.8	11,100.3	11,932.8	12,827.8	13,789.8	14,824.1
Net operating profits After tax	791.4	763.8	807.1	944.7	981.0	999.0	1,014.3	1,026.2	1,034.2	1,037.7
− Net interest expense after tax	−6.7	−6.8	−7.5	−9.2	−10.1	−10.8	−11.7	−12.5	−13.5	−14.5
= Net profit	**798.2**	**770.6**	**814.6**	**954.0**	**991.0**	**1,009.9**	**1,025.9**	**1,038.8**	**1,047.7**	**1,052.2**
Operating ROA	19.0%	18.2%	17.4%	16.5%	15.7%	14.9%	14.1%	13.2%	12.4%	11.6%
ROE	23.4%	22.4%	21.4%	20.4%	19.4%	18.3%	17.3%	16.3%	15.3%	14.3%
BV of assets growth rate	6.7%	0.9%	10.7%	22.9%	9.3%	7.5%	7.5%	7.5%	7.5%	7.5%
BV of equity growth rate	17.1%	0.9%	10.7%	22.9%	9.3%	7.5%	7.5%	7.5%	7.5%	7.5%
Net operating asset turnover	1.7	1.7	1.7	1.7	1.7	1.7	1.7	1.7	1.7	1.7
Free cash flow to capital	754.0	314.8	−256.7	413.7	512.9	495.9	473.4	444.8	409.2	365.7
Free cash flow to equity	767.4	402.2	−58.1	518.3	607.1	597.1	582.2	561.7	534.9	500.9

of the year times cost of equity, (2) abnormal ROE is the difference between ROE and cost of equity, (3) abnormal earnings growth is the change in net profit less prior year's retained earnings (here: the increase in equity) times cost of equity, (4) free cash flow to equity is net profit less the increase in operating working capital less the increase in net long-term assets plus the increase in net debt, (5) abnormal NOPAT is NOPAT less total net capital at the beginning of the year times the weighted average cost of capital, (6) abnormal operating ROA is the difference between operating ROA and the weighted average cost of capital (WACC), (7) abnormal NOPAT growth is the change in abnormal NOPAT, and (8) free cash flow to capital is NOPAT less the increase in operating working capital less the increase in net long-term assets.

As discussed earlier, to derive cash flows in 2015, we need to make assumptions about sales growth rate and balance sheet ratios in 2016. We discuss below three different sets of assumptions in this regard. The cash flow forecasts shown in Table 8.4 are based on the simple assumption that the sales growth and beginning balance sheet ratios in 2016 remain the same as in 2015. We relax this assumption later.

TABLE 8.4 Performance forecasts for Porsche for the fiscal years 2006 to 2015

Fiscal year	2006	2007	2008	2009	2010	2011	2012	2013	2014	2015
Equity valuation										
(€ millions)										
Abnormal earnings	514.9	484.9	498.3	565.2	566.1	553.1	534.9	510.9	480.2	442.1
Abnormal ROE	15.1%	14.1%	13.1%	12.1%	11.1%	10.0%	9.0%	8.0%	7.0%	6.0%
Free cash flow to equity	767.4	402.2	−58.1	518.3	607.1	597.1	582.2	561.7	534.9	500.9
Abnormal earnings growth		−30.1	13.4	66.9	0.9	−13.0	−18.2	−24.0	−30.6	−38.1
Asset valuation										
(€ millions)										
Abnormal NOPAT	471.2	440.7	449.4	505.1	500.4	482.5	459.0	429.3	392.5	347.8
Abnormal ROA	11.3%	10.5%	9.7%	8.8%	8.0%	7.2%	6.4%	5.5%	4.7%	3.9%
Free cash flow to capital	754.0	314.8	−256.7	413.7	512.9	495.9	473.4	444.8	409.2	365.7
Abnormal NOPAT growth		−30.5	8.7	55.7	−4.7	−18.0	−23.5	−29.7	−36.8	−44.7
Discount rates:										
Equity	0.923	0.853	0.787	0.727	0.671	0.620	0.572	0.528	0.488	0.451
Assets	0.929	0.862	0.800	0.743	0.690	0.641	0.595	0.552	0.513	0.476
Growth factors:[a]										
Equity	1.000	1.009	1.117	1.373	1.500	1.613	1.734	1.864	2.004	2.154
Assets	1.000	1.009	1.117	1.373	1.500	1.613	1.734	1.864	2.004	2.154

a. The growth factor is relevant only for calculating the present value for abnormal ROA and ROE.

TERMINAL VALUES

The forecasts in Tables 8.3 and 8.4 extend only through the year 2015, and thus we label 2015 the "terminal year." (Selection of an appropriate terminal year is discussed later.) Terminal value is essentially the present value of either abnormal earnings or free cash flows occurring beyond the terminal year. Because this involves forecasting performance over the remainder of the firm's life, the analyst must adopt some assumption that simplifies the process of forecasting. Below we discuss a variety of alternative approaches to this task.

Terminal values with the competitive equilibrium assumption

Table 8.2 projects a sales growth rate and return on equity declining gradually over time during the period 2009 to 2015 before stabilizing sometime during that period. What should we assume beyond 2015? Is it reasonable to assume a continuation of the same stable 2015 performance in 2016 and beyond? Is some other pattern more reasonable?

One thing that seems clear is that continuation of a sales growth that is significantly greater than the average growth rate of the economy is unrealistic over a very long horizon. That rate would likely outstrip inflation in the euro and the real growth rate of the world economy. Over many years, it would imply that Porsche would grow to a size greater than that of all other firms in the world combined. But what would be a suitable alternative assumption? Should we expect the firm's sales growth rate to ultimately settle down to the rate of inflation? Or to a higher rate, such as the nominal GDP growth rate? Or to something else?

Ultimately, to answer these questions, one must consider whether the rate of growth in industry sales can outstrip the general growth in the world economy, and whether and for how long Porsche's competitive advantages can enable it to grow faster than the overall industry. Clearly, looking 11 or more years into the future, any forecasts of sales growth rates are likely to be subject to considerable error.

Fortunately, in many if not most situations, how we deal with the seemingly imponderable questions about long-range growth in sales simply *does not matter very much!* In fact, under plausible economic assumptions, there is no practical need to consider sales growth beyond the terminal year. Such growth may be *irrelevant*, so far as the firm's current value is concerned!

How can long-range growth in sales *not* matter? The reasoning revolves around the forces of competition. Competition tends to constrain a firm's ability to identify, on a consistent basis, growth opportunities that generate supernormal profits. (Recall the evidence in Chapter 6 concerning the reversion of ROEs to normal levels over horizons of five to ten years.) Certainly a firm may at a point in time maintain a competitive advantage that permits it to achieve returns in excess of the cost of capital. When that advantage is protected with patents or a strong brand name, the firm may even be able to maintain it for many years, perhaps indefinitely. With hindsight, we know that some such firms – like Coca-Cola – were able not only to maintain their competitive edge but to expand it across dramatically increasing investment bases. But in the face of competition, one would typically not expect a firm to extend its supernormal profitability to new *additional* projects *year after year*. Ultimately, we would expect high profits to attract enough competition to drive the firm's return down to a normal level. Each new project would generate cash flows with a present value no greater than the cost of the investment – the investment would be a "zero net present value" project. Because the benefits of the project are offset by its costs, it does nothing to enhance the current value of the firm, and the associated growth can be ignored.

Of course, terminal value estimation does not necessarily *require* this "competitive equilibrium assumption." If the analyst expects that supernormal margins can be extended to new markets for many years, it can be accommodated within the context of a valuation analysis. At a minimum, as we will discuss in the next section, the analyst may expect that supernormal margins can be maintained on the existing sales base, or on markets that grow at the rate of inflation. However, the important lesson here is that the rate of growth in *sales* beyond the forecast horizon is *not* a relevant consideration *unless* the analyst believes that the growth can be achieved while generating supernormal margins – and competition may make that a difficult trick to pull off.

Assumption only on incremental sales

An alternative version of the competitive equilibrium assumption is to assume that Porsche will continue to earn abnormal earnings forever on the sales it had in 2015, but there will be no abnormal earnings on any incremental sales beyond that level. If we invoke the competitive equilibrium assumption on incremental sales for years beyond 2015, then it does not matter what sales growth rate we use beyond that year, and we may as well simplify our arithmetic by treating sales *as if* they will be constant at the year 2015 level. Then operating ROA, ROE, NOPAT, net profit, free cash flow to debt and equity, and free cash flow to equity will all remain constant at the year 2015 level.

Under this scenario, it is simple to estimate the terminal value by dividing the 2015 level of each of the variables by the appropriate discount rate. Under the abnormal earnings (NOPAT) growth valuation method, Porsche's abnormal earnings (NOPAT) growth beyond 2015 and its terminal value will be zero. As one would expect, terminal values in this scenario will be higher than those with no abnormal returns on all sales in years 2016 and beyond. This is entirely due to the fact that we are now assuming that Porsche can retain its superior performance on its existing base of sales indefinitely.

Terminal value with persistent abnormal performance and growth

Each of the approaches described above appeals in some way to the "competitive equilibrium assumption." However, there are circumstances where the analyst is willing to assume that the firm may defy competitive forces and earn abnormal rates of return on new projects for many years. If the analyst believes supernormal profitability can be extended to larger markets for many years, one possibility is to project earnings and cash flows over a longer horizon, until the competitive equilibrium assumption can reasonably be invoked. In the case of Porsche, for example, we could assume that the supernormal profitability will continue for five years beyond 2015 (for a total fore-casting horizon of 15 years from the beginning of the forecasting period), but after that period, the firm's ROE and operating ROA will be equal to its cost of equity and its weighted average cost of capital.

Another possibility is to project growth in abnormal earnings or cash flows at some constant rate. Consider the following. By treating Porsche as if its competitive advantage can be maintained only on the *nominal* sales level achieved in the year 2015, we will be assuming that in *real* terms its competitive advantage will shrink. Let's say that the analyst expects Porsche to maintain its advantage (through supplies of new and more advanced products to a similar customer base) on a sales base that remains constant in *real* terms – that grows beyond the year 2015 at the expected long-run inflation rate between 2 and 4 percent. The computations implied by these assumptions are described below. The approach is more aggressive than the one described earlier, but it may be more realistic. After all, there is no obvious reason why the *real* size of the investment base on which Porsche earns abnormal returns should depend on inflation rates.

The approach just described still relies to some extent on the competitive equi-librium assumption. The assumption is now invoked to suggest that supernormal profitability can be extended only to an investment base that remains constant in real terms. However, there is nothing about the valuation method that requires *any* reliance on the competitive equilibrium assumption. The calculations described below could be used with *any* rate of growth in sales. The question is not whether the arithmetic is available to handle such an approach, but rather how realistic it is.

Let's stay with the approach that assumes Porsche will extend its supernormal margins to sales that grow beyond 2015 at the rate of inflation (2 percent). How would abnormal earnings and free cash flows beyond 2015 behave?

Beyond our terminal year, 2015, as the sales growth rate remains constant at 2 percent, abnormal earnings, abnormal earnings growth, free cash flows, and book values of assets and equity also grow at a constant rate of 2 percent. This is simply because we held all other performance ratios constant in this period. As a result, abnormal operating ROA and abnormal ROE remain constant at the same rate as in the terminal year.

The above exercise shows that, when we assume that the abnormal performance persists at the same level as in the terminal year, projecting abnormal earnings (growth) and free cash flows is a simple matter of growing them at the assumed sales growth rate. Since the rate of abnormal earnings and cash flows growth is constant starting in 2016, it is also straightforward to discount those flows. For a given discount rate r, any flow stream growing at the constant rate g can be discounted by dividing the flows in the first year by the amount $(r–g)$.

Terminal value based on a price multiple

A popular approach to terminal value calculation is to apply a multiple to abnormal earnings, cash flows, or book values of the terminal period. The approach is not as ad hoc as it might at first appear. Note that under the assumption of no sales growth, abnormal earnings or cash flows beyond 2015 remain constant. Capitalizing these flows in perpetuity by dividing by the cost of capital is equivalent to multiplying them by the inverse of the cost of capital. For example, capitalizing free cash flows to equity at 8.3 percent is equivalent to assuming a terminal cash flow multiple of 12.05. Thus applying a multiple in this range is similar to discounting all free cash flows beyond 2015 while invoking the competitive equilibrium assumption on incremental sales.

The mistake to avoid here is to capitalize the future abnormal earnings or cash flows using a multiple that is too high. The earnings or cash flow multiples might be high currently because the market anticipates abnormally profitable growth. However, once that growth is realized, the PE multiple should fall to a normal level. It is that normal PE, applicable to a stable firm or one that can grow only through zero net present value projects, that should be used in the terminal value calculation. Thus multiples in the range of 7 to 12 – close to the reciprocal of cost of equity and WACC – should be used here. Higher multiples are justifiable only when the terminal year is closer and there are still abnormally profitable growth opportunities beyond that point. A similar logic applies to the estimation of terminal values using book value multiples.

Selecting the terminal year

A question begged by the above discussion is how long to make the detailed forecast horizon. When the competitive equilibrium assumption is used, the answer is whatever time is required for the firm's returns on incremental investment projects to reach that equilibrium – an issue that turns on the sustainability of the firm's competitive advantage. As indicated in Chapter 6, historical evidence indicates that most firms in Europe should expect ROEs to revert to normal levels within five to ten years. But for the typical firm, we can justify ending the forecast horizon even earlier – note that the return on *incremental* investment can be normal even while the return on *total* investment (and therefore ROE) remains abnormal. Thus a five- to ten-year forecast horizon should be more than sufficient for most firms. Exceptions would include firms so well insulated from competition (perhaps due to the power of a brand name) that they can extend their investment base to new markets for many years and still expect to generate supernormal returns. In 2006 U.S.-based coffee company Starbucks was still extending its brand name to untapped markets, and appears to be such a firm.

Estimates of Porsche's terminal value

Choosing terminal year   In the case of Porsche, the terminal year used is ten years beyond the current one. Table 8.3 shows that the ROE (and operating ROA) is forecasted to decline only gradually over these ten years, from the unusually high 23.4 percent in 2006 to 14.3 percent by 2015. At this level the company will earn an abnormal return on equity of 5.9 percent, since its cost of equity is estimated to be 8.3 percent.

If NOPAT margins could be maintained at the projected 7.0 percent on ever-increasing sales, this abnormal ROE could be achieved even on new investment in 2016 and beyond. Only a substantial decline in the NOPAT margin to about 4.5 percent would, in the face of continued sales growth, be enough to cause the return on the *incremental* investment to be very close to the cost of capital. Thus the performance we have projected for the terminal year 2015 is still far removed from a competitive equilibrium, and the choice for a terminal year is far from arbitrary.

Based on a strong belief in Porsche's continued competitive advantage, we could decide to fix the terminal year for Porsche as 2015 and attempt to estimate its terminal value at that time. Given Porsche's significantly large abnormal earnings in 2015, it would then be prudent to assume that Porsche's maintains its competitive advantage on a sales base that remains constant in real terms. Alternatively, we could extend the forecast horizon by a few more years, hold sales growth constant at 7.5 percent, but let Porsche's NOPAT margin gradually decline to 4.5 percent in 2020. In the terminal year, Porsche's abnormal earnings would then approach zero and we could introduce the competitive equilibrium assumption.

Terminal value under varying assumptions   Table 8.5 shows Porsche's terminal value under three scenarios. Scenario 1 of this table shows the terminal value if we assume that Porsche will continue to grow its sales at 7.5 percent beyond fiscal year 2015, and that it will continue to earn the same level of abnormal returns as in 2015 (that is, we assume that all the other forecasting assumptions will be the same as in 2015). Under this scenario, terminal values in the abnormal earnings model (TV_{AE}), the abnormal earnings growth model (TV_{AEG}), and the free cash flow model (TV_{FCF}) are as follows:

$$TV_{AE} = \frac{1.075 \times AE_{2015}}{(.083 - .075) \times (1.075)^{10}}$$

$$TV_{AEG} = \frac{075 \times AE_{2015}}{.083 \times (.083 - .075) \times (1.075)^{9}}$$

$$TV_{FCF} = \frac{1.075 \times FCFE_{2015}}{(.083 - .075) \times (1.075)^{10}}$$

where AE_{2015} and $FCFE_{2015}$ are expected abnormal earnings and free cash flow to equity for fiscal 2015, respectively.

Scenario 2 shows the terminal value if we assume that Porsche will grow at a lower rate, closer to the expected German inflation rate, at 2 percent in 2016 and beyond, but will maintain its competitive advantage and therefore its level of abnormal returns in 2015 forever. Scenario 3 shows the terminal value if we extend the forecast horizon to 2020, assume that the company will grow at 7.5 percent from 2016 to 2020, and will not have any significant abnormal returns in 2021 and beyond. In this third scenario, the terminal values are as follows:

$$TV_{AE} = 0$$

$$TV_{AEG} = -1 \times \frac{AE_{2020}}{.083 \times (1.075)^{15}}$$

$$TV_{FCF} = \frac{BVE_{2020}}{(1.075)^{15}}$$

where BVE_{2020} is Porsche's end-of-year book value of equity in fiscal 2020.

TABLE 8.5 Valuation summary for Porsche under varying scenarios*

Scenario 1	Beginning book value	Value from forecasts for 2006–2015	Value from forecasts beyond 2016 (terminal value)	Total value	Value per share (€)
Equity value (€ millions)					
Abnormal earnings	3,412.1	3,424.3	26,766.1	33,602.5	1,920.14
Abnormal ROE	3,412.1	3,424.3	26,766.1	33,602.5	1,920.14
Abnormal earnings growth	N.A.	9,236.3	24,366.2	33,602.5	1,920.14
Free cash flows to equity	N.A.	3,276.8	30,325.7	33,602.5	1,920.14
Asset value (€ millions)					
Abnormal NOPAT	4,159.3	3,084.3	89,040.4	96,283.9	N.A.
Abnormal ROA	4,159.3	3,084.3	89,040.4	96,283.9	N.A.
Abnormal NOPAT growth	N.A.	9,394.9	86,889.1	96,283.9	N.A.
Free cash flows to capital	N.A.	2,656.6	93,627.3	96,283.9	N.A.

Scenario 2	Beginning book value	Value from forecasts for 2006–2015	Value from forecasts beyond 2016 (terminal value)	Total value	Value per share (€)
Equity value (€ millions)					
Abnormal earnings	3,412.1	3,424.3	3,225.0	10,061.4	574.94
Abnormal ROE	3,412.1	3,424.3	3,225.0	10,061.4	574.94
Abnormal earnings growth	N.A.	9,236.3	825.1	10,061.4	574.94
Free cash flows to equity	N.A.	3,459.0	6,602.5	10,061.4	574.94
Asset value (€ millions)					
Abnormal NOPAT	4,159.3	3,084.3	2,964.4	10,207.9	N.A.
Abnormal ROA	4,159.3	3,084.3	2,964.4	10,207.9	N.A.
Abnormal NOPAT growth	N.A.	9,394.9	813.0	10,207.9	N.A.
Free cash flows to capital	N.A.	2,891.3	7,316.6	10,207.9	N.A.

(continued)

TABLE 8.5 Valuation summary for Porsche under varying scenarios* *(continued)*

Scenario 3	Beginning book value	Value from forecasts for 2006–2020	Value from forecasts beyond 2021 (terminal value)	Total value	Value per share (€)
Equity value (€ millions)					
Abnormal earnings	3,412.1	3,910.9	0.0	7,323.1	418.25
Abnormal ROE	3,412.1	3,910.9	0.0	7,323.1	418.25
Abnormal earnings growth	N.A.	7,697.2	−374.1	7,323.1	418.25
Free cash flows to equity	N.A.	3,893.0	3,430.1	7,323.1	418.25
Asset value (€ millions)					
Abnormal NOPAT	4,159.3	3,382.0	0.0	7,541.3	N.A.
Abnormal ROA	4,159.3	3,382.0	0.0	7,541.3	N.A.
Abnormal NOPAT growth	N.A.	7,401.7	139.6	7,541.3	N.A.
Free cash flows to capital	N.A.	2,996.8	4,544.5	7,541.3	N.A.

*Scenario 1: Sales growth of 7.5% in 2015 and beyond; constant NOPAT/Sales. Scenario 2: Sales growth of 2% in 2015 and beyond; constant NOPAT/Sales. Scenario 3: Extension of the forecast horizon to 2020; Sales growth of 7.5% and gradually declining NOPAT/Sales (from 7.0% to 4.5%) between 2016 and 2020; no abnormal earnings in 2021 and beyond.

COMPUTING ESTIMATED VALUES

Table 8.5 shows the estimated value of Porsche's assets and equity, each using four different methods. Value of assets is estimated using abnormal operating ROA, abnormal NOPAT, abnormal NOPAT growth, and free cash flows to debt and equity. Value of equity is estimated using operating ROE, abnormal earnings, abnormal earnings growth, and free cash flow to equity. These values are computed using the financial forecasts in Table 8.4 and the terminal value forecasts under different scenarios we discussed earlier.

Note that the cash flow forecasts in Table 8.4 are based on scenario 1 for 2016. When we change these assumptions, the cash flow forecasts for 2015 change. Therefore the present values of cash flows for years 2006 to 2015 also vary across the three scenarios.

In Table 8.5, present values of abnormal NOPAT (growth) and free cash flow to capital are computed using a WACC of 7.7 percent; present values of abnormal earnings (growth) and free cash flow to equity are computed using a cost of equity of 8.3 percent. Note that under the abnormal earnings (NOPAT) growth valuation approach, abnormal earnings (NOPAT) growth values in year t are multiplied by the corresponding discount factors in year $t-1$. To calculate the present values of abnormal operating ROA and abnormal ROE, the values for each year are first multiplied by the corresponding growth factor, as shown in the formulae in Chapter 7, and then they are discounted using a WACC of 7.7 percent and cost of equity of 8.3 percent.

Value estimates presented in each scenario show that the abnormal returns method, abnormal earnings method, abnormal earnings growth method, and the free cash flow method result in the same value, as claimed in Chapter 7. Note also that

Porsche's terminal value represents a significantly larger fraction of the total value of assets and equity under the free cash flow method relative to the other methods. As discussed in Chapter 7, this is due to the fact that the abnormal returns and earnings methods rely on a company's book value of assets and equity, so the terminal value estimates are estimates of incremental values over book values. Similarly, under the abnormal earnings growth method, the terminal value estimates reflect only the changes in abnormal earnings that are expected to occur beyond the terminal year. In contrast, the free cash flow approach ignores the book values, so the terminal value forecasts are estimates of total value during this period.

The primary calculations in the above estimates treat all flows as if they arrive at the end of the year. Of course, they are likely to arrive throughout the year. If we assume for the sake of simplicity that cash flows will arrive mid-year, then we should adjust our value estimates upward by the amount $\left[1 + \left(\frac{r}{2} \right) \right]$, where r is the discount rate.

Value estimates versus market values

As the discussion above shows, valuation involves a substantial number of assumptions by analysts. Therefore the estimates of value will vary from one analyst to another. The only way to ensure that one's estimates are reliable is to make sure that the assumptions are grounded in the economics of the business being valued. It is also useful to check the assumptions against the time-series trends for performance ratios discussed in Chapter 6. For example in the case of Porsche, the assumptions of scenario 1 are highly optimistic and likely to be disconnected from business reality. While it is quite legitimate for an analyst to make assumptions that differ markedly from normal time-series trends in any given case, it is important for the analyst to be able to articulate the business and strategy reasons for making such assumptions.

When a company being valued is publicly traded, it is possible to compare one's own estimated value with the market value of a company. When an estimated value differs substantially from a company's market value, it is useful for the analyst to understand why such differences arise. A way to do this is to redo the valuation exercise and figure out what valuation assumptions are needed to arrive at the observed stock price. One can then examine whether the market's assumptions are more or less valid relative to one's own assumptions. As we discuss in the next chapter, such an analysis can be invaluable in using valuation to make buy or sell decisions in the security analysis context.

For example in the case of Porsche, our estimated values of the firm's equity under scenarios 2 and 3 are significantly smaller than the observed value at the beginning of fiscal 2006. Our estimated value per share under the most optimistic terminal value assumptions (scenario 2) was about €575 per share, while the company's stock price at that time was €654. Clearly the market was making more optimistic assumptions than our own under these two scenarios. The differences in the two sets of assumptions might be related to growth rates, NOPAT margins, asset turns, or discount rates (primarily due to differences in assumed equity risk premium or capital structure). One could run different scenarios regarding each of these variables and test the sensitivity of the estimated value to these assumptions.

Other practical issues in valuation

The above discussion provides a blueprint for doing valuation. In practice, the analyst has to deal with a number of other issues that have an important effect on the valuation task. We discuss below three frequently encountered complications – accounting distortions, negative book values, and excess cash.

Dealing with accounting distortions

We know from the discussion in Chapter 7 that accounting methods per se should have no influence on firm value (except as those choices influence the analyst's view of future real performance). Yet the abnormal returns and earnings valuation approaches used here are based on numbers – earnings and book value – that vary with accounting method choices. How, then, can the valuation approach deliver correct estimates?

Because accounting choices must affect both earnings *and* book value, and because of the self-correcting nature of double-entry bookkeeping (all "distortions" of accounting must ultimately reverse), estimated values will not be affected by accounting choices, *as long as the analyst recognizes the accounting distortions.*[7] As an example, let's assume that managers are aggressive in their accounting choices, choosing to provide for a lower allowance for doubtful accounts even though they have information to the contrary, thus causing the current period's abnormal earnings and the ending book value to be higher by €100. For the time being, let's say the accounting choice has no influence on the analyst's view of the firm's real performance. That is, the analyst is assumed to recognize that management's current estimate of future customer defaults is artificially lower and can make accurate forecasts of future defaults.

Our accounting-based valuation approach starts with the current period's abnormal earnings, which are €100 higher as a result of the accounting choice. However, the choice also causes future abnormal earnings to be lower for two reasons. First, future earnings will be lower (by €100) in a later period, when the customer actually defaults on the payments and receivables will have to be written off. Second, in the meantime the benchmark for normal earnings, the book value of equity, will be higher by €100. Let's say the trade receivables are not written off until two years after the current period. Then assuming a discount rate of 13 percent and the impact of the current aggressive accounting, the subsequent write-down on our calculation of value is as follows:

	Euro impact	Present value
Increase in current abnormal earnings (and book value)	€100	€100.00
Decrease in abnormal earnings of year 1, due to higher book value (.13 × €100)	−13	÷ 1.13 = −11.50
Decrease in abnormal earnings of year 2, due to higher book value (.13 × €100)	−13	
due to lower earnings from trade receivables write-off	−100	
	−113	÷ 1.13² = −88.50
Impact of accounting choice on present value		€0.00

The impact of the higher current abnormal earnings and the lower future abnormal earnings offset exactly, leaving no impact of the current underestimation of the allowance for doubtful accounts on estimated firm value.

The above discussion makes it appear as if the analyst would be indifferent to the accounting methods used. There is an important reason why this is not necessarily true. When a company uses "biased" accounting – either conservative or aggressive – the analyst is forced to expend resources doing accounting analyses of the sort described in Chapter 3. These additional analysis costs are avoided for firms with unbiased accounting.

If a thorough analysis is not performed, a firm's accounting choices can, in general, influence analysts' perceptions of the real performance of the firm and hence the forecasts of future performance. In the above example, the managers' allowance and receivables estimates, if taken at face value, will influence the analyst's forecasts of future earnings and cash flows. If so, the accounting choice per se would affect expectations of future earnings and cash flows in ways beyond those considered above. The estimated value of the firm would presumably be higher – but it would still be the same regardless of whether the valuation is based on DCF or discounted abnormal earnings.[8]

An analyst who encounters biased accounting has two choices – either to adjust current earnings and book values to eliminate managers' accounting biases, or to recognize these biases and adjust future forecasts accordingly. Both approaches lead to the same estimated firm value. For example, in the above illustration a simple way to deal with managers' underestimation of current default allowance is to increase the allowance and to decrease the current period's abnormal earnings by €100. Alternatively, as shown above, the analyst could forecast the write-off two periods from now. Which of the two approaches is followed will have an important impact on what fraction of the firm's value is captured within the forecast horizon, and what remains in the terminal value.

Holding forecasting horizon and future growth opportunities constant, higher accounting quality allows a higher fraction of a firm's value to be captured by the current book value, earnings, and the abnormal earnings within the forecasting horizon. Accounting can be of low quality either because it is unreliable or because it is extremely conservative. If accounting reliability is a concern, the analyst has to expend resources on "accounting adjustments." If accounting is conservative, the analyst is forced to increase the forecasting horizon to capture a given fraction of a firm's value, or to rely on relatively more uncertain terminal values estimates for a large fraction of the estimated value.

Dealing with negative book values

A number of firms have negative earnings and book values of book equity. Firms in the start-up phase have negative equity, as do those in high technology industries. These firms incur large investments whose payoff is uncertain. Accountants write off these investments as a matter of conservatism, leading to negative book equity. Examples of firms in this situation include biotechnology firms, internet firms, telecommunication firms, and other high technology firms. A second category of firms with negative book equity are those that are performing poorly, resulting in cumulative losses exceeding the original investment by the shareholders.

Negative book equity and negative earnings make it difficult to use the accounting-based approach to value a firm's equity. There are several possible ways to get around this problem. The first approach is to value the firm's assets (using, for example, abnormal operating ROA or abnormal NOPAT) rather than equity. Then, based on an estimate of the value of the firm's debt, one can estimate the equity value. Another alternative is to "undo" accountants' conservatism by capitalizing the investment expenditures written off. This is possible if the analyst is able to establish that these expenditures are value creating. A third alternative, feasible for publicly traded firms, is to start from the observed share price and work backwards. Using reasonable estimates of cost of equity and steady-state growth rate, the analyst can calculate the average long-term level of abnormal earnings or abnormal earnings growth needed to justify the observed share price. Then the analytical task can be framed in terms of examining the feasibility of achieving this abnormal earnings (growth) "target."

It is important to note that the value of firms with negative book equity often consists of a significant option value. For example, the value of high tech firms is not only driven by the expected earnings from their current technologies but also the payoff from technology options embedded in their research and development efforts. Similarly, the value of troubled companies is driven to some extent by the "abandonment option" – shareholders with limited liability can put the firm to debt holders and creditors. One can use the options theory framework to estimate the value of these "real options."[9]

Dealing with excess cash and excess cash flow

Firms with excess cash balances, or large free cash flows, also pose a valuation challenge. In our projections in Table 8.2, we implicitly assumed that cash beyond the level required to finance a company's operations will be paid out to the firm's shareholders. Excess cashflows are assumed to be paid out to shareholders either in the form of dividends or stock repurchases. Notice that these cash flows are already incorporated into the valuation process when they are earned, so there is no need to take them into account when they are paid out.

It is important to recognize that both the accounting-based valuations and the discounted cash flow valuation assume a dividend payout that can potentially vary from period to period. This dividend policy assumption is required as long as one wishes to assume a constant level of financial leverage, a constant cost of equity, and a constant level of weighted average cost of capital used in the valuation calculations. As discussed in a later chapter, firms rarely have such a variable dividend policy in practice. However, this in itself does not make the valuation approaches invalid, as long as a firm's dividend policy does not affect its value. That is, the valuation approaches assume that the well known Modigliani-Miller theorem regarding the irrelevance of dividends holds.

A firm's dividend policy can affect its value if managers do not invest free cash flows optimally. For example, if a firm's managers are likely to use excess cash to undertake value-destroying acquisitions, then our approach overestimates the firm's value. If the analyst has these types of concerns about a firm, one approach is to first estimate the firm according to the approach described earlier and then adjust the estimated value for whatever agency costs the firm's managers may impose on its investors. One approach to evaluating whether or not a firm suffers from severe agency costs is to examine how effective its corporate governance processes are.

SUMMARY

We illustrate in this chapter how to apply the valuation theory discussed in Chapter 7. The chapter explains the set of business and financial assumptions one needs to make to conduct the valuation exercise. It also illustrates the mechanics of making detailed valuation forecasts and terminal values of earnings, free cash flows, and accounting rates of return. We also discuss how to compute cost of equity and the weighted average cost of capital. Using a detailed example, we show how a firm's equity values and asset values can be computed using earnings, cash flows, and rates of return. Finally, we offer ways to deal with some commonly encountered practical issues, including accounting distortions, negative book values, and excess cash balances.

DISCUSSION QUESTIONS

1. A spreadsheet containing Porsche's actual and forecasted financial statements as well as the valuation described in this chapter is available on the companion website of this book. How will the forecasts in Table 8.3 for Porsche change if the assumed growth rate in sales from 2006 to 2015 remains at 5 percent (and all the other assumptions are kept unchanged)?

2. Recalculate the forecasts in Table 8.3 assuming that the NOPAT profit margin declines by 0.7 percentage points per year between fiscal 2006 and 2015 (keeping all the other assumptions unchanged).

3. Recalculate the forecasts in Table 8.4 assuming that the ratio of net operating working capital to sales is 10 percent, and the ratio of net long-term assets to sales is 65 percent for all the years from fiscal 2006 to fiscal 2015. Keep all the other assumptions unchanged.

4. Calculate Porsche's cash payouts to its shareholders in the years 2006–2015 that are implicitly assumed in the projections in Table 8.3.

5. How will the abnormal earnings calculations in Table 8.4 change if the cost of equity assumption is changed to 10 percent?

6. How will the terminal values in Table 8.5 change if the sales growth in years 2016 and beyond is 5 percent, and the company keeps forever its abnormal returns at the same level as in fiscal 2015 (keeping all the other assumptions in the table unchanged)?

7. Calculate the proportion of terminal values to total estimated values of equity under the abnormal earnings method, the abnormal earnings growth method, and the discounted cash flow method. Why are these proportions different?

8. Under the competitive equilibrium assumption the terminal value in the discounted cash flow model is the present value of the end-of-year book value of equity in the terminal year. Explain.

9. Under the competitive equilibrium assumption the terminal value in the discounted abnormal earnings growth model is the present value of abnormal earnings in the terminal year times minus one, capitalized at the cost of equity. Explain.

10. What will be Porsche's cost of equity if the equity market risk premium is 6 percent?

11. Assume that Porsche changes its capital structure so that its market value weight of debt to capital increases to 30 percent, and its after-tax interest rate on debt at this new leverage level is 4 percent. Assume that the equity market risk premium is 7 percent. What will be the cost of equity at the new debt level? What will be the weighted average cost of capital?

12. Nancy Smith says she is uncomfortable making the assumption that Porsche's dividend payout will vary from year to year. If she makes a constant dividend payout assumption, what changes does she have to make in her other valuation assumptions to make them internally consistent with each other?

NOTES

1. One way to estimate systematic risk is to regress the firm's stock returns over some recent time period against the returns on the market index. The slope coefficient represents an estimate of β. More fundamentally, systematic risk depends on how sensitive the firm's operating profits are to shifts in economy-wide activity, and the firm's degree of leverage. Financial analysis that assesses these operating and financial risks should be useful in arriving at reasonable estimates of β.

2. See T. Copeland, T. Koller, and J. Murrin, *Valuation: Measuring and Managing the Value of Companies*, 2nd edition (New York: John Wiley & Sons, 1994). Theory calls for the use of a short-term rate, but if that rate is used here, a difficult practical question arises: how does one reflect the premium required for expected inflation over long horizons? While the premium could, in principle, be treated as a portion of the term $[E(r_m) - r_f]$, it is probably easier to use an intermediate- or long-term riskless rate that presumably reflects expected inflation.

3. The average return reported here is the arithmetic mean as opposed to the geometric mean. Ibbotson and Associates explain why this estimate is appropriate in this context (see *Stocks, Bonds, Bills, and Inflation*, 2002 Yearbook, Chicago). This estimate of the worldwide equity risk premium comes from E. Dimson, P. Marsh, and M. Staunton, "Global Evidence on the Equity Risk Premium," *Journal of Applied Corporate Finance* 15, No. 4 (2003): 8–19.

4. E. Dimson, P. Marsh, and M. Staunton (2003), op. cit., argue that when estimating future equity risk premiums, it is preferred to take a global approach than a country-by country approach. Reasons for taking a global approach are, for example, that many country-specific events that affected historical risk premiums are nonrecurring and that worldwide capital markets have integrated significantly. In their study "International Differences in the Cost of Equity Capital: Do Legal Institutions and Securities Matter," *Journal of Accounting Research* 44, No. 3 (2006): 485–531, L. Hail and C. Leuz provide evidence that international differences in the strictness of disclosure and securities regulation and enforcement also create international differences in firms' cost of equity. Harmonization of such regulations within, for example, the European Union may therefore also reduce the country variations in risk premiums.

5. See William R. Gebhardt, Charles M. C. Lee, and Bhaskaran Swaminathan,"Toward an Ex-Ante Cost of Capital," *Journal of Accounting Research* 39 (2001): 135–176; and James Claus and Jacob Thomas, "Equity Premia as Low as Three Percent? Evidence from Analysts' Earnings Forecasts for Domestic and International Stock Markets," *The Journal of Finance* 56 (October 2001): 1629–1666.

6. We estimated Porsche's equity beta by regressing the company's monthly stock returns on the monthly returns of the German market index during a period of 60 months prior to August 2006. A spreadsheet with Porsche's monthly returns and monthly market returns is available on the book's companion website.

7. Valuation based on discounted abnormal earnings does require one property of the forecasts: that they be consistent with "clean surplus accounting." Such accounting requires the following relation:

End-of-period book value =
Beginning book value + earnings – dividends ± capital contributions/withdrawals

Clean surplus accounting rules out situations where some gain or loss is excluded from earnings but is still used to adjust the book value of equity. For example, under IFRS, gains and losses on foreign currency translations are handled this way. In applying the valuation technique described here, the analyst would need to deviate from IFRS in producing forecasts and treat such gains/losses as a part of earnings. However, the technique does *not* require that clean surplus accounting has been applied *in the past* – so the existing book value, based on IFRS or any other set of principles, can still serve as the starting point. All the analyst needs to do is apply clean surplus accounting in his/her forecasts. That much is not only easy but is usually the natural thing to do anyway.

8. It is important to recognize that when the analyst uses the "indirect" cash flow forecasting method, undetected accounting biases can influence not only future earnings forecasts but also future free cash flow forecasts. In the current example, since accounts receivables are overstated, the analyst will assume that they will be collected as cash in some future period, leading to a higher future cash flow estimate.

9. If negative earnings are likely to be transitory, this may be a reason to extend the forecast horizon. P. Joos and G. Plesko find that the probability of losses being transitory is negatively related to the size of the loss and positively related to the size of the firm, sales growth, whether or not the loss is the first loss, and whether or not the firm pays out dividends. If a loss is likely to be permanent, the value of the firm is driven by the value of the abandonment option. See P. Joos and G. Plesko, "Valuing Loss Firms," *The Accounting Review* 80 (2005): 847–870.

Ryanair Holdings plc

R yanair is a low-cost, low-fare airline headquartered in Dublin, Ireland, operating over 200 routes in 20 countries. The company has directly challenged the largest airlines in Europe and has built a 20+ year track record of incredibly strong passenger growth while progressively reducing fares. It is not unusual for one-way tickets (exclusive of taxes) to sell on Ryanair's Web site for less than €1.00. See Exhibit 1 for an excerpt of Ryanair's Web site, where fares between London and Stockholm, for example, are available for 19 pence (approximately US$0.33). CEO Michael O'Leary describes the airline as follows: "Ryanair is doing in the airline industry in Europe what Ikea has done. We pile it high and sell it cheap. ... For years flying has been the preserve of rich [people]. Now everyone can afford to fly."[1,2] Having created profitable operations in the difficult airline industry, industry analysts and Ryanair itself have likened the airline to its U.S. counterpart, Southwest Airlines, and the common stock has attracted the attention of investors in Europe and abroad.

Low-fare airlines

Historically the airline industry has been a notoriously difficult business in which to make consistent profits. Over the past several decades, low-fare airlines have been launched in an attempt to operate with lower costs, but with few exceptions, most have gone bankrupt or been swallowed up by larger carriers (see Exhibit 2 for a list of failed airlines). Given the excess capacity in the global aircraft market in more recent years, barriers to entry in the commercial airline space have never been so low. Price competition in the U.S. and Europe, along with rising fuel costs, has had a deleterious affect on both profits and margins at most carriers. The current state of the industry can be described for most carriers as, at best, tumultuous.

The introduction of the low-fare sector in the United States predated its arrival in Europe. An open skies policy was introduced through the Airline Deregulation Act of 1978, which removed controls of routes, fares, and schedules from the control of the Civil Aeronautics Board.[3] This spurred 22 new airlines to be formed between 1978 and 1982, each hoping to stake their claim in the newly deregulated market.[4] These airlines maximized their scheduling efficiencies, which, in combination with lower staff-to-plane ratios and a more straightforward service offering, gave them a huge cost advantage over the big airlines. This led to the current two-tier industry structure, with the low-fare airlines waging fare wars with the larger established carriers.

Professor Mark T. Bradshaw prepared this case with the assistance of Fergal Naugton and Jonathan O'Grady (MBAs 2005). This case was prepared from published sources. HBS cases are developed solely as the basis for class discussion. Cases are not intended to serve as endorsements, sources of primary data, or illustrations of effective or ineffective management. Copyright © 2005 President and Fellows of Harvard College. HBS Case 9–106–003.

1. G. Bowley, "How Low Can You Go?" FT.com Web site, June 20, 2003.
2. Ibid.
3. U.S. Centennial of Flight Commission report, www.centennialofflight.gov/essay/Commercial_Aviation/Dereg/Tran8.htm.
4. N. Donohue and P. Ghemawat, "The US Airline Industry, 1978–1988 (A)," HBS No. 390-025.

This was, however, a challenging time for the new startups. First, the Federal Reserve raised the Funds Rate from 7.93% in 1978 to 12.26% in 1982. This had a dramatic effect on the financing costs for the start-up airlines, making financing of capital expenditures excessively costly. In addition, at this time the incumbent airlines were generally in relatively strong financial positions. Their deep pockets made it possible for them to run at a loss on certain routes in order to undercut the start-ups where necessary. As a result, many of the new companies failed.

One notable exception however was Southwest Airlines. By focusing on secondary airports, lightening-fast turnarounds, information technology, and a strong firm culture, they managed to gain passenger share and profitability. Within a decade, ticket prices in the U.S. had fallen by 33% and the volume of passengers had more than doubled.[5]

It was not until 1992, with the signing of the Maastricht Treaty, that years of protectionism by the governments of the so-called "flag" carriers began to be dismantled. In 1993, European Union (EU) national carriers were for the first time permitted to offer international services from other EU countries. By 1997, this was broadened to include domestic destinations and opened to any certified EU airline. Open skies had arrived in Europe.

Even before then, start-up airlines had begun to enter the European space. These companies would typically negotiate with their country's flag carrier for the right to fly to secondary airports only. Ticket sales were handled by agents and the resulting cost structure forced the start-ups to compete with the incumbents primarily on service. Because they were not competing to provide traffic for the major hubs, but rather targeting customers who had not previously considered flights for travel, they were in effect growing the size of the market, and were thus not seen as a major threat to the legacy carriers. However, with the signing of the Maastricht Treaty, the number of new airlines entering the industry greatly increased and these start-ups were now free to compete solely on cost, looking across the Atlantic to the Southwest Model.

Subsequently, as the new entrants vied for market space, prices fell, encouraging previously untapped demand. European passenger volumes had a strong upward trajectory (+5% CAGR between 1998 and 2003). However, while low-cost passenger numbers soared, the long-haul operators reduced traffic and higher fuel costs due to events like the SARS virus and September 11th attacks. The flag carriers, which were now financially constrained, were forced to renegotiate, and even cancel, contracts for the delivery of new aircraft from Airbus and Boeing. The two aerospace giants were left with significant numbers of planes needing to be delivered, for which the start-ups proved to be welcome customers.

Unlike the arrangements between legacy carriers and major airports, start-up airlines negotiated dramatically lower landing and facility charges with secondary airports. They argued that because they were bringing a significant number of passengers through these airports on a regular basis, the airports would be able to substantially increase the rents they received from concession stands and other retailers. As the low-fare airlines had no particular loyalty to one airport over another, the threat that they could simply stop flying to a particular airport was real.

Ryanair

Ryanair was Europe's first low-fare carrier, with an initial route between Waterford, Ireland and London. Initial cabin crew had to be no taller than 5' 2" because the

---

5. *"Freedom in the Air,"* The Economist, *April 3, 1997.*

aircraft being deployed were among the smallest being flown on commercial routes. The company immediately challenged incumbents, Aer Lingus and British Airways, and obtained approval for a Dublin-London (Luton) route, charging less than half of what the large carriers were charging. A price war ensued, but over the next decade Ryanair eventually overtook Aer Lingus and British Airways on this route, the largest international route in Europe at that time.[6] See Exhibit 3 for Ryanair's remarkable passenger growth from 1985 through 2004.

The company went public on May 9, 1997, and shortly thereafter was voted "Airline of the Year" by the Irish Air Transport Users Committee, "Best Managed National Airline" in the world by International Aviation Week magazine, "Best Value Airline" by the U.K. "Which" Consumer Magazine, and most popular airline on the web by Google. Relative to other airlines, Ryanair's common stock has performed reasonably well since going public, despite negative events like the Iraq war and significant increases in fuel prices.

See Exhibit 4 for the stock price performance of Ryanair and selected European airlines since Ryanair's initial public offering. Additionally, see Exhibit 5 for Ryanair's 2004 financial statements. These financial statements are prepared under Irish and U.K. accounting standards. Because the company has shares trading on the Nasdaq in the U.S., they also provide a reconciliation of major line items from Irish and U.K. accounting standards to U.S. accounting standards (see Exhibit 6).

Ryanair's objectives, as set forth in their annual report, include:

- Increasing passenger traffic by 20% each year;
- Reducing fares by 5% each year;
- Reducing costs by 5% each year; and
- Realizing a profit margin of 20% or more.

To date, there are numerous factors that have contributed to the company's profitability, including the following.

1. *Cut-price deals.* Ryanair will frequently sell a large number of seats in advance for a nominal fee, e.g. €1.00 or less. This attracts immense publicity as customers scramble to log in and purchase seats. For each seat purchased, tax and duties must also be paid. These can amount to €30–40. The tickets are sold on a non-refundable basis. Because they are so cheap, many buy multiple seats to gain flexibility. The "no show" rate is therefore much higher for these types of tickets. Ryanair only owes the tax and duty if the customer actually completes a flight. The average revenue per ticket is therefore not, say €1, but closer to the average of non-discounted ticket prices.

2. *Fly point-to-point.* Each route is a mini-business unit. Capacity is tailored to fit demand according to computer simulated models. If a route is unprofitable, it can simply be cut from the schedule. Passengers may not buy connecting flights, so must check-in for each Ryanair flight individually. This reduces the firm's liability in the event of a delay and reduces instances of lost baggage.

3. *Fly to secondary airports.* By avoiding the large hubs, Ryanair is able to negotiate reduced landing charges. There is the added benefit of lower congestion at such airports. This allows the aircraft to complete the journey in the shortest possible time. The downside to passengers is that sometimes these airports are located in

---

6. *Company Web site.*

locations far from the intended destination. For example, the company flies to Frankfurt-Hahn, not Frankfurt which is 100 km away. As O'Leary states, "For the price-sensitive customers, distance is no problem."[7]

4. *Quick turn-around*. Ryanair aircraft are expected to land and take off again from an airport inside 25 minutes. This is only possible because they fly into secondary airports. This allows the firm to maximize the number of flights per day.

5. *No over-nighting of staff*. By flying point-to-point, a Ryanair plane ends the day where it started. This means that crew can return to their homes and expensive hotel bills and per diems are avoided.

6. *Internet bookings*. The firm sells 97% of its tickets via the internet. This cuts out travel agent commission costs (averaging approximately 10% of the ticket cost) and gives the airline maximum control over scheduling and capacity. Mr. O'Leary is not bashful about this substantial source of cost savings, having stated, "Screw the travel agent. Take the [agents] out and shoot them. What have they done for passengers over the years?"[8]

7. *One class*. Ryanair does not offer passengers the choice of business and economy class, eliminating the requirement for food to be delivered to the aircraft when it lands, thus facilitating low turnaround times. Moreover, offering only one class of service furthers the goal of providing low fares, which the company believes is the ultimate in customer service. According to their Passenger Service and Lowest Fares Charter, "Ryanair believes that any passenger service commitment must involve a commitment on pricing and punctuality, and should not be confined to less important aspects of 'service' which is the usual excuse the high fare airlines use for charging high air fares."[9]

8. *One aircraft type*. The company flies Boeing 737 planes exclusively. This reduces maintenance training costs and allows for bulk buying of spare parts. The strong financial position of the company allowed it to purchase many of the aircraft that had been canceled by incumbent airlines. These new airplanes are more fuel efficient and have a higher passenger capacity.

9. *Personnel costs and incentives*. Because the aircraft that Ryanair pilots fly are new, the firm claims that their pilots' experience is of value to the competition. Therefore, it charges pilots for training, the cost of which is earned back by the pilots through years of service. Pilots have financial incentives for smooth landings, not so much for passenger comfort but for reduced maintenance costs. Additionally, the airline does not provide food or beverages for free, but does offer items for sale on each flight. Flight attendants are paid a commission based on the total of beverage and other sales in flight.

Ryanair has an entrepreneurial culture and takes great pride in breaking with old conventions. This spirit is disseminated from the top by the swashbuckling manner of CEO, Michael O'Leary. Irish business folklore has it that when he first decided to employ the internet to sell seats, O'Leary did not hire a firm of IT consultants and web-designers. He instead visited a local technical college and offered the project as a challenge to the eager students in the computer lab. They learned by doing, and

7. G. Bowley, *"How Low Can You Go?"*
8. Ibid.
9. Company Web site.

O'Leary got a Web site with the necessary functionality at a fraction of list price. He is also known for wild publicity stunts, such as driving a tank to easyJet's headquarters in England and broadcasting the theme to the television show The A-Team. He taunts the competition even with the painting of aircraft. One of Ryanair's airplanes is painted with the message, "Arriverderci Alitalia."[10]

Mr. O'Leary is not bashful of his company's achievements. He positions himself as a champion against inefficiencies and monopolies, while his manner has been described as arrogant and dismissive. Even in financial reports for investors, he often leads off with tirades against airports that charge too much or other issues that adversely affect Ryanair. For example, the 2005 road show included several slides titled "Stansted Airport: The Rip-Off," which highlighted costs of a cross-subsidization plan across airports run by the British Airport Authority.

Similarly, in discussing 2005 financial results, the company report stated "In Ireland, the situation at Dublin Airport has descended into a farce. The Dublin Airport Authority which is responsible for this third world facility is to be rewarded for its incompetence by being allowed to build the second terminal. This facility will not be available until 2009 at the earliest and in the mean time passengers at Dublin will be forced to endure long queues and intolerable overcrowding while the Government protects this failed monopoly by blocking competition. ... The [Prime Minister] recently demonstrated how hopelessly out of touch he is by claiming that the present overcrowded terminal has the capacity for 6 million more passengers per annum. It would appear that there aren't any queues at the VIP escort to the Government jet ... Had the Government heeded Ryanair's calls for a competing second terminal seven years ago, this current embarrassment for Irish tourism would have been avoided. As always in Ireland the ordinary passengers suffer, while the politicians fudge."[11]

Turbulence in 2004

Just after reporting third quarter profit increases of 10% (quarter ended December 31, 2003), Ryanair issued a profit warning in January 2004 for the company's upcoming full-year results for the fiscal year ending March 31, 2004. CEO Michael O'Leary stated, "While we now expect after tax profits for the current year to dip slightly, our annualized profit margin will still be in excess of 20% and Ryanair will continue to be the world's most profitable airline by margin." Ryanair's share price dropped 30% on the news (see Exhibit 7). The expected fall in profits for the fourth quarter was attributed to lower yields (i.e., average passenger fares) and lower load factors (i.e., seats with paying passengers as a fraction of total seats available). According to Mr. O'Leary, the lower yields are due to Ryanair's strategy of steadily lowering fares as part of its battle plan. He argues, "This is not due to overcapacity. It's the result of the ongoing fare wars under way across Europe, and we're winning them. It's like Southwest in the U.S. When they first went into California, their stock price fell by 40% to 50% due to fare wars with the likes of the United [Airlines] shuttle and other California carriers. Ten years later, Southwest owned California."[12]

More bad news followed immediately after the profit warning, when Ryanair received an unfavorable ruling from the European Commission (EC) regarding $18 million in financial incentives it had received from Charleroi airport in Belgium

10. G. Bowley, "How Low Can You Go?"
11. Company press release, May 31, 2005.
12. "Airing Ryanair's Beef with the EC," Business Week Online, February 16, 2004.

between 2001 and 2003. The Commissioners indicated that the ruling was an attempt to encourage economic growth while simultaneously ending state subsidies that have been declared illegal under the European Union. The ruling put additional pressure on Ryanair's stock price. In response, Mr. O'Leary explained "Any share price jumps up and down, and ours is no exception. But as long as the basic business model is sound and you're executing it properly, nothing will stop you – certainly not a bunch of EU commissioners who think everyone should pay higher fares."[13]

Financial performance

Prior to the profit warnings in early 2004, Ryanair had been profitable every quarter and reported annual increases in sales, operating profit, and net income in every year (see Exhibit 8). As forewarned in January 2004, despite an increase in sales for fiscal 2004, net income declined for the fiscal year ended March 31, 2004 relative to the fiscal 2003 level. This was the first reported year-over-year downturn in profits since going public.

Nevertheless, Ryanair continued to add capacity in 2004, increasing available seat kilometers by 64%. The overall load factor for 2004 exceeded 80%, relative to a break-even level of 59%. The company's fleet of planes have 189 seats, implying that on average, 111 seats must be filled to break even. Ryanair has the lowest cost structure of any comparable airline, as seen in Exhibit 9. Low-costs permit Ryanair to charge lower fares and still provide a high return on investment. See Exhibit 10 for average revenue per passenger, return on equity (ROE), and other financial metrics for fifteen airlines. Ryanair's average revenue per passenger (in $US) is just $49. The only other airlines with similar low fares include U.K.-based easyJet ($US 77 per passenger) and Southwest Airlines ($US 89). Nearly half of the airlines listed (all U.S.-based incumbent carriers) report losses and/or have meaningless ROE because the denominator of the calculation (i.e., book value of equity) is negative. For 2004, Ryanair reports the highest ROE, 17%. The only other airline with profitability approaching that of Ryanair is Japan Airlines, but the du Pont decomposition of ROE indicates that this is largely driven by Japan Airlines' use of significant leverage, relative to limited leverage at Ryanair. Even with the relatively strong profitability, the stock market values Ryanair at a just modest level relative to other airlines, trading at a P/E of 20.8 relative to 50.5 for newcomer JetBlue Airways and 40.7 for veteran low-fare airline Southwest.

Valuation

Following the series of bad news announcements in early 2004, the investor community split into two camps: those that saw the downturn in profits and cash flows as the end of Ryanair's strong performance run versus those that believed the stock price drop as an overreaction to a company that retained strong fundamentals. Exhibit 11 provides an analysis of Ryanair's profitability and operating, investment, and financing activities over the most recent three years. The overall picture is that of a financially healthy company with strong sales growth, high profitability, and negative net debt (i.e., interest bearing liabilities < cash and liquid resources).

Exhibit 12 summarizes equity analyst reports released during the first six months of 2004, which encompasses the profit warnings in January, the EU decision in February, and the announcement of earnings in June. The recommendations span the range from

---

13. BusinessWeek Online, *op. cit.*

Sell recommendations with target prices below the current trading price (e.g., target price of €4.40 when the current stock price was €4.65), to Buy recommendations with target prices at lofty levels up to 35% above current trading price (e.g., target price of €6.00 when the current stock price was €4.41). Standard earnings based valuations also provide disparate conclusions, depending on assumptions. Exhibit 13 provides just five scenarios, simplified to consider strong vs. slowing sales growth and controllable vs. increasing fuel/other costs. The resulting valuation estimates range from well below current trading price (€3.05) to well above (€7.57).

Clearly, the discrepancies in valuations reflect divergent opinions on numerous issues that plague the airline sector, such as fare competition, cost containment, regulation, and macroeconomic vulnerability. Perhaps not surprisingly, in contrast to many market observers in the airline industry, Ryanair continues to have a bullish outlook, signing purchase agreements for an additional 140 Boeing 737 aircraft in February 2005. Each aircraft will have an approximate cost of US$51 million. With the addition of these aircraft to the 91 in service already, the company expects to grow annual passenger traffic to 70 million by 2012, almost triple the number in 2004.

Ryanair

EXHIBIT 1   Ryanair web site excerpt

Fly from London (Stansted)
Fares are exclusive of taxes fees & charges which do not exceed £14.00

	from		from		from
Stockholm (NYQ)	£0.19	Knock	£0.99	Szczecin NEW	£3.19
Pescara	£0.19	Berlin (Schonefeld)	£1.19	Bydgoszcz NEW	£3.19
Karlsruhe-Baden	£0.19	Palermo	£1.19	Rzeszöw NEW	£3.19
Haugesund	£0.19	Ancona	£1.19	Gdańsk NEW	£3.19
Gothenburg	£0.19	Venice (Treviso)	£1.19	Biarritz	£3.19
Poitiers	£0.19	Santiago De Comp.	£1.19	Santander (Bilbao)	£3.19
Nimes	£0.19	Almeria	£1.19	Limoges	£3.19
Newquay	£0.19	Bologna (Forli)	£1.19	Valladolid	£3.19

Source: www.ryanair.com, July 8, 2005.

EXHIBIT 2   Failed airlines in the U.S. and Europe

U.S.	People's Express	**Italy**	Volare
	Frontier Airlines		Agent Air
	Texas Air		Air Freedom
	New York Air		Free Airways
			Windjet
Great Britain	Duo		
	Now	**Poland**	Air Polonia
			DreamAir
Ireland	Fresh Aer		GetJet
	JetMagic		Silesian Air
	JetGreen		White Eagle
	Skynet		
		Finland	Flying Finn
Germany	Berlinjet		
	Low Fare Jet	**Norway**	Goodjet
	V-Bird		
		Bosnia	Air Bosnia
France	Aeris		
	Air Littoral	**Spain**	Air Cataluyna
	Airlib Express		
	Fly Eco		

Source: Merrion Stockbrokers Irish Equity Research report, January 21, 2005.

Ryanair

EXHIBIT 3 **Annual Ryanair passenger traffic (number of passengers), 1985–2004**

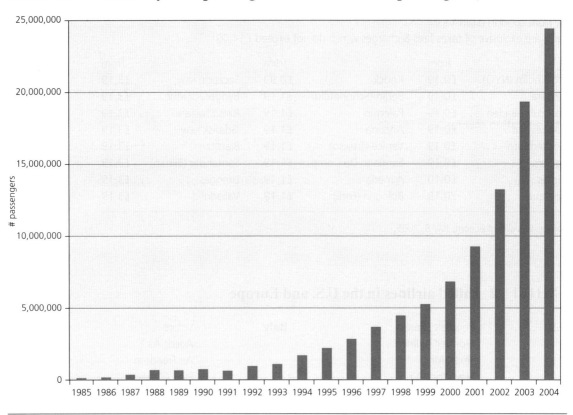

Source: Ryanair investor relations Web site.

EXHIBIT 4 **Relative stock price performance of selected European and U.S. airlines: 1997–2003**

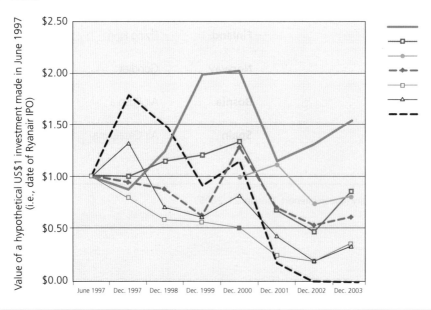

Source: Standard & Poor's Compustat Global database.

EXHIBIT 5 **Financial statements**

Consolidated profit and loss account (all amounts in € 000)

	2004	**2003**	**2002**
Operating			
Scheduled revenues	924,566	731,951	550,991
Ancillary revenues	149,658	110,557	73,059
Total operating revenue – continuing operations	1,074,224	842,508	624,050
Operating expenses			
Staff costs	(123,624)	(93,073)	(78,240)
Depreciation and amortization	(101,391)	(76,865)	(59,010)
Other operating expenses	(597,922)	(409,096)	(323,867)
Total operating expenses excluding goodwill	(822,937)	(579,034)	(461,117)
Operating profit – continuing operations before amortization of goodwill	251,287	263,474	162,933
Amortization of goodwill	(2,342)	—	—
Operating profit – continuing operations after amortization of goodwill	248,945	263,474	162,933
Other (expenses)/income			
Foreign exchange gains	3,217	628	975
(Loss) on disposal of fixed assets	(9)	(29)	527
Interest receivable and similar income	23,891	31,363	27,548
Interest payable and similar charges	(47,564)	(30,886)	(19,609)
Total other (expenses)/income	(20,465)	1,076	9,441
Profit on ordinary activities before tax	228,480	264,550	172,374
Tax on profit on ordinary activities	(21,869)	(25,152)	(21,999)
Profit for the financial year	206,611	239,398	150,375

Ryanair

Consolidated balance sheet (all amounts in € 000)

	2004	2003
Fixed assets		
Intangible assets	44,499	0
Tangible assets	1,576,526	1,352,361
Total fixed assets	1,621,025	1,352,361
Current assets		
Cash and liquid resources	1,257,350	1,060,218
Accounts receivable	14,932	14,970
Other assets	19,251	16,370
Inventories	26,440	22,788
Total current assets	1,317,973	1,114,346
Total assets	2,938,998	2,466,707
Current liabilities		
Accounts payable	67,936	61,604
Accrued expenses and other liabilities	338,208	251,328
Current maturities of long term debt	80,337	63,291
Short term borrowings	345	1,316
Total current liabilities	486,826	377,539
Other liabilities		
Provisions for liabilities and charges	94,192	67,833
Accounts payable due after one year	30,047	5,673
Long term debt	872,645	773,934
Total other liabilities	996,884	847,440
Shareholders' funds-equity		
Called-up share capital	9,643	9,588
Share premium account	560,406	553,512
Profit and loss account	885,239	678,628
Total shareholders' funds-equity	1,455,288	1,241,728
Total liabilities and shareholders' funds	2,938,998	2,466,707

Ryanair

Consolidated cash flow statement (all amounts in € 000)

	2004	2003	2002
Net cash inflow from operating activities	462,062	351,003	309,109
Return on investments and servicing of finance			
Interest received	26,292	30,171	30,193
Interest paid	(46,605)	(29,563)	(19,833)
Net cash (outflow)/inflow from return on investments and servicing of finance	(20,313)	608	10,360
Taxation			
Corporation tax paid	(2,056)	(3,410)	(5,071)
Capital expenditure			
Purchase of tangible fixed assets	(331,603)	(469,878)	(372,587)
Sale of tangible fixed assets	4	31	563
Net cash (outflow) from capital expenditure	(331,599)	(469,847)	(372,024)
Acquisitions			
Purchase consideration	(20,795)	—	—
Onerous lease payments	(11,901)	—	—
Net cash (outflow) from acquisition of subsidiary undertakings	(32,696)	—	—
Net cash inflow/(outflow) before financing and management of liquid resources	75,398	(121,646)	(57,626)
Financing			
Loans raised	187,035	331,502	175,746
Loans repaid	(71,278)	(44,779)	(27,886)
Issue of share capital	6,948	56	188,331
Share issue costs	—	—	(6,330)
Capital element of finance leases	—	(1)	(107)
Net cash inflow from financing	122,705	286,778	329,754
Management of liquid resources			
(Increase) in liquid resources	(249,220)	(166,329)	(251,241)
Net cash (outflow)/inflow from financing and management of liquid resources	(126,515)	120,449	78,513
Increase (decrease) in cash	(51,117)	(1,197)	20,887

Ryanair

Consolidated statement of changes in shareholders' funds-equity (all amounts in € 000)

	Called-up share capital	Share premium account	Profit and loss account	Total
Balance at March 31, 2002	9,587	553,457	439,230	1,002,274
Issue of ordinary equity shares (net of issue costs)	1	55	—	56
Profit for the financial year	—	—	239,398	239,398
Balance at March 31, 2003	9,588	553,512	678,628	1,241,728
Issue of ordinary equity shares	55	6,894	—	6,949
Profit for the financial year	—	—	206,611	206,611
Balance at March 31, 2004	9,643	560,406	885,239	1,455,288

Source: 2004 and 2003 Ryanair Annual Reports.

EXHIBIT 6 **Summary of differences between Irish/United Kingdom and U.S. GAAP (€ 000)**

	2004	2003	2002
Profit for financial year as reported in the consolidated profit and loss account and in accordance with Irish and U.K. GAAP	206,611	239,398	150,375
Adjustments			
Pensions	89	697	751
Derivative financial instruments (net of tax)	—	(4,189)	—
Amortization of goodwill	2,342	—	—
Employment grants	—	469	464
Capitalized interest regarding aircraft acquisition programme	7,213	5,262	5,027
Darley Investments Limited	88	88	88
Taxation – effect of above adjustments	(913)	85	(1,156)
Net income in accordance with U.S. GAAP	215,430	241,810	155,549
Total assets as reported in the consolidated balance sheets and in accordance with Irish and U.K. GAAP	2,938,998	2,466,707	1,889,572
Adjustments			
Pensions	3,200	3,111	2,414
Amortization of goodwill	2,342	—	—
Capitalized interest regarding aircraft acquisition programme	17,502	10,289	5,027
Darley Investments Limited	(151)	(239)	(327)
Total assets as adjusted to accord with U.S. GAAP	2,961,891	2,479,868	1,896,686
Shareholders' equity as reported in the consolidated balance sheets and in accordance with Irish and U.K. GAAP	1,455,288	1,241,728	1,002,274
Adjustments			
Pension	3,200	3,111	2,414
Amortization of goodwill	2,342	—	—
Employment grants	—	—	(469)
Capitalized interest regarding aircraft acquisition programme	17,502	10,289	5,027
Darley Investments Limited	(151)	(239)	(327)
Minimum pension liability (net of tax)	(2,631)	(2,656)	—
Unrealized (losses) on derivative financial instruments (net of tax)	(116,681)	(73,371)	12,448
Tax effect of adjustments (excluding pension and derivative adjustments)	(2,588)	(1,675)	(1,760)
Shareholders' equity as adjusted to accord with U.S. GAAP	1,356,281	1,177,187	1,019,607

Source: 2004 and 2003 Ryanair Annual Reports.

Ryanair

EXHIBIT 7 **Ryanair stock price: January–June 2004**

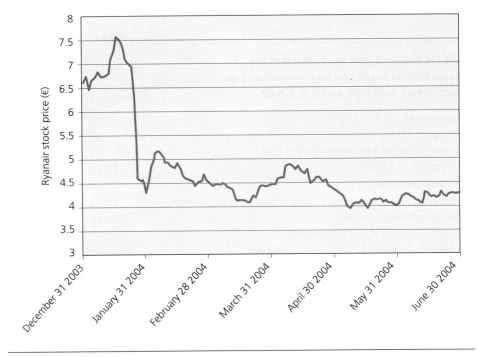

Source: Center for Research on Security Prices database.

EXHIBIT 8 **Ryanair financial performance 1997–2004 (€ 000)**

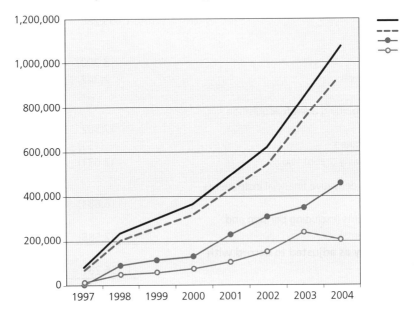

Source: Thomson Financial.

EXHIBIT 9 **Comparison of costs per available seat kilometer for various airlines**

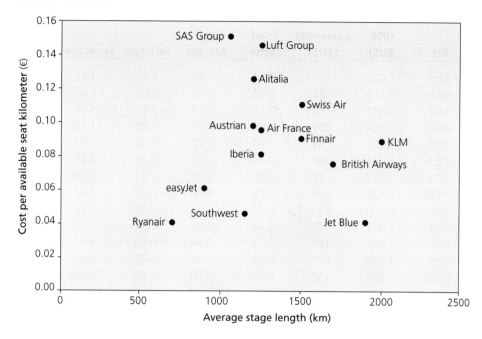

Source: Davy Stockbroker report on Ryanair, February 16, 2004.

EXHIBIT 10   **Financial and operating metrics for selected airlines**

	P/E	Market value (000 $US)	Average revenue/ passenger ($US)	Load factor	Margin	Turnover	Leverage	ROE
JetBlue Airways	50.5	2,420	104	0.83	0.04	0.45	3.70	0.06
Southwest Airlines	40.7	1,278	89	0.69	0.05	0.58	2.05	0.06
British Airways	24.2	5,501	330	0.73	0.03	0.67	4.60	0.10
Japan Airlines	24.2	6,752	201	0.64	0.01	0.98	11.10	0.15
Ryanair	20.8	4,273	49	0.74	0.20	0.44	1.99	0.17
Lufthansa	13.1	6,564	280	0.74	0.02	0.86	4.55	0.09
easyJet	12.4	917	77	0.85	0.04	0.82	1.68	0.05
Qantas Airways	9.8	4,526	208	0.78	0.06	0.62	3.02	0.11
Singapore Airlines	9.6	8,000	540	0.73	0.12	0.54	1.76	0.11
SAS	n.m.	1,486	137	0.64	−0.03	0.91	5.16	−0.15
American Airlines	n.m.	1,765	185	0.75	−0.04	0.65	n.m.	n.m.
Delta Air Lines	n.m.	1,046	125	0.75	−0.35	0.69	n.m.	n.m.
Northwest Airlines	n.m.	952	152	0.80	−0.08	0.80	n.m.	n.m.
United Airlines	n.m.	151	176	0.79	−0.10	0.79	n.m.	n.m.
US Airways	n.m.	60	151	0.76	−0.09	0.85	n.m.	n.m.

n.m. = not meaningful
Load factor = Revenue passenger miles (or kilometers)/Available seat miles (or kilometers)
Margin = Net income/Sales
Turnover = Sales/Total assets
Leverage = Total assets/Stockholders' equity

Sources: Jane's World Airlines, Company Annual Reports.

EXHIBIT 11 **Ratio analysis, 2002–2004**

DECOMPOSING PROFITABILITY: DUPONT ALTERNATIVE

	2002	2003	2004
Net operating profit after taxes (NOPAT)/Sales	0.230	0.284	0.212
× Sales/Net assets	1.384	1.278	1.053
= Operating return on assets (ROA)	0.318	0.363	0.224
Financial spread[a]	0.286	0.361	0.320
× Net financial leverage[b]	−0.327	−0.342	−0.179
= Financial leverage gain	−0.094	−0.124	−0.057
Return on equity (ROE = Operating ROA + Spread * Net financial leverage)	0.224	0.239	0.166

EVALUATING OPERATING MANAGEMENT

	2002	2003	2004
Key growth rates:			
Annual sales growth	28.0%	35.0%	27.5%
Annual net income growth	43.9%	59.2%	−13.7%
Key profitability ratios:			
Sales/Sales	1.000	1.000	1.000
Cost of sales/Sales	0.739	0.687	0.766
Gross margin	0.261	0.313	0.234
Investment income/Sales	0.000	0.000	0.000
Other income, net of Other expense/sales	0.002	0.001	0.001
Minority interest/Sales	0.000	0.000	0.000
EBIT margin	0.263	0.313	0.235
Net interest expense (Income)/Sales	−0.013	−0.001	0.022
Pre-tax income margin	0.276	0.314	0.213
Taxes/Sales	0.035	0.030	0.020
Unusual gains, net of Unusual losses (after tax)/Sales	0.000	0.000	0.000
Net income margin	0.241	0.284	0.192
EBITDA margin	0.263	0.433	0.371
NOPAT margin	0.230	0.284	0.212
Recurring NOPAT margin	0.228	0.283	0.212

Ryanair

EVALUATING INVESTMENT MANAGEMENT

	2002	2003	2004
Working capital management:			
Operating working capital/Sales	−0.212	−0.268	−0.241
Operating working capital turnover	−4.710	−3.738	−4.151
Accounts receivable turnover	71.771	81.551	71.758
Inventory turnover	28.865	33.812	36.113
Accounts payable turnover	15.372	12.378	13.358
Days' receivables	5.086	4.476	5.087
Days' inventory	12.645	10.795	10.107
Days' payables	23.745	29.488	27.323
Long-term asset management:			
Net long-term assets turnover	1.069	0.953	0.840
Net long-term assets/Sales	0.935	1.050	1.190
PP&E turnover	1.017	0.885	0.794
Depreciation & amortization/Sales	0.000	0.119	0.136

EVALUATING FINANCIAL MANAGEMENT

	2002	2003	2004
Short-term liquidity:			
Current ratio	3.278	3.043	2.952
Quick ratio	3.138	2.951	2.848
Cash ratio	3.095	2.918	2.808
Operating cash flow ratio	0.708	1.123	1.204
Debt and long-term solvency:			
Liabilities-to-equity	0.907	0.885	0.987
Debt-to-equity	0.609	0.555	0.675
Net-debt-to-equity	−0.327	−0.342	−0.179
Debt-to-capital	0.378	0.357	0.403
Net-debt-to-net capital	−0.485	−0.521	−0.217
Interest coverage ratio	9.791	9.565	5.804
Dividend payout ratio	0.000	0.000	0.000
Sustainable growth rate	0.224	0.239	0.166

a. Operating ROA – Effective after-tax interest rate.
b. Net debt/Net equity, where Net debt = Interest bearing liabilities – Cash and marketable equity securities.

Source: Ryanair Annual Reports.

Ryanair

EXHIBIT 12 **Equity analyst reports on Ryanair, January–June 2004**

Report date	Equity research firm	Report title	Recommendation	Price	Target price
				(€ per share, except where noted)	
28-Jan-04	ABN Amro	The Emperor Falls Off His Throne	Sell	4.75	5.15
29-Jan-04	UBS	More Questions Than Answers	Reduce2 (Sell)	4.72	6.25
29-Jan-04	BNP/Paribas	Reach for the Alka-Selzer? Buy Instead	Outperform	4.75	6.10
2-Feb-04	UBS	Business Model Under the Microscope	Reduce2 (Sell)	4.87	4.50
3-Feb-04	Deutsche Bank	Stop Talking and Do Your Business – Upgrade to Buy	Buy	4.66	5.70
3-Feb-04	Smith Barney Citigroup	Talk of Its Demise is Greatly Exaggerated	Hold (2)	4.95	5.50
4-Feb-04	BNP/Paribas	No Lasting Damage (But a Slap on the Wrist!)	Outperform	4.95	6.10
4-Feb-04	ABN Amro	Imperial Lather	Reduce	4.66	4.40
4-Feb-04	Raymond James	EU Decision Announced	Market Perform	$35.75	—
5-Feb-04	NCB Group	Commission Ruling Will Not Derail the Model	Buy	—	6.00
11-Feb-04	CSFB	Profits Shock	Underperform	5.20	4.42
12-Feb-04	Raymond James	Raising Rating to Outperform	Outperform	$37.68	$45.00
3-Mar-04	NCB Group	All to Play For in March	Buy	4.84	6.00
9-Mar-04	Raymond James	February Traffic Results; Establishing FY05 Quarterly Estimates	Outperform 2	$34.28	$40.00
6-Apr-04	ABN Amro	Yields Set to Improve	Add	4.97	5.50
3-May-04	NCB Group	It Isn't Broken – It's Just More Visibly Seasonal	Buy	4.80	6.00
6-May-04	Panmure Gordon	easyJet and Ryanair Passenger Growth and Load Factors	Hold	4.45	5.00
21-May-04	UBS	Full Year Results – June 1st	Reduce 2 (Sell)	4.65	4.40
21-May-04	CSFB	FY Results Preview	Underperform	4.55	4.42
25-May-04	Deutsche Bank	FY 03/04 Results Preview	Buy	4.53	5.70
27-May-04	Smith Barney Citigroup	FY04 Results Expectations – Outlook Uncertain	Hold (2)	4.39	5.50
1-Jun-04	Deutsche Bank	Good Results but Competition Remains Tough	Buy	4.38	5.70
1-Jun-04	Smith Barney Citigroup	Results in Line, Outlook Slightly Better	Hold (2)	4.38	5.50
1-Jun-04	William deBroe	Ryanair Results	Sell	4.45	—
2-Jun-04	ABN Amro	Walking a tightrope	Add	4.38	5.00
2-Jun-04	NCB Group	No Major Surprises – Forecasts Creep Up on Stronger Summer Trading	Buy	4.41	6.00
3-Jun-04	CSFB	Challenging Outlook	Underperform	4.41	4.42

Ryanair

Source: Investext.

Ryanair

EXHIBIT 13 **Ryanair valuations under various assumptions**

	2004 actual	Scenario #1	Scenario #2	Scenario #3	Scenario #4	Scenario #5
Description:	—	Slowing sales growth; increasing fuel/other costs	Slowing sales growth; controllable fuel/other costs	Strong sales growth; increasing fuel/othercosts	Moderate sales growth; controllable fuel/other costs	Strong sales growth; controllable fuel/other costs
Forecast horizon:	—	5 years	5 years	5 years	5 years	5 years
Forecast horizon assumptions:						
Annual sales growth rate	27.5%	20%, fading to 9%	20%, fading to 9%	25%, fading to 12%	25%, fading to 10%	25%, fading to 12%
Net operating profits after tax/Sales	21.2%	20%, fading to 15%	20.0%	20%, fading to 15%	21%, fading to 18%	21%, fading to 18%
Terminal value assumptions:						
Sales growth rate	—	7.0%	7.0%	9.0%	8.5%	9.0%
Net operating profits after tax/Sales	—	15.0%	17.5%	15.0%	17.0%	17.0%
Market risk premium	—	6%	6%	6%	6%	6%
Risk free rate	—	4.5%	4.5%	4.5%	4.5%	4.5%
Tax rate	—	10%	10%	10%	10%	10%
Cost of debt	—	2%	2%	2%	2%	2%
Common equity beta	—	1	1	1	1	1
Valuation per share (March 31, 2004)	**€ 4.65**	**€ 3.05**	**€ 4.50**	**€ 4.56**	**€ 6.14**	**€ 7.57**

Source: Casewriter calculations.

BUSINESS ANALYSIS AND VALUATION APPLICATIONS

Equity Security Analysis

Equity security analysis is the evaluation of a firm and its prospects from the perspective of a current or potential investor in the firm's shares. Security analysis is one step in a larger investment process that involves (1) establishing the objectives of the investor, (2) forming expectations about the future returns and risks of individual securities, and then (3) combining individual securities into portfolios to maximize progress toward the investment objectives.

Security analysis is the foundation for the second step, projecting future returns and assessing risk. Security analysis is typically conducted with an eye toward identification of mispriced securities in hopes of generating returns that more than compensate the investor for risk. However, that need not be the case. For analysts who do not have a comparative advantage in identifying mispriced securities, the focus should be on gaining an appreciation for how a security would affect the risk of a given portfolio, and whether it fits the profile that the portfolio is designed to maintain.

Security analysis is undertaken by individual investors, by analysts at brokerage houses (sell-side analysts), and by analysts that work at the direction of fund managers for various institutions (buy-side analysts). The institutions employing buy-side analysts include collective investment funds, pension funds, insurance companies, universities, and others.

A variety of questions are dealt with in security analysis:

- A sell-side analyst asks: How do my forecasts compare to those of the analysts' consensus? Is the observed market price consistent with that consensus? Given my expectations for the firm, does this security appear to be mispriced? Should I recommend this security as a buy, a sell, or a hold?

- A buy-side analyst for a "value share fund" asks: Does this security possess the characteristics we seek in our fund? That is, does it have a relatively low ratio of price to earnings, low price-to-book value, and other fundamental indicators? Do its prospects for earnings improvement suggest good potential for high future returns on the security?

- An individual investor asks: Does this security offer the risk profile that suits my investment objectives? Does it enhance my ability to diversify the risk of my portfolio? Is the firm's dividend payout rate low enough to help shield me from taxes while I continue to hold the security?

As the above questions underscore, there is more to security analysis than estimating the value of equity securities. Nevertheless, for most sell-side and buy-side analysts, the key goal remains the identification of mispriced securities.

INVESTOR OBJECTIVES

The investment objectives of individual savers in the economy are highly idiosyncratic. For any given saver they depend on such factors as income, age, wealth, tolerance for risk, and tax status. For example, savers with many years until retirement are likely to prefer to have a relatively large share of their portfolio invested in equities, which offer a higher expected return but high short-term variability. Investors in high tax brackets are likely to prefer to have a large share of their portfolio in shares that generate tax-deferred capital gains rather than shares that pay dividends or interest-bearing securities.

Collective investment funds (mutual funds, unit trusts, OEICs, SICAVs, or BEVEKs as they are termed in some countries) have become popular investment vehicles for savers to achieve their investment objectives.[1] Collective investment funds sell shares in professionally managed portfolios that invest in specific types of equity and/or fixed income securities. They therefore provide a low-cost way for savers to invest in a portfolio of securities that reflects their particular appetite for risk.

The major classes of collective investment funds include (1) money market funds that invest in commercial paper, certificates of deposit, and treasury bills, (2) bond funds that invest in debt instruments, (3) equity funds that invest in equity securities, (4) balanced funds that hold money market, bond, and equity securities, and (5) real estate funds that invest in commercial real estate. Within the bond and equities classes of funds, however, there are wide ranges of fund types. For example, bond funds include:

- *Corporate bond funds* that invest in investment-grade rated corporate debt instruments.[2]
- *Government bond funds* that invest in government debt instruments.
- *High yield funds* that invest in non-investment-grade rated corporate debt.
- *Mortgage funds* that invest in mortgage-backed securities.

Equity funds include:

- *Income funds* that invest in equities that are expected to generate dividend income.
- *Growth funds* that invest in equities expected to generate long-term capital gains.
- *Income and growth funds* that invest in equities that provide a balance of dividend income and capital gains.
- *Value funds* that invest in equities that are considered to be undervalued.
- *Short funds* that sell short equity securities that are considered to be overvalued.
- *Index funds* that invest in equities that track a particular market index, such as the MSCI World Index or the DJ Euro Stoxx 50.
- *Sector funds* that invest in equities in a particular industry segment, such as the technology or health sciences sectors.
- *Regional funds* that invest in equities from a particular country or geographic region, such as Japan, the Asia-Pacific region, or the U.S.

The focus of this chapter is on analysis for equity securities.

EQUITY SECURITY ANALYSIS AND MARKET EFFICIENCY

How a security analyst should invest his or her time depends on how quickly and efficiently information flows through markets and becomes reflected in security prices. In the extreme, information would be reflected in security prices fully and immediately upon its release. This is essentially the condition posited by the *efficient markets hypothesis*. This hypothesis states that security prices reflect all available information, as if such information could be costlessly digested and translated immediately into demands for buys or sells without regard to frictions imposed by transactions costs. Under such conditions, it would be impossible to identify mispriced securities on the basis of public information.

In a world of efficient markets, the expected return on any equity security is just enough to compensate investors for the unavoidable risk the security involves. Unavoidable risk is that which cannot be "diversified away" simply by holding a portfolio of many securities. Given efficient markets, the investor's strategy shifts away from the search for mispriced securities and focuses instead on maintaining a well-diversified portfolio. Aside from this, the investor must arrive at the desired balance between risky securities and short-term government bonds. The desired balance depends on how much risk the investor is willing to bear for a given increase in expected returns.

The above discussion implies that investors who accept that share prices already reflect available information have no need for analysis involving a search for mispriced securities. If all investors adopted this attitude, of course no such analysis would be conducted, mispricing would go uncorrected, and markets would no longer be efficient![3] This is why the efficient markets hypothesis cannot represent an equilibrium in a strict sense. In equilibrium there must be just enough mispricing to provide incentives for the investment of resources in security analysis.

The existence of some mispricing, even in equilibrium, does not imply that it is sensible for just anyone to engage in security analysis. Instead, it suggests that securities analysis is subject to the same laws of supply and demand faced in all other competitive industries: it will be rewarding only for those with the strongest comparative advantage. How many analysts are in that category depends on a number of factors, including the liquidity of a firm's shares and investor interest in the company.[4] For example, there are about 45 sell-side professional analysts who follow British Petroleum, a company with highly liquid shares and considerable investor interest. There are many other buy-side analysts who track the firm on their own account without issuing any formal reports to outsiders. For the smallest publicly traded firms in Europe, there is typically no formal following by analysts, and would-be investors and their advisors are left to themselves to conduct securities analysis.

Market efficiency and the role of financial statement analysis

The degree of market efficiency that arises from competition among analysts and other market agents is an empirical issue addressed by a large body of research spanning the last three decades. Such research has important implications for the role of financial statements in security analysis. Consider for example the implications of an extremely efficient market, where information is fully impounded in prices within minutes of its revelation. In such a market, agents could profit from digesting financial statement information in two ways. First, the information would be useful to the select few who receive newly announced financial data, interpret it quickly, and trade on it within minutes. Second, and probably more important, the information would be useful for gaining an understanding of the firm, so as to place the analyst in a better position to interpret other news (from financial statements as well as other sources) as it arrives.

On the other hand, if securities prices fail to reflect financial statement data fully, even days or months after its public revelation, there is a third way in which market agents could profit from such data. That is to create trading strategies designed to exploit any systematic ways in which the publicly available data are ignored or discounted in the price-setting process.

Market efficiency and managers' financial reporting strategies

The degree to which markets are efficient also has implications for managers' approaches to communicating with their investment communities. The issue becomes most important when the firm pursues an unusual strategy, or when the usual interpretation of financial statements would be misleading in the firm's context. In such a case, the communication avenues managers can successfully pursue depend not only on management's credibility, but also on the degree of understanding present in the investment community. We will return to the issue of management communications in more detail in Chapter 13.

Evidence of market efficiency

There is an abundance of evidence consistent with a high degree of efficiency in securities markets.[5] In fact, during the 1960s and 1970s, the evidence was so one-sided that the efficient markets hypothesis gained widespread acceptance within the academic community and had a major impact on the practicing community as well.

Evidence pointing to very efficient securities markets comes in several forms:

- When information is announced publicly, the markets react *very* quickly.
- It is difficult to identify specific funds or analysts who have consistently generated abnormally high returns.
- A number of studies suggest that share prices reflect a rather sophisticated level of fundamental analysis.

While a large body of evidence consistent with efficiency exists, recent years have witnessed a re-examination of the once widely accepted thinking. A sampling of the research includes the following:

- On the issue of the speed of share price response to news, a number of studies suggest that even though prices react quickly, the initial reaction tends to be incomplete.[6]
- A number of studies point to trading strategies that could have been used to outperform market averages.[7]
- Some related evidence – still subject to ongoing debate about its proper interpretation – suggests that, even though market prices reflect some relatively sophisticated analyses, prices still do not fully reflect all the information that could be garnered from publicly available financial statements.[8]

The controversy over the efficiency of securities markets is unlikely to end soon. However, there are some lessons that are accepted by most researchers. First, securities markets not only reflect publicly available information, they also anticipate much of it before it is released. The open question is what fraction of the response remains to be impounded in price once the day of the public release comes to a close. Second, even in most studies that suggest inefficiency, the degree of mispricing is relatively small for large firms.

Finally, even if some of the evidence is currently difficult to align with the efficient markets hypothesis, it remains a useful benchmark (at a minimum) for thinking about the behavior of security prices. The hypothesis will continue to play that role unless it can be replaced by a more complete theory. Some researchers are developing theories that encompass the existence of market agents who are forced to trade for unpredictable "liquidity" reasons, and prices that differ from so-called "fundamental values," even in equilibrium. Also, behavioral finance models recognize that cognitive biases can affect investor behavior.[9]

APPROACHES TO FUND MANAGEMENT AND SECURITIES ANALYSIS

Approaches used in practice to manage funds and analyze securities are quite varied. One dimension of variation is the extent to which the investments are actively or passively managed. Another variation is whether a quantitative or a traditional fundamental approach is used. Security analysts also vary considerably in terms of whether they produce formal or informal valuations of the firm.

Active versus passive management

Active portfolio management relies heavily on security analysis to identify mispriced securities. The passive portfolio manager serves as a price taker, avoiding the costs of security analysis and turnover while typically seeking to hold a portfolio designed to match some overall market index or sector performance. Combined approaches are also possible. For example, one may actively manage 20 percent of a fund balance while passively managing the remainder. The growing popularity of passively managed funds in Europe over the past 20 years serves as testimony to many fund managers' belief that earning superior returns is a difficult thing to do.

Quantitative versus traditional fundamental analysis

Actively managed funds must depend on some form of security analysis. Some funds employ "technical analysis," which attempts to predict share price movements on the basis of market indicators (prior share price movements, volume, etc.). In contrast, "fundamental analysis," the primary approach to security analysis, attempts to evaluate the current market price relative to projections of the firm's future earnings and cash flow generating potential. Fundamental analysis involves all the steps described in the previous chapters of this book: business strategy analysis, accounting analysis, financial analysis, and prospective analysis (forecasting and valuation).

In recent years, some analysts have supplemented traditional fundamental analysis, which involves a substantial amount of subjective judgment, with more quantitative approaches. The quantitative approaches themselves are quite varied. Some involve simply "screening" shares on the basis of some set of factors, such as trends in analysts' earnings revisions, price-earnings ratios, price-book ratios, and so on. Whether such approaches are useful depends on the degree of market efficiency relative to the screens.

Quantitative approaches can also involve implementation of some formal model to predict future stock returns. Longstanding statistical techniques such as regression analysis and probit analysis can be used, as can more recently developed computer-intensive techniques such as neural network analysis. Again, the success of these approaches depends on the degree of market efficiency and whether the analysis can exploit information in ways not otherwise available to market agents as a group.

Quantitative approaches play a more important role in security analysis today than they did a decade or two ago. However, by and large, analysts still rely primarily on the kind of fundamental analysis involving complex human judgments, as outlined in our earlier chapters.

Formal versus informal valuation

Full-scale, formal valuations based on the methods described in Chapter 7 have become more common, especially in recent years. However, less formal approaches are also possible. For example, an analyst can compare his or her long-term earnings projection with the consensus forecast to generate a buy or sell recommendation. Alternatively, an analyst might recommend a share because his or her earnings forecast appears relatively high in comparison to the current price. Another possible approach might be labeled "marginalist." This approach involves no attempt to value the firm. The analyst simply assumes that if he or she has unearthed favorable (or unfavorable) information believed not to be recognized by others, the share should be bought (or sold).

Unlike many security analysts, investment bankers produce formal valuations as a matter of course. Investment bankers, who estimate values for purposes of bringing a private firm to the public market, for evaluating a merger or buyout proposal, or for purposes of periodic managerial review, must document their valuation in a way that can readily be communicated to management and, if necessary, to the courts.

THE PROCESS OF A COMPREHENSIVE SECURITY ANALYSIS

Given the variety of approaches practiced in security analysis, it is impossible to summarize all of them here. Instead, we briefly outline steps to be included in a comprehensive security analysis. The amount of attention focused on any given step varies among analysts.

Selection of candidates for analysis

No analyst can effectively investigate more than a small fraction of the securities on a major exchange, and thus some approach to narrowing the focus must be employed. Sell-side analysts are often organized within an investment house by industry or sector. Thus they tend to be constrained in their choices of firms to follow. However, from the perspective of a fund manager or an investment firm as a whole, there is usually the freedom to focus on any firm or sector.

As noted earlier, funds typically specialize in investing in shares with certain risk profiles or characteristics (e.g., growth shares, "value" shares, technology shares, cyclical shares). Managers of these types of funds seek to focus the energies of their analysts on identifying shares that fit their fund objective. In addition, individual investors who seek to maintain a well-diversified portfolio without holding many shares also need information about the nature of a firm's risks.

An alternative approach to security selection is to screen firms on the basis of some hypothesis about mispricing – perhaps with follow-up detailed analysis of shares that meet the specified criteria. For example, one fund managed by a large insurance company screens shares on the basis of recent "earnings momentum," as reflected in revisions in the earnings projections of sell-side and buy-side analysts. Upward revisions trigger investigations for possible purchase. The fund operates on the belief that earnings momentum is a positive signal of future price movements. Another fund complements the earnings momentum screen with one based on recent short-term share price movements, in the hopes of identifying earnings revisions not yet reflected in share prices.

KEY ANALYSIS QUESTIONS

Depending on whether fund managers follow a strategy of targeting equities with specific types of characteristics, or of screening shares that appear to be mispriced, the following types of questions are likely to be useful:

- What is the risk profile of a firm? How volatile is its earnings stream and share price? What are the key possible bad outcomes in the future? What is the upside potential? How closely linked are the firm's risks to the health of the overall economy? Are the risks largely diversifiable, or are they systematic?

- Does the firm possess the characteristics of a growth share? What is the expected pattern of sales and earnings growth for the coming years? Is the firm reinvesting most or all of its earnings?

- Does the firm match the characteristics desired by "income funds"? Is it a mature or maturing company, prepared to "harvest" profits and distribute them in the form of high dividends?

- Is the firm a candidate for a "value fund"? Does it offer measures of earnings, cash flow, and book value that are high relative to the price? What specific screening rules can be implemented to identify misvalued shares?

Inferring market expectations

If the security analysis is conducted with an eye toward the identification of mispricing, it must ultimately involve a comparison of the analyst's expectations with those of "the market." One possibility is to view the observed share price as the reflection of market expectations and to compare the analyst's own estimate of value with that price. However, a share price is only a "summary statistic." It is useful to have a more detailed idea of the market's expectations about a firm's future performance, expressed in terms of sales, earnings, and other measures. For example, assume that an analyst has developed new insights about a firm's near-term sales. Whether those insights represent new information for the stock market, and whether they indicate that a "buy" recommendation is appropriate, can be easily determined if the analyst knows the market consensus sales forecast.

Around the world a number of agencies summarize analysts' forecasts of sales and earnings. Forecasts for the next year or two are commonly available, and for many firms, a "long-run" earnings growth projection is also available – typically for three to five years. Some agencies provide continuous online updates to such data, so if an analyst revises a forecast, that can be made known to fund managers and other analysts within seconds.

As useful as analysts' forecasts of sales and earnings are, they do not represent a complete description of expectations about future performance, and there is no guarantee that consensus analyst forecasts are the same as those reflected in market prices. Further, financial analysts typically forecast performance for only a few years, so that even if these do reflect market expectations, it is helpful to understand what types of long-term forecasts are reflected in share prices. Armed with the models in Chapters 7 and 8 that express price as a function of future cash flows or earnings, an analyst can draw some educated inferences about the expectations embedded in share prices.

For example, consider the valuation of British Petroleum (BP). On March 31, 2006, BP's share price was 661 pence. For the year ended December 31, 2005, the company reported that earnings per share increased from 49 pence the prior year to 63 pence, reflecting the increase of crude oil prices to previously unseen levels. BP's book value of equity per share was 226 pence. By the end of March analysts were forecasting that BP would experience a slowdown in earnings growth in 2006, with earnings projected to grow by 5 percent to 66 pence. Modestly higher growth was projected for following years: 9 percent in 2007 (72 pence) and 8 percent per year for 2008 to 2010.[10] Analysts expected BP to pay out approximately 35 percent of its annual earnings in dividends.

How do consensus forecasts by analysts reconcile with the market valuation of BP? What are the market's implicit assumptions about the short-term and long-term earnings growth for the company? By altering the amounts for key value drivers and arriving at combinations that generate an estimated value equal to the observed market price, the analyst can infer what the market might have been expecting for BP in March 2006. Table 9.1 summarizes the combinations of earnings growth, book value growth, and cost of capital that generate prices comparable to the market price of 661 pence.

BP has an equity beta of 1.2. Given long-term U.K. government bond rates of 4.5 percent and a market risk premium of 5–6 percent, BP's cost of equity capital probably lies between 10.5 and 11.7 percent. In addition, the company's growth in book value has been 4 percent for the last year, which is close to the historical long-term book value growth rate for the economy. Critical questions for judging the market valuation of BP are (1) how quickly will the company's earnings return to the level reported in 2004, and (2) how quickly will earnings growth revert to the same level as average firms in the economy, historically around 4 percent. The analysis reported in Table 9.1 presents three scenarios for BP's earnings growth that are consistent with an observed market price of 661 pence. The three scenarios assume that earnings growth reverts to the economy average after 2010 and that BP's dividend payout ratio between 2006 and 2010 is 35 percent.

Table 9.1 shows the implications for BP's earnings growth between 2008 and 2010 if a reduction in oil prices drives down earnings in 2006 and 2007. This analysis indicates that with an 11.7 percent cost of equity and a rapid return to pre-2005 performance (i.e., 10 percent decline in 2006 and 2007), earnings need to grow by more than 18 percent per year between 2008 and 2010 to justify the 661 pence share price. However, if growth is 5 and 9 percent in 2006 and 2007 respectively, as the consensus predicts,

TABLE 9.1 Alternative assumptions about value drivers for BP consistent with the observed market price of 661 pence

	2006	2007	2008	2009	2010	Implied earnings per share in 2010
Assumed equity cost of capital of 10.5% *Earnings growth:*						
Scenario 1	5.0%	9.0%	−0.3%	−0.3%	−0.3%	71 pence
Scenario 2	−10.0%	−10.0%	11.9%	11.9%	11.9%	72 pence
Scenario 3	2.5%	2.5%	2.5%	2.5%	2.5%	71 pence
Assumed equity cost of capital of 11.7% *Earnings growth:*						
Scenario 1	5.0%	9.0%	5.4%	5.4%	5.4%	84 pence
Scenario 2	−10.0%	−10.0%	18.4%	18.4%	18.4%	85 pence
Scenario 3	6.0%	6.0%	6.0%	6.0%	6.0%	84 pence

expected earnings growth is close to the economy average (of 4 percent) for the next three years. The 661 pence share price is also consistent with a scenario that predicts constant earnings growth of 6.0 percent between 2006 and 2010. The value of BP's equity is computed as in Table 9.2. Because one quarter of the fiscal year has passed on March 31, two adjustments must be made in the analysis. First, the present value factor for the first five years equals $(1 - r_e)^{-(t - 0.25)}$. Second, the book value on March 31 is set equal to the book value on January 1 times $(1 + r_e)^{0.25}$.

TABLE 9.2 Computing the value of BP's equity

Year	Beginning book value	Earnings (6.0% annual growth)	Abnormal earnings (11.7% cost of equity)	PV factor	PV of abnormal earnings
2006	226.0p	66.8p	40.3p	0.9200	37.1p
2007	269.4	70.8	39.3	0.8236	32.3
2008	315.4	75.0	38.1	0.7374	28.1
2009	364.2	79.5	36.9	0.6601	24.4
2010	415.9	84.3	35.7	0.5910	21.1
After 2010			37.1	7.6752	284.6
Cumulative PV of abnormal earnings					427.6
+ Book value on March 31, 2006					232.3
= Equity value per share					659.8p

Unless the analyst has good indications that oil prices will rebound after two years, given BP's 661 pence share price it is unlikely that the market anticipates that earnings will be hit by declining oil prices in 2006 and 2007. BP's share price more likely reflects the expectation that earnings growth will be moderate but stable in future years. This type of scenario analysis provides the analyst with insights about investors' expectations for BP, and is useful for judging whether the share is correctly valued. Security analysis need not involve such a detailed attempt to infer market expectations. However, whether the analysis is made explicit or not, a good analyst understands what economic scenarios could plausibly be reflected in the observed price.

KEY ANALYSIS QUESTIONS

By using the discounted abnormal earnings/ROE valuation model, analysts can infer the market's expectations for a firm's future performance. This permits analysts to ask whether the market is overvaluing or undervaluing a company. Typical questions that analysts might ask from this analysis include the following:

- What are the market's assumptions about long-term ROE and growth? For example, is the market forecasting that the company can grow its earnings without a corresponding level of expansion in its asset base (and hence equity)? If so, how long can this persist?
- How do changes in the cost of capital affect the market's assessment of the firm's future performance? If the market's expectations seem to be unexpectedly high or low, has the market reassessed the company's risk? If so, is this change plausible?

Developing the analyst's expectations

Ultimately, a security analyst must compare his or her own view of a share with the view embedded in the market price. The analyst's own view is generated using the same tools discussed in Chapters 2 through 8: business strategy analysis, accounting analysis, financial analysis, and prospective analysis. The final product of this work is, of course, a forecast of the firm's future earnings and cash flows and an estimate of the firm's value. However, that final product is less important than the understanding of the business and its industry that the analysis provides. It is such understanding that enables the analyst to interpret new information as it arrives and to infer its implications.

KEY ANALYSIS QUESTIONS

In developing expectations about the firm's future performance using the financial analysis tools discussed throughout this book, the analyst is likely to ask the following types of questions:

- How profitable is the firm? In light of industry conditions, the firm's corporate strategy, and its barriers to competition, how sustainable is that rate of profitability?
- What are the opportunities for growth for this firm?

- How risky is this firm? How vulnerable are operations to general economic downturns? How highly levered is the firm? What does the riskiness of the firm imply about its cost of capital?

- How do answers to the above questions compare to the expectations embedded in the observed share price?

The final product of security analysis

For financial analysts, the final product of security analysis is a recommendation to buy, sell, or hold the share (or some more refined ranking). The recommendation is supported by a set of forecasts and a report summarizing the foundation for the recommendation. Analysts' reports often delve into significant detail and include an assessment of a firm's business as well as a line-by-line income statement, balance sheet, and cash flow forecasts for one or more years.

In making a recommendation to buy or sell a share, the analyst has to consider the investment time horizon required to capitalize on the recommendation. Are anticipated improvements in performance likely to be confirmed in the near-term, allowing investors to capitalize quickly on the recommendation? Or do expected performance improvements reflect long-term fundamentals that will take several years to play out? Longer investment horizons impose greater risk on investors that the company's performance will be affected by changes in economic conditions that cannot be anticipated by the analyst, reducing the value of the recommendation. Consequently, thorough analysis requires not merely being able to recognize whether a share is misvalued, but being able to anticipate when a price correction is likely to take place.

Because there are additional investment risks from following recommendations that require long-term commitments, security analysts tend to focus on making recommendations that are likely to pay off in the short term. This potentially explains why so few analysts recommended selling dot-com and technology shares during the late 1990s when their prices would be difficult to justify on the basis of long-term fundamentals. It also explains why analysts recommended Enron's share at its peak, even though the kind of analysis performed in this chapter would have shown that the future growth and ROE performance implied by this price would be extremely difficult to achieve. It also implies that to take advantage of long-term fundamental analysis can often require access to patient, long-term capital.

PERFORMANCE OF SECURITY ANALYSTS AND FUND MANAGERS

There has been extensive research on the performance of security analysts and fund managers during the last two decades. We summarize a few of the key findings.

Performance of security analysts

Despite the recent failure of security analysts to foresee the dramatic price declines for dot-com and telecommunications shares, and to detect the financial shenanigans and overvaluation of companies such as Ahold, Enron, and Parmalat, research shows that analysts generally add value in the capital market. Analyst earnings forecasts are more accurate than those produced by time-series models that use past earnings to predict future earnings.[11] Of course this should not be too surprising since analysts can update their earnings forecasts between quarters to incorporate new firm and economy information, whereas time-series models cannot. In addition, share prices tend to respond positively to upward revisions in analysts' earnings forecasts and recommendations, and negatively to downward revisions.[12] Finally, recent research finds that analysts play a valuable role in improving market efficiency. For example, share prices for firms with higher analyst following more rapidly incorporate information on accruals and cash flows than prices of less followed firms.[13]

Several factors seem to be important in explaining analysts' earnings forecast accuracy. Not surprisingly, forecasts of near-term earnings are much more accurate than those of long-term performance.[14] This probably explains why analysts typically make detailed forecasts for only one or two years ahead. Studies of differences in earnings forecast accuracy across analysts find that analysts that are more accurate tend to specialize by industry and by country and work for large well-funded firms that employ other analysts who follow the same industry.[15]

Although analysts perform a valuable function in the capital market, research shows that their forecasts and recommendations tend to be biased. Early evidence on bias indicated that analyst earnings forecasts tended to be optimistic and that their recommendations were almost exclusively for buys.[16] Several factors potentially explain this finding. First, security analysts at brokerage houses are typically compensated on the basis of the trading volume that their reports generate. Given the costs of short selling and the restrictions on short selling by many institutions, brokerage analysts have incentives to issue optimistic reports that encourage investors to buy shares rather than to issue negative reports that create selling pressure. Second, analysts that work for investment banks are rewarded for promoting public issues by current clients and for attracting new banking clients, creating incentives for optimistic forecasts and recommendations. Studies show that analysts that work for lead underwriters make more optimistic long-term earnings forecasts and recommendations for firms raising equity capital than unaffiliated analysts.[17]

More recent evidence indicates that during the late 1990s there was a marked decline in analyst optimism for forecasts of near-term earnings.[18] One explanation offered for this change is that during the late 1990s analysts relied heavily on private discussions with top management to make their earnings forecasts. Management allegedly used these personal connections to manage analysts' short-term expectations downward so that the firm could subsequently report earnings that beat analysts' expectations. In response to concerns about this practice, in October 2000 the U.S. SEC approved Regulation Fair Disclosure, which prohibits management from making selective disclosures of nonpublic information. In Europe, the E.U. Transparency and Market Abuse Directives, adopted in 2004, may counter such practices, albeit less directly.

Performance of fund managers

Measuring whether collective investment and pension fund managers earn superior returns is a difficult task for several reasons. First, there is no agreement about how to estimate benchmark performance for a fund. Studies have used a number of approaches – some have used the capital asset pricing model (CAPM) as a benchmark, others have used multifactor pricing models. For studies using the CAPM, there are questions about what type of market index to use. For example, should it be an equal- or value-weighted index, an exchange-related index or a broader market index? Second, many of the traditional measures of fund performance abstract from market-wide performance, which understates fund abnormal performance if fund managers can time the market by reducing portfolio risk prior to market declines and increasing risks before a market run-up. Third, given the overall volatility of stock returns, statistical power is an issue for measuring fund performance. Finally, tests of fund performance are likely to be highly sensitive to the time period examined. Value or momentum investing could therefore appear to be profitable depending on when the tests are conducted.

Perhaps because of these challenges, there is no consistent evidence that actively managed collective investment funds generate superior returns for investors. While some studies find evidence of positive abnormal returns for the industry, others conclude that returns are generally negative.[19] Of course, even if collective investment fund managers on average can only generate "normal" returns for investors, it is still possible for the best managers to show consistently strong performance. Some studies do in fact document that funds earning positive abnormal returns in one period continue to outperform in subsequent periods. However, more recent evidence suggests that these findings are caused by general momentum in stock returns and fund expenses rather than superior fund manager ability.[20] Researchers have also examined which, if any, investment strategies are most successful. However, no clear consensus appears – several studies have found that momentum and high turnover strategies generate superior returns, whereas others conclude that value strategies are better.[21]

Finally, recent research has examined whether fund managers tend to buy and sell many of the same shares at the same time. They conclude that there is evidence of "herding" behavior, particularly by momentum fund managers.[22] This could arise because managers have access to common information, because they are affected by similar cognitive biases, or because they have incentives to follow the crowd.[23] For example, consider the calculus of a fund manager who holds a share but who, through long-term fundamental analysis, estimates that it is misvalued. If the manager changes the fund's holdings accordingly and the share price returns to its intrinsic value in the next quarter, the fund will show superior relative portfolio performance and will attract new capital. However, if the share continues to be misvalued for several quarters, the informed fund manager will underperform the benchmark and capital will flow to other funds. In contrast, a risk-averse manager who simply follows the crowd will not be rewarded for detecting the misvaluation, but neither will this manager be blamed for a poor investment decision when the share price ultimately corrects, since other funds made the same mistake.

There has been considerably less research on the performance of pension fund managers. Overall, the findings show little consistent evidence that pension fund managers either overperform or underperform traditional benchmarks.[24]

SUMMARY

Equity security analysis is the evaluation of a firm and its prospects from the perspective of a current or potential investor in the firm's shares. Security analysis is one component of a larger investment process that involves (1) establishing the objectives of the investor or fund, (2) forming expectations about the future returns and risks of individual securities, and then (3) combining individual securities into portfolios to maximize progress toward the investment objectives.

Some security analysis is devoted primarily to assuring that a share possesses the proper risk profile and other desired characteristics prior to inclusion in an investor's portfolio. However, especially for many professional buy-side and sell-side security analysts, the analysis is also directed toward the identification of mispriced securities. In equilibrium, such activity will be rewarding for those with the strongest comparative advantage. They will be the ones able to identify any mispricing at the lowest cost and exert pressure on the price to correct the mispricing. What kinds of efforts are productive in this domain depends on the degree of market efficiency. A large body of evidence exists that is supportive of a high degree of efficiency in stock markets, but recent evidence has reopened the debate on this issue.

In practice, a wide variety of approaches to fund management and security analysis are employed. However, at the core of the analyses are the same steps outlined in Chapters 2 through 8 of this book: business strategy analysis, accounting analysis, financial analysis, and prospective analysis (forecasting and valuation). For the professional analyst, the final product of the work is, of course, a forecast of the firm's future earnings and cash flows, and an estimate of the firm's value. But that final product is less important than the understanding of the business and its industry that the analysis provides. It is such understanding that positions the analyst to interpret new information as it arrives and infer its implications.

DISCUSSION QUESTIONS

1. Despite many years of research, the evidence on market efficiency described in this chapter appears to be inconclusive. Some argue that this is because researchers have been unable to link company fundamentals to share prices precisely. Comment.

2. Geoffrey Henley, a professor of finance, states: "The capital market is efficient. I don't know why anyone would bother devoting their time to following individual shares and doing fundamental analysis. The best approach is to buy and hold a well-diversified portfolio of shares." Do you agree? Why or why not?

3. What is the difference between fundamental and technical analysis? Can you think of any trading strategies that use technical analysis? What are the underlying assumptions made by these strategies?

4. Investment funds follow many different types of investment strategies. Income funds focus on shares with high dividend yields, growth funds invest in shares that are expected to have high capital appreciation, value funds follow shares that are considered to be undervalued, and short funds bet against shares they consider to be overvalued. What types of investors are likely to be attracted to each of these types of funds? Why?

5. Intergalactic Software Plc went public three months ago. You are a sophisticated investor who devotes time to fundamental analysis as a way of identifying mispriced shares. Which of the following characteristics would you focus on in deciding whether to follow this share?
   ■ The market capitalization.
   ■ The average number of shares traded per day.

■ The bid–ask spread for the share.

■ Whether the underwriter that took the firm public is a Top Five investment banking firm.

■ Whether its audit company is a Big Four firm.

■ Whether there are analysts from major brokerage firms following the company.

■ Whether the share is held mostly by retail or institutional investors.

6. There are two major types of financial analysts: buy-side and sell-side. Buy-side analysts work for investment firms and make recommendations that are available only to the management of funds within that firm. Sell-side analysts work for brokerage firms and make recommendations that are used to sell shares to the brokerage firms' clients, which include individual investors and managers of investment funds. What would be the differences in tasks and motivations of these two types of analysts?

7. Many market participants believe that sell-side analysts are too optimistic in their recommendations to buy shares and too slow to recommend sells. What factors might explain this bias?

8. Joe Klein is an analyst for an investment banking firm that offers both under-writing and brokerage services. Joe sends you a highly favorable report on a share that his firm recently helped go public and for which it currently makes the market. What are the potential advantages and disadvantages in relying on Joe's report in deciding whether to buy the share?

9. Intergalactic Software's shares have a market price of €20 per share and a book value of €12 per share. If its cost of equity capital is 15 percent and its book value is expected to grow at 5 percent per year indefinitely, what is the market's assessment of its steady state return on equity? If the share price increases to €35 and the market does not expect the firm's growth rate to change, what is the revised steady state ROE? If instead the price increase was due to an increase in the market's assessments about long-term book value growth rather than long-term ROE, what would the price revision imply for the steady state growth rate?

10. Joe states, "I can see how ratio analysis and valuation help me do fundamental analysis, but I don't see the value of doing strategy analysis." Can you explain to him how strategy analysis could be potentially useful?

NOTES

1. OEIC stands for "Open-Ended Investment Company" and is a U.K. collective investment fund. SICAV stands for "Société d'Investissement à Capital Variable" and is an open-ended collective investment fund in France and Luxembourg. BEVEK stands for "Beleggingsvennootschap met Veranderlijk Kapitaal" and is an open-ended collective investment fund in Belgium.

2. Investment-grade rated bonds have received a credit rating by Moody's of Baa or above and/or a credit rating by Standard & Poor's of BBB or above. We discuss these rating categories in more detail in Chapter 10.

3. P. Healy and K. Palepu, "The Fall of Enron," *Journal of Economic Perspectives* 17, no. 2 (Spring 2003): 3–26, discuss how weak money manager incentives and long-term analysis contributed to the share price run-up and subsequent collapse for Enron. A similar discussion on factors

affecting the rise and fall of dot-com shares is provided in "The Role of Capital Market Intermediaries in the Dot-Com Crash of 2000," Harvard Business School Case 9–101–110, 2001.

4. See R. Bhushan, "Firm Characteristics and Analyst Following," *Journal of Accounting and Economics* 11 (2/5), July 1989: 255–275, and P. O'Brien and R. Bhushan, "Analyst Following and Institutional Ownership," *Journal of Accounting Research* 28, Supplement (1990): 55–76.

5. Recent reviews of evidence on market efficiency are provided by E. Fama, "Efficient Capital Markets: II," *Journal of Finance* 46 (December 1991): 1575–1617; S. Kothari, "Capital Markets Research in Accounting," *Journal of Accounting and Economics* 31 (September 2001): 105–231; and C. Lee, "Market Efficiency in Accounting Research," *Journal of Accounting and Economics* 31 (September 2001): 233–253.

6. For example, see V. Bernard and J. Thomas, "Evidence That Stock Prices Do Not Fully Reflect the Implications of Current Earnings for Future Earnings," *Journal of Accounting and Economics* 13 (December 1990): 305–341.

7. Examples of studies that examine a "value share" strategy include J. Lakonishok, A. Shleifer, and R. Vishny, "Contrarian Investment, Extrapolation, and Risk," *Journal of Finance* 49 (December 1994): 1541–1578, and R. Frankel and C. Lee, "Accounting Valuation, Market Expectation, and Cross-Sectional Stock Returns," *Journal of Accounting and Economics* 25 (June 1998): 283–319.

8. For example, see J. Ou and S. Penman, "Financial Statement Analysis and the Prediction of Stock Returns," *Journal of Accounting and Economics* 11 (November 1989): 295–330; R. Holthausen and D. Larcker, "The Prediction of Stock Returns Using Financial Statement Information," *Journal of Accounting and Economics* 15 (June/September 1992): 373–412; and R. Sloan, "Do Stock Prices Fully Reflect Information in Accruals and Cash Flows about Future Earnings?" *The Accounting Review* 71 (July 1996): 298–325.

9. For an overview of research in behavioral finance, see *Advances in Behavioral Finance* by R. Thaler (New York: Russell Sage Foundation, 1993), and *Inefficient Markets: An Introduction to Behavioral Finance* by A. Shleifer (Oxford: Oxford University Press, 2000).

10. These forecasts were taken from multexinvestor.com.

11. Time-series model forecasts of future annual earnings are the most recent annual earnings (with or without some form of annual growth), and forecasts of future quarterly earnings are a function of growth in earnings for the latest quarter relative to both the last quarter and the same quarter one year ago. See L. Brown and M. Rozeff, "The Superiority of Analyst Forecasts as Measures of Expectations: Evidence from Earnings," *Journal of Finance* 33 (1978): 1–16; L. Brown, P. Griffin, R. Hagerman, and M. Zmijewski, "Security Analyst Superiority Relative to Univariate Time-Series Models in Forecasting Quarterly Earnings," *Journal of Accounting and Economics* 9 (1987): 61–87; and D. Givoly, "Financial Analysts' Forecasts of Earnings: A Better Surrogate for Market Expectations," *Journal of Accounting and Economics* 4, no. 2 (1982): 85–108.

12. See D. Givoly and J. Lakonishok, "The Information Content of Financial Analysts' Forecasts of Earnings: Some Evidence on Semi-Strong Efficiency," *Journal of Accounting and Economics* 2 (1979): 165–186; T. Lys and S. Sohn, "The Association Between Revisions of Financial Analysts' Earnings Forecasts and Security Price Changes," *Journal of Accounting and Economics* 13 (1990): 341–364; and J. Francis and L. Soffer, "The Relative Informativeness of Analysts' Stock Recommendations and Earnings Forecast Revisions," *Journal of Accounting Research* 35, no. 2 (1997): 193–212.

13. See M. Barth and A. Hutton, "Information Intermediaries and the Pricing of Accruals," working paper, Stanford University, 2000.

14. See P. O'Brien, "Forecasts Accuracy of Individual Analysts in Nine Industries." *Journal of Accounting Research* 28 (1990): 286–304.

15. See G. Bolliger, "The Characteristics of Individual Analysts' Forecasts in Europe," *Journal of Banking and Finance* 28 (2004): 2283–2309; M. Clement, "Analyst Forecast Accuracy: Do Ability, Resources, and Portfolio Complexity Matter?" *Journal of Accounting and Economics* 27 (1999): 285–304; J. Jacob, T. Lys, and M. Neale, "Experience in Forecasting Performance of Security Analysts," *Journal of Accounting and Economics* 28 (1999): 51–82; and S. Gilson, P. Healy, C. Noe, and K. Palepu, "Analyst Specialization and Conglomerate Stock Breakups," *Journal of Accounting Research* 39 (December 2001): 565–573.

16. See L. Brown, G. Foster, and E. Noreen, "Security Analyst Multi-Year Earnings Forecasts and the Capital Market," *Studies in Accounting Research*, No. 23, American Accounting Association (Sarasota, FL), 1985. M. McNichols and P. O'Brien, in "Self-Selection and Analyst Coverage," *Journal of Accounting Research,* Supplement (1997): 167–208, find that analyst bias arises

primarily because analysts issue recommendations on firms for which they have favorable information and withhold recommending firms with unfavorable information.

17. See H. Lin and M. McNichols, "Underwriting Relationships, Analysts' Earnings Forecasts and Investment Recommendations," *Journal of Accounting and Economics* 25, no. 1 (1998): 101–128; R. Michaely and K. Womack, "Conflict of Interest and the Credibility of Underwriter Analyst Recommendations," *Review of Financial Studies* 12, no. 4 (1999): 653–686; and P. Dechow, A. Hutton, and R. Sloan, "The Relation Between Analysts' Forecasts of Long-Term Earnings Growth and StockPrice Performance Following Equity Offerings," *Contemporary Accounting Research* 17, no. 1 (2000): 1–32.

18. See L. Brown, "Analyst Forecasting Errors: Additional Evidence," *Financial Analysts' Journal* (November/December 1997): 81–88, and D. Matsumoto, "Management's Incentives to Avoid Negative Earnings Surprises," *The Accounting Review* 77 (July 2002): 483–515.

19. For example, evidence of superior fund performance is reported by M. Grinblatt and S. Titman, "Mutual Fund Performance: An Analysis of Quarterly Holdings," *Journal of Business* 62 (1994), and by D. Hendricks, J. Patel, and R. Zeckhauser, "Hot Hands in Mutual Funds: Short-Run Persistence of Relative Performance," *The Journal of Finance* 48 (1993): 93–130. In contrast, negative fund performance is shown by M. Jensen, "The Performance of Mutual Funds in the Period 1945–64," *The Journal of Finance* 23 (May 1968): 389–416, and B. Malkiel, "Returns from Investing in Equity Mutual Funds from 1971 to 1991," *Journal of Finance* 50 (June 1995): 549–573.

20. M. Grinblatt and S. Titman, "The Persistence of Mutual Fund Performance," *Journal of Finance* 47 (December 1992): 1977–1986, and D. Hendricks, J. Patel, and R. Zeckhauser, "Hot Hands in Mutual Funds: Short-Run Persistence of Relative Performance," *Journal of Finance* 48 (March 1993): 93–130, find evidence of persistence in mutual fund returns. However, M. Carhart, "On Persistence in Mutual Fund Performance," *The Journal of Finance* 52 (March 1997): 57–83, shows that much of this is attributable to momentum in stock returns and to fund expenses; B. Malkiel, "Returns from Investing in Equity Mutual Funds from 1971 to 1991," *The Journal of Finance* 50 (June 1995): 549–573, shows that survivorship bias is also an important consideration.

21. See M. Grinblatt, S. Titman, and R. Wermers, "Momentum Investment Strategies, Portfolio Performance, and Herding: A Study of Mutual Fund Behavior," *The American Economic Review* 85 (December 1995): 1088–1105.

22. For example, J. Lakonishok, A. Shleifer, and R. Vishny, "Contrarian Investment, Extrapolation, and Risk," *Journal of Finance* 49 (December 1994): 1541–1579, find that value funds show superior performance, whereas M. Grinblatt, S. Titman, and R. Wermers, "Momentum Investment Strategies, Portfolio Performance, and Herding: A Study of Mutual Fund Behavior," *The American Economic Review* 85 (December 1995): 1088–1105, find that momentum investing is profitable.

23. See D. Scharfstein and J. Stein, "Herd Behavior and Investment," *The American Economic Review* 80 (June 1990): 465–480, and P. Healy and K. Palepu, "The Fall of Enron," *Journal of Economic Perspectives* 17, no. 2 (Spring 2003): 3–26.

24. For evidence on performance by pension fund managers, see J. Lakonishok, A. Shleifer, and R. Vishny, "The Structure and Performance of the Money Management Industry," *Brookings Papers on Economic Activity*, Washington, DC (1992): 339–392; T. Coggin, F. Fabozzi, and S. Rahman, "The Investment Performance of U.S. Equity Pension Fund Managers: An Empirical Investigation," *The Journal of Finance* 48 (July 1993): 1039–1056; and W. Ferson and K. Khang, "Conditional Performance Measurement Using Portfolio Weights: Evidence for Pension Funds," *Journal of Financial Economics* 65 (August 2002): 249–282.

The initial public offering of PartyGaming Plc[1]

On June 30, 2005, PartyGaming Plc offered 781,629,050 of its ordinary shares for public trading on the London Stock Exchange. The offer price of the shares was 116 pence per ordinary share. The number of shares offered for public trading represented approximately 19.5 percent of PartyGaming's 4 billion shares outstanding.

An investment in PartyGaming's shares was not without risks. In its prospectus, PartyGaming warned its prospective investors that they

> … should be aware that an investment in PartyGaming Plc involves a high degree of risk and that, if certain of the risks described in Part 3 occur, they may lose all or a very substantial part of their investment. Accordingly, an investment in the Shares is only suitable for investors who are particularly knowledgeable in investment matters and who are able to bear the complete loss of their investment.

PartyGaming and its industry[2]

PartyGaming was founded in 1997. Between 1997 and 2005 the company had become one of the largest online gaming suppliers in the world. In 2005, the company generated the largest proportion of its revenues from accommodating online poker games, partly by means of its own website PartyPoker.com – the world's leading online poker site. Specifically, online poker produced 92 percent of the company's revenues; the remaining 8 percent came from online casino and bingo games. The company had achieved its leading position in online poker through a timely entry into the online poker market, supported by effective online and offline sales and marketing, a reliable technology, and high-level customer support.

In 1997, Ruth Parasol started PartyGaming with the launch of the Starluck casino site, which was operated and managed from the Caribbean. Three years later, Anurag Dikshit and Vikrant Bhargava – who would later become the company's Operations and Marketing Directors – became investors in PartyGaming and started to develop the company's poker business. The poker site PartyPoker.com was launched in 2001 from Canada. With the help of famous poker player Mike Sexton, PartyGaming was able to attract a lot of publicity for its new website by organizing the "PartyPoker.com Million" tournament, for which the qualification rounds took place online. In 2002 and 2003, PartyGaming launched PartyBingo.com and moved its operations to Hyderabad (India) and its headquarters to Gibraltar.

The online gaming market had experienced rapid growth in the years just prior to 2005. Primary drivers of this growth were the increasing worldwide popularity of the internet as well as the increasing customer awareness of the sector's existence. Increasing customer awareness had resulted from greater television exposure and intensified marketing activities by the major industry players. In addition, online gaming companies had invested in their growth by developing new products and

---

1. Professor Erik Peek prepared this case. The case is intended solely as the basis for class discussion and is not intended to serve as an endorsement, source of primary data, or illustration of effective or ineffective management.
2. The material in this and the following sections largely draws from PartyGaming's IPO prospectus (June 14, 2005).

improving payment processing, transaction services, and customer support. Industry analysts did not expect this growth to stop in the near term. The online sector's share of the global gaming market was expected to increase from 3 to 8 percent between 2004 and 2009.

Industry analysts estimated the size of the global online and offline gaming market to be $243 billion (in revenues) in 2004 and $282 billion in 2009. The online gaming market was estimated to generate revenue of approximately $8.2 billion in 2004 and $22.7 billion in 2009. In 2004, online casino and bingo games accounted for 29 percent of the online gaming revenues, whereas online poker games accounted for 13 percent. Respectively 50 percent, 27 percent, and 15 percent of the global online gaming revenues had been generated from the U.S., Europe, and Asia. Industry analysts expected the U.S. share of the global online gaming market to decline to 40 percent in 2009 as a result of the above-average market growth in Europe and Asia. The key drivers of such growth would be the increasing number of internet users, the increasing popularity of gaming, increasing marketing investments made by the industry players, and the development of new distribution channels, such as mobile phones.

Poker had become more popular over the years mostly because of the increased television coverage of poker tournaments and the exposure of the game on popular television shows. Because many of the poker players around the world were still playing offline, the online poker market could potentially grow from the migration of offline players to online play. Analysts estimated that this migration, in combination with the attraction of new poker players, could make the online poker market's revenues grow from slightly more than $1 billion in 2004 to close to $6.4 billion in 2009 – representing 28 percent of the global online gaming market. In comparison, analysts estimated that the online casino market would grow from $2,157 million (in revenues) in 2004 to $5,587 million in 2009. According to PartyGaming's management there were a number of barriers to entry to the online poker market, creating a competitive advantage for the company:

- *Player liquidity.* To be able to organize games with a wide range of stakes at all times of players' choosing, online poker providers needed to have a large customer base.
- *Software control.* The leading online poker providers had invested significant amounts in software. Having control over their own software helped them to make the software improvements that were necessary for attracting and retaining customers.
- *Payment processing expertise.* To attract and maintain customers, online poker providers must be able to provide a wide range of payment methods (credit cards, e-checks, online wallets) and must have built a reputation for quick, efficient, and error-free payment processing.
- *Customer support.* Online poker providers must make significant investments in customer service operations.
- *Marketing and global reach.* Online poker providers needed to have significant market resources to penetrate new geographic markets and increase advertising expenditures as competition increased.

Having the mission to be the world's largest gaming company, with the most trusted brands, innovative technology, and high-level customer service, PartyGaming focused its strategy on the following areas: (1) sustain brand value and maintain leadership in its current markets, (2) expand to markets outside the U.S., first in Europe, later in Asia, (3) continue to provide innovative technology and high-level customer support, (4) stretch the "Party" brand to other games, either acquired or self-developed, and (5) make use of alternative delivery channels, such as mobile phones and interactive television.

In 2004, PartyGaming was the undisputed market leader in the online poker segment. Based on the average ring game rake – the amount of money the provider takes from the pot – the company had a market share of 54 percent. The five next-largest providers of online poker gaming all had market shares between 5 and 8 percent.

The risks

As pointed out, an investment in PartyGaming's ordinary shares involved substantial risks. The following risks were especially high:

- *Regulatory risks.* One apparent risk affecting the online gaming market in 2005 was that in many countries national gaming laws had been developed to govern offline gaming activities and were not particularly suited to govern online gaming activities. Consequently, in some of PartyGaming's geographical segments there was much uncertainty about whether the supply of online gaming was legal or not. In some countries, foreign suppliers of online gaming were not able to obtain a license and it was uncertain whether and how local regulators would bring actions against foreign suppliers who had no license but were not physically present. PartyGaming ran the risk that regulators would change their laws and take actions that would inhibit the company's ability to process payments and advertise in a particular country. The advantage of these regulatory risks was, however, that they prevented many other companies from entering PartyGaming's industry, thereby reducing competition.

- *Taxation risks.* PartyGaming and most of its group companies had their domicile in Gibraltar, where they were exempt from paying taxes because they offered no services to Gibraltarians or Gibraltar residents. However, in early 2005 the European Commission and the governments of Gibraltar and the U.K. had agreed to abolish the Gibraltar exempt company tax regime by the end of 2010. PartyGaming would even lose its tax exempt status – and become subject to a 35 percent tax rate – on December 31, 2007, if it had a change in ownership before June 30, 2006, and immediately lose its tax exempt status if it had a change in ownership after June 30, 2006. At the time of the IPO, it was still unclear what regulators would consider a "change in ownership." PartyGaming expected that the IPO would not be treated as a change in ownership. The company's principal shareholders had agreed not to dispose of their shares within two years of the IPO. Further, the decision to abolish the exempt company tax regime had been appealed to the European Court. Finally, the government of Gibraltar was seeking alternative ways to provide companies with an attractive tax regime.

- *Technology risks.* PartyGaming ran the risk that hackers would attempt to gain access to its systems and disrupt its services. Further, the growing demand for the company's online gaming services could lead to a situation in which its technological architecture as well as the technological architecture of its third-party providers was not developed enough to ensure the absence of errors, failures, interruptions, or delays in the provision of its services. Finally, PartyGaming needed to make investments in technology that facilitated the delivery of its online gaming services to customers who were not using personal computers but other devices such as mobile phones or television set-top devices.

- *Competitive risks.* Other companies in PartyGaming's industry offered formidable competition. At the time of the IPO there were more than 2,000 online gaming sites and more than 200 online poker sites competing for the same customers. An increasing proportion of PartyGaming's revenues came from "third-party skins" – third-party brands that used PartyGaming's platform and shared their revenues.

Third-party skins were competition to the company's own operations and brought significant risks of disputes and litigation.

■ *Intellectual property rights.* A substantial part of PartyGaming's technology and know-how was proprietary and any misappropriated or unauthorized disclosure of its technology and know-how could harm the company's competitive advantage. Similarly, the use of "Party" domain names or the "Party" brand by third parties without approval could harm the value of the company's brand. In some countries where PartyGaming operated, national laws did not sufficiently protect the company's intellectual property rights, or actions to enforce its intellectual property rights, were costly. PartyGaming also ran the risk that other technology companies would claim that their intellectual property rights were infringed by PartyGaming, which could result in litigation.

■ *Risks of international expansion.* Because of the legal uncertainties in the U.S., PartyGaming planned to expand internationally. Competition outside the U.S. was, however, stronger than within the U.S. Further, international expansion would bring a number of additional risks, such as legal, political, cultural, and currency risks. Operating on an international scale could also increase the company's transaction costs.

■ *Short operating history.* PartyGaming's short operating history made it difficult to assess the company's prospects. In its prospectus, the company reported that it did not expect that its rapid historic growth would persist in the future. In order to grow, PartyGaming should innovate new products and services, countering the declining growth of the online poker market. The company also expected that, when growth would decline, the cyclicality and seasonality (lower yields per active player day in the second quarter, higher yields in the first and fourth quarters) of its operations would become more pronounced.

■ *Principal shareholders.* After the IPO, the principal shareholders of PartyGaming would hold close to 73 percent of the company's ordinary shares. Consequently, they could have a decisive influence on the company's financial and operating decisions as well as the success of any takeover offer.

Although PartyGaming had no physical presence in the U.S., it did not block U.S. customers from signing up to the company's websites. The company generated almost 87 percent of its revenues from the U.S., where the regulatory risks were significant. It advertised its gaming sites in the U.S. and made use of the services of U.S. payment processors to collect from and pay out funds to its U.S. customers. At the time of the IPO, the U.S. Department of Justice considered the U.S. operations of PartyGaming illegal. Further, at least seven U.S. states had laws that explicitly prohibited online gaming, while many other states prohibited all forms of unlicensed gaming. U.S. federal laws were, however, inconclusive about whether online gaming was indeed illegal and the status of state laws in the matter was unclear. The company had not received an official notification from any U.S. authority that it sought to bring action against the company for its U.S. operations. Any future action by U.S. authorities to issue an injunction, impose fines or imprisonment, or seize gaming proceeds could, however, impose considerable (legal) costs upon the company and reduce the company's revenues and profits.

U.S. law enforcement officials targeted their enforcement activities at U.S.-based companies who provided services such as IT, payment processing, and advertising to PartyGaming. In particular, they alleged the violation of U.S. laws to discourage U.S. banks from processing online gaming transactions and U.S. media from advertising online gaming sites. As a consequence, several banks, such as Citibank, financial

PartyGaming

service companies, such as PayPal, and media companies, such as Discovery, had decided not to provide any services to PartyGaming. Another threat to PartyGaming's U.S. operations was posed by the proposals of the U.S. Congress to prohibit online gaming or the provision of payment processing services to online gaming companies. Over past years, several proposals were made but did not receive sufficient support to be passed. In 2005, the U.S. Congress would consider the "Kyl Bill", which sought to prohibit the processing of online gaming transactions. At the time of the IPO, this proposal seemed to lack sufficient support from the U.S. Congress.

PartyGaming's governance

In early 2005 PartyGaming's Board of Directors comprised four executive directors and four nonexecutive directors. All nonexecutive directors were denoted as independent. The company's board had established an audit committee, a remuneration committee, a nominations committee, and an ethics committee. The company's CEO was Richard Lawrence Segal, who had joined the company in August 2004, after having been the CEO of cinema operator Odeon Limited for seven years.

Two executive directors were also principal shareholders of PartyGaming. After the IPO, Anurag Dikshit, Operations Director, would own 31.6 percent of the company's shares; Vikrant Bhargava, Marketing Director, would own 16.3 percent. Two other principal shareholders were co-founder Ruth Parasol – owning 16.3 percent – and her husband, Russell DeLeon – owning 9.0 percent. Each of the principal shareholders had agreed not to sell any shares during the 12 months following the IPO. Principal shareholders owning more than 15 percent of the company's shares had the right to nominate one nonexecutive director. However, they also agreed that at any time at least half of the company's board would comprise independent directors.

PartyGaming's performance

At the time of the IPO, PartyGaming's management considered the company's key strengths to be its high-margin business model, its strong marketing program and brand name, its large active player base, its high-quality and innovative technology, its offering of a wide variety of pay-in and withdrawal methods, its high-level 24/7 customer support, its well-developed systems of risk management and fraud detection, and its strong management team.

To sustain brand value and attract active players, PartyGaming made significant investments in marketing. The company made use of a variety of marketing strategies such as television and radio advertising, affiliate marketing (sharing revenues with other sites that market PartyGaming sites), direct mail, sign-up bonuses, and sponsorships. In addition, PartyGaming invested in the retention of customers by organizing the PartyPoker.com Million Tournaments, for which the qualification rounds were held online, introducing player loyalty programs (award schemes), and awarding bonuses to existing players who pay in new funds.

As evidence of PartyGaming's marketing success stands the large increase in the company's registered poker and casino players prior to 2005. Exhibit 1 shows the number of registered and active poker and casino players by period, as well as the average yield per player day. The number of active players, the average daily active players, active player days (average daily active players times the number of days in a period), and yield per active player day were PartyGaming's key performance indicators. The yield per active player day followed a seasonal pattern. In 2003 (2004), the yield per active poker player day was $21.0 ($19.8), $18.1 ($18.7), $18.8 ($18.9), and $20.0 ($19.1) in the first, second, third, and fourth quarter, respectively. Although PartyGaming had a large player base, the company was reliant on a relatively small number of customers. For example, close to 10 percent of the active poker players contributed 70 percent of the company's revenues from poker games. Similarly, 5 percent of the active casino players contributed 82 percent of the company's revenues from casino games.

Exhibit 2 shows PartyGaming's financial statements for the fiscal years 2003 and 2004, as well as for three fiscal quarters. These figures illustrate PartyGaming's growth in revenues and profits. One apparent development was the strong decline in equity between 2003 and 2004. The reason for this decline was the acquisition of PartyGaming Holdings Limited by PartyGaming Plc in 2004. PartyGaming acquired its interest in PartyGaming Holdings Limited in a transaction under common control. An acquisition under common control occurs when the acquirer and the target firm are both controlled by the same party. As a result of this transaction, PartyGaming Plc became the group's ultimate parent company. International Accounting Standards did not require acquisitions under common control to be accounted for using the purchase method. Consequently, PartyGaming used the pooling method to account for the acquisition, and the deficit in equity reflected the group's cumulative profits as if the new group structure had always been in place.

Questions

1. The initial offer price of PartyGaming's ordinary shares was 116 pence per share. Which sales growth and net operating profit margin assumptions are consistent with an offer price of 116 pence?

2. Using your own assumptions, estimate the value of PartyGaming's ordinary shares at the time of the IPO. How do the risks that PartyGaming faced affect your value estimate?

PartyGaming

EXHIBIT 1 **Information about PartyGaming's registered and active players**

	Fiscal year ending December 31, 2002	Fiscal year ending December 31, 2003	Fiscal year ending December 31, 2004	Three months ending March 31, 2005
Total registered poker players	105,000	1,283,000	5,225,000	6,603,000
Total registered casino players	535,000	903,000	1,296,000	1,376,000
Registered real-money poker players	20,000	210,000	806,000	1,020,000
Of which active players (in the last month of the period)	6,000	125,000	324,000	411,000
Registered real-money casino and bingo players	282,000	320,000	374,000	388,000
Of which active players (in the last month of the period)	4,000	9,000	13,000	14,000
Average daily active poker players	1,297	17,043	77,094	121,570
Average yield per active poker player day	$20.8	$19.5	$19.1	$18.6
Average daily active casino and bingo players	580	832	1,797	1,875
Average yield per active casino and bingo player day	$90.7	$96.9	$73.9	$73.1

Source: PartyGaming's IPO prospectus (June 14, 2005). The item total registered players includes "play money" players who participate in games for free.

PartyGaming

EXHIBIT 2 **PartyGaming's consolidated income statements, balance sheets, cash flow statements, and pro forma income statement and segment information for two fiscal years and three fiscal quarters**

CONSOLIDATED INCOME STATEMENTS ($ MILLIONS)

	Three months ending March 31, 2005	Three months ending December 31, 2004	Three months ending March 31, 2004	Fiscal year ending December 31, 2004	Fiscal year ending December 31, 2003
Revenue – net gaming revenue	222.6	194.0	115.4	601.6	153.1
Other operating revenue/(expenses)	−0.3	0.4	0.0	0.1	0.4
Administrative expenses					
– other administrative expenses	−23.3	−21.6	−15.8	−73.1	−29.4
– share-based payments	−4.6	−2.3	0.0	−3.2	0.0
– strategic review costs	−1.5	0.0	0.0	0.0	0.0
Distribution expenses	−64.6	−48.8	−28.7	−142.2	−34.9
Profit from operating activities	128.3	121.7	70.9	383.2	89.2
Finance income	0.6	0.8	0.2	1.4	0.0
Finance costs	−3.0	−4.4	−0.1	−12.9	0.0
Share of losses of associate	−0.3	0.0	0.0	0.0	0.0
Profit before tax	125.6	118.1	71.0	371.7	89.2
Tax	−8.2	−7.4	−3.9	−21.6	−5.6
Profit after tax	117.4	110.7	67.1	350.1	83.6
Minority interest	0.0	0.0	−1.6	−1.6	−6.6
Profit from ordinary activities attributable to equity holders of the parent	117.4	110.7	65.5	348.5	77.0
Net earnings per share ($ cents)	3.11	2.93	1.73	9.23	2.04
Net earnings per share ($ cents) – diluted	3.09	2.91	1.72	9.16	2.02
Weighted average shares outstanding	3,776	3,776	3,776	3,776	3,776
Weighted average shares outstanding, diluted	3,803	3,803	3,803	3,803	3,803

PartyGaming

PartyGaming

PRO FORMA INCOME STATEMENT AND SEGMENT INFORMATION ($ MILLIONS)

	Three months ending March 31, 2005	Three months ending December 31, 2004	Three months ending March 31, 2004	Fiscal year ending December 31, 2004	Fiscal year ending December 31, 2003
Revenues					
– Poker	210.3	183.5	102.9	553.0	123.7
– Casino/Bingo	12.3	10.5	12.5	48.6	29.4
– Other	0.0	0.0	0.0	0.0	0.0
Administrative expenses					
– Transaction fees	−10.1	−8.9	−6.2	−29.3	−9.8
– Staff costs	−10.5	−8.0	−4.3	−21.8	−8.3
– Depreciation and amortization	−1.7	−1.4	−0.8	−4.6	−1.1
– Other overheads	−7.1	−5.6	−4.5	−20.6	−10.2
Distribution expenses					
– Affiliate fees	−23.6	−18.8	—	−53.7	−13.3
– Customer acquisition and retention (primarily advertising)	−24.1	−14.5	—	−37.6	−10.6
– Chargebacks (amounts unrecoverable from customers)	−11.6	−10.2	—	−36.7	−8.2
– Customer bonuses	−3.7	−4.1	—	−10.0	−1.6
– Web-hosting	−1.6	−1.2	—	−4.2	−1.2
Profit before tax					
– Poker	128.0	118.0	64.5	360.1	81.2
– Casino/Bingo	6.2	6.0	6.7	28.4	8.2
– Other	−8.6	−5.9	−0.2	−16.8	−0.2
Impairment losses – trade receivables	−11.7	−10.1	−10.3	42.2	−9.9
Impairment losses – other	0.0	0.0	0.0	0.0	−0.4

CONSOLIDATED BALANCE SHEETS ($ MILLIONS)

	Three months ending March 31, 2005	Three months ending December 31, 2004	Three months ending March 31, 2004	Fiscal year ending December 31, 2004	Fiscal year ending December 31, 2003
Intangible assets	7.7	7.7	8.0	7.7	0.0
property, plant, and equipment	25.4	13.3	9.1	13.3	5.7
Investment in associates	1.5	0.0	0.0	0.0	0.0
Total non-current assets	34.6	21.0	17.1	21.0	5.7
Trade and other receivables	132.9	107.8	76.5	107.8	53.2
Cash and cash equivalents	78.3	133.9	131.7	133.9	74.6
Short-term investments	3.5	0.0	0.0	0.0	0.0
Total current assets	214.7	241.7	208.2	241.7	127.8
Total assets	249.3	262.7	225.3	262.7	133.5
Bank overdraft	2.9	1.8	2.3	1.8	0.0
Trade and other payables	46.4	39.5	18.7	39.5	14.4
Shareholder loans	229.3	223.9	0.0	223.9	0.0
Income taxes	36.2	28.0	10.7	28.0	6.7
Client liabilities and progressive prize pools	124.1	104.6	49.1	104.6	35.4
Provisions	7.9	4.7	3.0	4.7	1.9
Total non-current liabilities	446.8	402.5	83.8	402.5	58.4
Trade and other payables	5.0	6.1	7.5	6.1	0.0
Shareholder loans	80.2	258.9	0.0	258.9	0.0
Total current liabilities	85.2	265.0	7.5	265.0	0.0
Share capital	0.1	0.0	0.0	0.0	0.0
Share premium account	0.4	0.4	0.4	0.4	0.4
Retained earnings	534.4	417.0	134.0	417.0	68.6
Other reserve	−825.4	−825.4	−0.4	−825.4	−0.4
Share option reserve	7.8	3.2	0.0	3.2	0.0
Equity attributable to equity holders of the parent	−282.7	−404.8	134.0	−404.8	68.6
Minority interest	0.0	0.0	0.0	0.0	6.5
Total liabilities and shareholders' equity	249.3	262.7	225.3	262.7	133.5

PartyGaming

CONSOLIDATED CASH FLOW STATEMENTS ($ MILLIONS)

	Three months ending March 31, 2005	Three months ending December 31, 2004	Three months ending March 31, 2004	Fiscal year ending December 31, 2004	Fiscal year ending December 31, 2003
Profit before tax	125.6	118.1	71.0	371.7	89.2
Adjustment for:					
Amortization of intangibles	0.0	0.1	0.0	0.3	0.2
Interest expense	3.0	4.4	0.1	12.9	0.0
Interest income	−0.6	−0.8	−0.2	−1.4	0.0
Depreciation of property, plant, and equipment	1.7	1.3	0.8	4.3	0.9
Gains on sale of property, plant, and equipment	0.0	0.0	0.0	0.0	0.1
Increase in share-based payments reserve	4.6	2.3	0.0	3.2	0.0
Loss on investment in associate	0.3	0.0	0.0	0.0	0.0
Operating cash flows before movements in working capital and provisions	134.6	125.4	71.7	391.0	90.4
Increase in trade and other receivables	−24.6	−15.3	−23.3	−54.6	−48.1
Increase in trade and other payables	26.5	31.3	15.2	89.9	43.4
Increase in provisions	3.2	−3.5	1.1	2.8	0.4
Income taxes paid	−0.8	0.0	0.0	0.0	0.0
Cash generated/(used) by working capital	4.3	12.5	−7.0	38.1	−4.3
Net cash from operating activities	138.9	137.9	64.7	429.1	86.1
Purchases of property, plant, and equipment	−13.8	−4.0	−4.1	−11.9	−5.9
Purchases of intangible assets	0.0	0.0	0.0	0.0	−0.2
Purchase of minority interest in subsidiary	0.0	0.0	−5.8	−5.8	0.0
Interest received	0.6	0.5	0.2	1.4	0.0
Purchase and cancelation of own shares	0.0	0.0	−0.1	−2.0	−3.1
Investment in associated undertaking	−1.8	0.0	0.0	0.0	0.0
Increase in short-term investments	−3.5	0.0	0.0	0.0	0.0
Net cash used in investing activities	−18.5	−3.5	−9.8	−18.3	−9.2
Issue of shares	0.0	0.0	0.0	0.9	0.0
Interest paid	−3.8	−4.6	−0.1	−11.0	0.0
Equity dividends paid	0.0	0.0	0.0	0.0	−8.1
Payments to shareholders	−173.3	−113.5	0.0	−343.2	0.0
Net cash used in financing activities	−177.1	−118.1	−0.1	−353.3	−8.1

Source: PartyGaming's IPO Prospectus (June 14, 2005). Note that at the time of the IPO, the total number of shares outstanding was 4,000,000,000.

PartyGaming

Credit Analysis and Distress Prediction

Credit analysis is the evaluation of a firm from the perspective of a holder or potential holder of its debt, including trade payables, loans, and public debt securities. A key element of credit analysis is the prediction of the likelihood a firm will face financial distress.

Credit analysis is involved in a wide variety of decision contexts:

■ A potential supplier asks: Should I sell products or services to this firm? The associated credit will be extended only for a short period, but the amount is large and I should have some assurance that collection risks are manageable.

■ A commercial banker asks: Should we extend a loan to this firm? If so, how should it be structured? How should it be priced?

■ If the loan is granted, the banker must later ask: Are we still providing the services, including credit, that this firm needs? Is the firm still in compliance with the loan terms? If not, is there a need to restructure the loan, and if so, how? Is the situation serious enough to call for accelerating the repayment of the loan?

■ A pension fund manager, insurance company, or other investor asks: Are these debt securities a sound investment? What is the probability that the firm will face distress and default on the debt? Does the yield provide adequate compensation for the default risk involved?

■ An investor contemplating purchase of debt securities in default asks: How likely is it that this firm can be turned around? In light of the high yield on this debt relative to its current price, can I accept the risk that the debt will not be repaid in full?

Although credit analysis is typically viewed from the perspective of the financier, it is obviously important to the borrower as well:

■ A manager of a small firm asks: What are our options for credit financing? Would the firm qualify for bank financing? If so, what type of financing would be possible? How costly would it be? Would the terms of the financing constrain our flexibility?

■ A manager of a large firm asks: What are our options for credit financing? Is the firm strong enough to raise funds in the public market? If so, what is our debt rating likely to be? What required yield would that rating imply?

Finally, there are third parties – those other than borrowers and lenders – who are interested in the general issue of how likely it is that a firm will avoid financial distress:

- An auditor asks: How likely is it that this firm will survive beyond the short run? In evaluating the firm's financials, should I consider it a going concern?

- An actual or potential employee asks: How confident can I be that this firm will be able to offer employment over the long term?

- A potential customer asks: What assurance is there that this firm will survive to provide warranty services, replacement parts, product updates, and other services?

- A competitor asks: Will this firm survive the current industry shakeout? What are the implications of potential financial distress at this firm for my pricing and market share?

THE MARKET FOR CREDIT

An understanding of credit analysis requires an appreciation of the various players in the market for credit. We briefly describe those players here.

Suppliers of credit

The major suppliers in the market for credit are described below.

Commercial banks

Commercial banks are very important players in the market for credit. Since banks tend to provide a range of services to a client, and have intimate knowledge of the client and its operations, they have a comparative advantage in extending credit in settings where (1) knowledge gained through close contact with management reduces the perceived riskiness of the credit and (2) credit risk can be contained through careful monitoring of the firm. This is even more so in countries where commercial banks also provide investment banking services to their clients. Examples of investment banking services are asset management, investment advice, and the underwriting of clients' securities. Banks that engage in investment banking sometimes hold substantial equity stakes in other companies, including their clients. The combination of commercial banking and investment banking services, which is called universal banking, therefore not only helps banks to become better informed about their clients' operations but also makes banks more influential over their clients through the equity stakes that they control. Universal banking activities are especially common among the larger banks in Continental European countries such as Germany and Switzerland.[1]

A constraint on bank lending operations is that the credit risk be relatively low so that the bank's loan portfolio will be of acceptably high quality to bank regulators. Because of the importance of maintaining public confidence in the banking sector and the desire to shield government deposit insurance from risk, governments have incentives to constrain banks' exposure to credit risk. Banks also tend to shield themselves from the risk of shifts in interest rates by avoiding fixed-rate loans with long maturities. Because banks' capital mostly comes from short-term deposits, such long-term loans leave them exposed to increases in interest rates, unless the risk can be hedged with derivatives. Thus, banks are less likely to play a role when a firm requires a very long-term commitment to financing. However, in some such cases they assist in providing a placement of the debt with, say, an insurance company, a pension fund, or a group of private investors.

Other financial institutions

Banks face competition in the commercial lending market from a variety of sources. Finance companies compete with banks in the market for asset-based lending (i.e., the secured financing of specific assets such as receivables, inventory, or equipment). Insurance companies are involved in a variety of lending activities. Since life insurance companies face obligations of a long-term nature, they often seek investments of long duration (e.g., long-term bonds or loans to support large, long-term commercial property and development projects). Investment bankers are prepared to place debt securities with private investors or in the public markets (discussed below). Various government agencies are another source of credit.

Public debt markets

Some firms have the size, strength, and credibility necessary to bypass the banking sector and seek financing directly from investors, either through sales of commercial paper or through the issuance of bonds. Such debt issues are facilitated by the assignment of a debt rating. Fitch, Moody's, and Standard and Poor's are three of the world's largest rating agencies. A firm's debt rating influences the yield that must be offered to sell the debt instruments. After the debt issue, the rating agencies continue to monitor the firm's financial condition. Changes in the rating are associated with fluctuation in the price of the securities.

Banks often provide financing in tandem with a public debt issue or other source of financing. In highly levered transactions, such as leveraged buyouts, banks commonly provide financing along with public debt that has a lower priority in case of bankruptcy. The bank's "senior financing" would typically be scheduled for earlier retirement than the public debt, and it would carry a lower yield. For smaller or start-up firms, banks often provide credit in conjunction with equity financing from venture capitalists. Note that in the case of both the leveraged buyout and the start-up company, the bank helps provide the cash needed to make the deal happen, but it does so in a way that shields it from risks that would be unacceptably high in the banking sector.

Sellers who provide financing

Another sector of the market for credit are manufacturers and other suppliers of goods and services. As a matter of course, such firms tend to finance their customers' purchases on an unsecured basis for periods of 30 to 60 days. Suppliers will, on occasion, also agree to provide more extended financing, usually with the support of a secured note. A supplier may be willing to grant such a loan in the expectation that the creditor will survive a cash shortage and remain an important customer in the future. However the customer would typically seek such an arrangement only if bank financing is unavailable because it could constrain flexibility in selecting among and/or negotiating with suppliers.

A mixture of credit types

The above described suppliers of credit are not equally important in every country. One source of differences across countries is the extent to which national bankruptcy laws protect the suppliers of credit. A stylized classification of bankruptcy laws involves two groups: laws that provide extensive creditor protection in the case of default versus laws that are oriented toward keeping the company in default a going concern and shielding the company from the influence of creditors. The former type of laws typically offer creditors a first right to repossess collateral and enforce other contractual rights when their borrower is in default. These laws therefore increase the probability that creditors recover their loans but reduce the probability that borrowers survive bankruptcy. The latter type of laws typically impose court-administered bankruptcy procedures on the borrower in default and its creditors as well as an automatic stay on the borrower's assets. An automatic stay on the assets means that creditors cannot repossess their collateral during the period in which the borrower's financial obligations are being restructured. The U.K. is an example of a European country that has strong creditor protection laws. Examples of European countries that have weak creditor protection laws, or borrower-friendly bankruptcy laws, are France, Italy, and Portugal. Germany takes a position in between these two extremes. In Germany, courts impose bankruptcy procedures on the borrower and its creditors, but there is no automatic stay on the borrower's assets and creditors have considerable influence on the borrower's reorganization process.[2]

In countries where the legal rights of banks are weakly protected and banks experience difficulties in repossessing collateral when a borrower defaults, they are likely to be hesitant in extending long-term credit. As an alternative, companies may borrow smaller proportions of debt from multiple banks. Because it is more difficult for a company in default to renegotiate its loans with multiple banks than with one bank, multiple-bank borrowing reduces the company's incentive to strategically default. Research has found that multiple-bank borrowing is most common in Belgium, France, Italy, Spain, and Portugal, where banks are indeed weakly protected in case of bankruptcy.[3]

Supplier financing is also an efficient alternative form of debt financing when creditor rights are weakly protected.[4] A reason for this is that suppliers are often well informed about their debtors' operations and they have a straightforward way to discipline their debtors. That is, in case of default of payment, suppliers can repossess the delivered goods and withhold future deliveries. In fiscal year 2005, public companies in Belgium, France, Italy, Spain, and Portugal had an average payables-to-sales ratio of 18.7 percent. The ratio ranged from 14.5 percent in Belgium to 24.3 percent in Italy. In contrast, public companies in Denmark, Finland, Germany, the Netherlands, Sweden, Switzerland, and the U.K. had an average payables-to-sales ratio of 9.6 percent.

Research has indicated that in countries where companies' access to bank debt or public debt is restricted or relatively expensive, companies may also resort to off-balance sheet financing.[5] One example of off-balance sheet financing is the factoring of receivables, where companies sell their customer receivables to a lender at a discount. In the first half of the 2000s, the use of factoring was fastest growing in eastern Europe, where bankruptcy laws were weak. Further, companies in Italy made relatively more use of factoring than companies in other parts of Europe.

Public debt markets are also not equally developed in all parts of the world. Table 10.1 shows the size of public debt markets as a percentage of national gross domestic product (GDP) in 10 European countries at the end of 1999. These percentages show that public debt markets were especially large in Denmark, Germany, the Netherlands, Switzerland, and the U.K. Table 10.1 also reports the size of public equity markets for comparison. The low correlation between the sizes of public debt and equity markets illustrates that in many countries public debt markets had developed independently from public equity markets. Unfortunately, more recent data on debt markets with a similar level of detail is not readily available. Illustrating

TABLE 10.1 The importance of public debt and public equity markets in the economy (end-1999 data)

Country	Total market value of public debt in the domestic private sector as a percentage of GDP	Total market value of public equity in the domestic private sector as a percentage of GDP
Belgium	1.4%	78.9%
Denmark	96.4%	60.5%
France	15.0%	111.1%
Germany	64.8%	72.1%
Italy	5.4%	66.1%
Netherlands	45.1%	187.7%
Portugal	9.1%	63.7%
Spain	2.8%	77.0%
Switzerland	35.0%	267.4%
U.K.	29.4%	198.3%

Source: World Federation of Exchanges.

the fact that country rankings in debt market importance have changed slightly over the first half of the 2000s, in May 2006 Standard and Poor's issued most of its ratings for public debt issues of companies from the U.K. (about 30 percent of its European ratings), France (18 percent), and Germany (17 percent).

THE CREDIT ANALYSIS PROCESS

At first blush, credit analysis might appear less difficult than the valuation task discussed in Chapters 7 and 8. After all, a potential creditor ultimately cares only about whether the firm is strong enough to pay its debts at the scheduled times. The firm's exact value, its upside potential, or its distance from the threshold of creditworthiness may not appear so important. Viewed in that way, credit analysis may seem more like a "zero-one" decision: either the credit is extended, or it is not.

It turns out, however, that credit analysis involves more than just establishing creditworthiness. First, there are ranges of creditworthiness, and it is important to understand where a firm lies within that range for purposes of pricing and structuring a loan. Moreover, if the creditor is a bank or other financial institution with an expected continuing relationship with the borrower, the borrower's upside potential is important, even though downside risk must be the primary consideration in credit analysis. A firm that offers growth potential also offers opportunities for future income-generating financial services.

Given this broader view of credit analysis, it should not be surprising that it involves most of the same issues already discussed in the prior chapters on business strategy analysis, accounting analysis, financial analysis, and prospective analysis. Perhaps the greatest difference is that credit analysis rarely involves any explicit attempt to estimate the value of the firm's equity. However, the determinants of that value are relevant in credit analysis because a larger equity cushion translates into lower risk for the creditor.

Below we describe a series of steps that is used by commercial lenders in credit analysis. Of course not all commercial lenders follow the same process, but the steps are representative of typical approaches. The approach used by commercial lenders is of interest in its own right and illustrates a comprehensive credit analysis. However, analysis by others who grant credit often differs. For example, even when a manufacturer conducts some credit analysis prior to granting credit to a customer, it is typically much less extensive than the analysis conducted by a banker because the credit is very short term and the manufacturer is willing to bear some credit risk in the interest of generating a profit on the sale.

We present the steps in a particular order, but they are in fact all interdependent. Thus, analysis at one step may need to be rethought depending on the analysis at some later step.

Step 1: Consider the nature and purpose of the loan

Understanding the purpose of a loan is important not just for deciding whether it should be granted but also for structuring the loan. Loans might be required for only a few months, for several years, or even as a permanent part of a firm's capital structure. Loans might be used for replacement of other financing, to support working capital needs, or to finance the acquisition of long-term assets or another firm.

The required amount of the loan must also be established. When bankruptcy laws provide a bank sufficient protection, it would typically prefer to be the sole financier of small and medium-sized companies, in which case the loan would have to be large enough to retire existing debt. The preference for serving as the sole financier is not just to gain an advantage in providing a menu of financial services to the firm. It also reflects the desirability of not permitting another creditor to maintain a superior interest that would give it a higher priority in case of bankruptcy. If other creditors are willing to subordinate their positions to the bank, that would of course be acceptable so far as the bank is concerned.

Often the commercial lender deals with firms that may have parent-subsidiary relations. The question of to whom one should lend then arises. The answer is usually the entity that owns the assets that will serve as collateral (or that could serve as such if needed in the future). If this entity is the subsidiary and the parent presents some financial strength independent of the subsidiary, a guarantee of the parent could be considered.

National bankruptcy laws in the country where the potential borrower is located also affect the maturity of the loan. When the bankruptcy laws provide weak protection to the commercial lender it may decide only to extend a loan with a short maturity. Short-term loans carry the advantage that the lender can frequently review the borrower and make adjustments to the terms of the loan when necessary.[6] Commercial lenders are inclined to shorten loan maturities especially when lending to firms with little collateral, such as intangible-intensive firms.[7]

Step 2: Consider the type of loan and available security

The type of loan considered is a function of not only its purpose but also the financial strength of the borrower. Thus, to some extent, the loan type will be dictated by the financial analysis described in step 3 in the process. Some of the possibilities are as follows:

- *Open line of credit.* An open line of credit permits the borrower to receive cash up to some specified maximum on an as-needed basis for a specified term, such as one year. To maintain this option, the borrower pays a fee (e.g., $\frac{3}{8}$ of 1 percent) on the unused balance in addition to the interest on any used amount. An open line of credit is useful in cases where the borrower's cash needs are difficult to anticipate.

- *Revolving line of credit.* When it is clear that a firm will need credit beyond the short run, financing may be provided in the form of a "revolver." Sometimes used to support working capital needs, the borrower is scheduled to make payments as the operating cycle proceeds and inventory and receivables are converted to cash. However it is also expected that cash will continue to be advanced so long as the borrower remains in good standing. In addition to interest on amounts outstanding, a fee is charged on the unused line.

- *Working capital loan.* Such a loan is used to finance inventory and receivables, and it is usually secured. The maximum loan balance may be tied to the balance of the working capital accounts. For example, the loan may be allowed to rise to no more than 80 percent of receivables less than 60 days old.

- *Term loan.* Term loans are used for long-term needs and are often secured with long-term assets such as plant or equipment. Typically, the loan will be amortized, requiring periodic payments to reduce the loan balance.

- *Mortgage loan.* Mortgages support the financing of real estate, have long terms, and require periodic amortization of the loan balance.

- *Lease financing.* Lease financing can be used to facilitate the acquisition of any asset but is most commonly used for equipment, including vehicles. Leases may be structured over periods of 1 to 15 years, depending on the life of the underlying asset.

Much bank lending takes place on a secured basis, especially with smaller and more highly leveraged companies. Security will be required unless the loan is short term and the borrower exposes the bank to minimal default risk. When security is required, one consideration is whether the amount of available security is sufficient to support the loan. The amount that a bank will lend on given security involves business judgment, and it depends on a variety of factors that affect the liquidity of the security in the context of a situation where the firm is distressed. It also depends on the extent to which creditor protection laws permit banks to quickly repossess collateral in the event of default. In countries where bankruptcy laws provide weak creditor protection, such as France, banks typically require more collateral for a given loan amount.[8] The following are some rules of thumb often applied in commercial lending to various categories of security:

- *Receivables.* Trade receivables are usually considered the most desirable form of security because they are the most liquid. An average bank allows loans of 50 to 80 percent of the balance of nondelinquent accounts. The percentage applied is lower when (1) there are many small accounts that would be costly to collect where the firm is distressed, (2) there are a few very large accounts, such that problems with a single customer could be serious, (3) bankruptcy laws are creditor-unfriendly and preclude the bank claiming and collecting the receivables while the borrower in default is being restructured, and/or (4) the customer's financial health is closely related to that of the borrower, so that collectibility is endangered just when the borrower is in default. On the latter score, banks often refuse to accept receivables from affiliates as effective security.

- *Inventory.* The desirability of inventory as security varies widely. The best-case scenario is inventory consisting of a common commodity that can easily be sold to other parties if the borrower defaults. More specialized inventory, with appeal to only a limited set of buyers, or inventory that is costly to store or transport is less desirable. An average bank typically lends up to 60 percent on raw materials, 50 percent on finished goods, and 20 percent on work in process.

■ *Machinery and equipment.* Machinery and equipment is less desirable as collateral. It is likely to be used, and it must be stored, insured, and marketed. Keeping the costs of these activities in mind, banks typically will lend only up to 50 percent of the estimated value of such assets in a forced sale such as an auction.

■ *Real estate.* The value of real estate as collateral varies considerably. Banks will often lend up to 80 percent of the appraised value of readily salable real estate. On the other hand, a factory designed for a unique purpose would be much less desirable.

When security is required to make a loan viable, a commercial lender will estimate the amounts that could be lent on each of the assets available as security. Unless the amount exceeds the required loan balance, the loan would not be extended.

Even when a loan is not secured initially, a bank can require a "negative pledge" on the firm's assets – a pledge that the firm will not use the assets as security for any other creditor. In that case, if the borrower begins to experience difficulty and defaults on the loan, and if there are no other creditors in the picture, the bank can demand the loan become secured if it is to remain outstanding.

Step 3: Analyze the potential borrower's financial status

This portion of the analysis involves all the steps discussed in our chapters on business strategy analysis, accounting analysis, and financial analysis. The emphasis, however, is on the firm's ability to service the debt at the scheduled rate. The focus of the analysis depends on the type of financing under consideration. For example, if a short-term loan is considered to support seasonal fluctuations in inventory, the emphasis would be on the ability of the firm to convert the inventory into cash on a timely basis. In contrast, a term loan to support plant and equipment must be made with confidence in the long-run earnings prospects of the firm.

KEY ANALYSIS QUESTIONS

Some of the questions to be addressed in analyzing a potential borrower's financial status include the following:

■ *Business strategy analysis*. How does this business work? Why is it valuable? What is its strategy for sustaining or enhancing that value? How well qualified is the management to carry out that strategy effectively? Is the viability of the business highly dependent on the talents of the existing management team?

■ *Accounting analysis*. How well do the firm's financial statements reflect its underlying economic reality? Are there reasons to believe that the firm's performance is stronger or weaker than reported profitability would suggest? Are there sizable off-balance sheet liabilities (e.g., operating leases) that would affect the potential borrower's ability to repay the loan?

■ *Financial analysis*. Is the firm's level of profitability unusually high or low? What are the sources of any unusual degree of profitability? How sustainable are they? What risks are associated with the operating profit stream? How highly leveraged is the firm? What is the firm's funds flow picture? What are its major sources and uses of funds? Are funds required to finance expected growth? How great are fund flows expected to be relative to the debt service required? Given the possible volatility in those fund flows, how likely is it that they could fall to a level insufficient to service debt and meet other commitments?

Ultimately, the key question in the financial analysis is how likely it is that cash flows will be sufficient to repay the loan. With that question in mind, lenders focus much attention on solvency ratios: the magnitude of various measures of profits and cash flows relative to debt service and other requirements. To the extent such a ratio exceeds 1, it indicates the "margin of safety" the lender faces. When such a ratio is combined with an assessment of the variance in its numerator, it provides an indication of the probability of nonpayment.

Ratio analysis from the perspective of a creditor differs somewhat from that of an owner. For example, there is greater emphasis on cash flows and earnings available to *all* claimants (not just owners) *before* taxes (since interest is tax-deductible and paid out of pretax euros). To illustrate, the creditor's perspective is apparent in the following solvency ratio, called the "funds flow coverage ratio":

$$\text{Funds flow coverage} = \frac{\text{EBIT} + \text{Depreciation}}{\text{Interest} + \dfrac{\text{Debt repayment}}{(1 - \text{tax rate})} + \dfrac{\text{Preference dividends}}{(1 - \text{tax rate})}}$$

We see earnings before both interest and taxes in the numerator. This measures the numerator in a way that can be compared directly to the interest expense in the denominator, because interest expense is paid out of pretax euros. In contrast, any payment of principal scheduled for a given year is nondeductible and must be made out of after-tax profits. In essence, with a 50 percent tax rate, one euro of principal payment is "twice as expensive" as a one-euro interest payment. Scaling the payment of principal by (1 – tax rate) accounts for this. The same idea applies to preference dividends, which are not tax-deductible.

The funds flow coverage ratio provides an indication of how comfortably the funds flow can cover unavoidable expenditures. The ratio excludes payments such as dividend payments to ordinary shareholders and capital expenditures on the premise that they could be reduced to zero to make debt payments if necessary.[9] Clearly, however, if the firm is to survive in the long run, funds flow must be sufficient to not only service debt but also maintain plant assets. Thus, long-run survival requires a funds flow coverage ratio well in excess of 1.[10]

It would be overly simplistic to establish any particular threshold above which a ratio indicates a loan is justified. However, a creditor clearly wants to be in a position to be repaid on schedule, even when the borrower faces a reasonably foreseeable difficulty. That argues for lending only when the funds flow coverage is expected to exceed 1, even in a recession scenario – and higher if some allowance for capital expenditures is prudent.

The financial analysis should produce more than an assessment of the risk of nonpayment. It should also identify the nature of the significant risks. At many commercial banks it is standard operating procedure to summarize the analysis of the firm by listing the key risks that could lead to default and factors that could be used to control those risks if the loan were made. That information can be used in structuring the detailed terms of the loan so as to trigger default when problems arise, at a stage early enough to permit corrective action.

Step 4: Utilize forecasts to assess payment prospects

Already implicit in some of the above discussion is a forward-looking view of the firm's ability to service the loan. Good credit analysis should also be supported by explicit forecasts. The basis for such forecasts is usually management, but, not surprisingly, lenders do not accept such forecasts without question.

In forecasting, a variety of scenarios should be considered – including not just a "best guess" but also a "pessimistic" scenario. Ideally, the firm should be strong enough to repay the loan even in the latter scenario. Ironically, it is not necessarily a decline in sales that presents the greatest risk to the lender. If managers can respond quickly to a sales dropoff, it should be accompanied by a liquidation of receivables and inventory, which enhances cash flow for a given level of earnings. The nightmare scenario is one that involves large negative profit margins, perhaps because managers are caught by surprise by a downturn in demand and are forced to liquidate inventory at substantially reduced prices.

At times it is possible to reconsider the structure of a loan so as to permit it to "cash flow." That is, the term of the loan might be extended or the amortization pattern changed. Often a bank will grant a loan with the expectation that it will be continually renewed, thus becoming a permanent part of the firm's financial structure. (Such a loan is labeled an "evergreen.") In that case the loan will still be written as if it is due within the short term, and the bank must assure itself of a viable "exit strategy." However, the firm would be expected to service the loan by simply covering interest payments.

Step 5: Assemble the detailed loan structure, including loan covenants

If the analysis thus far indicates that a loan is in order, it is then time to pull together the detailed structure: type of loan, repayment schedule, loan covenants, and pricing. The first two items were discussed above. Here we discuss loan covenants and pricing.

Writing loan covenants

Loan covenants specify mutual expectations of the borrower and lender by specifying actions the borrower will and will not take. Some covenants require certain actions (such as regular provision of financial statements); others preclude certain actions (such as undertaking an acquisition without the permission of the lender); still others require maintenance of certain financial ratios. Violation of a covenant represents an event of default that could cause immediate acceleration of the debt payment, but in most cases the lender uses the default as an opportunity to re-examine the situation and either waive the violation or renegotiate the loan.

Loan covenants must strike a balance between protecting the interests of the lender and providing the flexibility management needs to run the business. The covenants represent a mechanism for ensuring that the business will remain as strong as the two parties anticipated at the time the loan was granted. Thus, required financial ratios are typically based on the levels that existed at that time, perhaps with some allowance for deterioration but often with some expected improvement over time.

The particular covenants included in the agreement should contain the significant risks identified in the financial analysis, or at least provide early warning that such risks are surfacing. Some commonly used financial covenants include:

- *Maintenance of minimum net worth.* This covenant assures that the firm will maintain an "equity cushion" to protect the lender. Covenants typically require a level of net worth rather than a particular level of profit. In the final analysis, the lender may not care whether that net worth is maintained by generating profit, cutting dividends, or issuing new equity. Tying the covenant to net worth offers the firm the flexibility to use any of these avenues to avoid default.

- *Minimum coverage ratio.* Especially in the case of a long-term loan, such as a term loan, the lender may want to supplement a net worth covenant with one based on coverage of interest or total debt service. The funds flow coverage ratio presented above would be an example. Maintenance of some minimum coverage helps assure that the ability of the firm to generate funds internally is strong enough to justify the long-term nature of the loan.

- *Maximum ratio of total liabilities to net worth.* This ratio constrains the risk of high leverage and prevents growth without either retaining earnings or infusing equity.

- *Minimum net working capital balance or current ratio.* Constraints on this ratio force a firm to maintain its liquidity by using cash generated from operations to retire current liabilities (as opposed to acquiring long-lived assets).

- *Maximum ratio of capital expenditures to earnings before depreciation.* Constraints on this ratio help prevent the firm from investing in growth (including the illiquid assets necessary to support growth) unless such growth can be financed internally, with some margin remaining for debt service.

In addition to such financial covenants, loans sometimes place restrictions on other borrowing activity, pledging of assets to other lenders, selling of substantial parts of assets, engaging in mergers or acquisitions, and payment of dividends.

Covenants are included not only in private lending agreements with banks, insurance companies, and others, but also in public debt agreements. However, public debt agreements tend to have less restrictive covenants for two reasons. First, negotiations resulting from a violation of public debt covenants are costly (possibly involving not just the trustee, but also bondholders), and so they are written to be triggered only in serious circumstances. Second, public debt is usually issued by stronger, more creditworthy firms. (The primary exception would be high yield debt issued in conjunction with leveraged buyouts.) For the most financially healthy firms with strong debt ratings, very few covenants will be used – only those necessary to limit dramatic changes in the firm's operations, such as a major merger or acquisition.

Dividend payout restrictions are not only included in debt contracts, but may also be mandated by law. For example, in several Continental European countries firms are legally obliged to transfer a proportion of their profits to a legal reserve, out of which they cannot distribute dividends. The law then prescribes the minimum legal reserve that a company must maintain.

Loan pricing

A detailed discussion of loan pricing falls outside the scope of this text. The essence of pricing is to assure that the yield on the loan is sufficient to cover (1) the lender's cost of borrowed funds, (2) the lender's costs of administering and servicing the loan, (3) a premium for exposure to default risk, and (4) at least a normal return on the equity capital necessary to support the lending operation. The price is often stated in terms of a deviation from a bank's base rate – the rate charged to stronger borrowers. For example, a loan might be granted at base rate plus 2 percent. An alternative base is LIBOR, or the London Interbank Offered Rate, the rate at which large banks from various nations lend large blocks of funds to each other.

Banks compete actively for commercial lending business, and it is rare that a yield includes more than 2 percentage points to cover the cost of default risk. If the spread to cover default risk is, say, 1 percent, and the bank recovers only 50 percent of amounts due on loans that turn out bad, then the bank can afford only 2 percent of their loans to fall into that category. This underscores how important it is for banks to conduct a thorough analysis and to contain the riskiness of their loan portfolio.

FINANCIAL STATEMENT ANALYSIS AND PUBLIC DEBT

Fundamentally, the issues involved in analysis of public debt are no different from those of bank loans and other private debt issues. Institutionally, however, the contexts are different. Bankers can maintain very close relations with clients so as to form an initial assessment of their credit risk and monitor their activities during the loan period. In the case of public debt, the investors are distanced from the issuer. To a large extent, they must depend on professional debt analysts, including debt raters, to assess the riskiness of the debt and monitor the firm's ongoing activities. Such analysts and debt raters thus serve an important function in closing the information gap between issuers and investors.

The meaning of debt ratings

The two major debt rating agencies in the world are Moody's and Standard and Poor's. Using the Standard and Poor's labeling system, the highest possible rating is AAA. Proceeding downward from AAA, the ratings are AA, A, BBB, BB, B, CCC, CC, C, and D, where "D" indicates debt in default. Table 10.2 presents examples of firms in rating categories AAA through B, as well as the average interest expense as a percentage of total debt across all firms in each category. Only about 1 percent of the public non-financial companies rated by Standard & Poor's have the financial strength to merit an AAA rating. Among the few are the European firms Novartis and Nestlé – both among the largest, most profitable firms in the world. AA firms are also very strong and include British Petroleum, Royal Dutch Shell, and Siemens. Firms rated AAA and AA have the lowest costs of debt financing; in fiscal year 2005 their average interest expenses were roughly 2.8 and 3.3 percent of total debt.

To be considered investment grade, a firm must achieve a rating of BBB or higher. Many funds are precluded by their articles from investing in any bonds below that grade. Even to achieve a grade of BBB is difficult. Renault, one the largest car manufacturers in the world, was rated as "only" BBB – barely investment grade – in 2006. Fiat and Royal Ahold were in the BB category. Ahold was the third largest food retailer in the world. However, it had suffered from the effects of an accounting fraud at one of its U.S.-based subsidiaries, the economic slowdown in Europe, and price wars in its domestic market. The B category includes ASM International, Invensys, and Rhodia, all of which were facing financial difficulty. In Europe, none of the industrial companies rated by Standard & Poor's are in a category below the B category. An example of a Japan-based CCC rated

TABLE 10.2 Debt ratings: European example firms and average interest expense by category

S&P debt rating	Example firms in 2006	Percentage of European companies given same rating by S&P	Average interest expense to total debt, fiscal 2005 (%)
AAA	Nestlé	1.1	2.81
	Novartis		
AA	BASF	7.5	3.25
	British Petroleum		
	GlaxoSmithKline		
	Royal Dutch Shell		
	Siemens		
	Total		
A	Carrefour	29.5	4.31
	Deutsche Post		
	Groupe Danone		
	Nokia		
	Philips Electronics		
	Tesco		
	Volkswagen		
BBB	British American Tobacco	38.8	4.47
	Cadbury Schweppes		
	Electrolux		
	Moët Hennessy Luis Vuitton		
	Renault		
	Repsol YPF		
BB	British Airways	16.0	5.86
	Fiat		
	Pernod Ricard		
	Royal Ahold		
B	ASM International	7.1	7.54
	Invensys		
	Rhodia		

Source: Standard and Poor's 2006 and Thomson Worldscope.

firm is car manufacturer Mitsubishi Motors Corporation, which was close to bankruptcy following the overcapacity problems faced by the industry. U.S.-based Delta Airlines and Northwest Airlines were rated as D, since they had filed for bankruptcy in 2005.

Table 10.2 shows that the cost of debt financing rises markedly once firms' debt falls below investment grade. For example, in fiscal 2005 the interest expenses of companies with BBB rated debt were 4.5 percent of total debt, on average; interest rates for BB rated companies were 5.9 percent; and interest rates for firms with B rated debt were 7.5 percent.

Table 10.3 shows median financial ratios for firms by debt rating category. Firms with AAA and AA ratings have very strong earnings and cash flow performance as well as minimal leverage. Firms in the BBB class are only moderately leveraged, with about 45 percent of net capital coming in the form of debt. Earnings tend to be relatively strong, as indicated by a pretax interest coverage (EBIT/interest) of 4.9 and a cash flow debt coverage (cash flow from operations/total debt) of nearly 27 percent. Firms with B ratings, however, face significant risks: they typically report small profits or losses, have high leverage, and have interest coverage ratios close to 1.

Factors that drive debt ratings

Research demonstrates that some of the variation in debt ratings can be explained as a function of selected financial statement ratios, even as used within a quantitative model that incorporates no subjective human judgment. Some debt rating agencies rely heavily on quantitative models, and such models are commonly used by insurance companies, banks, and others to assist in the evaluation of the riskiness of debt issues for which a public rating is not available.

Table 10.4 lists the factors used by three different firms in their quantitative debt rating models. The firms include one insurance company and one bank, which use the models in their private placement activities, and an investment research firm, which employs the models in evaluating its own debt purchases and holdings. In each case profitability and leverage play an important role in the rating. One firm also uses firm size as an indicator, with larger size associated with higher ratings.

Several researchers have estimated quantitative models used for debt ratings. Two of these models, developed by Kaplan and Urwitz and shown in Table 10.5, highlight the relative importance of the factors.[11] Model 1 has the greater ability to explain variation in bond ratings. However, it includes some factors based on equity market data, which are not available for all firms. Model 2 is based solely on financial statement data.

The factors in Table 10.5 are listed in the order of their statistical significance in Model 1. An interesting feature is that the most important factor explaining debt

TABLE 10.3 Debt ratings: Median financial ratios by category

S&P debt rating	NOPAT to net capital	Pretax interest coverage	Median ratios for overall category in May 2006 (European non-financial companies only) Cash flow from operations to total debt	Net debt to net capital
AAA	10.0%	17.2 times	44.7%	15.0%
AA	7.9	15.9	36.2	29.9
A	6.8	7.0	24.9	43.6
BBB	5.6	4.9	23.2	44.8
BB	4.7	2.4	16.8	54.9
B	1.2	1.2	−3.6	57.5

Source: Thomson Worldscope.

TABLE 10.4 Factors used in quantitative models of debt ratings

	Firm 1	Firm 2	Firm 3
Profitability measures	Return on net capital	Return on net capital	Return on net capital
Leverage measures	Non-current debt to capitalization	Non-current debt to capitalization Total debt to total capital	Non-current debt to capitalization
Profitability and leverage	Interest coverage Cash flow to non-current debt	Interest coverage Cash flow to non-current debt	Fixed charge coverage Coverage of current debt and fixed charges
Firm size	Sales	Total assets	
Other		Standard deviation of return Subordination status	

ratings is not a financial ratio at all – it is simply firm size! Large firms tend to get better ratings than small firms. Whether the debt is subordinated or unsubordinated is next most important, followed by a leverage indicator. Profitability appears less important, but in part that reflects the presence in the model of multiple factors (ROA and interest coverage) that capture profitability. It is only the explanatory power that is *unique* to a given variable that is indicated by the ranking in Table 10.5. Explanatory power common to the two variables is not considered.

When applied to a sample of bonds that were not used in the estimation process, the Kaplan-Urwitz Model 1 predicted the rating category correctly in 44 of 64 cases, or 63 percent of the time. Where it erred, the model was never off by more than one category, and in about half of those cases its prediction was more consistent with the market yield on the debt than was the actual debt rating. The discrepancies between actual ratings and those estimated using the Kaplan-Urwitz model indicate that rating agencies incorporate factors other than financial ratios in their analysis. These are likely to include the types of strategic, accounting, and prospective analyses discussed throughout this book.

We have also estimated a debt ratings prediction model that is conceptually similar to the Kaplan-Urwitz model but includes the factors from Table 10.3 (plus firm size) as predictors. The sample of companies that we used to estimate the model is the sample of 251 European non-financial companies that were rated by Standard & Poor's in May 2006. Table 10.6 lists the factors and their coefficients in order of their statistical significance. Note that one important difference between this model and the Kaplan-Urwitz model is that this model predicts company-specific debt ratings instead of bond-issue-specific ratings. When applied to the sample of 251 European companies, the model predicted the debt rating category correctly for 55 percent of the companies. The model was off by one category for 41 percent of the companies and off by two categories for 4 percent of the companies. The model was never off by more than two categories.

In the "European" debt ratings prediction model, factors similar to those in the Kaplan-Urwitz model are most significant. That is, Standard and Poor's European debt ratings in May 2006 were primarily driven by firm size, profitability, riskiness of the profit stream, and leverage (in order of statistical significance). The variables cash

TABLE 10.5 Kaplan-Urwitz models of debt ratings

Firm or debt characteristic	Variable reflecting characteristic	Coefficients Model 1	Model 2
	Model intercept	5.67	4.41
Firm size	Total assets[a]	0.0011	0.0013
Subordination status of debt	1 = subordinated; 0 = unsubordinated	–2.36	–2.56
Leverage	Non-current debt to total assets	–2.85	–2.72
Systematic risk	Market model beta, indicating sensitivity of share price to market-wide movements (1 = average)[b]	–0.87	—
Profitability	Net profit to total assets	5.13	
Unsystematic risk	Standard deviation of residual from market model (average = .10)	–2.90	—
Riskiness of profit stream	Coefficient of variation in net profit over 5 years (standard deviation/mean)	—	–0.53
Interest coverage	Pretax funds flow before interest to interest expense	0.007	0.006

The score from the model is converted to a bond rating as follows:
If score > 6.76, predict AAA
   score 6.76–5.19, predict AA
   score 5.19–3.28, predict A
   score 3.28–1.57, predict BBB
   score 1.57–0.00, predict BB
   score < 0.00, predict B

a. The coefficient in the Kaplan-Urwitz model was estimated at .005 (Model 1) and .006 (Model 2). Its scale has been adjusted to reflect that the estimates were based on assets measured in U.S. dollars from the early 1970s. Given that $1 from 1972 is approximately equivalent to $4.67 in 2005, the original coefficient has been divided by 4.67. On December 31, 2005, $1 was approximately equal to £0.58, €0.84, DKK6.31, and SEK7.96.

b. Market model is estimated by regressing stock returns on the market index, using monthly data for the prior 5 years.

flow to total debt and interest coverage have low coefficients and are not statistically significant. We did not include equity market data in the model because a substantial proportion of the European companies rated by Standard and Poor's were not publicly listed. This may be one of the reasons why this model predicts debt ratings slightly less accurately than the Kaplan-Urwitz model.

Given that debt ratings can be explained reasonably well in terms of a handful of financial ratios, one might question whether ratings convey any *news* to investors – anything that could not already have been garnered from publicly available financial data. The answer to the question is yes, at least in the case of debt rating downgrades. That is, downgrades are greeted with drops in both bond and share prices.[12] To be sure, the capital markets anticipate much of the information reflected in rating changes. But that is not surprising, given that the changes often represent reactions to recent known events and that the rating agencies typically indicate in advance that a change is being considered.

TABLE 10.6 Debt ratings prediction model estimated on a sample of European companies

Firm or debt characteristic	Variable reflecting characteristic	Coefficients
	Model intercept	0.853
Firm size	Natural logarithm of total assets (in € billions)	0.601
Profitability	NOPAT to net capital (Operating ROA)	12.008
Riskiness of profit stream	Standard deviation of Operating ROA over 5 years	−5.247
Leverage	Net debt to net capital	−0.848
Interest coverage	EBIT to interest expense	0.003
Cash flow performance	Cash flow from operations to total debt	−0.041

The score from the model is converted to a debt rating as follows:
If score > 6.01, predict AAA
  score 6.01–4.31, predict AA
  score 4.31–2.78, predict A
  score 2.78–1.31, predict BBB
  score 1.31–0.00, predict BB
  score < 0.00, predict B

PREDICTION OF DISTRESS AND TURNAROUND

The key task in credit analysis is assessing the probability that a firm will face financial distress and fail to repay a loan. A related analysis, relevant once a firm begins to face distress, involves considering whether it can be turned around. In this section we consider evidence on the predictability of these states.

The prediction of either distress or turnaround is a complex, difficult, and subjective task that involves all of the steps of analysis discussed throughout this book: business strategy analysis, accounting analysis, financial analysis, and prospective analysis. Purely quantitative models of the process can rarely serve as substitutes for the hard work the analysis involves. However, research on such models does offer some insight into which financial indicators are most useful in the task. Moreover, there are some settings where extensive credit checks are too costly to justify, and where quantitative distress prediction models are useful. For example, the commercially available "Zeta" model is used by some manufacturers and other firms to assess the creditworthiness of their customers.[13]

Several distress prediction models have been developed over the years.[14] They are similar to the debt rating models, but instead of predicting ratings, they predict whether a firm will face some state of distress within one year, typically defined as bankruptcy. One study suggests that the factors most useful (on a stand-alone basis) in predicting bankruptcy one year in advance are:[15]

1. Profitability $= \left[\dfrac{\text{Net income}}{\text{Net worth}}\right]$

2. Volatility $= \left[\text{Standard deviation of}\left(\dfrac{\text{Net income}}{\text{Net worth}}\right)\right]$

3. Financial leverage $= \left[\dfrac{\text{Market value of equity}}{(\text{Market value of equity} + \text{Book value of debt})}\right]$

The evidence indicates that the key to whether a firm will face distress is its level of profitability, the volatility of that profitability, and how much leverage it faces. Interestingly, liquidity measures turn out to be much less important. Current liquidity won't save an unhealthy firm if it is losing money at a fast pace.

Of course, if one were interested in predicting distress there would be no need to restrict attention to one variable at a time. A number of multifactor models have been designed to predict financial distress. One such model, the Altman Z-score model, weights five variables to compute a bankruptcy score.[16] For public companies the model is as follows:[17]

$$Z = 1.2(X_1) + 1.4(X_2) + 3.3(X_3) + 0.6(X_4) + 1.0(X_5)$$

where X_1 = net working capital/total assets
X_2 = retained earnings/total assets
X_3 = EBIT/total assets
X_4 = market value of equity/book value of total liabilities
X_5 = sales/total assets

The model predicts bankruptcy when Z < 1.81. The range between 1.81 and 2.67 is labeled the "gray area."

The following table presents calculations for two companies, Invensys and AstraZeneca:

		Invensys Plc		AstraZeneca Plc	
	Model coefficient	Ratios	Score	Ratios	Score
Net working capital/assets	1.2	0.22	0.26	0.28	0.34
Retained earnings/Total assets	1.4	−1.80	−2.52	0.70	0.98
EBIT/Total assets	3.3	0.04	0.13	0.26	0.86
Market value of equity/Book value of total liabilities	0.6	0.32	0.19	6.90	4.10
Sales/Total assets	1.0	1.10	1.10	0.96	0.96
			−0.84		7.24

Invensys was created in 1998 through the merger of two engineering conglomerates, BTR and Siebe. Following the merger, analysts were critical of the conglomerate's lack of focus and its poor growth prospects. In the year ended March 31, 2003, Invensys reported a record loss of £1.4 billion. The loss was primarily attributable to losses on the disposal of discontinued operations, restructuring costs, and the company's £585 million write-down of its investment in Baan Company, an almost bankrupt company that Invensys had acquired in 2000. At that time, Invensys market value had dropped from £4.7 billion in March 2001 to £368 million in March 2003. In the year ended March 31, 2006, Invensys reported its first small net profit (excluding discontinued operations) of £22 million since 1998 and reached a market value of £910 million. It is not surprising to see that the model rates Invensys' likelihood of failure as high. AstraZeneca, an AA rated company, has much stronger financial performance and a much higher market valuation (£44.7 billion) than Invensys. AstraZeneca's score indicates that it has a very low likelihood of failure.

Such models have some ability to predict failing and surviving firms. Altman reports that when the model was applied to a holdout sample containing 33 failed and 33 nonfailed firms (the same proportion used to estimate the model), it correctly predicted the outcome in 63 of 66 cases. However, the performance of the model would degrade substantially if applied to a holdout sample where the proportion of failed and nonfailed firms was not forced to be the same as that used to estimate the model.

The Altman Z-score model was estimated on a sample of U.S. firms. When applying this model to a sample of non-U.S. firms, the following complications must be considered. First, accounting practices may differ from country to country. In particular, under some accounting systems total liabilities may be substantially understated because of firms' use of off-balance sheet financing. When comparing the Altman Z-scores of two firms with different accounting practices, the preferred approach would be to undo these firms' financial statements from accounting distortions and bring all off-balance sheet liabilities on the balance sheet before calculating the scores. Second, although the model may be equally useful across countries in predicting financial distress, the likelihood that financial distress leads to bankruptcy depends on national bankruptcy laws and thus varies from country to country.

One way to overcome the above problems is to use distress prediction models that were estimated in a particular firm's home country. An international survey of distress prediction models suggests that more than 40 variants of such models exist worldwide.[18] A common characteristic of these models is that they all include some measures of profitability and leverage. For example, one model that was developed by Taffler and is commonly used in the U.K. calculates Z-scores as follows:[19]

$$Z = 3.20 + 12.18(X_1) + 2.50(X_2) - 10.68(X_3) + 0.0289(X_4)$$

where X_1 = profit before tax/current liabilities
X_2 = current assets/total liabilities
X_3 = current liabilities/total assets
X_4 = no-credit interval (in days)

The no-credit interval is defined as immediate assets (current assets excluding inventories and prepaid expenses) minus current liabilities, divided by total operating expenses excluding depreciation and multiplied by 365 days. This variable measures how long the firm can finance its current operations when other sources of short-term finance are unavailable. The model predicts bankruptcy when $Z < 0$. In fiscal year 2005, the Taffler Z-scores for Invensys and AstraZeneca were 1.06 and 18.31, respectively.

Simple distress prediction models like the Altman and the Taffler models cannot serve as a replacement for in-depth analysis of the kind discussed throughout this book. But they do provide a useful reminder of the power of financial statement data to summarize important dimensions of the firm's performance. In addition, they can be useful for screening large numbers of firms prior to more in-depth analysis of corporate strategy, management expertise, market position, and financial ratio performance.

SUMMARY

Credit analysis is the evaluation of a firm from the perspective of a holder or potential holder of its debt. Credit analysis is important to a wide variety of economic agents – not just bankers and other financial intermediaries but also public debt analysts, industrial companies, service companies, and others.

At the heart of credit analysis lie the same techniques described in Chapters 2 through 8: business strategy analysis, accounting analysis, financial analysis, and portions of prospective analysis. The purpose of the analysis is not just to assess the likelihood that a potential borrower will fail to repay the loan. It is also important to identify the nature of the key risks involved, and how the loan might be structured to mitigate or control those risks. A well structured loan provides the lender with a viable "exit strategy," even in the case of default. A key to this structure is properly designed accounting-based covenants.

Fundamentally, the issues involved in analysis of public debt are no different from those involved in evaluating bank loans or other private debt. Institutionally, however, the contexts are different. Investors in public debt are usually not close to the borrower and must rely on other agents, including debt raters and other analysts, to assess creditworthiness. Debt ratings, which depend heavily on firm size and financial measures of performance, have an important influence on the market yields that must be offered to issue debt.

The key task in credit analysis is the assessment of the probability of default. The task is complex, difficult, and to some extent, subjective. A small number of key financial ratios can help predict financial distress with some accuracy. The most important financial indicators for this purpose are profitability, volatility of profits, and leverage. However, the models cannot replace the in-depth forms of analysis discussed in this book.

DISCUSSION QUESTIONS

1. What are the critical performance dimensions for (a) a retailer and (b) a financial services company that should be considered in credit analysis? What ratios would you suggest looking at for each of these dimensions?

2. Why would a company pay to have its public debt rated by a major rating agency (such as Fitch, Moody's or Standard & Poor's)? Why might a firm decide not to have its debt rated?

3. Some have argued that the market for original-issue junk bonds developed in the U.S. in the late 1970s as a result of a failure in the rating process. Proponents of this argument suggest that rating agencies rated companies too harshly at the low end of the rating scale, denying investment-grade status to some deserving companies. What are proponents of this argument effectively assuming were the incentives of rating agencies? What economic forces could give rise to this incentive?

4. Many debt agreements require borrowers to obtain the permission of the lender before undertaking a major acquisition or asset sale. Why would the lender want to include this type of restriction?

5. Betty Li, the Finance Director of a company applying for a new loan, states, "I will never agree to a debt covenant that restricts my ability to pay dividends to my shareholders because it reduces shareholder wealth." Do you agree with this argument?

6. A bank extends three loans to the following companies: an Italy-based biotech firm; a France-based car manufacturer; and a U.K.-based food retailer. How may these three loans differ from each other in terms of loan maturity, required collateral, and loan amount?

7. Cambridge Construction Plc follows the percentage-of-completion method for reporting long-term contract revenues. The percentage of completion is based on

the cost of materials shipped to the project site as a percentage of total expected material costs. Cambridge's major debt agreement includes restrictions on net worth, interest coverage, and minimum working capital requirements. A leading analyst claims that "the company is buying its way out of these covenants by spending cash and buying materials, even when they are not needed." Explain how this may be possible.

8. Can Cambridge improve its Z score by behaving as the analyst claims in Question 7? Is this change consistent with economic reality?

9. A banker asserts, "I avoid lending to companies with negative cash from operations because they are too risky." Is this a sensible lending policy?

10. A leading retailer finds itself in a financial bind. It doesn't have sufficient cash flow from operations to finance its growth, and it is close to violating the maximum debt-to-assets ratio allowed by its covenants. The Marketing Director suggests, "We can raise cash for our growth by selling the existing stores and leasing them back. This source of financing is cheap since it avoids violating either the debt-to-assets or interest coverage ratios in our covenants." Do you agree with his analysis? Why or why not? As the firm's banker, how would you view this arrangement?

NOTES

1. Some arguments that have been raised in other countries against universal banking are the following. First, because of their investment banking activities, universal banks may incur greater risks than other commercial banks and, consequently, jeopardize the stability of a country's financial system. Second, universal banks may become too powerful because of their size and hold back competition in the banking industry. Third, universal banks could potentially misuse inside information about clients that they obtained through their lending activities in securities trading. In the U.S., these concerns led to ban on universal banking until 1999. For a discussion of the potential advantages and disadvantages of universal banking, see, for example, George J. Benston, "Universal Banking," *Journal of Economic Perspectives* (1994): 121–143.
2. See Sergei. A. Davydenko and Julian R. Franks, "Do Bankruptcy Codes Matter? A Study of Defaults in France, Germany and the U.K.," working paper, University of Toronto and London Business School, 2005.
3. See Steven Ongena and David C. Smith, "What Determines the Number of Bank Relationships? Cross-Country Evidence," *Journal of Financial Intermediation* (2000): 26–56.
4. See Asli Demirgüç-Kunt and Vojislav Maksimovic, "Firms as Financial Intermediaries: Evidence from Trade Credit Data," working paper, World Bank and University of Maryland, 2001.
5. See Marie H. R. Bakker, Leonora Klapper, and Gregory F. Udell, "Financing Small and Medium-Sized Enterprises with Factoring: Global Growth and Its Potential In Eastern Europe," working paper, World Bank and Indiana University, 2004.
6. See Asli Demirgüç-Kunt and Vojislav Maksimovic, "Institutions, Financial Markets, and Firm Debt Maturity," *Journal of Financial Economics* 54 (1999): 295–336.
7. See Mariassunta Giannetti, "Do Better Institutions Mitigate Agency Problems? Evidence from Corporate Finance Choices," *Journal of Financial and Quantitative Analysis* 38 (2003): 185–212.
8. Sergei. A. Davydenko and Julian R. Franks, op. cit.
9. The same is true of preference dividends. However, when preference shares are cumulative, any dividends missed must be paid later, when and if the firm returns to profitability.
10. Other relevant coverage ratios are discussed in Chapter 5.
11. Robert Kaplan and G. Urwitz, "Statistical Models of Bond Ratings: A Methodological Inquiry," *Journal of Business* (April 1979): 231–261.

12. See Robert Holthausen and Richard Leftwich, "The Effect of Bond Rating Changes on Common Stock Prices," *Journal of Financial Economics* (September 1986): 57–90; and John Hand, Robert Holthausen, and Richard Leftwich, "The Effect of Bond Rating Announcements on Bond and Stock Prices," *Journal of Finance* (June 1992): 733–752.

13. See *Corporate Financial Distress* by Edward Altman (New York: John Wiley, 1993).

14. See Edward Altman, "Financial Ratios, Discriminant Analysis, and the Prediction of Corporate Bankruptcy," *Journal of Finance* (September 1968): 589–609; Altman, *Corporate Financial Distress,* op. cit.; William Beaver, "Financial Ratios as Predictors of Distress," *Journal of Accounting Research,* Supplement (1966): 71–111; James Ohlson, "Financial Ratios and the Probabilistic Prediction of Bankruptcy," *Journal of Accounting Research* (Spring 1980): 109–131; and Mark Zmijewski, "Predicting Corporate Bankruptcy: An Empirical Comparison of the Extant Financial Distress Models," working paper, SUNY at Buffalo, 1983.

15. Zmijewski, op. cit.

16. Altman, *Corporate Financial Distress,* op. cit.

17. For private firms, Altman, ibid., adjusts the public model by changing the numerator for the variable X_4 from the market value of equity to the book value. The revised model follows:

$$Z = .717(X_1) + .847(X_2) + 3.107(X_3) + 0.420(X_4) + .998(X_5)$$

where X_1 = net working capital/total assets
X_2 = retained earnings/total assets
X_3 = EBIT/total assets
X_4 = book value of equity/book value of total liabilities
X_5 = sales/total assets

The model predicts bankruptcy when $Z < 1.20$. The range between 1.20 and 2.90 is labeled the "gray area."

18. See E. Altman and P. Narayanan, "An International Survey of Business Failure Classification Models," *Financial Markets, Institutions and Instruments* (May 1997): 1–57, for an extensive description of various non-U.S. bankruptcy prediction models.

19. The Taffler model and tests of its predictive accuracy are described in R. Taffler, "The Assessment of Company Solvency and Performance Using a Statistical Model," *Accounting and Business Research* (1983): 295–307 and R. Taffler, "Empirical Models for the Monitoring of UK Corporations," *Journal of Banking and Finance* (1984): 199–227.

KarstadtQuelle AG[1]

Credit analyst Felix Brüggen glanced through the latest annual and quarterly reports of the German publicly listed company KarstadtQuelle AG. He was given the task to assess the creditworthiness of KarstadtQuelle, determine whether the company could bear the burden of another loan, and, if so, determine the maximum loan amount and set the appropriate interest rate on the new loan. KarstadtQuelle was a German diversified company that operated 90 German department stores and 32 German sport stores, provided European mail order services under the brand names neckermann.de and Quelle, held a 50 percent stake in tour operator Thomas Cook AG, and held investments in real estate through its subsidiary Karstadt Immobilien.[2] The company had been close to bankruptcy in 2004, but had shown a remarkable turnaround in 2005. In March 2006, KarstadtQuelle announced that it was debt-free, which suggested that the company had been able to substantially improve its creditworthiness.

KarstadtQuelle in 2004[3]

In the second half of 2004, KarstadtQuelle was on the verge of bankruptcy. The company did not reach its financial targets for that year and struggled under the debt load it had built up over the years, while lacking access to new long-term financing. The main reasons for the company's problems, which KarstadtQuelle's (new) management outlined in the company's 2005 Annual Report, were mismanagement and difficult market circumstances. The poor financial situation required drastic measures. In 2004, KarstadtQuelle's Management Board changed composition – by replacing the managing and finance directors – and the company reorganized the Management Boards of many of its subsidiaries. In addition, the company negotiated a new three-year credit facility of €1.75 billion with a syndicate of 16 banks, agreed with its current shareholders to issue new shares for an amount of approximately €500 million, and issued €140 million in convertible bonds. These capital increases were supported by the announcement of a new restructuring plan that was to be carried out in fiscal 2005. During 2004, KarstadtQuelle's share price decreased, however, by 61 percent, from €19.70 to €7.60.

KarstadtQuelle in 2005

Fiscal year 2005 was labeled by management "the year of restructuring." KarstadtQuelle's restructuring program had the following components:

■ *Divestments in retail.* The company would strengthen its 88 larger department stores – with sales space above 8,000 square meters and total revenues of €4.5 billion – and

1. Professor Erik Peek prepared this case. The case is intended solely as the basis for class discussion and is not intended to serve as an endorsement, source of primary data, or illustration of effective or ineffective management.
2. Thomas Cook AG has been proportionally consolidated in KarstadtQuelle's financial statements.
3. This and the following sections are primarily based on material from KarstadtQuelle's 2005 Annual Report, its Interim Reports of March 2006 and June 2006, and its press releases issued during 2004, 2005, and 2006.

divest its 77 smaller department stores – with sales space below 8,000 square meters and total revenues of €0.7 billion. It also planned to divest its specialty store chains, such as sports stores RunnersPoint and GolfHouse. These divestments should help KarstadtQuelle to expand its high-margin products in the department store business.

■ *Focus within mail order.* In the mail order business, KarstadtQuelle would focus its efforts on growth in the specialty mail order segment and in the e-commerce segment.[4] The company would further strategically reorient its traditionally strong universal mail order business in Germany.

■ *Cost savings.* KarstadtQuelle expected to be able to achieve €210 million in cost savings in its department store business and €150 million in cost savings in its universal mail order business by the year 2006.

■ *Real estate.* The company considered segregating its real estate business from its department store (retail) business.

■ *Reorientation of the group.* KarstadtQuelle would streamline its portfolio, abandon marginal operations and outsource some of its processes in the retail business.

Although the financial and operational state of the company's mail order business appeared worse than anticipated, KarstadtQuelle's management had been able to make some important changes to the segment in 2005. Mail order companies Quelle and neckermann.de were converted into limited liability companies and started to operate separately under their own management to improve these subsidiaries' decision processes. In the mail order segment the company also positioned Quelle and neckermann.de in the market as two sharply distinct brands and combined several separately operating service units into one to reduce costs.

KarstadtQuelle also sold several specialty stores as well as its small department stores. The divestiture program also resulted in the sale of Karstadt Hypothekenbank AG to the company's pension fund. After the sale, Karstadt Hypothekenbank AG took over from KarstadtQuelle's finance companies the financing of the company's hire purchase business in its mail order segment, thereby helping KarstadtQuelle to derecognize its discounted installment receivables (in accordance with IAS 39). The sale of Karstadt Hypothekenbank reduced KarstadtQuelle's net non-current liabilities by approximately €1 billion. The sale of the company's marginal operations and smaller department stores yielded close to €1.1 million. In addition, Kartstadt Quelle sold and leased back its mail order logistics real estate at a price of over €400 million. As a result of the restructuring, KarstadtQuelle was able to reduce its workforce by roughly one-fifth, or 25,000 employees.

In KarstadtQuelle's 2005 Annual Report, management reported that although performance in the mail order segment was still below plan, the company had reached its targets. In 2005, sales had declined from €17.2 billion to €15.8 billion, but the company had been able to cut its net loss from €1.6 billion to €316 million. During the fiscal year 2005, KarstadtQuelle's share price increased by 68 percent, from €7.60 to €12.74, to imply a market value of €2.69 billion.

KarstadtQuelle in the first half of 2006

After the financial restructuring of the company in 2005, KarstadtQuelle's management considered the company's equity position too vulnerable. To reduce

4. *Specialty mail order companies focus on selling one product type, such as baby products or fashion products, whereas universal mail order companies offer a broad assortment of product categories.*

leverage further, the company sold its real estate portfolio – consisting of department stores, car parks, sport stores, and office buildings – for an amount of €4.5 billion. The real estate was sold to and leased back from an entity that was jointly owned by a subsidiary of Goldman Sachs – the Whitehall Fund – and KarstadtQuelle. KarstadtQuelle had a participation of 49 percent in the joint entity but, as it reported, carried no other risks than arising from its equity contribution of €120 million. The operational management of the joint entity was in the hands of the Whitehall Fund. The first payment under the real estate transaction – €2.7 billion – was received on July 3, 2006. The second payment – the remaining €1.8 billion – would be received later in the year 2006.

According to KarstadtQuelle, the real estate transaction had several positive effects. First, it yielded a high short-term cash inflow that helped the company to quickly reduce its financial liabilities. Second, it improved important balance sheet ratios such as the equity-to-assets ratio. Third, it resulted in a high nonrecurring income component for fiscal 2006. Fourth and finally, it led to a lasting improvement in pretax profits to the order of €100 million.

The company continued to restructure its business. It repositioned its department stores by distinguishing "Premium" stores that sold high-margin products at prime locations from "Boulevard" stores that focused on selling brands in the middle to higher price segment. Further, KarstadtQuelle increased its purchase volume in Asia and set up local design centers in Europe and Asia to develop fashionable and timely products. To facilitate procurement in Asia, the company signed an agreement to cooperate with the Chinese export company Li & Fung. These actions aimed to reduce purchase expenses and increase inventory turnover, thereby reducing working capital by an estimated €500 million. The proceeds from the real estate transaction further helped KarstadtQuelle to invest another €200 million in restructuring its universal mail order business.

In the first half of 2006, KarstadtQuelle managed to report a net profit of €558.1 million. During this half year, KarstadtQuelle's share price increased by 62 percent, from €12.74 to €20.59, to reach a market value of €4.34 billion.

Questions

1. When preparing a report that summarizes the main factors affecting KarstadtQuelle's creditworthiness, which factors should the credit analyst focus on? How do these factors affect KarstadtQuelle's creditworthiness?

2. Assess whether KarstadtQuelle could bear the burden of another €500 million loan. If so, what would be the appropriate interest rate on this new loan?

EXHIBIT 1 KarstadtQuelle's consolidated financial statements

INCOME STATEMENTS (€ thousands)

	Half year ending June 30, 2006	Year ending December 31, 2005	Half year ending June 30, 2005	Year ending December 31, 2004
Sales	6,474,551	15,845,032	7,166,102	17,199,007
Cost of sales and expenses for tourism services	(3,614,132)	(8,911,823)	(3,911,755)	(9,631,912)
Gross income	2,860,419	6,933,209	3,254,347	7,567,095
Other capitalized own costs	13,987	50,691	22,242	53,519
Operating income	1,315,470	1,102,555	388,286	819,669
Staff costs	(1,180,843)	(2,630,323)	(1,382,563)	(3,109,417)
Operating expenses	(2,321,642)	(5,152,129)	(2,245,903)	(5,575,730)
Other taxes	(10,702)	(29,344)	(13,644)	(30,262)
Earnings before interest, tax and depreciation and amortization (EBITDA)	676,689	274,659	22,765	(275,126)
Depreciation and amortization (not including amortization of goodwill)	(145,297)	(343,329)	(171,828)	(425,115)
Impairment loss	(507)	(48,193)	(57,550)	(101,641)
Earnings before interest, tax and amortization of goodwill (EBITA)	530,885	(116,863)	(206,613)	(801,882)
Amortization of goodwill	0	(8,399)	205	(152,446)
Earnings before interest and tax (EBIT)	530,885	(125,262)	(206,408)	(954,328)
Income from investments	2,740	(9,454)	2,259	1,314
Income from investments in associates	4,259	16,681	8,535	12,481
Net interest income	(192,055)	(292,953)	(153,537)	(326,863)
Other financial results	19,634	15,783	(12,911)	(165,371)
Earnings before tax (EBT)	365,463	(395,205)	(362,062)	(1,432,767)
Taxes on income	194,500	81,180	117,053	178,008
Earnings from continuing operations	559,963	(314,025)	(245,009)	(1,254,759)
Result from discontinued operations	0	(258)	(25,352)	(370,531)
Net profit/loss before minority interests	559,963	(314,283)	(270,361)	(1,625,290)
Profit/loss due to minority interests	(1,847)	(2,199)	(1,515)	(24)
Net loss after minority interests	558,116	(316,482)	(271,876)	(1,625,314)

BALANCE SHEETS (€ thousands)

	Half year ending June 30, 2006	Year ending December 31, 2005	Half year ending June 30, 2005	Year ending December 31, 2004
Intangible assets	1,087,878	1,104,831	1,117,732	1,100,986
Tangible assets	1,061,660	2,452,839	2,659,840	2,786,185
Shares in associates	86,343	98,398	110,226	105,877
Other financial assets	624,494	535,220	1,032,739	1,405,772
Other non-current assets	96,764	94,167	129,746	116,313
Deferred taxes	220,891	228,249	283,529	164,914
Non-current assets	3,178,030	4,513,704	5,333,812	5,680,047
Inventories	1,547,838	1,621,095	1,700,643	1,823,904
Trade receivables	795,267	844,385	1,400,712	1,295,494
Tax receivables	127,316	50,430	89,381	61,800
Other receivables and other assets	1,011,858	1,139,128	1,046,039	911,201
Purchase price receivable from real estate transaction	2,690,203	0	0	0
Cash and cash equivalents and securities	770,550	707,163	657,504	661,156
Current assets	6,943,032	4,362,201	4,894,279	4,753,555
Assets classified as held for sale	481,506	262,658	1,942,263	1,209,587
Balance sheet total	10,602,568	9,138,563	12,170,354	11,643,189
Subscribed share capital	514,544	510,398	510,398	510,398
Reserves	790,711	(237,068)	(196,053)	58,663
Minority interests	12,192	16,745	31,595	26,783
Equity	1,317,447	290,075	345,940	595,844
Long-term capital of minority interests	0	0	53,203	58,983
Non-current financial liabilities	1,007,146	3,012,793	3,361,517	3,372,376
Other non-current liabilities	485,925	566,606	596,024	549,694
Pension provisions	886,923	906,756	859,101	891,911
Other non-current provisions	368,220	383,784	350,802	365,483
Deferred taxes	18,880	11,673	8,483	12,533
Non-current liabilities	2,767,094	4,881,612	5,229,130	5,250,980
Current financial liabilities	3,062,043	724,776	2,164,105	2,062,517
Trade payables	1,331,760	1,600,870	1,424,662	1,554,497
Current tax liabilities	180,695	201,746	151,775	229,840
Other current liabilities	1,405,913	768,855	1,286,692	799,186
Current provisions	506,277	609,677	564,313	626,136
Current liabilities	6,486,688	3,905,924	5,591,547	5,272,176
Liabilities from assets classified as held for sale	31,339	60,952	1,003,737	524,189
Balance sheet total	10,602,568	9,138,563	12,170,354	11,643,189

KarstadtQuelle

CASH FLOW STATEMENTS (€ thousands)

	Half year ending June 30, 2006	Year ending December 31, 2005	Half year ending June 30, 2005	Year ending December 31, 2004
EBITDA	676,689	274,659	22,765	(275,126)
Profit/loss from the disposal of fixed assets	(906,419)	(155,154)	(24,278)	(1,304)
Profit/loss from foreign currency	(4,457)	(1,907)	3,038	4,919
Decrease of non-current provisions (not including pension and tax provisions)	(2,178)	(95,099)	(18,760)	(59,880)
Addition to (Utilization of) restructuring provision	(130,367)	255,853	(84,830)	583,809
Other expenses/income not affecting cash flow	146,904	168,307	98,454	146,161
Gross cash flow	(219,828)	446,659	(3,611)	398,579
Changes in working capital	(68,114)	1,006,822	(173,859)	93,576
Changes in other current assets and liabilities	317,002	(231,280)	114,760	165,831
Dividends received	1,165	13,278	2,803	24,958
Payments/refunds of taxes on income	(46,068)	(8,253)	(37,395)	(46,452)
Cash flow from operating activities	(15,843)	1,227,226	(97,302)	636,492
Cash flow from acquisitions/divestments of subsidiaries less cash and cash equivalents disposed of	79,572	250,388	10,080	(3,060)
Purchase of tangible and intangible assets	(81,127)	(258,785)	(84,686)	(331,475)
Purchase of investments in non-current financial assets	(140,295)	(7,953)	(69,020)	(83,283)
Cash receipts from sale of tangible and intangible assets	62,133	703,648	133,560	119,356
Cash receipts from sale of non-current financial assets	8,522	43,723	40,665	32,835
Cash flow from investing activities	(71,195)	731,021	30,599	(265,627)
Interest received	72,957	134,202	62,773	131,533
Interest paid	(185,698)	(377,162)	(190,584)	(331,834)
Pension payments	(54,135)	(62,272)	(90,365)	(95,867)
Cash receipts/payments under mortgage bond program and for (financial) loans	334,309	(1,546,621)	297,971	(192,959)
Payment of liabilities due under finance lease	(9,729)	(47,264)	(16,208)	(39,489)
Cash payments/cash receipts for dividends and capital increase	3,979	(1,520)	(571)	473,006
Cash flow from financing activities	161,683	(1,900,637)	63,016	(55,610)
Changes in cash and cash equivalents affecting cash flow	74,645	57,610	(3,687)	315,255
Changes in cash and cash equivalents due to changes in exchange rates or other changes caused by the consolidated companies	(11,258)	(14,856)	(1,020)	(14,367)
Cash and cash equivalents at the beginning of the period	707,163	653,162	662,211	352,274
Cash and cash equivalents at the end of the period	770,550	695,916	657,504	653,162

KarstadtQuelle

EXHIBIT 2 **Excerpts from the notes to the consolidated financial statements – KarstadtQuelle's Annual Report 2005**

Consolidation

In the year under review the shares In Karstadt Hypothekenbank AG were exchanged for shares held by the II.KarstadtQuelle Pension Trust e.V. In Quelle Neckermann Versand Finanz GmbH & Co. KG and Karstadt Hypothekenbank AG deconsolidated. During the year the company was treated as a disposal group and its assets and liabilities recognized under Assets qualified as held for sale and Liabilities in connection with assets classified as held for sale. Impairment of €51,440 thousand resulting within the year from estimated sales proceeds from company assets has proved to be no longer necessary in connection with this exchange.

Sale of receivables

Individual group companies are selling trade receivables to Karstadt Hypothekenbank AG, which was transferred to the II.KarstadtQuelle Pension Trust e.V. under the CTA program. Karstadt Hypothekenbank AG at the end of the fiscal year took over from the finance companies the purchase of receivables being sold by these companies under the ABS programs. In this connection, the sale of receivables was classified as an actual derecognition under IAS 39. International companies in mail order are continuing to sell under asset-backed securitization (ABS) transactions their receivables to a finance company, which refinances the purchases on the capital market. Under the ABS program the purchasers of these receivables withhold part of the purchase price as security until receipt of the payments. If there is sufficient likelihood of realization, the anticipated payment is shown as a separate financial asset.

The vendors must assume responsibility for collecting the debts. At the balance sheet date adequate provisions are set aside for these commitments. For the assumption of the risks and interim financing the vendors pay a program fee, which, depending on the classification of the sales, is shown as a true sale or a sale which does not qualify for derecognition under other operating expenses or interest.

Operating income

Amounts shown in € thousands	2005	2004
Income from the disposal of assets classified as held for sale	167,613	12,949
Income from advertising cost subsidies	154,738	169,702
Earnings from rental income and commissions	131,155	103,239
Income from charged-on goods and services	57,800	55,283
Income from the disposal of non-current assets	52,080	11,885
Income from the reversal of other liabilities	37,514	27,883
Income from exchange rate differences	28,157	44,121
Income from the reversal of other provisions	27,697	19,851
Income from deconsolidation	20,471	10,659
Income from other services	18,779	21,569
Income from the reversal of allowances	9,783	8,310
Other income	396,768	334,218
	1,102,555	819,669

Operating expenses

Amounts shown in € thousands	2005	2004
Logistics costs	1,431,003	1,459,007
Catalog costs	893,853	861,938
Operating and office/workshop costs	693,058	777,016
Advertising	615,761	648,103
Administrative costs	559,386	479,393
Restructuring costs	269,342	651,455
Allowances on and derecognition of trade receivables	223,506	256,577
Losses from the disposal of assets classified as held for sale	60,050	1,894
Outside staff	32,435	23,632
Expenses due to currency differences and losses	26,250	49,040
Losses from the disposal of fixed assets	4,491	21,636
Other expenses	342,994	346,039
	5,152,129	5,575,730

Net interest income

Amounts shown in € thousands	2005	2004
Interest costs from pension expense	(133,384)	(137,104)
Other interest and similar income	254,790	217,699
Other interest and similar expenses	(414,359)	(407,458)
	(292,953)	(326,863)

The previous year's value included non-recurring charges of €51.9 million from restructuring.

Through application of the new IAS 39 the Group's receivables sales were classified as non-disposal of receivables. Accordingly, the corresponding expenses from prefinancing of receivables (so-called program fees) are recognized under interest expenses. These amount to €55,641 thousand (previous year: €41,165 thousand) for the 2005 financial year. The previous year's amounts were adjusted accordingly for better comparability.

KarstadtQuelle

Leases

Finance lease agreements have a firmly agreed basic leasing period of between 20 and 25 years and include a purchase option for the lessee after expiry of the basic leasing period. Assets under finance lease agreements have a carrying amount of €237,783 thousand (previous year: €262,686 thousand) at the balance sheet date. These assets relate to buildings, aircraft and reserve engines where the carrying value of the future minimum lease payments covers the material purchase costs. For aircraft financing normally a purchase option for the residual value plus an amount

equal to 25% of the amount by which the fair value exceeds the residual value exists after the expiry of the lease period. If the purchase option is not exercised, the aircraft is sold by the lessor. If the proceeds from the sale are lower than the residual value, the lessee must pay the difference to the lessor. The lessee is entitled to up to 75% of the amount by which the sales proceeds exceed the residual value.

The operating lease agreements comprise mainly building leases without purchase option or aircraft leases where the assessment of the criteria of IAS 17 resulted in classification as operating lease.

	Up to 1 year		1 to 5 years		Over 5 years	
Amounts shown in € thousands	**2005**	**2004**	**2005**	**2004**	**2005**	**2004**
Finance lease agreements:						
Lease payments due in future	38,328	65,875	320,653	185,498	138,313	131,161
Discount	(759)	(36,209)	(35,783)	(48,924)	(31,598)	(14,162)
Present value	37,569	29,666	284,870	136,574	106,715	116,999
Lease payments under subleases	1,152	0	4,606	0	5,758	0
Operating lease agreements:						
Lease payments due in future	343,359	311,629	919,291	863,627	1,221,619	842,697
Discount	(11,072)	(16,953)	(124,498)	(131,195)	(600,007)	(364,210)
Present value	332,287	294,676	794,793	732,432	621,612	478,487
Lease payments under subleases	23,847	22,694	63,318	43,098	75,363	15,940

Trade receivables

Breakdown of trade receivables by business segment (Amounts shown in € thousands)	2005	2004
Karstadt	82,441	41,324
Mail order	602,074	1,093,715
Thomas Cook	82,113	73,508
Services	76,626	79,287
Other	1,131	7,660
	844,385	1,295,494

In connection with the application of IAS 39 sales of receivables under ABS programs were not subject to any further disposals at the beginning of the 2005 financial year. Accordingly, the previous year's figures of €622 million have been adjusted to suit the

change in recognition. The reorganization of the receivables sale program at home with the sale of receivables amounting to €613 million to Karstadt Hypothekenbank AG at the end of the financial year, however, resulted in an actual disposal and thus to a marked reduction in trade receivables.

To secure claims under a global agreement for the sale of receivables, security was provided to Karstadt Hypothekenbank AG on existing and future trade receivables.

Under the syndicated loan agreement and the second lien financing amounts totaling €243,414 thousand owed by customers to various Group companies were assigned as security for debtors' liabilities.

Financial liabilities

Amounts shown in € thousands	Up to 1 year		1 to 5 years		Over 5 years	
	2005	**2004**	**2005**	**2004**	**2005**	**2004**
Bank loans and overdrafts	231,438	734,047	797,776	694,086	326,934	469,513
Liabilities under leasing agreements	18,800	33,249	244,719	145,809	68,013	163,177
Other financial liabilities	474,538	1,295,221	200,511	677,130	1,374,840	1,222,661
Total	724,776	2,062,517	1,243,006	1,517,025	1,769,787	1,855,351

Interest-bearing bank loans and overdraft loans are recognized at the amount paid out less directly assignable issue costs. Financing costs, including premiums payable as repayments or redemption, are allocated with effect for income. Liabilities under lease agreements are shown at present value.

The terms and conditions of the facility were adjusted in December 2005 mainly with regard to the conclusion of the secondary loan facility explained below with regard to adherence to financial ratios. €275 million of the loan facility had been utilized at the balance sheet date. The financial ratios to be adhered to relate to adjusted EBITDA, interest coverage, debt coverage and the level of equity. For the mail order segment there is a further financial ratio relating to adjusted EBITDA.

To secure the Group's finances for the long term, in December of the financial year the KarstadtQuelle Group also agreed a further secondary loan facility amounting to nominally €309 million, which had been fully utilized by the balance sheet date. The security provided for the liabilities is for the most part identical with the security underlying the syndicated loan facility, although ranking below the syndicated facility.

The loans secured by mortgage bear interest rates between 2.75% p.a. and 7.24% p.a. at the balance sheet date. The syndicated loan facility taken up the previous year and the recently concluded second-ranking loan facility bear interest on the basis of EURIBOR (or LIBOR, if drawing in currencies other than euros) plus margin and regulatory costs. In the case of the syndicated loan facility the bullet facility is initially subject to a margin of 3.5% p.a., which will rise to 4.5% p.a. in 2006 and to 5.5% p.a. in 2007. For the seasonal facility and the revolving loan facility initially a margin of 3.75% p.a. has been agreed from December 10, 2005, for the period of one year. Thereafter under certain circumstances it will rise to 4.75% p.a. The second-ranking loan facility bears interest with a margin of 12%.

Financial liabilities also include liabilities to customers of the KarstadtQuelle Bank from savings deposits, night money, balances on card accounts, promissory notes and savings certificates amounting to €77,642 thousand.

Of first-ranking financial liabilities €484,675 thousand (previous year: €742,172 thousand) are secured by mortgages and €350,372 thousand by other rights. In addition, there is first-ranking mortgage security amounting to €1,249,465 thousand (previous year: €1,419,737 thousand) under the Karstadt Hypothekenbank AG's (Essen) mortgage bond program. Liabilities of €91,238 thousand proportionate (previous year €74,060 thousand) arising from real estate financing at Thomas Cook are likewise supported by mortgage or similar security.

KarstadtQuelle AG has undertaken a guarantee to the Karstadt Hypothekenbank AG, Essen, for loans of Karstadt Finance B.V., Hulst, Netherlands, amounting to €1.8 billion, which translates to €1.3 billion at the balance sheet date.

Under the agreed syndicated loan facility a partial land charge assignment declaration was agreed with real estate management companies, and the creation of overall land charges and in some cases binding security pledges in respect of land charges was agreed. Furthermore, shares in Thomas Cook AG and various fully consolidated Group companies and amounts due from customers of the various Group companies were assigned. Furthermore, unrecognized brands held by KarstadtQuelle AG, Karstadt Warenhaus GmbH, Quelle GmbH and neckermann.de GmbH were assigned as security for liabilities of KarstadtQuelle AG.

Liabilities of €350,273 thousand (previous year: €391,850 thousand) arising from aircraft financing are secured by aircraft mortgages or are subject to availability limitations resulting from the financing structure.

Leasing liabilities carried as liabilities are effectively secured by the lessor's rights to buildings or aircraft specified in the finance lease.

KarstadtQuelle

Pension provisions

The recognized amount from pension obligations results as follows:

Amounts shown in € thousands	Commitments financed from funds	Commitments financed from provisions	2005	2004
Present value of future pension commitments (DBO)	1,564,743	1,019,941	2,584,684	2,602,586
Unrecognized actuarial gains/losses	(71,678)	(117,610)	(189,288)	(72,217)
Unrecognized past service costs	(119)	(336)	(455)	(634)
Fair value of plan assets	(1,485,424)	0	(1,485,424)	(1,504,939)
	7,522	901,995	909,517	1,024,796
Pension provisions in connection with disposal groups	0	(2,761)	(2,761)	(132,885)
	7,522	899,234	906,756	891,911

Pension costs are as follows:

Amounts shown in € thousands	Commitments financed from funds	Commitments financed from provisions	2005	2004
Service costs	3,856	8,378	12,234	15,126
Interest costs	70,151	39,009	109,160	141,735
Expected return on plan assets	(84,723)	0	(84,723)	(83,865)
Actuarial gains/losses with effect on income	32	305	337	113,424
Past service costs	1,255	2,386	3,641	99
Income from changes in plans/expenses from deconsolidation	4,987	3,201	8,188	351
	(4,442)	53,279	48,837	186,168

Whereas the cost of pension claims acquired during the financial year is shown under staff costs, the interest and the expected return on plan assets and the actuarial losses affecting plan assets are recorded with effect for income and shown under financial results.

The composition of plan assets is calculated from the following table:

Amounts shown in € thousands	2005	2004
Real estate, incl. dormant holdings	987,966	1,091,060
Corporate investments	351,000	348,674
Financial resources	146,458	65,205
	1,485,424	1,504,939

The Group utilizes parts of real estate assets itself. The lease payments are made on the basis of usual market estimates. Furthermore, under their articles of incorporation the pension trusts may lend up to 10% of their assets back to the Group in the form of cash and cash equivalents. An amount of €72,982 thousand (previous year: €26,971 thousand) results here at the balance sheet date.

KarstadtQuelle

Other non-current provisions

Amounts shown in € thousands	Staff	Guarantees/ warranties	Contingent losses resulting from pending transactions	Restructuring effects	Other
As at 01.01.2005	31,866	958	298	235,295	34,659
Changes in consolidated companies	(123)	0	0	(626)	(128)
Currency differences	(8)	(2)	0	8	0
Recourse	(705)	(642)	276	(43,444)	(1,804)
Reversal	(13,283)	(23)	(248)	(6,704)	(678)
Appropriation	965	647	0	72,227	11,660
Reclassification acc. to IFRS 5	(285)	(1)	0	8,694	(701)
As at 31.12.2005	18,427	937	326	265,450	43,008

Staff provisions include provisions for severance payments and jubilee payments and death benefits.

Other provisions relate mainly to litigation risks and restoration liabilities.

KarstadtQuelle

CHAPTER 11

Mergers and Acquisitions

Mergers and acquisitions have long been a popular form of corporate investment. There is no question that these transactions provide a healthy return to target shareholders. However, their value to acquiring shareholders is less understood. Many skeptics point out that given the hefty premiums paid to target shareholders, acquisitions tend to be negative-valued investments for acquiring shareholders.[1]

A number of questions can be examined using financial analysis for mergers and acquisitions:

■ Securities analysts can ask: Does a proposed acquisition create value for the acquiring firm's shareholders?

■ Risk arbitrageurs can ask: What is the likelihood that a hostile takeover offer will ultimately succeed, and are there other potential acquirers likely to enter the bidding?

■ Acquiring management can ask: Does this target fit our business strategy? If so, what is it worth to us, and how can we make an offer that can be successful?

■ Target management can ask: Is the acquirer's offer a reasonable one for our shareholders? Are there other potential acquirers that would value our company more than the current bidder?

■ Investment bankers can ask: How can we identify potential targets that are likely to be a good match for our clients? And how should we value target firms when we are asked to issue fairness opinions?

In this chapter we focus primarily on the use of financial statement data and analysis directed at evaluating whether a merger creates value for the acquiring firm's shareholders. However, our discussion can also be applied to these other merger contexts. The topic of whether acquisitions create value for acquirers focuses on evaluating motivations for acquisitions, the pricing of offers, and the methods of financing, as well as assessing the likelihood that an offer will be successful. Throughout the chapter we use France-based Alcatel's merger with U.S.-based Lucent Technologies in 2006 to illustrate how financial analysis can be used in a merger context.

MOTIVATION FOR MERGER OR ACQUISITION

There are a variety of reasons why firms merge or acquire other firms. Some acquiring managers may want to increase their own power and prestige. Others, however, realize that business combinations provide an opportunity to create new economic value for their shareholders. New value can be created in the following ways:

1. *Taking advantage of economies of scale.* Mergers are often justified as a means of providing the two participating firms with increased economies of scale. Economies of scale arise when one firm can perform a function more efficiently than two. For example, Alcatel and Lucent are both telecommunications equipment makers and had considerable overlap in management, information technology, sales, and research and development activities. The merger was expected to provide operating synergies from eliminating duplicate functions and excess capacity, and from reducing research, material, general and administrative costs. At the time of the merger, management estimated that it would save €1.4 billion over the first three years following the merger by cutting roughly 9,000 jobs, closing offices, trimming business overlap, and sharing research and development facilities, procurement budgets, and information technology. All told, management stated that it could realize cost savings with a present value of €10 billion through the merger.

2. *Improving target management.* Another common motivation for acquisition is to improve target management. A firm is likely to be a target if it has systematically underperformed its industry. Historical poor performance could be due to bad luck, but it could also be due to the firm's managers making poor investment and operating decisions, or deliberately pursuing goals that increase their personal power but cost shareholders. Lucent had reported losses and negative operating cash flows in the years 2001 through 2003. The company became profitable again in 2004. However, at the time of the merger announcement, Lucent's price-earnings ratio of 10.5 was substantially below the industry average. For the following fiscal year, analysts reckoned that Lucent's revenues and earnings per share would decline by 4 and 43 percent, respectively. Nonetheless, the merger agreement provided that Patricia F. Russo, who took over as Lucent's CEO in 2002, would also become the CEO of the combined company.

3. *Combining complementary resources.* Firms may decide that a merger will create value by combining complementary resources of the two partners. For example, a firm with a strong research and development unit could benefit from merging with a firm that has a strong distribution unit. In the Alcatel-Lucent merger, the two firms appeared to have complementary capabilities and resources. Alcatel had a strong market position in IP network transformation and triple play. Lucent was the global leader in building IP multimedia subsystems as well as spread spectrum networks for third-generation mobile communication systems such as UMTS. In addition, both firms had a strong market presence in different geographical areas. Alcatel generated close to 50 percent of its revenues in Europe, whereas 66 percent of Lucent's revenues came from its North American operations. The merger thus increased Alcatel's and Lucent's geographical reach. After the merger, the combined company would generate approximately one-third of its revenues in Europe and one-third of its revenues in North America.

4. *Capturing tax benefits.* Companies may obtain several tax benefits from mergers and acquisitions. The major benefit is the acquisition of operating tax losses. If a firm does not expect to earn sufficient profits to fully utilize operating loss carryforward benefits, it may decide to buy another firm that is earning profits, provided that these profits are made in the same tax jurisdiction as where the loss carryforwards arose. The operating losses and loss carryforwards of the acquirer can then be offset against the target's taxable profit. A second tax benefit often attributed to mergers is the tax shield that comes from increasing leverage for the target firm. That is, the interest expense on the additional debt is tax-deductible and lowers the target firm's tax payments. This was particularly relevant for leveraged buyouts in the 1980s.[2]

5. *Providing low-cost financing to a financially constrained target.* If capital markets are imperfect, perhaps because of information asymmetries between management and outside investors, firms can face capital constraints. Information problems are likely to be especially severe for newly formed, high-growth firms. These firms can be difficult for outside investors to value since they have short track records, and their financial statements provide little insight into the value of their growth opportunities. Further, since they typically have to rely on external funds to finance their growth, capital market constraints for high-growth firms are likely to affect their ability to undertake profitable new projects. Public capital markets are therefore likely to be costly sources of funds for these types of firms. An acquirer that understands the business and is willing to provide a steady source of finance may therefore be able to add value.[3]

6. *Increasing product-market rents.* Firms also can have incentives to merge to increase product-market rents. By merging and becoming a dominant firm in the industry, two smaller firms can collude to restrict their output and raise prices, thereby increasing their profits. This circumvents problems that arise in cartels of independent firms, where firms have incentives to cheat on the cartel and increase their output. At the time of the Alcatel-Lucent merger, telecom service providers such as AT&T, Vodafone, and Telefónica, who were the major buyers of Alcatel's and Lucent's equipment, were also in the midst of consolidation. The merger thus improved the combined company's bargaining power over its increasingly powerful customers.

While product-market rents make sense for firms as a motive for merging, the two partners are unlikely to announce their intentions when they explain the merger to their investors, since most countries have competition (antitrust) laws which regulate mergers between two firms in the same industry. For example, in the European Union large mergers must be approved by the European Commission, which examines whether mergers do not impede effective competition by creating a dominant market position. National mergers are generally reviewed by national competition authorities. In the U.S. there are three major antitrust statutes – The Sherman Act of 1890, The Clayton Act of 1914, and The Hart Scott Rodino Act of 1976.

Anti-competitive concerns were significant for the Alcatel-Lucent merger because the merger created the world's largest telecommunications equipment maker. Merger approval was required from both the U.S. Federal Trade Commission (FTC) and the European Commission.

While many of the motivations for acquisitions are likely to create new economic value for shareholders, some are not. Firms that are flush with cash but have few new profitable investment opportunities are particularly prone to using their surplus cash to make acquisitions. Shareholders of these firms would probably prefer that managers pay out any surplus or "free" cash flows as dividends, or use the funds to repurchase their firm's shares. However, these options reduce the size of the firm and the assets under management's control. Management may therefore prefer to invest the free cash flows to buy new companies, even if they are not valued by shareholders. Of course managers will never announce that they are buying a firm because they are reluctant to pay out funds to shareholders. They may explain the merger using one of the motivations discussed above, or they may argue that they are buying the target at a bargain price.

Another motivation for mergers that is valued by managers but not shareholders is diversification. Diversification was a popular motivation for acquisitions in the 1960s and early 1970s. Acquirers sought to dampen their earnings volatility by buying firms in unrelated businesses. Diversification as a motive for acquisitions has since been widely discredited. Modern finance theorists point out that in a well-functioning capital market, investors can diversify for themselves and do not need managers to do so for them. In addition, diversification has been criticized for leading firms losing sight of their major competitive strengths and expanding into businesses where they do not have expertise.[4]

KEY ANALYSIS QUESTIONS

In evaluating a proposed merger, analysts are interested in determining whether the merger creates new wealth for acquiring and target shareholders, or whether it is motivated by managers' desires to increase their own power and prestige. Key questions for financial analysis are likely to include:

- *What is the motivation(s) for an acquisition and any anticipated benefits disclosed by acquirers or targets?*
- *What are the industries of the target and acquirer?* Are the firms related horizontally (the firms are suppliers of similar products) or vertically (one firm is the other firm's supplier)? How close are the business relations between them? If the businesses are unrelated, is the acquirer cash-rich and reluctant to return free cash flows to shareholders?
- *What are the key operational strengths of the target and the acquirer?* Are these strengths complementary? For example, does one firm have a renowned research group and the other a strong distribution network?
- *Is the acquisition a friendly one, supported by target management, or hostile?* A hostile takeover is more likely to occur for targets with poor-performing management who oppose the acquisition to preserve their jobs. However, as discussed below, this typically reduces acquirer management's access to information about the target, increasing the risk of overpayment.
- *What is the premerger performance of the two firms?* Performance metrics are likely to include ROE, gross margins, general and administrative expenses to sales, and working capital management ratios. On the basis of these measures, is the target a poor performer in its industry, implying that there are opportunities for improved management? Is the acquirer in a declining industry and searching for new directions?
- *What is the tax position of both firms?* What are the average and marginal current tax rates for the target and the acquirer? Does the acquirer have operating loss carryforwards and the target taxable profits?

This analysis should help the analyst understand what specific benefits, if any, the merger is likely to generate.

Motivation for the Alcatel-Lucent merger

Several industry factors influenced Alcatel and Lucent to merge. At the time of the merger, the telecommunications services industry, to which Alcatel and Lucent supplied most of their equipment, was going through a wave of consolidation. For example, in 2005 U.S.-based SBC Communications acquired AT&T to become the world's largest telecom service provider. One year later, the company, which was named AT&T after the merger, strengthened its dominant market position even further by acquiring U.S.-based BellSouth. Similarly, in 2005 Spanish Telefónica agreed to acquire British O2. In the same year, Sweden-based Tele2 acquired Netherlands-based Versatel, a specialist in triple play. These mergers substantially impaired telecom equipment makers' bargaining power over their primary customers. The merger between Alcatel and Lucent therefore somewhat restored the balance of power between suppliers and buyers of telecom equipment. Other telecom equipment makers followed a similar strategy. For example, in 2006 Germany-based Siemens and Finland-based Nokia combined their telecom equipment units into a joint venture.

The fixed telecommunications networks market was also in a state of transition. At the end of the first half of the 2000s, fixed network operators started to combine telephone, internet, and video services, under the label "triple play." The great demand from customers for these converged services and networks allowed the fixed networks market to expand for the first time since the burst of the telecom bubble in 2001. The merger between Alcatel and Lucent could strengthen the companies' position in the fixed networks segment and improve the probability that Alcatel-Lucent would benefit from the segment's growth. Lucent's experience in building IP multimedia systems could become complementary to Alcatel's experience with triple play in becoming a leader in converged networks.

The management of Alcatel and Lucent argued that a merger would provide the new company with four significant benefits. First, as noted above, the combined firm would be able to reduce costs by €1.4 billion per year through efficiency improvements such as streamlining administrative overhead, eliminating excess capacity and duplicate facilities, using purchasing power to reduce material costs, and coordinating research and development in areas where the two firms operated separately. These savings were expected to be fully realized by the third year after the merger. Second, the merger increased Alcatel's and Lucent's geographical reach by creating a combined company that operated on a global scale. Third, management noted that the two companies had complementary expertise that would help increase productivity. For example, Alcatel was a leader in IP network transformation and triple play, which complemented Lucent's leadership in building IP multimedia systems and spread spectrum networks. The combined company would be better able to offer its customers telecom solutions that integrated telephone, internet, and video. Fourth, combining the companies' research and development budgets and patents portfolios helped Alcatel-Lucent to increase the scale of its global research and development and could make Alcatel-Lucent an industry leader in innovation.

Analysts and the financial media generally concurred with management's assessments of the economic benefits that potentially would be derived from the merger. Some analysts nevertheless expressed concern that the large size of the two companies might make it difficult for them to actually achieve these synergies. Because the companies' existing customers expected support for years to come, analysts feared that the combined company would not be able to eliminate duplicate products in its product portfolio.[5]

ACQUISITION PRICING

A well thought out economic motivation for a merger or acquisition is a necessary but not sufficient condition for it to create value for acquiring shareholders. The acquirer must be careful to avoid overpaying for the target. Overpayment makes the transaction highly desirable and profitable for target shareholders, but it diminishes the value of the deal to acquiring shareholders. A financial analyst can use the following methods to assess whether the acquiring firm is overpaying for the target.

Analyzing premium offered to target shareholders

One popular way to assess whether the acquirer is overpaying for a target is to compare the premium offered to target shareholders to premiums offered in similar transactions. If the acquirer offers a relatively high premium, the analyst is typically led to conclude that the transaction is less likely to create value for acquiring shareholders.

Premiums differ significantly for friendly and hostile acquisitions. Premiums tend to be about 30 percent higher for hostile deals than for friendly offers, implying that hostile acquirers are more likely to overpay for a target.[6] There are several reasons for this. First, a friendly acquirer has access to the internal records of the target, making it much less likely that it will be surprised by hidden liabilities or problems once it has completed the deal. In contrast, a hostile acquirer does not have this advantage in valuing the target and is forced to make assumptions that may later turn out to be false. Second, the delays that typically accompany a hostile acquisition often provide opportunities for competing bidders to make an offer for the target, leading to a bidding war.

Comparing a target's premium to values for similar types of transactions is straightforward to compute, but it has several practical problems. First, it is not obvious how to define a comparable transaction. European takeover premiums differ on various dimensions. As argued, average premiums are greater in hostile takeovers than in friendly takeovers. Further, takeover premiums vary by means of payment. Equity-financed acquisitions (share-for-share mergers) require lower premiums than cash-financed acquisitions because the former type makes the target firms' shareholders also shareholders of the new company. Target shareholders thereby keep benefiting – through capital gains – from the synergies created by the merger. Takeover premiums may also depend on the target firms' country of domicile. When a target firm is located in a country with strict takeover rules, the target firm's shareholders may have more power to negotiate higher premiums. Recent research has indicated that takeover premiums in the U.K., where hostile takeover are more common and takeover rules are stricter, are on average higher than in Continental Europe.[7]

A second problem in using premiums offered to target shareholders to assess whether an acquirer overpaid is that measured premiums can be misleading if an offer is anticipated by investors. The share price run-up for the target will then tend to make estimates of the premium appear relatively low. This limitation can be partially offset by using target share prices one month prior to the acquisition offer as the basis for calculating premiums. However, in some cases offers may have been anticipated for even longer than one month.

Finally, using target premiums to assess whether an acquirer overpaid ignores the value of the target to the acquirer after the acquisition. This value can be viewed as:

$$\text{Value of target after acquisition} =$$
$$\text{Value as independent firm} + \text{Value of merger benefits}$$

The value of the target before acquisition is the present value of the free cash flows for the target if it were to remain an independent entity. This is likely to be somewhat different from the firm's share price prior to any merger announcement since the pre-takeover price is a weighted average of the value of the firm as an independent unit and its value in the event of a takeover. The benefits of the merger include such effects as improvements in target operating performance from economies of scale, improved management, and tax benefits, as well as any spillover benefits to the acquirer from the acquisition. Clearly, acquirers will be willing to pay higher premiums for targets that are expected to generate higher merger benefits. Thus, examining the premium alone cannot determine whether the acquisition creates value for acquiring shareholders.

Analyzing value of the target to the acquirer

A second and more reliable way of assessing whether the acquirer has overpaid for the target is to compare the offer price to the estimated value of the target to the acquirer. This latter value can be computed using the valuation techniques discussed in Chapters 7 and 8. The most popular methods of valuation used for mergers and acquisitions are earnings multiples and discounted cash flows. Since a comprehensive discussion of these techniques is provided earlier in the book, we focus here on implementation issues that arise for valuing targets in mergers and acquisitions. We recommend first computing the value of the target as an independent firm. This provides a way of checking whether the valuation assumptions are reasonable, because for publicly listed targets we can compare our estimate with premerger market prices. It also provides a useful benchmark for thinking about how the target's performance, and hence its value, is likely to change once it is acquired.

Earnings multiples

To estimate the value of a target to an acquirer using earnings multiples, we have to forecast earnings for the target and decide on an appropriate earnings multiple, as follows:

- *Step 1: Forecasting earnings.* Earnings forecasts are usually made by first forecasting next year's net profit for the target assuming no acquisition. Historical sales growth rates, gross margins, and average tax rates are useful in building a pro forma earnings model. Once we have forecasted the profit for the target prior to an acquisition, we can incorporate into the pro forma model any improvements in earnings performance that we expect to result from the acquisition. Performance improvements can be modeled as:
  - ❏ Higher operating margins through economies of scale in purchasing, or increased market power.
  - ❏ Reductions in expenses as a result of consolidating research and development staffs, sales forces, and/or administration.
  - ❏ Lower average tax rates from taking advantage of operating tax loss carryforwards.
- *Step 2: Determining the price-earnings multiple.* How do we determine the earnings multiple to be applied to our earnings forecasts? If the target firm is listed, it may be tempting to use the preacquisition price-earnings multiple to value postmerger earnings. However, there are several limitations to this approach. First, for many targets earnings growth expectations are likely to change after a merger, implying that there will be a difference between the premerger and postmerger price-earnings multiples. Postmerger earnings should then be valued using a multiple for firms with comparable growth and risk characteristics (see the discussion in Chapter 7). A second problem is that premerger price-earnings multiples are unavailable for unlisted targets. Once again it becomes necessary to decide which types of listed firms are likely to be good comparables. Finally, if a premerger price-earnings multiple is appropriate for valuing postmerger earnings, care is required to ensure that the multiple is calculated prior to any acquisition announcement because the price will increase in anticipation of the premium to be paid to target shareholders.

Table 11.1 summarizes how price-earnings multiples are used to value a target firm before an acquisition (assuming it will remain an independent entity), and to estimate the value of a target to a potential acquirer.

TABLE 11.1 Summary of price-earnings valuation for targets

Value of target as an independent firm	Target earnings forecast for the next year, assuming no change in ownership, multiplied by its *premerger* PE multiple
Value of target to potential acquirer	Target *revised* earnings forecast for the next year, incorporating the effect of any operational changes made by the acquirer, multiplied by its *postmerger* PE multiple

Limitations of price-earnings valuation

As explained in Chapter 7, there are serious limitations to using earnings multiples for valuation. In addition to these limitations, the method has two more that are specific to merger valuations:

1. PE multiples assume that merger performance improvements come either from an immediate increase in earnings or from an increase in earnings growth (and hence an increase in the postmerger PE ratio). In reality, improvements and savings can come in many forms – gradual increases in earnings from implementing new operating policies, elimination of overinvestment, better management of working capital, or paying out excess cash to shareholders. These types of improvements are not naturally reflected in PE multiples.

2. PE models do not easily incorporate any spillover benefits from an acquisition for the acquirer because they focus on valuing the earnings of the target.

Discounted abnormal earnings, abnormal earnings growth, or cash flows

As discussed in Chapters 7 and 8, we can also value a company using the discounted abnormal earnings, discounted abnormal earnings growth, and discounted free cash flow methods. These require us to first forecast the abnormal earnings, abnormal earnings growth, or free cash flows for the firm and then discount them at the cost of capital, as follows.

■ *Step 1: Forecast abnormal earnings/abnormal earnings growth/free cash flows.* A pro forma model of expected future profits and cash flows for the firm provides the basis for forecasting abnormal earnings, abnormal earnings growth, and free cash flows. As a starting point, the model should be constructed under the assumption that the target remains an independent firm. The model should reflect the best estimates of future sales growth, cost structures, working capital needs, investment and research and development needs, and cash requirements for known debt retirements, developed from financial analysis of the target. The abnormal earnings (growth) method requires that we forecast earnings or net operating profit after tax (NOPAT), preferably for as long as the firm expects new investment projects to earn more than their cost of capital. Under the free cash flow approach, the pro forma model will forecast free cash flows to either the firm or to equity, typically for a period of five to ten years. Once we have a model of the abnormal earnings, abnormal earnings growth or free cash flows, we can incorporate any improvements in earnings/free cash flows that we expect to result from the acquisition. These will include the cost savings, cash received from asset sales, benefits from eliminating overinvestment, improved working capital management, and paying out excess cash to shareholders.

■ *Step 2: Compute the discount rate.* If we are valuing the target's postacquisition NOPAT or cash flows to the firm, the appropriate discount rate is the weighted average cost of capital for the target, using its expected *postacquisition* capital structure. Alternatively, if the target equity cash flows are being valued directly or if we are valuing earnings, the appropriate discount rate is the target's *postacquisition cost of equity* rather than its weighted average cost of capital (WACC). Two common mistakes are to use the acquirer's cost of capital or the target's *preacquisition* cost of capital to value the postmerger earnings/cash flows from the target.

The computation of the target's postacquisition cost of capital can be complicated if the acquirer plans to make a change to the target's capital structure after the acquisition, since the target's costs of debt and equity will change. As discussed in Chapter 8, this involves estimating the asset beta for the target, calculating the new equity and debt betas under the modified capital structure, and finally computing the revised cost of equity capital or weighted cost of capital. As a practical matter, the effect of these changes on the weighted average cost of capital is likely to be quite small unless the revision in leverage has a significant effect on the target's interest tax shields or its likelihood of financial distress.

Table 11.2 summarizes how the discounted abnormal earnings/cash flow methods can be used to value a target before an acquisition (assuming it will remain an independent entity), and to estimate the value of a target firm to a potential acquirer.

TABLE 11.2 Summary of discounted abnormal earnings/abnormal earnings growth/ cash flow valuation for targets

Value of target without an acquisition	(a) Present value of abnormal earnings/abnormal earnings growth/free cash flows to target equity assuming no acquisition, discounted at *premerger* cost of equity; or (b) Present value of abnormal NOPAT/abnormal NOPAT growth/free cash flows to target debt and equity assuming no acquisition, discounted at *premerger* WACC, less value of debt.
Value of target to potential acquirer	(a) Present value of abnormal earnings/abnormal earnings growth/free cash flows to target equity, *including benefits from merger,* discounted at *postmerger* cost of equity; or (b) Present value of abnormal abnormal NOPAT/abnormal NOPAT growth/free cash flows to target, *including benefits from merger,* discounted at *postmerger* WACC, less value of debt.

■ *Step 3: Analyze sensitivity.* Once we have estimated the expected value of a target, we will want to examine the sensitivity of our estimate to changes in the model assumptions. For example, answering the following questions can help the analyst assess the risks associated with an acquisition:

❑ What happens to the value of the target if it takes longer than expected for the benefits of the acquisition to materialize?

❏ What happens to the value of the target if the acquisition prompts its primary competitors to respond by also making an acquisition? Will such a response affect our plans and estimates?

KEY ANALYSIS QUESTIONS

To analyze the pricing of an acquisition, the analyst is interested in assessing the value of the acquisition benefits to be generated by the acquirer relative to the price paid to target shareholders. Analysts are therefore likely to be interested in answers to the following questions:

■ What is the premium that the acquirer paid for the target's shares? What does this premium imply for the acquirer in terms of future performance improvements to justify the premium?

■ What are the likely performance improvements that management expects to generate from the acquisition? For example, are there likely to be increases in the revenues for the merged firm from new products, increased prices, or better distribution of existing products? Alternatively, are there cost savings as a result of taking advantage of economies of scale, improved efficiency, or a lower cost of capital for the target?

■ What is the value of any performance improvements? Values can be estimated using multiples or discounted abnormal earnings/cash flow methods.

Alcatel's pricing of Lucent

The Alcatel-Lucent merger was structured as a share-for-share exchange. For each share they held, Lucent shareholders would receive almost one-fifth of an Alcatel ADR. ADRs, or American Depository Receipts, are certificates that are issued by U.S. banks and represent foreign shares that are held on deposit by these banks. The Alcatel ADRs were listed on the New York Stock Exchange and provided the former Lucent shareholders with a convenient way to invest in Alcatel. Alcatel's €11.2 ($13.5) billion price for Lucent represented a 7 percent premium to target shareholders over the market value on March 23, 2006, when Alcatel and Lucent disclosed their merger talks.

With average takeover premiums in share-for-share exchanges of 15 percent, the premium that Alcatel offered to Lucent shareholders was relatively low. In terms of traditional multiple forms of valuation, Alcatel's pricing of Lucent also appeared to be on the low side. For example, at the time of the announcement of Alcatel's offer, the average PE value for other firms in the U.S. telecom equipment industry that were comparable to Lucent was close to 30. Alcatel's premerger PE value was 19 and U.S.-based Cisco Systems, which was of similar size to the Alcatel-Lucent combination, traded at around 25 times current earnings. Alcatel's offer valued Lucent at 13 times current earnings and 20 times next year's expected earnings.

The market reaction to the acquisition announcement on April 2, 2006 suggests that analysts believed that the deal created value for Alcatel's shareholders – Alcatel's share price increased by 8.4 percent (adjusted for market-wide changes), or €1.37 billion, during the 11 days prior to the announcement through to the actual announcement day. By the tenth trading day after the announcement, Alcatel's share was up 8.8 percent, or €1.44 billion. Given the €0.73 ($0.88) billion premium that Alcatel paid for Lucent, investors believed that the merger would create value of €2.17 billion.

ACQUISITION FINANCING

Even if an acquisition is undertaken to create new economic value and is priced judiciously, it may still destroy shareholder value if it is inappropriately financed. Several financing options are available to acquirers, including issuing shares or warrants to target shareholders, or acquiring target shares using surplus cash or proceeds from new debt. The trade-offs between these options from the standpoint of target shareholders usually hinge on their tax and transaction cost implications. For acquirers, they can affect the firm's capital structure and provide new information to investors.

As we discuss below, the financing preferences of target and acquiring shareholders can diverge. Financing arrangements can therefore increase or reduce the attractiveness of an acquisition from the standpoint of acquiring shareholders. As a result, a complete analysis of an acquisition will include an examination of the implications of the financing arrangements for the acquirer.

Effect of form of financing on target shareholders

As noted above, the key financing considerations for target shareholders are the tax and transaction cost implications of the acquirer's offer.

Tax effects of different forms of consideration

Target shareholders care about the after-tax value of any offer they receive for their shares. In many countries, whenever target shareholders receive cash for their shares, they are required to pay capital gains tax on the difference between the takeover offer price and their original purchase price. Alternatively, if they receive shares in the acquirer as consideration, they can defer any taxes on the capital gain until they sell the new shares. To qualify for the deferral of capital gains taxes, governments may require additional conditions to be met.[8] In the U.K., taxes on capital gains from takeovers can only be deferred when the acquirer and the target firm operate in the same industry. In the U.S., the acquisition must be undertaken as a tax-free reorganization. Within the European Union, not only capital gains on national, within-border share-for-share exchanges can be deferred. The E.U. Merger Directive guarantees that the option to defer capital gains taxes, if allowed for national mergers, applies also to cross-border share-for-share exchanges.

Tax laws that allow the deferral of capital gains taxes appear to cause target shareholders to prefer a share offer to a cash one. This is certainly likely to be the case for a target founder who still has a significant stake in the company. If the company's share price has appreciated over its life, the founder will face substantial capital gains tax on a cash offer and will therefore probably prefer to receive shares in the acquiring firm. However, cash and share offers can be tax-neutral for some groups of shareholders. For example, consider the tax implications for risk arbitrageurs, who take a short-term position in a company that is a takeover candidate in the hope that other bidders will emerge and increase the takeover price. They have no intention of holding shares in the acquirer once the takeover is completed and will pay ordinary income tax on any short-term trading gain. Cash and share offers therefore have identical after-tax values for risk arbitrageurs. Similarly, tax-exempt institutions are likely to be indifferent to whether an offer is in cash or shares.

Transaction costs and the form of financing

Transaction costs are another factor related to the form of financing that can be relevant to target shareholders. Transaction costs are incurred when target shareholders sell any shares received as consideration for their shares in the target. These costs will not be faced by target shareholders if the bidder offers them cash. Transaction costs are unlikely to be significant for investors who intend to hold the acquirer's shares following a share acquisition. However they may be relevant for investors who intend to sell, such as risk arbitrageurs.

Effect of form of financing on acquiring shareholders

For acquiring shareholders the costs and benefits of different financing options usually depend on how the offer affects their firm's capital structure and any information effects associated with different forms of financing.

Capital structure effects of form of financing

In acquisitions where debt financing or surplus cash are the primary form of consideration for target shares, the acquisition increases the net financial leverage of the acquirer. This increase in leverage may be part of the acquisition strategy, since one way an acquirer can add value to an inefficient firm is to lower its taxes by increasing interest tax shields. However, in many acquisitions an increase in postacquisition leverage is a side effect of the method of financing and not part of a deliberate tax-minimizing strategy. The increase in leverage can then potentially reduce shareholder value for the acquirer by increasing the risk of financial distress.

To assess whether an acquisition leads an acquirer to have too much leverage, financial analysts can assess the acquirer's financial risk following the proposed acquisition by these methods:

- Assessing the pro forma financial risks for the acquirer under the proposed financing plan. Popular measures of financial risk include debt-to-equity and interest coverage ratios, as well as projections of cash flows available to meet debt repayments. The ratios can be compared to similar performance metrics for the acquiring and target firms' industries. Do postmerger ratios indicate that the firm's probability of financial distress has increased significantly?

- Examining whether there are important off-balance sheet liabilities for the target and/or acquirer that are not included in the pro forma ratio and cash flow analysis of postacquisition financial risk.

- Determining whether the pro forma assets for the acquirer are largely intangible and therefore sensitive to financial distress. Measures of intangible assets include such ratios as market to book equity and tangible assets to the market value of equity.

Corporate control and the form of financing

Ordinary shares carry voting rights that allow shareholders to exercise influence over company management. When an acquisition is being financed with equity, part of the acquiring shareholders' voting power will transfer to the target shareholders after the acquisition. Acquiring firms that are controlled by one large shareholder may therefore choose cash or debt as the primary form of financing to avoid their major shareholder losing control. Research has found that European acquirers whose primary shareholder controls between 40 and 60 percent of the equity votes indeed have a preference for cash as the primary form of consideration.[9] For shareholders who hold an equity stake between 40 and 60 percent, the threat of losing control after a share-for-share exchange is most imminent.

Information problems and the form of financing

As we discuss in Chapter 12, information asymmetries between managers and external investors can make managers reluctant to raise equity to finance new projects. Managers' reluctance arises from their fear that investors will interpret the decision as an indication that the firm's equity is overvalued. In the short term, this effect can lead managers to deviate from the firm's long-term optimal mix of debt and equity. As a result, acquirers are likely to prefer to use internal funds or debt to finance an acquisition, because these forms of consideration are less likely to be interpreted negatively by investors.[10]

The information effects imply that firms forced to use equity financing are likely to face a share price decline when investors learn of the method of financing.[11] From the viewpoint of financial analysts, the financing announcement may, therefore, provide valuable news about the preacquisition value of the acquirer. On the other hand, it should have no implications for analysis of whether the acquisition creates value for acquiring shareholders, since the news reflected in the financing announcement is about the *preacquisition* value of the acquirer and not about the *postacquisition* value of the target to the acquirer.

A second information problem arises if the acquiring management does not have good information about the target. Equity financing then provides a way for acquiring shareholders to share the information risks with target shareholders. If the acquirer finds out after the acquisition that the value of the target is less than previously anticipated, the accompanying decline in the acquirer's equity price will be partially borne by target shareholders who continue to hold the acquirer's shares. In contrast, if the target's shares were acquired in a cash offer, any postacquisition loss would be fully borne by the acquirer's original shareholders. The risk-sharing benefits from using equity financing appears to be widely recognized for acquisitions of private companies, where public information on the target is largely unavailable.[12] In practice it appears to be considered less important for acquisitions of large public corporations.[13]

KEY ANALYSIS QUESTIONS

The form of financing has important tax and transaction cost implications for target shareholders. It can also have important capital structure and information effects for acquirers. From the perspective of the analyst, the effect of any corporate tax benefits from debt financing should already be reflected in the valuation of the target. Information effects are not relevant to the value of the acquisition. However, the analyst does need to consider whether demands by target shareholders for consideration in cash lead the acquirer to have a postacquisition capital structure which increases the risk of financial distress to a point that is detrimental for shareholders. Thus, part of the analyst's task is to determine how it affects the acquirer's capital structure and its risks of financial distress by asking the following questions:

- What is the leverage for the newly created firm? How does this compare to leverage for comparable firms in the industry?

■ What are the projected future cash flows for the merged firm? Are these sufficient to meet the firm's debt commitments? How much of a cushion does the firm have if future cash flows are lower than expected? Is the firm's debt level so high that it is likely to impair its ability to finance profitable future investments if future cash flows are below expectations?

Alcatel's financing of Lucent

Alcatel offered Lucent shareholders 0.1952 Alcatel ADRs for each Lucent share. Given Lucent's 4,469 million shares outstanding, Alcatel issued 872 million shares, which at €12.85 per share implied a total offer of €11.2 billion. The merger was structured as a "tax-free reorganization" for federal tax purposes. This implied that Lucent shareholders would not recognize any gain or loss for federal tax purposes from exchanging their Lucent shares for Alcatel ADRs in the merger.

By using shares to finance the acquisition, Alcatel reduced its financial leverage. The market reacted positively to the offer, increasing Alcatel's share price by 1.1 percent (adjusting for market-wide returns) on the announcement date (March 23, 2006). This reaction suggests that investors did not interpret Alcatel's share offer as indicating that its equity was overvalued. Also, in the following ten days Alcatel's share price increased, albeit by a mere 0.4 percent.

ACQUISITION OUTCOME

The final question of interest to the analyst evaluating a potential acquisition is whether it will indeed be completed. If an acquisition has a clear value-based motive, the target is priced appropriately, and its proposed financing does not create unnecessary financial risks for the acquirer, it may still fail because the target receives a higher competing bid or because of opposition from entrenched target management. Therefore, to evaluate the likelihood that an offer will be accepted, the financial analyst has to understand whether there are potential competing bidders who could pay an even higher premium to target shareholders than is currently offered. They also have to consider whether target managers are entrenched and, to protect their jobs, likely to oppose an offer.

Other potential acquirers

If there are other potential bidders for a target, especially ones who place a higher value on the target, there is a strong possibility that the bidder in question will be unsuccessful. Target management and shareholders have an incentive to delay accepting the initial offer to give potential competitors time to also submit a bid. From the perspective of the initial bidder, this means that the offer could potentially reduce shareholder value by the cost of making the offer (including substantial investment banking and legal fees). In practice, a losing bidder can usually recoup these losses and sometimes even make healthy profits from selling to the successful acquirer any shares it has accumulated in the target.

> ## KEY ANALYSIS QUESTIONS
>
> The financial analyst can determine whether there are other potential acquirers for a target and how they value the target by asking the following questions:
>
> - Are there other firms that could also implement the initial bidder's acquisition strategy? For example, if this strategy relies on developing benefits from complementary assets, look for potential bidders who also have assets complementary to the target. If the goal of the acquisition is to replace inefficient management, what other firms in the target's industry could provide management expertise?
>
> - Who are the acquirer's major competitors? Could any of these firms provide an even better fit for the target?

Target management entrenchment

If target managers are entrenched and fearful for their jobs, it is likely that they will oppose a bidder's offer. Some firms have implemented "golden parachutes" for top managers to counteract their concerns about job security at the time of an offer. Golden parachutes provide top managers of a target firm with attractive compensation rewards should the firm get taken over. However, many firms do not have such schemes, and opposition to an offer from entrenched management is a very real possibility.

In some European countries the entrenchment of management is facilitated by legal provisions that allow a company to install various takeover defenses. For example, in most countries, firms can limit the number of votes that a shareholder can exercise at a shareholders' meeting. A voting cap effectively reduces the voting power that a potential acquirer can obtain. Another example of a takeover defense mechanism, which is commonly used in the Netherlands, is the issuance of depository receipts by an administrative office that is controlled by the firm whose shares the office holds.[14] Holders of depository receipts have the right to receive dividends but no voting rights. Instead, the administrative office retains and exercises the voting rights. This construction makes it difficult for an acquiring firm to obtain any voting power.

While the existence of takeover defenses for a target indicates that its management is likely to fight a bidding firm's offer, defenses do not often prevent an acquisition from taking place. Instead, they tend to cause delays, which increase the likelihood that there will be competing offers made for the target, including offers by friendly parties solicited by target management, called "white knights." Takeover defenses therefore increase the likelihood that the bidder in question will be outbid for the target, or that it will have to increase its offer significantly to win a bidding contest. These risks may discourage acquirers from embarking on a potentially hostile acquisition. Nonetheless, in recent years hostile takeovers have become more rather than less popular in Europe. For example, in 2006, steel producer Mittal Steel was engaged in a hostile takeover attempt for industry peer Arcelor. Arcelor called in the help of "white knight" Severstal, but eventually was forced by its shareholders to accept Mittal's offer. The takeover battle had caused a delay of five months and had driven up the takeover price by 49 percent, or €8.4 billion.

Takeover regulations have the objectives of preventing management entrenchment and protecting minority shareholders during European takeovers. During the 1990s, national takeover regulations in Europe began converging toward the U.K. regime model. In 2004 the European Commission issued a heavily debated Takeover

Directive, which applies to companies whose shares are traded on a (regulated) public exchange. The most important rules in this Directive (effective since May 2006) are the following:[15]

- The equal-treatment rule and the mandatory-bid rule aim at protecting minority shareholders in takeovers. The mandatory-bid rule prescribes that the acquiring firm makes an offer for all remaining shares, once its equity stake exceeds a predefined threshold. In Denmark, Italy, and the U.K., this threshold is, for example, 30 percent. The equal-treatment rule requires that the acquiring firm makes equally favorable offers to the controlling and minority shareholders of the target firm.

- Under the squeeze-out rule, the acquiring firm can force the remaining minority shareholders to sell their shares at the tender offer price, once the firm holds a predefined equity stake of, usually, between 80 and 95 percent. Under the sell-out rule, the remaining shareholders can force the acquiring firm to buy their shares at a fair price.

- The board-neutrality rule requires that during takeovers management will not take actions that may frustrate the takeover.

Another proposed rule, the breakthrough rule, did make it into the final Directive but can be opted out of by individual countries. The breakthrough rule mandates that a firm that has acquired a predefined percentage of shares can exercise votes on its shares *as if* all outstanding shares, including the firm's shares, carry one vote per share. For example, the breakthrough rule guarantees that an acquiring firm that owns 90 percent of the target firm's ordinary shares can exercise exactly 90 percent of the votes during a shareholders' meeting of the target firm, irrespective of the takeover defense mechanisms that are in place.

The rules in the E.U. Takeover Directive can affect the analysis of a takeover offer. For example, in some jurisdictions the laws prescribe that when the mandatory-bid rule comes into effect, the acquiring firm must offer the remaining shareholders no less than the highest price it has paid to other shareholders. This rule, of course, invites the investor to strategically wait until the last moment before accepting the offer. The board-neutrality rule reduces management entrenchment through postbid takeover defenses and therefore reduces the probability that a target firm will oppose an acquisition. The breakthrough rule, if implemented, can remove firms' prebid takeover defenses, such as voting caps.

KEY ANALYSIS QUESTIONS

To assess whether the target firm's management is entrenched and therefore likely to oppose an acquisition, analysts can ask the following questions:

- Does the target firm have takeover defenses designed to protect management? If so, do national takeover rules reduce the effect of such defenses? Further, do national takeover rules regulate that minority shareholders receive a fair price?

- Has the target been a poor performer relative to other firms in its industry? If so, management's job security is likely to be threatened by a takeover, leading it to oppose any offers.

- Is there a golden parachute plan in place for target management? Golden parachutes provide attractive compensation for management in the event of a takeover to deter opposition to a takeover for job security reasons.

Analysis of outcome of Alcatel's offer for Lucent

Analysts covering Lucent had little reason to question whether Lucent would be sold to Alcatel. The offer was a friendly one that had received the approval of Lucent's management and board of directors. There probably was some risk of another telecom equipment maker entering the bidding for Lucent. For example, following the merger announcement there were rumors that Sweden-based Ericsson would launch a competing bid to acquire Lucent. However, Ericsson's management explicitly denied that it had any interest in acquiring Lucent after already having acquired one of Lucent's U.K. competitors, Marconi. Eventually, none of Alcatel's competitors made a bid for Lucent.

SUMMARY

This chapter summarizes how financial statement data and analysis can be used by financial analysts interested in evaluating whether an acquisition creates value for an acquiring firm's shareholders. Obviously, much of this discussion is also likely to be relevant to other merger participants, including target and acquiring management and their investment banks.

For the external analyst, the first task is to identify the acquirer's acquisition strategy. We discuss a number of strategies. Some of these are consistent with maximizing acquirer value, including acquisitions to take advantage of economies of scale, improve target management, combine complementary resources, capture tax benefits, provide low-cost financing to financially constrained targets, and increase product-market rents.

Other strategies appear to benefit managers more than shareholders. For example, some unprofitable acquisitions are made because managers are reluctant to return free cash flows to shareholders, or because managers want to lower the firm's earnings volatility by diversifying into unrelated businesses.

The financial analyst's second task is to assess whether the acquirer is offering a reasonable price for the target. Even if the acquirer's strategy is based on increasing shareholder value, it can overpay for the target. Target shareholders will then be well rewarded but at the expense of acquiring shareholders. We show how the ratio, pro forma, and valuation techniques discussed earlier in the book can all be used to assess the worth of the target to the acquirer.

The method of financing an offer is also relevant to a financial analyst's review of an acquisition proposal. If a proposed acquisition is financed with surplus cash or new debt, it increases the acquirer's financial risk. Financial analysts can use ratio analysis of the acquirer's postacquisition balance sheet and pro forma estimates of cash flow volatility and interest coverage to assess whether demands by target shareholders for consideration in cash lead the acquirer to increase its risk of financial distress.

Finally, the financial analyst is interested in assessing whether a merger is likely to be completed once the initial offer is made, and at what price. This requires the analyst to determine whether there are other potential bidders, and whether target management is entrenched and likely to oppose a bidder's offer.

DISCUSSION QUESTIONS

1. During the early 1990s there was a noticeable increase in mergers and acquisitions between firms in different countries (termed cross-border acquisitions). What factors could explain this increase? What special issues can arise in executing a cross-border acquisition and in ultimately meeting your objectives for a successful combination?

2. In the 1980s leveraged buyouts (LBOs) were a popular form of acquisition in the U.S. In the late 1990s and early 2000s LBOs became increasingly popular in Europe. Under a leveraged buyout, a buyout group (which frequently includes target management) makes an offer to buy the target firm at a premium over its current price. The buyout group finances much of the acquisition with debt capital, leading the target to become a highly leveraged private company following the acquisition.

   a. What types of firms would make ideal candidates for LBOs? Why?

   b. How might the acquirer add sufficient value to the target to justify a high buyout premium?

3. Kim Silverman, Finance Director of the First Public Bank, notes: "We are fortunate to have a cost of capital of only 10 percent. We want to leverage this advantage by acquiring other banks that have a higher cost of funds. I believe that we can add significant value to these banks by using our lower cost financing." Do you agree with Silverman's analysis? Why or why not?

4. The Munich Beer Company plans to acquire Liverpool Beer Co. for £60 per share, a 50 percent premium over the current market price. Jan Höppe, the Financial Director of Munich Beer, argues that this valuation can easily be justified, using a price-earnings analysis. "Munich Beer has a price-earnings ratio of 15, and we expect that we will be able to generate long-term earnings for Liverpool Beer of £5 per share. This implies that Liverpool Beer is worth £75 to us, well above our £60 offer price." Do you agree with this analysis? What are Höppe's key assumptions?

5. You have been hired by GS Investment Bank to work in the merger department. The analysis required for all potential acquisitions includes an examination of the target for any off-balance sheet assets or liabilities that have to be factored into the valuation. Prepare a checklist for your examination.

6. Company T is currently valued at €50 in the market. A potential acquirer, A, believes that it can add value in two ways: €15 of value can be added through better working capital management, and an additional €10 of value can be generated by making available a unique technology to expand T's new product offerings. In a competitive bidding contest, how much of this additional value will A have to pay out to T's shareholders to emerge as the winner?

7. A leading oil exploration company decides to acquire an internet company at a 50 percent premium. The acquirer argues that this move creates value for its own shareholders because it can use its excess cash flows from the oil business to help finance growth in the new internet segment. Evaluate the economic merits of this claim.

8. Under current International Financial Reporting Standards, acquirers are required to capitalize goodwill and report any subsequent declines in value as an impairment charge. What performance metrics would you use to judge whether goodwill is impaired?

NOTES

1. In a review of studies of merger returns, Michael Jensen and Richard Ruback, "The Market for Corporate Control: The Scientific Evidence," *Journal of Financial Economics* 11 (April 1983): 5–50, conclude that target shareholders earn positive returns from takeovers, but that acquiring shareholders only break even.
2. See Steven Kaplan, "Management Buyouts: Evidence on Taxes as a Source of Value," *Journal of Finance* 44 (1989): 611–632.
3. Krishna Palepu, "Predicting Takeover Targets: A Methodological and Empirical Analysis," *Journal of Accounting and Economics* 8 (March 1986): 3–36.
4. Chapter 2 discusses the pros and cons of corporate diversification and evidence on its implications for firm performance.
5. See "Alcatel and Lucent: The Urge to Merge," *The Economist,* April 6, 2006.
6. See Paul Healy, Krishna Palepu, and Richard Ruback, "Which Mergers Are Profitable – Strategic or Financial?," *Sloan Management Review* 38, no. 4 (Summer 1997): 45–58. For empirical evidence on European target firms' cumulative stock returns around the takeover announcement, see Martina Martynova and Luc Renneboog, "Mergers and Acquisitions in Europe," Working Paper, Tilburg University, 2006. This study reports that 60 days after a hostile takeover announcement European target firms' share prices have run up by, on average, 45 percent since 60 days prior to the announcement. In contrast, after friendly takeover announcements, share prices have run up by, on average, 10 percent. The average difference in price run-up of 35 percent can be interpreted as the average difference in (expected) takeover premiums.
7. See, for example, Martina Martynova and Luc Renneboog, op. cit.
8. In several European countries, such as in Belgium, Denmark, and Germany, individual shareholders pay no or little taxes on the capital gains that they make from selling or exchanging their shares in a takeover, provided that they have held the shares for a defined period, typically being a period of one or two years. For these shareholders the after-tax value of a takeover offer does not depend on whether they receive cash or shares as consideration.
9. See Mara Faccio and Ronald W. Masulis, "The Choice of Payment Method in European Mergers and Acquisitions," *Journal of Finance* 60 (2005): 1345–1388.
10. See Stewart Myers and Nicholas Majluf, "Corporate Financing and Investment Decisions When Firms Have Information That Investors Do Not," *Journal of Financial Economics* (June 1984): 187–221.
11. For evidence see Nicholas Travlos, "Corporate Takeover Bids, Methods of Payments, and Bidding Firms' Stock Returns," *Journal of Finance* 42 (1987): 943–963.
12. See S. Datar, R. Frankel, and M. Wolfson, "Earnouts: The Effects of Adverse Selection and Agency Costs on Acquisition Techniques," *Journal of Law, Economics, and Organization* 17 (2001): 201–238.
13. See Mara Faccio and Ronald W. Masulis, op. cit.
14. See Rezaul Kabir, Dolph Cantrijn, and Andreas Jeunink, "Takeover Defenses, Ownership Structures, and Stock Returns in the Netherlands: An Empirical Analysis," *Strategic Management Journal* 18 (1997): 97–109.
15. Marc Goergen, Marina Martynova, and Luc Renneboog give a complete description of the most important rules in the E.U. Takeover Directive in their study "Corporate Governance Convergence: Evidence from Takeover Regulation Reforms in Europe," *Oxford Review of Economic Policy* 21 (2005): 243–268.

The Air France-KLM Merger[1]

We have always been convinced of the necessity of consolidation in the airline industry. Today, we announce a combination with KLM that will create the first European airline group, which is a milestone in our industry. This will bring significant benefits to customers, shareholders and employees. Capitalizing on the two brands and on the complementary strengths of both companies, we should, within SkyTeam, be able to capture enhanced growth opportunities.

Jean-Cyril Spinetta, Chairman and CEO of Air France

KLM has been pointing out the need for consolidation in light of the challenges facing our industry, and we have not made it a secret we were looking for a strong European partner. Through this innovative partnership with Air France and our subsequent expected participation in the SkyTeam alliance, we are confident that we have secured a sustainable future for our company. Our valuable Schiphol hub will be an integral part of the dual hub strategy of the new airline group, allowing us to build on what KLM and its staff have achieved over nearly 85 years.

Leo van Wijk, President and CEO of KLM

On September 30, 2003, Air France and KLM Royal Dutch Airlines – two European airlines that provided international passenger and cargo airline services – issued a press release that announced their planned merger. The merger envisaged the creation of the leading European airline Air France-KLM. In 2003, both airlines were the primary national ("flag carrying") airlines in their home countries, France and the Netherlands. However, poor industry conditions put pressure on the airlines' growth and operating margins. In the fiscal year ending on March 31, 2003, Air France, the larger of the two airlines, reported an increase in total sales of slightly more than one percent to €12,687 million and a net profit of €120 million (€0.55 per share). KLM performed worse than Air France. In the same fiscal year, KLM reported a decrease in total sales of slightly less than one percent to €6,485 million and a loss (before extraordinary items) of €186 million (€3.97 per share).

For a number of years, KLM had been searching for a strategic partner, which seemed to be of essential importance given the deteriorating industry conditions. Initially, KLM attempted to form an alliance with the Italian flag carrier, Alitalia. However, this alliance soon appeared to be unsuccessful because of the poor functioning of Milan Malpensa Airport, an unexpected delay in the privatization of Alitalia, and cultural incompatibilities between the Italians and the Dutch.[2] After breaking with Alitalia, KLM kept on searching for another partner. In early 2000, talks about joining forces with British Airways remained unfruitful, as KLM and its

1. Professor Erik Peek prepared this case. The case is intended solely as the basis for class discussion and is not intended to serve as an endorsement, source of primary data, or illustration of effective or ineffective management.
2. "KLM Ends Venture With Alitalia, Imperiling US Airline Alliance," Wall Street Journal, May 1, 2000; "Alitalia is Seeking Damages for Breakup with KLM," Wall Street Journal, August 2, 2000.

main shareholder, the Dutch state, were unwilling to hand over control to the British flag carrier.[3] In the second half of 2003, Air France came to the rescue.

KLM Royal Dutch Airlines[4]

KLM Royal Dutch Airlines was founded in 1919, which, at the time of the merger, made it the oldest continuously operating airline in the world. Landmarks in the company's history were its very first scheduled flight to London in 1920, its first intercontinental flight to Jakarta (formerly Batavia) in 1924, and its operating scheduled flights to New York from 1946.

Over the years, the core activities of KLM remained very much the same. The airline provided worldwide passenger and cargo transport, engineering and maintenance, and, in a later stage, charter and low-cost scheduled flights. KLM operated its charter and low-cost flights primarily through its subsidiaries Buzz and Transavia. In 1994, KLM served 153 cities in 81 countries on six continents and ranked eighth among the largest international airlines based upon ton-kilometer traffic on international flights. Nine years later, KLM served 350 cities in 73 countries on six continents and ranked fifth among the largest international airlines.

In its prospectus from 1994, which accompanied the issuance of 18.5 million additional ordinary shares, the airline summarized its most important operating risks. First, the airline operated in an industry that was cyclical and highly competitive. The cyclical nature could have a strong adverse effect on KLM's profitability because, as every other airline, it had a high degree of operating leverage (high fixed-to-variable cost ratio). Second, the airline's profitability depended strongly on exchange rate fluctuations as well as on fluctuations in aircraft fuel prices. Third, because in many parts of the world airlines and international air traffic were highly regulated, KLM's operations could be affected by foreign governments' actions of protectionism.

Within this uncertain economic environment, KLM's corporate objective was "… to position itself as an airline operating worldwide from a European base that provides quality service for passengers and cargo shippers at competitive cost levels." The strategy that KLM used to attain this objective was to:

- *Increase customer preference.* KLM focused on achieving a high level of customer satisfaction, for example, by closely monitoring customer demand and by expanding its "Flying Dutchman" frequent flyer program.

- *Strengthen its market presence around the world.* KLM strengthened its market presence in the world's major air transportation markets by expanding its hub-and-spoke operations at Schiphol Airport and by creating alliances with other European, American, and Asian airlines. For example, in 1989, KLM had acquired a 20 percent stake in Northwest Airlines, a North American airline having its operations hubs in Boston, Detroit, and Minneapolis. This acquisition helped KLM to gain better access to American destinations. The alliance between KLM and Northwest implied that both airlines operated as a joint venture on transatlantic flights, while KLM did all their marketing in Europe and Northwest in the U.S.

3. *"Europe's Flag Airlines: Going Nowhere,"* Business Week, *February 26, 2001.*
4. *Material in this section is drawn from KLM's 1994 prospectus, its 2002/2003 Annual Report, and its corporate website.*

■ *Reduce its costs to at least an internationally competitive level.* During the early 1990s, KLM launched a restructuring program that aimed to reduce its costs and increase its productivity. The program included spinning off noncore business units, network optimization, eliminating the first class section on intercontinental flights, redesigning business processes, and acquiring more efficient aircraft. KLM launched a second restructuring program, Focus 2000, in 1996, and a third one, Baseline, in 2000.

In 2003, KLM's shares were listed on the Amsterdam Euronext Exchange and on the New York Stock Exchange. Since early in KLM's history, the Dutch state had been KLM's primary shareholder. The state's ownership interest in KLM gradually decreased over the years, from 38 percent of the votes in 1994 to 14 percent in 2003. Nonetheless, the state remained able to effectively influence the airline's major (non-operating) decisions through various mechanisms. First, up to the date of the merger, the state had the option to obtain a 50.1 percent voting interest to prevent any unde-sirable accumulation of share ownership in the hands of others. This option was espe-cially important to prevent a country imposing restrictions on KLM exercising international traffic rights. Because such traffic rights were the result of bilateral treaties between governments and tied to domestically owned airlines, countries could deny these rights to KLM if in their view the airline was no longer in Dutch hands. Second, the articles of association offered the state the right to appoint a majority of the Supervisory Board. Third, the state held the majority of KLM's priority shares, through which it had a veto over important decisions such as the issuance of shares, payments of stock dividends, and changes in the articles of association.

The merger agreement[5]

During 2002, while renewed negotiations between British Airways and KLM reached deadlock, KLM representatives also started to meet with Air France representatives to talk about the possibilities of cooperation. Parallel to these meetings, Air France's North American alliance partners, Continental Airlines and Delta Airlines, discussed possible cooperation with KLM's North American alliance partner, Northwest Airlines. In August 2002, the three North American airlines signed a ten-year agreement to improve schedule connections between the airlines and to share codes, frequent flyer programs, and airport lounges. After the signing of the agreement, the three airlines encouraged Air France and KLM to start similar cooperation in Europe. However, because the French state was planning to privatize Air France (i.e., reduce its shareholdings to a level below 20 percent), Air France and KLM envisaged a closer form of cooperation. Initially, both parties discussed the option of creating a dual listed company structure. Air France and KLM would keep their separate listings but cross-hold 50 percent of the shares of each other's operating subsidiaries. Because Air France had a substantially greater market value than KLM, Air France would also become the direct owner of 52 percent of KLM's shares and certain of its assets would be excluded from the transaction. However, the idea of creating a dual listed company structure appeared too complex and both airlines soon opted for a simpler alternative, which they presented to their shareholders on September 30, 2003.

 The alternative proposal implied that the former shareholders of KLM and Air France became shareholders of the publicly listed holding company Air France-KLM, which would hold 100 percent of the shares of two private operating companies, Air

5. Material in this section is drawn from the Air France-KLM merger prospectus (April 5, 2004).

France and KLM. Former Air France shareholders would receive one Air France-KLM share for every Air France share that they held. In exchange for 10 KLM shares, former KLM shareholders would receive 11 Air France-KLM shares plus 10 Air France-KLM warrants. The warrants had a strike price of €20.00, were exercisable after 18 months and had an exercise period of 3.5 years. Three warrants gave the warrant holder the right to purchase two Air France-KLM shares.

Based on Air France's closing price on September 29, 2003, the estimated value of one warrant was equal to €1.68 (according to the Air France-KLM merger announcement). This warrant value was based on the following assumptions:

- The September 29 AIR-France(-KLM) share price was €13.69.
- The risk-free rate equaled 2.89 percent.
- The estimated future volatility of the AIR-France(-KLM) share price was 40 percent.
- Estimated dividends per share were €0.096, €0.144, and €0.188 during the exercise period (based on I/B/E/S estimates).

Based on the AIR France (-KLM) share price of €13.69 and a warrant value of €1.68, the total value of the offer for KLM shareholders equaled €16.74 per share (11/10 × €13.69 + €1.68), which implied a premium of 40 percent over KLM's closing share price on September 29, 2003. After the share exchange, former KLM shareholders would own 19 percent of the ordinary shares (and voting rights) of Air France-KLM. The share exchange offer would commence only after approval from the E.U. and U.S. competition authorities, and if no third party announced a public offer for either KLM's or Air France's shares.

The transaction between Air France and KLM was not a full-blown merger. The two private operating companies, Air France and KLM, remained separate entities, in particular because it was important to preserve the two established brand names. Further, the Dutch state retained the option to acquire a 50.1 percent voting interest in KLM (the operating company) if necessary to preserve KLM's landing rights.

Motivation for the merger

Airline industry analysts tend to distinguish two phases of evolution in a deregulated airline industry – i.e., the expansion phase and the consolidation phase. To illustrate, in the 1970s, the U.S. government deregulated the U.S. airline industry, which led to a serious expansion of supply from 1978 to 1990. In this expansion phase, U.S. airlines responded by cutting their costs, but their operating margins experienced a secular decline. In the early stages of consolidation, from 1986 onwards, mergers resulted in the elimination of several brands, but did not restrict or reallocate capacity. Since the mergers initially raised costs, profit margins remained under pressure. In the later stages of the consolidation phase, U.S. airlines reallocated their capacity from unprofitable (geographical) areas to profitable (geographical) areas. This significantly improved U.S. airlines' profit margins. In the mid-1990s, the European airline industry was in a different stage of development than the U.S. airline industry. At that time, European airlines had just entered into the earlier stages of consolidation by creating alliances. However, alliances made it difficult to reallocate capacity and improve profitability. Furthermore, government interference hindered efficient allocation of capacity.[6]

---

6. See "Global Airlines: Survival of the Fittest," Goldman Sachs Global Research, September 22, 1997.

During the late 1990s and the early 2000s, the profit potential of the European airline industry changed substantially. At the end of the 1990s, Europe had an increasing number of large and small airlines, many airports close together, and most governments supporting loss-making national airlines. Government support resulted in very few unprofitable companies leaving the market. At the same time, many airlines started downgrading their product by offering low levels of service on short-haul flights to compete on costs. All major airports had capacity constraints, which (in combination with their slot trading system that favored current slot-owners) made access to established airports difficult for new entrants. However, new entrants, such as Ryanair and easyJet were moving to smaller, local airports to avoid the capacity constraints of the major airports. These new entrants further intensified the competition (on costs) in the European airline industry. Finally, the use of web booking systems made the market more transparent. Customers were able to easily compare prices, which substantially reduced switching costs.

After 2000, the profit potential of the European airline industry improved slightly. The European Commission had allowed governments to cover insurance risks and costs faced by airlines after the September 11, 2001 terrorist attacks; however, other forms of government support were no longer allowed. Further, after September 2001, many airlines significantly reduced (fixed) capacity, which reduced competition. Finally, more and more countries signed bilateral "open skies" agreements with the U.S., implying that European airlines could fly to any place in the U.S., at any fare, at any time (but only from their home countries). In early 2004, a European agreement with the U.S. was being negotiated, implying that, for example, the German national airline Lufthansa would be allowed to fly from Milan to New York. Nonetheless, KLM's return on equity during the fiscal years ending in 2001, 2002, and 2003 was 3.7, –7.8, and –24.1 percent respectively.

Exhibit 1 reports KLM's and Air France's motivation for entering into the merger agreement, as it was set out at the merger presentation on September 30, 2003.

Response of the Dutch Investor Association

In early 2004, the Dutch Investor Association (VEB; Vereniging voor Effectenbezitters) began to oppose the merger proposal. The VEB was of the opinion that during the months following the merger, KLM's value had increased substantially due to changed circumstances, which would justify a higher takeover price. KLM shareholders had to decide before May 5, 2004 (just before KLM's publication of its 2003/2004 financial statements) whether or not they wished to offer their shares to Air France. The VEB claimed that KLM shareholders should be able to take these latest financial results into account when making their decision. Air France and KLM refused this, supported by a Dutch court decision on April 29, 2004. Exhibit 2 sets out the VEB's objections in detail.

On May 6, 2004, KLM announced that net profit, operating profit, and revenues for the fiscal year 2003/2004 were €24 million, €120 million, and €5,870 million, respectively.

Questions

1. Evaluate the motivating factors behind the Air France-KLM merger. Does the merger effectively address the strategic challenges faced by KLM and Air France?

2. Calculate the present value of the synergies. To what extent is the actual market response to the merger announcement consistent with the estimated value of the expected performance improvements?

3. To what extent can the premium be justified by the expected performance improvements (as presented in Exhibit 1)?

4. Critically analyze each of the VEB's (Dutch Investor Association) objections to the proposed takeover price (as presented in Exhibit 2). Do you have any evidence that Air France shareholders agree with the VEB?

5. If you were a shareholder of KLM, would you support this merger proposal?

The Air France-KLM merger

EXHIBIT 1 **Appendix to the offer document**

Strategic rationale of the transaction

The airline industry is fragmented and its current competitive structure, with national carriers for each individual country, is an inheritance from a former era. This has contributed to low profitability and lack of value creation for shareholders. The need for structural changes and consolidation in Europe is widely accepted, but has not yet commenced as a consequence of regulatory and political constraints.

The single European market and its current enlargement to some 455 million inhabitants reinforce the need for consolidation.

The evolution of the European regulatory framework highlighted by (i) the November 2002 European Court of Justice ruling and (ii) the mandate given in June 2003 to the European Commission to negotiate the open sky agreement with the US now creates an attractive environment for a value creating combination.

If commercial alliances have contributed over the past years to initiate the first steps towards consolidation, deeper cooperation is now needed to generate significant and sustainable synergies.

The proposed transaction between Air France and KLM is the first significant move in this context and will create a leading airline group in Europe with aggregated revenues of EUR 19.2 billion (2002/03 fiscal year).

The combination with KLM is a major step in Air France's strategy. In parallel, KLM's strategy over the years has consistently been built on two pillars: the strengthening of its own organization, as well as the participation in a global alliance, for which it seeks a strong European partner. The combination with Air France is the achievement of this strategy.

The transaction will benefit from the complementarities of the two airlines' operations:

- Two reputable and strong brands that will be further strengthened.
- Two operational hubs (Paris CDG and Amsterdam Schiphol) which are among the most efficient in Europe and provide significant development potential.
- Two complementary networks both in medium and long haul. In medium haul Air France has a strong position in Southern Europe and KLM has developed a strong position in Northern and North Eastern Europe, and both will be able to expand their positions in Central and Eastern Europe. The long haul networks currently consist of 101 destinations of

which only 31 are common (essentially the world's largest cities with high traffic volumes).

- A combined network of 226 destinations with 93 new destinations for KLM passengers and 48 new destinations for Air France passengers.
- A strong presence in cargo where Air France and KLM are the 4th and 11th largest in the world respectively but with complementary capabilities and expertise.
- A strong combination in the field of aircraft maintenance, creating one of the largest MRO providers worldwide.
- SkyTeam will eventually become the second largest global airline alliance and with its partners being able to offer passengers a more truly worldwide network.

Synergies

Potential synergies arising from the proposed transaction have been thoroughly assessed and quantified by a joint working group of Air France and KLM who has reviewed the feasibility and quantum of the synergies and their build-up over time.

Sales and distribution

By coordinating the two sales organizations the new group will have an improved presence around the world and will be able to offer a wider range of products to passengers. Cost savings could be achieved by coordinating the sales structures of the two companies. A joint negotiation position with catering and ground-handling partners could also lead to additional benefits.

Network / Revenue management and fleet

By full code sharing, harmonizing the flight schedules and optimizing common management revenue policy the two airlines will be able to offer more destinations, a larger number and more convenient connections for passengers and to improve sales performance.

Cargo

The offering of an improved product through a more extensive network in combination with coordinated freighter planning, should lead to an increase of revenues. Cost savings should also be possible by more efficient hub handling.

The Air France-KLM merger

Engineering and maintenance

The two airlines will be able to integrate purchasing of stock, to create centres of excellence in engineering and optimize the use of existing E&M platforms.

IT

Converging the IT applications used by both airlines should generate considerable cost savings in the medium term.

Other

Optimizing and harmonizing other activities such as simulator utilization and joint purchasing of goods should deliver further cost savings.

The identified potential synergies are expected to result in an annual improvement of the combined operating income (Earnings Before Interest and Tax) of between EUR 385 million and EUR 495 million, following a gradual implementation over a period of five years, with further upward potential thereafter.

Approximately 60 per cent of potential synergies are expected to be derived from cost savings.

This does not include additional expected synergies from marketing cooperation with respective partners. Furthermore, any improvement from the common fleet policy and lower capital expenditure requirements have not yet been determined and have not been taken into account in these estimates.

KLM restructuring plan

The KLM restructuring plan, which was announced in April 2003, with targeted annual operating income improvement of EUR 650 million by April 1, 2005, are additional to the synergies mentioned above. The KLM management remains fully committed to achieving this objective.

Estimated value of the synergies

Synergies by activity (Euro amounts in millions)

Activity	Main actions	Year 3 (2006/2007)	Year 5 (2008/2009)
Sales/Distribution	– Coordination of sales structures; – Sales cost improvements; – Handling and catering.	€40	€100
Network, revenue management, fleet	– Network/scheduling management; – Revenue management harmonization; optimization of fleet utilization; – Coordinated management.	€95–130	€30–195
Cargo	– Network optimization; – Commercial alignments; support services.	€35	€35
Maintenance	– Procurement; – Insourcing; pooling (stocks etc.).	€25	€60–€65
IT systems	Progressive convergence of IT systems	€20	€50–€70
Other	Procurement synergies	€5–€10	€10–€30
Total cost savings		€220–€260	€385–€495

Total expected synergies per year (Euro amounts in millions)

	2004/2005	2005/2006	2006/2007	2007/2008	2008/2009	Long-term
Total savings	65–75	110–135	220–260	295–370	385–495	>600

EXHIBIT 2 Press release of the Dutch Investor Association (VEB): "Air France Shareholders Get It on the Cheap", April 19, 2004[a]

After two postponements on 22 March and 31 March, KLM and Air France announced they intend to pursue their merger plans unchanged. This means that Air France will make an offer worth €784 million, whereby each KLM share will be worth 1.1 Air France shares plus a warrant. Far too low an offer.

Half a year has gone by since the merger was announced on 30 September 2003. In the intervening 6 months a number of circumstances have emerged that would justify a higher bid. The prospectus and the bid offer show that KLM is worth considerably more than was apparent until now. There are other questions that remain unanswered that would provide a clearer view of KLM's value. Here are ten reasons why the Air France bid is far too low.

Net equity per share is €34

KLM net worth (assets after debt) is €1,501 million, or €34.14 per share. At an Air France share price of €15 the offer amounts to €17.80 per KLM share. The bid is thus equivalent to just over its net equity value. Air France shareholders will obtain half KLM for free.

A further point is that KLM owns significant intangible assets that are not valued on the balance sheet. This includes the KLM brand name and the landing rights owned by KLM which have a definite economic value. Since these important intangibles are not valued at all in the balance sheet, a price in excess of net equity value stands to reason.

The bid is worth a mere 7 times earnings (2004) and 5 times earnings (2005)

Analysts forecast a substantial increase of profit for Fiscal 2004/2005 and the following Fiscal. They predict earnings in the €100–€110 million range in 2004. In the following year they could reach the €150–€170 million range. This equates to €2.50 and €3.60 per share. The bid is thus 7 times expected earnings for 2004 and 5 times expected earnings for 2005. Compared with other listed companies, whose average p/e ratio is 14, this is a very low valuation. Prices paid for other airline companies score are 17 times 2004 earnings and 11 times 2005.

Real estate assets include a surplus value of at least €248million, or €5.60 per share

The bid documentation (p. F-158) prepared by Air France and KLM reveals significant hidden reserves in KLM's stock of real estate. These are valued in KLM's balance sheet at €331 million. Price at purchase was €728 million, 55% of which has been written off. According to KLM these assets are now worth €248 million more. Put against 44.2 million shares on the market this corresponds to a surplus value of €5.60 per share. Specialists say the surplus value is closer to the €450–€650 million bracket!

Unlike Air France, KLM has accumulated a pension fund surplus of €2.4 billion

According to French GAAP (Generally Accepted Accounting Principles) KLM equity is worth about €3 billion, roughly double the equity according to Dutch GAAP and four times the value of the bid. Some significant modifications have been made to arrive at these figures. On the one hand the pension fund reserve has been added to shareholder equity. This is worth €2.4 billion. Against that a negative adjustment has to be made for contingent tax liabilities falling upon KLM of €811 million. French GAAP values equity per share at €69.

The exchange ratio is partly the result of operating results in 2002/2003 and 2003/2004: These were seriously depressed by the SARS health scare and the crisis in Iraq

KLM has been looking for years for a partner. There were several previous rounds of negotiation with British Airways. In 2001 a merger attempt with Alitalia failed. Processing the consequences of this failure were unpleasant. KLM was obliged to pay Alitalia €275 million, which was equivalent to €6 per KLM share. The media reported that KLM had refused an out of court settlement worth €50 million. The Alitalia costs appear as a charge in the 2002/2003 accounts. Last year operating results came under pressure as a result of the SARS health scare which significantly reduced

a. Reprinted with permission from the Vereniging van Effectenbezitters.

The Air France–KLM merger

passenger traffic to and from Asia. The first quarter of calendar 2003 put heavy pressure on both sales and profit as a result of the coming war in Iraq and the danger of terrorist attacks directed at aircraft. It is obvious that these factors depressed the price negotiations which clearly took account of current operational results. KLM would have been far better served by sitting it out until it could enter into negotiations from a more comfortable and more profitable situation.

The last two quarters show results significantly above the estimates of analysts

The merger and the price were announced on 30 September. In the intervening period KLM published its quarterly results, first on 23 October 2003 (Q2) and then on 22 January 2004 (Q3). KLM's results exceeded – even significantly – expectations. This has led to KLM anticipating a slightly positive result for 2003/2004 – despite SARS, Iraq, the low dollar and a poor economy. These improvements alone would have justified an adjustment of the price.

The earnings trend on the French side is less attractive. In the last 9 months Air France net profit has fallen from €143 million to €80 million.

Air France gets control of KLM without paying a premium

Air France will be the masters in the newly merged company. Previous Air France shareholders will hold onto an 81% share in the company. The CEO will be a Frenchman, Jean-Cyrille Spinetta. In both the Executive and the Supervisory Boards the Dutch will be in a minority. Of the eight Executive Board Directors four will be Dutch and four will be French. Although both companies pay lip-service to the mantra of a merger, it is in reality a takeover. Air France pitches a bid priced in its own shares for KLM and gains control. It might be that the changing of the guard will take place in stages to allow landing rights to be preserved, but after three years this formal structure will be dissolved as well. In cases of takeover, a control premium payable in addition to the standard economic valuation is the norm. Air France is not paying it.

KLM has started a cost savings programme worth €650 million, but KLM shareholders will get only 19% of the benefit

On 8 May 2003 KLM announced a cost cutting programme designed to yield €650 million in savings.

The major share of these cost reductions have still to be carried out. On 22 January KLM announced that €125 millions worth of savings had been achieved. Clearly, successful execution of the programme will lead to better profitability at KLM. If the cost reduction programme is implemented in full and half of the benefits are given back to the customer in the form of reduced fares, operational results will go up by €325 million. Stripping out 35% corporation tax, this leads to a contribution of €211 million to the bottom line. If the transaction goes through, KLM shareholders will own 19% of the joint company, as a result of which only 19% of these benefits will flow to KLM shareholders. But every single percentage point of the improvement will have come from the business they used to own.

Key factors show that KLM should obtain over 30% of the merged airline

On a total passengers carried basis KLM is the world's tenth largest airline and Air France is number three. Taken by sales, Air France with revenues worth €12.7 billion is about twice the size of KLM (revenues of €6.5 billion). A revenue criterion thus leads to a 66:34 ratio: KLM shareholders deserve a one third share in the merged airline. Other measures of size lead to the same ratio. Based on four criteria – sales, number of aircraft, shareholder equity and headcount – an average ratio comes out at 69:31. The figure means that the KLM figure should be 63% higher than the agreed 19%. If there are no signs of structural differences in profitability between Air France and KLM – and nothing has emerged to show this – these yardsticks can be used to make a reliable estimate of what the share swap ratio should be.

Benefits of synergy

The bid prospectus (p. 50) lists significant benefits of synergy the two companies expect to achieve if the merger goes through. Year One factors for €75 million in synergy benefits, rising to €450 million in Year Five. Clearly KLM shareholders should be compensated for these synergies in the form of a proper price offer, or share swap. It is scarcely an adequate response to claim that, because Air France has brought out an offer priced in shares, KLM shareholders will thereby participate in the benefits. For whatever reasons that they may consider relevant – let us say, for issues of control – KLM shareholders may decide to decline the offer to become Air France shareholders. If they accept the merger and do decide to become Air France share-holders they will share in the benefits of synergy to the tune of a mere 19%.

Key dates

Above are ten reasons why the offer for KLM is far too low. In terms of procedure there are two important dates. On Monday 19 April an Extraordinary General Meeting of Shareholders will be held. Information about the offer will be given, questions will be answered and a proposal to change the Articles of Association – which will permit the merger – will be put to the vote. At 11 a.m. on 3 May the offer will close. Prior to that KLM shareholders

will have to decide whether they want to accept or reject the bid. If less than 70% of the shares are tendered the transaction will be a dead letter. If less than 95% of shares are tendered, KLM's share listing will be maintained.

We have tried to shed light on the true worth of KLM. It is significantly higher than the current bid offer. This will not dispense KLM shareholders from taking their own decision. That can be based on other decisions such as enthusiasm over the prospects of Air France, a need for cash or whatever.

Peter Paul de Vries
Chairman of Vereniging van Effectenbezitters (Dutch Investor Association)

The Air France-KLM merger

EXHIBIT 3 **Abridged merger prospectus**

Unaudited condensed pro forma consolidated financial information

The following unaudited condensed pro forma consoli-dated financial information is being provided to give you a better understanding of what the results of operations and financial position of Air France-KLM might have looked like had the offer of Air France for KLM common shares occurred on an earlier date. The unaudited condensed pro forma financial information is based on the estimates and assumptions set forth in the notes to such information. The unaudited condensed pro forma consolidated financial information is preliminary and is being furnished solely for illustrative purposes and, therefore, is not necessarily indicative of the combined results of operations or financial position of Air France-KLM that might have been achieved for the dates or periods indicated, nor is it necessarily indicative of the results of operations or financial position of Air France-KLM that may, or may be expected to, occur in the future. No account has been taken within the unaudited condensed pro forma consolidated financial statements of any synergy or efficiency that may, or may be expected to, occur following the offer.

For accounting purposes, the combination will be accounted for as Air France's acquisition of KLM using the purchase method of accounting under both French and U.S. GAAP. Under French GAAP, this determination has been based on the assessment of effective control of KLM by Air France, primarily through the ability of Air France to control the significant decisions of KLM as a result of its deciding vote on the strategic management committee. Under U.S. GAAP, Air France believes that its ability to cast the deciding vote for majority matters of the strategic management committee, combined with its ownership of 49% of the voting share capital of KLM, and its ownership of all of the outstanding depositary receipts related to the administered share-holdings which will exist following the completion of the exchange offer, will provide Air France with a controlling financial interest in KLM, and that consoli-dation of KLM provides the most meaningful presen-tation of the combined financial position and results of operations of Air France-KLM. We have also concluded that Air France should initially measure all assets, liabil-ities and non-controlling interests of KLM at their fair values at the date of completion of the exchange offer.

As a result of the above considerations under French GAAP and U.S. GAAP, the accompanying unaudited pro forma financial information includes adjustments to

reflect the fair values of KLM's net assets as further described in the accompanying footnotes. The final combination will be accounted for based on the final determination of the transaction value and the fair values of KLM's identifiable assets and liabilities at the date of exchange of control. Therefore, the actual goodwill amount, as well as other balance sheet items, could differ from the preliminary unaudited condensed pro forma consolidated financial information presented herein, and in turn affect items in the preliminary unau-dited condensed pro forma consolidated income state-ments and balance sheet, such as amortization of intangible assets, income of equity affiliates, long-term assets, negative goodwill, pre-paid pension assets and related income taxes.

The following unaudited pro forma consolidated financial information gives pro forma effect to the offer, after giving effect to the pro forma adjustments described in the notes to the unaudited pro forma consolidated financial information. The unaudited condensed pro forma consolidated income statements for the financial year ended March 31, 2003 and for the six months ended September 30, 2003 give effect to the offer and the business combination as if they had occurred on April 1, 2002. The unaudited condensed pro forma consolidated balance sheet as of September 30, 2003 gives effect to the offer and the business combination as if they had occurred on September 30, 2003. The unaudited condensed pro forma consoli-dated financial information of Air France-KLM is based on the historical consolidated financial statements of Air France, which are included elsewhere in this prospectus, and on the historical consolidated financial statements of KLM, which are included in KLM's Annual Report on Form 20-F for the year ended March 31, 2003, as amended, and in the unaudited interim condensed consolidated financial statements for the six months ended September 30, 2003 filed by KLM on Form 6-K dated December 30, 2003, incorporated by reference in this prospectus. The historical financial statements of Air France and KLM are prepared in accordance with French GAAP and Dutch GAAP, respectively. Dutch GAAP differs in some respects from French GAAP. Accordingly, the historical financial state-ments of KLM have been adjusted to French GAAP for all periods presented in this unaudited condensed pro forma consolidated financial information.

Air France has presented the unaudited condensed pro forma consolidated financial information in accor-dance with both French GAAP and U.S. GAAP for the year ended March 31, 2003 and as of September 30, 2003 and for the six-month period then ended in order to fulfill regulatory requirements in the United States. The combined entity will continue to prepare its consolidated financial statements in accordance with French GAAP until application of IFRS becomes mandatory within the European Union for financial years beginning on or after January 1, 2005. Air France

will also provide additional information in accordance with U.S. GAAP in order to fulfill regulatory requirements in the United States.

These unaudited condensed pro forma consolidated financial statements are only a summary and should be read in conjunction with the historical consolidated financial statements and related notes of Air France and KLM.

UNAUDITED CONDENSED PRO FORMA COMBINED INCOME STATEMENT
FOR THE SIX-MONTH PERIOD ENDED SEPTEMBER 30, 2003

| (euro amounts in millions) | French GAAP | | |
	Air France	KLM	Pro forma combined
Net sales	€6,193	€3,036	€9,229
Salaries and related costs	(2,025)	(922)	(2,947)
Depreciation and amortization	(618)	(218)	(806)
Aircraft fuel	(657)	(396)	(1,053)
Landing fees and other rents	(654)	(268)	(922)
Aircraft maintenance materials and outside repairs	(186)	(263)	(449)
Aircraft rent	(239)	(133)	(372)
Selling expenses and passenger commissions	(533)	(191)	(724)
Contracted services and passenger revenues	(533)	(286)	(819)
Other operating expenses	(660)	(264)	(924)
Income (loss) from operations	88	95	213
Restructuring costs	(11)	(75)	(86)
Interest expense	(71)	(53)	(124)
Interest income and other financial income, net	65	26	91
Other income (expense), net	0	7	7
Gain on sale of stock subsidiaries	0	12	12
Income of equity affiliates	22	7	32
Income (loss) before taxes and minority interests and goodwill amortization	93	19	145
Income tax	(32)	4	(38)
Minority interest	(1)	0	(1)
Goodwill amortization and impairment	(8)	(2)	115
Income (loss) from continuing operations	€52	€21	€221

The accompanying notes are an integral part of the unaudited condensed pro forma consolidated financial statements.

The Air France-KLM merger

**UNAUDITED CONDENSED PRO FORMA COMBINED INCOME STATEMENT
FOR THE YEAR ENDED MARCH 30, 2003**

| (euro amounts in millions) | French GAAP | | |
	Air France	KLM	Pro forma combined
Net sales	€12,687	€6,367	€19,054
Salaries and related costs	(3,856)	(1,714)	(5,570)
Depreciation and amortization	(1,310)	(528)	(1,776)
Aircraft fuel	(1,369)	(866)	(2,235)
Landing fees and other rents	(1,362)	(525)	(1,887)
Aircraft maintenance materials and outside repairs	(477)	(642)	(1,119)
Aircraft rent	(521)	(256)	(777)
Selling expenses and passenger commissions	(1,157)	(486)	(1,643)
Contracted services and passenger revenues	(1,086)	(594)	(1,680)
Other operating expenses	(1,357)	(663)	(2,020)
Income (loss) from operations	192	93	347
Restructuring costs	(13)	0	(13)
Interest expense	(161)	(140)	(301)
Interest income and other financial income, net	76	(4)	72
Other income (expense), net	0	(42)	(42)
Gain on sale of stock subsidiaries	4	6	10
Income of equity affiliates	29	(4)	31
Income (loss) before taxes and minority interests and goodwill amortization	127	(91)	104
Income tax	13	30	22
Minority interest	(4)	0	(4)
Goodwill amortization and impairment	(16)	(4)	230
Income (loss) from continuing operations	€120	€(65)	€352

The accompanying notes are an integral part of the unaudited condensed pro forma consolidated financial statements.

UNAUDITED CONDENSED PRO FORMA COMBINED BALANCE SHEET, SEPTEMBER 30, 2003

(euro amounts in millions)	French GAAP		
	Air France	KLM	Pro forma combined
Current assets:			
Cash and cash equivalents	€1,202	€55	€1,257
Short-term investments and restricted cash	169	475	644
Accounts receivables	1,574	728	2,302
Inventories	209	145	354
Prepaid expenses and other	559	2,511	1,981
Total current assets	3,713	3,914	6,538
Flight and ground equipment, net	6,353	2,350	8,674
Flight and ground equipment under capital lease, net	1,515	2,592	3,708
Investment in equity affiliates	312	216	484
Investment in securities	103	0	66
Deferred income taxes	76	53	657
Other non-current assets	154	10	164
Intangible assets	159	48	207
Goodwill	103	12	103
Total assets	€12,488	€9,195	€20,705
Current liabilities:			
Current maturities of long-term debt	€223	€16	€239
Short-term obligation (other)	297	148	445
Current obligation under capital leases	113	151	265
Trade payables	1,204	546	1,750
Deferred revenue on ticket sales	807	471	1,278
Taxes payable	4	11	15
Accrued salaries, related benefits and employee-related liabilities	559	236	795
Other current liability	626	329	955
Total current liabilities	3,833	1,908	5,741
Long-term debt	2,349	591	2,940
Non-current obligation under capital leases	1,204	2,453	3,657
Pension liability	601	4	641
Provisions	450	223	1,906
Other non-current liability	0	212	212
Deferred tax liability, non-current	0	747	747
Minority interest	29	0	29
Total stockholders' equity	4,022	3,058	4,833
Total liabilities and stockholders' equity	€12,488	€9,195	€20,705

The accompanying notes are an integral part of the unaudited condensed pro forma consolidated financial statements.

The Air France-KLM merger

Excerpts from the notes to the pro forma financial statements – significant differences between Dutch GAAP and French GAAP (euro amounts in millions, except per share data)

KLM prepares its consolidated financial statements in accordance with Dutch GAAP, which differ in certain material respects from French GAAP. For purposes of preparing the unaudited condensed pro forma consolidated financial information, KLM's historical consolidated financial statements have been adjusted to conform to French GAAP as applied by Air France for each period presented. These adjustments have been made based on estimates of the management of Air France and KLM. These adjustments are unaudited, and may not fully reflect the application of French GAAP for the periods presented as if KLM had prepared its financial statements using French GAAP. Upon completion of the exchange offer, Air France and KLM will perform a detailed review of their accounting policies and financial statement classifications, and additional adjustments may be required to conform the KLM financial statements to Air France-KLM's financial statements as presented under French GAAP.

Although Air France and KLM do not expect that this detailed review will result in material changes to accounting policies or classifications other than noted below, no such assurance can be given at this time. The table below summarizes the net effect of French GAAP adjustments on KLM's stockholders' equity as of September 30, 2003:

Note	Differences	Stockholders' equity at September 30, 2003
1	Pension benefits	€2,355
2	Derivative instruments	11
4	Accounting for treasury stock	23
7	Frequent flyer program	(16)
5	Deferred income taxes	(811)
	Stockholders' equity without tax	€1,562

Note 1 Pension benefits

Under Dutch GAAP, pension costs for KLM's defined benefit pension plans are generally expensed on the basis of the actuarially determined contributions that KLM is required to pay under various worldwide pension schemes. Air France accounts for the costs and obligations of its pension plans in accordance with French GAAP, which does not significantly differ from IAS 19.

This French GAAP adjustment provides for the costs and obligations related to KLM's pension plans as if these amounts had been determined using IAS 19 as

applied on a historical basis of accounting. This adjustment, reflected in the "French GAAP adjustment" third column of the condensed pro forma income statements resulted in a decrease in Salaries and related costs by €45 million and €170 million for the six months ended September 30, 2003 and for the year ended March 31, 2003, respectively. The KLM balance sheet at September 30, 2003 was adjusted as follows in this respect: an increase in the "Prepaid expenses and other" caption of €2,336 million and a decrease in Provisions by €19 million resulting in an increase in stockholders' equity before tax by €2,355 million.

Note 2 Derivative instruments

Under Dutch GAAP, derivatives are recorded separately on the balance sheet and are accounted for at fair value. Changes in the fair value of derivatives which meet certain criteria for cash flow hedge accounting may be deferred and recognized in other comprehensive income until such time as the hedged transaction is recognized. Ineffective portions of hedges are recognized immediately in earnings. Under French GAAP qualifying hedge instruments are presented on the balance sheet net of the hedged item. For cash flow hedges, changes in values of derivative instruments are deferred, as no separate presentation of other comprehensive income is included under French GAAP.

Certain derivatives do not meet the criteria for hedge accounting under Dutch GAAP, but do meet criteria for hedge accounting under French GAAP. As a result, changes in fair values of certain derivatives have been included in income under Dutch GAAP but would have been deferred under French GAAP. The French GAAP adjustment gives effect to reclassifications to reflect net presentation of qualifying hedges, and reverses the effects of changes in fair values of cash flow hedges that had been included in other comprehensive income under Dutch GAAP. In addition, the impacts on income of some non-qualifying derivatives under Dutch GAAP which meet French GAAP criteria have been reversed. The September 30, 2003 balance sheet impacts are described in the following table (in € millions):

Flight equipment	€ (110)
Other non-current assets	(409)
Long-term debt	(291)
Capital lease obligation	(239)
Stockholders' equity before tax	11

Before tax, the income (loss) statement adjustment amounts to €(13) million and €(11) million for the six months ended September 30, 2003 and the year ended March 31, 2003, respectively.

Note 3 Recognition of restructuring costs

Under Dutch GAAP, €75 million (with a €26 million tax effect) arising from decisions made by KLM's Board of Managing Directors have been classified as extraordinary items in the unaudited condensed pro forma consolidated financial information. Under French GAAP, the expense of €49 million relating to the restructuring provision would have been recognized as the actual costs were incurred. The provision balance at March 31, 2003 is reversed in the balance sheet as a Dutch GAAP to French GAAP adjustment. During the six months ended September 30, 2003, the restructuring costs did qualify for French GAAP purposes and consequently were recorded in the Dutch GAAP to French GAAP reconciliation, with an impact of €75 million on restructuring costs with a related tax impact of €26 million.

Note 4 Accounting for treasury stock

Under French GAAP, treasury shares held by Air France to fulfill commitments under employee stock option plans are accounted for as an asset. Provisions are recorded in order to record the shares at the lower of cost or market value, with related gains and losses recognized in the income statement. Under Dutch GAAP, the purchase price of these shares is deducted from stockholders' equity. The French GAAP adjustment reclassifies €23 million of KLM's acquired treasury shares to short-term investments and recognizes a realized income on the sale of those shares for an amount of €13 million for the six month period ended September 30, 2003 and a loss of €(16) million in the income statement for the year ended March 31, 2003.

Note 5 Deferred income taxes

These adjustments reflect the deferred tax impacts of the French GAAP adjustments listed above, except for treasury stock adjustments which are tax exempted in the Netherlands. Income tax effect has been calculated using the KLM current tax rate of 34.5%. The net tax effect of French GAAP adjustments is a decrease in stockholders' equity of KLM of €811 million (an increase by €747 million of the deferred tax liabilities and a decrease by €64 million of the deferred tax assets).

For the year ended March 31, 2003, the deferred income taxes caption also reflects the French GAAP reclassification, from operating income and income tax to extraordinary items, net of tax, of the outcome of the dispute between KLM and Alitalia.

Note 6 Lease deposits

Under Dutch GAAP, lease deposits are either classified as investments in debt securities or other noncurrent assets, or deducted from financial debt, while under French GAAP lease deposits are offset with financial debt (obligation under capital leases). This reclassification leads to the decrease of financial debt and lease deposits by €475 million.

Note 7 Frequent flyer program

Under Dutch GAAP, the liability recorded for the accrued costs related to flight awards earned by members of the frequent flyer program is classified as a long-term liability. Under French GAAP, amounts accrued related to the Fréquence Plus frequent flyer program are included in advance ticket liability in the consolidated balance sheet of Air France and classified as a current liability for purposes of the pro forma financial information. The French GAAP adjustment reclassifies €42 million provision recorded by KLM under Dutch GAAP to unearned revenue in accordance with French GAAP as applied by Air France. This reclassification impacts provision for €26 million, stockholders' equity for €10 million and deferred tax assets for €6 million.

Note 8 Inventory

Under Dutch GAAP, certain rotable and exchangeable parts have been classified in inventories. Under French GAAP, these items are classified as flight equipment. The net book value of these rotable parts and exchangeable components is €66 million at September 30, 2003.

Note 9 Other

Under French GAAP, unrealized foreign exchange gain or loss on working capital elements is classified in financial income or expense. This reclassification amounts to €17 million and €22 million for the six months ended September 30, 2003 and the year ended March 31, 2003, respectively. In addition, as required under French GAAP, the Goodwill amortization or impairment caption has been reclassified to a separate line item below operating income. This reclassification amounts to €2 million and €4 million for the six months ended September 30, 2003 and the year ended March 31, 2003, respectively.

The Air France-KLM merger

Note 10 Discontinued operation and extraordinary items

Under French GAAP, KLM would have presented the disposal of its business "Buzz" as a discontinued operation in the income statement. This disposal was consummated during the six months ended September 30, 2003.

In addition, the outcome of the dispute between KLM and Alitalia would have been presented as an extraordinary item net of tax under French GAAP. This results in a reclassification of €(276) million and €95 million from operating income and income tax to extraordinary items, respectively, in the KLM pro forma French GAAP income statement for the year ended March 31, 2003. Discontinued operation net of tax, extraordinary items net of tax and cumulative effect of change in accounting principles are captions below income (loss) from continuing operations and are not presented in the pro forma condensed income statements.

Excerpts from the notes to the pro forma financial statements – pro forma adjustments (euro amounts in millions, except per share data)

Under French GAAP, Air France is the acquirer of KLM and will account for its acquisition of KLM using the purchase method of accounting. Under the purchase method, Air France will allocate the total purchase price of KLM to the acquired assets and liabilities (including previously unrecognized items) based on their relative fair values as determined on the date of the transaction. This unaudited condensed pro forma consolidated financial information has been prepared and presented assuming that Air France will acquire a 100% controlling economic interest in KLM following the completion of the combination and the conditional acquisition of the Cumulative Preference Shares A. Under French GAAP, the estimated aggregate purchase price has been calculated as follows (in € millions, except number of shares and per share data):

KLM common shares outstanding	46,810,000
Exchange ratio into Air France's shares	1.10
Equivalent number of Air France's shares	51,491,000
Air France's share price	13.34
Estimated fair value of Air France shares issued	686.9
Estimated fair value of Air France warrants issued	73.5
Estimated fair value of preferred and priority shares	35.5
Estimated transaction-related expenses	15.1
Total estimated purchase price consideration	811.0

The preliminary allocation of its purchase price reflected herein presents preliminary estimates of fair values as determined at September 30, 2003. Such estimates are based on an independent appraisal. The actual allocation of the purchase price will be based on the fair values determined at the date of the transaction, which may differ, in some respects, from those presented below. The estimated excess of purchase price consideration over the approximate value of KLM's net assets, the estimated fair value adjustments and the estimated negative goodwill are as follows (in € millions):

Total estimated purchase price consideration	811
Less: KLM's net assets under French GAAP	(3,058)
Consideration of fair values of acquired assets and liabilities:	
Reduction in fair value of aircraft	(675)
Reduction in reported value of intangible assets	(12)
Incremental fair value of buildings and lands	248
Reduction in fair value of equity investment	(44)
Reduction in fair value in pension and post-retirement plans and increase in pension provision	(1,125)
Deferred tax adjustments	528
Other items, net	66
Excess of the fair value of net assets acquired over purchase consideration	(1,233)

Preliminary estimates of fair values and the final purchase price allocation may materially differ from preliminary amounts and allocations provided in this section. This analysis presents a preliminary allocation of purchase price to the assets and liabilities of KLM, based on independent appraisals conducted at September 30, 2003. The final allocation of purchase price will be completed at the latest at the end of the fiscal year following the acquisition fiscal period, and will be based on valuations and appraisals conducted as of the date of the exchange offer closing date, as specified under French GAAP. We have identified aircraft and pension plans valuations as the most significant areas for potential material discrepancies between pro forma and final purchase price allocation.

Aircraft market value references are principally U.S. dollar-based and therefore, the euro-denominated fair value of the KLM fleet may fluctuate significantly based on €/$ exchange rate fluctuations. The exchange rate retained for the purpose of the pro forma purchase price allocation was $1.13 per €1.00. Should this exchange rate fluctuate to $1.18 for €1.00 or $1.24 for €1.00, the downward fair value adjustment to the KLM fleet would increase by €140 million or €270 million, respectively. Should the exchange rate fluctuate oppositely to $1.07 for €1.00, the downward fair value adjustment to the KLM fleet would decrease by €155 million.

The purchase price allocation may also differ significantly from our preliminary estimates, based on market conditions and assumptions prevailing to the pension plans valuation, mainly based on long term discount rates, anticipated inflation, stock market current valuation, overall economic prospects, and changes in agreements applicable to pensions in the Netherlands and to KLM employees. As further discussed below, the purchase price allocation may also need to be revised in case the overfunded pension plan assets recognition would be limited by the asset ceiling rules introduced by IAS 19.

Under French GAAP, in accordance with the accounting rules governing the purchase method of accounting, Air France is not allowed to recognize intangible assets, such as KLM's trademark or certain take-off and landing slots, when a negative residual goodwill amount results from the purchase price allocation.

KLM sponsors a number of pension benefit plans across the various locations where it operates. As of September 30, 2003, total obligations in respect of these plans amount to €7,055 million, and available pension funds assets have been fair valued at €8,260 million. Benefit plans for employees outside the Netherlands account for less than 5% of total obligations. In the Netherlands, pension benefits consist of final or average career salary plans which are funded through separate legal entities to which employees also contribute. Other post-employment benefits consist of sponsored medical coverage for some retirees, resulting in an estimated obligation ("PBO") for these plans of €67 million with no related assets. The adjustment to the carrying value of the KLM pension plans is based on this preliminary assessment of PBO and current values of plan assets. As of September 30, 2003, some plans have assets in excess of the PBO estimated by external actuaries. Under French GAAP, the amount of net asset which can be recognized is limited by the asset ceiling rules introduced by IAS 19. These rules limit the amount of net asset which can be recognized on the employer's balance sheet to the present value of any economic benefits available in the form of refunds from the plans or reductions in future contributions to the plans. Following the proposed transaction, the asset ceiling limitation will also consider amounts of cumulative unrecognized actuarial losses and past service costs in determining the maximum asset to be recorded by the combined companies. As of September 30, 2003, the amount of net asset recognized is €1,247 million.

Following the completion of the transaction Air France will perform a full valuation of the acquired KLM plans, in order to determine the actual amount of pension assets to be included in the allocation of purchase price to the acquired plans of KLM. This valuation will occur as of the closing date for the proposed transaction. It is not possible to predict at this time what the final value of the pension asset will be or whether the amount of such asset to be recorded by Air France will need to be reduced by a provision as a result of the asset ceiling restrictions. As a result, the final value to be allocated to the acquired plans could be subject to significant change. Furthermore, the amount of net pension asset recorded would be subject to reconsideration of the asset ceiling test, which could result in significant increases or decreases of the provision/non-cash impacts to Air France's results of operations.

For purposes of the presentation of the pro forma condensed consolidated income statements, the adjustments listed above have been presented as if the transaction had occurred on the first day of the first period presented. The impacts of the pro forma allocation of purchase consideration affect the results of operations for the six-month period ended September 30, 2003 and the year ended March 31, 2003 as follows:

- **Note 11 Tangible assets.** Reflects adjustments to the reported depreciation of KLM based on the reduction in the fair value of the fixed assets.

- **Note 12 Investments in equity affiliates.** Reflects adjustments to the carrying value of KLM's investments in affiliates, primarily KLM's 50% investment in Martinair. For purposes of the pro forma income statements, the decrease in the carrying value of Martinair has been attributed to the fleet assets having an estimated remaining useful life of seven years. The amortization of these adjustments results in an increase to the reported income from this equity investee of €3 million and €6 million for the six months ended September 30, 2003 and the year ended March 31, 2003, respectively.

- **Note 13 Goodwill.** This adjustment reflects the elimination of the amounts of historical goodwill and goodwill amortization of €2 million for the six-month period ended September 30, 2003 and €4 million for the year ended March 31, 2003.

- **Note 14 Negative goodwill.** For French GAAP purposes, the excess of the purchase consideration over the fair value of the individual assets and liabilities recognized above results in residual negative goodwill of €1,233 million. Under French GAAP, the residual negative goodwill is allocated to the income statement on a straight line method over a period that reflects assumptions made and management plans as of the acquisition date. On a preliminary basis, Air France's management has estimated that a five-year period would satisfy these criteria. Therefore, for pro forma purposes, the negative goodwill amount has been amortized over a five year period which results in a positive adjustment to net income of €246 million per year ended March 31, 2003 and €123 million for the six months ended September 30, 2003.

The above list is not exhaustive, and there may be other assets and liabilities which may have to be adjusted to fair value when both final valuations and allocations are made following the completion of the exchange offer.

Air France will complete the determination of fair values and the allocation of the purchase price after the completion of the exchange offer. French GAAP allows Air France to complete the purchase price allocation no later than the end of the fiscal year subsequent to the fiscal year in which the exchange offer was completed. The determination of fair values will be based on an independent appraisal.

The exchange ratio agreed between Air France and KLM implicitly valued KLM at less than KLM's net asset value. KLM performs an impairment test whenever there is an indication that the carrying amounts of its assets may not be recoverable. KLM has performed impairment tests on its owned and financially leased aircraft in a manner consistent with Statement of Financial Accounting Standards No. 144 (SFAS 144) under U.S. GAAP as well as in accordance with the Guideline of the Council for Annual Reporting No. 121 (RJ 121) under Netherlands GAAP. SFAS 144 requires the recognition of an impairment loss if the carrying amount of a long-lived asset or group of assets is not recoverable and exceeds its fair value. The carrying amount of an asset or group of assets is generally not recoverable if it exceeds the sum of the undiscounted, pre-tax, future cash flows expected to result from the use and eventual disposition of the asset or group of assets. Assets must be grouped at the lowest level for which identifiable cash flows are largely independent of the cash flows of other assets. Under Netherlands GAAP, KLM compared the carrying amount of each asset group (cash generating unit) to its recoverable amount, which is defined as the higher of the net selling price and its value in use.

In conducting its impairment tests, KLM grouped its fleet assets into four groups:

- KLM's wide body fleet,
- KLM's 737 fleet,
- KLM's regional fleet, and
- Transavia's fleet.

KLM's wide body fleet, which is used for long-haul destinations, consists of a total of five different kinds of aircraft. Impairment tests for KLM's wide body fleet were conducted for each of these kinds of aircraft, because KLM monitors and optimizes its employment of, and revenues from, each of these kinds of aircraft separately. Therefore, KLM considers this the lowest level for which identifiable cash flows are largely independent of the cash flows of other assets. Impairment tests for KLM's 737 fleet, KLM's regional fleet and Transavia's fleet were conducted at the fleet level instead of by aircraft type or subtype level because in KLM's operations the aircraft composing those fleets are generally interchangeable and therefore cash flows of types or subtypes are not meaningfully identifiable. In its impairment tests KLM:

- calculated total cash flows during the estimated economic life of each type of asset by multiplying the estimated annual cash flows from that asset type by the remaining average economic life of that asset type,

- estimated future cash flows based on historical cash flows and KLM's business plan for 2004–2005,

- estimated the residual asset value at the end of each aircraft's estimated economic life by reference to KLM's depreciation calculations, the Aircraft Value Reference Guide (published by the Aircraft Value Reference Company) and KLM's historical sales experience,

- considered the estimated residual asset value as a cash inflow at the end of the asset's economic life,

- assumed that KLM would replace each of its aircraft at the end of its economic life, and

- did not take into account expected changes in yields.

Based on undiscounted cash flows, the asset groups described above passed the recoverability test under SFAS 144 and RJ 121. Although KLM assumed that its aircraft would be replaced at the end of their economic life, KLM also considered the potential scenario involving a gradual decline in operations, under which KLM would be unable to invest in replacement aircraft, and concluded that such a scenario would take decades to transpire and is remote within the timeframe covered by KLM's estimated future cash flows.

KLM's management and supervisory boards agreed to accept Air France's offer at a significant discount to KLM's net asset value after they reviewed all of the strategic options available to KLM, including remaining an independent company, and concluded that at that time there was no superior strategic alternative to the combination. In assessing the offer in light of the fact that the consideration offered by Air France was below KLM's net asset value, the KLM management and supervisory boards considered certain factors, including the benefits that KLM believed may arise from combining certain complementary features of Air France's and KLM's businesses, KLM's expectation that cost savings and revenue-increasing synergies could be realized following completion of the offer, and the benefits associated with KLM's expected admission into the SkyTeam alliance (subject to KLM's fulfilling the admission criteria) following completion of the offer. The factors that the KLM management and supervisory boards considered in arriving at their decisions to approve and recommend the offer to holders of KLM's common shares are described in KLM's Solicitation/Recommendation Statement on Schedule 14D-9, which has been filed with the Securities and Exchange Commission and which is being mailed to KLM's shareholders together with this prospectus.

The Air France-KLM merger

EXHIBIT 4 **KLM-Air France merger announcement, September 30, 2003**

A: KLM share price from June 30, 2003 to May 5, 2004

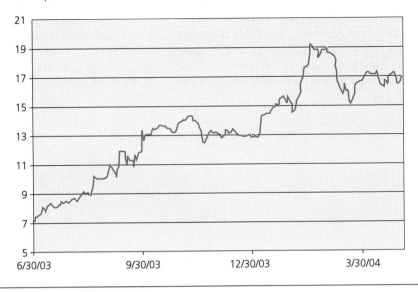

Source: Thomson Datastream.

B: Air France share price from June 30, 2003 to May 5, 2004

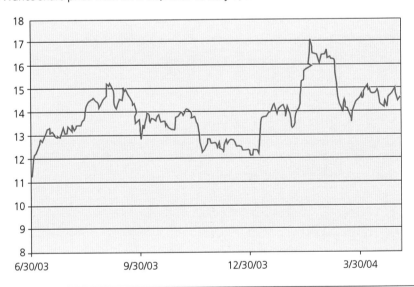

Source: Thomson Datastream.

C: Stock returns (and prior day's closing share prices) surrounding the merger announcement

	KLM return (previous closing price)	Dutch AEX Index	Air France return (previous closing price)	French CAC40 Index
3 days before announcement (day −3)	−2.81% (on 11.75)	−1.24%	−1.66% (on 14.45)	−1.02%
2 days before announcement (day −2)	3.85% (on 11.42)	−1.34%	−4.86% (on 14.21)	−0.43%
1 day before announcement (day −1)	0.84% (on 11.86)	−0.46%	1.26% (on 13.52)	−0.87%
Day of the announcement (day 0)	12.54% (on 11.96)	−1.84%	−4.16% (on 13.69)	−1.68%
1 day after announcement (day +1)	−5.69% (on 13.46)	1.56%	−1.75% (on 13.12)	1.79%
2 days after announcement (day +2)	3.47% (on 12.68)	0.93%	4.58% (on 12.89)	0.06%
3 days after announcement (day +3)	-0.30% (on 13.12)	2.87%	−1.48% (on 13.48)	3.24%
From day −10 to day +10	14.78% (on 11.91)	−1.54%	−4.62% (on 14.50)	0.18%
From day −5 to day 5	16.06% (on 11.27)	−2.68%	−5.67% (on 14.64)	−0.35%
From September 30, 2003 to May 5, 2004	45.90% (on 11.96)	10.60%	6.50% (on 13.69)	16.96%

Source: Thomson Datastream.

D: Valuation data and other information

	KLM	Air France
Closing price on September 30, 2003	11.96	13.69
Number of ordinary shares outstanding on September 30, 2003	46,809,699	219,780,887
Beta	1.63	1.36
Yield on government bonds with 10 years' maturity on September 30, 2003	4.14%	4.13%
Statutory tax rate in 2003	34.5%	35.43%
Effective tax rate in 2003	32.0%	13.27%

The Air France-KLM merger

Corporate Financing Policies

In this chapter we discuss how firms set their capital structure and dividend policies to maximize shareholder value. There is a strong relation between these two decisions. For example, a firm's decision to retain internally generated funds rather than paying them out as a dividend can also be thought of as a financing decision. It is not surprising, therefore, to find that many of the factors that are important in setting capital structure (such as taxes, costs of financial distress, agency costs, and information costs) are also relevant for dividend policy decisions. We examine how these factors affect capital structure and dividend policy, as well as how the financial analysis tools, discussed in Part 2 of this book, can be used to evaluate capital structure and dividend policy decisions.

A variety of questions are dealt with in analysis of corporate financing policies:

■ Securities analysts can ask: Given its capital structure and dividend policy, how should we position a firm in our fund – as a growth or income share?

■ Takeover specialists can ask: Can we improve shareholder value for a firm by changing its financial leverage or by increasing dividend payouts to owners?

■ Management can ask: Have we selected a capital structure and dividend policy that supports our business objectives?

■ Credit analysts can ask: What risks do we face in lending to this company, given its business and current financial leverage?

Throughout our discussion we take the perspective of an external analyst who is evaluating whether a firm has selected a capital structure and dividend policy that maximize shareholder value. The topic obviously also applies to management's decisions about what debt and dividend policies it should implement.

FACTORS THAT DETERMINE FIRMS' DEBT POLICIES

As discussed in Chapter 5, a firm's debt policy can be represented by comparing its net debt, defined as interest-bearing debt less excess cash and marketable securities, and its equity. In practice, since it is difficult to estimate excess cash and marketable securities, analysts typically use total cash and marketable securities as a proxy. For example, consider the debt policies for Novartis AG, a large Swiss pharmaceutical company, and Enel SpA, a large Italian utility company, for the year ended December 31, 2005, reported in Table 12.1.

TABLE 12.1 Net interest-bearing debt for Novartis and Enel for the year ended
December 31, 2005

(millions, except for net debt to equity ratio)	Novartis	Enel
Interest-bearing debt	$12,658	€14,896
Less: cash and marketable securities	10,933	476
Net debt	1,725	14,420
Book shareholders' equity	32,990	19,057
Net interest-bearing debt to book equity	5%	76%

Novartis' liquid assets (cash and marketable securities) are comparable to its interest-bearing debt. As a result, its net debt is only 5 percent of its book equity. In contrast, Enel has a ratio of net debt to book equity of 76 percent. Throughout the chapter we will examine factors that are relevant to the financing differences for these firms.

When financial analysts evaluate a firm's capital structure, two related questions typically emerge. First, in the long term, what is the best mix of debt and equity for creating shareholder value? And second, if managers are considering new investment initiatives in the short term, what type of financing should they use? Two popular models of capital structure provide help in thinking about these questions. The static model of capital structure examines how trade-offs between the benefits and costs of debt determine a firm's long-term optimal mix of debt and equity. And the dynamic model examines how information effects can lead a firm to deviate from its long-term optimal capital structure as it seeks financing for new investments. We discuss both models because they have somewhat different implications for thinking about capital structure.

THE OPTIMAL LONG-TERM MIX OF DEBT AND EQUITY

To determine the best long-term mix of debt and equity capital for a firm, we need to consider the benefits and costs of financial leverage. By trading off these benefits and costs, we can decide whether a firm should be financed mostly with equity or mostly with debt.

Benefits of leverage

The major benefits of financial leverage typically include corporate tax shields on interest and improved incentives for management.

Corporate interest tax shields

In many countries tax laws provide a form of government subsidy for debt financing which does not exist for equity financing. This arises from the corporate tax deductibility of interest against profits. No such corporate tax shield is available for dividend payments or for retained earnings. Debt financing therefore has an advantage over equity, since the interest tax shields under debt provide additional income to debt and equity holders. This higher income translates directly into higher firm values for leveraged firms in relation to unleveraged firms.

Some practitioners and theorists have pointed out that the corporate tax benefit from debt financing is potentially offset by a personal tax disadvantage of debt.[1] That is, since in some countries the holders of debt must pay relatively high tax rates on interest income, they require that corporations offer high pretax yields on debt. This disadvantage is particularly severe when interest income is taxed at a higher rate than capital gains on equity. In countries where personal tax rates on interest income are higher than on long-term capital gains, personal tax effects at least partially offset the corporate tax benefits of debt. However, most financial managers and financial economists believe that there is a corporate tax advantage to debt financing.

Therefore, the corporate tax benefits from debt financing should encourage firms with high effective tax rates and few forms of tax shield other than interest to have highly leveraged capital structures. In contrast, firms that have tax shield substitutes for interest, such as depreciation, or that have operating loss carryforwards and hence do not expect to pay taxes, should have capital structures that are largely equity.

KEY ANALYSIS QUESTIONS

To evaluate the tax effects of additional debt, analysts can use accounting, financial ratio, and prospective analysis to answer the following types of questions:

- What is a firm's average tax rate? How does this rate compare with the average tax rate and financial leverage for its major competitors?
- What portion of a firm's tax expense is deferred taxes versus current taxes?
- What is the firm's marginal corporate tax rate likely to be?
- Does the firm have tax loss carryforwards or other tax benefits? How long are they expected to continue?
- What noninterest tax shields are currently available to the firm? For example, are there sizable tax shields from accelerated depreciation?
- Based on pro forma income and cash flow statements, what are the estimates for the firm's taxable profit for the next five to ten years? What noninterest tax shields are available to the firm? Finally, what would be the tax savings from using some debt financing?

Management incentives for value creation

A second benefit of debt financing is that it focuses management on value creation, thus reducing conflicts of interest between managers and shareholders. Conflicts of interest can arise when managers make investments that are of little value to shareholders and/or spend the firm's funds on perks, such as overly spacious office buildings and lavish corporate jets. Firms are particularly prone to these temptations when they are flush with cash but have few promising new investment opportunities, often referred to as "free cash flow" situations. These firms' shareholders would generally prefer that their managers pay out any free cash flows as dividends or use the funds to repurchase shares. However, these payouts reduce the size of the firm and the assets under management's control. Management may therefore invest the free cash flows in new projects, even if they are not valued by shareholders, or spend the cash flows on management perks.

How can debt help reduce management's incentives to overinvest and to overspend on perks? The primary way is by reducing resources available to fund these types of outlays, since firms with relatively high leverage face pressures to generate cash flows to meet payments of interest and principal.

The debt introduced as a result of the 1988 leveraged buyout of RJR Nabisco was viewed by many as an example of debt creating pressure for management to refocus on value creation for shareholders. Under this view, the incentive problems facing the company stemmed from the high cash flows it generated in the tobacco business and the low investment opportunities in this line of business given the decline in popularity of smoking in the U.S. The increased debt taken with the LBO forced RJR Nabisco's management to eliminate unnecessary perks, such as corporate jets and parties with famous sports stars, to slow diversification into the food industry, and to cancel unprofitable projects such as the smokeless cigarette.

As a more recent example, in 2004 Italy-based yellow pages publisher Seat Pagine Gialle followed many of its international industry peers, such as Yell, TeleMedia, and QwestDex, by being acquired in a leveraged buyout for €5.65 billion. The acquisition, which was one of the largest leveraged buyouts in Europe, was financed for about €3.2 billion with senior debt and €1.15 billion with high yield bonds, which Standard and Poor's had rated at BB. The company's industry, the telephone directories advertising market, was characterized by stable cash flows because the demand for advertising in directories was much less cyclical than the demand for advertising in, for example, daily newspapers. The industry's investment opportunities were, however, limited, which made it attractive for LBOs. The Seat Pagine Gialle LBO was followed by other LBOs in the same industry, such as Dutch VNU's sell-off of its yellow pages business unit.

KEY ANALYSIS QUESTIONS

Financial ratio and prospective analysis can help analysts assess whether there are currently free cash flow inefficiencies at a firm as well as risks of future inefficiencies. Symptoms of excessive management perks and investment in unprofitable projects include the following:

- *High ratios of general and administrative expenses and overhead to sales.* If a firm's ratios are higher than those for its major competitors, one possibility is that management is wasting money on perks.

- *Significant new investments in unrelated areas.* If it is difficult to rationalize these new investments, there might be free cash flow problems.

- *High levels of expected operating cash flows (net of essential capital expenditures and debt retirements) from pro forma income and cash flow statements.*

- *Poor management incentives to create additional shareholder value,* evidenced by a weak linkage between management compensation and firm performance.

Costs of leverage: Financial distress

As a firm increases its leverage, it increases the likelihood of financial distress, where it is unable to meet interest or principal repayment obligations to creditors. This may force the firm to declare bankruptcy or to agree to restructure its financial claims.

Financial distress can be expensive, since restructurings of a firm's ownership claims typically involve costly legal negotiations. It can also be difficult for distressed firms to raise capital to undertake profitable new investment opportunities. Finally, financial distress can intensify conflicts of interest between shareholders and the firm's debt holders, increasing the cost of debt financing.

Legal costs of financial distress

When a firm is in serious financial distress, its owners' claims are likely to be restructured. This can take place under formal bankruptcy proceedings or out of bankruptcy, depending on the jurisdiction in which the firm operates. Restructurings are likely to be costly, since the parties involved have to hire lawyers, bankers, and accountants to represent their interests, and they have to pay court costs if there are formal legal proceedings. These are often called the *direct* costs of financial distress.

Costs of forgone investment opportunities

When a firm is in financial distress, and particularly when it is in bankruptcy, it may be very difficult for it to raise additional capital for new investments, even though they may be profitable for all the firm's owners. In some cases bankrupt firms are run by court-appointed trustees, who are unlikely to take on risky new investments – profitable or not. Even for a firm whose management supports new investment, the firm is likely to be capital constrained. Creditors are unlikely to approve the sale of nonessential assets unless the proceeds are used to first repay their claims. Potential new investors and creditors will be wary of the firm because they do not want to become embroiled in the legal disputes themselves. Thus, in all likelihood the firm will be unable to make significant new investments, potentially diminishing its value.

Costs of conflicts between creditors and shareholders

When a firm is performing well, both creditors' and shareholders' interests are likely to coincide. Both want the firm's managers to take all investments that increase the value of the firm. But when the firm is in financial difficulty, conflicts can arise between different classes of owners. Creditors become concerned about whether the firm will be able to meet its interest and principal commitments. Shareholders become concerned that their equity will revert to the creditors if the firm is unable to meet its outstanding obligations. Thus managers are likely to face increased pressure to make decisions which serve the interests of only one form of owner, typically shareholders, rather than making decisions in the best interests of all owners. For example, managers have incentives to issue additional debt with equal or higher priority, to invest in riskier assets, or to pay liquidating dividends, since these actions reduce the value of outstanding creditors' claims and benefit shareholders. When it is costly to completely eliminate this type of game playing, creditors will simply reduce the amount they are willing to pay the firm for the debt when it is issued, increasing the costs of borrowing for the firm's shareholders.

Overall effects of financial distress

The costs of financial distress discussed above offset the tax and monitoring benefits of debt. As a result, firms that are more likely to fall into financial distress or for which the costs of financial distress are especially high should have relatively low financial leverage. Firms are more likely to fall into financial distress if they have high business risks – that is, if their revenues and earnings before interest are highly sensitive to fluctuations in the economy. Financial distress costs are also likely to be relatively high for firms whose assets are easily destroyed in financial distress. For example, firms with human capital and brand intangibles are particularly sensitive to financial distress since dissatisfied employees and customers can leave or seek alternative suppliers. In contrast, firms with tangible assets can sell their assets if they get into financial distress, providing additional security for lenders and lowering the costs of financial distress. Firms with intangible assets are therefore less likely to be highly leveraged than firms whose assets are mostly tangible.

These factors probably largely explain why Novartis and Enel, the two companies discussed at the beginning of the chapter, have such different financing policies. Novartis probably keeps its leverage low because many of its core assets are intangibles, such as research staff and sales force representatives. These types of assets can easily be lost if Novartis gets into financial difficulty as a result of too much leverage. In all likelihood, management would be forced to cut back on R&D and marketing, allowing their most talented researchers and sales representatives to be subject to offers from competitors. Novartis can reduce these risks by having very low leverage.

In contrast, Enel is a utility company. It has very stable cash flows since its revenues come from services with stable and predictable demand, such as the delivery of electricity. In addition, its major assets are power plants, which are less likely to diminish in value if it gets into financial distress. If the debt holders ended up as the new owners of the firm following financial distress, they could continue to use the existing assets. Enel can therefore take advantage of the tax benefits from corporate debt without bearing a high cost of financial distress.

KEY ANALYSIS QUESTIONS

The above discussion implies that a firm's optimal financial leverage will depend on its underlying business risks and asset types. If the firm's business risks are relatively high or its assets can be easily destroyed by financial distress, changing the mix of debt and equity toward more debt may actually destroy shareholder value. Analysts can use ratio, cash flow, and pro forma analysis to assess a firm's business risks and whether its assets are easily destroyed by financial distress. Their analysis should focus on these activities:

■ *Comparing indicators of business risk for the firm and other firms in its industry with the economy.* Popular indicators of business risk include the ratio of fixed operating expenses (such as depreciation on plant and equipment) to sales, the volatility of return on assets, as well as the relation between indicators of the firm's performance and indicators of performance for the economy as a whole.

■ *Examining competition in the industry.* For firms in a highly competitive industry, performance is very sensitive to changes in strategy by competitors.

■ *Determining whether the firm's assets are largely intangible and therefore sensitive to financial distress,* using ratios like market-to-book equity.

Determining the long-term optimal mix of debt and equity: Firm factors

The above discussion implies that the optimal mix of debt and equity for a firm can be estimated by trading off the corporate interest tax shield and monitoring benefits of debt against the costs of financial distress. As the firm becomes more highly leveraged, the costs of leverage presumably begin to outweigh the tax and monitoring benefits of debt.

However there are several practical difficulties in trying to estimate a firm's optimal financial leverage. One difficulty is quantifying some of the costs and benefits of leverage. For example, it is not easy to value the expected costs of financial distress or any management incentive benefits from debt. There are no easy answers to this problem. The best that we can do is to qualitatively assess whether the firm faces free cash flow problems, and whether it faces high business risks and has assets that are easily destroyed by financial distress. These qualitative assessments can then be used to adjust the more easily quantified tax benefits from debt to determine whether the firm's financial leverage should be relatively high, low, or somewhere in between.

A second practical difficulty in deciding on a firm's level of financial leverage is quantifying what we mean by high, low, and medium. One way to resolve this question is to use indicators of financial leverage, such as debt-to-equity ratios, for the market as a whole as a guide on leverage ranges. To provide a rough sense of what companies usually consider to be high and low financial leverage, Table 12.2 shows median debt-to-market equity and debt-to-book equity ratios for selected European industries for the fiscal year 2005. Median ratios are reported for all listed companies and for large companies (with market capitalizations greater than €300 million) only.

Median debt-to-book equity ratios are highest for the hotel, air transportation, heavy construction, water supply, and electric services industries. The core assets for firms in these industries include physical equipment and property that are readily transferable to debt holders in the event of financial distress. Surprisingly, the hotel and air transportation industries have higher leverage than the electric services industries, even

TABLE 12.2 Median net interest-bearing debt-to-book equity and net interest-bearing debt-to-market equity for selected European industries in 2005

Industry	Net interest-bearing debt-to-book equity		Net interest-bearing debt-to-market equity	
	All listed firms	Large listed firms	All listed firms	Large listed firms
Computer programming and data processing	–34%	–25%	–9%	–6%
Pharmaceutical	–26%	–12%	–7%	–3%
Computer integrated systems design	–17%	–3%	–6%	–1%
Electric services	24%	63%	10%	22%
Heavy construction	44%	62%	18%	19%
Air transportation	63%	65%	25%	36%
Hotels and motels	81%	47%	51%	38%
Water supply	141%	156%	66%	72%

though the latter industry is typically much less sensitive to economy risk. One potential reason for this is that in 2005 the market and book values of equity in the highly cyclical hotel and air transportation industries may have been temporarily depressed because of the European economic downturn. In 2005, the median return on assets in these two industries was 0.8 and 2.7 percent, versus 3.9 percent in the electric services industries. Because equity is the denominator in our leverage ratios, temporarily depressed equity values result in temporarily inflated leverage ratios. In 1998, prior to the economic downturn, net interest-bearing debt-to-book equity was substantially lower than in 2005; 49 percent in the hotel industry and 30 percent in the air transportation industry.

The software and pharmaceutical industries' core assets are their research staffs. Ownership of these types of assets cannot be easily transferred to debt holders if the firm is in financial distress. Researchers are likely to leave for greener pastures if their budgets are cut. As a result, firms in this industry have relatively conservative capital structures.[2]

It is also interesting to note that large firms tend to have higher leverage than small firms in the same industries. This probably reflects the fact that larger firms tend to have more product offerings and to be more diversified geographically, reducing their vulnerability to negative events for a single product or market, and enabling them to take on more debt.

The net debt-to-market equity ratios by and large tell a similar story to the debt-to-book equity ratios. They reflect the fact that most firms have market-to-book equity ratios greater than 1 because companies generally invest in projects that add value for shareholders and because some types of assets, such as R&D, are typically not reflected in book equity.

Determining the long-term optimal mix of debt and equity: Country factors

In the previous discussion, we pooled all countries and ignored the fact that the optimal degree of leverage can systematically differ across countries. Recall our discussion on the influence of national bankruptcy laws on the types of credit that firms prefer. In summary, we concluded in Chapter 10 that in countries with borrower-friendly, creditor-unfriendly bankruptcy laws:

■ Creditors require more collateral for a given loan amount.

■ Creditors extend more short-term debt because this allows them to frequently review the borrower's financial position and adjust the terms of the loan when necessary.

■ Companies make greater use of supplier financing.

■ Companies make greater use of off-balance sheet financing such as the factoring of customer receivables.

■ Public debt markets tend to be less developed.

The net effect of these country differences in loan maturity, off-balance sheet financing, supplier financing, and public debt markets importance on country differences in leverage is unfortunately anything but straightforward. For example, we showed that Belgian, French, and Italian companies have, on average, greater amounts of trade payables on their balance sheets. In these three countries, however, equity markets are still not as well developed as in some other parts of Europe. Thus, supplier financing might just as well serve as a substitute for long-term debt and equity, leaving the net debt to net capital ratio unchanged.

To provide a rough indication of how the mix of debt and equity financing varies across Europe, Table 12.3 shows median debt-to-equity, cash-to-equity, and net

TABLE 12.3 Median cash and marketable securities holdings and leverage for 12 European countries in 2005

Country	Interest-bearing debt-to-book equity	Cash and marketable securities-to-book equity	Net interest-bearing debt-to-book equity	Net interest-bearing debt-to-market equity
Portugal	140%	18%	104%	58%
Spain	87%	23%	63%	25%
Italy	70%	26%	42%	22%
Belgium	51%	23%	36%	20%
France	56%	30%	29%	11%
Denmark	45%	18%	27%	12%
Finland	45%	20%	27%	10%
Netherlands	45%	26%	25%	11%
Switzerland	32%	27%	9%	4%
Germany	35%	28%	4%	2%
Sweden	21%	27%	3%	1%
U.K.	17%	28%	−4%	−2%

debt-to-equity ratios for 12 European countries in 2005. Germany, Sweden, and the U.K. tend to have the lowest net debt-to-equity ratios. Cash and marketable securities holdings of the median company in these countries are, on average, almost as large as its interest-bearing debt. Maybe surprisingly, the net interest-bearing debt-to-equity ratios are highest in countries with borrower-friendly, creditor-unfriendly bankruptcy laws, such as Italy, Portugal, and Spain. Two reasons may explain this.

First, in countries where bankruptcy laws shield management from its creditors in situations of financial distress, the threat of creditors intervening in the company's operations and repossessing collateral is less severe. Consequently, managers in these countries may feel comfortable with taking on more debt. As argued, despite being weakly protected, creditors are willing to extend debt because they can force borrowers to borrow smaller proportions of debt from multiple banks and can choose to extend loans with short maturities.

Second, the net debt-to-equity ratios are lowest in the countries where equity markets are most developed, such as the U.K., the Netherlands, and Switzerland. Companies from these countries can more easily use equity financing as an alternative to debt financing than companies from countries with weakly developed equity markets, such as Portugal and Italy.

THE FINANCING OF NEW PROJECTS

The second model of capital structure focuses on how firms make new financing decisions. Proponents of this dynamic model argue that there can be short-term frictions in capital markets that cause deviations from long-run optimal capital structure. One source of friction arises when managers have better information about their firm's future performance than outside investors. This could lead managers to deviate from their long-term optimal capital structure as they seek financing for new investments.

To see how information asymmetries between outside investors and management can create market imperfections and potentially affect short-term capital structure decisions, consider management's options for financing a proprietary new project that it expects to be profitable. One financing option is to use retained earnings to cover the investment outlay. However, what if the firm has no retained earnings available today? If it pays dividends, it could perhaps cut dividends to help pay for the project. But as we see later, investors usually interpret a dividend cut as an indication that the firm's management anticipates poor future performance. A dividend cut is therefore likely to lead to a share price decline, which management would probably prefer to avoid. Also, many firms do not pay dividends.

A second financing option is to borrow additional funds to finance the project. However, if the firm is already highly leveraged, the tax shield benefits from debt are likely to be relatively modest and the potential costs of financial distress relatively high, making additional borrowing unattractive.

The final financing option available to the firm is to issue new equity. However, if investors know that management has superior information on the firm's value, they are likely to interpret an equity offer as an indication that management believes that the firm's share price is higher than the intrinsic value of the firm.[3] The announcement of an equity offer is therefore likely to lead to a drop in the price of the firm's shares, raising the firm's cost of capital, and potentially leading management to abandon a perfectly good project.

This discussion implies that if the firm has internal cash flows available or is not already highly leveraged, it is relatively straightforward for it to arrange financing for the new project. Otherwise, management has to decide whether undertaking the new project is worthwhile given the costs of cutting dividends, issuing additional debt, or issuing equity to finance the project. The information costs of raising funds by these means lead to a "pecking order" for new financing. Managers first use internal cash to fund investments, and only if this is unavailable do they resort to external financing. Further, if they have to use external financing, managers first use debt financing. New equity issues are used only as a last resort because of the difficulties that investors have in interpreting these issues.[4]

One way for management to mitigate the information problems of using external financing is to ensure that the firm has financial slack. Management can create financial slack by reinvesting free cash flows in marketable securities so that it doesn't have to go to the capital market to finance a new project. It could also choose to have relatively low levels of debt, so that the firm can borrow easily in the future.

In summary, information asymmetries between managers and external investors can make managers reluctant to raise equity to finance new projects. Managers' reluctance arises from their fear that investors will interpret the decision as an indication that the firm's equity is overvalued. In the short term, this effect can lead managers to deviate from the firm's long-term optimal mix of debt and equity.

KEY ANALYSIS QUESTIONS

The above discussion implies that in the short term management should attempt to finance new projects primarily with retained earnings. Further, it suggests that management would be well advised to maintain financial slack to ensure that it is not forced to use costly external financing. To assess a firm's financing options, we would ask the following types of questions:

- What is the value of current cash reserves (not required for day-to-day working capital needs) that could be used for new capital outlays? What operating cash resources are expected to become available in the coming few years? Do these internal resources cover the firm's expected cash needs for new investment and working capital?

- How do the firm's future cash needs for investment change as its operating performance deteriorates or improves? Are its investment opportunities relatively fixed, or are they related to current operating cash flow performance? Investment opportunities for many firms decline during a recession and increase during booms, enabling them to consistently use internal funds for financing. Therefore firms with stable investment needs should build financial slack during booms so that they can support investment during busts.

- If internal funds are not readily available, what opportunities does the firm have to raise low-cost debt financing? Normally, a firm which has virtually zero debt could do this without difficulty. However, if it is in a volatile industry or has mostly intangible assets, debt financing may be costly.

- If the firm has to raise costly equity capital, are there ways to focus investors on the value of the firm's assets and investment opportunities to lower any information asymmetries between managers and investors? For example, management might be able to disclose additional information about the value of existing assets, and the uses and expected returns from the new funds.

Summary of debt policy

There are no easy ways to quantify the best mix of debt and equity for a firm and its best financing options. However, some general principles are likely to be useful in thinking about these questions. We have seen that the benefits from debt financing are likely to be highest for firms with:

- high marginal tax rates and few noninterest tax shields, making interest tax shields from debt valuable;

- high, stable profits/cash flows and few new investment opportunities, increasing the monitoring value of debt and reducing the likelihood that the firm will fall into financial distress or require costly external financing for new projects; and

- high tangible assets that are not easily destroyed by financial distress.

The financial analysis tools developed in Part 2 of the book are useful in rating a firm's interest tax shield benefits, its business risk and investment opportunities, and its major asset types. This information can then be used to judge whether there are benefits from debt or whether the firm would be better off using equity financing to support its business strategies. The analyst must beware, however, that optimal debt levels can differ substantially across countries because of international differences in, for example, legal institutions.

FACTORS THAT DETERMINE DIVIDEND POLICIES

To assess a firm's dividend policy, analysts typically examine its dividend payout, its dividend yield, and any share repurchases. Dividend payout is defined as cash dividends as a percentage of profit available to ordinary shareholders, and it reflects the extent to which a company pays out profits or retains them for reinvestment. Dividend yield is dividends per share as a percentage of the current share price, and indicates the current dividend return earned by shareholders. Finally, share repurchases are relevant because many companies use repurchases of their own shares as an alternative way of returning cash to shareholders. Table 12.4 provides information on these variables for Novartis and Enel.

Novartis appears to be following a more conservative dividend policy. It has a lower payout than Enel and a lower dividend yield. However, in 2005 Novartis returned $0.2 billion to shareholders through share repurchases, whereas Enel made no share repurchases. If this distribution is included with dividends, Novartis paid out 36 percent of net profit in 2005.

What factors should a firm consider when setting its dividend policy? Do investors prefer firms to pay out profits as dividends or to retain them for reinvestment? As we noted above, many of the factors that affect dividends are similar to those examined in the section on capital structure decisions. This should not be too surprising, since a firm's dividend policy also affects its financing decisions. Thus, dividends provide a means of reducing free cash flow inefficiencies. They also have tax implications for investors and can reduce a firm's financial slack. Finally, lending contracts that are designed to protect lenders' interests can affect a firm's dividend payouts.

Below we discuss the factors that are relevant to managers' dividend decisions and how financial analysis tools can be used in this decision process.

Dividends as a way of reducing free cash flow inefficiencies

As we discussed earlier, conflicts of interest between managers and shareholders can affect a firm's optimal capital structure; they also have implications for dividend policy decisions. Shareholders of a firm with free cash flows and few profitable investment opportunities want managers to adopt a dividend policy with high payouts. This will deter managers from growing the firm by reinvesting the free cash flows in new projects that are not valued by shareholders or from spending the free cash flows on

TABLE 12.4 Dividend policy for Novartis and Enel for the year ended December 31, 2005

	Novartis	Enel
Dividend payout	33%	100%
Dividend yield	1.7%	9.3%
Cash ordinary dividends	$2.0 billion	€3.9 billion
Share repurchases	$0.2 billion	€0 billion

management perks. In addition, if managers of a firm with free cash flows wish to fund a new project, most shareholders would prefer that they do so by raising new external capital rather than cutting dividends. Shareholders can then assess whether the project is genuinely profitable or simply one of management's pet projects.

> ### KEY ANALYSIS QUESTIONS
>
> Earlier we discussed how ratio and cash flow analysis can help analysts assess whether a firm faces free cash flow inefficiencies, and how pro forma analysis can help indicate the likelihood of future free cash flow problems. The same analysis and questions can be used to decide whether a firm should initiate dividends.

Tax costs of dividends

What are the implications for dividend policy if dividends and capital gains are taxed, particularly at different rates? Classical models of the tax effects of dividends predict that if the capital gains tax rate is less than the rate on dividend income, investors will prefer that the firm either pays no dividends, so that they subsequently take gains as capital accumulation, or that the firm undertakes a share repurchase, which qualifies as a capital distribution. Even if capital gains are slightly higher than dividend tax rates, investors may prefer capital gains to dividends since they do not actually have to realize their capital gains. They can delay selling their shares and thereby defer paying the taxes on any capital appreciation. Of course, if capital gains tax rates are substantially higher than the rates on ordinary income, investors are likely to favor dividend distributions over capital gains.

Today many practitioners and theorists believe that taxes play only a minor role in determining a firm's dividend policy since a firm can attract investors with various tax preferences. Thus a firm that wishes to pay high dividend rates will attract shareholders that are tax-exempt institutions, which do not pay taxes on dividend income. In contrast, a firm that prefers to pay low dividend rates will attract shareholders who have high marginal tax rates and prefer capital gains to dividend income.

Dividends and financial slack

We discussed earlier how managers' information advantage over dispersed investors can increase a firm's cost of external funds. One way to avoid having to raise costly external funds is to have a conservative dividend policy that creates financial slack in the organization. By paying only a small percentage of net profit as dividends and reinvesting the free cash flows in marketable securities, management reduces the likelihood that the firm will have to go to the capital market to finance a new project.

Managers of firms with high intangible assets and growth opportunities are particularly likely to have an information advantage over dispersed investors, since accounting information for these types of firms is frequently a poor indicator of future performance. Accountants, for example, do not attempt to value R&D, intangibles, or growth opportunities. These types of firms are therefore more likely to face information problems and capital market constraints. To compound this problem, high-growth firms are typically heavily dependent on external financing since they are not usually able to fund all new investments internally. Any capital market constraints are therefore likely to affect their ability to undertake profitable new projects.

Because paying dividends reduces financial slack and is thus costly, a firm's dividend policy can help management communicate effectively with external investors. Investors recognize that managers will only increase their firm's dividend rate if they anticipate that the payout does not have a serious effect on the firm's future financing options. Thus, the decision to increase dividends can help investors appreciate management's optimism about the firm's future performance and its ability to finance growth.[5]

KEY ANALYSIS QUESTIONS

As noted earlier for debt policy, the financial analysis tools discussed in Part 2 of the book can help analysts assess how much financial slack a firm should maintain. The same analysis and questions are relevant to dividend policy analysis. Based on the answers to the earlier questions, analysts can assess whether the firm's projected cash needs for new investments are stable in relation to its operating cash flows. If so, it makes sense for management not to pursue too high a dividend payout and to build financial slack during boom periods to help fund investments during busts. Similarly, if the firm's ability to raise low-cost debt is limited because it is in a volatile industry or has mostly intangible assets, management is likely to avoid high dividend payouts to reduce the risk that it will have to raise high-cost external capital in the future or even forgo a profitable new project.

Lending constraints and dividend policy

One of the concerns of a firm's creditors is that when the firm is in financial distress, managers will pay a large dividend to shareholders. This problem is likely to be particularly severe for a firm with highly liquid assets, since its managers can pay a large dividend without selling assets. To limit these types of ploys, managers agree to restrict dividend payments to shareholders. Such dividend covenants usually require the firm to maintain certain minimum levels of retained earnings and current asset balances, which effectively limit dividend payments in times of financial difficulty. However these constraints on dividend policy are unlikely to be severe for a profitable firm.

Legal dividend restrictions

In many European countries corporate law mandates restrictions on firms' dividend payouts, primarily with the objective of protecting the rights of creditors. Such legal dividend restrictions replace or complement the restrictions that creditors may impose on borrowers by means of debt covenants.[6] Legal dividend restrictions typically require that companies transfer a fixed percentage of their current profits to a legal reserve, unless the legal reserve exceeds a certain percentage of total capital. Companies then can distribute dividends out of the remainder of current profits plus the current amount of retained earnings. Legal dividend restrictions of this kind can be found in most western European countries, although mandated transfers to legal reserves do not exist in Finland, Ireland, the Netherlands, and the U.K.

Determining optimal dividend payouts

One question that arises in using the above factors to determine dividend policy is defining what we mean by high, low, and medium dividend payouts. To provide a rough sense of what companies usually consider to be high and low dividend payouts and yields, Table 12.5 shows median dividend payout ratios and dividend yields for selected European industries for the fiscal year 2005. Median ratios are reported for all listed companies and for large listed companies (market capitalizations greater than €300 million) only.

It is interesting to note that many European listed companies do not pay any dividends. This is particularly true for small firms, which probably have more attractive growth opportunities. The highest payouts tend to be made by utility companies, such as companies providing natural gas, water, and electric services. For these firms the median payouts tend to be roughly 35–55 percent and yields are between 2.5 and 4 percent. In contrast, firms in highly competitive industries with substantial reinvestment opportunities, such as computer programming and pharmaceuticals, tend to have low dividend payouts and dividend yields.

Returning to the cases of Novartis and Enel, it is interesting to see that Novartis has a higher dividend payout ratio than its industry median (33 percent versus 0 percent). When share repurchases are included, Novartis actually paid out 36 percent of its 2005 profits. Apparently the company believes that it does not have to reinvest all of its profits to maintain its high rate of success in drug development. It is also interesting to note that Novartis uses share repurchases as a way to return funds to shareholders. One potential explanation for this is that Novartis does not want to commit to the current rate of payout indefinitely. Its dividend payout therefore represents its long-term payout commitment, and repurchases are used for temporary increases in that rate. Also, Novartis' use of share repurchases is probably tax effective for its Swiss and U.S. shareholders since capital gains rates on repurchased share gains are lower than ordinary income rates on dividends.

TABLE 12.5 Median dividend payout ratio and dividend yield for selected European industries in 2005

	Dividend payout ratio		Dividend yield	
Industry	All listed firms	Large listed firms	All listed firms	Large listed firms
Computer programming and data processing	0%	19%	0%	1%
Computer integrated systems design	0%	40%	0%	1%
Pharmaceuticals	0%	30%	0%	1%
Hotels and motels	0%	28%	1%	2%
Electric services	32%	34%	2%	2%
Air transportation	34%	21%	1%	1%
Heavy construction	34%	38%	2%	2%
Water supply	61%	64%	3%	4%

A summary of dividend policy

Just as it is difficult to provide a simple formula to compute a firm's optimal capital structure, it is difficult to formalize the optimal dividend policy. However, we can identify several factors that appear to be important:

- High-growth firms should have low dividend payout ratios, and they should use their internally generated funds for reinvestment. This minimizes any costs from capital market constraints on financing growth options.

- Firms with high and stable operating cash flows and few investment opportunities should have high dividend payouts to reduce managers' incentives to reinvest free cash flows in unprofitable ventures.

- Firms should probably not be too concerned about tax factors in setting dividend policy. Whatever their policy, they will be able to attract a clientele of investors. Firms that select high dividend payouts will attract tax-exempt institutions or corporations, and firms that pay low or no dividends will attract individuals in high tax brackets.

- Firms' financial covenants can have an impact on their dividend policy decisions. Firms will try to avoid being too close to their constraints in order to minimize the possibility of cutting their dividend. In addition to financial covenants, legal dividend restrictions can further limit firms' discretion in setting dividends.

SUMMARY

This chapter examined how firms make optimal capital structure and dividend decisions. We show that a firm's optimal long-term capital structure is largely determined by its expected tax status, business risks, and types of assets. The benefits from debt financing are expected to be highest for firms with (1) high marginal tax rates and few non-interest tax shields, making interest tax shields valuable; (2) high, stable profits/cash flows and few new investment opportunities, increasing the monitoring value of debt and reducing the likelihood that the firm will fall into financial distress; and (3) high tangible assets that are not easily destroyed by financial distress.

We also show that, in the short term, managers can deviate from their long-term optimal capital structure when they seek financing for new investments. In particular, managers are reluctant to raise external financing, especially new equity, for fear that outside investors will interpret their action as meaning that the firm is overvalued. This information problem has implications for how much financial slack a firm is likely to need to avoid facing these types of information problems.

Optimal dividend policy is determined by many of the same factors – firms' business risks and their types of assets. Thus, dividend rates should be highest for firms with high and stable cash flows and few investment opportunities. By paying out relatively high dividends, these firms reduce the risk of managers investing free cash flows in unprofitable projects. Conversely, firms with low, volatile cash flows and attractive investment opportunities, such as start-up firms, should have relatively low dividend payouts. By reinvesting operating cash flows and reducing the amount of external financing required for new projects, these firms reduce their costs of financing.

Financial statement analysis can be used to better understand a firm's business risks, its expected tax status, and whether its assets are primarily assets in place or growth opportunities. Useful tools for assessing whether a firm's current capital structure and dividend policies maximize shareholder value include accounting analysis to determine off-balance sheet liabilities, ratio analysis to help understand a firm's business risks, and cash flow and pro forma analysis to explore current and likely future investment needs.

DISCUSSION QUESTIONS

1. Financial analysts typically measure financial leverage as the ratio of debt to equity. However, there is less agreement on how to measure debt, or even equity. How would you treat the following items in computing this ratio? Justify your answers.
   - revolving credit agreement with bank
   - cash and marketable securities
   - deferred tax liabilities
   - preference shares
   - convertible debentures
   - non-current provisions.

2. Finance theory implies that the debt-to-equity ratio should be computed using the market values of debt and equity. However, most financial analysts use book values of debt and equity to compute a firm's financial leverage. What are the limitations of using book values rather than market values for comparing leverage across industries, countries, or firms? For what types of industries/firms are book values likely to be most misleading?

3. One important driver of a firm's capital structure and dividend policy decisions is its business risk. What ratios would you look at to assess business risk? Name two industries with very high business risk and two industries with very low business risk.

4. European public companies with "low" leverage have an interest-bearing net debt-to-equity ratio of –15 percent or less, firms with "medium" leverage have a ratio between –15 and 40 percent, and "high" leverage firms have a ratio of 40 percent or more. Given these data, how would you classify the following firms in terms of their optimal debt-to-equity ratio (high, medium, or low)?
   - a successful pharmaceutical company
   - an electric utility
   - a manufacturer of consumer durables
   - a commercial bank
   - a start-up software company.

5. A rapidly growing internet company, recently listed on the London Stock Exchange, needs to raise additional capital to finance new research and development. What financing options are available, and what are the trade-offs between each?

6. The following table reports (in millions) earnings, dividends, capital expenditures, and R&D for U.S.-based Intel for the period 2001–2005:

Year	Net Profit	Dividends	Capital expenditures	R&D
2001	$1,291	$538	$7,309	$3,796
2002	3,117	533	4,703	4,034
2003	5,641	524	3,656	4,360
2004	7,516	1,022	3,843	4,778
2005	8,664	1,958	5,818	5,145

What are the dividend payout rates for Intel during these years? Is this payout policy consistent with the factors expected to drive dividend policy discussed in the chapter? What factors do you expect would lead Intel's management to increase its dividend payout? How do you expect the equity market to react to such a decision?

7. European public companies with low dividend payouts have payout ratios of 0 percent, firms with medium payouts have ratios between 1 and 33 percent, and high payout firms have a ratio of 33 percent or more. Given these data, how would you classify the following firms in terms of their optimal payout policy (high, medium, or low)?

- a successful pharmaceutical company
- an electric utility
- a manufacturer of consumer durables
- a commercial bank
- a start-up software company.

8. In this chapter we argued that international differences in bankruptcy laws and equity market development are a potential cause of international differences in financial leverage. Can you think of other factors that might explain differences in capital structure and dividend policy across countries?

9. In 2005, the French corporation tax rate on ordinary profits was 33.33 percent. If shares were held by a corporation for more than two years, the tax rate on capital gains was about 15 percent. The tax rate on capital gains decreased in 2006 to close to 8 percent and in 2007 to 0 percent. What implications do these changes in the tax rate on capital gains have for corporate dividend policy and capital structure?

NOTES

1. See Merton Miller, "Debt and Taxes," *Journal of Finance* 32 (May 1977): 261–276.
2. Rahim Bah and Pascal Dumontier provide empirical evidence that R&D-intensive firms in Europe, Japan, and the U.S. have lower debt and pay out lower dividends than non-R&D firms. See Rahim Bah and Pascal Dumontier, "R&D Intensity and Corporate Financial Policy: Some International Evidence," *Journal of Business Finance and Accounting* 28 (June/July 2001): 671–692.
3. Paul Healy and Krishna Palepu in "Earnings and Risk Changes Surrounding Primary Stock Offers," *Journal of Accounting Research* 28 (Spring 1990): 25–49, find that announcements of equity issues are interpreted by investors as a signal from management that the firm is riskier than investors expected.

4. These matters are discussed by Stewart Myers and Nicholas Majluf in "Corporate Financing and Investment Decisions When Firms Have Information That Investors Do Not Have," *Journal of Financial Economics* (June 1984): 187–221.
5. Findings by Paul Healy and Krishna Palepu in "Earnings Information Conveyed by Dividend Initiations and Omissions," *Journal of Financial Economics* 21 (September 1988): 149–175, indicate that investors interpret announcements of dividend initiations and omissions as managers' forecasts of future earnings performance.
6. See Christian Leuz, Dominic Deller, and Michael Stubenrath, "An International Comparison of Accounting-Based Payout Restrictions in the United States, United Kingdom and Germany," *Accounting and Business Research* 28 (1998): 111–129.

CUC International, Inc. (A)[1]

In March 1989 Stuart Bell, Executive Vice President and CFO of CUC International, Inc., was concerned that the company's stock was seriously undervalued. He attributed the undervaluation to the investment community's concern about the quality of CUC's earnings:

I am afraid our accounting is misunderstood by many investors. Recently, we have been forced to spend a lot of top management time and energy defending our policy in analysts' meetings. As a result we have been unable to focus investors' attention on our innovative business strategy and the tremendous cash-flow generating potential of our business. Concerns about our earnings quality are scaring new institutional investors from investing in our business. Many money managers tell me that they love our business concept but are afraid to buy our stock because they are worried about our accounting. The accounting is also giving short sellers an excuse to scare our current investors and drive down the stock price.

While Bell was convinced that CUC's accounting was appropriate, he wondered whether it was actually hurting, rather than helping, the company. What, if anything, should CUC do to shore up investors' confidence in the company?

Business history and operations

CUC International, located in Stamford, Connecticut, was a membership-based consumer services company. CUC marketed its membership programs to credit card-holders of major financial, retailing, and oil companies, including Chase Manhattan, Citibank, Sears, JC Penney, and Amoco. The company was formed in 1973 as Comp-U-Card of America, went public in 1983, and was renamed CUC International in 1987. As a result of its strong performance, the company was included in *Inc.* magazine's list of the fastest growing public companies in 1984 and 1986.

CUC's most popular product was Shoppers Advantage, introduced in 1981. Consumers paid an annual membership fee for this service, which entitled them to call the company's operators on a toll-free line, or to use on-line computer access seven days a week to inquire about, price, and/or buy brand-name products. Shoppers Advantage offered more than 250,000 brand-name and specialty items. Many members used the service principally as a reference for comparison pricing, not necessarily to purchase items directly. The company's large membership base allowed it to negotiate attractive discounts on the products offered in its catalog. As a result, the company guaranteed its subscribers the lowest prices available on goods it sold. If a member, after purchasing merchandise through CUC, sent an advertisement from an authorized dealer with a lower price within 30 days of placing an order, the company agreed to refund the difference. Members' purchase orders were executed through

1. Professor Paul Healy and Professor Krishna Palepu prepared this case. The case is intended solely as the basis for class discussion and is not intended to serve as an endorsement, source of primary data, or illustration of effective or ineffective management. Copyright © 1992 by the President and Fellows of Harvard College. HBS Case 9–192–099.

independent vendors who shipped the merchandise directly to customers, enabling the company to carry no inventory.

The firm acquired a large share of its new members through agreements with major credit card issuers, who provided CUC access to its list of cardholders. These individuals were solicited by three direct marketing approaches: billing statement inserts, solo mailings, and telemarketing. In billing statement insert programs, membership applications were enclosed in the monthly billing statements of credit card issuers. Solo mailings were membership offers mailed directly. Telemarketing involved following up mailings with telephone calls to explain membership offers further. CUC paid 10 to 20 percent of initial and renewal membership fees as a commission to the credit card company.

CUC incurred a large one-time cost for new member solicitations. Because only a small fraction of people reached through direct mail solicitations purchased the service, membership acquisition costs typically exceeded membership fees in the first year. For example, in 1989 the annual membership fee for Shoppers Advantage was $39, the average solicitation cost per new member was $29.37, commissions to the credit card companies were $6.63, and the average operating service cost per member was $5.00. Thus on average for each new member acquired, CUC incurred a cash outflow of $2 in the first year.

Members subscribed to Shoppers Advantage for a single year at a time. Renewals were automatically billed each year through the credit card company, and members could elect to cancel the service. There were thus no direct solicitation costs for renewing members. In 1989 CUC had a net cash inflow of $27.37 for each renewing member – membership fees were $39, and the commissions to the credit card companies and operating service costs totaled $11.63.[2] Membership renewal rates were therefore a key determinant of the profitability of the Shoppers Advantage program. The average annual renewal rate for Shoppers Advantage in recent years was 71 percent, making the program very profitable. This average was based on eight years' experience with the product since 1981.

CUC capitalized on its Shoppers Advantage experience by introducing a variety of other membership-based products. These included: (1) Travellers Advantage – a travel membership created in 1988 to provide subscribers access to database information and reservations on discount airline travel, hotels and auto rental, tours, and cruises; (2) AutoVantage – to provide subscribers with new car price and performance summaries, used car valuations, and parts and service discounts; and (3) Premier Dining – a service introduced in 1989 offering subscribers two-for-one dining at mid- to upscale restaurants in major U.S. cities. The company made large marketing investments to build memberships in these new programs.

CUC's management explained the key elements of its business strategy as follows:

The company's expansion has been built on a foundation of creating, developing, and marketing a broad array of valuable services to consumers....Aggressive marketing is an important strength. We sell our goods and services directly to millions of customers of major credit card issuers. Because our consumer services are a natural enhancement to personal financial services, more than 40 of the top 50 money center banks and a growing number of retailers and oil companies find it advantageous to work with CUC....As competition heats up in the financial services industry, demand for CUC's services is likely to increase. Credit card issuers rely

2. *The figures in this and the previous paragraph are from an analyst report by Brian E. Stack of Advest, Inc. dated October 30, 1989.*

upon our services to draw new customers, increase card use, and raise average balances. They also use our services to differentiate their cards from others, and to tailor what they offer to appeal to different life-style and geographic preferences. Finally, card issuers benefit from the stream of membership commissions they receive from CUC.[3]

By December 1988, CUC had approximately 12 million members enrolled in its programs. Revenues had grown from $45 million in the year ending January 31, 1984 (fiscal year 1984) to $198 million in the year ending January 31, 1988 (fiscal 1988), and earnings had grown from $3 million to $17 million during this period. Exhibits 3 and 4 present the financial statements for the year ended January 31, 1988, and for the nine months ended October 31, 1988. Management expected the company to continue its rapid growth in the future, with revenues for the fiscal year ending January 31, 1989 projected to be approximately $270 million.

The financial reporting controversy

CUC's management decided that because current marketing outlays provided significant future benefits, the company should capitalize membership solicitation costs in its financial statements, and amortize them over three years at rates of 40 percent, 30 percent, and 30 percent. This choice was endorsed by Ernst & Whinney, the company's auditors, and by the Securities and Exchange Commission when the company went public.

While it was unusual to capitalize marketing costs, CUC's managers believed that this decision was justified given the nature of the company's business and their confidence in future renewal rates. Bell explained the rationale behind CUC's accounting choice:

Many companies spend money on acquiring plant and equipment, and they capitalize these costs. Our business does not require major investments in plant and equipment. Instead, it requires investments in membership acquisitions. Because our membership renewal rates are so high and steady, I believe that it is important for accounting to reflect future benefits from spending money on membership acquisition in the current period. While expensing these costs is conservative, it fails to reflect their true nature.

In its accounting choice, CUC's management could not obtain much guidance from other companies' practices. Magazine publishers typically expensed costs of acquiring new subscribers, whereas insurance companies capitalized policy acquisition costs. Safecard Services, Inc., a credit-card registration company which also incurred large outlays for membership acquisition, capitalized its membership acquisition costs and amortized them over a ten-year period.

When CUC made the initial public stock offering, it had only a limited following among analysts and institutional investors. As the company grew larger, it sought to broaden its investor base. Some analysts, however, were concerned that capitalized marketing costs would subsequently have to be written off as losses because of high uncertainty about future renewal rates. They argued that deferring current marketing costs lowered the firm's earnings quality.

Analysts' concerns about the firm's accounting for marketing costs may have arisen from their experience with Safecard Services, Inc. Safecard's capitalization of

---

3. *Source: CUC's 1988 Annual Report.*

membership acquisition costs had been the subject of considerable controversy in the financial press. Safecard's decision to write off deferred marketing costs in 1987 may have heightened analysts' concerns about the value of CUC's capitalized marketing costs.

By early 1989 the company's stock had become a target of short sellers and its price began to suffer. As shown in Exhibit 1, short positions in the company rose from approximately 157,000 in November 1988 to more than 2,000,000 in March 1989.[4] While the stock market was generally on the upswing, CUC's stock price declined from $19.3 at the beginning of January 1988 to $16.3 at the beginning of March 1989. Exhibit 2 shows the stock price performance for CUC relative to the performance of the value-weighted OTC market index between January 4, 1988, and March 9, 1989. During this period CUC's stock price declined by 50 percent relative to the market. *Value Line Investment Survey* commented in its report on CUC dated March 17, 1989:

> *CUC International shares have taken a beating. The stock has fallen more than 35% since our last report three months ago. Wall Street's concern over the company's accounting methods ... contributed to the stock price decline.*

Management believed that the decline in CUC's stock performance could not be explained by either disappointing current operating performance or by forecasts of slower growth. Quarterly revenues and earnings grew steadily throughout 1988, and were consistent with *Value Line* analyst forecasts. In its March 18, 1988, report, *Value Line* forecasted that the company would have earnings of $5.5 million, $6 million, and $6.6 million in the quarters ending in April 1988, July 1988, and October 1988. Actual earnings in these quarters were $6 million, $6.6 million, and $6.9 million, respectively. The company projected that its growth would continue in the future – sales were projected to grow by 30 percent per year and operating cash flows would grow by 60 percent per year during the next five years. Finally, the firm was able to fund its substantial marketing outlays solely from operating cash flows during this period.

Possible management responses

At least three options were available to CUC's management in responding to investors' concerns. One approach would be to adopt a more conservative policy to account for membership acquisition costs. By writing off previously capitalized expenses and adopting a policy of expensing future outlays as incurred, the firm would eliminate the major source of analysts' criticisms. However, such a move would seriously affect the company's balance sheet and income statement. More important, the accounting change would be unlikely to help management convince investors that current marketing outlays have future benefits.

An alternative strategy would be to provide expanded disclosure to justify the firm's capitalization of membership acquisition costs. This approach would involve identifying what type of information is likely to be most relevant and credible to investors. Further, it would require assessing whether the additional disclosures would provide proprietary information to competitors.

Finally, CUC could use corporate finance policies to enhance its stock price. Investors typically interpret cash payouts in the form of dividends and share repurchases as an indication of management's optimism about the firm's future cash flows. Such payouts, however, need to be planned in the context of the firm's investment needs for membership acquisitions.

---

4. *Source:* Barron's Financial Weekly *(Dow Jones News Service).*

One of the items on the agenda of CUC's upcoming board meeting was to consider proposals for dealing with the firm's communication challenge. Stu Bell was wondering which of the above options he should recommend.

Questions

1. Evaluate CUC's business model. What are the key value drivers and risks in this business?

2. Why do you think the investors are so concerned about CUC?

3. CUC's CFO Stu Bell was considering a large stock repurchase or one-time dividend payment, financed by debt, as a way to improve investor confidence. Do you think this is a good idea? What is the maximum amount the company can borrow to finance this initiative without taking undue financial risk? Under your recommendation, what will CUC's interest coverage and cash flow available for servicing interest and principal payments on the debt be for the next two years?

4. Assuming CUC implements the stock repurchase or dividend payment plan, should the company do anything with respect to its accounting for membership acquisition costs?

CUC International

EXHIBIT 1 **CUC International shares sold short from January 1988 to March 1989**

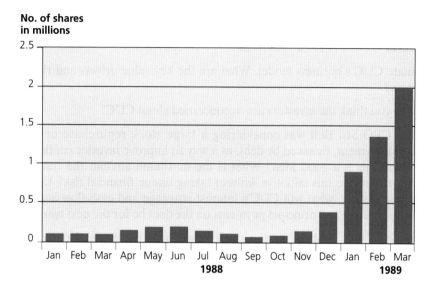

EXHIBIT 2 **Cumulative difference in stock returns for CUC International and the OTC market index in the period January 4, 1988, to March 9, 1989**

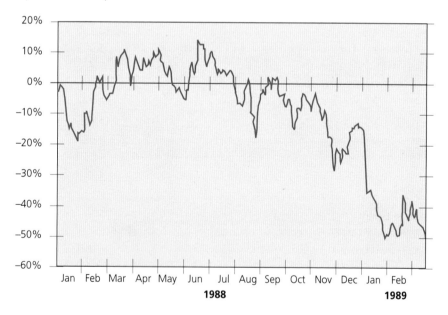

EXHIBIT 3 **CUC International, abridged annual report for the year ended January 31, 1988**

Consolidated financial statements

CONSOLIDATED BALANCE SHEET

(Dollar amounts in thousands)	January 31 1988	1987
ASSETS		
Current assets		
Cash and cash equivalents	$25,953	$14,810
Receivables, less allowance of $613 and $405	33,201	24,209
Prepaid expenses and other	3,468	3,288
Total current assets	62,622	42,307
Deferred membership charges, net	22,078	13,112
Prepaid solicitation costs	17,089	4,915
Prepaid commissions	6,267	8,127
Contract renewal rights, net	27,944	30,443
Excess of cost over net assets acquired, net	33,301	19,066
Properties, net	16,048	10,074
Other	1,519	4,416
Total assets	$186,868	$132,460
LIABILITIES AND SHAREHOLDERS' EQUITY		
Current liabilities		
Members' deposits	$4,997	$4,340
Accounts payable and accrued expenses	36,063	16,446
Federal and state income taxes	423	
Current portion of long-term obligations	1,404	5,011
Total current liabilities	42,887	25,797
Convertible subordinated debentures	12,000	22,000
Long-term obligations	3,767	5,120
Deferred income taxes	14,624	6,073
Other	1,229	1,268
Total liabilities	74,507	60,258
Shareholders' Equity		
Common stock-par value $.01 per share; authorized 50 million shares; issued 19,683,567 and 17,820,338	197	178
Additional paid-in capital	82,271	59,550
Retained earnings	32,420	14,997
Treasury stock – 398,230 and 398,091 shares, at cost	(2,527)	(2,523)
Total shareholders' equity	112,361	72,202
Total liabilities and shareholders' equity	$186,868	$132,460

CUC International

CONSOLIDATED STATEMENT OF INCOME

(Dollar amounts in thousands, except per share amounts)	Year Ended January 31		
	1988	**1987**	**1986**
Revenues			
Membership and service fees	$195,277	$138,149	$84,123
Other	3,180	3,610	3,342
Total revenues	198,457	141,759	87,465
Expenses			
Operating	64,092	43,248	26,729
Marketing	68,937	56,496	35,042
General and administrative	31,729	23,342	14,572
Interest	2,259	2,663	1,507
Total expenses	167,017	125,749	77,850
Operating income	31,440	16,010	9,615
Acquisition costs			2,348
Income before income taxes and extraordinary credit	31,440	16,010	7,267
Provision for income taxes	14,017	7,350	4,435
Income before extraordinary credit	17,423	8,660	2,832
Extraordinary credit-utilization of tax loss carryforwards		1,041	3,589
Net income	$17,423	$9,701	$6,421
Income per common share			
Income before extraordinary credit	$.90	$.49	$.18
Extraordinary credit		.06	.23
Net income per common share	$.90	$.55	$.41

CONSOLIDATED STATEMENT OF CASH FLOWS

(Dollar amounts in thousands)	1988	1987	1986
Operating activities			
Net income	$17,423	$9,701	$6,421
Adjustments to reconcile net income to net cash provided by operating activities:			
Amortization of membership acquisition costs	44,641	35,501	20,237
Amortization of prepaid commissions	1,860	2,029	2,081
Amortization of contract rights and excess cost	3,423	2,199	
Deferred income taxes	11,712	5,553	442
Depreciation	2,506	2,582	1,969
Extraordinary credit and loss from discontinued operations			(1,475)
Change in operating assets and liabilities, net of acquisitions:			
Net (increase) decrease in receivables	(8,049)	(6,747)	3,795
Net increase (decrease) in members' deposits, accounts payable and accrued expenses and federal and state income taxes	12,755	(3,649)	(586)
Deferred membership income	9,629	14,366	9,052
Membership acquisition costs	(63,236)	(43,720)	(42,564)
Prepaid solicitation costs	(12,174)	(4,915)	
Prepaid commissions			(409)
Other, net	2,576	(1,748)	39
Net cash from (used in) operating activities	23,066	11,152	(998)
Investing activities			
Acquisitions, net of cash acquired	(4,625)	(18,341)	
Acquisitions of properties	(7,586)	(5,078)	(4,345)
Proceeds from disposal of properties net of $3.2 million note receivable		783	
Disposals of marketable securities		1,933	2,724
Other, net			240
Net cash from (used in) investing activities	(12,211)	(20,703)	(1,381)
Financing activities			
Issuance of common stock	5,326	6,220	613
Issuance of convertible subordinated debentures			15,000
Purchase of treasury stock		(2,377)	
Repayments of long-term obligations	(4,960)	(2,955)	(795)
Other, net	(78)		
Net cash from financing activities	288	888	14,818
Net increase (decrease) in cash and cash equivalents	11,143	(8,663)	12,439
Cash and cash equivalents at beginning of year	14,810	23,473	11,034
Cash and cash equivalents at end of year	$25,953	$14,810	$23,473

CUC International

Notes to consolidated financial statements

Note 1. Summary of significant accounting policies

Principles of Consolidation: The consolidated financial statements include the accounts of CUC International Inc. (formerly Comp-U-Card International Incorporated) and its wholly-owned subsidiaries. The Company operates in one business segment, providing a variety of services through individual, financial institution, credit union and group memberships. All significant intercompany transactions have been eliminated in consolidation.

Deferred Membership Charges, Net: Deferred membership charges is comprised of (in thousands):

January 31,	1988	1987
Deferred membership income	$(52,834)	$(43,205)
Unamortized membership acquisition costs	74,912	56,317
Deferred membership charges, net	$22,078	$13,112

The related membership fees and membership acquisition costs have been between $30 and $39 per individual member during the years ended January 31, 1988 and 1987. In addition, the annual renewal costs have remained between ten and twenty percent of annual membership fees for the same period.

Renewal costs consist principally of charges from sponsoring institutions and are amortized over the renewal period. Individual memberships are principally for a one-year period. These membership fees are recorded, as deferred membership income, upon acceptance of membership, net of estimated cancellations, and pro-rated over the membership period. The related initial membership acquisition costs are recorded as incurred and charged to operations as membership fees are recognized, allowing for renewals, over a three-year period. Such costs are amortized commencing with the beginning of the membership period, at the annual rate of 40%, 30% and 30%, respectively. Membership renewal rates are dependent upon the nature of the benefits and services provided by the Company in its various membership programs. Through January 31, 1988, membership renewal rates have been sufficient to generate future revenue in excess of deferred membership acquisition costs over the remaining amortization period.

Amortization of membership acquisition costs, including deferred renewal costs, amounted to $44.6 million, $35.5 million and $20.2 million for the years ended January 31, 1988, 1987, and 1986, respectively.

Prepaid Solicitation Costs: Prepaid solicitation costs consist of initial membership acquisition costs pertaining to membership solicitation programs that were in process at year end. Accordingly, no membership fees had been received or recognized at year end.

Prepaid Commissions: Prepaid commissions consist of the amount to be paid in connection with the termination of contracts with the Company's field sales force ($4.9 million and $5.8 million at January 31, 1988 and 1987, respectively) and the termination of special compensation agreements with an officer and former officer ($1.3 million and $1.6 million at January 31, 1988 and 1987, respectively). The amount relating to the termination of the field sales force is being amortized, using the straight-line method, over eight years and the amount relating to the termination of the special compensation agreement is being amortized ratably over ten years.

Contract Renewal Rights: Contract renewal rights represent the value assigned to contracts acquired in acquisitions and are being amortized over 9 to 16 years using the straight-line method.

Excess of Cost Over Net Assets Acquired: The excess of cost over net assets acquired is being amortized over 15 to 25 years using the straight-line method.

Earnings Per Share: Amounts per share have been computed using the weighted average number of common and common equivalent shares outstanding. The weighted average number of common and common equivalent shares outstanding was 19.4 million, 17.8 million and 15.8 million for the years ended January 31, 1988, 1987, and 1986, respectively. Fully diluted earnings per share did not differ significantly from primary earnings per share in any year.

Statement of Cash Flows: The Company adopted Financial Accounting Standards Board (FASB) "Statement of Cash Flows" in its fiscal 1988 financial statements and restated previously reported statements of changes in financial position for fiscal years 1987 and 1986. For purposes of the consolidated statement of cash flows, the Company considers all investments with a maturity of three months or less to be cash equivalents.

Financial highlights

(In thousands, except per share amounts)

Year Ended January 31	1988	1987	1986	1985	1984
Total revenues	$198,457	$141,759	$87,465	$65,947	$45,468
Net income	17,423	9,701	6,421	4,214	3,184
Per common share:					
Net income	$.90	$.55	$.41	$.28	$.23
Book value	5.83	4.14	2.33	1.94	1.70
Shareholders' equity	$112,361	$72,202	$34,859	$28,673	$24,806
Number of active members	10,000	8,400	4,700	1,200	450

Report of independent auditors

Ernst & Whinney
Six Landmark Square, Suite 500
Stamford, Connecticut 06901

Board of Directors and Shareholders
CUC International Inc.
Stamford, Connecticut

We have examined the consolidated balance sheet of CUC International Inc. as of January 31, 1988 and 1987, and the related consolidated statements of income, shareholders' equity and cash flows for each of the three years in the period ended January 31, 1988. Our examinations were made in accordance with generally accepted auditing standards and,

accordingly, included such tests of the accounting records and such other auditing procedures as we considered necessary in the circumstances.

In our opinion, the consolidated financial statements referred to above present fairly the consolidated financial position of CUC International Inc. at January 31, 1988 and 1987, and the consolidated results of operations and cash flows for each of the three years in the period ended January 31, 1988, in conformity with generally accepted principles applied on a consistent basis.

Ernst & Whinney
Stamford, Connecticut
March 30, 1988

CUC International

EXHIBIT 4 **CUC International, abridged interim financial statements for nine months ended October 31, 1988**

CONSOLIDATED BALANCE SHEET

(Dollar amounts in thousands)	October 31, 1988 (unaudited)	January 31, 1988
ASSETS		
Current assets		
Cash and cash equivalents	$32,003	$25,953
Receivables	38,118	33,201
Other	4,164	3,468
Total current assets	74,285	62,622
Deferred membership charges, net	37,223	22,078
Prepaid solicitation costs	25,538	17,089
Prepaid commissions	5,397	6,267
Contract renewal rights and intangible assets, net	64,419	61,245
Properties, net	19,805	16,048
Other	2,040	1,519
Total assets	$228,707	$186,868
LIABILITIES AND SHAREHOLDERS' EQUITY		
Current liabilities		
Members' deposits	$4,485	$4,997
Accounts payable and accrued expenses	50,017	36,063
Federal and state income taxes	1,264	423
Current portion of long-term obligations	1,494	1,404
Total current liabilities	57,260	42,887
Convertible subordinated debentures	12,000	12,000
Long-term obligations	2,673	3,767
Deferred income taxes	16,844	14,624
Other	1,402	1,229
Total liabilities	90,179	74,507
Shareholders' equity		
Common stock	203	197
Other shareholders' equity	138,325	112,164
Total shareholders' equity	138,528	112,361
Total liabilities and shareholders' equity	$228,707	$186,868

CUC International

CONSOLIDATED INCOME STATEMENT (unaudited)

(In thousands, except per share amounts)	Three months ended October 31		Nine months ended October 31	
	1988	1987	1988	1987
Revenues				
Membership and service fees	$70,131	$50,696	$192,016	$143,409
Other	938	386	2,297	1,693
Total revenues	71,069	51,082	194,313	145,102
Expenses				
Operating	24,320	16,258	64,123	47,608
Marketing	23,524	17,761	65,647	50,625
General and administrative	11,787	8,721	32,363	25,097
Total expenses	59,631	42,740	162,133	123,330
Operating income	11,438	8,342	32,180	21,772
Provision for income taxes	4,577	3,672	12,854	9,591
Net income	$6,861	$4,670	$19,326	$12,181
Net income per common share	$.33	$.24	$.93	$.63
Weighted average number of common and common equivalent shares outstanding	20,752	19,665	20,870	19,231

CUC International

13

Communication and Governance

Corporate governance has become an increasingly important issue in capital markets throughout the world following financial market meltdowns in the European and U.S. markets. These market collapses exposed problems of accounting misstatements and lack of corporate transparency, as well as governance problems and conflicts of interest among the intermediaries charged with monitoring management and corporate disclosures.

The breakdowns have increased the challenge for managers in communicating credibly with skeptical outside investors, making it more difficult than ever for new (and in some cases even established) firms to raise capital. Financial reports, the traditional platform for management to communicate with investors, are viewed with increased skepticism following a number of widely publicized audit failures and the demise of Arthur Andersen.

The market crashes have also raised questions about improving the quality of governance by information and financial intermediaries. New regulations, such as the Eighth Company Law Directive in the E.U. and the Sarbanes-Oxley Act in the U.S., attempt to increase accountability and financial competence of audit committees and external auditors, who are charged with reviewing the financial reporting and disclosure process.

This chapter discusses how many of the financial analysis tools developed in Chapters 2 through 8 can be used by managers to develop a coherent disclosure strategy, and by corporate board members and external auditors to improve the quality of their work. The following types of questions are dealt with:

- Managers ask: Is our current communication strategy effective in helping investors understand the firm's business strategy and expected future performance, thereby ensuring that our share price is not seriously overvalued or undervalued?

- Audit committee members ask: What are the firm's key business risks? Are they reflected appropriately in the financial statements? How is management communicating on important risks that cannot be reflected in the financial statements? Is information on the firm's performance presented to the board consistent with that provided to investors in the financial report and firm disclosures?

- External auditors ask: What are the firm's key business risks, and how are they reflected in the financial statements? Where should we focus our audit tests? Is our assessment of the firm's performance consistent with that of external investors and analysts? If not, are we overlooking something, or is management misrepresenting the firm's true performance in disclosures?

Throughout this book we have focused primarily on showing how financial statement data can be helpful for analysts and outside investors in making a variety of decisions. In this chapter we change our emphasis and focus primarily on management and governance agents. Of course an understanding of the management communication process and corporate governance is also important for security analysts and investors. The approach taken here, however, is more germane to insiders because most of the types of analyses we discuss are not available to outsiders.

GOVERNANCE OVERVIEW

As we discuss throughout this book, outside investors require access to reliable information on firm performance, both to value their debt and equity claims and to monitor the performance of management. Investors require that managers provide information on their company's performance and future plans when they agree to provide capital to the firm.

However, left to their own devices, managers are likely to paint a rosy picture of the firm's performance in their disclosures. There are three reasons for manager optimism in reporting. First, most managers are genuinely positive about their firms' prospects, leading them to unwittingly emphasize the positive and downplay the negative.

A second reason for management optimism in reporting arises because firm disclosures play an important role in mitigating "agency" problems between managers and investors.[1] Investors use firm disclosures to judge whether managers have run the firm in investors' best interests or, on the other hand, have abused their authority and control over firm resources. Reporting consistently poor earnings increases the likelihood that top management will be replaced, either by the Board of Directors or by an acquirer who takes over the firm to improve its management.[2] Of course managers are aware of this and have incentives to show positive performance.

Finally, managers are also likely to make optimistic disclosures prior to issuing new equity. Recent evidence indicates that entrepreneurs tend to take their firms public after disclosure of strong reported, but frequently unsustainable, earnings performance. Also, seasoned equity offers typically follow strong, but again unsustainable, share and earnings performance. The strong earnings performance prior to IPOs and seasoned offers appears to be at least partially due to earnings management.[3] Of course rational outside investors recognize management's incentives to manage earnings and downplay any bad news prior to a new issue. They respond by discounting the shares, demanding a hefty new issue discount, and in extreme cases refusing to purchase the new shares. This raises the cost of capital and potentially leaves some of the best new ventures and projects unfunded.[4]

Financial and information intermediaries help reduce agency and information problems that face outside investors by evaluating the quality of management representations in the firm's disclosures, providing their own analysis of firms' (and managers') performance and making investment decisions on investors' behalf. As presented in Figure 13.1, these intermediaries include internal governance agents, assurance professionals, information analyzers, and professional investors. The importance of these intermediaries is underscored by the magnitude of the fees that they collectively receive from investors and entrepreneurs.

Internal governance agents are responsible for monitoring a firm's management. In Europe there exist two different governance systems. In a one-tier board system, such as prevailing in the U.K., non-executive directors are members of the same corporate

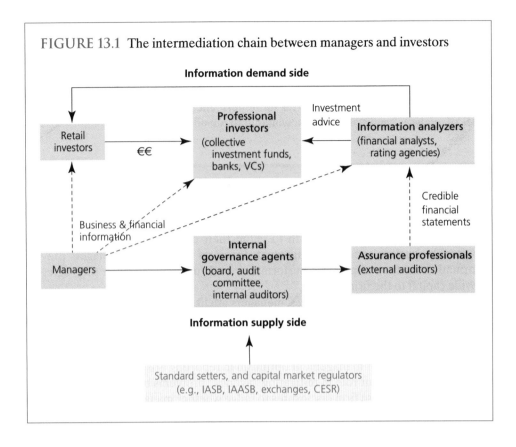

FIGURE 13.1 The intermediation chain between managers and investors

board as firm management (executive directors), whom they monitor. In a two-tier board system, such as prevailing in Continental Europe, the task of monitoring the Management Board has been delegated to a separate Supervisory Board. In many Continental European countries, the law explicitly requires the members of the Supervisory Board to act in the interests of all stakeholders, not just the shareholders. In large German firms, up to half of the members of the Supervisory Board are representatives of the firm's employees. The functions of Corporate or Supervisory Boards include reviewing business strategy, evaluating and rewarding top management, and assuring the flow of credible information to external parties.

Assurance professionals, such as external auditors, enhance the credibility of financial information prepared by managers. Information analyzers, such as financial analysts and rating agencies, are responsible for gathering and analyzing information to provide performance forecasts and investment recommendations to both professional and retail individual investors. Finally, professional investors (such as banks, collective investment funds, insurance, and venture capital firms) make investment decisions on behalf of dispersed investors. They are therefore responsible for valuing and selecting investment opportunities in the economy.

In this framework, management, internal governance agents, and assurance professionals are charged with supplying information; individual and professional investors and information analyzers make up the demand side. Both the supply and demand sides are governed by a variety of regulatory institutions. These include public regulators, such as the European securities and bank regulators, as well as private sector bodies, such as the International Accounting Standards Board, the International Auditing and Assurance Standards Board, and stock exchanges.

The level and quality of information and residual information and agency problems in capital markets are determined by the organizational design of these intermediaries and regulatory institutions. Key organizational design questions include the following: What are the optimal incentive schemes for rewarding top managers? What should be the composition and charter of Corporate Boards? Should auditors assure that financial reports comply with accounting standards or represent a firm's underlying economics? Should there be detailed accounting standards or a few broad accounting principles? What should be the organizational form and business scope of auditors and analysts? What incentive schemes should be used for professional investors to align their interests with individual investors?

A variety of economic and institutional factors are likely to influence the answers to these design questions. Examples include the ability to write and enforce optimal contracts, proprietary costs that might make disclosure costly for investors, and regulatory imperfections. The spectacular rise and fall of Enron suggests that these limitations could have a first-order effect on the functioning of capital markets.

While it is interesting to speculate on how to improve the functioning of capital markets through changes in organizational design, that issue goes beyond the scope of this chapter. Instead, we discuss how the financial analysis tools developed in Chapters 2 through 8 can be used to improve the performance of some of the information intermediaries who have been widely criticized following revelations of financial reporting fraud and misstatements at companies such as Ahold, Enron, and Parmalat.[5]

We have already discussed the application of financial analysis tools to equity and credit analysts and to professional investors in Chapters 9 and 10. In the remainder of this chapter, we discuss how these tools can be used by managers to develop a strategy for effective communication with investors, by members of Boards of Directors or Supervisory Boards and audit committees in overseeing management and the audit process, and by audit professionals.

MANAGEMENT COMMUNICATION WITH INVESTORS

Some managers argue that communication problems are not worth worrying about. They maintain that as long as managers make investment and operating decisions that enhance shareholder value, investors will value their performance and the firm's shares accordingly. While this is true in the long run, since all information is eventually public, it may not hold in the short or even medium term. If investors do not have access to the same information as management, they will probably find it difficult to value new and innovative investments. In an efficient capital market, they will not consistently overvalue or undervalue these new investments, but their valuations will tend to be noisy. This can make share prices relatively noisy, leading management at various times to consider their firms to be either seriously overvalued or undervalued.

Does it matter if a firm's shares are overvalued or undervalued for a period? Most managers would prefer to not have their shares undervalued, since it makes it more costly to raise new financing. They may also worry that undervaluation is likely to increase the chance of a takeover by a hostile acquirer, with an accompanying reduction in their job security. Managers of firms that are overvalued may also be concerned about the market's assessment, since they are legally liable for failing to disclose information relevant to investors.[6] They may therefore not wish to see their shares seriously overvalued, even though overvaluation provides opportunities to issue new equity at favorable rates.

A word of caution

As noted above, it is natural that many managers believe that firms are undervalued by the capital market. This frequently occurs because it is difficult for managers to be realistic about their company's future performance. After all, it is part of their job to sell the company to new employees, customers, suppliers, and investors. In addition, forecasting the firm's future performance objectively requires them to judge their own capabilities as managers. Thus many managers may argue that investors are uninformed and that their firm is undervalued. Only some can back that up with solid evidence.

If management decides that the firm does face a genuine information problem, it can begin to consider whether and how this could be redressed. Is the problem potentially serious enough that it is worth doing something to alter investors' perceptions? Or is the problem likely to resolve itself within a short period? Does the firm have plans to raise new equity or to use equity to acquire another company? Is management's job security threatened? As we discuss below, management has a wide range of options in this situation.

KEY ANALYSIS QUESTIONS

We recommend that before jumping to the conclusion that their firms are undervalued, managers should analyze their firms' performance and compare their own forecasts of future performance with those of analysts, using the following approach:

- *Is there a significant difference between internal management forecasts of future earnings and cash flows and those of outside analysts?*

- *Do any differences between managers' and analysts' forecasts arise because of different expectations about economy-wide performance?* Managers may understand their own businesses better than analysts, but they may not be any better at forecasting macro-economic conditions.

- *Can managers identify any factors that might explain a difference between analysts' and managers' forecasts of future performance?* For example, are analysts unaware of positive new R&D results, do they have different information about customer responses to new products and marketing campaigns, etc.? These types of differences could indicate that the firm faces an information problem.

Example: Communication issues for Royal Dutch Shell

Royal Dutch Shell Plc is the world's third largest energy and petrochemical group, operating in 140 countries and employing more than 110,000 people. At the beginning of the 2000s the group had a complicated ownership structure. The service and operating companies of the Royal Dutch Shell group were owned by two holding companies: Shell Petroleum N.V. and the Shell Petroleum Company Ltd. These two companies were, in turn, owned by two exchange-listed companies: Netherlands-based Royal Dutch Petroleum Company, which held a 60 percent equity stake, and U.K.-based Shell Transport and Trading Company, which held a 40 percent equity stake. Together, Royal Dutch and Shell were named the Royal Dutch Shell group. Royal Dutch and Shell had their shares listed on their domestic exchanges as well as on the New York Stock Exchange. Both exchange-listed companies had their own

Management Boards but coordinated many of their decisions and activities by means of explicit arrangements and joint conferences. In the period from 2000 to 2002, the Royal Dutch Shell group reported gradually declining returns on its assets between 19.5 and 14.0 percent. Both exchange-listed holding companies experienced share price declines of about 30 and 20 percent, respectively, reaching a combined market capitalization of €148.6 billion.

By the end of 2002, Royal Dutch Shell had estimated that its "proved reserves" were 10.1 billion barrels of crude oil and natural gas liquids and 53.4 trillion standard cubic feet of natural gas. Proved reserves were the estimated quantities of oil and gas that Royal Dutch Shell expected to recover from its current reservoirs with a reasonable degree of certainty. Following U.S. accounting principles, Royal Dutch Shell had estimated that the present value of these proved reserves was almost €63 billion. The calculation of this present value incorporated the future costs of extraction, production, and distribution activities but was based on current price levels, current tax rates, and a fixed discount rate of 10 percent. The company reported in its financial statements that "oil and gas reserves cannot be measured exactly since estimation of reserves involves subjective judgment and arbitrary determinations. Estimates remain subject to revision." In addition, Royal Dutch Shell assured that "a substantial but unknown proportion of future real cash flows from oil and gas production activities is expected to derive from reserves which have already been discovered but which cannot yet be regarded as proved."

On January 9, 2004, Royal Dutch Shell surprised investors with the announcement that its proved oil and gas reserves were about 20 percent smaller than it had previously disclosed. Specifically, the company reclassified 2.7 billion barrels of oil and natural gas liquids as well as 7.2 trillion standard cubic feet of natural gas as "probable but not proved." The estimated value of the reclassified reserves was close to €6 billion. The market value of Royal Dutch Shell decreased by 7.5 percent, or €10.6 billion, upon the announcement. In February and March, two exchange regulators, the U.S. Securities and Exchange Commission (SEC) and the U.K. Financial Services Authority (FSA), started their investigations into the matter. On April 30, 2004, the company's market value had decreased by 8.9 percent (adjusted for changes in the FTSE All-World Oil & Gas Price Index), or €12.6 billion since the day before the announcement. By that time, rating agency Standard & Poor's had also downgraded Royal Dutch Shell's debt from AAA to AA.

The lasting decline in Royal Dutch Shell's market value exceeded the present value of the change in the company's proved reserves. On April 30, 2004, the company had a price-earnings ratio of 7.6, which was substantially lower than the price-earnings ratios of its competitors, such as British Petroleum (12.1), Exxon Mobil (11.0), and Total (10.4). The market's negative response to the announcement contrasted with management's view on the matter. On April 19, 2004, management reported that they expected to "book nearly all of these volumes as proved over time, some 85 percent within the next decade." The question therefore arises whether the market was further discounting the reserves of Royal Dutch Shell and undervaluing the firm because the firm had lost some of its credibility. Before this can be concluded, a number of questions need to be answered:

■ What are the assumptions that analysts made when calculating the present value of Royal Dutch Shell's oil and gas reserves. Did they use lower discount rates? How did analysts value the discovered but unproved oil and gas reserves? Had analysts also revised their value estimates of unproved reserves?

■ Did analysts see the unexpected announcement as a confirmation of their concerns that the oil and gas industry experienced severe difficulties in replacing its reserves? Were analysts truly more pessimistic than management about the future profitability and riskiness of the oil and gas industry?

■ What was the value that analysts attached to the losses that potentially arose from penalties in lawsuits and settlements with exchange regulators? What was the value loss attributed to Standard & Poor's downgrading the company's debt?

■ What other events may explain the company's sudden drop in market value? The primary question for investors was probably the quality of the firm's reserve disclosures. However, management needs to have a deeper understanding of these issues.

■ If management believes that the firm is actually undervalued, what options are available to correct the market's view of the company?

COMMUNICATION THROUGH FINANCIAL REPORTING

Financial reports are the most popular format for management communication. Below we discuss the role of financial reporting as a means of investor communication, the institutions that make accounting information credible, and when it is likely to be ineffective.

Accounting as a means of management communication

As we discussed in Chapters 3 and 4, financial reports are an important medium for management communication with external investors. Reports provide investors with an explanation of how their money has been invested, a summary of the performance of those investments, and a discussion of how current performance fits within the firm's overall philosophy and strategy.

Accounting reports not only provide a record of past transactions, they also reflect management estimates and forecasts of the future. For example, they include estimates of bad debts, forecasts of the lives of tangible assets, and implicit forecasts that outlays will generate future cash flow benefits that exceed their cost. Since management is likely to be in a position to make forecasts of these future events that are more accurate than those of external investors, financial reports are a potentially useful way of communicating with investors. However, as discussed above, investors are also likely to be skeptical of reports prepared by management.

Factors that increase the credibility of accounting communication

A number of mechanisms mitigate conflicts of interest in financial reporting and increase the credibility of accounting information that is communicated to shareholders. These include accounting standards, auditing, monitoring of management by financial analysts, and management reputation.

Accounting standards and auditing

Accounting standards, such as those promulgated by the International Accounting Standards Board (IASB), provide guidelines for managers on how to make accounting decisions and provide outside investors with a way of interpreting these decisions. Uniform accounting standards attempt to reduce managers' ability to record similar economic transactions in different ways, either over time or across firms. Compliance with these standards is enforced by external auditors who attempt to ensure that managers' estimates are reasonable. Auditors therefore reduce the likelihood of earnings management.

Monitoring by financial analysts

Financial intermediaries such as analysts also limit management's ability to manage earnings. Financial analysts specialize in developing firm- and industry-specific knowledge, enabling them to assess the quality of a firm's reported numbers and to make any necessary adjustments. Analysts evaluate the appropriateness of management's forecasts implicit in accounting method choices and reported accruals. This requires a thorough understanding of the firm's business and the relevant accounting rules used in the preparation of its financial reports. Superior analysts adjust reported accrual numbers, if necessary, to reflect economic reality, perhaps by using the cash flow statement and the footnote disclosures.

Analysts' business and technical expertise as well as their legal liability and incentives differ from those of auditors. Consequently, analyst reports can provide information to investors on whether the firm's accounting decisions are appropriate or whether managers are overstating the firm's economic performance to protect their jobs.[7]

Management reputation

A third factor that can counteract external investors' natural skepticism about financial reporting is management reputation. Managers that expect to have an ongoing relationship with external investors and financial intermediaries may be able to build a track record for unbiased financial reporting. By making accounting estimates and judgments that are supported by subsequent performance, managers can demonstrate their competence and reliability to investors and analysts. As a result, managers' future judgments and accounting estimates are more likely to be viewed as credible sources of information.

Limitations of financial reporting for investor communication

While accounting standards, auditing, monitoring of management by financial analysts, and management concerns about its reputation increase the credibility and informativeness of financial reports, these mechanisms are far from perfect. Consequently there are times when financial reporting breaks down as a means for management to communicate with external investors. These breakdowns can arise when (1) there are no accounting rules to guide practice or the existing rules do not distinguish between poor and successful performers, (2) auditors and analysts do not have the expertise to judge new products or business opportunities, or (3) management faces credibility problems.

Accounting rule limitations

Despite the rapid increase in new accounting standards, accounting rules frequently do not distinguish between good and poor performers. For example, current accounting rules do not permit managers to show on their balance sheets in a timely fashion the benefits of investments in quality improvements, human resource development programs, research and development (with the exception of development expenditures of which the future benefits can be reliably measured), and customer service.

Some of the problems with accounting standards arise because it takes time for standard setters to develop appropriate standards for many new types of economic transactions. Other difficulties arise because standards are the result of compromises between different interest groups (e.g., auditors, investors, corporate managers, and regulators).

Auditor and analyst limitations

While auditors and analysts have access to proprietary information, they do not have the same understanding of the firm's business as managers. The divergence between managers' and auditors'/analysts' business assessments is likely to be most severe for firms with distinctive business strategies, or firms that operate in emerging industries. In addition, auditors' decisions in these circumstances are likely to be dominated by concerns about legal liability, hampering management's ability to use financial reports to communicate effectively with investors.

Finally, conflicts of interest faced by auditors and analysts make their analysis imperfect. Conflicts can potentially induce auditors to side with management to retain the audit, or to enable the audit firm to sell profitable non-audit services to the client. They can also arise for analysts who provide favorable ratings and research on companies to support investment banking services, or to increase trading volume among less informed investors.

Limited management credibility

When is management likely to face credibility problems with investors? There is very little evidence on this question. However, managers of new firms, firms with volatile earnings, firms in financial distress, and firms with poor track records in communicating with investors should expect to find it difficult to be seen as credible reporters.

If management has a credibility problem, financial reports are likely to be viewed with considerable skepticism. Investors will see financial reporting estimates that increase income as evidence that management is padding earnings. This makes it very difficult for management to use financial reports to communicate positive news about future performance.

Example: Accounting communication for Royal Dutch Shell

Royal Dutch Shell's key financial reporting estimates are for proved oil and gas reserves. The company makes these estimates using geological information about each reservoir, reservoir production histories, and reservoir pressure histories. The distinction between proved and unproved reserves is important. Accounting standards consider oil and gas reserves to be proved when the company has government and regulatory approval for the extraction of reserves and is able to bring the reserves quickly to the market in a commercially viable manner. Although Royal Dutch Shell discloses the size and present value of its proved reserves outside the financial statements instead of recording the reserves as an on-balance sheet asset, proved reserves estimates can affect net income. First, depreciation, depletion, and amortization of production plants are calculated using the unit-of-production method, where the expected production capacity is derived from the proved reserves. Second, the company capitalizes exploration drilling costs for one year, after which it chooses between continued capitalization and immediate amortization based on whether the exploration has successfully led to the booking of proved reserves. Third, the company recognizes provisions for the decommissioning of production facilities over the life of its proved reserves. Hence, despite the fact that the estimation of proved oil and gas reserves is a fairly subjective exercise, several important accounting choices are unavoidably based on the exercise's results. The inherent uncertainty of establishing proved oil and gas reserves thus also introduces substantial uncertainty into Royal Dutch Shell's income numbers. In addition, any attempt to distinguish proved from unproved reserves is bound to be artificial. Royal Dutch Shell repeatedly indicated that the reclassified reserves had been discovered and remained under the company's control, but only could not be brought to the market quickly enough to be classified as proved.

External auditors did not scrutinize the proved reserve disclosures as part of their annual audit. One reason why external auditors do not audit the reserves estimates is likely to be that they lack the expertise to do so. Some oil companies, especially those from the emerging markets, voluntarily hired outside experts to provide independent verification of reserves. This helped them to signal the accuracy of their estimates to outside investors and reduce potential information problems. In 2004, Royal Dutch Shell also decided to let outside experts certify the quality of its reserves disclosures. However, prior to 2004, this had not been its practice.

The overstatement of proved oil and gas reserves had likely impaired management credibility. To restore credibility, Royal Dutch Shell undertook the following steps:

- In March 2004, the current and the previous Managing Directors of Royal Dutch Shell's exploration and production unit stepped down from their positions. One month later, the company's Finance Director also resigned. These three directors were principally accountable for the overstatements of oil and gas reserves.

- Royal Dutch Shell abandoned its practice of evaluating business unit's performance and calculating managers' bonuses based on reserve bookings. Although the fraction of bonuses related to reserve bookings had been small, investors could have perceived this compensation practice as a potential cause of the reserves overstatements.

- Management concluded that there had been material weaknesses in the company's internal control procedures. To address these weaknesses, the company reviewed its global reserve portfolio, revised its guidelines for booking reserves, established a committee that should oversee the implementation of the reserves guidelines, and increased the independence of the internal auditor who was responsible for auditing the company's reserves. Management announced that "the controls we now have in place will be rigorously enforced and will be subject to far greater levels of scrutiny within Shell. Despite the difficulties of recent months Shell is a sound and profitable business. We are making the changes to our reserves practices to ensure that that remains the case."

- In October 2004, management decided to unify Royal Dutch Petroleum and Shell Transport and Trading under a single parent company, Royal Dutch Shell Plc. The combined company would have a single Board of Management. According to management the simplification of the board and company structure would improve managers' decision-making processes, accountability, and leadership.

KEY ANALYSIS QUESTIONS

For management interested in understanding how effectively the firm's financial reports help it communicate with outside investors, the following questions are likely to provide a useful starting point:

■ What are the key business risks that have to be managed effectively? What processes and controls are in place to manage these risks? How are the firm's key business risks reflected in the financial statements? For example, credit risks are reflected in the bad debt allowance, and product quality risks are reflected in allowances for product returns and the method of revenue recognition. For these types of risks, what message is the firm sending on the management of these risks through its estimates or choices of accounting methods? Has the firm been unable to deliver on the forecasts underlying these choices? Alternatively, does the market seem to be ignoring the message underlying the firm's financial reporting choices, indicating a lack of credibility?

■ How does the firm communicate about key risks that cannot be reflected in accounting estimates or methods? For example, if technological innovation risk is critical for a company, it is unable to reflect how well it is managing this risk through research and development in its financial statements. But investors will still have questions about this business issue.

OTHER FORMS OF COMMUNICATING WITH INVESTORS

Given the limitations of accounting standards, auditing, and monitoring by financial analysts, as well as the reporting credibility problems faced by management, firms that wish to communicate effectively with external investors are often forced to use alternative media. Below we discuss three alternative ways that managers can communicate with external investors and analysts: meetings with analysts to publicize the firm, expanded voluntary disclosure, and using financing policies to signal management expectations. These forms of communication are typically not mutually exclusive.

Analyst meetings

One popular way for managers to help mitigate communication problems is to meet regularly with financial analysts that follow the firm. At these meetings management will field questions about the firm's current financial performance as well as discuss its future business plans. In addition to holding analyst meetings, many firms appoint a director of public relations, who provides further regular contact with analysts seeking more information on the firm.

In the last ten years, conference calls have become a popular forum for management to communicate with financial analysts. Recent research finds that firms are more likely to host calls if they are in industries where financial statement data fail to capture key business fundamentals on a timely basis.[8] In addition, conference calls themselves appear to provide new information to analysts about a firm's performance and future prospects.[9]

While firms continue to meet with analysts, new rules, such as the E.U. Market Abuse Directive, have changed the nature of these interactions. Under these new rules, which became effective in 2004, all E.U. countries must have regulations and institutions in place that prevent unfair disclosure. Specifically, countries must ensure that exchange-listed companies disclose nonpublic private information promptly and simultaneously to all investors. This can reduce the information that managers are willing to disclose in conference calls and private meetings, making these less effective forums for resolving information problems.

Voluntary disclosure

Another way for managers to improve the credibility of their financial reporting is through voluntary disclosure. Accounting rules usually prescribe minimum disclosure requirements, but they do not restrict managers from voluntarily providing additional information. These could include an articulation of the company's long-term strategy, specification of nonfinancial leading indicators that are useful in judging the effectiveness of the strategy implementation, explanation of the relationship between the leading indicators and future profits, and forecasts of future performance. Voluntary disclosures can be reported in the firm's annual report, in brochures created to describe the firm to investors, in management meetings with analysts, or in investor relations responses to information requests.[10]

One constraint on expanded disclosure is the competitive dynamics in product markets. Disclosure of proprietary information on strategies and their expected economic consequences may hurt the firm's competitive position. Managers then face a trade-off between providing information that is useful to investors in assessing the firm's economic performance, and withholding information to maximize the firm's product market advantage.

A second constraint in providing voluntary disclosure is management's legal liability. Forecasts and voluntary disclosures can potentially be used by dissatisfied shareholders to bring civil actions against management for providing misleading information. This seems ironic, since voluntary disclosures should provide investors with additional information. Unfortunately, it can be difficult for courts to decide whether managers' disclosures were good-faith estimates of uncertain future events which later did not materialize, or whether management manipulated the market. Consequently many corporate legal departments recommend against management providing much in the way of voluntary disclosure.

Finally, management credibility can limit a firm's incentives to provide voluntary disclosures. If management faces a credibility problem in financial reporting, any voluntary disclosures it provides are also likely to be viewed skeptically. In particular, investors may be concerned about what management is not telling them, particularly since such disclosures are not audited.

Selected financial policies

Managers can also use financing policies to communicate effectively with external investors. Financial policies that are useful in this respect include dividend payouts, share repurchases, financing choices, and hedging strategies. One important difference between this type of communication and additional disclosure is that the firm does not provide potentially proprietary information to competitors. The signal therefore indicates to competitors that a firm's management is bullish on its future, but it does not provide any details.

Dividend payout policies

As we discussed in Chapter 12, a firm's cash payout decisions can provide information to investors on managers' assessments of the firm's future prospects. This arises because dividend payouts tend to be sticky, in the sense that managers are reluctant to cut dividends. Thus, managers will only increase dividends when they are confident that they will be able to sustain the increased rate in future years. Consequently, investors interpret dividend increases as signals of managers' confidence in the quality of current and future earnings.[11]

Share repurchases

In some countries, such as the U.S. and the U.K., managers can use share repurchases to communicate with external investors. Under a share repurchase, the firm buys back its own shares, either through a purchase on the open market, through a tender offer, or through a negotiated purchase with a large shareholder. Of course a share repurchase, particularly a tender offer repurchase, is an expensive way for management to communicate with outside investors. Firms typically pay a hefty premium to acquire their shares in tender offer repurchases, potentially diluting the value of the shares that are not tendered or not accepted for tender. In addition, the fees to investment banks, lawyers, and share solicitation fees are not trivial. Given these costs, it is not surprising that research findings indicate that share repurchases are effective signals to investors about the level and risk of future earnings performance.[12] Research findings also suggest that firms that use share repurchases to communicate with investors have accounting assets that reflect less of firm value and have high general information asymmetry.[13]

Financing choices

Firms that have problems communicating with external investors may be able to use financing choices to reduce them. For example, a firm that is unwilling to provide proprietary information to help dispersed public investors value it may be willing to provide such information to a knowledgeable private investor – which can become a large shareholder/creditor – or a bank that agrees to provide the company with a significant new loan. A firm with credibility problems in financial reporting can sell shares or issue debt to an informed private investor such as a large customer who has superior information about the quality of its product or service.

Such changes in financing and ownership can mitigate communication problems in two ways. First, the terms of the new financing arrangement and the credibility of the new lender or shareholder can provide investors with information to reassess the value of the firm. Second, the accompanying increased concentration of ownership and the role of large block holders in corporate governance can have a positive effect on valuation. If investors are concerned about management's incentives to increase shareholder value, the presence of a new block shareholder or significant creditor on the board can be reassuring. This type of monitoring arises in leveraged buyouts, start-ups backed by venture capital firms, and in firms with equity partnership investments. In Japanese and German corporations, it may also arise because large banks own both debt and equity and have close working relationships with firms' managers.

Of course, in the extreme, management can decide that the best option for a firm is to no longer operate as a public company. This can be accomplished by a management buyout, where a buyout group (including management) leverages its own investment (using bank or public debt finance), buys the firm, and takes it private. The buyout group hopes to run the firm for several years and then take the company public again, hopefully with a track record of improved performance that enables investors to value the firm more effectively.

Hedging

An important source of mispricing arises if investors are unable to distinguish between unexpected changes in reported earnings due to management performance and transitory shocks that are beyond managers' control (e.g., foreign currency translation gains and losses). Managers can counteract these effects by hedging such "accounting" risks. Even though hedging is costly, it may be valuable if it reduces information problems that potentially lead to misvaluation.

Example: Other communications for Royal Dutch Shell

During the first half of the 2000s, the strong rise in crude oil prices had had a significantly positive impact on oil companies' profits and free cash flows. Because of a lack of investment opportunities and to restrict management from investing in unprofitable projects, oil companies frequently repurchased shares from their investors or paid out special dividends. In fiscal years 2001 and 2002, Royal Dutch Petroleum and Shell Transport and Trading both had repurchased 2.8 percent of their outstanding shares. In 2003, no shares were repurchased. On April 29, 2004, Royal Dutch Shell announced that it would immediately relaunch its share repurchase program. The company would return close to €1.4 billion to its shareholders in 2004 and €3.6 billion in 2005.

KEY ANALYSIS QUESTIONS

For management considering whether to use financing policies to communicate more effectively with investors, the following questions are likely to provide a useful starting point for analysis:

- Have other potentially less costly actions, such as expanded disclosure or accounting communication, been considered? If not, would these alternatives provide a lower cost means of communication? Alternatively, if management is concerned about providing proprietary information to competitors, or has low credibility, these alternatives may not be effective.

- Does the firm have sufficient free cash flow to be able to implement a share repurchase program or to increase dividends? If so, these may be feasible options. If the firm has excess cash available today but expects to be constrained in the future, a share repurchase may be more effective. Alternatively, if management expects to have some excess cash available each year, a dividend increase may be in order.

- Is the firm cash constrained and unable to increase disclosure for proprietary reasons? If so, management may want to consider changing the mix of owners as a way of indicating to investors that another informed outsider is bullish on the company. Of course another possibility is for management itself to increase its stake in the company.

AUDITOR ANALYSIS

In Europe, the auditor is responsible for providing investors with assurance that the financial statements are prepared in accordance with an identified set of accounting standards, such as IFRS. This requires the auditor to evaluate whether transactions are recorded in a way that is consistent with the rules produced by regulators (including the IASB and local exchange regulators) and whether management estimates reflected in the financial statements are reasonable. However, audits are required to not only assess whether the financial statements are prepared in accordance with IFRS, but also to judge whether they fairly reflect the client's underlying economic performance. This additional requirement is explicitly mentioned in the Fourth E.U. Company Law Directive, which regulates firms' financial reporting within the E.U., as well as in International Accounting Standard 1.[14] IAS 1 requires "an entity, in extremely rare circumstances in which management concludes that compliance with a requirement in a Standard or an Interpretation would be so misleading that it would conflict with the objective of financial statements…, to depart from the requirement unless departure is prohibited by the relevant regulatory framework." This additional assurance requires more judgment on the part of the auditor but also increases the value of the audit to outside investors.

The results of the audit are disclosed in the audit report, which is part of the financial statements. If the firm's financial statements conform to the IFRSs and give a true and fair view of the assets, liabilities, and performance, the auditor issues an unqualified report. However, if the financials do not conform to the IFRSs or unfairly present the firm's financial position, the auditor is required to issue a qualified or an adverse report that provides information to investors on the discrepancies. Finally, if the auditor is uncertain about whether the firm can survive during the coming year, a going concern report is issued that points out the firm's survival risks.

The key procedures involved in a typical audit include (1) understanding the client's business and industry to identify key risks for the audit, (2) evaluating the firm's internal control system to assess whether it is likely to produce reliable information, (3) performing preliminary analytic procedures to identify unusual events and possible errors, and (4) collecting specific evidence on controls, transactions, and account balance details to form the basis for the auditor's opinion. In most cases client management is willing to respond to issues raised by the audit to ensure that the company receives an unqualified audit opinion. Once the audit is completed, the auditor presents a summary of audit scope and findings to the firm's audit committee.

It is worth noting that the audit is not intended to detect fraud. Of course in some cases it may do so, but that is not its purpose. The detection of fraud is the domain of the internal audit.

Challenges facing audit industry

During the 1980s and 1990s, the large audit firms in some European countries started to develop more and more consulting services because they decided that the profit margins on regular audits were too thin in a world of standardized audits. This diversification strategy deflected top management energy and partner talent from the audit side of the business to the more profitable consulting part. In addition, the audit firms were sometimes aggressively pursuing a high volume strategy, and so audit partner compensation and promotion became more closely linked to a cordial relationship with top management that attracted new audit clients and retained existing clients. This made it difficult for partners to be effective watchdogs.

In the early 2000s, the accounting debacles of companies like Ahold, Enron, and Parmalat, made regulators and users of financial statements question the independence of auditors from their clients and the quality of the audit. Since then, several regulatory changes have been passed to correct the structural problems facing the industry. In the E.U., the revised Eighth Company Law Directive has forced member countries to implement changes in their national regulations to improve auditor independence and audit quality. The Directive has set minimum educational qualifications for admission to the profession and requires European auditors to participate in continuing professional development programs. All audits must be carried out in accordance with the International Auditing Standards (ISA), as promulgated by the International Auditing and Assurance Standards Board (IAASB) and endorsed by the E.U. This requirement should standardize the quality of audits across the E.U. Furthermore, the Directive prescribes that the external auditor does not provide any non-audit services to the audited company if this may compromise his independence. To maintain independence, the auditor (the person, not the firm) must also not audit the same company for more than five consecutive years. To enforce these rules, every E.U. country must install a public oversight system. These requirements are all likely to improve the dynamics of the audit industry.

Role of financial analysis tools for auditing

How can the financial analysis tools discussed in this book be used by audit professionals? The four steps in financial analysis are strategy analysis, accounting analysis, financial analysis, and prospective analysis. We discuss how each of these is relevant to the audit.

Strategy analysis

One of the fundamental challenges facing auditors is how to narrow the scope of their work. Large corporations undertake millions of transactions each year. It is not possible for any audit to review all of these. So the auditor has to decide where to focus attention and time.

Strategy analysis can help identify those few key areas of the business that are critical to the organization's survival and future success. These are the areas that investors want to understand so that they can evaluate the firm's value proposition and how well it is managing key success factors. They are also likely to be areas worth further testing and analysis by the auditor, to assess their impact on the financial statements. For example, the key success factor for a conglomerate that pursues a strategy of acquisitions in a variety of industries is managing acquisitions. The key success factor for a financial services firm is managing loan risks, and the key risk for a pharmaceutical firm is its research and development.

Strategy analysis is critical to the first stage of the audit, understanding the client's business, industry, and risks. It is important that the auditor develop the expertise to be able to identify the one or two key risks facing their clients.

Accounting analysis

For the auditor, accounting analysis involves two steps. First, the auditor must understand how the key success factors and risks are reflected in the financial statements. For the conglomerate, for example, they are reflected in the valuation of goodwill. If the conglomerate fails to manage its acquisitions successfully, it will have to take a write-down of goodwill. For financial services companies the key success factors and risks are reflected in the provision for loan losses. If a firm fails to manage its loan process properly, it will begin making loans to more risky clients, leading to higher future default rates and requiring higher loan loss estimates. In contrast, for a pharmaceutical firm, accounting rules treat its key success factor, product development, in a mechanical way by requiring that it expense most R&D outlays when they are incurred. While this probably makes the audit easier to perform, it implies that the pharmaceutical firm's financial statements are not a very timely source of information on the company's research activities, and the auditor's service is less valuable. Firm management will have to use other ways of providing credible information to investors on its research.

The second step in accounting analysis is for the auditor to evaluate management judgment reflected in the key financial statements items. For example, for a financial services company where provisions for loan losses are critical, the auditor will need to design tests and collect evidence to evaluate management's forecasts of future loan losses implicit in the provision. The auditor must assess whether these forecasts are reasonable given the company's historical performance, the current economic climate, and the credit review and collection process in place in the firm. For a conglomerate where goodwill valuations are critical, the auditor must judge whether the current performance of acquired companies meets forecasts made by management at the time of the acquisition and is reflected in the price that the conglomerate paid for the target.

Financial analysis

Auditors use financial ratio analysis as part of their analytic review. Financial ratios help auditors judge whether there are any unusual performance changes for their client, either relative to past performance or relative to their competitors. Such changes merit further investigation to ensure that the reasons for the change can be fully explained, and to determine what additional tests are required to satisfy the auditor that the reported changes in performance are justified.

For example, financial ratio analysis of U.S.-based WorldCom's financial performance should have revealed a significant decline in the company's cost structure that was not matched by any of its competitors. Such analysis should have been a red flag for the auditor that prompted a detailed examination of WorldCom's costs and capitalization policies, and might have led the auditor to detect the massive fraudulent change in capitalization of network costs at WorldCom.

Careful ratio analysis can also reveal whether clients are facing business problems that might induce management to conceal losses or keep key obligations off the balance sheet. Such information should alert auditors that extra care and additional detailed tests are likely to be required to reach a conclusion on the client's financial statements.

Prospective analysis

Auditors use prospective analysis to assess whether estimates and forecasts made by management are consistent with the firm's economic position. They typically do not concern themselves with the equity market's valuation of their client. Yet there is valuable information for auditors in the market's valuation. The market's perception of a client's future performance provides a useful benchmark for affirming or disconfirming the auditor's assessment of the client's prospects. If the auditor reaches a different conclusion about a client than the market, it is worth exploring reasons for the differences. Is the client failing to disclose some critical information known to the auditor? Or is the auditor too optimistic or pessimistic?

If the auditor concludes that the market is overly optimistic about a client, is additional disclosure required to help investors get a more realistic view of the company's prospects? Are the estimates and forecasts made by management in preparing the financial statements realistic, or do they seek to avoid disappointing the market?

Alternatively, if the auditors decide that the market is overly pessimistic about their client's prospects, what additional information, if any, can be disclosed to increase transparency? Is the company too conservative in its financial statement estimates and forecasts?

KEY ANALYSIS QUESTIONS

The following questions are likely to provide a useful starting point for auditors in their analysis of a client's financial statements:

- What are the key business risks facing the firm? How well are these risks managed?

- What are the key accounting policies and estimates that reflect the firm's key risks? What tests and evidence are required to evaluate management judgment that is reflected in these accounting decisions?

- Do key ratios indicate any unusual changes in client performance? What tests and evidence are required to understand the causes of such changes?

- Has firm performance deteriorated, creating pressure on management to manage earnings or record off-balance sheet transactions? If so, what additional tests and evidence are required to provide assurance that the financial statements are consistent with GAAP and fairly represent the firm's financial position?

- How is the market assessing the client's prospects? If different from the auditor, what is the reason for the difference? If the market is overly optimistic or pessimistic, are there implications for client disclosure or accounting estimates?

Example: Auditing Royal Dutch Shell

For Royal Dutch Shell, how well the company manages its oil and gas reserves is one of its most critical success factors. Surprisingly, in 2004 regulators did not require oil companies to have their oil and gas reserves reviewed by an independent auditor. Some oil companies had their reserves voluntarily reviewed but Royal Dutch Shell only started to do that in 2004, after an internal investigative report advised it to do so.

The auditor most likely lacks the expertise to closely scrutinize the quality of the oil company's reserves estimates. Nonetheless, because the estimates of proved reserves also affect Royal Dutch Shell's accounting numbers, the auditor could at least ask the following questions:

- Are there any unusual changes in the speed with which the company replaces its currently extracted reserves? If so, does the change reflect a change in the scope of the company's exploration or extraction activities?

- Does the change reflect excessive overstatement of reserves by the client in earlier periods? If so, why did the auditors approve this earlier policy? Why did management select this year to revise those estimates?

- Is the change in reserve estimates justifiable, or is management simply responding to pressure to meet unrealistic market expectations?
- What information is available about the size of reserves and which procedures are followed to produce such information? Are geological reports, production histories, and pressure histories for each reservoir produced using reliable procedures? Which internal control procedures are in place to minimize the possibility that reserves estimates are managed?
- Does the company have the necessary regulatory approvals for the extraction of its proved reserves? Is there any reason to question the commercial viability of pending extraction activities?
- If the change in reserves estimates appears to be reasonable, what additional information can the firm provide to investors to address their concerns? Will this information need to be audited?

AUDIT COMMITTEE REVIEWS

Audit committees are responsible for overseeing the work of the auditor, for ensuring that the financial statements are properly prepared, and for reviewing the internal controls at the company. Audit committees, which are mandated by many stock exchanges as well as the E.U. Eighth Company Law Directive, typically comprise three to four outside directors or Supervisory Board member who meet regularly before or after their full board meetings.

According to the Eighth Directive, the audit committee monitors the company's reporting process and internal audit and control procedures. Next to overseeing the auditor's work, the audit committee must make sure that the auditor acts with independence from management. Finally, the audit committee makes a selection of auditors at the time that an auditor must be appointed.

In the U.S., stricter audit committee requirements have been created after the collapse of Enron. In 1999, the SEC, the national stock exchange(s), and the Auditing Standards Board issued new audit committee rules that defined best practices for judging audit committee members' independence and their qualifications. The Sarbanes-Oxley Act of 2002 further required that audit committees take formal responsibility for appointing, overseeing, and negotiating fees with external auditors. Audit committee members are required to be independent directors with no consulting or other potentially compromising relationship to management. It is recommended that at least one member of the committee have financial expertise, such as being a Finance or Managing Director, or being a retired audit partner.

Ideally the audit committee is expected to be independent of management and to take an active role in reviewing the propriety of the firm's financial statements. Committee members are expected to question management and the auditors about the quality of the firm's financial reporting, the scope and findings of the external audit, and the quality of internal controls.

In reality, however, the audit committee has to rely extensively on information from management as well as internal and external auditors. Given the ground that it has to cover, its limited available time, and the technical nature of accounting standards, audit committees are not in a position to catch management fraud or auditors' failures on a timely basis.

How then can the audit committee add value?[15] We believe that many of the financial analysis tools discussed in this book can provide a useful way for audit committees to approach their tasks. Many of the applications of the financial analysis steps discussed for auditors also apply for audit committees.

In its scrutiny of financial statements, the committee should use the 80–20 rule, devoting most of its time to assessing the effectiveness of those *few* policies and decisions that have the *most* impact on investors' perceptions of the company's critical performance indicators. This should not require any additional work for committee members, since they should already have a good understanding of the firm's key success factors and risks from discussions of the full Board.

Audit committee members should also have sufficient financial background to identify where in the financial statements the key risks are reflected. Their discussions with management and external auditors should focus on these risks. How well are they being managed? How are the auditors planning their work to focus on these areas? What evidence have they gathered to judge the adequacy of key financial statement estimates?

The audit committee also receives regular reviews of company performance from management as part of their regular Board duties. Committee members should be especially proactive in requesting information that helps them evaluate how the firm is managing its key risks, since this information can also help them judge the quality of the financial statements. Audit committee members need to ask: Is information on company performance we are receiving in our regular Board meetings consistent with the picture portrayed in the financial statements? If not, what is missing? Are additional disclosures required to ensure that investors are well informed about the firm's operations and performance?

Finally, audit committees need to focus on capital market expectations, not just statutory financial reports. In today's capital markets, the game begins when companies set expectations via analyst meetings, press releases, and other forms of investor communications. Indeed, the pressure to manage earnings is often a direct consequence of investors' unrealistic expectations, either deliberately created by management or sustained by their inaction. Thus it is also important for audit committees to oversee the firm's investor relations strategy and ensure that management sets realistic expectations for both the short and long term.

Example: Royal Dutch Shell's audit committee

Royal Dutch Shell had established an audit committee in 1976. The audit committee advised both the Supervisory Board of Royal Dutch and the Board of Directors of Shell.[16] Royal Dutch Shell reported that its audit committee frequently assessed the effectiveness of the company's internal control procedures and risk management processes. The committee further evaluated internal and external audit reports and assessed the performance of the internal and external audits. The Supervisory Board of Royal Dutch and the Board of Directors of Shell each had three members on the audit committee. In 2004, the audit committee met 23 times, compared with six times in 2003. The substantial increase in the number of meetings highlights the important role that the committee played during Royal Dutch Shell's reporting crisis.

Following the announcement of Royal Dutch Shell on January 9, 2004, the company's audit committee appointed an independent law firm to perform an investigation into the facts that had given rise to the reclassification. One of the recommendations that were made by the report was that in the future, the internal auditor who was responsible for the audit of the oil and gas reserves estimates should report directly to the Internal Audit Department, which, in turn, should report directly to the audit committee. This communication structure ensured that the audit committee gained better and timelier access to crucial information about the company's reserves estimates. In addition, the report recommended that the frequency and depth of internal reserves audits be increased.

KEY ANALYSIS QUESTIONS °

The following questions are likely to provide a useful starting point for audit committees in their discussions with management and auditors over the firm's financial statements:

- How are the key business risks facing the firm reflected in its financial statements? How are these risks being managed?

- How are the firm's key risks reflected in the financial statements – what are the key accounting policies and estimates? What was the basis for the external auditor's assessment of these items?

- Is information on the key value drivers and firm performance presented to the full Board consistent with the picture of the firm reflected in the financial statements and Management Report?

- What expectations are management creating in the capital market? Are these likely to create undue pressure to manage earnings?

SUMMARY

This chapter discussed how many of the financial analysis tools developed in Chapters 2 through 8 can be used by managers to develop a coherent disclosure strategy, and by Corporate Board members and external auditors to improve the quality of their work.

By communicating effectively with investors, management can potentially reduce information problems for outside investors, lowering the likelihood that the shares will be mispriced or unnecessarily volatile. This can be important for firms that wish to raise new capital, avoid takeovers, or whose management is concerned that its true job performance is not reflected in the firm's shares.

The typical way for firms to communicate with investors is through financial reporting. Accounting standards and auditing make the reporting process a way for managers to not only provide information about the firm's current performance, but to indicate, through accounting estimates, where they believe the firm is headed in the future. However, financial reports are not always able to convey the types of forward-looking information that investors need. Accounting standards sometimes do not permit firms to capitalize outlays, such as research expenditures, that provide significant future benefits to the firm.

A second way that management can communicate with investors is through nonaccounting means. We discussed several such mechanisms, including meeting with financial analysts to explain the firm's strategy, current performance, and outlook; disclosing additional information, both quantitative and qualitative, to provide investors with similar information as management's; and using financial policies (such as share repurchases, dividend increases, and hedging) to help signal management's optimism about the firm's future performance.

In this chapter we have stressed the importance of communicating effectively with investors. But firms also have to communicate with other stakeholders, including employees, customers, suppliers, and regulatory bodies. Many of the same principles discussed here can also be applied to management communication with these other stakeholders.

Finally, we examined the capital market role of governance agents, such as external auditors and audit committees. Both have recently faced considerable public scrutiny following a spate of financial reporting meltdowns in Europe and the U.S. Much has been done to improve the governance and independence of these intermediaries. We focus on how the financial analysis tools developed in the book can be used to improve the quality of audit and audit committee work. The tools of strategy analysis, accounting analysis, financial analysis, and prospective analysis can help auditors and audit committee members to identify the key issues in the financial statements to focus on and provide commonsense ways of assessing whether there are potential reporting problems that merit additional testing and analysis.

DISCUSSION QUESTIONS

1. In December 2004, Denmark-based Danske Bank experienced a share price decline of 6 percent upon its announcement that it planned to acquire the Irish bank National Europe Holdings. The Danish bank's Finance Director explained that "the market perception of us changed from being a high-yield equity story, because we'd been paying a huge amount of dividends and doing massive share buybacks, to being a growth-oriented, cross-border story." What actions could the Finance Director take to restore investor confidence?

2. a. What are likely to be the long-term critical success factors for the following types of firms?
   - A high technology company, such as semiconductor equipment maker ASM Lithography.
   - A large, low-cost retailer such as Aldi.

   b. How useful is financial accounting data for evaluating how well these two companies are managing their critical success factors? What other types of information would be useful in your evaluation? What are the costs and benefits to these companies from disclosing this type of information to investors?

3. The International Financial Reporting Standards permit management to revalue fixed assets that have increased in value. Revaluations are typically based on estimates of realizable value made by management or independent valuers. Do you expect that these accounting standards will make earnings and book values more or less useful to investors? Explain why or why not. How can management make these types of disclosures more credible?

4. Under a management buyout, the top management of a firm offers to buy the company from its shareholders, usually at a premium over its current share price. The management team puts up its own capital to finance the acquisition, with additional financing typically coming from a private buyout firm and private debt. If management is interested in making such an offer for its firm in the near future, what are its financial reporting incentives? How do these differ from the incentives of management that are not interested in a buyout? How would you respond

to a proposed management buyout if you were the firm's auditor? What about if you were a member of the audit committee?

5. You are approached by the management of a small start-up company that is planning to go public. The founders are unsure about how aggressive they should be in their accounting decisions as they come to the market. The Managing Director, asserts, "We might as well take full advantage of any discretion offered by accounting rules, since the market will be expecting us to do so." What are the pros and cons of this strategy? As the partner of a major audit firm, what type of analysis would you perform before deciding to take on a new start-up that is planning to go public?

6. Two years after a successful public offering, the Managing Director of a biotechnology company is concerned about equity market uncertainty surrounding the potential of new drugs in the development pipeline. In his discussion with you, the Managing Director notes that even though they have recently made significant progress in their internal R&D efforts, the shares have performed poorly. What options does he have to help convince investors of the value of the new products? Which of these options are likely to be feasible?

7. Why might the Managing Director of the biotechnology firm discussed in Question 6 be concerned about the firm being undervalued? Would the Managing Director be equally concerned if the shares were overvalued? Do you believe that the Managing Director would attempt to correct the market's perception in this overvaluation case? How would you react to company concern about market undervaluation or overvaluation if you were the firm's auditor? Or if you were a member of the audit committee?

8. When companies decide to shift from private to public financing by making an initial public offering for their shares, they are likely to face increased costs of investor communications. Given this additional cost, why would firms opt to go public?

9. In some Continental European countries firms are traditionally financed by banks, which have representatives on the companies' Boards. How would communication challenges differ for these firms relative to U.K. firms, which rely more on public financing?

NOTES

1. M. Jensen and W. Meckling, "Theory of the Firm: Managerial Behavior, Agency Costs, and Capital Structure," *Journal of Financial Economics* 3 (October 1976): 305–360, analyzed agency problems between managers and outside investors. Subsequent work by B. Holmstrom and others examined how contracts between managers and outside investors could mitigate the agency problem.
2. Kevin J. Murphy and Jerold L. Zimmerman, "Financial Performance Surrounding CEO Turnover," *Journal of Accounting and Economics* 16 (January/April/July 1993): 273–315, find a strong relation between CEO turnover and earnings-based performance.
3. See S. Teoh, I. Welch, and T. Wong, "Earnings Management and the Long-Run Market Performance of Initial Public Offerings, *The Journal of Finance* 63 (December 1998): 1935–1974, S. Teoh, I. Welch, and T. Wong, "Earnings Management and the Underperformance of Seasoned Equity Offerings," *Journal of Financial Economics* 50 (October 1998): 63–99, and L. Shivakumar, "Do Firms Mislead Investors by Overstating Earnings Before Seasoned Equity

Offerings?," *Journal of Accounting and Economics* 29 (June 2000): 339–371. The latter study explains why managers may overstate earnings prior to seasoned equity offerings despite the possibility that rational investors undo such earnings management.

4. This market imperfection is often referred to as a "lemons" or "information" problem. It was first discussed by G. Akerlof in relation to the used car market (see "The Market for 'Lemons': Quality Uncertainty and the Market Mechanism," *Quarterly Journal of Economics* 90 (1970): 629–650. Akerlof recognized that the seller of a used car knew more about the car's value than the buyer. This meant that the buyer was likely to end up overpaying, since the seller would accept any offer that exceeded the car's true value and reject any lower offer. Car buyers recognized this problem and would respond by only making low-ball offers for used cars, leading sellers with high quality cars to exit the market. As a result, only the lowest quality cars (the "lemons") would remain in the market. Akerlof pointed out that qualified independent mechanics could correct this market breakdown by providing buyers with reliable information on a used car's true value.

5. Of course, improved analysis alone is unlikely to be sufficient to improve market intermediation if the structural reforms implemented by the Eighth E.U. Directive, the Sarbanes-Oxley Act, and the stock exchanges fail to correct the serious conflicts of interest for intermediaries that we have witnessed in the past few years.

6. Douglas J. Skinner, "Earnings Disclosures and Stockholder Lawsuits," *Journal of Accounting and Economics* (November 1997): 249–283, finds that firms with bad earnings news tend to predisclose this information, perhaps to reduce the cost of litigation that inevitably follows bad news quarters.

7. For example, G. Foster, "Briloff and the Capital Market," *Journal of Accounting Research* 17, no. 1 (Spring 1979): 262–274, finds firms that are criticized for their accounting by Abraham J. Briloff on average suffer an 8 percent decline in their share price.

8. See Sarah Tasker, "Bridging the Information Gap: Quarterly Conference Calls as a Medium for Voluntary Disclosure," *Review of Accounting Studies* 3, no. 1–2 (1998): 137–167.

9. See Richard Frankel, Marilyn Johnson, and Douglas Skinner, "An Empirical Examination of Conference Calls as a Voluntary Disclosure Medium," *Journal of Accounting Research* 37, no. 1 (Spring 1999): 133–150.

10. Recent research on voluntary disclosure includes Mark Lang and Russell Lundholm, "Cross-Sectional Determinants of Analysts' Ratings of Corporate Disclosures," *Journal of Accounting Research* 31 (Autumn 1993): 246–271; Lang and Lundholm, "Corporate Disclosure Policy and Analysts," *The Accounting Review* 71 (October 1996): 467–492; M. Welker, "Disclosure Policy, Information Asymmetry and Liquidity in Equity Markets," *Contemporary Accounting Research* (Spring 1995); Christine Botosan, "The Impact of Annual Report Disclosure Level on Investor Base and the Cost of Capital," *The Accounting Review* (July 1997): 323–350; and Paul Healy, Amy Hutton, and Krishna Palepu, "Stock Performance and Intermediation Changes Surrounding Sustained Increases in Disclosure," *Contemporary Accounting Research* 16, no. 3 (Fall 1999): 485–521. This research finds that firms are more likely to provide high levels of disclosure if they have strong earnings performance, issue securities, have more analyst following, and have less dispersion in analyst forecasts. In addition, firms with high levels of disclosure policies tend to have a lower cost of capital and bid-ask spread. Finally, firms that increase disclosure have accompanying increases in stock returns, institutional ownership, analyst following, and share liquidity. In "The Role of Supplementary Statements with Management's Earnings Forecasts," working paper, Harvard Business School, 2003, A. Hutton, G. Miller, and D. Skinner examine the market response to management earnings forecasts and · find that bad news forecasts are always informative but that good news forecasts are informative only when they are supported by verifiable forward-looking statements.

11. Findings by Paul Healy and Krishna Palepu in "Earnings Information Conveyed by Dividend Initiations and Omissions," *Journal of Financial Economics* 21 (1988): 149–175, indicate that investors interpret announcements of dividend initiations and omissions as managers' forecasts of future earnings performance.

12. See Larry Dann, Ronald Masulis, and David Mayers, "Repurchase Tender Offers and Earnings Information," *Journal of Accounting and Economics* (September 1991): 217–252, and Michael Hertzel and Prem Jain, "Earnings and Risk Changes Around Stock Repurchases," *Journal of Accounting and Economics* (September 1991): 253–276.

13. See Mary Barth and Ron Kasznik, "Share Repurchases and Intangible Assets," *Journal of Accounting and Economics* 28 (December 1999): 211–241.

14. The actual wording of the Fourth E.U. Directive is that financial statements "shall give a true and fair view of the company's assets, liabilities, financial position and results." This provision in the Fourth Directive has, however, not been equally accepted by all E.U. member states and has influenced accounting especially in Denmark, the Netherlands, and the U.K. For a discussion of the impact of the "true and fair view" provision on European accounting, see the *European Accounting Review*, Volume 6, Issue 4, 1997. The coming years will show whether and how the "true and fair view" provision in IAS 1 will affect European accounting practices.

15. See P. Healy and K. Palepu, "Audit the Audit Committees: After Enron Boards Must Change the Focus and Provide Greater Financial Transparency," *Financial Times,* June 10, 2002, p. 14.

16. Royal Dutch and Shell had different governance structures. Royal Dutch had a two-tier board structure in which the Supervisory Board monitored the Management Board. Shell had a one-tier board structure in which outside directors monitored the inside directors, but in which outside and inside directors were members of one and the same Board of Directors.

Investor relations at Total

Jérôme Schmitt knew not to surprise. As head of Investor Relations (IR) at Total, the world's fourth largest publicly-traded oil and gas company and France's flagship enterprise, he had seen first-hand how fast the financial markets and the company's many other stakeholders could change their views of Total based on unexpected news. It was the fundamental task of the IR-group, though, to maintain long-term relationships with investors and avoid short-term sensibilities.

As an integrated oil and gas company, Total was involved both in exploration and production as well as in refining, shipping and marketing. Present in over 130 countries, the company produced oil and gas in 27 countries,[1] ran 28 refineries worldwide[2] and managed over 16,000 gas stations – and the nature and mere size of its operations made Total a natural focal point for many interested parties. Providing pertinent information to such a diverse group – consisting of employees, investors (both institutional and individual), customers, partners, environmentalists, governments and the general public, especially in the company's home market France – complicated Total's communication approach, especially as the groups all called for different types of information. Still, the communication had to be consistent. "It is the same story we have to tell everyone," said Schmitt.

Total believed it had a successful communication policy based on being consistent and on never over-promising. In September 2005, however, the system was being put to the test. While Total wanted to save money and create buffers against future bad times – against increasing oil prices and to ensure that the French corporate beacon did not become a take-over target – it also showed a €5.8 billion profit for the first half year 2005.[3] Telling the public both about strong earnings and about a need to save made for a complex communication situation; especially within the socio-political context in France, where Total employed half of its 110,000 employees. Total received further media attention when France's finance minister on September 9 announced that he would hit the oil majors with extra taxation unless they increased refining capabilities and cut petrol prices in France. The executive management, Schmitt and his IR team had some communication challenges ahead of them.

Total: The company, its history and its communication

Total was founded in 1924 as Compagnie Française des Pétroles (CFP) on initiative from the French president and in order for France to develop an oil industry. With no domestic oil reserves, CFP immediately ventured abroad, using a stake that the French state had in a Turkish petroleum company. CFP also set about opening new oil production fields, starting 1927 in Iraq, and grew both in scope (adding refining, transporting and marketing) and geographical size (prospecting in places such as

Professor Gregory S. Miller, Executive Director of the HBS Europe Research Center, Vincent Dessain, and Research Associate Anders Sjöman prepared this case. HBS cases are developed solely as the basis for class discussion. Cases are not intended to serve as endorsements, sources of primary data, or illustrations of effective or ineffective management. Copyright © 2005 President and Fellows of Harvard College. HBS Case 9–106–023.

Venezuela, Algeria, Indonesia and the North Sea.) The word "Total", which originally was a brand introduced in 1954, became part of the company name in 1985 and the sole moniker in 1991. That year, Total listed ADRs (American Depository Receipts) on the New York Stock Exchange. Said CFO Robert Castaigne,

> *1991 in a way marks the beginning of our financial communication. We were still unknown in the U.S. and U.K. We were a relatively small company, which had to set large targets and establish a "capital of trust" with the financial community.*

Listed on the French stock exchange since 1929, CFP's main shareholder for many years was the French state. However, the government sold off large parts of its holdings in the mid-1990s to hold less than 1% (and later divested this remaining interest in 1998). Also in the mid-1990s, Total was reorganized by then CEO Serge Tchuruk, who wanted to turn a bureaucratically run company into a world oil major. Said Castaigne, "Tchuruk woke up the company and brought new impetus." Tchuruk was in turn succeeded in 1995 by Thierry Desmarest, who continued Total's revitalization. Described as preferring to let action speak louder than words, Desmarest made a few "loud" decisions early on. For instance, he braved U.S. sanctions and developed two large oil fields in Iran, a country that U.S.-based Conoco Oil just abandoned for political reasons.[4] The investment in Iran followed Total's over 70 years of involvement in the region. Total under Desmarest was also not shy of investing in other politically charged locations, such as Libya and Myanmar (former Burma.)[5]

In the late 1990s, Total's portfolio of exploration and production operations gave the oil and gas company a decidedly "upstream" look, as industry observers put it. Selling the North American subsidiary had even further streamlined the company by divesting downstream activities such as refineries and gas stations. Total emphasized that it would concentrate on the upstream segment while rationalizing downstream operations in mature markets. Exploration and production were the more profitable parts of the oil business and where Total would continue to have its focus.

The acquisitions in 1999 and 2000

Investors and industry observers were therefore taken aback when on December 1, 1998 Total announced it would acquire Belgian group Petrofina, a downstream-heavy company with refineries, chemical plants and gas stations.[6] The sudden downstream move surprised analysts, who cringed at the 37% premium[7] over the Petrofina share price that Total would pay. Total's stock price dropped 11% the day after the announcement;[8] several analysts abruptly downgraded Total; and others claimed the merger's benefits only added up to half the premium Total had paid.[9] In the following week, Total shares dropped a total of 22%.[10] Desmarest and his team found themselves having to fly to the financial centers of the world to make their case directly to investors.[11] Said Castaigne, "It was necessary. Our message until then had always been 'Total is upstream, only upstream.' We decided to visit the financial community and investors to explain the strategy. They were very upset." Total could understand the market's reaction, commented Ian Howat, Senior Vice President of Strategy,

> *We massacred the implicit contract we had with the investors and the analysts. They thought we were one type of animal and now all of a sudden we were another. But sometimes you have to do things you know the markets will not like. There wasn't an alternative. We had about 4% market share in a mature R&M [refining and marketing] market in most European countries. There is no way to grow out of that situation unless you make some acquisitions.*

The message that Desmarest and his team now kept repeating was that Total had to make external acquisitions to grow in a maturing – and also consolidating – market in order to avoid becoming a take-over target or a niche player. The industry was already seeing similar examples: Exxon and Mobil had announced plans to merge, and BP and Amoco Corp had already joined in the summer.[12] Acquiring Petrofina gave Total downstream assets such as oil refining and marketing in northwest Europe and parts of the U.S.[13] Investors argued that the company did not need the downstream market and also brought up the fact that Petrofina's chemical operations almost fully overlapped with Total's.[14] Upstream, however, analysts agreed that the two companies were complementary: Total was strong in the Middle East, Latin America and Southeast Asia, and Petrofina in the North Sea and North America.[15] Ten days after the announcement, Total's share price was still 17% below its November-level.[16] (See Exhibit 1 for Total's share price between October 1998 and December 1999.) More calculations were presented, showing even larger cost savings due to synergies, but it would be time consuming to help the financial markets overcome their surprise. Said Castaigne,

> This is a good example of how you learn as a company to be consistent in your message. [When you present to the financial community,] you are in front of people who take notes of everything you say – and next time, they will of course try to see what is different between what you said before and what you say now. So it is important to be consistent. For us, this surprise change of strategy meant we had to slowly rebuild the trust with the financial markets by visits, visits and more visits, and also by listening more to our investors. We were helped somewhat in this phase by one financial institution who quickly understood our strategy. They invested when others were selling off their shares in Total.

It took Total seven months to complete the acquisition process and on July 1, 1999, the new company, named TotalFina, was officially formed. "And the following Monday," said Castaigne, "we moved on Elf Aquitaine."

Interestingly, thought Castaigne, the financial markets appreciated this second acquisition more than the first one. Going after rival Elf was seen as a sign that Total stood firm by its new aggressive growth strategy. TotalFina was the world's sixth largest oil company with a market capitalization of $40 billion,[17] but it was still too small to be a "major". Merging Total with Elf made sense to analysts, if Total wanted to end up on equal footing with industry giants. The match also looked good geographically: TotalFina was a west-east company and Elf's focus was north-south.

The move, however, came as a complete surprise to previously state-run Elf Aquitaine (it was privatized in 1995). The hostile takeover bid of €42 billion[18] (15% over Elf's share price)[19] was turned down by an infuriated Elf management. The French government, which held a "golden share" in Elf with veto rights against any takeover,[20] could have blocked the deal. It announced however that it would not oppose a merger – which made Elf, led by CEO Philippe Jaffre, make a counteroffer to buy TotalFina for €49 billion.[21] As a response, TotalFina upped its offer by almost 10%, arguably both to appease Elf share holders and also to serve as a warning to other potential suitors such as Italy's ENI.[22] By September 1999, Desmarest and Jaffre agreed to merge and create the world's fourth-largest oil company after Exxon Mobil, Shell and BP/Amoco. Desmarest was to lead the new group with Jaffre leaving the group. The new entity, named TotalFinaElf, became the largest company in the Eurozone and on the French stock market with a market capitalization of €95.47 billion, ahead of telecom group France Telecom and the food retailer Carrefour.[23]

The disasters in 2000 and 2001

The two high-profile acquisitions raised awareness of the Total group both in the industry and for the general public. Said Yves-Marie Dalibard, VP Corporate Communication, "Unfortunately, though, the Total story with the public and the media since 1999 is more about two serious accidents than these two acquisitions."

The first accident happened as the Elf merger was concluding. On December 12, 1999, the oil tanker Erika, a vessel that Total had chartered to carry heavy fuel oil, broke into two off the coast of Brittany after heavy storms. No lives were lost, but the sinking ship leaked about 15,000 tons of oil. At first, officials predicted that the rough weather would break up the oil slick before reaching land. However, by Christmas Day oil hit the French Biscay coastline. Eventually over 10,000 tons came ashore, killing over 120,000 seabirds.[24] Total was made the media's focal point and journalists hung to the company's first comment that the tanker did not actually belong to Total.[25] Said Dalibard,

> Top management had been working 7 days a week for 18 months with our mergers. So when the wreckage happened, it did not receive our full dedication, especially when the maritime department told us that the oil spill would not be that severe. People left for Christmas. Then, two–three days later, we have 10,000 tons on the shores. So yes, our reaction was late. Also, the words we used did not show appropriate compassion. Legally speaking we were not responsible but the public needed someone that could be assigned responsibility. So the public opinion, fueled by our lack of timely response, decided we were the responsible ones.

Eventually, Total agreed to finance all oil removal operations from the wreck. It also helped to clean the coastline, pump out the remaining cargo from the sunken tanker, and process over 230,000 tons of waste.[26] By 2005, the French courts were still a year away from assigning legal responsibility and Total and five employees were still under investigation. Legal repercussions aside, however, Total knew that the oil spill heavily influenced the company in its home market. Said Dalibard,

> When we conduct brand surveys, 44% say that "Erika" or "oil spills" are important parts of the Total story. Surprisingly, they also think that the Total story consists of the Prestige wreckage, when a tanker chartered by a Russian oil company sank off the Spanish coast in 2002. Total was not a party in any shape or form to that oil spill.

While Total handled the Erika-effects and also still integrated Petrofina and Elf, another disaster occurred: On September 21, 2001 a plant belonging to the group blew up in Toulouse, France. The AZF factory was part of the group's chemical division Grande Paroisse and specialized in nitrogen chemistry, especially for fertilizers. An accident in a stockpile of ammonium nitrate pellets caused an explosion which killed 30 people and injured over 2,500. As the plant was located within the city boundaries, a portion of the city was also significantly damaged.[27] Said Dalibard,

> It was very sad and very dramatic. This is ten days after 9/11, so terrorism is of course on our mind, but it may also have been a pure accident. This time, the company reacted completely different compared to Erika. One hour after the blast, our chairman flew to Toulouse and two hours after he was on site. He expressed all his sorrow and support to the community and directly took full responsibility on behalf of Total.

Going silent until 2003

Total's quick response positively affected the company image. "In our branding surveys now, there is no sign of people remembering AZF as a disaster for Total," said

Dalibard. "Very strange, because for us it was a horrendous event." In fact, the two accidents combined made Total's management take a drastic decision: they stopped all corporate communication to the general public. The "black-out" lasted until 2003, and did not include financial communication. Dalibard explained,

> *The executive committee concluded that we had no right to speak. We had to solve the problems of the people suffering from the wreckage and the explosion. Advertising or sponsoring would be completely unsuitable. "We have to be attentive to the people of the area," is what we said – and then be silent for the rest, keep a low profile, just hold our breath.*

The decision was not limited to France but was applied worldwide, even in countries where the public opinion hardly knew of Total. Dalibard explained, "I think it reflects the state of mind of the executive committee. It is not totally rational to do this across the board, but it is linked to what happened to these people personally. It was a trauma." The company did continue with standard press relations and financial communication. Limited so-called "commercial communication" was also allowed. Explained Dalibard,

> *We separated between a person's relationship to the institution and to the commerce. The commercial relationship was somewhat kept, through for instance our "You know where to turn"-campaign for our filling stations. But institutional messages were forbidden. So although the company was successful, we did not tell the public of our growth. (Exhibit 2 shows Total's stock price development between 1991 and 2005, and Exhibit 3 compares Total's stock during the first nine months of 2005 with the other oil majors.)*

Commented Schmitt, "Of course, the IR activities continued: we did tell our shareholders and the financial community about our strategy and objectives." In 2003, Total decided it was time to lift the ban on corporate communication. At the same time, the group was renamed from TotalFinaElf back to just Total and a new visual identity was introduced. The group also launched an advertising campaign to re-establish a relationship with the public. The campaign ran on the motto "Our energy is your energy" (or in French, "Pour vous, notre énergie est inépuisable", literally translated as "For you, our energy is inexhaustible"; see Exhibit 4 for an ad sample.) Said Dalibard,

> *The campaign explains the job of an oil group: refine existing resources, find new resources, do this in good conditions while preserving the environment, and all to the benefit of the customer. We run customized campaigns in different regions, but they are all based on the same concept and all try to restore the image and understanding for what an oil group does.*

Total in 2005

Total could by 2005 present itself as the world's fourth largest publicly-traded oil and gas integrated company. It operated in more than 130 countries, covering the entire oil and gas chain from exploration to distribution, and also held large operations in chemicals manufacturing. 2004 sales reached €123 billion, up from €104 billion the year before. Ninety-five percent of Total's profit came from outside of France. (Exhibit 5 shows Total's 2004 financials.) In 2004, Total had over 110,000 employees worldwide with 44% working in France. Employees held 4% of the shares. (See Exhibit 6 for Total's shareholder and employee base in 2004.)

Total divided its activities into three segments. The first segment, *Upstream*, encompassed exploration and production (E&P) of oil and natural gas, along with some other gas and power activities. Total had E&P activities in 44 countries and produced oil and gas in 27 countries. Europe stood for 32% of the group's production, Africa 31%, North America 2%, South America 9%, Asia-Pacific 9% and the Middle East 16%. As a country, Norway was the largest contributor with 406 thousand barrels of oil equivalent (kboe) per day in 2004. (Exhibit 7 shows production by region.) New exploration opportunities were evaluated based on geological, technical, political and economic factors as well as on projected oil and gas prices.[28]

The second segment, *Downstream*, covered trading and shipping, refining and the marketing of TOTAL and Elf brand petroleum products, automotive and other fuels, and specialties such as LPG (Liquefied Petroleum Gases), aviation fuel and lubricants, through both the retail network and other outlets worldwide. Total had in 2004 refinery capacity of 2.7 million barrels per day (b/d) and nearly 17,000 service stations, 2,700 of them in France under the Total and Elf brands.

The third segment, *Chemicals*, included petrochemicals, fertilizers and specialty chemicals. It also housed Arkema, a new legal entity which Total intended to spin-off in spring 2006 and which included vinyl products, industrial chemicals and performance products.[29]

The three operational segments were each built around an organizational pole (Exhibit 8 shows the organizational chart.) The segments were then supported by functions such as finance, strategy, legal affairs, HR and corporate communications. An executive Committee (COMEX) managed the company and answered to its Board of Directors. COMEX worked with an extended Management Committee (CODIR), which included all COMEX members plus 22 senior managers. (Exhibit 9 shows all committee members.) The extended board consisted of French and Belgian nationals, with the exception of Scottish Howat. He described the company, "Total is basically a bunch of engineers with a few hard-nosed finance people at the top – who by the way also happen to be engineers. Their job is to make sure the ingenuity of the engineers is set to create shareholder value."

In 2001, Total formed an Ethics Committee to coordinate Total's ethics practices, described in the company's 26-page long Code of Conduct. The committee organized educational and auditing resources and also handled the procedure for answering employee concerns. This included accepting so-called "whistle blowers" or employees which anonymously reported perceived conduct violations. Richard Lanaud, head of the Ethics Committee, reported directly to the CEO Desmarest. He said,

> *The code of conduct guides our business principles and individual behavior as they link to the environment, to people, to sustainable development. It is a top-driven initiative that the CEO decided to implement. It is also not targeted to one stake-holder group over another. External pressures may play a role in developing an ethics policy, but more important are the rewards it brings for the internal organization: creating a common language of shared values, satisfaction among employees, and growth for the company by protecting its name.*

Lanaud believed that the code of conduct only had a limited impact on persuading investors to invest in Total stock. Personally, he spent 80% of his time on internal activities over external.

Organizational units could also use a self-assessment procedure to determine themselves how well they complied with the code.[30] Total further worked with the U.K.-based accreditation company GoodCorporation to conduct ethical assessments of subsidiaries. GoodCorporation had turned Total's code into 84 points of control which they used as a check list when assessing subsidiaries. Lanaud explained,

> *We don't ask GoodCorporation to give our subsidiaries an accreditation although they handle the assessment. You couldn't give an accreditation to Total on a group*

level and it doesn't make sense on a subsidiary level. Also, we didn't want to create a race between our subsidiaries. We just wanted to find our weaknesses and also our good practices. To use an external party for this was fundamentally easier than doing it ourselves; they had an existing methodology and could also meet our stakeholders to get an outsider's more impartial view. Their job is important: you cannot set an efficient ethics policy without checking.

Financial communication

Financial communication at Total consisted of several formal processes, such as issuing the annual report, preparing the quarterly result publications, managing the conference calls that went with these, organizing investor "road shows", and managing the shareholders' Annual General Meeting. In addition, financial communication also included the daily activities of keeping the company's stakeholders up-to-date with the strategy, the results and the activities of the company.

The annual report

The most technical piece of communication that Total delivered was its annual report. It was also the document that was the most code-driven since it had to abide by financial rules and regulations. Thierry Reveau de Cyrières, General Legal Counsel to the board of directors, said, "Our accounts must give an image of the company's financial situation which is true. As a lawyer, I check that nothing significant has been omitted – to the extent I am aware of it of course." The actual process of drafting the annual report involved some 50 people. Among those, three participants stood out, explained Reveau de Cyrières, "There are three key players: IR, legal function and the communications group. We of course also involve people in accounting and treasury. Naturally, the people in the divisions make a very significant contribution as well, since they are the major part of the report."

Once the annual report had been put together it went through a detailed release process. It started with the disclosure committee made up of the group's main functional executives which checked that there were no outstanding issues. It then went to the audit committee, consisting of three independent directors with more time to examine risks more broadly, who made a final report to the board of directors. The board then received the report and not until their approval was it made public. With Total's financial year following the calendar year, the annual report was published in early spring. It then formed the discussion basis for the annual shareholders' meeting, thought of as "a true discussion between shareholders and the CEO".

Road shows

Twice a year (once in September and once in February), Total went on "road shows" where a group of senior executives visited around 35 cities[31] and met with institutional investors and analysts. Four teams traveled the world, led by CEO Desmarest, CFO Castaigne, Head of Strategy and Risk Assessment Bruno Weymuller and Ian Howat, Senior Vice President of Strategy. Overall, Total had in 2004 organized about 400 investor and analyst meetings.[32] The message that the teams presented during those presentations was crafted throughout the year by the Investor Relations group together with Desmarest, Castaigne as well as the strategy and planning group and the operational business team. Said Schmitt, "Management has to be deeply involved in crafting the message because they will have to deliver it." The end result was a slide show of some 30–35 slides. Schmitt expanded,

> *In an ideal world, IR should not exist. Thierry Desmarest could talk once or twice a year and tell the company's strategy. But it doesn't work that way. We are dealing with an audience that is also tracking a lot of other companies which means they have time and attention constraints. So we on our end have to be both clear and simple in our message – which we then have to repeat over and over again.*

Dalibard emphasized that consistency was key to making sure Total's message was received and taken at face value. He said,

> *The most important here is to use the same criteria and targets between each presentation and between road shows. Otherwise the analysts won't trust you. For four–five years now, we have had the same strategy and criteria to measure our success. We have changed the targets one or twice, based on changes in the external environment, but we have continued to use the same strategy and criteria, which make our presentations very coherent over time.*

Schmitt further explained,

> *Total doesn't change the broad message that everyone is getting. What might change is how deep you get into certain issues. More and more investors walk in the room and they already know the broad message and want answers to some very specific questions. Obviously Total must be prepared to answer them in a detailed way. But generally speaking, consistency and transparency of the broad message is crucial though because if there were message differences investors would find out quickly as they are bound to talk with each other – and that would hurt the company's credibility.*

During the road shows, however, the company did not provide valuation multiples or other calculations of firm value. Said Castaigne, "It is not our job to calculate these numbers. They are for the financial community to create. We give them the information they need, but we let them value the company. In the end, the market sets the share price."

Day-to-day communication

Although Total's main message was built once or twice a year, it issued press releases year-round. Press releases were issued for one of three reasons: material events where the company by law or regulation was obliged to inform; events that were related to the main IR crafted story; or happenings that were in Total's interest to inform on but coincidental to the main message, such as opening a new facility or sponsoring a sports event. All press releases, regardless of their purpose, were reviewed by the investor relations team to make sure that they were consistent with the overall message that Total wanted to spread. As a matter of standard, every press release also referred systematically to the geographic location and gave the environmental dimension of the event.

In Schmitt's view, in addition to spreading the corporate message, the IR group also had a function of being receptive to and understanding the expectations of the market participants. He said,

> *IR must be able to understand a trend even before it becomes apparent. For example, how would the investors react to Total's dividend's policy or share buyback strategy. Or about mergers and acquisitions in 2005? Before putting out the story, we need to have an idea of whether it will be valid for our shareholders – and for all stakeholders in general.*

Investors' sentiments towards Total, or their general assessment of a situation, could often be gauged through their ratings of a company or by simply picking up the phone and talking with them. However, the general public's views were harder to assess than the investors. To help in this, Total ran frequent market surveys, measuring both the public's awareness of Total as a company and their sentiments towards it. Said Dalibard,

> *The surveys show us how quickly views can change. In January [2005], surveys showed overall positive results for Total. Then came February with three different incidents. First, our financial results were very good – which is actually not that accepted by the French public. It is a very specific aspect of this country. Second, we had a small legal problem connected to Erika, which gave our opponents a new chance to stress Total's involvement in the story. Finally, we also had a social situation in a subsidiary in the south of France. So from a 68% positive rating in January, we dropped to 48% in February. Only to rebound two months later, back to 63% – which I think shows that the public in France is very sensitive to any event concerning Total.*

Interestingly, the surveys seemed to indicate the French public separated between Total, the company, and Total, the gas stations. The gas stations consistently received higher ratings than the company with the same name; Total interpreted this as the public having a "warmer" relationship with the gas stations and a "colder" relation with the company itself.

Given the impact any information about the company – financial, corporate or otherwise – seemed to have on the general sentiment towards Total, IR worked closely with the company's internal media group to make sure they all conveyed the same story. Said Dalibard,

> *Press relation links completely with financial communication since journalists of course will look at how we talk to investors. We have to maintain a strong internal relationship between our media and financial people to "keep the same tempo". Actually, every new press officer we hire has to be trained on the rules of financial communication. For media relations, we have processes and rules – but in terms of financial communication we as a company have legal commitments to be transparent, fair... Our media people have to take all these rules into consideration. Journalists and analysts cross-check what we tell them to get the full presentation. So even if we may differ in the emphasis on pieces between the two audiences, the overall message has to be the same.*

However, working with two types of audiences presented its own problems. Dalibard continued,

> *Most journalists work like analysts: they are their papers' specialists in the oil and gas business. If we have problems, it is not with them but with the general journalists that do not understand our business. But they are just as powerful [in shaping public opinion], probably more, since few in the general public read the specialist section of the newspaper and instead read the front page or main section articles where these generalists write.*

Investor relations: Communicating with stakeholders

The Financial Communication team at Total consisted in 2005 of about 10 people in Paris, with an additional team in New York of three people. The group's job, as described by its head Schmitt, could be divided into three main areas: communicating with retail investors, with institutional analysts and shareholders, and with ethical or environmental analysts and investors. The last area was newly established in order to match the growing number of specialized analysts on the investor side who looked specifically into the corporate social responsibility (CSR) aspects of a company. (See Exhibit 10 for the formal mission statement of the Financial Communication Group.)

Members of the IR-group attended some executive committee meetings, long term planning meetings, budget meetings etc. and also met regularly with the CEO. In order to understand the business issues, the IR team members all had operational backgrounds within Total. The IR group under Jérôme Schmitt reported to the CFO Castaigne. (See Exhibit 11 for the organization of the IR and Financial Communication group.) Commented Castaigne, "In the financial reports of any company, there are strategic messages that are very important. So the financial communication office is placed at the highest level internally."

Communicating with institutional investors

During the two 2004 road shows, members of the Group's management met, as they did every year, with portfolio managers and financial analysts in the leading financial centers of the world. In addition, institutional investors could download material on the Total corporate website and the CFO conducted three telephone conferences during the year. (Exhibit 12 shows the 2005 IR calendar.)[33] To Schmitt, the bulk of the IR work was to deal with institutional investors and convey the company's strategy. Howat further commented on the role of IR vis-à-vis institutional investors,

> *Contrary to the popular belief that the financial markets are always short-sighted, we are fortunately in an industry which investors like for its long term perspectives and development potential. Most of our presentations and most of the market's interest are on the company's long-term plans. Specifically for our E&P [exploration and production] activities we give a five year indication of production targets. We should not disappoint the market, so our five year numbers come out of our own planning but with prudence built into them.*

Not disappointing the market was a recurring theme in internal discussions, said Howat,

> *This was really drummed into us by our previous CEO. Financial communication is an exercise in honesty. Like the old saying, "You can fool some people all of the time, you can fool some of the people all of the time, but you can't fool all the people all the time." You can't fudge. Everything you choose to say should be the truth, the whole truth and nothing but.*

Communicating with retail investors

As Elf Aquitaine had had many more individuals as shareholders than Total, the merger meant that Total now had to cater to a large number of retail investors, a number that continued to grow. By 2005, Total had 520,000 retail investors, or 9% of the shareholder base. About 40% of these had less than 30 shares; about 40% between 30 and 99; 10% between 100 and 200 shares; and the remaining 10% had more than 200 shares. About 90% of all retail investors were French and about 60% of the shareholders had held their Total shares for more than 10 years and 25% between 5 and 10 years. Valérie Laugier was head of Retail Investor Service for four years and was responsible for all communication that went to this group. She said,

> *After the merger, my unit was attached directly to the financial communication group as it had been at Elf. It is not attached to the corporate communication, sustainable development or general secretary. Instead, since we belong to the*

financial communication group, we are linked directly to the CFO, which makes it easier for us to all communicate the same message. Even if the message I bring to my retail investors may have been simplified or made more pedagogical – since my audience is not made up of "petrol pros" like the oil analysts – it is the same exact message as the "pros" get. Although I may spend my days thinking about retail needs, I sit next to people that "swim" daily, so to speak, in the main message.

While the basic message and information conveyed were the same as with institutional investors Laugier pointed out that the approach used to communicate with Total's retail investor was based on very different strategies,

We base our retail investor communication on techniques that come from consumer communication. I was nine years with Total's gas station network, working with consumer services, and it felt natural to use the same approach when talking with our retail investors. These are individuals with which we have a relationship, just like with our gas station clients. I installed, for instance, a CRM [customer relationship management] system to keep a history of all communication with each shareholder. Before we did not know if someone who wrote or called us had ever been in contact with us – but now the CRM system can tell us that and also provide information about the person, such as how many Total shares they own, etc. Each individual shareholder has a file in our CRM system, to which we link all communication with that person. It allows us to not only trace previous communication but also to personalize it.

Another change Laugier brought was to limit the number of publications created for retail investors, while at the same time increasing the distribution of the remaining printed material. She said, "My argument was that nobody will hear us unless we turn up the volume, regardless of how many times we change the CD. I wanted to reach more retail investors more often." Thus, by 2005, Total communicated with its retail investors in carefully selected diffusion channels. One was the shareholders journal, *Journal des Actionnaires*, which 300,000 shareholders (the ones holding a minimum of 10 shares) received four times a year. Once a year, at the time of the annual report, all 520,000 individual shareholders received the journal.[34] Other channels were the company's web site and the toll-free number through which shareholders could obtain information about the company. The toll-free number received 80,000 calls annually and was run by an interactive voice server. The callers who did not find their answer in the preset menu were connected with a staff member (that reported to Laugier) who since early 2004 had been dedicated to answering shareholder questions, whether by telephone, e-mail, fax or regular letters.

As another channel, Total invited shareholders with more than 30 bearer shares or one registered share to join the "Shareholders' Circle", which organized events such as visits to industrial or cultural sites. For this group, Total also ran one-day training programs on "Understanding Total Financial Statements" which since its inception in May 2003 had attracted about 700 participants. About 100 shareholders had also attended a new program called "Moving to IFRS Norm Accounting". The training programs had so far been held in Paris (twice), Nice and in Clermont-Ferrand.

Another channel for communication was a schedule of about four annual information sessions for individual shareholders, which were held in Paris and in other regions. CEO Desmarest led the session in Paris; the others were chaired by Schmitt. These sessions were open to all individual shareholders. In addition, Total participated at the annual Actionaria Trade Show held in Paris. In 2004, Desmarest had participated in a question-and-answer session with two journalists in front of 1,200 individual shareholders.[35]

The year's largest retail investor event was however the shareholders' meeting or annual general meeting (AGM). The 3.5 hours long meeting was prepared by several Total teams: IR, Corporate Communication, legal, security and logistics. In 2004, the AGM was held on May 15 at the Paris Convention Center at Porte Maillot in central Paris. Personal invitations were sent to all shareholders holding 100 shares or more, about 100,000 people. Said Laugier,

> *A few years ago, we only sent out invitations to people with more than 10,000 shares. This basically meant nearly no invitations were sent at all. We then changed that to a minimum of 100 shares – and for the next year we will set the limit even lower at 50 shares.*

In 2002, the AGM had seen 1,900 attendants; by 2005 this number had grown to 2,300 shareholders, with many more attending from outside of the Paris region. Commented Laugier,

> *The shareholders' meeting is one of the most important things we do. But when I discuss this with any Anglo-Saxon colleague, they don't understand the need. In their cultures, especially the American, it is so much more common for individuals to invest in shares. But for us, the French, it is still not established and the people who do invest need the attention.*

Since many retail shareholders were both investors and French citizens, many of the issues with the general public were also of concern for retail shareholders. For example, Laugier commented about the Erika and AZF disaster in Total's past and about the decision to freeze corporate communication for a while,

> *At the time, people were ashamed to hold Total shares. They told us time after time that we needed to stand up and defend ourselves – but what they were really asking for was for us to defend them and their choice to hold Total shares. They want to be shareholders – but they also want to have a good conscience and even build their personal image by owning Total shares. We also see this reflected in the increasing number of questions on how we behave socially, ethically and environmentally.*

In order to better understand how retail investors perceived Total both as a company and as an investment opportunity, Total had a 12-person strong Shareholders Advisory Committee (in French, *Comité Consultatif*). The committee was appointed for a specific time and the incoming committee members were picked by Total in cooperation with an external recruitment agency. Said Laugier,

> *Earlier we could end up with an unrepresentative committee, consisting of too many retirees, too many Parisians and in fact also people who sat on similar boards almost for a living. So we hired this recruitment agency to help us make a more representative selection – and also find committee members more likely to argue with us on issues they don't agree with.*

The committee met four times a year in meetings that Schmitt and Laugier chaired. After a short presentation of the latest financial results by Schmitt, the meetings would quickly turn into a workshop where the members would criticize the latest financial publication or other official communication piece, and also work with benchmark exercises to come up with suggestions for Total to improve its communication.

Communicating with employee investors

A special category of retail investors were the company's own employees, who owned 4% of Total. Said Dalibard,

Since our staff follows media we have to be attentive to the message coming from the outside. Every press release we issue for investors and media is put on the intranet, with comments added for specific business areas. We need to manage the rhythm of communication to the financial community, to media and internally. They have to be done at the same time. When the rhythm breaks, you have problems. So internal communication is linked to financial communication, absolutely. Take for instance the issue of share buy-back. The shareholders like it since it is a way of increasing the value of each share. However, it means that this money is not distributed to staff or invested back into the company, so employees will argue that "if Total is successful enough to buy back shares, why can't we take part of that success?"

Some employees would try to use the annual shareholders' meeting as a platform for their views, whether they were shareholders or not. For instance, at the 2004 meeting, employees upset with the company's decision to spin off part of its chemical business into a separate company attempted – unsuccessfully – to march onto the meeting stage.

Communicating with ethical investors

As the financial markets had more analysts dedicated to ethical issues, as well as certain funds only investing in "ethical companies", Total had adapted its IR organization. Eve Gautier was now responsible for Corporate Social Responsibility information. Previously in the corporate communication and internal audit departments at Total, she had for the last six months been in charge of Total's relationship with CSR analysts. Schmitt commented on her role within the IR group,

Previously, I'd say that mainstream analysts often ignored these concerns, but the concerns didn't go away. The business of analysts is to pick the stock that will appreciate in the shortest amount of time; their bonus is calculated on that capital gain; so if any corporate social responsibility issues appear, they want them to go away as fast as possible. That is when they contact us directly.

One specific example involved a large Scandinavian investor. Said Gautier,

We got a contact from a Scandinavian investment fund. They said they were considering dropping our stock because of our presence in Myanmar. So for the analyst in that fund to be able to justify keeping our stock, we need to explain to him why we are in Myanmar and why this is in accordance with our ethical charter.

Retail shareholders also took a direct interest in Total's ethical policies, explained Gautier,

For retail shareholders, CSR is important, as is respecting the environment. The fact that we invest in bio diesel and solar energy renewables, for instance, is significant for retail investors. Retail shareholders want to be able to go to a dinner and say that they are proud to have invested in a socially responsible company.

Overall, Total saw how the importance of ethical and socially responsible continued to grow. A recent example came from the kick-off meeting on the 2005 fall road show: The first question from the first analyst did *not* deal with the company financials, as normally was the case, but targeted the company's sustainable development activities.

Presenting a balanced message

Although the IR group at Total could point to a successful track record (they were for instance given four awards by IR Magazine in 2004, including the Grand Prize for Best

Financial Communication), its corporate communication efforts were growing increasingly complicated. The task of staying with "only one message" was more challenging than ever, especially given the large variety of stakeholders. Commented Schmitt,

> *How we communicate our financial results is a key issue. We want to be confident with analysts and the financial community and say "Look how well we have done…" but at the same time, we have to be modest and show both them and others that although we did a good job we have to prepare for the future. It is all about semantics: how blunt do you want to be? Everything has to be in the message but the fine tuning happens in the subtleties. It is obvious that with an institutional investor we will spend more time dwelling on dividend policy. In other situations, with other audiences, we don't speak much about the dividend, only a short sentence, and instead we go deeper on different issues.*

Continued Dalibard,

> *For our upcoming September road show, we know people will ask "What do you do with all your money?" We have prepared descriptions of our investments and projects to make both investors and the public understand how difficult, expensive and time consuming it is to prepare the future of the company. Also, a number we like to emphasize is that we only represent 14% of the world's oil production when our share of the oil industry investments is approximately 23%. And by "we" I don't mean Total alone, but all the five biggest oil majors. Most production activity actually lies with national oil companies. Many don't know this.*

The topic of share buybacks was also expected to come up at the road-show. In 2004, Total bought back 22.44 million of its own shares at a cost of €3.6 billion. The buybacks involved 3.5% of the company's capital. For 2005, Total had announced that share buybacks would continue, adjusted for the financial environment and asset sales.[36] Commented Schmitt,

> *There is a real tension here: investment analysts want us to talk about dividend policy, share buybacks, restructuring; but employees and unions prefer to hear that Total is investing more for the future, hiring more people etc. This is why we spend quite a lot of time detailing our cash allocation policy which consists first of carefully selected investments projects, then dividends and share buybacks, all of this with a gearing comprised between 25% and 30%.*

The volatile nature of oil and gas prices complicated both setting the strategy and then communicating it. CFO Castaigne summarized the approach,

> *There are really three important factors when it comes to financial communication. The first is that it is a long-term process. You build your reputation over time. Second, be consistent. Third, don't sell your results, sell your performance. Since we are in a business where external conditions affect us heavily, we must distinguish between the impact of the environment and our own performance. If the environment changes drastically and we cannot meet our targets, we have to be clear in our communication about the link between the target and the change. We have to sell to the market that which is under our control, for instance costs, projects to increase production, the efficiency of our explorations or the advantage of our technologies. But it is hard for us to guess on, say, oil taxes that countries may or may not introduce.*

He then added,

> *You have to remember that in the life of a company, you have good times and bad times. So when reporting in good times, you have to keep in mind that tomorrow*

might be bad. You have to caution for things that may go wrong – because you know your own weaknesses. So over time, we have managed to sell the evolution of Total compared to our targets. That builds a good capital of trust with the investors, which allows them to plan long term and for us also translates into an increased share price.

Total's emphasis on a message that was consistent over time seemed to be appreciated by the financial analyst community. Wrote one analyst after Total's road show in September 2005, "Total's mid-year review contained no major surprises and represented a continuation and extension of its successful strategy and equity story, in our view." Given that consistency, minor modifications to the overall strategy then appeared to be acceptable, as evidenced by another analyst report: "Small changes in strategic outlook we consider to be the hallmark of a high quality major running the business for the long-term." (See Exhibit 13 for a summary of analyst reports after the September 2005 road show.)

The balance in communication between rejoicing in good results while still emphasizing the need to save for future downturns was not an easy one to strike. Desmarest said in a press interview that French critics might "have difficulty in understanding the size of the company. They wonder, perhaps it is too big."[37] Expanded Howat,

In a French political context, vis-à-vis the trade unions and the politicians, this type of message is a bit controversial. First, in France, nobody has ever seen a company that makes a net profit of €1 billion a month – so that immediately gets people's attention. And when they look at our level of dividend and the fact that we have typically been buying back 3%–4% of the company every year and in the context of France's culture and politics… it is not that simple.

A surprise windfall tax?

As if to prove Howat's point, the apparent contradiction of Total's message became the focus of a debate that erupted in late 2005. On September 8, French finance minister Thierry Breton told reporters that France might adopt a windfall tax on the "exceptional profits" of the oil companies.[38] The government was worried that high oil prices would deter consumer spending and so Breton called on "all the actors of the oil sector" to "behave as citizen businesses and make proposals, such as one could imagine them lowering prices at the petrol pump." If not, the French state would put in place new taxation on the oil companies, in addition to the taxes that already accounted for two-thirds of French petrol prices and more than half of diesel prices.[39]

In a meeting with Breton the following week, CEO Desmarest reiterated what he had already announced at Total's "First Half 2005 Financial Results"-presentation in early September: that Total would boost investments in French refineries and renewable energy research. Total would also wait about three weeks every time oil prices rose before raising consumer prices, while they on the other immediately would lower petrol prices if oil prices dropped. Although apparently satisfied with the outcome, Desmarest did tell reporters that some Total shareholders had asked the company to move its tax domicile abroad to avoid similar threats in the future. A spokesperson for the finance ministry emphasized emphatically that oil groups "should not just consider their shareholders but all stakeholders."[40]

Schmitt and the IR group at Total knew that all too well.

EXHIBIT 1 **Price development October 1998–December 1999: Total share price (Paris Stock Exchange) against Dow Jones Industrial Index and CAC 40 Index**

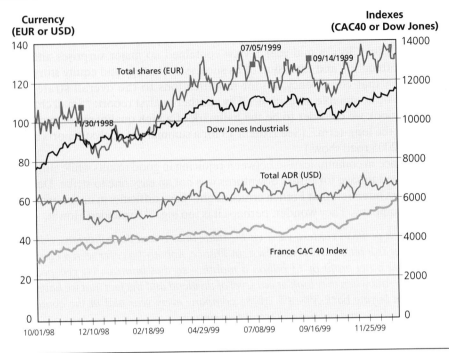

Note: 11/30/1998: Last day before Total announced acquisition of Petrofina.
07/05/1999: Total announces take-over plans of Elf Acquitaine.
09/14/1999: Press release: TotalFina and Elf Aquitaine reach amicable accord on merger.

In 2005, Total was listed in Paris, Brussels, London and New York. It was included in the French stock index CAC 40 (weight of 13.71%) and the Dow Jones Stoxx 50, Dow Jones Euro Stoxx 50 (weight of 6.24%), Dow Jones Global Titans 50 Index (Source: Total Annual Report 2004, page 38).

Left Y-axis: USD- or EUR-value of Total stock.
Right Y-axis: Index value.

Source: Datastream International.

EXHIBIT 2   **Price development January 1991–June 2005: Total share price and oil barrel**

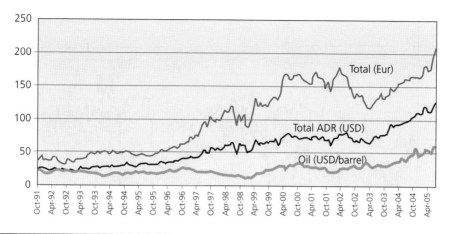

Source: Datastream International for Total share price, Global Financial Data for oil barrel price.

EXHIBIT 3   **Total's stock development vs. the top 6 oil companies, 1 January–9 September 2005**

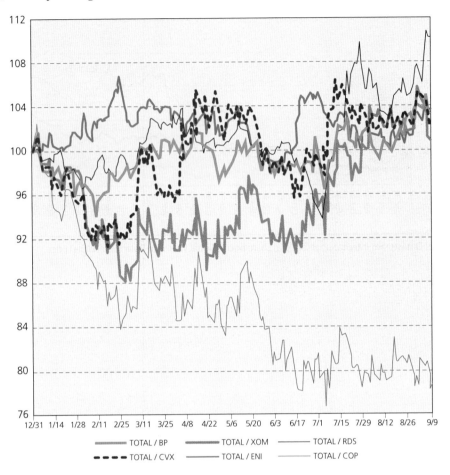

Note: Each line represents Total's share value over the share value of another oil major. The differential is assigned an index value of 100 for January 1, 2005. A downward sloping line then indicates that Total's share value is lower in value relative to the other oil major, compared to the starting date. An upward sloping line indicates that Total's share is appreciating in value vis-à-vis the other stock.

Company abbreviations: BP = British Petroleum (U.K.)
XOM = Exxon Mobil (USA)
RDS = Royal Dutch Shell (Netherlands)
CVX = Chevron (USA)
ENI = Ente Nazionale Idrocarburi (Italy)
COP = Conoco Philips (USA)

Source: Total.

EXHIBIT 4   Ad in Total's 2005 corporate image campaign – "Our Energy Is Your Energy"

Source: Company document.

EXHIBIT 5 **Total financials 2002–2004**

a. Financial highlights

(in millions of Euros, except earnings per share, dividends)	2004	2003	2002
Sales	−122,700	104,652	102,540
Operating income from business segments	17,123	13,004	10,995
Net operating income from business segments	8,792	6,973	5,868
Net income (Group share)	9,039	7,344	6,260
Earnings per share (in €)	14.68	11.56	9.4
Dividend per share (in €)	5.4	4.7	4.1
Net debt-to-equity ratio	27%	26%	29%
Return on equity	31%	26%	20%
Cash flow from operating activities	14,429	12,487	11,006
Total expenditures	8,668	7,728	8,657

b. Sales by segment 2004 and 2003

(in millions of Euros)	Upstream	Downstream	Chemicals
For year ended Dec 31, 2004			
Total sales	36,203	83,476	20,741
Operating income adjusted for special items	12,820	3,217	1,086
Net operating income adjusted for special items	5,834	2,302	656
Expenditures	6,170	1,516	905
For year ended Dec 31, 2003			
Total sales	30,250	70,947	17,850
Operating income adjusted for special items	10,476	1,970	558
Net operating income adjusted for special items	5,259	1,460	254
Expenditures	5,302	1,235	1,115

c. Consolidated statement of income

(in millions of Euros)	2004	2003	2002
Sales	122,700	104,652	102,540
Operating expenses	−101,141	−86,905	−86,622
Depreciation, depletion and amortization of tangible assets	−5,498	−4,977	−5,792
Operating income			
Corporate	−215	−209	−210
Business segments	16,276	12,979	10,336
Total operating income	**16,061**	**12,770**	**10,126**
Interest expense, net	−234	−232	−195
Dividend income on non-consolidated companies	164	152	170
Dividends on subsidiaries' redeemable preferred shares	−6	−5	−10
Other income (expense), net	2,174	−1,060	243
Provision for income taxes	−8,316	−5,353	−5,034
Equity in income (loss) of affiliates	337	1,086	866
Income before amortization of acquisition goodwill	**10,180**	**7,358**	**6,166**
Amortization of acquisition goodwill	−308	−139	−212
Consolidated net income	**9,872**	**7,219**	**5,954**
Of which minority interests	260	194	13
Net income	**9,612**	**7,025**	**5,941**
Earnings per share (euros)	**15.61**	**11.06**	**8.92**

d. Consolidated balance sheet

(in millions of Euros)	2004	2003	2002
Assets			
Non-current assets			
Intangible assets, net	1,908	2,017	2,752
Property, plant and equipment, net	36,422	36,286	38,592
Equity affiliates: investments and loans	9,874	7,833	7,710
Other investments	1,090	1,162	1,221
Other non-current assets	3,239	3,152	3,735
Total non-current assets	**52,533**	**50,450**	**54,010**
Current assets			
Inventories, net	7,053	6,137	6,515
Accounts receivable, net	14,025	12,357	13,087
Prepaid expenses and other current assets	5,363	4,779	5,243
Short-term investments	1,350	1,404	1,508
Cash and cash equivalents	3,837	4,836	4,966
Total current assets	**31,628**	**29,513**	**31,319**
TOTAL ASSETS	**84,161**	**79,963**	**85,329**
Liabilities and shareholders' equity			
Shareholders' equity			
Common shares	6,350	6,491	6,872
Paid-in surplus and retained earnings	33,266	30,408	30,514
Cumulative translation adjustment	−4,653	−3,268	−830
Treasury shares	−3,703	−3,225	−4,410
Total shareholders' equity	**31,260**	**30,406**	**32,146**
Subsidiaries' redeemable preferred shares	**147**	**396**	**477**
Minority interest	**629**	**664**	**724**
Long-term liabilities			
Deferred income taxes	6,063	5,443	6,390
Employee benefits	3,600	3,818	4,103
Other long-term liabilities	6,449	6,344	6,150
Total long-term liabilities	**16,112**	**15,605**	**16,643**
Long-term debt	**9,734**	**9,783**	**10,157**
Current liabilities			
Accounts payable	11,672	10,304	10,236
Other creditors and accrued liabilities	11,084	8,970	9,850
Short-term borrowings and bank overdrafts	3,523	3,835	5,096
Total current liabilities	**26,279**	**23,109**	**25,182**
TOTAL LIABILITIES AND SHAREHOLDERS' EQUITY	**84,161**	**79,963**	**85,329**

Note: Totaling the sales by segment in panel b does not match the sales total in panel a due to corporate and intercompany sales that are not reported on panel b.

Source: All financials taken from Total Annual Report 2004.

EXHIBIT 6 **Total shareholder and employee base 2004**

a. Shareholder base		b. Employees	
By region		**By region**	
France	33%	France	44%
United Kingdom	18%		
Rest of Europe	24%	Rest of Europe	27%
North America	23%		
Rest of World	2%	Rest of World	29%
By type		**By segment**	
Institutional shareholders	87%	Upstream	13%
Group employees	4%	Downstream	31%
Individual shareholders	9%	Chemicals	55%
		Holding	1%

Source: Total Annual Report 2004.

EXHIBIT 7   **Production by geographic area 2004**

Geographic area	Liquids	Natural Gas	Total
	(kb/d)	**(Mcf/d)**	**(Kboe/d)**
Europe	**424**	**2,218**	**832**
France	9	143	35
Norway	263	775	406
Netherlands	1	330	59
United Kingdom	151	970	332
Africa	**693**	**440**	**776**
Algeria	42	160	72
Angola	159	27	164
Cameroon	13		13
Congo	87	21	90
Gabon	99	27	104
Libya	62		62
Nigeria	231	205	271
North America	**16**	**241**	**61**
United States	16	241	61
Asia	**31**	**1,224**	**245**
Brunei	3	58	14
Indonesia	22	854	177
Myanmar		110	14
Thailand	6	202	40
Middle East	**110**	**39**	**117**
Iran	26		26
Qatar	31	1	31
Syria	30	32	36
U.A.E.	16	6	17
Yemen	7		7
South America	**128**	**474**	**213**
Argentina	11	325	70
Bolivia	3	82	18
Colombia	24	32	30
Venezuela	90	35	95
Others	**9**		**9**
Russia	9		9
Total production	**1,411**	**4,636**	**2,253**
Equity and non-consolidated affiliates			
Africa	37	4	37
Middle East	247	254	295
Total equity and non-consolidated affiliates	**284**	**258**	**332**
Worldwide production	1,695	4,894	2,585

Note: kb/d   = thousands of barrels per day
Mcf/d = million cubic feet per day
Kboe/d = thousands barrel of oil equivalent per day

Source: Total Annual Report 2004, page 62.

EXHIBIT 8 **Total organizational chart (1 April, 2005)**

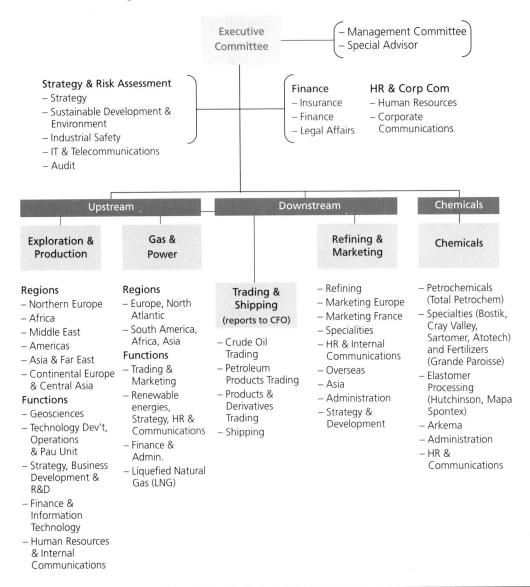

Source: Adapted by case writer from Total Annual Report 2004.

EXHIBIT 9 **Total Executive Committee (COMEX) and Management Committee (CODIR)**

The Executive Committee (COMEX)

- Thierry Desmarest — Chairman and Chief Executive Officer
- François Cornélis — Vice-Chairman, President of Chemicals
- Robert Castaigne — Chief Financial Officer
- Yves-Louis Darricarrère — President of Gas & Power
- Christophe de Margerie — President of Exploration & Production
- Jean-Paul Vettier — President of Refining & Marketing
- Bruno Weymuller — President of Strategy & Risk Assessment

The Management Committee (CODIR)

All Executive Committee members, plus:

Holding Company	Upstream	Downstream	Chemicals
■ Patrick de la Chevardière	■ Michael Bénézit	■ Alain Champeaux	■ Pierre-Christian Clout
■ Jean-Pierre Cordier	■ Philippe Boisseau	■ Jean-Claude Company	■ Philippe Goebel
■ Jean-Marc Jaubert	■ Jean-Marie Masset	■ François Groh	■ Jean-Bernard Lartigue
■ Jean-Michel Gires	■ Charles Mattenet	■ Pierre Klein	■ Thierry Le Hénaff
■ Jean-Jacques Guilbaud	■ Jean Privey	■ Eric de Menten	■ Hugues Woestelandt
■ Ian Howat		■ André Tricoire	

Source: Total Annual Report 2004.

EXHIBIT 10 **Mission statement for Total Financial Communication Department**

The Financial Communication Department has as its mission to establish, develop and maintain the Total Group's relationships with both its shareholders and the financial analysts that follow the oil sector. This mission entails in particular:

- Managing the Group's daily relationship with institutional investors and financial analysts;

- Writing and editing of financially related press releases and the creation of strategic presentation/conference calls made by the management for the financial communication, most notably for results presentations (accounts, strategies for each activity sector, group perspective);

- Organizing and carrying out road shows;

- Validating and/or creating (as needed), in close liaison with the Communications and Legal Departments, reference documents (annual report, 20-F);

- Organizing sector presentations, conference participations and field trips for investors and analysts;

- Managing the relationship with individual shareholders and, in particular, manage the Shareholders Advisory Committee and the Shareholders' Circle, participations at meetings and shareholder conventions;

- Writing and editing documents with general financial information targeted at the financial community and individual shareholders (fact book, shareholder letter);

- Managing the Group's relationship with analysts and investors in the CSR (Corporate Social Responsibility) domain;

- More generally, together with the Communication Department, distribute financial information published by the Group.

To carry out its obligations, the Financial Communication Department can turn to all other Group entities and will be associated, when needed, to the work carried out by the operational departments.

The Director of Financial Communication report to the Chief Financial Officer.

Jérôme Schmitt, Director of Financial Communication
Robert Castaigne, Chief Financial Officer

Source: Total internal document, translated from the French original by case writer.

EXHIBIT 11 **Investor Relations and Financial Communications Group: Organizational overview**

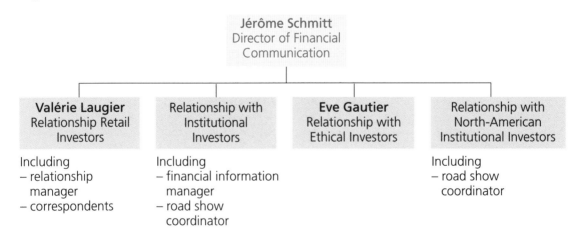

Note: Managers mentioned in case indicated by name in chart above.
Source: Total.

EXHIBIT 12   **Investor relations calendar 2005–2006**

Date	Event
2005	
17 Feb	Results for 4th quarter, 2004
13 Apr	Telephone conference on the shift to IFRS standards
14 Apr	Meeting of the shareholders in Strasbourg
4 May	Results for 1st quarter 2005
17 May	Shareholders' Meeting at the Paris Convention Center
24 May	Payment of the cash dividend
20 Jun	Meeting of shareholders in Montpellier
4 Aug	Results for 2nd quarter and 1st half 2005
7 Sep	Presentation of mid-2005 outlook
12 Oct	Meeting of shareholders in Bordeaux
4 Nov	Results for the 3rd quarter 2005
18–19 Nov	Actionaria Trade Show in Paris
2006	
15 Feb	Presentation of 2005 Results
12 May	Shareholders' Meeting in Paris

Source: Total Annual Report, page 47.

Total

EXHIBIT 13 **Summary of analyst reports after Total's September 2005 road show**

	Sector*	Total	BP	RD Shell	Exxon Mobil	Chevron Texaco	ENI	Repsol-YPF	Conoco Phillips
Anglo-Saxon analysts									
Banc of America		2	2	3	3	2			2
Bernstein	3	2	3	3	2	3	3		3
BBVA	2	2	3	4			4	2	
Bear Stearns	3	2	2	4	2	4			2
BNP Exane	4	3	2	4			2	3	
SCH	2	2	3	3			2	2	
Cazenove	3	3							
Citigroup Smith Barney	3	2	3	3	2	2	2	3	3
CSFB	2	2	3	3	3	2	2	4	3
Daiwa Securities	3	3	3	2			2	3	
Deutsche Bank	3	2	2	3	2	2	2	3	2
Dresdner KW		2							
Friedman Billings Ramsey	2	3	3	4	3	2			2
Goldman Sachs	3	2	3	2	2	3	2	3	3
HSBC	4	2	2	4			3	3	
ING	3	2	2	4			2	3	
JP Morgan	3	3	2	2	3	2	3	4	2
Lehman Brothers	4	2	4	3	2	2	2	3	2
Merrill Lynch	2	2	3	2	2	2	3	3	2
Morgan Stanley Dean Witter	2	3	3	2	2	3	4	2	2
Simmons	2	2	2	2	2	2	2	3	2
UBS Warburg	4	2	2	3	2	3	3	2	
Williams de Bröe	3	2	2	3			3	3	
Average	2.86	2.26	2.57	3.00	2.29	2.43	2.56	2.88	2.31
French analysts									
Cheuvreux	3	2	1	4			1	3	
Ixis	2	1	2	2			2	2	
CM – CIC Securities		1	2	3			3	3	
Dexia Securities	3	2		3			2	4	
KBC Securities	2	2	4	3			2	2	
Kepler Equities	2	2		3			2	4	
Natexis	3	2	2	3			3	3	
Société Générale	3	2	2	3			3	3	
Average	2.57	1.75	2.17	3.00			2.13	3.00	
Overall Average	**2.79**	**2.13**	**2.48**	**3.00**	**2.29**	**2.43**	**2.42**	**2.92**	**2.31**

Note: Sector grading: Company grading
                                            (1) Strong buy, Recommended list, Select list, Buy (ABN Amro)
        (2) Overweight/Positive   (2) Buy, Add, Accumulate, Market outperform, Outperform, Overweight
        (3) Neutral/Cautious   (3) Neutral, Market perform, Hold, Equal weight
        (4) Underweight/Negative   (4) Reduce, Underperform, Underweight
                                            (5) Sell

Source: Total's internal compilation of analyst reports.

Endnotes

1. Total Annual Report 2004, page 58.
2. From Hoover's coverage of Total, http://premium.hoovers.com/subscribe/co/overview. xhtml?ID=12393, accessed September 2005.
3. Total press release, "Total Second Quarter 2005 results," Paris, August 4, 2005, available at http://www.total.com/static/en/medias/topic1126/Total_20050804_en_PR_2Q_Results.pdf, accessed 3 October 2005.
4. "France Total CEO/Oil –5: Snapshot," *Dow Jones International News*, 9 January 1998, accessed via Factiva, September 2005.
5. Stanley Reed in London, with Stan Crock in Washington, "Total loves to go where others fear to tread – The Iran deal is just the latest of Desmarest's shrewd moves," 13 October 1997, *Business Week*, accessed via Factiva, September 2005.
6. John Tagliabue, "A French Oil Company That Doesn't Act the Part," 13 December 1998, *The New York Times*, accessed via Factiva, September 2005.
7. Marcel Michelson, "Total plugs merger, says profit slip limited," *Reuters News*, 6 January 1999, accessed via Factiva, September 2005.
8. John Tagliabue, "A French Oil Company That Doesn't Act the Part," 13 December 1998, *The New York Times*, accessed via Factiva, September 2005.
9. Bhushan Bahree and Martin Du Bois, "Total Will Buy Belgium's Petrofina at Big Premium," 2 December 1998, *The Wall Street Journal Europe*, accessed via Factiva, September 2005.
10. Case writer interview with Total CFO Robert Castaigne, August 2005, La Defense, Paris, France.
11. John Tagliabue, "A French Oil Company That Doesn't Act the Part," 13 December 1998, *The New York Times*, accessed via Factiva, September 2005.
12. Bhushan Bahree and Martin Du Bois, "Total Will Buy Belgium's Petrofina at Big Premium," 2 December 1998, *The Wall Street Journal Europe*, accessed via Factiva, September 2005.
13. Bhushan Bahree and Martin Du Bois, "Total Will Buy Belgium's Petrofina at Big Premium," 2 December 1998, *The Wall Street Journal Europe*, accessed via Factiva, September 2005.
14. "Upstream Focus," 31 January 1999, accessed via Factiva, September 2005.
15. "All The Way," 31 January 1999, *International Petroleum Finance*, accessed via Factiva, September 2005.
16. "A wise move by Total," 6 January 1999, *Petroleum Economist*, accessed via Factiva, September 2005.
17. "Petrofina and Total catch merger mania", *Petroleum Review*, 5 January 1999, accessed via Factiva, September 2005.
18. "TotalFina at stalemate with Elf Aquitaine over merger," 1 September 1999, *Process Engineering*, accessed via Factiva, September 2005.
19. "Oil Giant Launches Hostile Takeover France's Total Fina Bids for Elf Aquitaine," *Associated Press*, 6 July 1999, accessed via Factiva, September 2005.
20. Ibid.
21. "TotalFina at stalemate with Elf Aquitaine over merger," 1 September 1999, *Process Engineering*, accessed via Factiva, September 2005.
22. Lara Marlowe, "TotalFina, Elf Aquitaine agree terms for merger," 14 September 1999, *Irish Times*, accessed via Factiva, September 2005.
23. Ibid.
24. Presentation from Organization Cetacea's website, www.orcaweb.org.uk/downloads/Erikaoilspill. doc, accessed September 2005.
25. Peter Gumbel, "Operation Total Makeover", *Time Europe*, December 8, 2003, http://www.time. com/time/europe/magazine/article/0,13005,901031208-552068-2,00.html, accessed September 2005.
26. Compiled from Total corporate website, information available at http://www.total.com/en/ group/corporate_social_responsibility/special_reports/Erika/total_actions, accessed September 2005.
27. Total Annual Report 2004, page 176, "Risk Factors". Number 2,500 injured taken from company website.
28. Total Annual Report 2004, pages 58–75.
29. Total corporate website, http://www.total.com/en/group/activities/, accessed September 2005.
30. Total Corporate Social Responsibility Report 2004, page 10.
31. In 2004, meetings were held in Europe (Paris, Brussels, Amsterdam, the Hague, Rotterdam, London, Dublin, Edinburgh, Frankfurt, Munich, Cologne, Düsseldorf, Zurich, Geneva, Lausanne, Stockholm, Helsinki, Copenhagen, Milan and Madrid), North America (New York,

Boston, Philadelphia, Chicago, Denver, Atlanta, Houston, Austin, Des Moines, Miami, San Francisco, Los Angeles, San Diego, Montreal and Toronto), and Asia (Tokyo). (Source: Total Annual Report 2004, page 47.)

32. Total Annual Report 2004, page 38.
33. Total Annual Report 2004, page 47.
34. Total Annual Report 2004, page 43, and Interview Valérie Laugier, 27 September 2005, Total headquarters, Paris, France.
35. Total Annual Report 2004, page 44.
36. Total Annual Report 2004, page 40.
37. Carl Mortished, "Empire builder who plays a waiting game," *The Times*, 21 February 2005.
38. Several sources: Martin Arnold, "France threatens oil majors with windfall tax," *Financial Times*, 9 September 2005; Martin Arnold, "Threat of French oil windfall tax," *Financial Times*, 16 September 2005; Martin Arnold, "Investors ask Total to move tax domicile," *Financial Times*, 21 September 2005; Frédéric de Moincault, Jacques-Olivier Martin, Philippe Reclus, "Le débat sur la taxe exceptionnelle n'aurait jamais dû avoir lieu," *Le Figaro*, 20 September 2005.
39. Martin Arnold, "Threat of French oil windfall tax," *Financial Times*, 16 September 2005.
40. Martin Arnold, "France threatens oil majors with windfall tax," *Financial Times*, 9 September 2005.

INDEX

AUTHOR INDEX